Ruth F

D0721972

361-

Publications of

THE AMERICAN INSTITUTE

UNIVERSITY OF OSLO

In coöperation with the

DEPARTMENT OF AMERICAN CIVILIZATION

Graduate School of Arts and Sciences

UNIVERSITY OF PENNSYLVANIA

THE NORWEGIAN
LANGUAGE IN
AMERICA

THE NORWEGIAN LANGUAGE IN AMERICA

A STUDY IN BILINGUAL BEHAVIOR

EINAR HAUGEN

VOL. I

THE BILINGUAL
COMMUNITY

VOL. II

THE AMERICAN DIALECTS
OF NORWEGIAN

INDIANA UNIVERSITY PRESS

BLOOMINGTON   LONDON

First edition published by University of Pennsylvania Press,
subsidized by Norges Almenvitenskapelige Forskningsråd and
the Norwegian Ministry of Church and Education

Copyright ©1969 by Einar Haugen
Reprinted 1969 by Indiana University Press by arrangement with University
of Pennsylvania Press and the American Institute, University of Oslo
All rights reserved

No part of this book may be reproduced or utilized in any form
or by any means, electronic or mechanical, including photocopying
and recording, or by any information storage and retrieval system,
without permission in writing from the publisher. The Association of
American University Presses Resolution on Permissions constitutes
the only exception to this prohibition.

Library of Congress catalog card number: 70-85187
Standard Book Number: 253-34115-9
Published in Canada by Fitzhenry & Whiteside Limited, Don Mills,
Ontario
Manufactured in the United States of America

To my Mother and Father
Kristine and John Haugen
Who First Introduced me to the
Pleasures and Problems
of Bilingualism

Slekt etter slekt måtte seile
i trekkfugledrift over sjøen,
til gjensyn med landet de tapte;
forske det, spore dets skjebne.
Klarere så de enn andre,
med øynene kjærlighets-bitre.

Nordahl Grieg (1943).

PREFACE TO FIRST EDITION

When, at length, the happy day has come that a book based on years of patient collection can appear, one's thought go back to those who have helped to make it possible. The first grants in support of this research were made as far back as 1936 and 1937 by the University of Wisconsin Research Committee, which has continued to contribute small annual sums for equipment, assistance, and travelling. In 1942-43 the John Simon Guggenheim Foundation granted me a fellowship; and in 1949 the Committee on American Civilization at the University of Wisconsin used Rockefeller Foundation Funds to assist me to a semester's leave for writing. The same committee made available the services of Magne Oftedal as research associate in 1947-48. The authorities of the University of Wisconsin, among whom I would like to mention President E. B. Fred and Dean Mark Ingraham, have looked with benevolent eye on the project and have variously assisted in making time available for research.

But the roots of this work go back even farther. The idea that such homely materials could become the subject of scientific study was first implanted when H. L. Mencken's *The American Language* fell into my hands; there I first learned of the writings of George T. Flom, who later became my teacher. To Professor Flom I owe special gratitude for his pioneering work in this field. A new stimulus to the work came from discussions with Didrik Arup Seip and Ernst W. Selmer of the University of Oslo during their travels and studies in the United States in 1931-32.

Those who have given me the most have, of course, been my informants; even though they are not named in this book, they are not forgotten. Beyond them I am grateful to all my Norwegian-American friends, whose speech has been grist to my mill. My wife, Eva Lund Haugen, has not only contributed directly through her bilingual capacities and interests, but has also offered me that patience and moral encouragement without which no scholar can operate. Many others have been called upon for specific material that has gone into the book, too many to mention; most of them will be found in the footnotes. Magne Oftedal's contribution is too important to be left to footnotes, however; his year's activity as field worker not only added to the breadth of this study, but also contributed many acute observations and valuable linguistic insights. I am grateful also to my colleagues in the Linguistic Circle of the University of Wisconsin, past and present, of whom the following have shown a particular interest in this project: M. L. Hanley, W. F. Twaddell, Martin Joos, Frederic G. Cassidy, and Lester W. Seifert. Dean Theodore C. Blegen of the University of Minnesota has followed the work from the beginning with warm interest and encouragement. Hans Kurath of the University of Michigan stimulated my work by organizing the Committee on Non-English Languages in America and by asking me to teach a course in Bilingualism at the Linguistic Institute in 1949. The maps prepared by George W. Hill of Wisconsin nationality groups have been very helpful, and I wish to thank him for permitting me to use them as the basis for some of the maps here included. These have been prepared by Andrew Burghardt of the Wisconsin Department of Geography, under the direction of Arthur Robinson. Among the student workers and secretaries who have assisted in various ways are Liese von Oettingen, Olaf Holmer-Spetland, and Irene Ulvestad.

But the immediate delivery of the work is above all due to Sigmund Skard, of the University of Oslo, without whose enthusiasm and friendly intervention more years might have passed before the joyous event. I am especially grateful that he made it possible for the book to appear in his American Series, and wish to thank the Norwegian institutions which, at his suggestion, so generously assisted in defraying the costs of printing: Norges Almenvitenskapelige Forskningsråd, and the Norwegian Ministry of Church and Education. I am grateful also to the University of Pennsylvania Press for its aid in publication.

It is a pleasure to acknowledge the kindness of the following authors in permitting the use of quotations from their writings: Joran Birkeland, Borghild Dahl, Lowry Nelson, and Ted Olson; and to the holders of their copyrights E. P. Dutton Co., The Macmillan Company, and the American Book Company.

It has been my intention throughout this book to treat language as a social phenomenon, in such a way that it might offer something of value to students of history and sociology. At the same time I have not wished to neglect the more purely linguistic aspects of the topic, which have found their place especially in the second volume. The topic is a large one, and there are many phases of the subject which have here been discussed either sketchily or not at all. But most readers will probably find the book big enough already; some of the gaps I hope to fill in later publications.

March 10, 1952.

PREFACE TO SECOND EDITION

In the decade and a half since the original appearance of this book, very little has occurred to change the facts on which it is based or the judgments passed in its pages. Norwegian is still, like most other immigrant languages, slowly receding; it is nourished by only a slight trickle of immigration and home use by a small number of traditional-minded people. Thanks to a general revival of interest in foreign travel and foreign-language instruction, Norwegian has enjoyed a highly satisfactory academic expansion. (For details, see Bronner and Franzén's reports,* continuing the discussion on page 140 of this book.) The Oslo (and now the Bergen) International Summer Schools have attracted hundreds of Americans and have taught them at least a smattering of the language. In the United States a handful of newspapers are still appearing in Norwegian, including *Decorah-Posten* in Iowa and *Nordisk Tidende* in Brooklyn, New York. The emphasis among Norwegian-Americans is more than ever on the historical aspects of Norwegian immigration, with continued activity by the Norwegian-American Historical Association (now under the editorship of Kenneth Bjork of St. Olaf College) and the Norwegian-American Historical Museum in Decorah, Iowa. There is no longer any "Norwegian Lutheran Church in America," its organization having long since been absorbed into a larger American Lutheran church organization. (The tables have even been turned with the erection of an American-language Lutheran church by this organization in Oslo, Norway.)

The author has therefore ventured to reissue this book without

* The latest of them occurs in *Scandinavian Studies*, vol. 39 (1967), pp. 345-367.

substantive change, acting on requests received for copies since it went out of print. The title may suggest that the book is primarily or even exclusively of interest to Norwegians and their descendants or to students of Norwegian. I sincerely hope that these may be attracted to it in this new issue, now that a new generation of them has grown up. But it was apparent even to the first reviewers that the detailed study here given to Norwegian and its fate in America was intended as a paradigmatic analysis of a bilingual community in dynamic linguistic transition. The subtitle of the book was intended to suggest this more general goal, but it is to be feared that some non-Scandinavianists found the mass of detail about this one language and its dialects too formidable to extract the general ideas contained in it.

In order to remedy this weakness, if that is what it was, I wrote a more general book, surveying the whole American scene (even expanding it to include the whole hemisphere). This was *Bilingualism in the Americas: An Introduction and a Bibliography,* published in 1956 as Publication No. 26 of the American Dialect Society (reprinted 1964). Here the emphasis was on terminology and problems of research: how should one look upon such linguistic situations and how should they best be described in order to give full insight into their development and consequences? The bibliography attempted to include everything relevant, and each chapter concluded with a set of propositions to be tested by further research. In both books central emphasis was placed on linguistic data as illustrative of social and psychological developments of the speakers. The books could therefore be read with profit not only by professional linguists, but also by sociologists, anthropologists, and psychologists. *Bilingualism in the Americas* also had the advantage of appearing after Uriel Weinreich had published his excellent *Languages in Contact* (New York: The Linguistic Circle of New York, 1954), so that some of the terminology proposed in his book (e.g., "interference") could be incorporated with that which I had proposed as early as 1950 ("importation," "substitution," "loanshifts," "loanblends") in an article in *Language* (vol. 26, pp. 210-231); now reprinted in C. Scott and J. Erickson, *Readings for the History of the English Language* (Boston: Allyn and Bacon, 1968). I further refined the terminology by comparison with that of Werner Betz in Germany in reviews of works by his pupils, especially in *Language*, vol. 28 (1952), pp. 397-401, and vol. 32 (1956), pp. 761-766.

Aside from the correction of misprints, the present reissue makes only one significant change; a list is inserted at the back of Volume II in which the informants are listed by name instead of being identified only by number. The fear of embarrassment which led to omission of the names should no longer apply, now that many of them have passed on, and for the historical record it is well that they be listed. The recordings of their voices (as listed on pp. 618-635) have all been transferred to tape (though the quality is not that of modern tape recordings). One set of tapes is deposited at the World Linguistic Archives at Indiana University, while the other is in my possession at Harvard University. In addition, I have all the original field records, plus an elaborate classification of the materials found.

Among the topics which were not adequately treated in the book was the speech of urban and cultivated immigrants, aside from some discussion of the literary language (chapters 6-7). Another was the English spoken by my informants, since this was not part of the original plan; hence I was not able to analyze in detail the gradual shift from one language to another and the face-to-face situations which promoted it (though there is some information on the topic in chapters 3-5 and 10-11). No single, unified dialect is treated comprehensively, although I have enough materials for at least two such dialect monographs (Solør, Oppdal). Articles in which I have exploited some of the materials not used in this book or developed themes more fully are "The Impact of English on American-Norwegian Letter Writing" (*Studies in Honor of Albert Morey Sturtevant,* Univ. of Kansas Press, 1952, pp. 76-102) ; "Some Pleasures and Problems of Bilingual Research," *International Journal of American Linguistics,* vol. 20 (1954), pp. 116-122; "Problems of Bilingual Description," *Georgetown University Monograph Series on Languages and Linguistics,* vol. 7 (1954), pp. 9-19; "The Phoneme in Bilingual Description," *Language Learning,* vol. 7 (1956-57), pp. 17-23; "Language Contact," *Proceedings of the Eighth International Congress of Linguists* (Oslo, 1958), pp. 772-785; plus various reviews, of which only the one of Weinreich's book should be mentioned (*Language,* vol. 30, 1954, pp. 380-388).

No further work on the Norwegian language in America has been done since my researches, except for an unpublished study of Texas Norwegian by Kjell Johansen (M.A., Univ. of Texas, 1961). American Swedish has been the object of a large-scale collection of materials on tape (1962, 1964, 1966) by the Swedish Dialect Archives at Uppsala University under the direction of Folke Hedblom (*Svenska Landsmål,* 1965, 1-34). Aspects of American Swedish have been treated by Nils Hasselmo in a thesis (Harvard, 1961) and several articles. Under the direction of Glenn Gilbert a major project of study in the field of Texas German has been initiated (Harvard Dissertation, 1963), in cooperation with the German Dialect Archives at Marburg. A study of American Ukranian by J. O. Zhluktenko appeared in Kiev (1964), etc. Meanwhile the problem of linguistic retention by American immigrant groups was made the theme of a major socio-psychological study directed by Joshua Fishman, some results of which have been presented in his book *Language Loyalty in the United States* (The Hague: Mouton, 1966). Fishman has also published a portion of his results in a separate volume, *Yiddish in America (International Journal of American Linguistics,* Publication 36, 1965). A study under his leadership of the Puerto Ricans of New York, entitled *Bilingualism in the Barrios* (U.S. Dept. of Health, Education, and Welfare, 2 vols., 1968) further establishes his pre-eminence in this field of study, which he has denominated "language maintenance and language shift."

Fishman is only one of a group of younger Americans who have been concerned about developing the field of sociolinguistics (alongside psycholinguistics), in which bilingualism has played a large role. Others are Susan Ervin-Tripp, John J. Gumperz, and (in Canada) Wallace E. Lambert, whose numerous articles may be found in the journals; a representative collection is that edited by the Irish psychologist John Macnamara and forming the April, 1967, issue of *The Journal of Social Issues.* Stimulating contributions have also been made by A. Richard Diebold, Jr. (Ph.D. diss., Yale, 1961), e.g., in his article "Incipient Bilingualism" (*Language,* vol. 37, pp. 97-112, 1961). J. Vernon Jensen's *Effects of Childhood Bilingualism* (National Council of Teachers of English, 1962) contains a useful bibliography. The leader of all North American work in the field today has become William F. Mackey of Laval University in Quebec, where he has established an International Center of Bilingualism, from which numerous publications may be expected. Under his direction an International Seminar on the Description and Measurement of Bilingualism was held at the University of Moncton, New Brunswick, Canada, June 6-14, 1967, the proceedings of which will be published. Further interesting materials from Canada may be expected as the *Report of the Royal Commission on Bilingualism and Biculturalism* continues to appear; at the present writing only "A Prelminary Report" and "Book I" of the full report have appeared. Although Australia is not part of the Western hemisphere, it is not inappropriate to mention that continent as an area of immigration and consequent linguistic problems. An important study has appeared on the language assimilation of postwar German-speaking migrants there by Michael G. Clyne entitled *Transference and Triggering* (The Hague: Nijhoff, 1967).

Any further account of what has happened in the field since 1953 would require space that cannot justifiably be taken here. It is my hope that the reader will find that this later work has not made my book entirely superfluous.

Harvard University
October 21, 1968.   E.H.

TABLE OF CONTENTS
VOLUME I.

TABLE OF CONTENTS
VOLUME II.

LIST OF MAPS AND TABLES
VOLUME I.

Page

LIST OF MAPS AND TABLES
VOLUME II.

THE NORWEGIAN LANGUAGE IN AMERICA

Vol. I.

THE BILINGUAL COMMUNITY

Chapter 1.

THE BILINGUAL'S DILEMMA.

> No man fully capable of his own language ever masters another.
>
> *George Bernard Shaw (1903)*

The United States has probably been the home of more bilingual speakers than any other country in the world. Ever since the beginning of the great Atlantic migration, wave upon wave of non-English speakers has inundated the American shore.[1] A vivid appreciation of the need for survival caused most of the immigrants to learn as much English as was necessary to make their way in the new environment. But at the same time most of them continued to use their old language whenever occasion offered. More than that: many of them passed their language on to their descendants, thereby making them also bilingual. So it has come about that millions of Americans have been predestined by birth to a more or less pronounced bilingualism. As late as the census of 1940 some 21,996,240 white Americans reported that the language of their childhood home was not English.[2] Some of these were perhaps monolinguals, but the overwhelming majority were in some degree bilingual. The inescapable facts of the time and place of their birth made them bilingual whether they would or no.

1. *The Bilingual Problem.*

One might expect that a phenomenon so prominent in the lives of millions of Americans would have called forth study upon study from the pens of leading scholars and scientists. This has not been true. Instead, scholars have generally ignored it, feeling perhaps that it was beneath them, that it was a passing stage of no permanent importance to the national future. Americans have tended to take it for granted that 'foreigners' should acquire English, and that a failure to do so was evidence by implication of a kind of disloyalty to the basic principles of American life. In general, they have not even found the problem interesting, much less vital. It has seldom been recognized that the bilingual might have problems of adjustment which called on the best efforts of students and scholars for their solution. Even linguists have rarely exploited the possibilities of immigrant bilingualism for its bearing on problems of linguistic theory. Bilingualism has been treated as a necessary evil, a rash on the body politic, which time might be expected to cure without the need of calling in the doctors.

As for the bilinguals themselves, some have accepted their lot with enthusiasm, others with resignation, but many more have sought to evade it by becoming anglicized as soon as possible. However prominent bilingualism may be as a trait of American life, it is eclipsed by the continual flight of the bilinguals themselves from bilingualism. Very little prestige has been attached to the having of bilingual capacities. It has not usually been considered good form to make much of one's European background, particularly not of the accompanying linguistic accomplishments. Even before the Colonies had made their compact, and when the States were not yet united, the pressure of English speakers was causing Hollanders on the Hudson and Swedes on the Delaware to slough off their native languages so that they might enter the main stream of Anglo-Saxon communication. A keen-eared observer from Sweden who studied his Delaware countrymen in 1750, a century after their arrival, predicted that their Swedish would shortly die. It was already so mixed with English terms, he wrote, that it had become a new tongue.[3]

This situation has been duplicated again and again in American life. The immigrant bilingual has been living in an uncertain twilight zone, somewhere between the old country and the new. The problem that for others was not even present has assumed rather considerable dimensions in his life. His problem has not been merely one of syntax and grammar, but has entered into the very structure of his personality. Where others have been simple, he has been complex. Where others could rely on deeply ingrained habits of speech, he has had to make choices between approximately equivalent responses. Recent sociologists have made some excursions into this field, and they conclude that the bilingual is required to integrate a 'dual social situation' which the monolingual never even quite envisages.[4] In a study of Greek-Americans made in a large Eastern city it was found that their lives consist 'of a shuttling back and forth between their internal Greek relations and their external American relations.' This rather self-evident generalization is supported with much interesting data. But the situation can be duplicated from the experience of every immigrant group in this country. Millions of Americans have been oriented in childhood toward a tradition containing elements at variance with, sometimes even in conflict with the culture of the Anglo-Saxon majority. In the language of their parents they have often enjoyed their most intimate and valuable experiences. For these people English has been a language of the pocketbook and the outer shell of life, without depth or warmth.

It is evident that there is far more to this problem than meets the careless eye. It is not just a question of broken English, or a foreign brogue, which might safely be left to time and the speech clinics. Whole social structures have grown up in America to meet the demand for bilingual living. We have already referred to the growing concern of sociologists with these structures. An eminent rural sociologist has pointed out that 'in many instances the melting pot has never reached the melting point'.[5] By this he means that the optimistic American attitude that all immigrants would inevitably be assimilated into one great social structure has failed to materialize. Even when the bilingualism is gone, its effects linger on, frequently through the medium of church organizations that were originally created for the religious needs of bilingual groups. Many culture patterns which set Americans off from Englishmen are derived from non-English traditions that have been infused into our national culture. There are numerous groups whose purpose it is to stimulate special cultural interests of a bilingual nature. Foreign-language newspapers and radio programs bring more of the overseas touch to American life than do the usual American newspapers and programs. It is even possible that the stress on 'correct English' in our schools, with its accompanying schoolmam subservience to the dictionary as the bible of good usage, may be a reaction to the deep-seated bilingualism of American life.

Whatever may be the practical implications, the value of bilingual observations to a science of human behavior cannot be questioned. The political scientist will note that bilinguals often vote and respond to slogans differently from their monolingual fellow citizens. The social geographer will discover a tendency to clustering in certain areas by people of similar linguistic background. The psychologist will sometimes find evidence for personality splits that are tied up with bilingual responses. Above all, however, this is a problem for the linguist, to whom the study of bilinguals will bring choice morsels of observation bearing on practically all phases of linguistic analysis. If his primary emphasis is on linguistic change, he can here witness a more rapid flux in linguistic behavior than anywhere else. If he wishes to study linguistic structure, he can here find a veritable laboratory for the interaction of competing linguistic patterns.

2. *The Linguistic Deposit.*

It would seem that one of the most widespread effects of bilingualism is the deposit it leaves on the languages involved. The mastery of Latin as a second language by learned men in the Middle Ages has left a residue of Latin words and influences in all the languages of Europe. The use of Low German as a language of trade in Scandinavian cities over some centuries has given the Scandinavian languages a vocabulary shot through with expressions for handicraft and trade drawn from the language of northern Germany. English itself reveals in every sentence some of the many languages that Englishmen were forced to learn at one time or another in their history — Old Norse, Norman-French, Latin, Greek. It is an axiom of linguistic study that wherever such influences of one language upon another can be traced (which is everywhere) bilinguals have been its medium.[6] It would, indeed, be hard to conceive in what other way influence between languages could be transmitted except through individuals or groups who mastered at least some words of more than one language. But is the opposite necessarily true? Does bilingual mastery inevitably leave an influence on the languages spoken? That is a question which has not been settled, and for which we need more evidence than is yet at hand. As a practical observation we may say that while it seems to be possible for some individuals to speak two languages so that natives of both accept them without comment, this is not possible for whole groups of individuals. Paradoxical as this may seem, it will be illustrated from our materials, and one can find some justification for it from a consideration of the nature of language and language learning.

The mastery of *one* language in early childhood appears to be a universal human accomplishment. Some have even seen in it the chief distinguishing trait of human behavior. The mastery of *two or more* languages, though common enough, is by comparison a far more specialized achievement. Within a single, cohesive social group the use of a single language is the rule, and the maintenance of a second language the exception. The language itself becomes at once a means of communication and a cultural trait, which binds the group together and sets it off from other groups.[7]

But no group can live completely unto itself, and when individuals of different groups meet, the situation is ripe for bilingualism. Those who learn the language of the other group become carriers of intergroup relations, but from the point of view of the group their behavior is *marginal* rather than *central*. They are not indulging in an activity that all can share, but are developing a skill that is in the class of woodcarving or acrobatics or pianoplaying. This does not reduce its importance for the survival of the individual and even the group in certain situations, but it clearly limits the situations in which it is likely to be demanded. It is not, like monolingualism, a skill that is asked of all, or that is acquired by all without specialized effort. The psychological process seems to demand a more precise adjustment of motor skills, a more delicate balance of neural responses, which differs from that of ordinary monolingual speaking in ways that may be described as qualitative and not merely quantitative. Once acquired, an extra language is like swimming or dancing or bicycling, in not being easily forgotten even in disuse. But for successful and skillful performance, it requires, like these, constant practice and effort.

3. *Defining the Bilingual.*

We may well ask just how much mastery of another language is required before one can be said to be bilingual. It would be foolish to suppose, for instance, that most of the pupils in language classes, whose smattering of language learning is the despair of their teachers, could be called bilingual. Very few of them get beyond a stage that I have chosen to call *pre-bilingual:* a person who is no longer monolingual, but who has not acquired the power of uttering more than single words in the other language. The definition of bilingualism is actually dependent on our definition of language. In the widest sense, bilinguals come into being wherever differing dialects meet, even within the same overall language. Children brought up in households where father and mother speak different dialects often learn to speak both dialects. They grow up to be dialect imitators who can shock or amuse or bore their listeners by performing on several instruments of dialect patterning.

In the larger and more inclusive groups built up by modern means of communication such multidialectal relationships may become very complex. Most speakers become in some degree multidialectal, mastering several modes of speech according to the groups in which they happen to find themselves. We here shade off into the problems of style, which are not ordinarily thought of as being identical with those of bilingualism. But in a scientific sense it is not possible to draw any hard and fast line between these phenomena and the more obvious kind of bilingualism.[8] Interlingual learning and influence is after all only a special case of that learning which goes on between all human beings who communicate with one another. But it is undeniable that the situation is greatly complicated when communication has to leap the hurdle of mutually incomprehensible dialects. Bilingualism (which in this book is used to include multilingualism as well) may be of all degrees of accomplishment, but it is understood here to begin at the point where the speaker of one language can produce *complete, meaningful utterances* in the other language.] From here it may proceed through all possible gradations up to the kind of skill that enables a person to pass as a native in more than one linguistic environment.

As suggested above, bilingual speakers constitute a potent mode of binding different linguistic groups together. They form a link, a bridge, perhaps we should say a channel of communication between groups. Groups which would otherwise centrifugally part company and rotate around axes of their own are kept in contact by bilinguals who span the linguistic borders. Such links are increasingly important in a larger world of discourse. The need for them has been recognized by school systems in all ages which have aimed at national or international group cohesion. The formal teaching of foreign languages and even of the standardized mother tongue is the crystallized by-product of a more informal kind of bilingualism that has developed everywhere at the intersection of linguistic groupings. Such teaching and learning may be the very heart of a larger grouping into which the smaller group enters, and in such a case the term 'marginal' is clearly inadequate. The teaching of Latin in the Middle Ages was a case in point: bilingualism became the expression of a supralocal unity corresponding to the spiritual domain of the medieval Roman church. The Latin language was not the only link in this unity, but it was (and is) of high importance. Margins may then be of more than one kind: some, if not all, are also links, tying groups together that would otherwise be mutually isolated.

The number of bilinguals making up such links may be very small, or it may be great enough so that they come to constitute a group of their own. But it appears to require considerable *social pressure* for such a group to remain bilingual for any length of time. As long as the group is a true link between monolinguals, this pressure exists. But if the monolinguals on the one side disappear, becoming bilinguals or going over to the other language entirely, the reason for bilingualism disappears and its functional importance is reduced. Immigrant groups in Anglo-Saxon America are in this position; bilingualism usually disappears when the core of monolinguals who made its existence necessary has been dissipated.

The bilinguals might then be compared to links that have been torn loose at one end. From being intergroup ties they have become a merely marginal appendage and their members tend to disperse into the new group with which they have become affiliated.

4. *On Language Learning.*

We may now return to the question of what happens to the languages that take part in a bilingual communication. This is essentially the problem of whether individuals can keep two languages distinct. Is it possible to keep the patterns of two (or more) languages absolutely pure, so that a bilingual in effect becomes two monolinguals, — each speaking one language perfectly but also perfectly understanding the other and able to reproduce in one the meaning of the other without at any point violating the usages of either language? On the face of it one is inclined to say no. Hypothetically it is possible, just as a perfectly straight line or perfect beauty or perfect bliss are theoretically possible, but in practice it is necessary to settle for less. In some degree one or both languages will be bound to receive some transfer of patterns from the other. It may be a *phonetic* carry-over, in which case we say that the speaker has an 'accent'. It may be *grammatical*, so that the speaker, say, uses the singular where he should use the plural, or forms a past tense with a regular ending instead of some exceptional form that natives use. It is practically certain also to be *lexical*, for here the habits of each language are more arbitrary and less amenable to learnable rules than anywhere else. Every language groups the experiences of life into classes on the basis of more or less fanciful likenesses and differences; some have dignified this practice by calling it an 'analysis of experience'. It hardly deserves the name of analysis, for it is in effect the accumulated mass of more or less irrational comparisons which the speakers of a language over untold thousands of years have layered into the lexicon of every human form of speech now extant. To demand that this should be acquired anew in its total and (actually) infinite complexity is asking the superhuman. When Hugo Schuchardt, the great German linguist, was asked how many languages he knew, his standing answer was: 'Kaum meine eigene,' — scarcely my own.[9]

The learning of language is closely tied to the learning of cultural behavior of all kinds. Any process that is not instinctive in man and that cannot be learned purely by imitation, must be accompanied by the learning of words. Even if no absolutely new words happen to be involved, the old words acquire new meanings by being involved in new contexts. I may know what it is to *deal* the cards in a card game, and it then requires no great effort to learn what a *deal* is in politics; but it does require learning, which in effect here means a regrouping of familiar vocabulary. But it is very rare indeed that learning a new activity does not require also the learning of wholly new words. The special problem of the bilingual is that to be fully such he must accompany his learning of cultural *behavior* with the learning of a new set of *terminology*. Ideally this would require that he duplicate every experience he has had in speaking one language with speakers of his other language. Every emotion, every harrowing occurrence, every accomplishment would have to be lived through in the company of two different groups of speakers.

It is possible to attain a good deal of this sort of duplication by associating actively with speakers of both languages. But even those who acquire two languages in childhood and use them consistently in later life develop areas of experience in which one or the other language is preferred. A classic example in linguistic literature is that of the French professor, Louis Ronjat, whose son spoke German to his mother and French to his father, and was to all appearances completely bilingual. But in later life it was apparent to him that the language of his emotions was German, that of his thinking was French.[10]

Most monolinguals imagine that it is primarily a matter of learning single words. But languages differ not only in the specific terms they use for specific objects and actions; they differ even more in the kind of linguistic and social contexts in which these terms can be used. Even after one has mastered perfectly the grammatical situations, there are rigid limitations on the use of terms to describe classes of objects. It is easy enough to learn word X and the fact that it is appropriate in situations A and B.

But it is not enough to learn about word X_1 in another language that it means the same as X in situation A. For it does not follow that it is also usable in situation B. The fact that it is, or is not, has to be learned separately, as another cultural fact; violations of this principle are among the commonest errors of bilinguals in handling the languages they command. It is a law of general validity that one's experience in one language must necessarily lag behind one's experience in another.

5. *The Confounding of Patterns.*

We may assume, then, as a basis for discussion, that bilingualism leads inevitably to a certain confusion of patterns, at least when it is carried on by its less skilled or less highly trained practitioners, who after all constitute the great majority in every social group. This raises a host of questions which have been discussed by linguistic scientists for generations. Can we also assume that there is a correlation between the amount of bilingualism and the amount of confusion, so that the more bilinguals, the more confusion? Are both languages equally affected, or is the influence likely to be one-sided? Are the influences permanent or evanescent? Under what circumstances can language mixture really disturb the essential core or basic patterns of a language? Why are some forms adopted and not others? Is there such a thing as a 'hybrid' or 'mixed' language, in which the mixture is comparable to that of two animal breeds which are coupled into a new species? We need a realistic approach to the problems faced by the speaker of two languages, from whom stem all the changes in either language that come under the head of language 'mixture'. What is the dilemma he faces, and how can he most conveniently make his peace with that dilemma?

The answer is writ large in the languages of the world, but the evidence is complex and often contradictory. Scholars have come up with answers that differed according to the phases of the problem that interested them the most. Two phenomena that have awakened popular interest have been the *foreign accent* and the adoption of *foreign words*. On the former have been erected learned theories about *substrata*, or the influence of submerged on surviving languages. On the latter has hinged a long and vehement discussion of the *loanword*. Substratum theory has been used to explain the divergence of related idioms, e.g. the splitting off of the Romance languages from the Latin unity. This is not the place for a discussion of the validity of these theories, which usually operate with so many unknowns that a skeptical observer is likely to despair of finding the truth that undoubtedly is involved in them. The loanword, on the other hand, has been used as evidence for cultural diffusion, on the assumption that cultural influence inevitably leads to a borrowing of terminology. In practice we discover that the use of loanwords may far exceed the actual cultural novelties introduced by one group to another, and on the other hand, it may reflect very inadequately the actual extent of influence, since it is only one of the possible ways in which one language reacts under the influence of another. Any transfer of patterns that a bilingual individual can make from one of his languages to the other can also be made by the group which comes under his influence. Only by observing closely the behavior of bilinguals, and giving them the same kind of detailed and objective study that other speakers have received can we draw valid conclusions about the theories that have been advanced to account for the many strange phenomena of interlingual imitation.

It is against a background of this discussion, which involves some of the fundamental problems of linguistic behavior, that we must see the events that are going to be discussed in this book. The immigrants from non-English speaking countries who overflowed into the wide spaces of America became potential bilinguals from the moment that English-speaking dominance was established in the northern part of this continent. They came, speaking for the most part a local dialect that had developed in some particular community of Europe, where isolation had been the rule since medieval times. For self-evident reasons they sought others with whom they could speak, and formed settlements where they could communicate freely with each other in the tongue that was familiar and therefore dear to them. But the larger community of the new nation encroached upon them, and their isolation was threatened, particularly after the coming of industrial society and mass commu-

nication. They were forced into bilingualism and began immediately
to show all the effects of bilingual living that we have outlined in
the preceding pages. There is evidence here for substratum influence, for loanword diffusion, for all the more or less subtle dilemmas
that bilinguals have been forced to solve in all ages. In these respects the Norwegians are no different than all others; their profile
in America is in general terms that of all immigrant groups, though
of course no two are identical. In this book we shall try to describe
the dilemma of the Norwegian-American bilingual in terms that
can apply to the problems of all bilinguals.

This has not been the usual approach of writers who have happened to notice the phenomena connected with immigrant languages
in America. Many have been the scornful expressions used by observers about the 'mongrelian' languages, as the popular publicist
Brander Matthews once called them.[11] Even so competent a linguist as A. J. Ellis referred to Pennsylvania German in 1871 as
'debased German with English intermixture'.[12] This opinion has
been shared to a high degree by the more educated members of
each immigrant group, who have lashed their less fastidious
countrymen for their treatment of the native tongue. Each critic
has usually been familiar with his own group only, and has assumed
that some personal or national perversity was the underlying cause.
Observers fresh from overseas have been the most vehement in
their critique, for to them the phenomenon has often seemed particularly conspicuous. It is noticeable that some years of sojourn
among their fellow bilinguals have usually softened many of these
judgments, and led even the most puristic to temper their speech
to the winds of mongrelianism.

6. *Approach to an Understanding.*

It remained for an unprofessional and unorthodox student of
language, the well-known H. L. Mencken, to bring together for the
first time evidence concerning the universality of speech mixture
among immigrant Americans. In the second edition of his *American
Language* (1921) he set out a veritable smörgåsbord of commentaries
on Americanized immigrant languages, from the relatively respectable Pennsylvania German to the socially outcast gypsies. Even

though Mencken did not draw any significant conclusions from this material, any one who reads it will not only be entertained; he can hardly help but be impressed also by the similarity of the patterns that emerge in these various groups. A failing which is common to Jugo-Slavs, Finns, Lithuanians, Spaniards, Russians, Hollanders, Germans, and Scandinavians, to mention only a few, can hardly be attributed to a *national* weakness. All appear to be in the same boat, borne along by the same undertow.

The influence of bilingualism on a speaker is not one that has to await a deeper familiarity with the other language. It is evident from the observations made by early travellers among the Norwegians that it took only a very short time for these phenomena to develop. One of the first and most illuminating comments on AmN speech is that made by Ole Munch Ræder, Norwegian jurist, who visited his emigrated countrymen in Wisconsin for some months in 1847.[13] 'They do not bother about keeping the two languages separate,' he wrote, 'so that they may speak Norwegian to their own countrymen and English to others. Instead, they eliminate one word after the other from their Norwegian and substitute English words in such a way that the Norwegian will soon be completely forgotten.'

The settlements he visited had then been in existence a bare seven years, and most of the immigrants had not been in America for more than four or five years. Yet the sample he gives shows a number of the loanwords already being used in the forms they have preserved ever since: 'They have a "fæns" about their "farms" and have probably "digget" a well near the house so that they need not go so far to get water to use on their "stoven". Such a well is generally necessary, even if there is a "læk" or a "river" in the vicinity, because the water is generally too warm. Near the houses there is frequently a little garden, where they grow "pompuser" [pumpkins] among other things, and a little beyond is "fila".' He explains to his readers that the last word means the field, and then adds: 'When a Norwegian goes to town, it is generally to sell his wheat or his "flour", as well as to buy what he needs at the "store". The worst trouble he has in this strange country is "ægeren" (fever and ague).' Even the place names had already assumed the form they maintained in common speech for a long time: Espen for Ashippun, Koskelænd for Kosh-konong, Kolmiwok for Oconomowoc. As we shall see, these phenomena have formed the subject of alternately severe and amused comments by Norwegians and Norwegian-Americans throughout the existence of a Norwegian-speaking group in this country.

The regularity and consistency of these phenomena made it inevitable that attempts would be made sooner or later to study them and arrive at some kind of deeper understanding. Norwegian has been unusually fortunate in comparison with most other immigrant tongues in finding early interpreters with genuine scientific competence. The occasional contributions of such men as Peter Groth, a Norwegian-born linguist who spent some years in New York in the nineties, and Nils Flaten, an American-born linguist who grew up in a Minnesota settlement, were valuable and thoughtful summaries of the situation. But most important were the numerous contributions to the subject by the Wisconsin-born George T. Flom, who first published a word-list of American Norwegian in 1902, and returned to the theme repeatedly in his later writings.[14] Only Pennsylvania German had previously (1884-9) received, at the hands of M. D. Learned, a treatment even approaching the competence of Flom's analysis.[15] The present study is deeply indebted to Flom's work, which it seeks to supplement and complete.

With the coming of a genuinely scientific approach to the study of American English, it became possible to project an advance in the field of American bilingualism. Close upon the publication of the first results of the Linguistic Atlas of the United States came a renewed stimulus for a survey of non-English speech as well. In the summer of 1940 a conference of interested scholars at the University of Michigan brought together for the first time men equipped and eager to engage in work on the scientific description of immigrant speech. The bulletin that resulted from this conference is fundamental in the further pursuit of this topic.[16] Recent years have seen an increasingly active staff of younger men exploring the phenomena of bilingual speech in America, including particularly Pennsylvania German, Canadian and Louisiana French, but also the more recent immigrations of Germans and Scandinavians in the Middle West.[17]

7. *A Plan of Study.*

We may conclude this introductory chapter by saying that the writer's plan is to treat the linguistic experiences of the Norwegians in America with the same seriousness that is accorded the so-called 'standard' languages of civilization. Such languages are usually described for the purpose of creating grammars and dictionaries that can be used to impose these languages on children and other less fortunate members of the social order. The present book is not such a *prescriptive* study, for no one will care to learn the language herein described. But it is a fact that American Norwegian did become the speech of most of the nearly one million people who emigrated from Norway and many of their uncounted descendants. It has been in full and active use for better than a century and is still by no means dead. The descendants of the first immigrants have lost it, but others have taken their place; *their* descendants will also certainly lose it, and there will be no one to take their place. But in the meanwhile a mode of behavior that is highly typical of American life will be forgotten unless it is preserved in a full and precise description. The people who speak this immigrant tongue have escaped from any academic straitjacketing of their speech, and in some degree even from the regulating influence of a socially stable environment. But their development, we may hope to show, has not been wild or haphazard, however many occasional vagaries there may be. They are still behaving as social human beings must.

The division of the work into two parts is a concession to the needs of general readers. Under the overall title of *The Bilingual Community* the first volume tells the story of the bilingual world in which the Norwegian immigrants have lived. It is essentially a historical sketch with an emphasis on linguistic behavior. It tells of how the immigrants learned their English, how the new language created problems in their use of Norwegian, how they established institutions to preserve the Norwegian language, how they taught their children to read and write Norwegian, how they adjusted their names to the new culture, how they struggled among themselves on the problem of maintaining the mother tongue, and how they finally gave up the struggle and succumbed to English.

This volume is based on both written and oral sources, and on the writer's personal experiences. The second volume is more definitely linguistic, being a description of the internal life of the Norwegian dialects in America. It is based primarily on the writer's analysis of spoken Norwegian in the rural communities of Wisconsin and other middle western states. It includes a study of the changes in the dialects resulting from their dispersal in the new country, as well as the effect of English on their total structure. Samples of the American Norwegian dialects are presented, and the volume is concluded with a representative vocabulary of loanwords.[18]

Chapter 2.

NORWEGIAN MIGRATION TO AMERICA.

I Oleana der er det godt at være,
i Norge vil jeg inte Slavelænken bære!
Ole—Ole—Ole oh! Oleana!
Ole—Ole—Ole oh! Oleana!

(In Oleana, that's the place I'd like to be,
And not in Norway drag the chains of slavery!
Ole—Ole—Ole oh! Oleana!
Ole—Ole—Ole oh! Oleana!)

Ditmar Mejdell (1853), in a satirical ballad.

Throughout the better part of a century many thousands of Norwegians were deeply stirred by the call of American opportunity. Their response to the alluring future that beckoned from this side of the sea was thought by more sober observers to bear the marks of madness. It was commonly said that they suffered from 'America fever,' a highly contagious disease which spread with epidemic speed from man to man, from valley to valley, until it had enveloped all Norway and deeply changed the destinies of her people. In 1843 Henrik Wergeland, one of her great poets, wrote that 'it is the most virulent disease of our times, a national bleeding to death, a true madness, since those whom it possesses will listen neither to their own nor others' reason; they scorn all examples, they toss aside the present in favor of a still more threatening, uncertain, darkling future, and let themselves be driven into a maelstrom of unknown sufferings.' The pioneers of Norwegian emigration permitted themselves to differ with this and many other judgments in similar vein. Little by little they beat a path through the prejudices and difficulties that surrounded emigration, with the result that Norway became one of the countries which contributed most liberally of its brain and brawn to the building of America's new Northwest.

1. *Incitements to Emigration.*

Many penetrating studies have been made of the causes and backgrounds of this movement. But the entire complex of causes which historians have analyzed was compressed by the emigrants themselves into a single idea: the hope of *social betterment*. This hope could mean different things to different men: into it were woven strands of religious dissent, escape from personal problems, adventurousness, a dream of political freedom. But economic advantage counted for most. To the first Norwegian emigrants this was synonymous with the ownership of land, the only basis of social prestige which they thoroughly understood. As the tide of emigration swelled and the character of Norwegian society changed, America also came to mean gold. But in either case the decision to emigrate was not exclusively based on a cold calculation of economic advantage. It was a break with tradition, a gamble with the future, a cutting of social ties which one might almost term a revolutionary act. Those who were well adjusted and only stood to lose in social prestige naturally did not emigrate. Those, on the other hand, who were too ignorant or sluggish to have their imaginations fired by the hope of America also stayed at home. Economic considerations alone might easily have driven 95 per cent of the Norwegian people to emigrate; instead we find that Norway's population actually tripled during the period of emigration.[1]

No major social catastrophe, such as famine, persecution, revolution, or war was responsible for touching off the movement of emigration. It began, as one early writer put it, 'prosaically and unconsidered, like the great changes in the earth's surface...' Shortly after the Napoleonic wars, which brought Norwegian independence in their train, intimations came to Norway that other peoples were finding an increasingly attractive haven in America. The Irish had begun swarming to America from 1816 on, driven

by famine, overpopulation, and misrule. Close on their heels came
the Germans, eager to escape from the Metternich reaction and to
pioneer on the rich farm lands of the Mississippi valley. It is
known that German writings on America helped to spread the dream
of emigration in Norway. But the immediate impulse came to
Norway from England, which had been sending a steady stream
of new settlers to America. The first migration from Norway began
in Stavanger, in that corner of the country which faces England;
its leader was a man who had been converted to Quakerism in
England.

These stimuli found their response in Norway earlier than in
the rest of Scandinavia. In part this was due to Norway's position
as an Atlantic nation, which eased the problem of transportation.
In the days of sailing vessels most emigrants were carried in Norwegian ships. But it was also a direct consequence of growing
dissatisfactions which we shall have to consider more closely.

The Norway of the first emigrants was a far less democratic
and progressive nation than it has since become. It was, in fact,
a rural, secluded, pre-industrial country. In 1825 nine out of ten
Norwegians lived in the countryside, making their livelihood from
dairying, farming, lumbering, or fishing. Most of the farms were
self-contained economic units, which since time immemorial had
had to do the entire job of feeding, clothing, and housing their
inhabitants. The whims of nature were more significant to these
people than international market conditions. The rural folk were
a proud, free-holding peasantry, literate and Lutheran, but without
much share in the government of their country. Their horizon
was restricted, but they were gradually awakening to their potential political strength.

The administration of the country was almost wholly in the
hands of the official class — a well-educated, conscientious caste
of public servants. They prided themselves on their democracy,
for they were not a titled nobility, and they had given their country
the most liberal constitution in Europe. But there was nevertheless
a canyon of social difference between them and the rural population
they administered. Their culture was urban and European, and
their speech avoided the local 'vulgarisms' of the common people.
The contrast was sharply pictured by an emigrant who had chafed

under the restrictions imposed on his own advancement: 'I grew up in a place where I had the opportunity of seeing the young sons of the pastor, the judge, the captain, and the storekeeper being educated by a private tutor, and it was undoubtedly the sight of these well-dressed, carefree, lighthearted lads, who had nothing to do but play and gather knowledge, which first caused the painful question to force its way into my heart like sharp steel: "What have I done, and what have they done, that there should be so great a difference between us?" And when they sneered at my torn clothes and laughed and pointed at me and cried, "My, look at him!" as I plodded along, bent under some heavy burden with my nose towards the ground, then I wept and swore and boiled.'[2]

Around 1830 a rural opposition reared its head in the national parliament, challenging the established privileges of the officials. The countryfolk also got a religious hero in Hans Nilsen Hauge, a lay preacher whose religious dissent had brought him persecution and a long prison confinement. Equalitarian ideas were seeping into Norway and weakening the position of the upper class; the humility which the peasant was supposed to show was no longer being offered with the same willingness as before. In 1837 the countryfolk were granted local self-government, the first great forward step in their political education.

A crucial stimulus to change was the startling jump in population after 1815. Vaccination, improved sanitary conditions, the potato and other factors reduced infant mortality to such an extent that between 1815 and 1865 the Norwegian population doubled in numbers. But the country was ill prepared to support over 835,000 new inhabitants. The number of farm-owners increased only 27 per cent during this period, and the country lacked capital for large-scale industrial development. Meanwhile the number of landless agricultural laborers tripled. Statistics show that in 1845 there was an abnormally high proportion of young people of working age, 20—30. A vast reservoir of manpower was being created, potentially dissatisfied persons who were attached to Norway by no ties of land ownership, security of employment, or social influence. To them the liberal constitution of 1814 had somehow failed to bring the social and economic elysium which its creators had envisaged.[3]

At the middle of the century the tide began to turn. A series of general European stimuli helped to set Norwegian society in motion. With the revolutions of 1848, the repeal of the British Navigation Acts in 1849, and the Crimean War in 1854 began a phenomenal expansion of shipping and a rapid industrialization of Norwegian society. Within the decade after 1845 Norway got such modern institutions as railroads, telegraph lines, general mail service, public agricultural schools, textile mills, commercial banks, and insurance companies. She also got her first labor movement and the stirrings of a liberal political party. The farmers ceased producing everything for themselves and began sending their products to market. They were no longer little kings in their domain, but were becoming slaves of the business cycle. Education and the new mobility led to increased demands on life, to difficulties of financial adjustment, and a regrouping of population. Money grew in importance; debts and taxes began accumulating; prosperity was followed by depression. The land was full of new problems, both for the landless laborer who was no longer wanted, and for the small farmer whose soil lacked the productivity which the new age demanded.

The note of restlessness is clearly to be heard in the writings of Norwegian authors from the 50's and 60's. It finds vigorous expression in the novels of Bjørnson which were widely read by Norwegian country people both at home and after their emigration. The hero of his story *Arne* (1859) expressed his dissatisfaction in a poem which became the theme song of many an emigrant:

> Out would I, out — oh, so far, far, far
> Over the highest mountains.
> Wherever I turn, my path they bar...

Bjørnson wanted his readers to stay in Norway, and he taught his hero to find himself a niche in the homeland. But another poet was less complacent: Aasmund Vinje was himself a cotter's son and knew the grinding effect of poverty. He not only thought of emigrating himself, but seriously recommended it to others. 'As long as people are ignorant,' he wrote, 'they sit at home and grow on the same spot like grass and trees. But when they get to learn something and think about things, they pull up stakes and look for a better home. They don't always find it, but they have to try. That is why emigration is a sign of enlightenment and intelligence... As I began to learn, I felt a mighty urge to leave my valley, go to America or anywhere, just so I didn't have to stay at home where I found nothing to do. If I had not learned anything, I might have hired out to the parson, or gotten me a wife and a measly patch of a farm. I don't deny that this might have been just as good for me. But it was impossible. Thought had cast its fiery spark into me.'[4]

Horizons were opening up for the Norwegian people. The country lad of 1820 had accepted as a matter of course the cultural and economic traditions of his community. He had spoken the speech of his parish, and observed its ways from birth to death. But by 1870 he was being endowed with more freedom and less security. Even if he wished to stay on the farm, he might not be able to do so. Very often he did not want to, for he was stirred by the promise of brighter lights: he might go to school, learn a handicraft, or work in an office; he might live in town, or go to sea; with luck he might even rise to prominence in the affairs of his country; or he might gamble with America for a share in her fabled surplus. Emigration became one of the many expressions of the peaceful social revolution that transformed Norwegian society in the nineteenth century.

It seems clear, then, that Norwegians did not emigrate primarily because they were oppressed, or persecuted, or poverty-stricken. It is true that many of them were under-privileged; but so had their ancestors been and had humbly accepted it as the will of God. Economic and social conditions in Norway were actually better than in most European countries; and it was not the poor alone who emigrated. But the men of the nineteenth century were like Adam and Eve after they had tasted the apple of knowledge: they suddenly discovered that they were hungry. The apple they ate was the news of America which came to them through their newly-founded newspapers, their improved school systems, their previously migrated relatives, the letters and books about America. They emigrated because they had learned to be dissatisfied, and because a changing world had provided them with a hope of escape from their dissatisfaction.

⌊Neither did they emigrate because they were sons of the sea-faring vikings of old.⌉ The earliest emigrants were men who chafed under an economy which offered them and their sons little hope of social betterment. From their meager holdings they looked over to the untouched land on the American frontier. In this new society the rewards would not all be won by such capriciously distributed qualifications as wealth, birth, or genius. Comfort and distinction might be gained by the more democratically widespread qualities of a strong arm, a determined will, and a strict husbandry. These hard-headed sons of the soil could for the first time allow themselves the luxury of being dissatisfied with what fate had allotted them. Their turn had come to join the movement to America which one authority has called 'mass proletarian emigration.'[5]

2. *A Century of Migration.*

The Mayflower of the Norwegians bore the resounding name of the 'Restauration,' but she was no impressive vessel: less than forty tons, a mere fifty-four feet long. When she docked in New York harbor on October 9, 1825, she was loaded to the gunwales with a cargo of iron, seven sailors, forty-five religious dissenters, and a new-born babe. She made good copy for a New York reporter, who found her 'a novel sight.' 'The appearance of such a party of strangers,' he wrote, '..from so distant a country...in a vessel of a size apparently ill calculated for a voyage across the Atlantic ...argues a good deal of boldness...as well as an adventurous spirit in the passengers...' His piece was reprinted in so many papers that a week later he came back with more information: they were bound for the state of New York, where an agent had been sent to buy land. 'They belong to a religion called the Saints, corresponding in many points to the principles of the Friends... We understand...that they will shortly be succeeded by a much larger body of emigrants.'[6]

It took eleven years before this promise was fulfilled. Norwegians were not in a hurry to believe the tales of America. It was not until results were clearly available from this first group experiment that they were ready to venture across in any numbers. The pathfinder of the Stavanger settlers of 1825 had been Cleng Peerson, the mercurial, irrepressible, vagabond-like Daniel Boone of Norwegian migration. When they decided that New York was not to their liking, he sought out rich, unoccupied soil for them in north central Illinois. He caught up with the American frontier as it was about to round the southern tip of Lake Michigan, and made this frontier the Promised Land of Norwegians for sixty years to come. Six of the Stavanger families moved to Illinois in 1834 and became the advance guard of hundreds of thousands.

Within the year these settlers were writing letters to their friends and kin in Norway, letters which were copied and circulated by the hundreds. In 1835 one of their number visited Norway; when he came back in 1836, he brought with him close to two hundred farmers from his immediate neighborhood. After this year there was no cessation. One can trace on a map of Norway the spread of 'America fever' from district to district, as news of the experiences of the settlers spread outward from Stavanger in ever-widening circles. What had been but a remote rumor now became credible fact, when men of the farmers' own class, their own neighbors and friends whom they trusted, told them by letter and word of mouth of the new possibilities. In this way one can trace the strands of human influence which reached from the first emigrants down to the mass migration of later years.

Statistically regarded, the course of Norwegian migration has not been a smooth one. It presents the familiar picture of a series of camel's humps, with the largest in the middle. The movement may be compared to a pageant in five acts, where the intermissions were created by two wars and two depressions. The general picture will appear from the accompanying chart, and will find confirmation in the figures of Table 1. It corresponds well with the general curve of European migration to the United States, and it shows a close dependence on American business cycles.[7]

Act I, down to the Civil War, was the period of beginnings, with many fumbling settlements which had to be abandoned, until trial and error had established the main course of migration and located the old Norwegian settlements of Illinois, Wisconsin, and Minnesota, which became mother settlements to the rest. The settlers were drawn largely from the southwest and central moun-

Table 1. *The Course of Norwegian Emigration 1836-1928.*
According to Norwegian Figures.

In thousands.

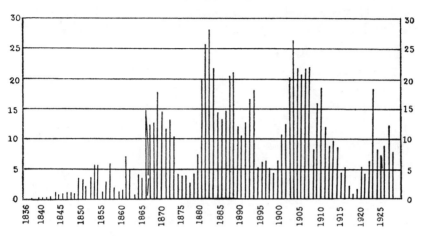

Period of Migration

	Low Migration				High Migration		
Years	Total number	Annual average	Rate per thousand population	Years	Total number	Annual average	Rate per thousand population
I 1836/48	10,500	808	0.63	1849/62	57,920	4,137	2.8
II 1863/65	9,400	3,133	1.9	1866/73	109,469	13,684	8.0
III 1874/78	20,878	4,176	2.3	1879/93	262,273	17,485	9.0
IV 1894/99	34,179	5,696	2.7	1900/14	224,541	14,970	6.9
V 1915/22	30,277	3,785	1.6	1923/30	52,655	6,582	2.6

tain regions of Norway; they were family men, who had ventured into the great unknown in a period when migration was attended by extraordinary perils on sea and land. In 1850, Wisconsin was the home of two-thirds of the Norwegian settlers; ten years later her share had fallen to one half, although the number had doubled. In this period was built the first Norwegian church (1844) and was published the first Norwegian newspaper (1847); the first

Norwegian member of a state legislature was elected (1849), and the first Norwegian volunteer regiment in an American war, the Fifteenth Wisconsin, was organized (1861).

Act II was opened by the Homestead Act of 1862, which made free land available to every sincere settler. Now the Norwegians

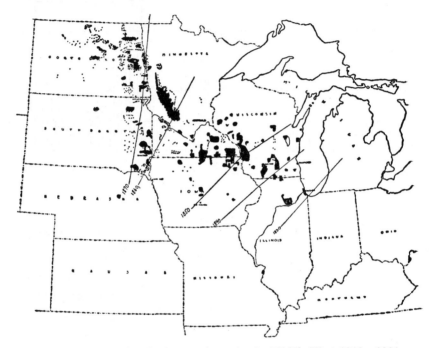

Plate 1. *Norwegian Settlement Areas in the Middle West 1830—1880.*

were really ready to come. Well-established settlements of their own people assured them of bases from which they could investigate the unknown lands on the frontier. The early comers had grown prosperous enough to send tickets home. English steamship lines and American frontier states sought to entice as many immigrants as possible. American railroads were pushing lines in all directions over the prairie. Norwegian society had been set in motion by the industrial transformation which began in the fifties so that large portions of her farming population went scurrying either to the cities or to America. Wisconsin's Norwegians were again doubled, but Minnesota was now close behind, and the first thrusts into Dakota had begun. The church was so greatly strengthened that it established a series of higher schools. The first really enduring newspapers were founded and grew apace on the crest of this great second wave of Norwegian immigration. The Panic of 1873, however, brought the second act to a close and frightened many would-be emigrants out of their resolve.

Act III began around 1879, when confidence in America was once more restored, and for the next fourteen years, in spite of good times and the extension of political democracy in Norway, America drew off every year two thirds of Norway's population increase, or more than at any other period. Settlement flowed relentlessly westward; from southern Minnesota and northern Iowa the settlers jumped right into the Red River Valley, making western Minnesota and the Dakotas their very own land. All parts of Norway were now giving up their share, city and country alike in unprecedented numbers; but the American frontier was petering out, and soon the immigrants were no longer seeking it with the same glad abandon. Urban colonies began to spring up in such mid-western centers as Chicago and Minneapolis, and land had lost much of its lure in comparison with city wages. These later immigrants were children of a new age in Norway, an exciting era of industrial expansion, democratic agitation, and broadening education. For the first time the Norwegian-American world saw also a true cultural flowering in its midst: novels of immigrant life, the beginnings of historical study, English translations of famous Norwegian writers.

Again a depression intervened to slow the stream of immigration; but in 1899 the fourth great wave set in. This wave was a part of that pre-war urban exodus which also brought to America huge numbers from southern and eastern Europe. There was now only one frontier left, the mountain regions of the Northwest and the plains of western Canada. For the first time the mountaineers of Norway sought the mountains of America; Idaho, Montana, Oregon, and especially Washington received some thousands of land-seekers each. But the pickings were thin, and the mass of the immigrants overflowed into the cities. Brooklyn on the East Coast and Seattle on the West rose into prominence as cities with large

Norwegian populations. These immigrants were, more than ever, unmarried persons, ambitious to make money and in many cases determined to go back home when they had made their pile. Their roots were less deep, more urban, than those of an earlier vintage; they had less of the high seriousness of the early pioneers. These years brought with them the most flourishing period in Norwegian-American culture, a period of great undertakings in literature and journalism, which reached its culmination in the centennial celebration of Norwegian independence in 1914, on the eve of the First World War.

Act V was the last, hardly more than a post-war aftermath. American immigration restrictions reflected a new fear that more immigration would mean a lowering of living standards. The immigrants of this period consisted more of women and older people; it was a family migration, bringing families together which had been separated, or making families which had been planned before emigration. In Norwegian-American life there was a marked retreat from the flourishing state of pre-war days. Americanization hysteria induced by the war acted to hasten the natural urge of the American-born to abandon their special traditions. The restriction of immigration was the handwriting on the wall, which is strongly reflected in the literature and historical writing that fills this last period. Institutions like the church rapidly turned to English, while foreign-language newspapers gradually lost strength. A century of bilingual living was about to be written off, but not before witnessing the greatest united effort of Norwegians in America, the Norse-American centennial of 1925 in Minneapolis.

A glance at the figures in Table 1 will reveal the magnitude of this century-long migration. Between 1836 and 1930 the authorities of Norway counted 852,142 emigrants. Through a period of ninety-five years an average of 9,033 Norwegians sailed across the sea every year. These did not all go to the United States; they scattered over the entire globe, some 3,000 to Australia, 40,000 to Canada, a handful everywhere. But the overwhelming bulk of them did enter the United States — at least 810,000 by 1930. Since less than ten per cent of these returned to Norway, this means that Norway has contributed a good three-quarter million to the American melting pot.

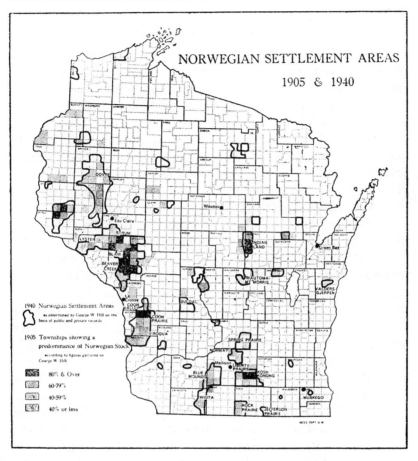

NORWEGIAN SETTLEMENT AREAS

1905 & 1940

1940 Norwegian Settlement Areas
as determined by George W. Hill on the
basis of public and private records

1905 Townships showing a
predominance of Norwegian Stock
according to figures gathered by
George W. Hill

80% & Over

60-79%

40-59%

40% or less

Plate 2. *Norwegian Settlement Areas in Wisconsin (1905 and 1940).*

When this is compared with the contribution of other European nations, it does not bulk too large. Even at its height, in the 80's, the Norwegian stream was no more than 3.1 per cent of the total European migration. But no country except Ireland had a higher *rate* of emigration: in the 80's eleven out of every thousand Norwegians were leaving annually, compared to sixteen Irishmen, six Englishmen, six Swedes, and four Germans. An even more startling way of regarding it is to note that through a century of huge population growth, Norway lost one third of her natural increase, or altogether a number nearly equal to her total population in 1800.

3. *The Norwegian Community in America.*

Norwegian migration has left its clear impress on the composition of the American people, especially in the Middle West. As late as 1940 there were still 658,220 Americans who declared Norwegian as the language of their childhood home. The number of first-generation Norwegians in the United States reached a high point of 403,858 in 1910 and declined to 262,088 by 1940. The number of their American-born children reached a high point of 752,236 in 1930 and declined to 662,600 in 1940. We can only guess at the number of their children's children. But we can hardly be far wrong in estimating the Norwegian stock at close to *two and a half million*, or more than twice the entire population of Norway at the time when emigration began.[8]

Behind these statistics we glimpse a myriad of men and women with the most varying personal characteristics. Nothing that one could say about any one of them would be true of all. For one thing, they are not nearly so blonde or blue-eyed as common belief makes them. Most of them did, however, bring into American life an overwhelming sturdiness and intensity of purpose. This was an indispensable asset to immigrants who were at once assigned the heaviest labor and the hardest tasks. In the earlier days of immigration, seven out of eight were from the countryside; three out of five were men; the bulk of them were unmarried and in their best working years. They came from agriculture and sailing, later from industry as well. They were not the poorest of their people and they were not without schooling. Most of them were orthodox Lutherans, but inclined to their own opinions on interpretation. A taste for hard liquor among some was offset by strongly Puritanic traditions among many.

They took hold of the wind-swept prairie of Illinois, Iowa, Wisconsin, Minnesota, and Dakota with little more than their bare hands. Their first shelter was the lowly sod hut or the ramshackle log cabin, and their nearest neighbors were the timber wolf and the Indian. They cleared their claims with simple tools and they hauled their grain to market behind a pair of oxen. Cholera and the ague attacked them along with a host of other plagues of primitive life. In winter many of them had to leave their families to earn cash for next year's seed corn in logging camps, canal construction, railroad gangs. Fear, hunger, loneliness were part of their regular diet, thousands of miles away from their own kin and the fond, familiar places of childhood. They grew out of these conditions into more comfortable days; one might almost say they grew up with the country. As for the later immigrants who chose the city, they had fewer hardships, but a no more enthusiastic welcome, for there was no free soil for them. They found their work where they could get it, and they won their place by patience, strength, and thrift.

Location of the Norwegians in the United States.
Census 1940.

States with greatest percentage of first and second generation Norwegians in total population:

	%	Number
1. N. Dakota	15.08	96,897
2. Minnesota	8.19	228,965
3. S. Dakota	6.5	41,908
4. Montana	4.46	24,996
5. Washington ...	4.24	73,569
6. Wisconsin.....	3.37	105,611
7. Oregon........	1.87	20,429
8. Iowa	1.75	44,362
9. Idaho	1.22	6,277
10. Wyoming	.91	2,296
11. Illinois	.79	62,148
12. Utah	.76	4,166
13. California	.71	49,064

Cities with greatest number of foreign-born Norwegians:

1. Brooklyn (in whole N. Y. metropolitan district 39,161)..............	20,214
2. Chicago..............	14,938
3. Minneapolis	11,777
4. Seattle (metr. distr.)....	9,854
5. Tacoma	3,592
6. Los Angeles..........	3,435
7. Duluth...............	3,251
8. San Francisco.........	2,951
9. Portland	2,355
10. Milwaukee	1,480
11. Spokane	1,276
12. Detroit	1,137
13. La Crosse............	1,134

American statistics show that half of them are still living on the soil or in towns of less than 2500; that in the cities they are most frequently found as skilled laborers; that they have developed a respectable number of professional and educated men; that they stand high in home ownership, in naturalization, in freedom from poverty and crime. On the American seaboard, east and west, they have contributed to the advancement of sailing and fishing. In their agricultural progress they have been thrifty; their willingness to shift from a failing wheat crop to dairying, tobacco raising, and other newer forms of agriculture suggests alertness and enterprise. Their well-kept, prosperous-looking farms dot the prairies of the Middle West. Grasshoppers, hail, and prairie fire could not drive them from the soil. Even the years of the dust bowl have come and gone, only to leave the Norwegians still the leading foreign element in North and South Dakota.

Fortunately the Norwegian immigrants also numbered in their midst individuals who possessed gifts beyond the dream of the valuable, but less exciting personalities which constitute the general run. A steady procession of highly and partially educated men, of cranks and geniuses, of fiddlers and storytellers, of saints and sinners have enlived the scene of the Norwegian-American world. Many remarkable comedies and some pitiful tragedies have been enacted among these immigrants. Norwegian-American society has not been one to treat budding genius tenderly or cater to the more delicate aspects of culture. Those who had the toughness to survive frequently reached fame. Among these one feels impelled to mention one of America's most original economic thinkers, Thorstein Veblen, who first learned to look with suspicion on the 'conspicuous waste' of American society as a lad on his Norwegian-American father's farm. Another was Andrew Furuseth, who as president of the Seamen's Union fought for livable conditions for American seamen.

It would be pointless to go on and enumerate 'famous Norwegians' in America, as is so often done in apologias for foreign groups. It is a matter of course that among all these citizens of normal and solid accomplishment there have been many with outstanding talents and a few who nourished the spark of genius. There are to-day admirals, senators, governors, congressmen, scholars, actors, inventors, manufacturers, judges — indeed every species of distinction among those of Norwegian stock. What these men have done they have usually done as Americans. But the fact that they have done it has been a source of pride to the immigrants, because it somehow made them feel as if they thereby belonged in a more real sense to America. Lutheran Norwegians were pleased that Notre Dame, a Catholic school, won football games — because the coach was Knute Rockne; they enjoyed pseudo-Norwegian films because Sonja Henie skated in them; they listened to difficult

German operas because Kirsten Flagstad sang them; and they repeated with undiluted pride that if Minnesota's late Senator Knute Nelson had only been born in America, 'he might have been president.'

4. *Immigrant Institutions.*

This sense of national pride has been strongly nourished by the accomplishments of the institutions which have grown out of Norwegian group life in America. Many Norwegians were readily dispersed into American life, with comparatively rapid effacement of their native personality. But most of them found it neither easy nor appealing to plunge headlong from one culture into another. Even when the immigrant's outward life was regulated to conform exactly with that of his American neighbor, he could not at once find full satisfaction for his cultural and spiritual needs. He could not toss his old self, the memories of home and school and friends, overboard when he walked down the gangplank.

So he sought the company of his fellow countrymen, where his own personality could unfold and the accents of speech were familiar and beloved. Americans have often complained at the clannishness of foreign groups, overlooking, in the words of H. H. Boyesen, that 'the immigrant, of whatever nationality, has no choice but to be clannish, unless he chooses to associate with those who look down upon him...'[9]. The Norwegians chose to live near one another and to create churches, newspapers, and societies which might minister to their own special needs. These they patronized to whatever extent they felt a craving for a common bond with one another and with their Norwegian past. Statistics point to a heightened incidence of insanity among immigrants, and the immigrant social order served the purpose of sheltering the immigrant's personality while it was being transferred from the old soil to the new.[10]

The first and the most persistent of the immigrant's institutions was the Lutheran church. America invited experimentation in religious matters, and many of the earliest settlers succumbed to the 'lures' of non-Lutheran churches. Within ten years of the founding of the first settlement in Illinois, however, there were three

Lutheran preachers on the scene, ready to organize Norwegian Lutheranism on a free church basis among their 'misguided and perverted countrymen.' Here the Norwegian pioneer found a natural center for his social and religious cravings. In the words of one writer, 'it was the only general meeting place for the whole settlement... If one did not come to worship God, one might come for other purposes, such as trading horses, assigning road work, hiring thrashers, or hearing the latest news...'[11] The church provided an outlet for much of the social energy of the immigrants. It gave full play to a certain streak of contentiousness which is part of the individualism of the Norwegian. Again and again the Norwegian world was rocked by violent religious controversy, bringing into the open an opposition between low and high church which in Norway had dwelt comfortably within the folds of the state church. It is very likely that much of this could have been avoided had not a group of the most conservative Norwegian church leaders fallen under the influence of the German Missouri Synod and taught views which were distasteful to the mass of the Norwegian laity. In any case the energy with which the battle was fought bore testimony to the earnestness of religious interests among the immigrants, and their unwillingness to accept dictation from above. Its effectiveness in arousing churchly loyalty is shown by the fact that the more numerous Swedes have only 396,999 members in their leading Lutheran church body, while the Norwegians have 661,355 in theirs.[12] Hospitals, orphanages, old peoples' homes, and a host of other charitable enterprises are churchly by-products which testify to the piety of the laymen and the enterprise of their leaders.

One of the chief tasks that faced the church was the training of competent pastors and laymen in the local congregations. The first successful solution was the establishment of Luther College, now at Decorah, Iowa, in 1861. This school was wholly in the spirit of the Norwegian Latin School, and provided a severely classical and linguistic training. It was followed by other schools, notably St. Olaf College, at Northfield, Minnesota, which was co-educational and less severely classical; it dates from 1875 and has grown to be the outstanding Norwegian-American church college, with national fame for its A capella choir under F. Melius Christiansen, and for its great author of pioneer novels, O. E. Rölvaag. These colleges and the many others established by Norwegian church leaders have gradually fallen into the pattern of the American liberal arts college, retaining only as much of the religious and national tinge as their constituents require. Courses in Norwegian established in American state universities are evidence that some members of the group also took an interest in these institutions.[13]

There have been secular societies a-plenty, though most of them seem destined to less permanence than the church. Many a local community has had its musical fare enriched by the Norwegian tradition of male chorus singing, which was transplanted to America in 1869. All America has reason to be grateful for the pioneer work done in the eighties by Norwegian ski clubs and ski manufacturers in introducing and nurturing the sport until America was ready to adopt it as her own. Perhaps the chief secular organization to-day is the Sons of Norway, a fraternal organization closely modelled on similar American brotherhoods. In general, the Norwegians have quickly learned the American habit of 'joining'; in the years since 1900 and particularly in the cities these organizations have provided the chief cohesive force among emigrants from Norway. Their programs and performances have not always been impressive; but they have provided shelter and training for Americans in the making.

The same has been true of the immigrant press. Several hundred newspapers have ministered to the Norwegians with more devotion than financial reward. In general the press has made it possible for a secular intelligentsia to exist among the immigrants. Men with some academic training were thus frequently enabled to devote themselves to writing; many of them were gifted with poetic and literary talent. Today only two newspapers of general distribution survive the falling by the wayside that has struck the press in recent years. One is *Decorah-Posten*, of Decorah, Iowa, which makes its strongest appeal to the old immigration of the Middle West; the other is *Nordisk Tidende*, of Brooklyn, an organ of the newest immigration.[14]

Many efforts have been made to depict the peculiar quality of the bilingual world in which the immigrants and many of their children have lived. Gifted and observant story tellers have tackled the job of portraying that inner conflict of personalities which is part of the immigrant's special problem. They have emphasized again and again the note of yearning for the lost homeland, which mingles with a quite different note of self-assertion. There is a pride of accomplishment which sustains the immigrant through all difficulties and provides a corrective to his nostalgia. The classic example of literary treatment is O. E. Rølvaag's *Giants in the Earth*, which raised the conflicts of pioneering out of the moment into a perspective of the eternal.[15] Historians have also assessed the problem, delving into the story of immigration and pioneering in a determined search for underlying trends and causes. The compilation of data began in the 60's, while the first pioneers were still alive, and has never ceased. Since the organization in 1925 of a vigorous historical society, the Norwegian-American Historical Association, a period of genuinely fruitful historical research has been inaugurated.[16] It is safe to say that more is known today about the history of the Norwegian group than any other immigrant nationality in the United States.

In the chapters that follow, an approach to the same problem has been attempted from a new point of view, the one of linguistic behavior. A prime factor and an ever-present problem in the life of most non-English-speaking immigrants is the problem of language. It is of course not their only problem and it cannot by itself be taken as a reliable index of assimilation; but it enters into their whole attitude to life, and determines many aspects of their behavior.[17]

Chapter 3.

THE LEARNING OF ENGLISH.

Læra Spraaket va nokot, som leitte,
Ofta stod me mæ skamfulle Fjæs;
Naar ein Yankee deg sporde, ka du heitte,
Raakte jamt, at du svara honom: Yæs!

('Twas a long pull learning the language,
And our spirits were often downcast;
When a Yankee would ask what our names were,
We most often would answer him, 'Yas!')

The Wisconsin Ballad (1878)[1]

The earliest immigrants were compelled by sheer necessity to
acquire some minimum of the English language, since they had no
countrymen with whom they could commune.[2] Books were available
in Norway that promised to teach the language, but they
were neither very numerous nor very helpful.[3] Most of the immigrants
followed the advice of Ole Rynning in his *Truthful Account
of America* (1838) to rely on 'daily association with Americans,'
which he believed would teach them enough in two or three months
so that they could get along.[4] Rynning regarded ignorance of
English as a handicap for the immigrants, particularly on their
trip to the interior, and he warned them that 'before having learned
the language fairly well, one must not expect to receive as large
daily or yearly wages as the native-born Americans.'

1. *The First Enthusiasm.*

A few of the leaders of the immigrants, such as the half-Scotch
James Denoon Reymert, had learned some English before leaving

Norway.[5] But in general a knowledge of English was at that time
an exclusive possession of the well-educated, and limited to only
a few of these. Reymert vigorously urged on his countrymen the
importance of learning English so that they might take part in
the affairs of the new country. In his newspaper *Nordlyset* he
warmly recommended the learning of English as a duty the immigrants owed their children. He warned them that they should
learn from the difficulties they themselves had had. 'Is it not
enough that *we* have been strangers and foreigners?' If their
children were to 'avail themselves of the privileges which the
institutions of our adopted country grant every inhabitant,' and
were not to remain 'hewers of wood and drawers of water all their
days,' they would have to gain a good knowledge of the English
language.[6] Another writer in *Nordlyset*, Knud Langeland, who
later became an editor of the leading Chicago paper *Skandinaven*,
wrote in much the same vein, warning the Norwegians that their
own ignorance was the chief barrier to equality with the native
Americans.[7] *Nordlyset* advertised an English-Norwegian and Nor-
wegian-English dictionary for sale, and did its utmost to acquaint
its readers with American institutions by printing basic American
documents like the Declaration of Independence, though to be
sure in Norwegian, the only language most of them could master
as yet.

A newspaper called *Friheds-Banneret*, which followed *Nordlyset*
a few years later, was also vociferous in its pleading for English.
The editor, John Mauritzon, and several contributors were agreed
that 'instruction in the English language, as carried on in the
public schools, is and remains the foremost means of advancing
the enlightenment of the younger generation.'[8] There is abundant
evidence that such advice was heeded, for the Norwegians did not
maintain any attitude of aloofness to the American public school.
The efforts that were made from some quarters to establish Norwegian day schools were almost wholly unsuccessful.[9]

Immigrant letters from the first period and the reports of such
observers as Søren Bache and Johan R. Reiersen agree that the
learning of English came easily to most Norwegians and that they
were ready and eager to take their place in the communities where
they settled.[10] An early immigrant from Voss attributed the dis-

satisfaction of some newcomers with American conditions to their ignorance of the language, for sharpers were eager to fasten upon such as could not speak for themselves.[11]

2. *The Norwegian Enclaves.*

In the course of the first decades of immigration the establishment of large all-Norwegian settlements in Illinois, Iowa, Wisconsin, and Minnesota led to a radical change in the linguistic situation. Once an immigrant had managed to reach such an area, he might manage very well without learning too much English. Kristofer Janson, a Norwegian writer and clergyman, commented on how 'the Norwegians had succeeded in secluding and bunching themselves together in colonies and in maintaining their Norwegian memories and customs. I often had to pinch my arm to realize that I really was in America. ...One heard nothing but Norwegian speech, and it never occurred to me to address people on the road except in Norwegian. I actually started when they answered, "What do you say?" — but of course, you're in America now.'[12] The organization of Norwegian Lutheran churches under the leadership of Norwegian clergymen developed an inner cohesiveness which obviously made for the preservation of the mother tongue. The pastors saw it as a practical matter for the preservation of their religious faith. They were severely criticised by some secular leaders, including the journalists quoted above, whose exhortations to the immigrants to learn English were partly intended as a criticism of the pastors. A pioneer physician, Dr. J. C. Dundas, accused the latter of wishing to establish a Norwegian theocracy in America; he wrote in *Friheds-Banneret* shortly after his arrival in America: 'They wish to continue here as in Norway to hinder the enlightenment of the people, to preach incomprehensible traditions as infallible truths, and deny the children of Norwegians the right to go to American schools before they are confirmed...'[13]

A contributor to the same paper, writing from Cambridge, Wisconsin, deplored the neglected state of the American schools in the Norwegian areas, and hinted that this was due to certain sinister influences.[14] Whatever the reason, it was undoubtedly true that in the early years the public school was not particularly effective in the pioneer areas. The second generation often grew up with less knowledge than the first, and the English learned in school was meagre enough. This observation, made to the writer by various informants, is confirmed in an article by Professor Knut Gjerset, who believed that the second generation was worse off than the first: 'Their childhood and youth came in the most desolate part of the pioneer period, when all forces, both physical and spiritual, had to be applied to the bitter struggle for existence. Of schools there were still but few, and so they had to find their spiritual nourishment where there was none.'[15]

3. *Bilingual Contacts.*

Nevertheless the schools were slowly making bilinguals out of the second generation. Meanwhile, the first generation was having to meet American society on its own terms. New immigrants kept coming in ever-increasing numbers, and the problem of the new language was always having to be met. Even those who were able to stave it off by joining their countrymen in the rural settlements had to face it in certain situations. We can classify these situations according to the kind of activities they involved as *economic, official*, or *social*. To these might be added *educational*, at least for the younger generation.

The economic activities were of two kinds: getting money, and spending it. Even after government land was given away by the Homestead Act of 1862, the Norwegian immigrant rarely had enough money to build houses or buy seed, animals, or implements to till the soil. His first task was to earn enough ready cash to make the first investments in land. There were certain standard openings available for healthy young Norwegians: as hired men on 'Yankee' farms, as workers on railroad and canal projects, as lumberjacks in the north woods. In Wisconsin they split rails and worked in lead mines, while in South Dakota some of them worked at the government forts.[16]

A characteristic account is found among the pioneer narratives gathered by Thor Helgeson; this one is told by a Telemark immi-

grant of 1843 from the Pine Lake Settlement in Wisconsin: 'When
we had fairly well recovered from the ague, my brothers and sisters
had to go out to the Americans and get work. But since they didn't
understand the Yankee language, their pay was not large. The
first winter father cut cordwood for 50 cents a cord on his own board.
At that he didn't get his pay in cash, but had to take the goods
the Yankees wanted to give him.'[17] We get a hint concerning the
kind of English learned in a story from the Wisconsin lumber
camps: 'The first we newcomers learned was to swear in English.
But we soon learned to understand something more than swearing
too. When we left the woods the next spring, we could chatter a
little English for bare necessity, and the second and third winters
we learned to talk fairly well.'[18] A third story tells of a man who
during the Civil War undertook to tell his friends about the war
on the basis of his reading of Norwegian and English papers: 'He
told about all the battles in a mixture of Norwegian and English..
Most of us didn't understand much of the Yankee language, but
a couple of fellows in the thrashing crew had been out among the
Americans and learned English, and when the speaker called a
battle a "bottle," the two yankee-learned thrashers burst out laugh-
ing.'[19]

[Even when the immigrant was able to dispense with wage-
earning and devote himself to tilling the soil, he was not exempt
from meeting the American world.] He still got his money from
people who spoke English, in this case the grocers, buyers, whole-
salers and others who bought his produce. His contacts were more
sporadic, and he could live more whole-heartedly for his own little
world of family, neighborhood, and church, where Norwegian became the language of common discourse. But his whole practice
of farming had to be organized along lines that were dictated
largely by the American market which he helped to supply. He
had to learn American methods of cultivating and harvesting, buy
American seeds to plant, and learn the American classification of
his products into various grades.

[As American agriculture changed from a self-contained economy
to a market economy, — a good deal more rapidly than the corresponding changes in Norway, — he was faced with a greater and
greater disparity between Norwegian and American farming meth-

ods. He had to buy American machinery to compete with his American neighbors, and from them he had to learn how to operate them. The village and the city became centers of radiation for American influences in his life, particularly their stores, through which passed all the solid improvements as well as the glitter and baubles which American life could offer him. Many are the stories of the perplexity of the American-Norwegian at 'the store.' Röl- vaag's Per Smevik was unable to make the clerk understand that he was asking for 'pens' when he clearly said 'pants'. A favorite story is told of the newcomer who in desperation got down on all fours and grunted like a pig to make the storekeeper understand he wanted pickled pig's feet, whereupon the storekeeper broke out in Norwegian, 'Well, why didn't you say you wanted pickled pig's feet?' But the Norwegian storekeeper was rather the exception than the rule in the early years; the following story is more typical: the newcomer goes in to buy some pork, and shouts the Norwegian word 'flesk,' but without results. Then the storekeeper finally says, 'Maybe it's *pork* you want?' At this the newcomer turns away in disgust, saying in his Trønder dialect, 'I didn't think I'd have to buy a whole sow (*purk*) just to get a piece of pork.'[20] While these stories may not be entirely authentic, they do exemplify one of the crucial points of contact between the immigrant and Ameri- can society, where new experiences and a new language crowded in upon him. Much of his food and all of his clothing, tools, and implements came from this source.

The *official* side of American life was first brought home to the immigrant (if we leave aside his experiences at the port of entry) when he filed on land. Here he met the terms of American land tenure, the section, quarter, and acre, which were to be the guiding framework of his living from then on. But the government did not leave him alone; it assessed his land and taxed it when the time came, and it asked him to get out and vote on how the taxes should be spent. He might well have had some experience with local government in Norway, but never in so absolute and sovereign a way as in this pioneer society which he was helping to build.

All this he had to learn, in the first instance, from Americans; he might well go on and instruct his fellow countrymen, but only by somehow finding equivalents in Norwegian for the new patterns he was being initiated into in America. He was shortly being elected a member of the town board, or the legislature, or even the congress; his vote was solicited by seekers for office. If he campaigned among his countrymen, he had to tell about it in Norwegian. If he went outside, he had to talk English; so bilingualism was, as the previously quoted editors declared, necessary to him in all his contacts with the political structure into which he had been placed. Similarly whenever he had occasion to go to court and seek justice. However tolerant the courts and the government might be of occasional language deficiencies, he was and felt himself to be at a strong disadvantage as long as he could not handle English well.

The immigrant's *social* life was less integrated with American groups than his economic life, but the isolation was far from complete. The edges of most settlements were extremely ragged, and many settlers had American or Irish neighbors. No matter how separated these might be at first by the language barrier, the time came when common interests and plain neighborliness overcame this barrier and friendships were formed across the fences. If nothing else, the schoolground became a common meeting place for the growing youngsters, and American social life made its first faint thrusts into the lives of the immigrants. American games were learned and soon displaced many of the old Norwegian ones. American customs like the shivaree and the surprise party were acquired, and American square dances and schottisches became a firm part of the amusement life of the community. This was true even while the immigrants associated principally with each other.

But of course many Norwegian social customs carried on, both for better and worse. Norwegian foods were retained, or revived, but principally as holiday fare, while the daily dishes were those which Americans also ate. There was only one place they could have learned to cook these, namely from Americans. New devices for cooking, and new dishes came from the American cuisine. When new houses were to be built, as wealth increased, they were modelled on American patterns and intended to impress neighbors who either had or wanted to have similar houses. One might say that the very concept of social innovation as a desirable thing was new to the Norwegian countryman, in whose life all had been static for so many centuries.

One of the most vivid accounts available of the pressure which even a rather indifferent neighbor might exert on the non-English-speaking immigrant is found in a book by the writer Joran Birkeland, who grew up in a bilingual home in Montana. She speaks of 'the strange psychological attitude of the Norwegian-American community in which I was born — a mingling of shame at being Norwegian, with a consequent feeling of inferiority, and an inability to feel satisfied with what it thought was American. The people who lived across the road from us, for instance, were American. At least they were not Norwegian. Perhaps they were Irish, though my father called them "Yankees." Everyone not Norwegian was, to him, a Yankee. Their children, black-eyed and boisterous, derided us for being "towheads", and my father felt embarrassed if Old Tom happened to be down by the road when Father came driving past so that he had to stop and pass the time of day with him. For English was Old Tom's native tongue and to my father even broken English was an effort. This made my father feel a lesser person than Old Tom. And yet, when Father looked at Old Tom's place, he lost his respect for him. The house was unpainted, the barn was little more than a shack, the farm machinery stood out in the rain and all sorts of weather the year around, and there seemed to be no *plan* to anything he did.' Concerning a Norwegian neighbor she reports: 'My father and John would stand for hours down by the road talking politics and crops in Norwegian, or in English that was also Norwegian. But if a "Yankee" drove up they would stop at once and become withdrawn and awkward. They were ashamed to display their native speech and ways, with him looking on.'[21]

That phase of life which he succeeded most definitely in shieldding from the impact of the American environment was his *religion.* There were American Lutherans, but they were hardly of any importance in the Middle West, and there were considerable doctrinal and liturgical differences between the Norwegian and the American Lutheran churches in this period.[22] Reports from the early Illinois settlements tell of widespread defection from Lutheranism, before the work of the newly founded church became effective.[23] A strain of lay activity which was especially strong in the regions in southwest Norway where the first immigrants came from led to a rapprochement with the low-church American groups in the same area. Later this controversy was moved into the Lutheran church and became one of the principal seeds of dissension in the growing synods. But in general the Norwegians remained loyal to the Norwegian Lutheran church, and established a ritual, a hymnary, and a church order that where as near to those of the state church of Norway as possible. But even here there were innovations: a church that got no subsidy from the state needed new financial organs. Boards of trustees came into being, and with them followed all the money-raising devices of American churches, from the Ladies' Aid to the Box Social. Basements were built under the churches as meeting places; young peoples' societies were organized, and the churches were soon well started on the road that gradually led them closer and closer to other American Protestant churches.

The degree of bilingualism in the Norwegian settlements varied greatly according to their size and contact with the outside world. Farmers who chose to restrict their contact with the English-speaking world to a minimum could live an entire life here as monolinguals. Even among the informants observed for this study there were a few whose English was practically non-existent. These were people who took no interest in political life, nor in the wordly pleasures of big cities, and who were content to till their soil and deal with such merchants as had learned Norwegian. As long as the church and their neighbors remained Norwegian, they found their principal needs satisfied. By others in the community they were sometimes laughed at for their inability to speak English, and stories were current about their helplessness in meeting bilingual situations. As respected members of a household, however, their influence on younger members of the family might be very considerable. Many an informant has attributed his knowledge of Norwegian to a grandparent who never learned English and who had to be talked to in Norwegian. But as a group they were not able to maintain the kind of a pressure that is exerted by a large, cohesive group of monolinguals. Their own Norwegian was if anything more mixed than that of the bilinguals around them.

There are no figures on the proportion of such speakers in the average Norwegian-American community, but observation suggests that they never constituted a majority of the community after the first half-dozen years in this country. Farm women, whose round of duties kept them closely tied to the farm and the Norwegian social group, were probably more often monolingual than the men. It is said to have happened that when Americans came to the door, the Norwegian women would rather hide than face the ordeal of the strange language.[24] In the second generation the tables were often turned, with the women becoming socially ambitious before their men, and adopting English as a ladder to social prominence.[25] A more detailed discussion of the relation between monolinguals and bilinguals in the community will be given in Chapter 14.

4. *The Immigrant's English.*

The extent of the English learned through the contacts sketched above was naturally limited to the words used in such situations. Those who went on to an education beyond the common school acquired wider areas of vocabulary, but the great mass of the population spoke no more English than necessity demanded. Stories are current about the errors in idiom committed by those who were not, as one informant put it, 'very agile in English.'[26] One Coon Valley pioneer worked for an American named Perry. One day when he had gone out to look for the cows, the bell cow came home alone without the bell. In trying to explain this to his employer, he said, 'It has lost him voice.'[27] A Spring Grove man, when offered the sugar at table, said, 'No, I'll take some behind,' (i.e., later).[28] A Waterloo Ridge man who was working with the thrashing crew, heard a loud crack in the thrashing rig, and said, 'I tink I hear someting smelling!' (Norwegian *smelle* 'crack').[29] From Upper Coon Valley the story comes of the man whose wife had been given a ride in a neighbor's automobile; he said to the neighbor: 'Thank you for riding on my woman' (Norwegian *køyra på* 'give someone a ride').[30] A Nelson, Wisconsin informant reported that as a boy he had answered a stranger who asked for his father, 'Oh, he's in the stove' (Norwegian *stova* 'living room').[31]

These stories, all told by the writer's informants, illustrate the awareness which exists among them of the problems faced by a bilingual speaker of English. One of them added this comment to her story: 'It hasn't always been so pleasant for us to be criticized for our speech. Even though we thought we talked just as good English as other Americans, we've been accused of talking "Norwegiany", and many of our best Norwegian-American pastors and speakers have been criticized for a "Norwegian twang" in their English language'.[32] A third-generation speaker from Blair, Wisconsin, said in Norwegian, 'Oh, you know I don't talk plain English, talk too much Norwegian — but there are many who talk worse than I do.' (Å du vet, je talar itte plein engelsk, talar før mie nårst — men dæ mange som talar værre enn je).[33] Although the informants consulted in this study were not subjected to an analysis of their English, the writer can testify that most of them did retain some slight trace of Norwegian in their speech, either in intonation or articulation.

One detailed study of this phenomenon has been made, by Anne Simley, at the time she taught at Crookston in northern Minnesota.[34] Her results check entirely with the writer's observations and have the advantage that they are statistical. She examined 115 youngsters of Norwegian background and found only 10 without traces of Norwegian accent. The errors made can be divided into five groups according to their approximate frequency:

(1) Nearly universal (82.5 %): failure to voice z and zh [rosəs] 'roses', [plɛshər] 'pleasure.'
(2) About half (52.1 %): stops for dental spirants [bot] 'both', [idər] 'either.'
(3) Less than half (39—42 %): a): advanced dentals (l, t, d, n), giving 'light' instead of dark effect; b) Norwegian tone-stress pattern, i.e. low pitch under stress and doubling of medial consonants after short vowels [littəl] 'little.'
(4) Uncommon (10—20 %): Norwegian vowels, monophthongal and with displaced quality, esp. o, e, æ, u, i.
(5) Sporadic (under 10 %): Confusions of similar sounds, esp. [j] alternating with [dzh], [v] — [w], [tsh] — [sh], [ʌ] — [a], [ʊ] — [u].

The most interesting conclusion reached by Miss Simley is that the error which is commonly associated with Scandinavian speech in popular humor, the confusion of 'y' and 'j' (Yonny Yonsen), is actually quite rare. The most persistent difficulty of Norwegian Americans is the inability to pronounce a proper z, especially at the ends of words. But even these lingering traces are disappearing, and we may expect that they will be overcome in time. They are limited today almost wholly to those who have grown up in rural Norwegian-American communities.

The dialect of English heard by the immigrants from their midwestern neighbors was of course the common vulgate of the rural regions. This is a remarkably uniform dialect throughout the region investigated, though with local variations in vocabulary. To any one who is familiar with present-day midwestern, however, it is striking to hear from the lips of older American-Norwegian speakers certain sounds and forms which are now uncommon in Wisconsin English. The loanwords adopted in an earlier period reflect a state of the language that is gone. Other forms, though they may be common enough, are at least not a part of standard American English. Some of these will be listed here in order to give a picture of the kind of English which exerted its influence on the speech of the early immigrants, especially in Wisconsin.

(1) Pronunciations

cordeen 'accordion'

ager 'ague'[35]

whippletree 'whiffletree'

injine 'engine'

git 'get'

spile 'spoil'

figger 'figure'

punkin 'pumpkin'

barel 'barrel'

paster 'pasture'

fasset 'faucet'

fills 'thills'

crost 'across'

overhalls 'overalls'

sig 'sick' (verb)

hosspower 'horsepower'

gool 'goal'

[a] for [ɔ] in watermelon, off, automobile.

(2) Words

squire 'judge' (esp. justice of the peace)

horn v. 'to shivaree' (only in Koshkonong and Iola); the term is common in New York, but has

not been reported from Wisconsin.[36]

buttery 'pantry'

two shillings 'quarter'

stoop 'porch'

tavern 'hotel'

travel 'walk' (this meaning is inferred from a widespread usage of the lw. *travla;* it has not been reported for AmE, but is very common in England, according to Wright's *English Dialect Dictionary*, and cannot be easily explained by any Norwegian usage)

jag 'short load of hay'

bent 'section of a barn'

citron 'watermelon'

the off and on horse 'right' and 'left'

spider 'skillet'

pieplant 'rhubarb'

salt rising 'home made yeast'

meeting 'a religious service'

yankee 'any American'

The loanwords which are based on these American usages are generally so thoroughly assimilated that the speakers are unable to identify them as English words, since they often do not occur in their own English. This is true, e.g. of buttery, which some speakers have described as the Norwegian word, in contrast to pantry. A number of the words listed above can be traced back to New York and western New England, where the American settlers of early Wisconsin originated.[37]

5. *Teaching Texts.*

Not all the immigrants remained satisfied with the kind of English they could pick up by oral contact. In the mid-seventies Norwegian-American publishers found it profitable to meet the demand for books of instruction specially prepared for their countrymen. O. M. Peterson's *100 Timer i Engelsk* was subtitled 'directions on how to learn to read, speak and write the English language in six months.'[38] Published in Chicago in 1874, when the second wave of Norwegians had just rolled in, this went through many editions and was certainly a great improvement on the earlier books published in Norway.[39]

The same could not be said of the one that appeared in the same city five years later, entitled *Den lille Amerikaner, en lærer og tolk for skandinaverne i Amerika.*[40] This was probably a reprint of a work appearing in Norway many years earlier, and showed complete unsuitability for American use. The author seems to have been innocent of any knowledge of American English, for he recommends phrases like these: 'Whence do you come? What o'clock is it? Pray, strike a light. I should be glad if it were situated on a salubrious spot of ground, and did not lie in a marshy soil.' The prize, however, is his discussion of the soil: 'It must be dunged now and then. I have a mind to drain this marsh and make a meadow of it. What corn do you sow this year? Summer corn, that will soon sprout, wheat, barley, oats and pease.' The pronunciations suggested are highly misleading, e.g. It iss teim to reis (It is time to rise).

A third textbook, published in 1882, also in Chicago, was entitled *Praktisk Lærebog i det engelske Sprog, med fuldstændig Udtalebetegnelse* (Practical Textbook in the English Language, with complete indication of pronunciation). It claimed to be 'a reliable guide for beginners, immigrants or others, who in a short time wish to teach themselves to read, write, and speak the English language.'[41] The anonymous author criticises earlier textbooks for their exclusive devotion to English conditions and for their stereotyped sentences. In this book the pronunciation was based on Webster's dictionary and the contents were intended to be practical and give information about American conditions. In spite of this, the pronunciation of such words as *half* (hahf) and *hot* (haatt) are entirely British (or Eastern); and he makes no distinction in transcription between *z* and *s*.

In 1882 the market was still further enriched by Allan Sætre's *Engelsk og skandinavisk Konversationsbog*, which claims to be a collection of daily expressions, 'particularly intended for the Scandinavian servant girl and the American housewife.'[42] It is chiefly an alphabetical list of E and N equivalents with some stilted conversations of a domestic nature. Curious, in view of the 'Scandinavian' in the title, is a conversation in which a girl applying for a position says she is Swedish, but the mistress replies that she wants a Scandinavian girl, after which the girl has to explain that there are three nationalities in Scandinavia. Just why a Swedish girl would be talking DN to her mistress is not made clear.

An entirely new departure is made in Martin Ulvestad's *Selvhjelp i engelsk* of 1892.[43] The author advises immigrants to learn English as quickly as possible, since 'knowledge of English is the first condition for success in America.' Apparently believing that teaching is made less deadly by humor, he devotes practically all his space for reading materials to current anecdotes from the so-called humorous magazines of his time. Ulvestad followed it up in 1895 with a large dictionary based on an earlier work published in Copenhagen by Svend Rosing.[44] He added pronunciations from Webster, with 'short' *a* and *o* still having their Eastern values, though he granted in a footnote that *a* becomes *æ* in 'the Western United States.' Ulvestad's dictionary was certainly the largest and most useful English-Norwegian one published in this country. The last was a pocket dictionary by Haldor J. Hanson, first appearring in 1909, entitled *English-Norwegian-Danish dictionary*.[45]

If the learner of English wanted still more textbooks, he was required to import them from Norway, though these rarely showed even the slightest accommodation to American conditions or American English. Perhaps educated Norwegians of that period generally shared the opinion expressed by Johan Schrøder in 1867 concerning American speech: 'That the breath of life was blown into us not through the mouth, but through the nostrils, is proved by the nose of the true American. When he speaks, he allows the greatest possible stream of air to pass out through this channel instead of following the words through the mouth. In Europe this nasal sound is called "snuffling" and is regarded as an unpleasant natural defect. In America it is fashionable and natural to snuffle. The nose serves the American not only for blowing, but also as a safety valve through which in the course of speaking he can empty his brain of its excess mental steam.'[46]

If this attitude to American English was at all common among the more educated immigrants, we can understand why they sometimes had more difficulty adjusting themselves than their humbler brethren. Professor Thrond Bothne once made the comment that common folk from the country or the towns of Norway generally learned English faster and better than those who had studied English in school in Norway.[47] But then this may have been only a reflection of old-fashioned methods and inadequate textbooks, such as many of those here described.

6. *The Bilingual Situation.*

While the learning of English thus went on, slowly but surely encroaching on the domain of Norwegian, a relatively stable situation had been achieved in the larger settlements. Norwegian had been established as the language of the family, the church, and the neighborhood, spoken to all who showed any inclination to speak it back, and carrying with it a fund of wit and wisdom from the native land. English, on the other hand, was the language spoken to outsiders, those with whom the immigrants were required to deal commercially and officially, in school and larger social groups. This situation persisted to the turn of the century, and had hardly begun to show important signs of deterioration before the outbreak of World War I. This was the truly bilingual period. But it was a special kind of bilingualism, in which the advantages were all on the side of the language that was being learned.

The conclusion emerges that the learning of English took place precisely in those fields where American culture had the most to offer that was new and unfamiliar. Norwegian became the vehicle of all that was old and familiar, traditional and precious; but it lacked the power of renewal which a living language must have. The group was not large enough nor isolated enough to have possibilities for internal innovation, and the developments in Norway were too remote to be influential. Instead of developing by constantly learning more of their own language, as they would have done at home, they were compelled to develop by learning a new language. In becoming bilinguals they were so to speak grafting a new stem on an old tree, and their further development proceeded partly in obedience to the habits of the old language, but much more in response to those of the new.

Chapter 4.

THE CONFUSION OF TONGUES.

> My friend, if I remember rightly,
> There is a tribe in far Morocco,
> Orangutangs amid the jungles,
> Who have no singers or interpreters.
> Their language sounded malebaric!
>
> *Ibsen, Peer Gynt, Act 4 (1867)*.

The learning of English proved to have a quick and disastrous effect on the Norwegian spoken among the immigrants. We have many testimonials from the very earliest years of settlement to the 'corrupting' influence of English. Ole Munch Ræder, the Norwegian jurist whose comment was quoted earlier, aptly described the process as a failure to keep the two languages apart.[1] But he was badly informed when he suggested that the Norwegians 'seemed to have a special knack for it'; it was only that he knew them best. His examples were accurate enough, and his observations can be confirmed by studying the letters which some of the earliest pioneers wrote to their relatives and friends at home.[2] They must often have been difficult to decipher for those who knew no English. A Norwegian rural poet who published a poem in 1853 about returned emigrants declared that

Dæ døm snakka va vont aa   What they said was hard to grasp;
  skjønne,   They mixed it so with English.[3]
de va saa my Engelst ibland.

The confusion of patterns which resulted in what is popularly known as 'mixing the languages' is so prominent a feature of all immigrant life in America that it has excited endless comment both inside and outside the immigrant group.

In this chapter we shall make a detailed study of the social responses called forth by 'mixing.' This will include the comments of outside observers, which range from the amused to the indignant and very rarely show any understanding of the immigrant's peculiar situation. It will include also the more or less conscious responses of the speakers themselves, those in which they have given expression to certain attitudes toward their own behavior. We shall examine the responses with an eye to answering the question of whether 'mixing' fulfills a social function. Since the chief function of language is communication, we may ask whether the confusion of two linguistic patterns also leads to confused or inadequate communication.

1. *Norwegian Observers Speak their Mind.*

Those who were freshly arrived from Norway, particularly if they were well educated men, seem to have agreed from the beginning that the speech of their countrymen in America was both barbarous and confusing. Clergyman Olaus Duus shook his head at what he heard in Scandinavia, Wisconsin, and wrote to his father in Norway in 1859, 'Such Norwegian as they talk here! It is so mixed with English phrases that I was quite annoyed when I first arrived. You never hear the word "hvedemeel" any more, just *flour;* never "gjerde," but *fence;* never "lade," but *barn;* never "stald," but *stable*.'[4] His colleague Johan Storm Munch, who served parishes around Wiota, Wisconsin, from 1853 to 1859 before returning to Norway, wrote in his memoirs: 'The language of the Norwegians over there is famous. They make haste to mix it with English, and the more they can mix the language, the better.' The good pastor was particularly astonished that 'they also freely decline and conjugate the English words with Norwegian endings, not rarely with *dialect* endings, whereby the most amusing combinations arise.' He exemplifies the practice with such forms as *filatn* 'the fields,' *fencom* 'to the fences,' *at fide piggom* 'to feed the pigs.' In concluding he remarks that many more examples could be found of this 'gibberish' (Kaudervelsk).[5] A rather severe critic of America, the journalist Johan Schrøder, published a description of his emigrated countrymen in which he declared that he often found it difficult to understand them when they 'mix Norwegian and English words'.[6]

Norwegian writers of fiction have occasionally introduced emigrants or their descendants, usually for humorous purposes, and made merry with their language, which they pepper with English expressions in the most unlikely ways. The earliest example of this practice is probably a story by the popular writer Harald Meltzer from 1860 entitled *Til og Fra Amerika* (To and From America).[7] The narrator visits an American settlement of Norwegians and there meets a character from Hadeland: 'We discovered a tendency in this good man, which later grew more and more visible, or rather audible, namely a zealous effort to mix into his speech as many English words as possible. He had *settled* land and was now a *farmer*. He travelled on the *railway* and on the *steamboat*. He shot *woodpigeons* and *wild-ducks*. He had *two dogs* and *three boys*. He sowed 22 *bushels* of wheat annually and drove seven *miles* an hour with his horses. In short, he was so far along that it clearly would not take many years before he was a perfect American, and the children were obviously following their father's example.'[8]

The opinion expressed by several of these writers, that the emigrants mixed in as many English words as possible, became the basis of the classic portrait drawn by the Norwegian satirist Jacob Hilditch in his *Trangviksposten*. This satire of small-town life in Norway would not be complete without a returned emigrant, a Mr. Jens Træby, who impresses everyone with his inevitable American fur coat. But the language he uses is a true hodge-podge, without rhyme or reason; his first words to the editor of the local paper are: 'Do you gjenkjende mig?' (Do you recognize me?). Another sample sentence is this impossible product: 'Well jeg started deirekt for the far West, hvør jeg hæd en Ønkel i Wisconsin, han hæd e Farm hvør jeg tuk tu vork...'[9] While this is not the way emigrants usually talk, it may serve as an example of how Norwegian observers think they talk. The writer Bjørnson introduced a returned emigrant in his novel *Magnhild* (1877); he de-

scribed her as speaking three languages, viz., English, country dialect, and some standard Norwegian. But in her conversation he
presented her as mingling these in wild disarray: 'My dear! I am
here bærre for di skuld. I wil seje deg, at all those years I have
tænkt meget på denne stund. My dear Magnhild... I have spoken
norsk bærre a couple of months only og kan inkje tale godt...
What hejter'n? Grong. Have you tålå ve'n?...Vil du rejse mæ
meg op gjønno lande in this — i denne vogn, Magnhild?...Dine
rum up stairs are they to be let?'[9a] In a modern detective thriller
an American of Norwegian extraction is made to talk as follows:
'God damn — min nevø! such rascal — og jeg som tenkte på å ta
that crook in my business — in my business! Never!...You kan
la henne gå.'[10] It is significant that all of the writers here cited
attribute the use of the pronoun *you* to their speakers, something
which has at least not occurred in the experience of this writer,
and which he considers improbable *a priori* for reasons that will
be developed later.

Some observers have included a note of regret in their comments,
with a more or less pointed admonition to their emigrated countrymen to mend their linguistic ways. In 1893 the Reverend H. J. S.
Astrup wrote that in 'some places they have accustomed themselves
to mix the languages quite terribly. It is not pretty to hear a conversation like the following: "You'll have to *jumpe fencen, krosse
fila,* and follow *roaden.*" If this ever comes before the eyes of my
friends in Illinois and other places where such things go on, I hope
they will not be offended if I say that it would be even more pleasant
to enjoy their hearty hospitality, their "pie" and their "sas," if
they would make an effort to do somewhat less of this "mixing."
It reminds one a little of "mixed pickles."'[11] A writer of Valdres
dialect, O. K. Ødegaard, issued a similar admonition to his emigrated dalesmen; he expressed his admiration of their success in
maintaining their Norwegian speech, but could not refrain from
adding 'that I have also heard a few who, on their visits home,
have mixed their Valdres dialect with American words and expressions, even in the wrong places. This is sad to hear for one with an
ear for his native tongue; it is sad to see a man making himself
small when he thinks he is making himself big.'[12] The theological
professor Absalon Taranger wrote in 1925, after a visit to America,

'It cannot be denied that the Norwegian-American written and spoken language is nearly always polluted by English words and expressions. And the Norwegian-American pronunciation of Norwegian is harsh and offensive to the Norwegian ear.'[13]

In sharp contrast with these loving-severe admonitions is the all-out criticism of journalist Thoralv Klaveness, who in 1904 lighted into 'that which first attracts a stranger's attention, because it has both a comic and an unpleasant effect: the language. It is frightful, particularly in the interior. Strictly spoken, it is no language whatever, but a gruesome mixture of Norwegian and English, and often one does not know whether to take it humorously or seriously. ...What have I not seen in letters of this Norwegian-American volapük! They could make even the strongest nerves shudder! ...Now there would be no objection if this strange tongue, as yet undiscovered by the learned, were spoken to Americans. ...But the sad fact is that it is used in communication among countrymen. In other words: Norwegians often use for mutual communication a language that they do not master. Their own language they do not seem to consider good enough.'[14]

It seems to be the almost unanimous opinion of educated visitors from Norway that the emigrants' treatment of Norwegian is either comical or offensive. They appear to think that the emigrants adopt English words as a matter of prestige, as an expression of scorn for the mother tongue. Their efforts to imitate it show that they think it is done in a haphazard way, without rhyme or reason, resulting in a hash or gibberish which may be compared with the chattering of orangutangs, a comparison hinted at by Ibsen in the passage from Peer Gynt quoted at the head of this chapter. The contemporary poet Herman Wildenvey, who spent some time among his countrymen in Brooklyn, refers to their speech as 'a linguistic crazy quilt.' He specifically stated that 'usually there are no laws of language among the city dwellers here.'[15] The laws he appears to be thinking of are the laws of rhetoric and style which are applicable to well-established standard languages in the centers of modern civilization. They are certainly not linguistic laws, for as we shall see, there are underlying regularities in the behavior of bilingual speakers which determine their linguistic expression, and which certainly deserve the name of laws if any statements about language do. The view that immigrant language is a comical gibberish is hardly based upon any real understanding either of immigrant life or the nature of language.

Among the small number of Norwegian observers who have perceived this fact we may single out the Reverend S. Sondresen, who spent the years from 1890 to 1911 as a pastor among the immigrants. His little book on the linguistic development of Norway, cited below, is evidence that he understood more than most people do of the nature of linguistic behavior. In a study of the Norwegian-Americans published many years after his return to Norway, he devoted a few pages to a discussion of the speech of his one-time parishioners. The conclusion at which he arrived was that 'many unthinking judgments have been passed on the poor Norwegian-Americans for their language-mixing.' He declared roundly that the mixing was 'not done in order to be affected, but came so naturally that one simply does not notice it. Even we pastors and others who might regard ourselves as "cultured" often fall into this sin of "mixing."' He turned to his countrymen at home and said, 'It is easy enough for us here in Norway to smile at these words and expressions; but when one lives among these people and learns to understand the circumstances under which they live, one will forgive them.'[16]

Sondresen's views are the exception rather than the rule. There can be no doubt that the rise of a special American type of Norwegian created a barrier between the emigrant and his non-emigrated countrymen.

2. *The Newcomer's Embarrassment.*

Those emigrants who arrived in an AmN community after its characteristic speech forms had been established often had a considerable adjustment to make. They had naively assumed that their countrymen would speak the same language as they, and were often shocked to discover the differences. Here are some characteristic samples from the reports of informants. A Madison man who arrived as an immigrant in 1911 called up his brother from the station; he got the following directions: 'Du skal taka stritkarsen til Schenk's Corner' (take the *streetcar* to Schenk's *Corner*). He had no idea of what kind of vehicle this might be, so he decided to walk.[17] An immigrant who came to a farm in Crawford County, Wisconsin was told by his uncle to 'ta håltradn og gå ne i pastre ette hestadn' (take the *halters* and go down in the *pasture* after the horses). When the lad registered complete lack of comprehension, another uncle said, 'Remember he's a newcomer.' So he translated it for him, 'Ta grimadn og gang ut i havnegangen ette gampadn.'[18]

A late comer to the Coon Valley settlement in Wisconsin reported on some of the troubles she had had as a newcomer: 'They told me to go over to the *fence*, chase the cattle away from the *fence;* but I had no idea what a 'fence' was, so I walked in the wrong direction.'[19] Several informants have spoken of their difficulties in understanding the terms of everyday life used in the settlements on their first arrival. One of the most detailed is the following by an immigrant of 1908, who found himself in a farming community of western Wisconsin where the dialect of his native valley was universally spoken: 'There they were, talking genuine Suldal, and they all talked alike. But whether they talked Suldal or they talked French made no difference at all to me, for I did not understand a word. They were chatting about 'baren' and 'fila' and 'sheden' and 'malkeshantie', 'vinnmøllo' and 'pompo' and all those words. I couldn't understand a single thing they were talking about, even though I understood about ninety per cent of all the words they used. I couldn't understand it because all the names were half or wholly English. They talked about 'mekar' (makes) and 'fiksar' (fixes) and so forth... But when I went to church, the preacher preached so fine, you see, just as they did in Norway, and I understood every word.'[20]

Just such an experience must have befallen O. E. Rølvaag on his arrival in South Dakota, for he reproduces it in his first literary effort, *Amerika-breve*.[21] His central figure Per Smevik is awakened on his first morning in his uncle's South Dakota farm home by the call to 'breakfast.' He has no idea of what this might be, unless it were the syrup on the breakfast table, which is the only object whose name he does not know. After a number of such experiences, he wrote home that 'this practice makes it harder for me than you could imagine. When uncle asks me to do something, I stand there like a fool, a regular numbskull, and understand nothing.'

Everyone agrees, however, that the newcomers learned fast. Even though they had their troubles at first, they quickly accepted the new lingo and practiced it with due diligence. Some of those who had grown up in the AmN dialect even felt that the newcomers went too far in their readiness to adopt English terms. They were so eager that they overshot the mark; a woman born in the Kosh-konong settlement averred that where she and her family used the Norwegian *jolegaoena* 'the Christmas presents,' the newcomers sometimes said *krismespresense!*[22] A man from Lodi, Wisconsin, told of a newcomer girl who was heard exclaiming to a friend whom she met outside the church: 'Eg va so glad når eg luk ju koming.'[23] In spite of such difficulties, however, it appears that they were quickly assimilated, and accepted the norms of the new community. In the meanwhile they acted as something of a brake on the anglicizing tendencies of the older group.

3. *Bilingual Norms.*

It is time now that we consider the question of whether we can properly speak of linguistic norms or laws in the bilingual community, and in what sense they may be said to exist. Because of the constant pressure of English there is a more rapid flux than in older and more stable communities. Any norms that exist are certainly more fluid than in an isolated rural dialect in an older country or in a standardized literary language. But the careful observer of AmN life cannot help but discover the remarkably high degree of uniformity of practice with respect to the adoption of English materials in the various settlements. There is individual variation, of course, but the variation cancels out in a common usage which makes it possible for everyone to be understood.

The writer has to some extent tested this uniformity by subjecting a number of speakers to oral questioning on their usage with respect to specific words. His questionnaire included several hundred items to which the response might be either Norwegian or English. A comparison of the results for different informants shows a remarkable <u>uniformity</u> of response. For example, three informants from Coon Valley, Wisconsin, differed on only 30 words.

Informant	11C2	11C1	11C4
Norwegian	17	7	5
N and E		4	1
English		19	24
No response	13		

The most 'puristic' informant, 11C2, was also a speaker of standard Norwegian with a strong opposition to 'mixing'; but even so she was unable to produce Norwegian words for more than seventeen of the doubtful thirty.

Another group of informants (all speaking the same dialect) were compared for a specific number of items in the questionnaire for which comparable responses were available. There were 231 words in this investigation; five speakers of Sogn dialect in two different communities agreed in 165 instances, or 72.4 % of the cases, in giving a Norwegian word for 47 and an English word for 118. The remaining 69 on which they disagreed were divided as follows:

Informant	17Q2	17Q3	17Q4	12Q1	17Q1
Year of Birth	1873	1890	1886	1884	1874
N responses	42	39	32	31	28

The difference between the most 'puristic' and the least is only fourteen words, or 6 % of the vocabulary investigated. Nor is the difference directly related to the age of the informants. It appears, however, that 17Q2 and 17Q3 were less active in their use of Norwegian than the others. One informant commented that she used more Norwegian words in talking to older people, by which of course she meant people who used more Norwegian.[24] But the relatively narrow margin of difference from speaker to speaker suggests that we may have to agree with the informant who said: 'They will all be more or less the same in mixing: if they can't think of the word, they will use the English.'[25]

We may conclude from these examples that there is considerable agreement among speakers of AmN on the words adopted from English, and that any variation that may take place falls within a limited number of words which everyone in the community understands in either language. As we shall see later, there is also a common practice in the technique of adaptation which these words undergo in becoming Norwegian.

One of the forces making for the relative uniformity of speech is the resistance to excessive adoption of English terms by some members of the community. The force of what we may call linguistic purism in the community is hard to measure, but its presence has been reported by some informants. A Koshkonong woman reported that her father thundered against the use of *travla* from English *travel* instead of the proper Norwegian *gao;* when others spoke of *joists*, he clung to the Norwegian *svidl*.[26] Another Koshkonong woman asserted that her parents never mixed, 'if they knew it.'[27] Such awareness was not universal, for I have had informants who did not become conscious of the English element in their speech until my questions forcibly called their attention to it. But a number of informants have shown by their unwillingness to answer questions which required English responses that they felt a certain sense of shame at not being able to remember the Norwegian word.

Children growing up in the bilingual community were often not aware of the situation until someone called their attention to it. Professor Nils Flaten, who grew up in Goodhue County, Minnesota, wrote that he was ten years old before he realized that such words as *påtikkele, stæbel,* and *fens* were 'not Norse, but mutilated English.'[28] But the point is that he did realize it during his growing years. A Koshkonong woman had the same fact brought home to her by a Norwegian storekeeper when she was still a child. She told him, 'Je vil ha den disjen' (I want that dish). He replied, 'I thought you were Norwegian.' Only then did she realize for the first time that she had used an English word in a Norwegian context.[29]

It seems probable that the greater mastery of English by most members of the second generation led to a puristic reaction in their use of Norwegian. Their knowledge of English made them more conscious of the presence of originally Norwegian words in their elders' speech. After a discussion of the various words for 'rug', 'carpet', and the like, an American-born informant said: 'There are a lot of these words I just can't use in Norwegian.'[30] Another declared that 'to use *keep* for *ha* would make me feel ashamed, as if I were blundering.'[31] A third made the flat statement that 'people who are born in this country try to keep their Norwegian pure.'[32] The explanation is suggested by one informant who said, 'We don't talk enough Norwegian to say "yard".'[33] Paradoxical as this may sound, it is simply due to the fact that the completely bilingual speakers felt no hesitation at switching to English when their Norwegian vocabulary was inadequate. Rather than incorporate their lws. singly, they found it easier to switch to the other language.

4. *The Awareness of 'Mixing'.*

In any case there is no doubt that most adult speakers of AmN are aware of the need for resorting to English in order to fill out their Norwegian vocabulary. In his interviews with them the writer has noted many remarks like the following: 'We mix so much English into our speech…it's terribly mixed up…we switch over so easily…you know we have to mix, for nobody can remember all the Norwegian words…'[34] They comment somewhat scornfully on their own language as 'Yankee-Norwegian.' Even more characteristic is its localization in some neighboring American state: Iowa-norsk, Illinois-norsk, Minnesota-norsk.[35] Possibly because most of his material was collected in Wisconsin, the writer has not happened to hear of 'Wisconsin-Norwegian'; but he has been told of 'Westby-Norwegian' by residents of that town.

The awareness of many speakers of AmN of what they are doing and the feeling of some that they ought not to be doing it does not prevent them from actually doing it when necessity arises. Even the unwillingness of some informants to give an English response to the writer's inquiry about specific words does not in the least mean that they would avoid the use of that word in a natural situation where it was demanded. But it is typical that many pay their respects to the decencies by making some facetious or apologetic remark when introducing a particularly flagrant example of English.

Among the typical phrases used in this situation are *som me seier* 'as we say' (or *dei* 'they'), or *me kaller* 'as we call it,' often with the addition of 'in English' or 'in this country.' The following examples are part of a large collection: Eg ha hatt alle — ka di kalla 'taonsjips-embeder' (I have had all — what they call 'township offices').[36] Kek so dai kadla her i Amerika (cake, as they call it here in America).[37] Då e vart distsjardsja som di seie frå armeen (when I was discharged, as they say, from the Army).[38] ..Tok opp som me sæie kålæksjen (took up, as we say, a collection).[39] Så har vi lånsosjel· dai kalla pao ængelsk (then we have a lawn social as they call it in English).[40] Some find more original ways of saying it, calling it 'jænkispråk' (Yankee language); or saying, 'da e vi jenkiar att' (then we're Yankees again); or adding, 'Dæ engelsk, men vi snur litt på dæ (it's English, but we twist it a little).[41] The idea of twisting appears also in these remarks: 'Kattaren — dai ha rængt da'; 'reparen — di ha krengt da te sjøle' (the 'cutter' — they have twisted this; the 'reaper' — they fixed this up themselves).[42]

A common whimsy is to apologize for one's use of an English word by pretending it is really Norwegian: 'Ain jænkinabo so me saie no pao gott norsk' (a 'Yankee' neighbor as we say in good Norwegian).[43] After using an English word, one informant commented 'Da vert no purketysk' (that gets to be pig German).[44]

The informant who has been put to the test by being asked what he says for this or that shows in many cases a deliberate effort to avoid the English word. This appears in some cases where the Norwegian word comes as an afterthought, after he has already given the English word. When the Norwegian word comes to mind first, it is felt as a triumph. Dei svella opp — trotna mao eg vel seia (they swelled up — 'trotna' I suppose I should say).[45] Silingen — på ril nosk æ dæ læmen (the ceiling — in real Norwegian it's 'læmen').[46] En røvver — elv [er] sjire norsk (a river — 'elv' is the pure Norwegian).[47] Hanklæ — dem sier taol mæst ('handklæ' — they say 'towel' mostly).[48] Pao vossamaol kadla mi da fjos, hær kadla mi da barne (in the Voss dialect we call it 'fjos', here we call it 'barn').[49] In these cases we may take it for granted that in most natural situations the speaker would use the English word. As a Spring Prairie informant said after he had uttered the word 'town treasurer': 'Da skulle vel vå pao nårsk, taon-kasserar, men da e nett so atte da inkje høve gått te saia da' (I suppose it should have been in Norwegian, 'town-kasserar,' but it just doesn't seem to fit so well to say that).[50]

The phrases which speakers use to set off some of their loans from English are comparable to the use of quotation marks in writing. Self-conscious speakers may sometimes use the phonetic device of a slight hesitation pause before the word. This is even more common before a *switch*, which is the term used here to designate a clean break between the use of one language and the other. Such switches rarely occur within a single breath group; it is generally necessary to break the breath group by a pause. An example is the sentence: 'Da venter di på atte di ska få — "treat"' (then they expect to get a — 'treat').[51] The dash stands for a momentary hesitation, followed by a single word in English. Switching is done with such frequency and ease by many speakers that we may regard it as typical for certain stages in the bilingual process. Switching is different from borrowing, in that the two languages are not superimposed, but follow one another.

Examination of a few typical recordings made of such speakers shows that the leading factors in switching are the need of quoting English-speaking people and of using English terms which it is not desired to adapt to Norwegian. A recording of a Beaver Creek informant lasting about fifteen minutes shows four switches, each time suggested by quotations from English, but sometimes persisting beyond the quotes.[52] An Iola recording of about the same length shows four switches also: (1) to show he can speak English; (2) to describe an illness of his pastor; (3) to describe certain symptoms of his own health; and (4) to quote an English-speaking person.[53] He ends his first switch in the middle of a sentence: 'But when it comes right down to it — nårst æ bæst for mæi' (Norwegian is best for me). Anecdotes are often told in this way: they start in English, but as the narrator gets under way, he switches back to Norwegian in order to lead up to the untranslatable and inimitable punch line.

Speakers will often be quite unaware that they are switching back and forth; they are accustomed to having bilingual speakers before them, and know that whichever language they use, they will be understood.

5. *Bilingual Humor.*

The awareness of 'mixing' as a social problem is expressed also in its use as a humorous device. Many good-natured stories are current about the use of English in Norwegian contexts which show that even the ordinary speakers of AmN sometimes find their own language amusing. They do not find it funny in the same way that outsiders do, but there are two ways in which their language amuses them. We shall give examples of this under two headings: the exaggerated mixture, and the bilingual pun.

The fact that many speakers notice mixture only when it is exaggerated is in itself evidence that there is a certain norm. Informants have mentioned certain individuals who amused them by using loanwords which they themselves did not use, e.g. one who laughed because a friend of hers said 'garden' for Norwegian *have*.[54] Stories were told in the Waterloo Ridge community in Iowa about a man who used English and Norwegian words side by side, e.g. 'Dæ sprang en hårrå-ræbbit åver råden-trækken-væien; så bynte filleponien kikke-spænne-slå' (A *hårrå*-rabbit ran across the road-track-*væi*; then the good-for-nothing pony began to kick-*spenne-slå*).[55] Most of the anecdotes told about mixing are of this unusual or exaggerated variety, and these form the basis of some of the samples found in print. They are characterized by a great step-up of frequency in loanwords over that which is normal in everyday speech; this may be done by picking contexts in which loanwords are naturally high and by turning into English every wordthat any speaker might conceivably anglicize, and even some which they wouldn't. The results are unreal, but funny even to an AmN speaker by virtue of the exaggeration.

One sample will suffice; it may be compared with the authentic samples of AmN speech in Chapter 19. There are no obviously incorrect forms in it, but the passage as a whole is unlikely; loans from English are italicised:

Han Ola, som *lever kross raaden* fraa mei, hadde *bæd løkk* igaar, saa dæ var *funny*, han itte *lusa* live sit. Han skulle *hala* noen *pigga* te *toun* me *kultan*. Dæ var *keind af muddy*, aa *æ regla blizzard*, som *mæka* saa mye *nois*, atte han itte *notisa træne*, som kom *runnandes* me full *spid*. Han var *putty klos* te *trække*, da dei *visla*, aa *kultan*, som er *skittlis* ta sei, blei *skærd* aa *jumpa* i *ditsen*, *bøsta leinsa*, *kikka* ut *dasjbore*, *pulla* ut *bolten* i *tanga* aa hadde et *rægla smæsop* for ei *runnaway*. Han Ola *futta* hjem *kross fila*, *just about* saa fort som *kultan runne* etter *raaden*. *Mississen* aa *kidsa* ble *keind af* nervøs, men *komforta* sei me dei *aidien*, at det var Guds *løkk*, ingen var *killa* eller *hørta*.[56]

The *bilingual pun* results when a word is adopted which happens to coincide in sound with a previous Norwegian word of quite different meaning, e.g. English clean > AmN *klina*, which coincides with Norwegian *klina* 'smear'. At this point one might expect that linguistic confusion could arise, but in practice the difficulty is always solved by context, as with other homonyms. Only when the meanings are grotesquely different and the words can occur in similar contexts does the possibility of humorous confusion arise. Examples are listed below for each of the words that are most commonly found in such jokes.[57] Even these, which have been worked to death by would-be humorists, are usually quite inexact and largely based on spelling rather than sound. Significantly, they are usually presented as having occurred in letters written to Norway; only a person unfamiliar with English could possibly misunderstand the words in question.

barn n. vs. Norwegian barn 'child'; i Amerika så maler dom alle barna røue (in America they paint all the *children* red)[58]; eg myste barn min (I lost my *child*).[59] The lw. is m., the N n., and they practically always differ in phonetic form; besides, the N word yields to *unge* in many dialects. The pun is thus based purely on spelling identity.

car n. vs. Norwegian kar 'man, fellow'; alt dæi behøvde å jøra nå dæi ville ne i byen va å hoppe på ein kar (all they needed to do when they wanted to go to town was to jump on a *fellow*).[60] Here, too, the pun is usually inexact, since most speakers use *kars* for English 'car'.

crop n. vs. Norwegian kropp 'body'; sidste harvest blev min krop ganske liden, men naar jeg faar brækket mere fil, skal jeg kunne sælge saa meget af min krop, at jeg kan klare mig (last harvest my *body* became quite small, but when I get more field broken up, I shall be able to sell enough of my *body* so that I can get along).[61] Most speakers pronounce English crop as 'krapp', not 'kropp'.

cutter n. vs. Norwegian kattar pl. 'cats'; dæi kjørde te kjærka på juledagen me katter (they drove to church on Christmas day with *cats*).[62] The pun is here exact, but quite unusual; the cutter was a type of sleigh commonly used in former days.

grease n. and v. vs. Norwegian gris 'pig' and grisa 'make dirty'; '"Tag Grisen, John, og sæt i Vognen." Hvorpaa Tjeneren, efter en Stund at have seet forundret paa sin Husbond, fjernede sig og kom tilbage med en Gris i Armene.' (Take the grease, John, and put in the wagon. Whereupon the servant, after having looked wonderingly at his master, went away and came back with a pig in his arms).[63] The servant is supposed to be a newcomer, the master an older arrival. Most speakers use the words in these meanings quite unaware of their collision with the Norwegian homonyms.

lose v. vs. Norwegian lusa 'delouse'; often used with *crop* (see above): dei syntes de va harmeli, dei måtte sitta der i fire år å lusa kråppen (they felt it was a shame that they had to sit there for four years *delousing* their *bodies*.)[64] The writer has heard it seriously used in the phrase lusa presten 'lose one's minister'.

river n. vs. Norwegian røver (-ar) 'robber'; døtter hennes sa at lanne doms låg imellem to røvere (her daughter said that their land lay between two *robbers*).[65] The pun is purely a spelling pun, for in speech *river* almost always has short ø, *røvar* long ø.

6. *Confusion of Identity.*

Once the words were adopted and given a form which did not markedly distinguish them from other Norwegian words, it was not always possible for the speakers to identify them as English. They became as much a part of the Norwegian language as those loanwords which had been accepted into the language in previous centuries in the homeland. The effort to distinguish them was hampered by the great number of cognates already existing in the two languages. Even so, a few informants made shrewd observations concerning the ultimate English origin of such well-disguised words as *hyppe* from English whip.[66] But most of them were confused by such authentically Norwegian words as *potet* 'potato', *panne* 'pan', *kløver* 'clover,' *april* 'April,' *mai* 'May'; all of these have been described as English words by one or more informants.[67] The rough-and-ready rule seems to be that when two synonyms or closely similar phonetic forms of the same word are available to the speaker, he identifies the one with the most Norwegian sound as Norwegian. In most cases this works; but the following instances show how it can go astray. Some of them belong to the type discussed earlier (Chapter 3) of English words now gone out of use:

(1) Near synonyms, the first of which was identified as Norwegian, the second as English (though both words are actually from English):

Norwegian	English	
brendi 'brandy'	viski	5H4
brikkstein 'brick'	brikk	5L4
båttri 'buttery'	pentri	14D3
fæm og tjuge sent '25 cents'	kvart	5G1
grusråd 'gravel road'	grevelråd	5G1
horna 'to horn (shivaree)'	sjøverera	10C1
pæne 'pen'	yard	12R1
slua 'slough'	marsh, fen	5G1
stup 'stoop'	porch	5L2
		5H3 (wife); 15P3
tånga '(wagon) tongue'	wægenpol	19A1

(2) Phonetically adapted lws., described as Norwegian (in contrast to English forms of the same): grønnri 'granary' 14D21; guffert 'gopher' 10C1; karter 'cutter' 10C1; kornfil 'corn field' 10C1; lånmovarn 'the lawnmower' 19A1; røvver 'river' 10C1; saverar 'surveyor' 5G1, 5L5; sjøvring 'shivaree' 20C1; skvætil 'squirrel' 10C1.

7. *An Interpretation of 'Mixing'.*

In none of the behavior patterns so far discussed have we seen anything approaching a breakdown of communication. The failure of recent arrivals from Norway to grasp the full significance of AmN speech is similar to that which any speaker of one dialect experiences in having to communicate with speakers of another. The amusement and indignation of some educated observers stems largely from their application of rigid standards of linguistic purity derived from literary and esthetic doctrine. Their shock at finding that their language has had to be adapted to be suitable for American conditions is largely the shock of any linguistic novelty. No native speaker of English feels any esthetic or emotional revulsion over the 'mixed' character of his language, which far exceeds that of most immigrant Norwegian speech. The conclusion by some critics that 'mixing' is an expression of snobbish contempt for the native tongue does not agree well with the fact that the very speakers who borrow are the ones who have clung persistently to the Norwegian language and passed it on to their children. Contempt would rather appear in a refusal to speak the language and an effort to forget it as rapidly as possible.

Reports are sometimes heard of individuals who 'speak no language whatever' and confuse the two to such an extent that it is impossible to tell which language they speak. No such cases have occurred in the writer's experience, in spite of many years of listening to AmN speech. He cannot deny that they might occur, but believes that most of the cases reported are the result of inaccurate observation. He has heard individuals of low-grade intelligence who have larded their Norwegian speech with an excessive amount of English; and Norwegian monolinguals or pre-bilinguals who interpersed Norwegian in their efforts to speak English. There is no reason why pidgin-like sequences could not occur among the immigrants; but they are in no way typical of the AmN community. In a study of 288 letters written by the subscribers to an AmN newspaper, reported on below, he found only two very short, illiterate notes in which a pidginized style occurred.

The fact that neither ridicule nor the admonitions of their betters have stopped the speakers of Norwegian in America from borrowing English patterns should be evidence to support our contention that there is an underlying necessity in the process. In becoming bilingual within the American cultural environment they were forced to modify their Norwegian if they wished to continue using it. At practically every point they maintained the basic phonetic and grammatical structures of their native dialects; but they filled in the lexical content of these structures from the vocabulary of English. This is a time-honored method in all linguistic development, whether bilingual or not. In the immigrant community it was an inevitable part of the assimilation to American life.

As long ago as 1909 this was pointed out by Professor A. A. Veblen (a brother of the famous economist), a mathematician and a connoisseur of Norwegian dialects. After discussing in some detail the reasons for certain loans in the dialects, he concluded: 'Even the most awful Norwegian-American spoken is a completely natural growth and development. Words and phrases owe their being to natural, easily explained circumstances and causes. ...We do not believe that this linguistic confusion is due to scorn of the mother tongue or to any effort to abandon it as quickly as possible so they may get something better and more resplendent instead. There are, to be sure, wretched individuals who are foolish enough to think it a great feat to throw overboard what they have gotten from their ancestors, particularly in something so everyday as language. But it may be doubted that such people have had much to say in the matter. This curious linguistic phenomenon is due quite simply to the fact that it is so easy and practical a way of getting along.'[68]

Our study of the confusion of tongues in the immigrant community has led us to the conclusion that it is not identical with a confusion of communication. The language used may seem barbarous and baffling to the outside observer, but those who join the social group soon discover that they have to follow the customary norm if they wish to be understood. There exists within the group a general sense of purism, which keeps the movement from proceeding too rapidly. Individuals who go too far in the direction of English are laughed at. A special word was coined to make fun of them: they were said to be *engelsk-sprengt* or *yankee-*

sprengt 'anglified' or 'yankeefied', one of the very few original AmN creations. Stories are current about the excesses of 'mixing,' and the speakers show a certain self-consciousness about it when they know that potential critics are listening. But most of them show relatively uniform behavior with respect to the usual loanwords, which means that the adoption of the words leaves the main structure of their Norwegian untouched. They think they are speaking Norwegian, even though they admit it may be a 'Minnesota-Norwegian', and in these contentions they are right. American Norwegian is indeed Norwegian, though we may wish to designate it as a *bilingual dialect* of that language.

In an article published in 1938, shortly after the initiation of these studies, the writer outlined an interpretation which seemed then and still seems to him a broader perspective than the one adopted by the critics previously quoted. The great vocabulary shift of the immigrant was there interpreted as an inevitable accompaniment of his changing personality. 'In learning the new language he was doing more than just acquiring new phrases. He was absorbing a new social and linguistic outlook, and this outlook also influenced his native tongue. ...In all his linguistic floundering we perceive his struggle to achieve again a unified cultural personality. His Norwegian approaches his English, because both are required to function within the same environment and the same minds.'[69] In contrast to the writers who have emphasized the rootlessness of the immigrant, his loss of contact with the old home and inability to find a home in the new, it seemed worth while to point out that for the immigrant the hyphenated group has played the role of a home in passage. 'The social life of his native group has given him a home and a standing in the new nation and has been a solid protection to his mental health.'

These ideas were expanded and suggestively developed by Theodore C. Blegen in his chapter on 'Language and Immigrant Transition' in the second volume of *Norwegian Migration to America*.[70] 'The immigrants,' he wrote, 'did not remain wholly apart from the people they came to — they were not wholly torn off from those they forsook. ...The immigrant neither gave up his old language nor, though he learned some English, did he master the new, but he was nevertheless not left helpless or frustrated.

What he did was to create, by gradual and normal processes of change, adaptation, and growth, something like an intermediate language — Norwegian-American, which combined both languages, broke the shock of his new-world plunge, and on the whole served his needs effectively.... He took the English language into his system, not in a mighty gulp, but bite by bite. He adjusted himself to American ways, not by some instantaneous and magical transformation, but idea by idea.... It appears that what, upon superficial retrospect, has the character of linguistic confusion was in reality a struggle of large numbers of people toward some kind of intellectual, or cultural unity; in this struggle Norwegian-American played a mediating role.'

Chapter 5.

THE GREAT VOCABULARY SHIFT.

> In the case of many words the younger genera-
> tion cannot tell whether they are English or Norse.
> I was ten or twelve years old before I found out that
> such words as *paatikkele* (particular), *stæbel* (stable),
> *fens* (fence) were not Norse but mutilated English
> words. I had often wondered that *poleit, trubbel,*
> *søppereter* were so much like the English words *polite,*
> *trouble, separator*.
>
> *Nils Flaten (1900)*[1]

The process of borrowing was also a process of learning. The
new words did not necessarily represent new objects or experiences,
but they inevitably brought with them new attitudes toward
experience. As the immigrants learned the catchwords of American
culture, they were bound to find them useful, even while they were
still speaking Norwegian. But at the other end of their vocabulary
a loss was simultaneously going on, an atrophy of terms no longer
needed or heard. As old-world customs and topics of conversation
fell away, the words associated with them tended to be forgotten.
Older informants were often eager to dwell on words and expressions which they had heard from their elders, but which they and
their descendants no longer used. Even those who had succeeded in
maintaining a remarkably faithful pronunciation could not escape
the necessity of a lexical adaptation to their environment. In our
study of the causes of borrowing in chapter 14 we shall find that
borrowing is correlated with the learning situations. Those learning
situations were investigated by the writer through his use of a
questionnaire which will be described in chapter 12. It was not

possible to be exhaustive, but representative words were chosen for each human activity in which the rural immigrants and their children were engaged. In this chapter we shall go through these activities and try to show for each one the new words that were introduced and some of the old ones that were lost. We shall again adopt the division into official, economic, and social life, with some more general terms at the end. We shall describe the activities, using the terms most commonly met with among the writer's informants. The loans are given in a N spelling which represents the oldest or most characteristic AmN pronunciation, according to principles explained in Appendix 2. In chapter 20 the reader can also find more information about the forms and frequencies of many of the words used here. Such technical terms as 'loanblend', 'loanshift', and 'loanword' are defined in chapter 15.

1. *The Usages of Official Life.*

The pattern of American administration was firmly founded long before the arrival of N immigrants. They had no choice but to adopt it *in toto.* N words like *herred* and *amt* had to give way to *tæun* (or *tæunsjipp*) and *kæunti*. In Norway *staten* had been 'the state', the government of the whole country; but over here *stat* was extended to mean the American state in which one happened to live. In Norwegian usage America as a whole was a *land*, but alongside this word the AmN speakers might also refer to it as a good *kontri*. They took active part in its political life, something which had been denied to many of them at home, and the whole terminology of American politics rapidly entered their speech: *vota, elekta, eleksjen, rønna for åffis*, and with morphemic substitution *tæunbord* 'town board' and *kjærmann* 'chairman'. The town *tresjerer* was sometimes known as *kasserar*, but this was a rare instance. The N *parti* carried on, but was extended to cover the same ground as E 'party'.

While it was much the same with the judiciary, the N terms seemed to have more vitality in this sphere. *Kort* 'court' replaced *rett* and *jødsj* 'judge' the *dommar*, though a few informants remembered the latter terms as well. The *skvær* 'squire', later known as *jøstis åv de pis*, was a new kind of judicial person. The man who pleaded your case was known as a *låiert*, but a large number of informants also used the N *prokurator* or *sakførar*. A suit was called a *sak* by many, but *låsut* 'law suit' and *kes* 'case' were even more common. A fine was often called a *mult*, as well as a *fein*, but the verb was always E *feina*. Whether in reference to marriages or dogs, the *leisen* 'license' replaced whatever N equivalents there may have been. A loanshift extension came into being for the place where one got it, however, the *korthus* (lit. 'house of cards'). Anyone who committed an offense would risk being put in *jeil*, though some remembered a Norwegian word *slaveri*. ' While the E terms were dominant in each case, the experience of the immigrants with courts before emigration would seem to have been somewhat greater than with politics.

Their first and most important contact with government came in their acquisition of land. By filing a *kleim* they were entitled to a *homstedd* if they would *settla* on the land for a prescribed period and till it. The *settlar* then acquired a *did* 'deed' to the homestead, which became the *heimfarm* or *heimplass* 'home place' because it had been *dida* 'deeded' to the owner by *gåvvemente* 'the government'. The land had been *savera* 'surveyed' by a *saver*, who measured it up into *seksjonar* or square *mil* 'miles'. One fourth of the section was a *kvart*, and smaller still was an *åtteti* 'eighty' or a *førti* 'forty'. All of these measures were N terms, extended in meaning to cover the E equivalents; the same was true of the basic measure, the *fot*. But E furnished the longer units of *jard* 'yard' and *rad* 'rod'. Once the land had been improved, its value was *sessa* 'assessed' by a *sessar*, and *skatt* or *tekks* was levied; here it seems that the N *skatt* was more common than the E word.

In all fields of official activity, the immigrants thus adopted the E terminology, shifting their own terms when possible to agree with E meanings, and retaining only a very small number of their old words, viz. *sak*, *prokurator*, and *skatt*, alongside the E terms.

2. *Economic Pursuits.*

In order to *mæka ei levving* they had to scratch about for a *jabb*, which often meant that they had to join a *kru* 'crew' of some kind and work under a *bas*. The word *boss* was well-known in Norway, but its meaning was here extended to include the same as in AmE. Many Norwegians found work in the *lomberkempar* which were located in the *peinri* 'pineries' or pine forests of northern Wisconsin and Minnesota. Their chief implement, the *sag* 'saw', retained its N name. This kind of work was only a temporary expedient for most of them, however, and as soon as they could, they acquired a *farm* which it never occurred to them to call a *gard*, as they had done in Norway. With the word came all its derivatives, *farma* 'to farm', *farmar*, and *farming*. If they could not afford to buy a farm, they might *renta* and live as *rentarar* 'renters', which entirely replaced the N *leiga* and *leilending*. In the tobacco raising areas of Wisconsin a very common arrangement was to farm on *sjær* 'share'. A person who did this was a *sjærmann* in some places (reported from Dane and Juneau counties), a loan-blend creation based on E *shareman*, but more frequently *sjær-brukar*, a hybrid creation based on N *gardbrukar* 'farmer'. In western states, esp. the Dakotas and Montanas, the *rensj* 'ranch' replaced the farm as a source of income.

The topography of the *kontri* in which they settled was far different from the one they had known before. It was simpler in its contours, and few of the terms used in Norway could be applied to it. There was a *præri*, broken at least in Wisconsin by an occasional *grov* and some *brusk* 'brushland' (a N term of small distribution and rather different meaning). One might call the hills by the N words *bakke* and *haug*, but most of them were *blåffar* 'bluffs' rising above the *røvver* 'river', for which N *elv* entirely vanished. Near the *krikk* (never N *bekk*) and the *leik* (never N *sjø*) there might be a *batom* with a *slu* or a *svamp*. The lake might contain an *ailen* 'island', but more people called it by its N name *øy* and several used the dialect cognate of the E word, *øyland*. Water was secured from a *spring*, which in Norway had referred to a tap, but here issued from the ground. The *dust* that blew in dry years retained its N names among many speakers, such picturesque dialect words having been reported as *gyft*, *gøyva*, *føykja*, *dumba*, *gøyv*, *ryk*, *dust*, and *støv*. But the usual term was the loanword *døst*.[2] The characteristic N word *dal* 'valley' was not forgotten, but *vælli* was also common. They never gave up the word *skog* 'forest', but what they cut down was no longer *tømmer*, 'timber', but *lågg* 'logs'.

The immigrants had known only an old and well-tilled soil, but were now faced with the laborious job of making new land. They had to *brekka* 'break' the soil with a special *brekkingsplog* 'breaking plow', and then *grubba* 'grub' so that it was *klira* 'cleared' of roots. N *rydja* 'clear' was not used; *brekka* was N, but its meaning in America was an extension. Only *plog* remained N; *harv* 'harrow' was also used, but the E *drag* took its place. The other instruments adopted were all E, from the *hå* 'hoe' to the *kåltevetar* 'cultivator' and the *disk* 'disc harrow'. Most speakers preferred to say *digga* 'dig' rather than N *grava*, but instead of *kålteveta* they used N *pløgja* 'plow' about cultivating the corn. Once the soil was prepared, it would be *fensa* with a *relsafens* 'rail fence', consisting of *påstar* 'posts' connected by *splitta rels;* other kinds of *fens* were substituted later on. In this way *filer* 'fields' came into being, where crops were sowed; these were distinct from the *paster* 'pasture' which was not plowed. Then came the time to *planta siden* 'plant the seed', for which few said *frø* or *såkorn* as in Norway. At first it was planted by hand, later by a *drill* or a *sider* 'seeder'. Words like *påst* 'post' and *planta* 'plant' were N, but their AmN meanings were extensions from the N meanings.

It was common enough to refer to the crop as *kroppen,* a N word meaning 'body', but N *avling* was also used. When it was *reip* 'ripe' (for which the informants preferred one of several N words, e.g. *skjær, gjord, mogen* etc.), it was *harvista* (rarely N *hausta*). This was the *harvist,* for which only a few remembered the N *slått* or *skurd.* The grains that in Norway were called *korn* were here called *grøn,* a N dialect usage that became general under influence of English 'grain' and generated numerous new terms, such as *smågrøn* 'small grains', *grønhus* 'grain loft', *grønri* 'granary'. But the individual grains were mostly called by their N names, *bygg* (also *barli*), *havre* (also *ots*), and *kveite* 'wheat'. In the earliest years the N instruments *skjera* 'sickle' and *ljå* 'scythe' were so called, but as harvesting implements they were replaced very early by the American cradle, known among the AmN as *krill.* The process was called *skjera* in Norway, but came to be known as *katta* 'cut' in America. Grain sheaves were often known by their N names of *band* or *bundel* (also anglicized from E bundle as *båndel*), but the American practice of setting up shocks of grain to dry in the field was less common in Norway. The word *sjakk* 'shock' and *sjakka* 'to shock' were in universal use, displacing the N *rauk, skruv,* etc.[3] But the N words for stack and stacking were kept, being wholly analogous with the E: *stakk* and *stekkja.*

With the invention of more elaborate instruments for the harvest, the E terminology continued to expand: the *riper* (also called *ripper, ripar,* and *rippert*) made it possible to *ripa grøne* 'reap the grain'. It was followed by the *bindar* or *sjølvbindar* 'self-binder', loanshifts which were later created anew in Norway for the same instrument. *Treskja* 'thrash' remained Norwegian; the *fœningmylla* 'fanning mill' was a loanblend. The common word for maize being corn, the N used their own *korn* as a loanshift substitute. The words for its parts and its cultivation were drawn from E as follows: *kabb* 'cob', *stokk* 'stalk' (an extension), *haska* (or *harska*) 'husk', *kornsjeddar* 'corn shredder', *kåltevetar* 'cultivator' (also called *kornplog* 'corn plow', a loanshift creation). The raising of tobacco became a N specialty in Wisconsin. The name of the crop remained N *tobakk.* But all the terms of its cultivation came from E: *freim* 'frame', *spir* 'spear', *toppa* 'top' (an extension), *kjura* 'cure', etc. Other crops with E names were *alfalfa, timmoti, fleks* (also N *lin*), *bins.* Peas were spoken of by their N name *erter,* except by those who began selling *pis* to the *fekteri.* Hay also remained N *høy,* but its handling was E; they *mova* 'mowed' it with a *movar* 'mower' which had a *sikkel* on it; then they used a *pitsj-fork* on it to *pitsja* the *høy* into the *høystakk.*

The most important motive power on the early farms were the *uksar* 'oxen' and *hestar* 'horses' which served as draft animals. These animals and the common implements like *vogn* 'wagon', *sele* 'harness', *slede* 'sleigh', *beksel* 'halter' remained N. But the operation of *hitsja upp* 'hitching up' the horses was no longer the N *spenna for. Svepa* 'whip' gave way to the loanblend *hyppa, humul* to *hyppeltre* 'whippletree' and *singeltre* 'single tree', *stong* to *tång* 'tongue' (an extension from the meaning of tong), *skåk* to *fils* 'thills', *køyra* to *driva* 'drive' (extension from meaning of 'drift'), *ok* to *jok* or *jug* 'yoke', *eika* to *spåk* 'spoke'. New E terms were *lombervogn* (lbl. from 'lumber wagon'), *båggi* 'buggy', *kattar* 'cutter', *kløvis* 'clevis', *bæka* 'to back', and *tim* 'team' (replacing N *spand*).

The left animal of a team was called the *nærvon* 'near one' and the right animal the *avon* 'off one'. Oxen were directed by *ha* 'haw' to the left, *jy* 'gee' to the right. Horses were told to go and stop by *gidapp* 'get up' and *ho* 'whoa'. The E distinctions were adopted between ox (AmN *ukse*), a castrated draft animal, bull (AmN *bull*, replacing N *stut*), a breeding animal, and steer (AmN *stir*), a castrated beef animal. As the years passed, the animals became less important for motive power, being replaced by the *trekter*. Other mechanical devices were the *håsspæuer* 'horsepower engine', the *innjein* 'engine', and the *planta* 'plant', all powered by *gæselin*. The *reidskap* 'tools' were also called *tuls*, and included the N *hamar* and *tong* 'pliers' (also *pleiers*). But others were entirely E, such as the *(kro)bar*, the *rensj* (or *rins*) 'wrench' and the *monkerins* 'monkey wrench'.

Other implements involved in general work on the farm included such common instruments with N names as the *kniv* 'knife', *spade* 'spade', *stige* 'ladder', etc. *Fork* was a N word also, but not usually in the sense of E fork which it acquired in America; N *skyffel* was extended to mean 'shovel'. The N *reip* and *taug* competed with *rop* 'rope', while *murstein* generally yielded to the loan *brikk* and the hybrid creation *brikkstein*. The N word for animal fodder *for* became less common than *fid*, and the process was called *fida* 'to feed'. Older persons spoke of taking care of the animals as *stella* or *stulla*, with corresponding nouns *stell* and *stull;* but the noun *kjårs* 'chores' prevailed, and many began to use a new creation *kjårsa* 'to do chores'. The more familiar farm animals all preserved their N names, including the *ku* 'cow', *kalv* 'calf', *gris* 'pig', *høna* 'chicken', *hane* 'rooster'; but occasionally one could hear of *pigsa* 'the pigs', and when eaten, the *høna* might easily become *kjikken*. Of course, the rare N word *kalkun* could not compete with *tørki* (or *tørkis*). Among the various nuisances that came to plague the settlers, the N *grashoppa* was enough like E *grasshopper* to remain, but *miskit* (or *moskit*) displaced *myhank* and *mygg* 'mosquito' except among some of the older speakers. The snake was usually called *orm*, but the new and dangerous varieties like the *ratel* 'rattler' or *rætelsneik* 'rattlesnake' were all E. They were troubled also by *guffert* 'gophers' and *bågg* 'bugs', the worst of which was the *kjens-bågg* 'chinchbug' which ruined their entire wheat crop.

The geography of the farm yard was determined almost entirely by AmE models. General terms like *hus* 'house' and *hytta* 'hut, cabin' remained, but the very material out of which the first ones were built was no longer *tømmer* 'timber', but *lågg* 'logs'. Professor A. A. Veblen described the development of the immigrant barns as follows: 'After the shanty to house the people, came the quarters for the cow, which naturally was called *fjøs*, and as long as they used oxen as draft animals, the oxen, too, could stay in the *fjøs*. But as soon as they got horses, these had to be housed in a *stald* or stable. If separate buildings were built, these were called *fjøs* and *stald* according to Norwegian custom. But if a common building was erected for cows and horses, then a common expression was needed for *fjøs* and *stald;* for this purpose the E word *stable* [stæbel] was conveniently available. But in the wooded areas a distinct building would often be erected for the grain and the feed, with the name of *laave*. But when they reached the point where they could build properly, the *fjøs* and the *stald* and the *laave* came under one roof, in a building with the easy, handy name of *barn*.'[4] Veblen added that the *stæbel* in such a *barn* was often said to be in the *beisment*. Informants have used the word *låve* (or *løa*) for the hayloft in the second story, while the meaning of *stald* has sometimes been extended to the meaning of E *stall*. But the word *fjøs* was rarely heard; those who did remember it, thought of it as equivalent to *stæbel*, while they regarded *låve* as equivalent to *barn*. In modern Norway the word *låve* has been extended to approximate equivalence with *barn*.

Other structures on the American farm were the *sjante* 'shanty' (with loanblending from N *hytte*), *kornkrubba* 'corn crib' (loanshift creation), *grønnri* 'granary', *geradj* 'garage', *seilo* 'silo', *grisepenn* 'pig pen' (and other kinds of pens), and several *sjedd* 'sheds' (*krøtter-* 'cattle', *høy-* 'hay', *masjin-* 'machine' etc.). The modifiers describing the kinds of pens or sheds are all N, but the nuclei are E. A few speakers use such E words as *bækhus* 'back house' (loanblend), but mostly this institution remains N (*dass, vetlahus, vannhus, uthus*, etc.). The family dwelling, which advanced in one generation from *sadhytte* 'sod hut' to *låggsjante* 'log shanty' and then to *freimhus* 'frame house' showed the effect of E models at each turn, but *hytte* and *hus* were substituted for hut and house. A hybrid creation came into being by a crossing of E *living* and N *house*, though there was no E word 'living house'; rather, *levvingshus* must be a reverse substitution from N *våningshus*.

The early word for the yard between the houses was *tun* or *gard*, but these yielded to *jard*. In this yard there might be a *vasstenk* 'water tank', a loanblend, but *vinnmylla* 'windmill' was entirely N. A well was known as a *brunn*, but some called it *well;* later on, a *sistern* 'cistern' was dug. After some years the farmer might fix up a *lån* 'lawn' around his house and buy a *lånmovar* to cut it. The earliest gardens were fruit orchards, which were known by the N word *hage*. But the later vegetable gardens were regularly the E *garden*. New plants, not familiar to the immigrants before emigration, included *grips* 'grapes' (though many informants knew the N words *druer* or *vindruer*), *paiplanta* 'pie plant' (i.e. rhubarb), *panki* 'pumpkin', *vattermylna* 'watermelon', *blækkberis* 'blackberries', *hikrill* 'hickory', and *blakkvalnot* 'black walnuts.' Substitution of N *planta* 'plant' and *not* 'nut' have occurred here, as well as one erroneous substitution of *mylna* 'mill' for *melon*.

The houses were arranged in ways that had little in common with those of Norway. There was a *besment*, which took the place of the N *kjeller* after it had been cemented in. In it was installed a *førnis*. Junk was kept in the *ætik*, which somehow was roomier than the N *loft*. The *freimhus* was constructed of such novel parts as *jåisar* 'joists', *sjingel* 'shingles', and *skrin* 'screens' (in pioneer days they used *miskitbar*, a kind of cheese cloth). The rooms comprised such American distinctions as *beddrom, dainingrom, klasett, båttri* (later known as *pentri*); in front and behind there was either a *stup* (a small, uncovered veranda) or a *portkj*. Only the *levingrom* might bear a N name, *stova*. When the farmer became elegant enough so that he also had a decorative *parler*, some referred to this room as *storstova* or *finstova* (also *finrom, framrom*).[5] Anyone who walked up the stairs was going *uppstærs* (a loanblend); but he walked *ne* 'down' more often than *nestærs* 'downstairs'. Some informants replied that they said they were going *uppå loftet*, but this did not always mean quite the same thing. The floor was usually N *golv*, the wall N *vegg*, but the ceiling was quite often called *siling* instead of *tak* (or *lem, rot*) because some people associated *tak* with the roof only. The E distinction was thus introduced into AmN also.

The furnishings within the house were evenly divided between N and E. Simpler objects like *benk* 'bench', *bord* 'table', *hylla* 'shelf', *seng* 'bed', *speil* 'mirror', *stol* 'chair', and *vogga* 'cradle' remained N, except in some compounds. The N *kommode* (called *dragkista* by some) was used, but was replaced by the more specific *dressar* 'bureau with dressing table' and *bjuro* 'chest of drawers'. Handles on doors were called *dørnabbar* (a reproduction of *door knobs*). Alarm clocks were called *vekkjarklokka* (*vekkjar, ringarklokka*) by some, but mostly it was *larmklokka*. For books they had a N *bokhylla* 'book shelf' or *bokskåp* 'book case', though a few called it *bokkeis*. In more recent times they acquired a *reidio*. On the floor was a *matta*, but this had given way to the more specific E *karpet* and *rågg*. On the windows many still had a *gardina* (in some dialects *umheng*), but the prevailing word was *kørten* (or *kørtens*). Towels were about evenly divided between N *handklæ* and E *tæul*. The bed sheet tended to remain N *laken*, but the bedcoverings were gradually reorganized into the Am pattern: the early, homemade spreads called *kviṭel, åklæ*, and *tæpen* gave way to *kvilt, blenket*, and *beddspredd*, at least after people had begun buying them at the stores.

The rooms were heated by a *ståv*, which replaced N *omn;* but the latter remained as the equivalent of E *oven*, a room in the stove where bread was baked. A draft in the stove was called *dreft*, but also *trekk* and *spjeld*. A. A. Veblen comments on the terms for stove as follows: 'In the pioneer shanties..they got along with a primitive *pais* (fireplace) until they could get hold of the more convenient stove, which was *not* the same as the N *kakkelovn*. The N *komfyr* (cook stove) was not known to the farmers in Valdres before they got both the name and the thing through "culture."'[6] The rooms were lighted by *lys* (*ljos*) 'candles' at first, then by a *karosinlampe* (a loanblend), and finally by an electric *bålb*. In school, home, and church there were *sitar* 'seats' which might have been either a *stol* 'chair', a *benk* 'bench' or a *sæte* 'seat' in Norway, but handily gathered under the E term in this country.

The immigrants quickly took after their Am neighbors in the matter of dress.[7] They put on *overols* and dressed their women in *katten*. For more formal wear they could retain their N *vest*, but the N *frakk* or *trøya* did not exactly correspond to the E *kot*, and so the latter prevailed, together with the heavier *overkot*. Many garments were spoken of in N by some, but grew more and more E, as in the case of *snøreliv* which changed to *korsett*, *kåpa* to *klok*, *halsklut* to *nekktai*, *tøffel* to *slippers*, *klænning* to *sut*. Entirely new was the moccasin, which was thoroughly Norwegianized as *magis* or *magus*. Even so about three fourths of the words for clothing remained N: *hatt* 'hat', *klær* 'clothes', *bukse* 'trousers', *fille* 'rag', *forkla* 'apron', *hanske* 'glove', *hose* 'hose', *kjole* 'dress', *knapp* 'button', *lumma* 'pocket', *luva* 'cap', *skjorta* 'shirt', *strømpe* 'stocking', etc. A person who dressed for everyday use would call it *å klæ seg;* but for special occasions he might be *uppdressa* 'dressed up'.

Housekeeping, even though it was the woman's domain, also received its quota of fresh impulses from the American world. The housewife lifted the *lokk* 'lids' from the stove with a *ståvhendel* and she stirred the fire with a *pokar*. She burned *kårdved* (loan-blend from E cordwood), but she usually spoke of the fire in N as *varmen*, though some adopted *feier*. She got water from the *fæsset*, and she set the table with *disjis*, including *pleitar* and *skålar* 'saucers'. Older people spoke of *tallikar* for plates, while a very few adopted the E *saser*. The cup also remained N (*kopp*), as did the knife and the spoon; but the *fork* replaced *gaffel* with all WN and many EN speakers. *Fork* needed only to be extended a bit, while *gaffel* was a recent implement and a foreign term in many N communities. Larger containers were almost all E in terminology: *bærill* (only 3 inf. said *tunna*, one *kagge*), *beis* 'basin', *besket* (66 inf., compared to 22 for *korg*), *baks* 'box' (with a great many compounds), *båkket* 'bucket', *dipper* (also *dippert*; only 7 said *ausa*), *jugga* 'jug' (61 inf., vs 50 *krukka*), *pæl* 'pail' (with many compounds), *tåbb* 'tub', and *vasketåbb* 'wash tub'. The N term was favored for *panna* 'pan' or *steikjepanna* 'frying pan', but many also used the term *speidar* 'spider' for a pan with feet. Baking bread was a familiar N occupation which retained its N expression *baka brød;* but the *saltreis* 'salt rising' was something they learned about from American neighbors, and later they began buying readymade *jist* at the store. The housewife had an ever-recurring task in the *husklining* 'housecleaning', an expression which was common in spite of the conflict in meaning of *klina* with a native N word meaning to smear. American ways of cleaning came in with the *mapp* 'mop',

the *bromm* 'broom', and the *brøsj* 'brush'. N words for brooms and
brushes such as *kost, lime, sopling, sodel, sopill* were given often
enough so that they must also have been widely used, but less so
than the E words. Dishwashing had been called *vaska upp* in N,
but the E *vaska disjis* tended to displace it.

'Food here is not the right sort for the newcomers,' wrote Søren
Bache in his diary for December 4, 1843, 'since the usual food here
is pork, beef, and wheat bread, whereas in Norway they were accustomed to coarse rye bread, milk, and cheese.'[8] Nevertheless it
did not take long to adjust their 'porridge and flatbread stomachs,'
as Meidell called them, to the American diet. N foods were rele-
gated to holiday occasions, if they were used at all. American
foods that came in by purchase or from cookbooks were *bisketar*
'biscuits', *kek* 'cake', *kendi* 'candy', *kokkis* 'cookies', *krekkers*
'crackers', *fraidkeik* 'friedcake' (a kind of doughnut), *greve* 'gravy',
malases 'molasses', *pai* 'pie', and *sas* 'sauce'. Cheese they had known
and called it *ost* as long as they made it themselves; but later the
word *kjis* came in. The N word *mjøl* 'flour' gave way universally
to *flæur*, which was white where the N had often been dark; only
in *kornmjøl* 'cornmeal' was the N word preserved. The E series
of *milling* 'midlings', *sjårts* 'shorts', and *brand* 'bran' were new to
the immigrants; their own word for coarse flour, *kli*, disappeared.
Homemade drinks might also retain their N names, whether *øl*
'beer' or *brennevin* 'brandy'; but before long they were buying
bir and *brendi*, not to speak of *viski*.

The N meals sometimes ran as high as five or six in a day, but
these were generally reduced in America to *brekkfest, middag*, and
såpper. Older informants remembered N words for the first, but
did not use them (*bisk, dugurd*); more people used the N *kveldsmat;*
nearly everyone said *middag* for the noon-day meal, the heaviest
one of the day. N custom was often followed with the mid-morning
and mid-afternoon coffee, which might be called N *øykt* or E
lønsj, but mostly just *formiddags-* or *ettermiddagskaffe* (sometimes
eftasverd). The word *såpper* was also applied to the church suppers,
including those famous *lutefisksåppers* so popular in recent years,
where Am and N customs were curiously mingled. Those who did
not have a family of their own had a choice between *å borde* 'board'
with someone or *å bætsla det* 'to bach it'. All in all, the terms relating

to food and its preparation remained N, except for those products and customs which came in from the outside world.

In selling his produce, the farmer had to transport it to the stores of his neighborhood or the nearest village. These were named in E regardless of the existence of corresponding N terms: the *kjisfektri*, the *krimeri*, the *eleveiter*, the *fektri*, and the *står*. He would start preparing his *mjølk* 'milk' by using the *mjølkeseppereitar* 'milk separator' (a loanblend) to bring out the *fløyte* 'cream'. His produce was measured and weighed in the common units of the land, the *kvart*, the *gallon*, the *busjel*, the *kård*, all new (*kvart* is an extension). He was paid in *sent* and *daler* (an extension). In the early years he was accustomed to speak of *skilling* also, a N term which was extended to some 13 times its old value because two shillings made a quarter; gradually also the *nikkel* or *femsent* (a hybrid creation) and the *deim* or *tisent* came in.

His contact with business had not been very intense in Norway; but in America he soon learned to value the importance of *bisnes*, and to study the movement of the *market*. He generally spoke of *kontant* 'cash', but also said *kæsj;* he learned alternately to *seiva pengar* 'save money' and to *spenna* 'spend' (the latter a homophonous loanshift). Small coins could be used to *veksla* 'change', but he also spoke of *kjeinja*. He learned what it meant to *kæsja kjekkar* 'cash checks', to *seina nøter* 'sign notes', and to take out *morgisar* 'mortgages' on his property. He learned to trade at a variety of stores or shops called *gråsseristår* and *hardværstår*, *barbersjapp* and *lomberjard* and *værhus* 'warehouse'. In these places he met the *stårkipar* and the *klørk*, while outside of them he might get acquainted with a *pedlar* now and then. An occasional informant gave the N words for these phenomena, but for the most part they were forgotten. *Innsjurings* 'insurance' was new to him, but somewhere he must have heard N *forsikring*, since he smuggled the suffix *-ing* into the word.

When he was doing good business, the temptation was great to enter a *salon* 'saloon', after repeal known as a *tævern*, go up to the *bar* and have a *drink* (also known by the N word *dram*). If this went on long enough, he would be likely to wind up in the *purhus*. But the *tavan* 'tavern' which was known in the old days was not a *salon;* it was an inn, where travellers put up and where even a respectable man might allow himself to be seen! In general the immigrant stayed away from cities in those days, and had few words for its life. Those he did have were mostly E, aside from the word *by* 'city' itself: he spoke of a *blakk* 'block', a *seidvåk* 'sidewalk' and a *strit* 'street'. A few inf. claimed they said *gata* for the last-named, but this has not occurred in the writer's experience in connected speech.

3. *Social Experiences.*

Many immigrants had travelled widely, either as sailors or fishermen or even peddlers, but the journey to America was usually the most extensive ever undertaken. E expressions from this field also seeped into the immigrant's speech; he started using his own word *gå* in the E sense of 'go', regardless of with what conveyance; and he adopted 'travel' (as *travla*) in the sense of 'walk', as the opposite of *køyra* 'ride'. He took a *tripp*, if he could afford it, and he might *stoppa* or *stå* 'stay' (both loanshift extensions) with relatives. He no longer carried his baggage in a *kista* or a *koffert*, but in a *tronk* and a *sutkeis*. He travelled from place to place on a main *råd* 'road', and only smaller, less pretentious roads were called as in N *vegar*. At a *kårna* (blending *corner* and *hyrna*) there might be a *kråssråd*, and he had no hesitation in saying that he would *kråssa* it. He bought himself a *tikket* to ride on the *kars*, as the *træn* was called in an earlier day. The *rellråd* had a fine *trekk*, with two straight *rells* (which some knew were called *skjena* in N, but they never called it that) laid on many wooden *teis*. It stopped at the *dipo*, which he also called by the N name of a *stasjon*. Other means of transportation were the *stritkars* and the *stimbåt*, the *baisikkel* and the *åtomobil*, but mostly the latter was called a *kars* 'car'. Everything relating to a car was of course E: the *bætri*, the *brekk*, the *gir*, the *geradj*, and the *trøkk*. He might *sjippa* goods by *træn* or *trøkk*, but he would just as often say N *frakt* as E *fret*. *Post* was familar from Norway and usually kept its N name, but some were beginning to use *meil* instead; the *poståffis* and the *meilmann* tended to follow the E model, but one could also say *postmann*.

Within the *setlament* was concentrated the major part of the social life of the rural immigrant; here he could retain a sense of living in a N *bygd*. Around him were scattered *indi* 'Indians' at first, but *nykommarar* 'newcomers' (a loanshift extension) kept arriving and the *indi* did not find it congenial. The N *setlament* was gradually surrounded by other nationalities such as the *jenki* (all native Americans with English mother tongue), the *eiris* 'Irish', the *bohimi* 'Bohemians', and the *polender* 'Poles'. But those nationalities with which he had been familiar before retained their N names, the *tyskar* 'Germans', the *danskar* 'Danes' and the *svenskar* 'Swedes'. Parallel to the singulars of these, *danske* and *svenske*, he adopted as his favorite term for himself a dialectal word, *norske*, pl. *norskar*, instead of the more literary and official term, *nordmann*.[9] There were also outcasts who travelled around as *tremps;* they were rarely called *fant* or *tiggar*.

Words like *jåina* 'to join', a *kræud* 'crowd', *visita* 'to visit', suggest American social customs and were easily picked up. But many N social occasions were also carried on, particularly those associated with Christmas, such as the *julebukk* 'Christmas fooling' and the *juletrefest* 'Christmas tree festival'. American neighbors taught them a whole new series of possibilities for merriment, the *fårt åv julai*, the *piknik*, the *suppreisparti*, the *besketsosjel* (or *-sosjebel*), the *sjøvri* or *horning* 'shivaree', the *sørkis* 'circus', the *fær* 'fair', and the *prograem*. Within the framework of these events, however, the words for social life remained largely N; all kinds of social relationships and attitudes kept their N terminology.

Worldly amusements were frowned on by some, but there was still a sufficient number of young people to organize dances (N *dans*). The N *fele* 'fiddle' bore the burden of providing the music in the early days, but later on the E *kårdin* 'accordion' came in to supplement it. As time went on, the *mjusik* was furnished by a *bæn* 'band' or an *årkestra* (all E words). Another new instrument was the *gittar*, which also came to be well known in Norway; but it was followed by a series of other instruments right down to the *sæksofon*. The dances included old Norwegian favorites like the *halling* and the *springdans*, as well as the livelier couple dances such as the *vals* and the *reinlender*. But alongside these came the Am *kotiljen*, *kådrill*, and other *skværdansar*, the *sjattis* 'schottische', the *tu-stepp*, and the *fakstratt*.

For all kinds of sports and games the E word *pleia* gradually supplanted N *spela* and *leika*, which were more specific in their meanings. Anyone who bet, however, would be almost as likely to say *våga* as *betta*, except, of course, in the expression *ju bett!* They learned many new *gemar* 'games', such as *beisbål, besketbål,* and *fottbål,* together with all their technical terms. Card games like *juker* and *poker* came in, together with some new names for the cards, esp. the *dus* 'deuce' and the *jekk* 'jack' (now and then the *kvin* also, though *dama* prevailed). Otherwise the *kortstokk* or *kortleik* 'deck of cards' kept its Norwegian names, though some called it a *dekk.* N games like *holoball* were gradually forgotten or limited to schoolboys, while the passion for American games grew. Among these were also fishing and hunting, which grew more sportslike as their economic value decreased. In fishing the E terms were dominant, aside from such obvious words as *fisk* 'fish', *fiskar* 'fisherman', *lina* 'line', and *krok* 'hook'. *Fiskarpåle* (a loanblend) was used oftener than the N words, and *beit* tended to push out the N *agn* (though there are N dialect words so similar to *beit* that they may have influenced it). The fish were mostly given E names, obviously for new fish like *bæs* 'bass' and *såkker* 'sucker', but even for familiar N fish like *træut* (N *aure*) and *pikril* (N *gjedde*). For *hunting* the very word *jakt* had almost disappeared; and the immigrants always spoke of *hunta* 'hunt' and *huntar* 'hunter'. They retained the N words *skyta* 'shoot' and *børsa* 'gun', but *soks, glefsa, fella* for 'trap' were less common than the E *træpp.* Among the animals hunted the E *rabit* was in strong competition with N *hare,* some regarding the latter as equivalent to its E analogue *hare.* The squirrel was generally called *skværill,* though many knew the N word *ikonn* also.

As we shall see in Chapter 6, there were two kinds of school in most settlements, the English winter school and the N summer school. The latter was known as the *norskskule* or *religionsskule,* and the teacher known as *skulelæraren.* But the terminology referring to *kammenskulen* was wholly E: the *titsjer* or the *skulemamma* (a loanshift creation) was in charge and usually had to teach all the subjects in the *tørm* until *vekesjen* came. They included such topics as *ritmetikk, djagrefi,* etc. The objects used in instruction were the *blekkbord,* the *kjåk,* and the *pensel.* For the simpler slate the N *tavla* was used, and many preferred *krit* 'chalk' and *blyant* 'pencil' to the E words. The words for higher education were wholly E, from the *ækædemi* and the *kaledj* to the *junivørsiti*. Only the high school was sometimes Norwegianized as *høgskule*, an extension from its N sense.

An interesting contrast can be noted between the vocabulary relating to the parts of the body and the ills that affect them. The former were entirely N, but many of the latter were E. Such general terms as *frisk* 'well', *sjuk* 'sick', *blø* 'bleed', *hoste* 'cough' and the like were kept. But the experiences of the new country and conversations with Am physicians were reflected in such new words as *æger* 'ague', *pennesaitis* 'appendicitis', and *numonia* 'pneumonia' (though *lungefeber* and *lungebetendelse* were also known). Among the patent medicines that won high favor were the *linnement* and the *peinkillar*. The extension of the word *kulde* 'cold' to include the common infection appears to be found among many immigrant groups.[10] The E expression to have or to catch (get) a cold was as infectious as the disease itself; the N construction was radically different, lit. 'to become cold-ed' (*bli forkjølet*).

The doctor himself was called *doktor*, a N term which replaced the more specific terms such as *læge* (*lækjar*) 'physician' or *kirurg* 'surgeon'. But the *dentist* acquired the E name; he had an *åffis*, not a *kontor* any longer. When a medical man talked to his patients, he learned how they *fila* 'felt', where they were *hørta* 'hurt', what they were *trubla* by, and why they *vørria*. Most of these single terms correspond to phrases or markedly different constructions in N. Certain other terms of sensation which did not seem to be replaceable by any N terms were *bader* and *badra* 'bother', *figra* 'figure', and *suppreisa* 'surprised'. Similarly with *kæra* 'care', though here *bry seg* managed to hold its own in certain meanings. In general, the N terms are predominant in the field of sensation, perhaps in a proportion of ten to one.

The same is true of words relating to the life of the family. Such a word as *bebi* 'baby', which has won wide use in modern Norway, was certainly in use among AmN speakers, but was generally rejected by informants in favor of *unge* or *barn*. The term *bætslar* was less common than *ungkar* (also *lausakar, peparsvein, sveinkall*), except in the specific meaning of 'one who does his own housekeeping' (cf. *bach* v. above). Many N terms for kinship were lost in reference to the distinction between the father's and mother's side of the family, e.g. *farbror* and *morbror* for 'uncle'. Some of the kin were described by E terms, especially the *kåssen*, the *ænti*, and the *brådder-in-lå*, though some used the N equivalents for these also. Older informants always referred to their parents as *far* and *mor*, but the younger ones had begun to adopt more informal ways of speaking, the *pa*, *papa*, or even *dæd*, and the *ma* or *mama* of American children.

The church and its teaching remained N longer than any other phase of AmN life. But even here there was a slow infiltration from the general American environment. Low church circles among the immigrants began referring to their services as a *midden* or *miting* 'meeting', presumably to get away from the Catholic-sounding *høymesse* 'high mass'. As long as members were buried in the churchyard immediately surrounding the church, it was customary to call it a *gravplass* or *kyrkjegard;* but the more American practice of having distinct burial plots led to the introduction of the *gravjard* (a loanblend) and the *semmeteri*. In Norway the church had been supported by taxes; but over here the collection of funds came to be a prominent part of its activity. There had to be *sosjels*, including *besketsosjels*, as well as all kinds of *prograems*, all held in the *besment*. But the Ladies Aid remained solidly Norwegian with the name *kvinneforening* for its Thursday afternoon rendezvous. In this use of *forening* for 'society', a rather bookish word, we may see the influence of the pastors and the church organization in general.

4. *General Terms.*

There are some words that are used in so many different life contexts that they do not fit in any one of the groupings made so far. We shall begin with the less numerous word classes, the prepositions, adverbs, interjections, and the like. The only preposition that seems to be rather commonly taken over from E is *kross* 'across'; an adverb that is fairly frequent is *ehedd* 'ahead', especially in such expressions as *han kom ut ehedd, hvem er ehedd?* Popular were also such adverbs as *ennivei* 'anyway', *ætål* 'at all', *iven* 'even', and *kårs* 'of course'. Any one of these would usually require a reworking of the N sentence to give the same meaning if a N adverb were to be used. The interjection *nå* 'no' has largely replaced the N *nei*, but the N *ja* has rarely been replaced by *jess*. Since *yah* is the usual midwestern word for *yes* in AmEng, possibly through German-Scandinavian influence, the result is that the yes-no system in AmN is exactly like that of AmEng. Interjections such as *sjur* 'sure', *vell* 'well', and *gudbai* 'goodbye' were universally used in place of their N equivalents. Other expressions for goodbye were used as variations, however, so that one could also hear speakers say *farvel, du får leva så vel*, etc. But it is apparent that interjections, as expressions conveying complete meanings not easily translated into other languages, are easily accepted by speakers.

The number of adjectives borrowed was not, as we shall see, too large, but it included a number of very common terms: *ål reit, bæd, bissi, klos, kamen, different, isi, hendi* (an extension), *lykkelig* 'lucky' (an extension), *nekst, nais, plein, plenti, regler* 'regular', *råff* 'rough', *sekken* 'second', *smart, ståkk* 'stuck', *tåff* 'tough'. A number of these were borrowed in longer combinations, such as *fila bæd*, or *sekken kåssen*. Others make trouble for a literal translation because they occur in different contexts from the corresponding N words, e.g. *bissi, klos, plenti*, or *ståkk*. Some are characteristic of new-world patterns of living and thinking, such as *ål reit, hendi, nais, plein, regler, råff, smart, tåff*. The displacement of the similar-sounding *nest* 'next' by E *next* is rather puzzling; it is probably due to frequent occurrence in such contexts as *next week*.

There were also some nouns of the same general nature, such as *kjens* 'chance', *pis* 'piece', *risk, stail* 'style', *trikk, vei* 'way' (a loanshift extension). Each of these occurs in expressions which are of rather common occurrence, like take a chance, a piece of pie, a big risk, it's the style, do tricks, do it this way, etc. In trying to say these phrases, the speaker found it difficult to transpose them or to analyze them into N equivalents. An example is the frequent occurrence in AmN of the expression 'piece of cake': *en pis e kek*.

Some commonly borrowed verbs of a general cast were the

following: *æda* 'add', *alaoa* 'allow', *maonta* 'amount', *bita* 'beat', *båsta* 'bust', *ta kær ta* 'take care of', *ketsja* 'catch', *kjeinja* 'change', *klema* 'claim', *kåvra* 'cover', *finnisja* 'finish', *fiksa* 'fix', *getta lång* 'get along', *hepna* 'happen', *kipa* 'keep', *lesta* 'last', *liva* 'leave', *leva* 'live' (dwell, an extension), *lusa* 'lose', *mæka* 'make', *meinda* 'mind', *miksa* 'mix', *pikka* 'pick', *peila* 'pile', *putta* 'put', *reisa* 'raise' (an extension), *riska* 'risk', *råbba* 'rub', *rønna* 'run', *sjøtta* 'shut', *sleida* 'slide', *sæunda* 'sound' (also the N *høyrast, lydast, låta*), *starta* 'start', *stikka* 'stick', *tenda* 'tend', *tikla* 'tickle', *tippa* 'tip', *trøsta* 'trust' (an extension), *tørna* 'turn'. Some of these are handy words of all use, like fix, make, put, run, which fit in a variety of expressions that would be hard to render in other languages. Most of them occur in favorite contexts, e.g. it doesn't amount to anything (dæ mæunta itte te no), take care of yourself, catch a cold, they don't get along (dem getta itte lång), mind your own business, etc. Very few of them displace any N words completely, though they do usurp certain contexts.

5. *The Incidence of Borrowing.*

Our detailed analysis of the chief loanwords in AmN by spheres of activity shows the importance of the learning situations. Official terms are seen to be overwhelmingly English, as are the economic terms. In these the contacts of the immigrants with the English-speaking world were necessarily intimate, and their behavior had to be guided by English precedents. In the field of social relations this was less true, since they were able to maintain a considerable degree of internal social life. The chief foci of influence were the store, the government, and the American neighbor. But in home and family life, in church and religion, the English expressions penetrated more slowly; nor did they affect the immigrant's emotional and general behavior to the same extent as his economic life.

The evidence for this conclusion has here been drawn chiefly from the limited vocabulary included in the writer's questionnaire (which is described in more detail in chapter 12 and Appendix 3). It would be helpful if one could supplement this evidence with analyses of more nearly complete vocabularies, but the size and fluidity of a speaker's vocabulary is such as to make this kind of study extremely difficult. One informant, Dr. Odin Anderson (14D3), went to the trouble of making as complete a list of his AmN vocabulary as he could recall, including both the native words and the loanwords from English. The writer has selected from this list the uncompounded stems, a total of 4,257 words, of which 72.1 % were N and 27.9 % were of E origin, in common use among the Solør speakers around Blair, Wisconsin. In Table 2 this list is analyzed with respect to the spheres of activity and the relative proportion of English lws. in each. The spheres range from 100

Table 2. *Percentage of English Loanwords in Various Fields of Activity.*

PREDOMINANTLY ENGLISH
(50-100 %)

Autos and bicycles	100.0
City life	78.8
Sports and games	73.8
Machinery	72.7
Communications	68.7
Social affairs	65.3
Horsedrawn vehicles	63.2
Government, politics	55.6
Farming	53.2
Business and trade	50.3

STRONGLY MIXED
(30-50 %)

Buildings and grounds	43.8
Schooling and books	43.8
Exclamations	43.5
Furniture, furnishings	39.0
Food and drink	35.6
Housekeeping	32.0
Heat and light	31.5
Trees and plants	31.4
Miscellaneous abstracts	30.0

PREDOMINANTLY NORWEGIAN
(00-30 %)

Physical activity	28.0
Health and medicine	27.6
Music, dancing	26.8
Fishing, hunting	26.0
Clothing	24.3
Tools, implements	23.4
Social relations	21.1
Material relations	20.7
Animals	20.0
Quality	18.8
Colors	14.6
Weather	13.3
Character	12.2
Groups, classes	11.0
Quantity	10.0
Condition	9.9
Substances	9.3
Sensations, thoughts	9.0
Man and environment	8.6
Church	7.3
Shape	5.3
Home and family	4.9
Time, place, direction	0.0
Parts of body	0.0
Folklore	0.0
Form words	0.0

per cent English terms referring to autos and bicycles to 0 per cent referring to parts of the body and to folklore.

The writer has also made an investigation of the terms used in one particular sphere of farming, the harvesting of grain.[11] He found here that of 32 words connected with the harvest in Norway, only 17 were carried on in America. Two of these were shifted in meaning to agree with E analogues, while two others were already so close to the E that they could hardly have been changed. Thirteen new E words were adopted, making a total of 30 words, or nearly the same as in Norway. Of these we may say that 15, or exactly 50 %, are importations from E, which agrees well with the figure of 53.2 given for farming in Table 2. By this change the distance from N to E was shortened by one half. But the cultural shift was actually complete, for the E and AmN vocabulary structure in this area was now identical, with a one-to-one correspondence between them.

This feature of one-to-one correspondence which the naive speakers of the language appear to strive for is a potent factor in many loans. Not only does it appear as above in the number of terms available in any given sphere, but it appears also in the tendency to make whole expressions as similar as possible in the two languages. Expressions such as 'have a cold', in which a cold is presented as the object of a verb, are often reproduced in full because the speaker gets started on them before he realizes that in his language the corresponding expression is a participial adjective *forkjølet*.

In spite of the many temptations that thus are offered to import foreign materials, the actual number of loans in any given utterance is usually not as large as some think. The number is of course dependent on the nature of the subject treated. An attempt was made to determine the approximate proportion of lws. in various kinds of running texts as actually spoken by the writer's informants on phonograph recordings. The following table shows the results.

The passages are seen to vary from no loanwords to one in twelve, with an average of less than one in twenty-five. The same speaker may vary from 0.5 to 7.6 % according to subject matter, which is clearly the determining factor. The writer's impression is that individual differences are not too significant. In PaGer M.

D. Learned found a variation from none to 12-15 %, while
A. F. Buffington counted 2.5-5.0 % for literary and 5-8 % for
oral material.[12] This seems in good agreement with the AmN situation. The writer has included loanshifts as well as loanwords in
the number above. The passages counted are all quite unaffected
in manner and represent oral narration at its best.

Table 3. *Percentage of Loanwords in Running Text.*

Inf.	Subject	No. of lws.	Total words	Percent lws. of Total
4L4	Wedding	5	167	3.0
6P2	Pioneer days	8	275	3.0
6Q3	Farm life	9	214	4.2
23A2	Travels	18	204	8.8
14D3	Killing cats	9	148	6.1
5L1	Milking	1	186	0.5
5L1	Character	3	170	1.8
5L1	Farming	13	171	7.6
8M2	Courting	16	315	5.0
10C2	Fishing	6	346	1.7
14D4	Lynching	22	419	5.2
20Q2	Folklore	0	286	0.0
		110	2901	3.8

In spite of all inroads from E ways of speaking, the main body
of the N vocabulary remained intact. Nils Flaten once wrote that
any English word could get into the Norwegian language that
could 'stand the treatment it was apt to get.'[13] This might be
true in certain situations, when the speaker momentarily could
not recall the N word and so adopted the E as a makeshift. But
we have seen repeatedly how certain very common terms like *kniv*
'knife' and *skei* 'spoon' were not displaced, while others apparently
equally common were, such as *gaffel* 'fork'. The E words *wall*,
elbow, *head*, *chair*, and *light* were not usually borrowed. But all
of them could appear in compounds, when these comprised meanings for which it was not natural to substitute the N equivalents,
e.g. *retaining wall*, *elbow grease*, *head of cattle* (or *bullhead*), *rocking
chair*, *headlight*. The word *bed* was not generally borrowed in its

basic meaning, but in the transferred meanings of a *seedbed* or *flower bed* it was regular.

It is thus quite impossible to predict with any confidence that a given word cannot be borrowed. One can only say that it is highly probable that words of high frequency in the native language are less likely to be displaced than those of low frequency. Of the thousand most frequent words in the writer's N word count, only 47 or less than one in twenty, are ever displaced by E words. Most of these are terms referring to very specific aspects of N geographical or social life, e.g. *gård, elv, låve, li, ås, øy, bekk*, etc. But individually and sporadically any word can be borrowed; the writer has even heard the conjunctions *and* and *but* used in a N context by some speakers. But in general the speakers of AmN were not borrowing beyond the number of words that one might expect; the core of their language was wholly Norwegian, and in no way the kind of non-descript pidgin that some have suggested.

Chapter 6.

THE TRADITION OF WRITING.

> It has often been said in books that the Norwegians have the same language as the Danes; and it might really seem as if this were true. Our books and publications show the same language form as the Danish; an article from a Danish newspaper can be printed without change in Norwegian newspapers and vice versa.
>
> *Ivar Aasen (1864)*[1]

The Norwegians who settled in America brought with them something more than the spoken dialects of their local communities. A tradition of writing had been established among them, so that nearly all of them were sufficiently literate to read the books of Scripture and many of them could write the letters which reported on their adventures in the new land. While the spoken dialects were many, the tradition of writing was single. It corresponded precisely to no one kind of speech, though it resembled the speech of urban and educated people more than that of rural speakers. Like other traditions of writing in Europe, it had grown up around the centers of political and cultural power and served as an instrument of government. In Norway, united as she was with Denmark from 1380 to 1814, the official language of writing had become Danish.

1. *Primary Education in Norway.*

Not until the 18th century was any serious attempt made to spread a knowledge of this written language among the common people of Norway. This was one of the primary functions of the universal school system which the government first tried to establish in 1739. In 1827 a law was finally passed requiring the setting up of an effective system of rural schools.[2] This first foundation of democratic institutions was modest enough, being limited to a two or three months' course during each of seven or eight years. The subjects taught, in order of importance, were religion, reading, writing, and arithmetic; the last two were taught in only a few schools. The reading material was wholly religious, and the immediate goal was preparation for confirmation around the age of 14. As late as 1840, on the threshold of mass emigration, 91 % of the rural school children were being taught by ambulatory teachers who did their schoolmastering in private homes.[3] Only about a fourth of the children were then being taught to write.

A new law of 1860 tried to put an end to the ambulatory school and widen the horizon of instruction. By 1870 81.9 % of the children were being taught in permanent school buildings.[4] The legal minimum of instruction was set at eighteen weeks, but in favored districts it might reach as high as twenty-seven or more weeks per year.[5] Previous to this time teachers had been chosen among the best confirmands, but now they were required to have passed some sort of examination. Even so, the state school inspectors complained that 'instruction has been largely confined to reading from the book and to learning religious materials' and that 'the instruction in reading has consisted rather in giving the child a certain rapidity of tongue movement than in giving it the ability to read clearly, with proper intonation and understanding.'[6]

Not until 1869 was a law adopted which made both the rural and the urban school a common public school designed for the education of the entire citizenry and a foundation for higher training in public life.[7] In the meanwhile the old school had done its work, and it is evident from the many newspapers and periodicals that sprang into being among the emigrants that the reading skill was well established. AmN informants agree that a Norwegian pioneer who could not read was a rare sight indeed. There were some who never learned to write, or whose writing was limited to a signature. But by 1890 there was no excuse even for this failing anywhere in Norway; and the later emigrants were all able to read and write, Norway being among the earliest countries in the world where literacy was made universal.

2. *The Church School.*

[In America the fathers of the Norwegian Church made the teaching of reading and writing one of their first tasks.] The Reverend
J. W. C. Dietrichson had scarcely arrived in Koshkonong settlement
in 1844 before he engaged a parochial school teacher. He wished
to make sure that the immigrant children would carry on in the
faith of their fathers. The salary was modest, being only ten dollars
a month for three months of the year, but the example was important. It was followed by many, perhaps most of the congregations,
and [in 1851 the principle of religious education in the Norwegian
language was written into the first constitution of the Norwegian
Synod.[8] The assembled pastors declared that the children should
learn to read Norwegian first; English could wait until they were
thirteen years of age.] Rules were enacted for the examination of
prospective parochial school teachers, and so a program of religious
education was under way.

In 1852 the directors of the Skandinavisk Presseforening announced that they were printing the necessary schoolbooks, including a Norwegian ABC, Luther's Catechism, Pontoppidan's
Explanation to the Catechism, and Wexels' Bible Stories.[9] Five
years later a contact was made with the German Missouri Synod
which led to renewed emphasis on parochial education. Conferences
held at Coon Prairie and Rock Prairie in 1858 were attended by
parochial school teachers and pastors. Here was defined a more
precise policy for the Synod, which led to the first public controversies over the problem of parochial versus secular education
among the Norwegians. A lively discussion arose when it became
apparent that the leaders of the Synod contemplated making the
parochial schools a full-fledged educational system, replacing the
American common school. In this case the Synod leaders had
apparently miscalculated the temper of their parishioners, for
their agitation met with widespread opposition from laymen and
clerics alike, as may be gathered from the illuminating account in
Blegen's *Norwegian Migration.*[10] [Norwegian immigrants were
simply not willing to make the financial sacrifices necessary to
build a religious school system parallel to the American secular
school.]

The result was a compromise whereby many congregations supported a supplemental church school, which met from one to three months in the summer or at other times when the public school was not in session. The curriculum was simple enough: it consisted chiefly of a rote memorization of the Catechism, the Explanation to the Catechism, and the Bible Stories, with some singing of hymns. The medium of instruction was Norwegian, so that some time had to be devoted to teaching the children to read the language. As pointed out for a similar practice among Swedish immigrants by George M. Stephenson, this made the school in effect a language as well as a religious school.[11] On some occasions further material may have been introduced by the teachers, as recommended in 1858 by the teacher at Koshkonong, J. Agerholm, who warned against 'an unvaried diet of religion.' But in popular speech the parochial school was known as *religionsskulen* 'the religious school' and as *norskskulen* 'the Norwegian school'. Its importance as a factor in keeping alive the ability to read Norwegian may be gauged by the fact that as late as in 1917, 82.6 % of the pupils in parochial schools were being taught in Norwegian, while only 37.2 % of those in Sunday schools were being taught in that language. The three synods which united to form the Norwegian Lutheran Church in America in 1917 reported that week-day or vacation instruction was being given by 1,796 teachers to 41,716 children.[12]

No full account is available of the history and influence of the parochial school among the N immigrants, in spite of the significance of this institution.[13] This is regrettable for our study, since the parochial school appears to have done a great deal to preserve a familiarity with the written language of Norway. Practically all of the informants interviewed for this study had attended the 'Norwegian school' and had there received their only instruction in Norwegian reading and writing. The schools did not usually have to teach the children to speak the language; they merely taught speakers of AmN to read and write the official Dano-Norwegian norm of the religious textbooks.

The teachers in these schools were in some cases qualified by instruction received in the teachers' seminaries of Norway. The school reports in Norway for 1869 and 1870 show that of 151 teachers reported as leaving the profession, 44, or more than a fourth, were emigrating.[14] Some of these certainly eked out a meager income with some months of parochial teaching after emigration. The best of them, men like Peder P. Hektoen at Coon Prairie, or Thor Helgeson in Iola, became figures of significance in their communities, whose influence might rival and even exceed that of the pastors. S. Sondresen, himself a pastor, reports that some pastors were reluctant to have permanently resident school-teachers for fear that the latter might lead factions against them.[15] But in general the schoolteacher's life was no bed of roses. His salary was small, for the parishioners did not always care to open their purses too widely for educational purposes. The periods of instruction were irregular, and in the early years most of the schools were ambulatory, as they had been in Norway. One pupil reports: 'Teacher and children had to stay in the kitchen-living room, where the housewife was busy with her domestic duties.'[16] Most of the teachers had other occupations from which they derived their major support, usually farming. As time went on, students of theology or even ordinary college students from the N-A church schools replaced the Norwegian *seminarister*, thereby picking up some extra cash and experience in the summers.

The pupils, for their part, did not always make life too easy for the teachers. One informant reported: 'We figured it was unfair, robbing us of vacation... in parochial school we were devils incarnate.'[17] This view was of course not unanimous; another informant declared, 'Those were our best days.'[18] A vivid passage illustrating the less favorable aspects of the religious school is found in a story by Waldemar Ager: 'His childhood had been darkened by the Norwegian religious school. In his home nothing but English had been spoken; but his father, who was a very serious Lutheran of the old school, had demanded that he should attend the Norwegian school and learn the Catechism and the Explanation in Norwegian. So he had memorized them in the shadow of the switch. First there were the ten commandments and the switch. Then there were the Articles or the switch and the Lord's Prayer and the switch or threats of the switch. He had chewed and chewed on long words like "Nidkjærhed" (zeal), "Miskundelse" (mercy), "Vederkvægelse" (comfort), "Retfærdiggjørelse" (justification),

"Vederstyggelighed" (abomination), and the like until it almost made him ill. No sooner had he learned them than they changed places and danced around in all the questions and answers like living beings which maliciously stuck in his throat just so he should get a scolding or a beating.'[19]

A criticism in the same vein was expressed by the author O. E. Rølvaag in 1922 when he wrote: 'We teach our children to talk a little Norwegian; then we thrust an impossible ABC-book in their hands; after that the Catechism and Pontoppidan's Explanation. If we take them along to the Norwegian services and send them to a four weeks' religious school to a teacher who perhaps knows very little Norwegian himself, we think that is all that is needed.... It is surprising how much Norwegian some of the brightest children have acquired in this way. But one thing is lacking: love. And in many cases it has become neither fowl nor flesh, neither Norwegian nor religion. It has no doubt happened that the child in this way has gotten a distaste for both. The long, heavy words, and even more the abstract concepts in Catechism and Explanation choked the interest for the language.'[20] Rølvaag wished to see the textbooks modernized and simplified, and the teaching method he advocated was one of story-telling and singing, to capture the emotions and the imagination of the children.

3. *Dano-Norwegian and the Dialects.*

⌈The problem of teaching Norwegian spelling to speakers of AmN dialects was aggravated by the wide difference between this speech and the Dano-Norwegian norm which they were required to read and write.⌉ Words like those cited by Ager in the preceding passage had no natural association with the daily speech of the pupils. This difficulty was accentuated as English became more prevalent among the immigrants. One pastor is said to have asked his pupils to bring him some wild grapes (*druer*). At the next meeting of the class he was astounded to receive a gift of wild pigeons. His pupils had understood him to say *duer* 'doves', since *druer* was to them a purely literary word; in AmN speech the word is usually *grips* from English 'grapes'.[21]

The official book language was a straitjacket in which rural speakers could recognize but few features of the dialects that were their mother tongue. M. B. Landstad, well-known hymnist and ballad collector, once wrote that 'when the child begins to read our books, he must practically learn a new language, a circumstance that has a more hampering influence on our schools than people are accustomed to think.'[22] This situation was probably paralleled in most European countries where a centralized government had succeeded in imposing its form of writing on an entire country. But in Norway there was a special poignancy in the situation because the orthography had been imposed during Norway's national impotence, the centuries of her political submergence in the Dano-Norwegian kingdom. Once her independence had been won in 1814, patriots were not slow in discovering that written Danish and written Norwegian were as 'like as two peas,' while the spoken languages were quite divergent. Ardent discussion arose concerning this apparent lack of a truly Norwegian language, but few were prepared to take the consequences of a radical break in Dano-Norwegian orthographic unity.

This was the more true because the inconvenience of the spelling was least for those who had the most power. The ruling class, a strong and self-conscious bourgeois-bureaucracy, regarded itself as the guardian of culture and tradition. One of the instruments of this culture was the Dano-Norwegian orthography, a medium of that higher education which led to positions of influence and power. The orthography was more than a reflection of speech; it had become a symbol of authority which was widely held to be a model for proper speaking.

Under the pressure of this ideal a form of speech had sprung into being in the upper classes which was neither locally restricted nor slavishly bookish. It was not local — because intermarriage and migration from post to post gave this class a mobility which the country people lacked. It was not bookish — because Norwegian speech habits were too powerful to be entirely uprooted, and the requirements of everyday life made a rigid application of Danish norms impossible. That such a cultivated speech norm existed was not clearly recognized until the mid-century, when linguist-reformer Knud Knudsen gave it a name and a local habitation.[23] His favorite term for it was one that might be rendered as 'cultivated colloquial speech' (den dannede dagligtale), though he also described it as 'urban' (byfolkets talesprog) and 'nation-wide' (den landsgyldige norske uttale). In his time the school-masters generally did not regard this form of speech as in any way ideal: to them it was little more than a mutilated version of the sacred *skriftsprog*, or written language. Any one who should read aloud or speak in public on elevated topics was counselled to follow the spelling zealously. It took great courage to assert, as did Knud-sen, that Norwegians ought to reform their spelling to make it agree with this cultivated colloquial norm.

4. *Reading and Spelling.*

[The average country lad who came to school was thus practi-cally predestined to learn a pronunciation that served no one as a means of everyday communication.] All accounts agree that pronunciation was taught letter by letter; each word was spelled out, and then given as literal a pronunciation as possible. The result was not Danish, which differed widely from Norwegian pronunciation as well as its own spelling. The written form of Danish was highly conservative, reflecting probably most closely the Danish pronunciation of around 1200.[24] Nor was the result 'cultivated colloquial,' for the schoolmaster was usually of rural origin himself and had rarely heard anyone talk this language except possibly the local pastor. There was no published·guide to pronunciation other than that furnished by the spelling itself. Knudsen wrote in 1850: 'The opinion that in cases of doubt the book is the best authority on pronunciation is quite widespread, no matter how superficial it may be, and no matter how little it can bear scrutiny.'[25] P. Chr. Asbjørnsen, who had had extensive contact with country schoolmasters while collecting folklore, commented on the 'strange schoolmaster style, a stilted, comical imitation of obsolete book language, into which huge chunks of the forthright local dialect were occasionally dumped by accident.'[26] The writer has heard just this style of speech among some of his AmN informants who were schoolmasters or influenced by them.

However amusing this style might sound to city dwellers, nothing else was available to country people who had little opportunity for contact with upper-class urban speakers. One of the strongest arguments for reform of the spelling was precisely, as leading linguists declared in 1892, that 'no one born in the country can discover the cultivated pronunciation from the spelling, nor can one who knows the cultivated pronunciation discover the spelling.'[27]

A vivid illustration of the respect in which the spelling was held may be found in the columns of an organ published for the common-school teachers of Norway in 1861.[28] John Stenersen, instructor at a teachers' training school, mildly suggested some minor reforms in the teaching of reading. To get away from the mechanical rigidity of the usual pupil reading, he advised teachers not to insist on such difficult and utterly obsolete pronunciations as *dst* (for *st*) or *dt* (for *t*) or *hv* (for *v*), nor such purely orthographic signs as the double *u* in *huus* 'house' and *e* in *foer* 'went'. In the reading of conversational materials, particularly in folk tales, he advocated such natural speech forms as *far* for *fader* 'father', *sa* for *sagde* 'said', and *mei* for *mig* 'me'.[29] For this he was pounced upon by two fellow-teachers in the columns of the same journal. One of them ironically declared: 'In the whole country people read mig, dig, sig according to the letter, and this should be "un-natural," "strange," "affected" !'[30] In his reply Stenersen expressly declared that of course he had not intended such radical forms for beginners, or indeed for all styles of reading.[31] But his second colleague insisted that no freedom whatever should be permitted; he could see no difficulty in pronouncing the jawbreaker combinations that Stenersen wished to avoid. The *d* in *vendte*, he declared, might be 'only slightly audible' so that the word sounded like *vente*, but pronouncing it had the advantage 'that it prepares and shapes a steady and confident orthography.'[32] So long as the orthography remained as foreign to the mass of Norwegians as it was, there is no denying that this view had a certain force: for pupils who had no access to cultivated colloquial speech, a good spelling pronunciation became a reminder of the spelling itself.

⌈Rather than continue the teaching of an artificial spelling pronunciation, the Norwegians chose to reform the spelling.⌉ In 1862, the very next year after the discussion just quoted, the agitation of the indefatigable Knudsen bore fruit in the acceptance by the Ministry of Church and Education of his proposal for the abandonment of certain obsolescent and inconsistent spellings. Among these changes were the dropping of silent vowels intended to show vowel length, e.g. *ie, ae, oe* (for *i, a, o*) or *ee, ii, uu* (for *e, i, u*); *c, ch,* and *q* for *k;* and *ph* for *f*.[33] This was a great triumph for the rational principles of spelling advocated a generation earlier by the Danish linguist Rasmus Rask.[34] His ideas had found a willing ear among various Norwegian rebels, but in 1838 their efforts had been quashed by the Ministry of Church and Education.[35] Knudsen was not satisfied to stop with this relatively innocuous reform. In 1869 he helped promote an inter-Scandinavian conference at Stockholm where a number of common Scandinavian changes were proposed, changes that were actually followed for a time by some writers like Ibsen and Bjørnson. Official spelling rules began to appear under the editorship of Jacob Aars. During the 70's small reforms were gradually introduced in these; in 1870, *x* became *ks;* in 1877 the capitalization of common nouns was officially abandoned.

But the wave of democratic nationalism that swept the nation during the 70's demanded more vigorous action. The first major break came in 1879, when a bill was passed requiring the teachers to use the children's own dialect in the elementary grades. A program of energetic linguistic reform was a prominent plank in the platform of the Liberal Party — the party that carried most of the remaining elections in the 19th century. A language that was at once more Norwegian and more democratic became one of the major goals of the liberal movement. Considerable support was growing up for an entirely new language, the Landsmaal of Ivar Aasen, first launched in 1853, a written norm based on the more conservative rural dialects and intended to supplant the DN norm completely. The time was ripe for further advances, if the DN were not to fall behind. In 1887 the Ministry of Church and Education issued an order instructing teachers in the grades that 'the norm for pronunciation and reading is the "cultured colloquial speech," i. e. that pronunciation which in each section of the country is the usual one in the careful, but natural daily speech of cultured people.'[36] Spelling pronunciation was abandoned for good, which did not necessarily ease the teachers' problem. Now they had to teach their pupils two new languages instead of one, and it was not long before they were clamoring for spelling reforms that might again bring the two together.

In 1892 a new official school reader by Nordahl Rolfsen adopted a great number of colloquial spellings. In 1894 many of these were included in the new edition (the 11th) of Aars's spelling rules, which made them official for the schools.[37] The schools were now well ahead of the general public, and the confusion of spellings was beginning to claim the attention of the press. A discussion held at a teachers' meeting in Drammen as late as 1904, however, showed that many teachers were still teaching the old spelling pronunciation.[38] But the separation from Sweden in 1905, with its attendant national enthusiasm, provided the impetus for a final break with the Dano-Norwegian orthography. In 1907 the Storting adopted a new official orthography for DN in accord with the principles for which Knud Knudsen had so long contended. The leading features of the cultivated colloquial were established in writing, and all adherence to Danish precept or example was given up for good.

5. *Primers on the Prairie.*

The textbooks which, as Rølvaag put it, were 'thrust into the hands' of the parochial school pupils were largely reprints of texts used in Norway, if they were not simply imported. But the special circumstances of immigrant life soon made it both necessary and desirable to print original texts made in this country. An ABC was so imperative that the directors of the Scandinavian Press Association announced a contest for the best one 'suited to our school conditions and otherwise adapted to circumstances here.'[39] The winner of this contest was none other than the first president of the Norwegian Synod, the Reverend A. C. Preus. His *ABC for Begyndere*, published in Madison, Wisconsin, in 1857 was the first Norwegian textbook in this country. Others followed, and some of these came to be thumbed by successive generations until they and their drawings were as familiar to Norwegian-American readers as McGuffey's to an earlier generation of Americans.

The first book which faced the beginning pupil was always the ABC. After Preus's early effort the following titles appeared; the list is as complete as the writer could make it: *Billed ABC for Børn* (LaCrosse, Wis., 1866); *Norsk-amerikansk A.B.C.* (Chicago, Illinois, n.d.); *A.B.C.* (Decorah, Iowa, 1877; 16p.); Hallvard Roalkvam, *A.B.C. Læsebog for børn med billeder* (Decorah, Iowa, 1882; 32p.); H. Grousdal, *A.B.C. med Stave- og Læseøvelser* (Decorah, Iowa, 1884; 48p.); Johannes Jøssendal, *Billed-A.B.C.* (Decorah, Iowa, 1888?; many editions, one completely revised and marked '150th thousand' in 1897; 48p.); *A.B.C.-bog med läse og staveövelser* (Minneapolis, Minn., n.d.); Knute O. Løkensgaard, *Læsebog for børn*, 1ste trin (Wittenberg, Wis., 1891; many editions).[40]

In all of these books the orthography was of course traditional Dano-Norwegian, at least until 1890. The same was true of Knud Thronsen's *Norsk læsebog for børn og ungdom* (Decorah, Iowa, 2v., 1876—80; new ed. 1894). This was published by the Norwegian Synod and intended to give the pupils reading material beyond that which was found in their Bible histories and catechisms. A similar effort was *Norsk Læsebog for Menighedsskoler* (Minneapolis, 1889). After 1890 these books generally abandoned the use of verb plurals and capital letters for nouns. One of them was Knute O. Løkensgaard's *Læsebog for børn, 2det trin* (Minneapolis, 1896). Thronsen's second edition of 1894 even went so far as to recommend the adoption of the cultured colloquial pronunciation, such as saying *jei* and *mei* for the spellings *jeg* 'I' and *mig* 'me'. The first books to show any considerable effort to include material of special interest to American readers were Olav Refsdal, *Barnebogen* (Minneapolis, Minn., 1898; 7. printing, 1906; 74 p.) and Ole Nilsen, *Læsebog for menighedsskolen* (Chicago, 1909; 258p.).

A supplement to the textbook material began appearing when the various synods published special periodicals in Norwegian which were distributed to the young. In 1875 the Norwegian Synod started its *Børneblad;* followed by Hauge Synod in 1877 with its *Børnevennen.* After 1917 these were combined in a publication of the united church under the name *Barnevennen;* this carried on until 1933, and showed a reformed (1907) spelling for the first time in the history of such publication. At certain periods there were even enough parochial teachers to carry on a society, at least within

the Norwegian Synod, the so-called Synodens Lærerforening.
From 1880—1881 two volumes of a journal appeared called *Luthersk
Skoleblad, Maanedsskrift for Kristelig Opdragelse og Undervisning.*[41]
In the years 1905 to 1914 appeared another journal called simply
Skoleblad.

6. *The Evidence of Spelling.*

⌐The problems which were faced by teachers of DN spelling in
America can best be studied by observing the results in written
documents produced by the immigrants and their children. The
chief use to which they put their skill was the writing of letters
to friends and family here and in Norway. Now and then they also
had to compose a more official document, such as the letter of
call issued by Norwegian settlers in Lemonweir, Juneau County,
Wisconsin, to the Rev. H. A. Preus on May 22, 1854.[42] This letter
shows great uncertainty about the use of capitals (...Hvorpaa
Hvi kunde Muntligen tales Ved...) and the division of words (et
Skole Hus, tilstede Værende), as well as a number of typical
spelling confusions (hv/v, w/v, e/æ, gj/j, dt/t). The purely literary
verb plurals are mostly overlooked (ære and erre occur beside the
singular er), but in spite of a generally awkward usage there are
very few examples of dialect intrusion (kjærkegaard for Kirkegaard
'churchyard'; helser for hilser 'greets'). Another fascinating
example of popular spelling habits is the accompanying printed
placard composed at Manitowoc, Wisconsin, in 1876.[43] Its chief
failings are uncertainty concerning word division (For friskning,
Taler Stolen) and failure to geminate consonants (Eftermidag,
Hura). It is less surprising that the special Norwegian letters æ
and ø are eliminated, since these were probably not available in
the typesetter's font.

⌐A special aspect of the tradition of writing among the immigrants is their treatment of English words and names in a Norwegian context.⌐ Before they had gained any considerable acquaintance with English spelling they often attempted to render the
new words in their writing. The placard above shows what could
happen to a word like *picnic:* Pik Nik! Letters written by early

Placard from a Norwegian Picnic held at Manitowoc,
Wisconsin, July 4, 1876.

1776.   **1876.**

SKANDINAVISK
PIK NIK!

═══ 4 JULY! ═══

PAA MR. WOOD'S LAND.

PROGRAM:

Deltagerne samles ved Prestegaarden Kl. 2 Eftermidag. Sangchoret Luren afsynger en Vandresang, "Fra Ostens Veld." Med Sangchoret i spidsen Macherer's til Pik Nik'n.

"Luren" afsynger en Indlednings-sang paa Pladsen, Med Sommerlov, o. s. v.

Uafhengegheds Erklaringen paa Norsk oplees af Foreningens Formand, M. Ornes.

3 gange 3 Hura for Amerikas Folk og Frihed. Sang af "Luren." Hoiest Lofter jeg da Guld Pokalen.

Festtale for dagen af Pastor L. M. Bjorn.
Sang af Luren, "Hil dig vor Fostermor."
For friskning. Ingen Bordsetning. Enhver spiser hvad han selv har med bragt.

TALER STOLEN FRI

Sang af Luren, til Slutning, "Solnedgang."
Beer og Limonede Besorges af Foreningen frit.
En talrig Deltagelse onskes.
Adgang 25c: Damer og Born fri.

SKANDINAVISKE FORENING.

immigrants in Illinois and Missouri who had emigrated from Voss
show some amazing transformations:[44]

Illinois	Elernoes	buckwheat	bug qveite
Beaver Creek	Boverkrik	hickory	hekri
Shelbyville	Skiel Bevil	steamboat	stimbaad
Shelby County	Skiel Be conti	pint	paint
Ottawa	Attevei, Advei	acre	æger
New York	Nyørk	bushel	Bushiel
Ohio River	Ohaia Rover	barrel	barel
Hannibal	Hennebaal	one gallon	en Galle
Little Indian Creek	Lille indgienkrik	halfbreeds	hafbrids
St. Francisville	Sant Fransvil		

[Most of these spellings resulted from the more or less accurate
application of Norwegian spelling rules to the current AmN pronunciations of English words.] But in all their naiveté they do show
that the work of the Norwegian school teachers had not been entire-
rely in vain.

[A systematic study of naive spellings in a group of immigrant
letters was made by the writer for the purpose of determining the
relation between speech and writing in immigrant communities.[45]]
The editors of *Decorah-Posten* were kind enough to turn over a
batch of letters received from their subscribers between January
1 and July 1, 1936. The 289 letters included seemed to the writer
to be a fair index of the writing skills of AmN speakers in the Middle
West. The states chiefly represented were Minnesota with 36.2 %,
Wisconsin 13.2 %, North Dakota 12.1 %, South Dakota 7.3 %,
Washington 5.2 %, and Iowa 4.5 %, but there were scattered contributors throughout the Middle and Far West all the way to Alaska.
Of the 229 who wrote in Norwegian only 68 stated their places
of origin in Norway; these were predominantly in Eastern Norway:
the Eastern Lowlands account for 35.4 % and the Eastern Valleys,
especially Gudbrandsdal, for another 25 %. Only 25 stated the
date of their emigration: this ranged from 1880 to 1924, with the
median at 1886. Eighteen correspondents gave their ages, which
ranged from 67 to 92, with the median 76. Twelve stated how
long they had subscribed to the paper, the median being 47 years.
While it is not strictly valid to combine these figures, they do give

us an idea of the nature of the typical correspondent here studied: a man or woman born in Eastern Norway about 1860, who emigrated to America in 1886, settled in the Middle West, and began subscribing to Decorah-Posten in 1889. The education received by most of them came before the time when the schools began experimenting with spelling and the teaching of cultured colloquial pronunciation. Only the oldest set of changes had been made, those which were also adopted by the N-A press at an early period.

It was necessary to study these letters in manuscript form, since their printed forms would give no idea of the original spellings. Extensive editing of subscriber's letters is a regular practice of N-A newspapers, at least as far as their spelling is concerned. In general the conclusion emerges that the writers were trying to write the DN norm used in the paper, but that many factors interfered with their success. The three chief types of variations from standard DN were: 1) Phonetic substitutions within the DN norm; 2) Non-standard intrusions from the writers' speech; and 3) Anglicisms of all kinds. We shall see in the following how these were distributed in the material studied.

We are not surprised to find that all but 17 of the 229 Norwegian letters were cast in the forms of DN orthography from 1870 to 1890. Of the remaining 17, only 9 were consistently written in one of the later, reformed spellings, and 2 in Aasen's New Norse or dialect. Not included in the 229 are 11 Danish letters and 2 Swedish (or partly Swedish) ones. It is easy to see that some of these writers were ill at ease in the written DN language. One correspondent asked the editor to correct his errors, adding: 'Voxte op I meget smaa kaar saa jeg fik gaa I Arbeidssælen da jeg var I 9 a 10 Aars Alderen og her blev det I Skogen paa Driven og Sagmøllerne det var en god skole.' (Grew up in very hard circumstances so I had to go to work at age 9 or 10 and here I had to work in the woods and sawmills that was a good school). In view of the age and limited education of the correspondents it is more surprising that they wrote as well as they did than they they made a number of errors. In a rough estimate based on a standard size writing paper of 5 × 8 inches the number of errors per page was as follows:

Errors per page	0	1-5	6-10	11-15	16-20	21-25	26-30	Total
Number of writers	12	108	74	28	4	1	2	229
Percent of writers .	5.3	47.2	32.3	12.2	1.7	0.4	0.9	100.0

Very few wrote perfectly, but more than half made fewer than six errors to the page.

A goodly number of these errors consisted of pure punctuational mistakes. Capitalization of nouns was a stumbling block to many; but only 56 % of the writers made any effort at all to carry out this practice, and of these only about one fifth, or 25 writers, succeeded. The rest showed a tendency to capitalize verbs and adjectives, or even adverbs and prepositions, about as often as nouns. The use of periods and commas was satisfactory only in about a third of the letters (73); many tended to use only one of these marks, inserted to mark the flow of ideas rather than any grammatical unit. Excessive word spacing is characteristic of 96 or 42 % of the writers. English separation of compounds has probably accentuated this tendency, as in reise penge 'travel money', farmer kjæring 'farm woman', kvinde forenings formand 'Ladies' Aid chairman'; but some go far beyond even English usage, writing Liver Poll 'Liverpool', a ligge veld 'anyway' (for alligevel). The opposite error of writing words together is much less common, being found only in 12 writers and quite sporadically; enstund 'a while', sligen 'such a'. Improper use of the hyphen is rare: jerte-Rum 'heart-room', der-borte 'over-there'.

Among the very common errors are those which can only be described as pure miswritings or lapses. In letters dashed off hastily this is only what one may expect; they can be detected because they result in combinations which have no apparent relation to the speech of the writers. A total of 256 such lapses have been counted in 116 different writers, distributed as follows: omissions 54.7 % (skrv for skrev 'wrote', bldet for bladet 'the paper'), intrusions 5.9 % (runiner for ruiner 'ruins', redraktør for redaktør 'editor'), substitutions 30.4 % (spalpe for spalte 'column', persolale for personale 'office force'), malformations 9.0 % (hagelt for hyggeligt 'pleasant', torskifske for torskefiske 'cod fishing'). The great preponderance of omissions shows that economy of effort has been at work; the substitutions and intrusions are mostly anticipations or dittographs, while the malformations are mostly metatheses.

Those remaining errors which appear to have some correlation to the problems of language and spelling are listed in the accompanying table of naive spellings. For each type the number of letters is given in which the error occurred; the figures are only suggestive, since they are not based on a complete count of both correct and incorrect forms. One example of each error is given.

Table 4. *Naive Spellings within the DN norm.*

POSITIONS	ALTERNATIVES	
1 *Gemination of Consonants*	*Omission*	*Intrusion*
a) Between vowels after stress	86 (maa*t*e 'had to')	37 (spis*s*e 'eat')
b) Between vowels after non-stress	34 (ka*s*erer 'treasurer')	16 (ho*tt*el 'hotel')
c) Finally	2 (he*r* 'Mr.')	10 (a*ll* 'all')
d) In clusters		10 (va*kk*re 'pretty')
2 *Voicing of Stops* (p t k)	*Unvoicing*	*Voicing*
a) Medially and finally after vowels	30 (ma*t* 'food')	6 (rø*g*ed 'smoked' p.p.)
b) Before voiceless consonants	16 (di*k*t 'poem')	18 reda*g*tør ('editor')
3 *Assimilated* (*'silent'*) *Consonants*	*Omission*	*Intrusion*
a) d after vowels	10 (me 'with')	
b) d after l	47 (snil 'nice')	2 (aldt 'all')
c) d after n	98 (en 'than')	7 (end 'one')
d) d after r	13 (or 'word')	
e) d before s	11 (plas 'place')	
f) d before st	36 (best 'best')	
g) d before t	39 (got 'good')	4 (sludt 'ended')
h) t in the suffixed def. art.	13 (blade 'the paper')	
i) g in some words	10 (osaa 'also', aldri 'never')	
j) h before v	62 (vad 'what')	4 (hved 'by')

4 *The palatalized velars*

	Omission	Intrusion	Substitution
a) voiced palatal fricative (g before i, y; j, gj, hj, lj elsewhere)	33 (jerne 'gladly') 1 (Gøvig 'Gjøvig')	5 (gjik 'went') 1 (gjernbanen 'the RR.')	6 (jik 'went') 2 (gjemme 'at home') 3 (hjeld 'debt')
b) voiceless palatal fricative (k before i, y; kj elsewhere)		5 (Kjina 'China')	
c) palatal sibi- lant (sk be- fore e, i, y; sj, skj else- where)	3 (forskeligt 'different') 1 (forsjellige 'different ones')	1 (skjer 'hap- pens') 1 (skjelden 'rare')	1 (sjik 'custom')

5 *Foreign letters and clusters*

	Omission	Intrusion	Substitution
a) t/th	3 (Luterske 'Lutheran')	5 (eftther 'after')	
b) k/c/ch/ck/q		1 (chritiserer 'criticizes') 4 (pollitick 'politics')	17 (clima 'climate') 4 (Krookston 'Crookston')
c) v/w			23 (wi 'we') 5 (Vausau 'Wausau')
d) sj/si/ch/ti/sch			1 (mis*j*on 'mission') 1 (suskrip*si*on 'subscription') 1 (Komferma*si*on 'confirmation 3 (pen*ti*on 'pension')
(e) s/c/z			2 (desember 'December') 2 (spice 'eat') 1 (Airsona 'Arizona') 1 (influenca 'influenza')

6 *The Mid-vowels*

	Simple for digraph	Digraph for simple
a) e/æ before r	65 (ere 'honor')	23 (hær 'here')
b) e/æ not before r	73 (tre 'tree')	36 (kjænde 'know')
c) o/aa	30 (nor 'when')	45 (faar 'for')

7 *Potentially syllabic e*

	Omission	Intrusion
a) Before l	17 (mennesklig 'human')	33 (nogele 'some')
b) Before n	(mensker 'people')	(svundene 'vanished')

c) Before r	(tempratur 'temperature')	(mindere 'less')
d) Before other consonants	(ligsaa 'just as')	(agetet 'respected')

8 *Shortened word forms*	*Short forms*	
bli/blive, ha/have, far/fader etc.	11 (blir 'becomes')	

9 *Miscellaneous*		
og 'and'/at 'to', both pronounced [å]	10 og for at	4 at for og
v/f	11 av 'of' for af	14 haft 'had' for havt
ng before gn and k	5 (songn 'parish', tængte 'thought')	
mf for nf	6 (komfermeret 'confirmed')	

The kind of errors made are of interest as showing the particular obstacles that faced these writers in conforming to the DN norm. Most of them can be described as *an erroneous choice among alternative spellings for the same phoneme.* The rules for the use of the alternatives were often complex, in some cases arbitrarily characteristic of individual words. Long consonants were written double between vowels after stress, but not finally or in clusters; short consonants were geminated between vowels after non-stress in some words of foreign origin. In such words as *kasserer* and *hotel* it was necessary to memorize the written images of the words; the correct number of consonants could not be reconstructed from the pronunciation. The same was true of stops before voiceless consonants, as in *digt* vs. *redaktør.* Silent *t*'s, *d*'s, *g*'s, and *h*'s had to be memorized for each word, as did the foreign letters and clusters in such words as *luthersk, mission, pension,* and *influenza.* The use of *e/æ* and *o/aa* followed no rule of N pronunciation; Aars required 7 of the 39 pages in his spelling rules of 1878 to expound the use of *e/æ* alone. The palatalized velars offer a number of complications because of the coalescence of palatalized *g* with older *j, gj, hj,* and *lj* (all pronounced *j*, like E *y* in *yes*) and of *sk* with *sj, skj, si, ch,* and *sch* (all pronounced like E *sh*). Norwegian speakers had a special problem in the use of voiced stops (*b, d, g*) after vowels instead of the spoken *p, t, k;* yet examples of substitution of *p, t, k* for *b, d, g* are found in only thirty writers. Only the word *like* 'like' is consistently written with *k* (14); but this spelling was authorized at least as early as 1878.[46] Similarly, the shortened word forms which were adopted in 1907 are found in only eleven writers, though this may partly be due to the failure of many writers to use the particular words in question. It is interesting to note that many of these errors are still prevalent in the Norwegian schools even after the various spelling reforms. Loss of silent *d* and *h,* confusion of *o* and *å, e* and *æ,* single and geminated consonants, *og* and *å,* are still very common, according to an investigation made by Hans Bergersen.[47]

In general, it is obvious that⌐when faced with alternative spellings, writers who are uncertain about the appearance of the spelled word tend to choose the shorter alternative.⌐The only apparent exception, the insertion of syllabic *e,* may represent an actual pronunciation with *e,* or possibly the pronunciation of the letters (*l, r, n*) as the writers spell out the words to themselves. The number of so-called 'reverse' spellings (*sønd* for *søn*) is very small, compared to the simplifications. In a few cases the writers have preferred the spelling that is most distinctive e.g. *aa* for *o* when representing the sound [å] or *kj* for *k* in words like *Kina, gj* for *g* in words like *gik.* The presence of alternative foreign spellings makes for their introduction even in native words, as when *vi* is spelled *wi.*

Traces of the older orthography, preceding 1870, are also found. The use of two vowels to mark vowel length is found in 17 writers: *see* 'see' (4), *riis* 'spanking', *troer* 'believes', *nye* 'new', etc.

7. Significant Deviations from the Spelling Norm.

Non-standard forms and pronunciations occur in less than half of the letters (107), usually no more than one per letter. Only two writers, both apparently from Western Norway, use their dialects in a serious way, approaching that of the NN norm. Four have used dialect forms for humorous effect, as the writer who declares about the cold weather: 'det rent ut smæld i Vægga' (there's a regular crackling in the walls). Even if we did not have the writers' statements concerning their prevailingly EN origin, it would not be hard to identify the majority as having come from this part of the country. The following are unmistakably EN, though they cannot be precisely localized within that area: døft 'baptized', samre 'same', tel 'to', kjærke 'church', vaarønna 'spring work', trøkke 'print', kørja 'the basket', vores 'our', demses 'their', dem 'they' (36 writers), vetta 'know'. Other forms which are used in various parts of the country and often by urban speakers of non-standard N are: strakst 'at once', vist 'if', skynte 'hurry', engels 'English', dusing 'dozen', antereret 'excited', kaffi 'coffee', ner 'down', fameli 'family', arbet 'worked', relion 'religion', katesere 'catechize', maane 'month', hu 'she', naar (for da, in the past) 'when'. Rural forms which have since been adopted in either the NN or DN norm or both are: skog 'woods', kveite 'wheat', sakne 'miss', hukse 'remember', helse 'health', veg 'way', heim 'home', snø 'snow', morosam 'fun', kald 'cold', hard 'hard', frå 'from', trøtt 'tired', gauk 'cuckoo', namn 'name', trufast 'faithful', skule 'school', nå 'now'. Grammatical forms which are similarly widespread in the dialects are the feminine definite article -a (8 writers), plurals in -ar or -er (3), infinitives or weak preterites in -a (3), preterites or past participles in -e (12), reflexives in -st (3), strong preterites like saag 'saw' (10), togg 'chewed', bles 'blew', fek 'got'.

Only when a number of such forms are concentrated in one letter or when some feature of highly limited geographical distribution occurs, does it become possible to identify the origin of the writers more precisely. Among our letters a group of writers from upper Gudbrandsdal and another from Solør stand out in this respect. The occurrence of the following features identifies writers from upper Gudbrandsdal: fornøigd 'satisfied', veil 'well', ai for ei in words like jait 'goat', vaik 'weak'.[48] Of six letters known to be written by natives of Solør four have everywhere i for y (and ei for øy); only one writes the y's correctly (the sixth happens to contain no words in y). While an occasional writing of i for y may occur elsewhere (and of course other dialects have also delabialized the y), the concomitant use of nuk (for nok) 'enough' makes Solør origin almost certain.[49] In general the writers from Solør, Gudbrandsdalen, Trøndelag, and northern Norway show a higher proportion of dialect forms than the rest, apparently reflecting a greater difficulty in writing standard DN.

A very small number of non-standard words is found in the letters. They scarcely amount to more than a score, some of which are really only phonetic variants of standard words: alder 'never', blome 'flower', døl 'dalesman', garnhespel 'reel of yarn', god for 'able', helsing 'greeting', håssen 'how', inkun 'some one', inte 'not', mysmergryn 'a dish made of whey cheese', papperslanter 'bills', regla 'story', snøge 'to snow', ta 'of', tess 'worthwhile', tusse 'goblin', varmkule 'warm spell', veive 'crank', værmor 'mother-in-law'. All of these (except regla) come from EN writers, many of them specifically from Gudbrandsdalen.

8. *The Impact of English.*

⌈The impact of English is much more in evidence than that of the local dialects.[50]⌋ In the first place about one sixth of the letters were written in English, often with an apology and a request for translation into N before publication. Many of them are obituaries or other public announcements, and show little individuality. ⌈A few of the N letters show by their obvious anglicisms of construction and idiom that they were written by members of the younger generation whose N is rather shaky.⌋ Typical is the request of one writer that the editor correct her letter, as she 'har ikke gaaet paa norsk skole saa at sige untagen hvad Jeg har lært av min mor' (haven't gone to Norwegian school so to speak except for what I learned from my mother).

⌈But even in the letters written by the great majority who do master N in speech and writing, there are numerous anglicisms.⌋ They are relatively fewer in the short letters renewing subscriptions, more numerous in letters of commentary, narrative, or public announcement, where a wider vocabulary is required. Of the total number of 229 letters, 60.4 % contained one or more anglicism. Only 23.6 % contained more than one anglicism per page, the absolute maximum for any writer being eight. If we estimate 100 words per page, we see how modest the actual number of anglicisms is in relation to the total. Only in two letters was anything found that approached linguistic confusion; these were brief and illiterate.[51] But even they are nothing like the supposedly N-A letter made up by the Norwegian writer Oskar Braaten which begins as follows: 'Dir modder. Ai will naa kom bæk tu Norwei. Amerika is et lusekøntri som naabaaddi skulde gaa tu....'⁵²

The American influence is pervasive enough to be apparent in the handwriting; less than 100 of the letters show any conspicuous trace of the more angular type of Norwegian school hand. Dates are often given in American form, e. g. June 1st for 1ste juni. Anglicized spellings of N words sometimes occur: femty 'fifty', minde dag 'memorial day'. An occasional E word order is found: og derfor jeg ønsker at have det (inst. of ønsker jeg) 'and therefore I wish to have it.' E phrases have been reproduced by combinations of Norwegian words, as in tage in 'take in, i. e. attend'. New N words have been created on the model of E compounds or phrases: indkomme 'income', sengefasthed 'being bedfast'. N words have been shifted in meaning in response to E uses of similar-sounding words: bank 'river bank' (paa Banken af midl rever), bunke 'bunk, camp bed' (fikse op vores Bed eller Bonke), vel av 'well off' (vi er vel av), papir 'newspaper' (jeg saa i Papiret), parti 'party' (det blev et parti for helle Nilse Slækten), plads 'place' (Byen LaCrosse er en fin liden Plas), gaa 'go' (saa solgte jeg mit Hus og jik til Amerika), spænde 'spend' (vor jeg spænte mine lit over 30 Aar), stoppe 'stop' (han stoppede hos Ole Elstad).

The loanwords proper are 229 in number, of which 156 nouns, 6 pron., 16 adj., 5 num., 32 verbs, 11 adv., 2 prep., and 1 conj. They are of the same kind as are generally heard in speech, words like acre, block, bushel, business, cake, clerk, dollar, farm, feed, flour, flu etc. A few such words are found which (by chance) have not occurred in the writer's notation of spoken AmN, e.g. cookee 'cook's helper' (vilde da at jeg skulde blive Koken's hjelper eller Koki), drive 'logs driven' (i skogen paa Driven og Sagmøllerne), grandchildren (og saa har han 3 Grænkjilderen). Sporadic use of E form words is found, though usually only in the most illiterate writers, e. g. the pronouns I, him, and what in the previously cited letters, this (des Papir), some (det snøga som), something (naar saa tankerne kommer i arbeide finder man somting man aldri har rigti forstaaet), the adverb where (vær han Havde sit Hjæm), the conjunction and (her en der, Mr. end Mrs.).

Lws. are often adapted to N spelling rules, reflecting current

AmN pronunciations. Among the more common changes are: (1) gemination, as in Rappit Chiti 'Rapid City', or simplification, as in faagi 'foggy'; (2) omission of silent letters, as in suprise 'surprise', guvementet 'the government', sirvis 'service'; (3) substitution of equivalent spellings, as in picknick, releaf, saive, valy, zerow; (4) substitution of N spellings, as in brik 'brick', grænkjilderen 'grandchildren', relif 'relief', mounten 'mountain', badra 'bothered', koki 'cookee', Norve 'Norway', vækæsjen 'vacation', tørkey 'turkey', saidvalken 'the sidewalk', feiermand 'fireman', kanty 'county', taun 'town', taaf 'tough'. Such spellings are especially conspicuous when they are applied to proper nouns: Vilmar 'Willmar', Walwort 'Walworth', Julen 'Ulen', Mantene 'Montana', Græn Forks 'Grand Forks', Fergus Faals 'Fergus Falls', and Ragbi 'Rugby'.

The grammatical forms given to the lws. are parallel to those used in speech except that the feminine gender and other popular grammatical features are rare. The only example of a feminine is fila 'the field'. Of 176 nouns, 84.8 % are masculine, the rest neuter. N plurals are regularly added, but in some cases plurals in -s are also found: roads, blocks, baraks, nieces, respects, gangsters, visiters, pallbearers. The verbs are all weak, using preterites in -ede or -et and participles in -et (very rarely in -a): bordede 'boarded', fixet 'fixed', huntet 'hunted', meket 'made', sætlede (setla) 'settled'.

9. *Summary.*

In this chapter we have traced the establishment of a tradition of writing among the N immigrants. Even though the actual extent of training in Norway was not very great for most rural children, it was sufficient to implant habits of reading in all and writing in most of the immigrants. Once arrived in this country, they established supplementary parochial schools in which the religious and linguistic instruction of the Norwegian rural school was continued. In this way even the second generation learned to read and write Norwegian, and a medium of communication by writing was etablished between them and others of Norwegian background. In spite of its brief and fragmentary character, the parochial school was probably the greatest single force in keeping alive a knowledge of written Norwegian. There were, to be sure, many obstacles in the way of the immigrants' acquisition of this language form, since their own dialects were generally at variance with it, and they had little opportunity to hear it spoken except from the pulpit. The DN spelling norm was actually a Danish norm, and it was not until 1907 that the Norwegians at home abandoned their dependence on Danish models. A study of letters written by a representative group of rural immigrants shows, however, that they had mastered the main features of this norm. It met them in their ABC's, their religious textbooks, and their newspapers, and the errors they made were largely inherent in the inconsistencies of the norm itself and the comparatively short schooling which most of them had enjoyed. To this we must add the confusion resulting from the impact of English, which was greater by far than the influence of their native, dialectal speech.

Chapter 7.

THE LITERARY LANGUAGE.

> No one knows what a magnificent cultural achieve-
> ment Norwegian-American literature is until he
> has himself lived on the Western prairies and felt
> the language imperceptibly withering away in a new
> natural setting, a new social environment, under the
> pressure of a strange cultural and linguistic world,
> and without a constant cultural interchange with
> Norway.
>
> *Sigurd Folkestad (1925)*[1]

In spite of the many obstacles which hampered the emigrants
in their handling of the written Dano-Norwegian, this language
became the unquestioned medium of nearly all their serious writing
in the new country. Their very existence as an immigrant group
was in part conditioned on the acceptance of this language as an
instrument of church, press, and literature. Hundreds of periodical
publications, books, and pamphlets poured from the presses.
The quality in this deluge was hardly proportionate to its mass,
but it represented every kind of theme and every species of cultural
aspiration which could possibly find a voice in such a group. Many
gained a hearing who would not have been listened to in the homeland, and others turned into crying voices in the vast wilderness.
Those who wrote Norwegian in America with the purpose of being
read by their emigrated countrymen were beset by certain problems
which were non-existent or less acute back home. In the early
years the simplest aids to writing and printing were missing; and
as these were supplied by a growing educational and literary
interest, there was the never-ending struggle against the dominant

patterns of English. As if this were not enough, Norwegian turned into a fluid, unstable language norm as the nationalists succeeded in breaking the mold into which it had been poured by a century-long Dano-Norwegian tradition. Our theme in this chapter will be a study of some typical phases of the linguistic problems which faced the editors, teachers, and authors who tried to weld the Dano-Norwegian language into an instrument of immigrant writing.

1. *Before the Civil War: the Early Press.*

During the first generation of Norwegian settlement nearly all original writing was concentrated in the immigrant press.[2] The men who shouldered the task of founding the early newspapers had no precedents to guide them, other than their familiarity with newspapers in the homeland and whatever slight contact they may have had with American or possibly German-American newspaper practice. Not one of them was a professional journalist, though some of them became so in due course. They included school teachers and clergymen, but were mostly laymen, the sons of farmers and merchants, with little education beyond the common school. The modest equipment of most would-be editors was well described by Knud Langeland, an editor of *Nordlyset*, the first Norwegian newspaper, when he introduced himself as follows: 'We have neither high learning nor brilliant talents; we have never set foot within the walls of a higher institution of learning; Greek and Latin are not among our literary treasures. But the editor relies on good intentions, an honest will, and tireless work to enable him to convey to his countrymen the most important and interesting news of the day in simple, straightforward, but not quite barbarous Norwegian.'[3] It must be confessed that not all of his successors or colleagues achieved this last-named goal. But there is no doubt of their good intentions.

Like so many other immigrant leaders they had a two-fold perspective. They had the tremendous task of enlightening their immigrated countrymen about the ways of America, and at the same time they wished to keep them informed about developments in the homeland. News from Norway came in the form of letters and newspapers, which were vigorously excerpted in the immigrant press. But the news of America, which dominated the greater part of the newspapers, had to be translated out of English. An analysis of four representative issues of *Nordlyset* from 1847 shows that more than three fifths of the material had originated in English.[4] Of 970 column inches only 314 were original, while 49 were reprinted from Norwegian sources; all the rest was translated, including 240 inches of advertising. The material from Norwegian sources was unusually skimpy in these issues because the editor had difficulty in securing Norwegian newspapers in the early days. But otherwise the proportion is representative of the general situation in most of the immigrant press.

The strain of accommodating all the phenomena of the new land was often more than the Norwegian language could stand. Even if English-Norwegian dictionaries had been available to these early editors, as they were later on, they would still have failed to include many of the neologisms of the frontier. In all those spheres of life where the immigrants came into most immediate contact with their American environment, there was need for a new vocabulary, whether in public administration, economic life, or social customs. There was no way out of using such words as bill, convention, ticket, vote, legislature, Whig, Democrat, town, county seat, school fund, sheriff, township. In their adjustment to American farming the newcomers were forced to speak in terms of breaking soil, claiming land, shelling corn, of settler, settlement, prairie, farmer, creek, fence, field, log house, lot, shingle, farm, steer, hoe, yoke, team, acre, bushel, cord, rod, corn meal, flour, spring wheat. American advertisers created special problems of vocabulary with their long lists of American products and the ecstatic language used to describe their virtues. Words like drygoods, drugs, groceries included types of goods which were not classified in quite the same way back home. Proper names and addresses formed foreign bodies in the Norwegian context, for it might have been misleading to turn them into Norwegian. Rather than risk misunderstandings of the new institutions of American life, the editors mostly chose the easier and safer path of using their American names and letting stylistic consistency go hang.

They had enough trouble just meeting the mechanical problems of getting out a foreign-language newspaper in the wilderness. Printing in the Gothic type was perhaps not too difficult in a state where German newspapers were already established; but Norwegian required at least two characters not in the German font, and we note that in the first issue of *Nordlyset* the editor, James Denoon Reymert, apologized to his readers for having to use the German *ä* and *ö* instead of *æ* and *ø*.[5] He evidently anticipated criticism, for he asked the indulgence of his readers toward all possible shortcomings: 'A number of small errors in the typesetting are due to the fact that we have not been able to secure a printer acquainted with the Norwegian language, but this will all be corrected very shortly.' Three issues later he again made a resigned, but facetious appeal: 'After repeated readings and corrections, so many that our feeble talent for discovery was quite exhausted, we had to let the issue go out into the world. ...Too late we discovered that the date of this issue should be August 26 instead of August 29.' Conversations with immigrant editors have led this writer to believe that the problem of typographical inexpertness was a persistent one, especially in the smaller newspapers. Waldemar Ager, editor of *Reform* in Eau Claire, told the author that much of the time he had to write out in a plain hand every contribution that went into his paper because the typographer understood no Norwegian. In larger newspapers, which could afford to hire competent typographers, it was possible to give them poor copy, such as letters from the subscribers, and expect them to normalize the spelling and punctuation as they went along.

Nordlyset in the hands of Reymert certainly took its task of enlightening the readers as seriously as one could expect. Reymert printed the American Declaration of Independence in the first issue and followed it up in the second with the first installment of the Constitution.[6] These were weighty materials, difficult to render into satisfactory Norwegian, and there was no let-up during the fall as he printed a series of lives of famous Americans, the state constitutions of Illinois and Wisconsin, the President's inaugural address, the Mexican peace treaty, and the like. It is no wonder that he ran afoul of the Norwegian language in trying to render the frequently complicated and redundant expressions of these documents. What can one do in a foreign language with 'a decent respect for the opinions of mankind'? At least one cannot render it into Norwegian as 'en anstændig Respect for Menneskehedens Meninger' without awakening something of a smile from a connoisseur of Norwegian. The same is true of his translation of the passage beginning 'We assume these truths to be self-evident...': 'Vi antage disse Sandheder udisputeerlige: At alle Mennesker ere skabte lige; at de ere af Skaberen udstyrede med visse uadskillelige Rettigheder; at iblandt disse ere Liv, Frihed og Trakten efter Lyksalighed.'[7] One wonders how much the readers understood of such bombastic sentences as the one from Daniel Webster: 'Jeg anraaber paa det alvorligste, om Betragtningen af vor Stilling og vor Character blandt Jordens Nationer forat vi skulle rigeligen være istand til at bedømme vort Stand-punct og vore Pligter...' Perhaps it should be attributed to haste that the following sentence from a presidential message violates many elementary usages of the Norwegian language: 'Formegen Roos, kan ikke blive bestrøet, over vore regulaire og volenteure Officerers og Soldaters Tapperhed, Discipline, mageløs Mod og Standhaftighed; Alle søgende de farligste Poster og veiede sig med hverandre til Døden, i den hvemodigske Uforfærdenhed.'[8] There is a sort of translator's hypnosis, which seems to cause even good writers to be transfixed by the word order or constructions of a foreign language. Nothing else could explain the creation of a word like Foretagelsesaand for the American 'spirit of enterprise' in a language where Foretagsomhed was already available.[9]

Nordlyset was certainly not alone in making such desperate shift with the language. *Friheds-Banneret*, a brief and flighty venture of 1852-3 in Chicago, was even less skilled in its adaptation of American rhetoric. In printing the national platform of the Free Democrats its editor had some grievous moments. This is a bouquet of samples from that document: 'ved Udstædelsen af den uretfærdig, trykkende og ukonstitutionel "Flygtige Slavelov" [i. e. Fugitive Slave Law]...ved at gjøre en suveren Stats Indlemmelse i Unionen tilfældig [i. e. dependent] af andre Forholdsreglers Antagelse...at det fri-demokratiske Parti er ikke organiseret for at hjælpe hverken Whig eller demokratiske Vinge af Unions store Slave-Kompromis-Parti, men for at tilintetgjøre dem begge, ved at forskyde og forlade dem som haabløse, fordær-

vede, og uværdige af al Tiltro.'[10] A more satisfactory level of translation was not attained until the appearance of *Emigranten* in
1853, which became the chief organ of the pre-Civil War period.
Its first editor, C. L. Clausen, was academically trained and a good
writer, while his leading successor, C. F. Solberg, became one of
the really outstanding AmN editors. Even here the advertisements
remained a constant source of howlers, where it was easy to detect
the less successful results of the language struggle. One merchant
announced that 'I Salget af Varer til daglig Brug taaler dette
Etablissement ingen Medbeiler, men kan og vil undersælge ethvert
andet, stort eller lille, Vest for New-York.' The use of Medbeiler
for 'competitor' and the creation of undersælge to render English
'undersell' are typical of the awkward devices adopted to render
American commercialese.

Criticism was not lacking in the press of that time, and the
editors were sometimes given the lash for their linguistic sins. An
anonymous critic of 1853 surveyed the Norwegian immigrant press
down to that date.[11] The language in *Friheds-Banneret* he simply
described as 'barbaric English-Norwegian.' Of this and another
paper he unkindly said that their spiritual kinship was revealed by
their identical capacity for murdering their mother tongue. 'I
recently read an article on child training which was supposed to
have been translated from English. Its three columns contained
94 errors in language, without counting errors of spelling and punctuation!' As a general comment on the defunct papers he wrote
that 'the influence of these papers was weakened and they were
made less attractive to their countrymen by the poor Norwegian
in which they were edited. The translations from English were
particularly bad, so much so that they could very well have been
used as exercises for schoolboys to correct. The words were Norwegian, to be sure, but the phrases were English. Sometimes there
were even words that did not exist in Norwegian, as when *over-
toges* was used in the sense of English "was overtaken" [its real
meaning is "was taken over"]. At first, before I had learned some
more English, I had difficulty in understanding certain sentences.
But this could be excused in men who had not learned their mother
tongue grammatically.' This final concession on the part of the
critic is significant: the environment was non-academic and the

readers were practical men. As they had learned the elements of life in the new country, its terminology came to be the only right and natural one, however much it might differ from that of the original language.

The editors showed their awareness of the problem in the way they incorporated the new English terms into their Norwegian sentences. Each English expression for which no Norwegian equivalent was immediately available represented either an orthographic or grammatical problem.

(1) In many cases the words were marked as foreign bodies by some device like the following: (a) Quotation marks, e. g. Vort "team" bestaaer nu i 4 Yoke Oxer og en Hest; Oprettelsen af et "Meeting House" i Milwaukee; at vi ikke bruger Guds Ord som en "Stepping-Stone".[12] (b) A Norwegian gloss, e. g. en liden Hvede Field (Ager); vote eller stemme Abolitionticket; Fever and Ague (Koldfeberen); det Sjel- og Legemsfordervende Whiskey (Brænde-viin); Trustees (Edsvorne Personer); Comptoir eller Office; en Office eller Embede; en Maadeholds eller Temperance Forening; Beveræge eller Drik. (c) Parentheses, perhaps representing an afterthought to the effect that the English word was more precise than the Norwegian equivalent: Lovforsamlingen (Legislaturen); En Aarsgammel Oxecalv (Steer); Friheds-Partiet (The Liberty Party); en Fredsdommer (Justice of the Peace). In many instances the Norwegian and English words were used in the same issue or even article, e. g. Post Office side by side with Postkontor.

(2) Various accommodations to Norwegian usage helped to make some words more familiar: (a) Respellings (possibly misspellings) reflecting Norwegian pronunciation: Jankee or Jenkee, Beveræge, Grocerier, Yoget [the yoke], Indien, Akre. (b) Inflectional suffixes, fitting the words into a Norwegian context: Whiger (but also Whigs), plural Bushel (but also Bushels). (c) Assignment of gender: et Team, en Beveræge, en Office (but in one case et Post Office, perhaps due to N Postkontor). Neuter words recorded from *Nordlyset* were: team, yoke, fence, settlement, assortment, meeting house, school fund, and township.

(3) Norwegian words were pressed into use as equivalents of some similar-sounding English terms: (a) Simple terms such as brække 'break' in the sense of breaking land (25 Acres opbrækket),

klæmme 'squeeze' in the sense of claiming land (han har klæmt sit Land), simpel 'vulgar' for E simple (Maaden at gjøre Meel af Korn er meget simpelt), ordinere 'ordain' for E order; ˏ(b) Compounds with part Norwegian and part English constituents, such as Boarding-Huus, Korn-Meel, Spring-Hvede, Loghuse, Skolefund, County Sædet, Town Møde (also: Town Skriveren, Town Affairer, Town Committee, Town Regjering, Town Valg); (c) Pseudo-Norwegian words, containing suffixes similar to the English, e.g. Volontør for E volunteer, employerer for employs, etc.

The practices here exemplified from *Nordlyset* more or less set the pattern for later newspapers as well. In part the usages were transferred from speech; in part they were peculiar to writing and may even have influenced speech. Many of the later comers must have learned the English words first in the half-Norwegian form which they often assumed in print. The editors varied in the extent to which they yielded to the English pressure of the environment, and within the same newspaper it is possible to find many inconsistencies. Even a carefully edited paper like *Emigranten* will furnish abundant examples: an article on Indian corn used the word korn for this plant throughout, excepting in the title and twice in the text where the 'correct' Norwegian word mais was used.[13] In an ad headed De Norskes Krambod i Beloit 'the store of Norwegians in Beloit' the subhead ran: Den Billigste Store Vestenfor Milwaukee.[14] The word 'store' was avoided in an editorial, but 'clerk' slipped in instead: han har faaet en Norsk Clerk i sin Boutik.[15] In one article the writer couldn't make up his mind between det Stille Ocean and det Stille Hav for the Pacific Ocean.[16] The columns containing contributors' letters usually show more colloquial admixture of English than the rest, though even these were edited. One contributor was permitted to use N gaa in a usage imitated from E go and write, as he no doubt would have said, that he 'agtede at gaae opad Riveren og tage Arbeide.'[17] But the same usage occurred in a regular article where it was said: 'I kortere Tid end der før udfordredes til at gaae fra New-York til Columbus...'[18]

These examples will suffice to show the⌐pressure of English patterns on the early journalists and the extent to which they yielded to it. Their language was created in constant struggle and bears the marks of a hybrid environment. But the growing response of their readers shows that it met the needs of the situation, however inadequate by the standards of native grammarians.

2. *Anglicisms and the Later Press.*

The years that followed the Civil War brought with them a new wave of immigration which vastly expanded the number of Norwegians and their spread throughout the Middle West. A whole bevy of new journals sprang up to cater to their needs. *Emigranten* was absorbed by a LaCrosse rival and appeared after 1868 as *Fædrelandet og Emigranten*. In the meanwhile *Skandinaven* had appeared in Chicago in 1866 and rapidly grew to become the chief organ of political republicanism. Newspapers bobbed up in Minnesota too, the most significant being the Minneapolis *Budstikken* from 1873. In the following year came two important papers, the *Norden* in Chicago and the *Decorah-Posten* in Decorah, Iowa, the latter destined to absorb all the others as the last surviving major newspaper in the Middle West. Beause of the much larger circulation attained by many of these and the improved methods of typography, they were able to overcome some of the mechanical weaknesses of the early press. But throughout the history of the immigrant press the editor's life consisted of a day-to-day battle against the English patterns which threatened the very heart of his Norwegian style.

Succeeding generations of immigrated editors brought with them from Norway a fresh sense of the changing linguistic norms of the homeland and a renewed enthusiasm for the task of writing 'good' Norwegian. But it can safely be said that no one succeeded entirely in keeping his linguistic path inviolate, and extremely few were so ambitious or perhaps foolish as to attempt a task which would have opened a chasm between them and their subscribers. In the words of a correspondent to Decorah-Posten of 1930: 'The so-called common people are so used to our characteristic language mixture that what may possibly be regarded as language sins are fully and completely understood precisely because they are written in this way.'[19]

A cursory examination of *Decorah-Posten* around the turn of the century shows that this must indeed have been so, or that journal would not have attained its commanding position among AmN papers. The news columns in an issue of 1900 shows precisely the same type of anglicised terminology, only slightly more sophisticated, as in the earlier *Nordlyset*.[20] No one could read as much as a single column without knowing that the material had been written in America: han pumpede en Tilstaaelse ud af Estergren; en ignoreret Lov; en Auditør [Norw. revisor]; amendere Billen; en første Dividende; Statsanstalternes Lemmers Klæder [i.e. the clothes of inmates at state institutions]; en Injunktion som blev exekveret; Prospektering efter Kobber; Larmen af den undvigende Gas [i.e. the noise of the escaping gas]; Arbeiderunioner; Rapporter fra Baglandet [i.e. reports from the hinterland, in California]; lægge i Stoven; ingen høie Bluffs; en god Mule [N mulesel]; vi "Lumberjacks"; Temperancestat; Landet vil uden Tvil stige i Pris, eftersom det bliver opsettlet. Conspicuous as these expressions undeniably would be to a Norwegian stylist, their total number on two full pages containing ab. 9000 words did not amount to more than 100, or about 1 word in 90. Now and then a real howler comes along, resulting more from a misguided attempt to make Norwegian expressions out of English than from a frank giving up, as in the following case: De ledende Kjøbmænd... kappes med hverandre i sund Konkurrance om de bedste Skuevinduer [i.e. show windows].[21] Comparison with an issue from 1922 showed rather a reduction than an increase of anglicisms since 1900; but even within a single issue there was a variation from the columns written by one staff member to those of another. The careful reader could not avoid noticing the erroneous usage in such a phrase as this: Indianer imødegaar Livsstraf 'Indian faces life sentence.' In Norway imødegaar can only mean 'contradict'; it should have been written gaar Livsstraf imøde. But in view of the fact that the context made any real confusion impossible, the average reader no doubt accepted the meaning without cavilling about the phrasing.

Criticism of the language used in the immigrant press did not come from the average subscribers, but in the later as in the earlier press it came from the more critical members of the editorial staffs themselves.⌉ The severest and at the same time most amusing indictment was made by one of the associate editors of *Decorah-Posten* who for a short time conducted a column consisting entirely of linguistic specimens culled from the pages of the Norwegian (and Danish) immigrant press. The column ran from December 10, 1929 to April 15, 1930 under the ironical heading of *Sprogets Vildblomster* (Wildflowers of the Language). The author preserved a rather transparent anonymity by signing himself Botanicus, but the specimens he exhibited were held up as weeds rather than as flowers. He poked fun at his fellow editors by picking out stylistic boners, chiefly those which were due to unsuspected English influences. Any one whose ear was attuned to native Norwegian or Danish usage would be greatly amused by such sentences as he found his contemporaries using: hun vinkede med Øinene 'she winked with her eyes' (vinke in N means 'wave one's hands'); Elias som blev født av Ravnene 'Elijah who was fed by the ravens' (født in N means 'born'); uden at der var blit tilføiet ham nogen Harm 'without any harm having been done him' (in N harm means 'angry'). He found them creating new constructions modelled on English ones: levere en Tale 'deliver a speech'; løbe for office 'run for office'; en hel Hær af Journalister dækket Kampen 'a whole army of journalists covered the fight'; opp til oss 'up to us'; gaa ned i Historien 'go down in history'; naar han smiler, da varmer du op til ham 'when he smiles, you warm up to him.'

The collection is amusing indeed to the connoisseur and invaluable to a student of AmN, since it brings useful examples of all the typical confusions of pattern that are part of the immigrant's dilemma. It shows conclusively that editors in the twentieth century were behaving in much the same way as Reymert and his followers in the nineteenth. But the Botanizer's colleagues were not amused. Waldemar Ager, who probably felt himself exposed to the implied criticism, wrote in *Reform* that 'it is most unfortunate to start making fun of the Norwegian which is commonly used in our Norwegian-American press. We all know that we can not measure up to those who have had an opportunity to form their language in the higher schools in the old country.'[22] Another, Franklin Petersen, wrote that Botanicus might as well try to stop Niagara Falls as to weed out the many luxuriant and colorful wildflowers of the Norwegian-American language. 'For a hundred years the emigrants have shaped the tongue they took with them over the sea until it has become a language all its own which it is difficult for others to understand. When the Norwegian-American has stayed here a while, he discovers that there are many English words which express his thoughts in an easier and more effective way than those he possesses in his mother tongue. Therefore he trims up the English words a little, adds a Norwegian ending to the word to give it a familiar sound, and includes it in his vocabulary.'[23]

Botanicus was placed in the position of having to defend his critical attitude, which he did with the plea that professional writers had a responsibility towards the language. It was their duty to maintain a standard of purity and correctness, for 'the language that is most purely spoken is also the most comprehensible.' 'No one expects that Norwegian-American speech should be free of mixture, but newspapers, which should be leaders in this field, ought to avoid to the best of their ability and as long as possible any turns of phrase that are too bad.'[24] The editor-in-chief of his paper, Kristian Prestgard, took the question up in an editorial, and expressed his gratitude to Botanicus for keeping a critical eye on the doings of the writers. 'He has shown that far too many of those who work in the Norwegian language think in English when they write Norwegian or imagine they do, which may be something quite different.' At the same time Prestgard warned him that words were living organisms, which could not be squeezed into grammatical rules without serious danger of mayhem.[25]

Those subscribers who took an interest in the discussion were strongly divided. Some came to his support, thanking him for his efforts to clean out the linguistic 'weeds'.[26] Now and then they even added samples of their own to his collection. But the most typical reaction was that of a subscriber who wrote in a strongly defensive way that poor people who had emigrated from Norway some 40 to 50 years earlier lacked schooling and had had to spend their time in the new country working, eating, and sleeping. 'Therefore we are willing to put up with anything as long as we can understand it...'[27] This feeling among the average subscribers may have been the reason for the discontinuance of the column at the end of the first season. They did not share the writer's enthusiasm for the purity of rhetorical standards; perhaps in most instances they were unable to see anything funny in the examples quoted. This was their language, and it was no more funny to them than any language is to those who use it. Those who are highly trained in the rhetoric of a given language tend to acquire a static view of the language, assuming that its models and its norms are inviolable. But a historical and social view of language must lead to a realization that a language responds to social change. AmN could not remain true to the arbitrary norms of old-world DN if it were to function adequately in exile.

This view was clearly expressed as early as 1879 by an anonymous writer who edited the *Norsk-amerikansk Haandbog* for *Skandinaven:* he may have been Svein Nilsson, then editor of that paper.[28] He recognized the use of English in immigrant Norwegian and defended its introduction in reasonable quantities into the written language. Any one who would avoid the use of English terms would have to make up new Norwegian words, which would not be understood over here; or else use Norwegian words of approximately equivalent meaning. But this could be quite misleading, as when the word Borgermester was used for mayor, Raadmand for a member of the common Council, Auditør for an auditor, etc. 'Any one who is at all acquainted with the administration of these countries must know that the functions of the American officials mentioned have little or no similarity to those of the Scandinavian officials whose titles are equated to theirs.' He also pointed out that many of the 'correct' Norwegian words were French or German loanwords in Norwegian anyway: 'then it is most natural to prefer the English words which are used here in daily speech to the French or German words which are in use in Scandinavia but are unknown to most people over here.'

A study of current practice in the surviving newspapers would show that the most carefully edited ones, such as *Decorah-Posten* and *Nordisk Tidende,* approximately follow this moderate norm. Of the two, *Nordisk Tidende* carries less American news and maintains a style somewhat closer to that of present-day Norwegian (referring now to word-choice, but true also of orthography). It is also more liberal in its inclusion of English-language material in its columns. In both newspapers the chief trouble-spot linguistically is the advertising, while the news columns and editorials generally make more effort to maintain a pure Norwegian.[29] But the editors recognize realistically that neither they nor their readers would be served by a rigid exclusion of the key terms of American social structure.[30]

3. *The Teaching of Norwegian.*

Guidance in the writing of Norwegian on an adult level was available from the time of the founding of Luther College in 1861. Its early catalogs were printed in Norwegian, and all instruction except in English literature and language took place in Norwegian. As late as 1905/6 a section of its catalog was printed in Norwegian. Students received a thorough linguistic training modelled on the classical courses in Norway; most of them went out as pastors in the Norwegian Lutheran Church and played a dominant role in the creation of a clerical literature. There were also students who led in the creation of a secular literature, such as Rasmus B. Anderson and Peer Strømme. Other Norwegian-American institutions were established, the most prominent of which was St. Olaf College in 1875 (though it did not become a college until 1890). Even when these schools became predominantly English in their language of instruction, a faculty of Norwegian was retained and for many years students were required to take courses in which they could learn at least a smattering of the language. Some of the teachers of Norwegian were able writers and lecturers, who played a prominent role in the cultural life of the group. The most eminent of these were P. J. Eikeland of St. Olaf College and his pupil and colleague, O. E. Rølvaag.[31]

As early as 1869 an effort was made to organize a society for the establishment of Scandinavian professorships at American universities. One of the prime movers was Rasmus B. Anderson, who in that year became an instructor at the University of Wisconsin. He introduced instruction in Norwegian into the curriculum in 1870 and was made professor of Scandinavian Languages in 1875.[32] The Universities of Minnesota and North Dakota followed this example in 1883 and 1891, as a result of resolutions passed by the respective State Legislatures.[33] In 1912 the University of Washington established a Department of Scandinavian, in which courses in Norwegian were regularly offered. Many other universities have established single courses and professorships, but these are the only ones where the Norwegian language has been taught continuously down to the present time.[34]

⌈The demand for Norwegian instruction led naturally to the production of teaching materials. The earliest teachers at Luther College used textbooks imported from Norway. Their students had a foundation of reading knowledge from their parochial school training, as we have seen in the preceding chapter.⌉ At the University of Wisconsin, also, the earliest announcements by R. B. Anderson show that he was using literary texts like Bjørnson's *Synnøve Solbakken* in imported editions. But two years after he had started teaching Norwegian, a grammar of the language appeared in Chicago, and five years later Anderson included it for the first time in his catalog announcements. This was the first book of its kind in America. The author was a clergyman, C. J. P. Peterson, and the title was: *A Norwegian-Danish Grammar and Reader, with a Vocabulary; designed for American students of the Norwegian-Danish language.*[35] This text, which was widely used for a generation, was thoroughly traditional in its approach. The orthography included such conservative features as capitalized nouns and plural verb forms, and even some silent *e*'s. The grammar was nothing but a schoolbook sketch; it was followed by reading selections from Danish and Norwegian authors, and a vocabulary.

In 1875 another Peterson, with the initials O. M., published a Norwegian grammar as part of a letter-writer for the immigrants; the year after, it appeared independently under the title of *Kortfattet norsk sproglære indeholdende retskrivningslære formlære og sætningslære, tilligemed exempler og øvelser, samt anvisning til at analysere.*[36] The orthography used was the one then coming into use in Norway: no capitalized nouns and no verb plurals; but he advised pronouncing the silent *d*'s and *t*'s in such words as haard 'hard' and bordet 'the table'. A section on grammar was also included in a *Norsk-amerikansk Haandbog* published by John Anderson in Chicago in 1879; but here the capitals *were* used, in conformity with the spelling of *Skandinaven*, which was published by the same concern. A 'first reader' in Norwegian by O. M. Peterson came in 1885; in the preface he noted that 'Norwegian orthography has for some time been in a state of great confusion, every author of note, and every would-be author, having devised an orthography of his own.'[37] His own spelling, he wrote, was one that agreed 'substantially with the orthography of all modern authors of note.'

The Nineties saw a new burst of activity in Norwegian textbooks, possibly stimulated by the awakened Anglo-Saxon interest in Ibsen and other Norwegian authors. Grammars appeared in Oxford (England), and in New York; but more widely used in American classes was the *Norwegian Grammar and Reader* by Julius E. Olson of 1898.[38] A pupil of Olson's, George T. Flom, followed this up in 1905 with the first annotated text; he chose the most popular novel written in Norwegian up to that time, Bjørnson's classic tale of country life, *Synnøve Solbakken*.[39] In textbooks, as in other cultural activities among the immigrants, the years from the liberation of Norway to the end of the First World War were the most productive. Four grammars and seven reading texts appeared, reflecting the great expansion of college teaching, especially in the Norwegian-American colleges:

(1) Grammars. Peter J. Eikeland, *Norsk grammatik med eksempler og opgaver for skolen og til selvstudium* (Kristiania, 1908); Johan Andreas Holvik, *Beginners' Book in Norse* (Minneapolis, Minn., 1910); Maren Michelet, *First Year Norse* (Minneapolis, Minn., 1912); Peter J. Eikeland, *Haandbok i norsk retskrivning og uttale til skolebruk og selvstudium* (Minneapolis, Minn., 1916).

(2) Reading texts. Henrik Ibsen, *Brand, et dramatisk digt*, ed. with introduction and notes by Julius E. Olson (Chicago, 1912); J. A. Holvik, *Second Book in Norse; literary selections* (Minneapolis, Minn., 1912); Bjørnstjerne Bjørnson, *En glad gut*, ed. for school use by J. A. Holvik (Minneapolis, Minn., 1915); the same, ed. by Guy R. Vowles (Minneapolis, Minn., 1915); Bjørnson, *En fallit*, ed. by J. A. Holvik (Minneapolis, Minn., 1919); Jonas Lie, *Selected Stories and Poems*, ed. by I. Dorrum (Minneapolis, Minn., 1914); Henrik Ibsen, *Terje Viken*, ed. by M. Michelet and Guy R. Vowles (Minneapolis, Minn., 1918).

World War I delivered a body blow to the study of Norwegian, especially in the high schools, where it had been widely introduced. As a result, few works were published during the twenties, the chief ones being Rølvaag and Eikeland's *Norsk Læsebok* in three volumes and an edition of Jonas Lie, *Lodsen og hans hustru*.[40] The present writer made a contribution to the field in the thirties with his *Beginning Norwegian*, which appeared in mimeographed form in 1934 and in print in 1937.[41] This was followed by *Reading Norwegian*, a book of easy selections in reading, and *Spoken Norwegian*, a beginners' guide to conversational Norwegian produced for the United States Armed Forces during World War II.[42]

The texts which appeared after the turn of the century were not intended to give learners full mastery of the written language. They were aimed at Americans who wished to learn something about Norwegian, not at speakers of Norwegian who might wish to perfect their mastery of the written language.

The persistence of Norwegian as an academic subject can be gauged by the facts presented in the previously[34] cited survey for 1950-51 by Bronner and Franzén. In that year courses in the Norwegian language were being offered at the Universities of California (Berkeley and Los Angeles), Chicago, Georgetown, Harvard, Kansas, Michigan, Minnesota, North Dakota, Pennsylvania, South Dakota, Utah, Washington, and Wisconsin; at the colleges (mostly operated by the Lutheran church) named Augsburg, Augustana (Sioux Falls, S. D.), Bethany, Concordia (Moorhead, Minn.), Iowa State Teachers, Luther, Pacific Lutheran, St. Olaf, and Waldorf; at the high schools in Brooklyn, N. Y. (Bay Ridge), Chicago (College Prep. School), Everett, Wash., Grand Forks, N. D., Minneapolis, Minn. (Roosevelt, South), and Fargo, N. D. (Oak Grove Seminary). The total number of students enrolled in these institutions was 147 in the universities, 594 in the colleges, and 298 in the high schools, making altogether 1,039 Norwegian language students in the United States.

The post-war drop of 17 per cent revealed by this figure may not be too significant. But the trend was not encouraging, particularly in the high schools and colleges, where group loyalties were obviously weakening. Norwegian teaching faced the possibility that instruction might some day be limited to the rarefied air of the universities.

4. *The Problem of Orthography.*

The problem of orthography was not acute in the earliest press, at least not before the Civil War. The spelling used in *Nordlyset* and *Emigranten* was essentially that of school and press in Norway at the time, conspicuous to later readers because of the widespread use of silent vowels to mark length, e.g. *steen* 'stone', *overgaaer* 'exceeds', and such superfluous letters as *c, ph, q,* and *x.* Developments sketched in the preceding chapter led to the abandonment of these forms by 1870. The new immigrant press of the 70's accepted most of these changes. In Norway this relatively standardized DN spelling was under continual fire and was sharply modified after 1890. But in the immigrant press it remained standard, at least in the most widely read organs, a great deal longer.

A study of *Skandinaven* for the year 1874 shows that verb plurals were quite irregularly used. Within the same story the following forms occur after plural subjects: udviser, ville, har, have, ere, har, i.e. exactly 50-50. The more conservative *Fædrelandet og Emigranten* showed a more consistent use of the plurals. As stated above, C. J. P. Peterson used them in his grammar of 1872. But in general this grammatical rather than orthographic feature of older DN disappeared in the AmN press. On the other hand those changes that were made in the successive school orthographies after 1875 found no response in the press. This was conspicuously the case with the capitalization of nouns, which was officially abandoned in Norwegian schools in 1877, though it did not penetrate the homeland press until some years later. The writer P. P. Iverslie agitated for this change in the columns of *Skandinaven* as early as 1874, but without success. 'It makes the orthography more convenient,' he declared, 'more handsome, and what may be of considerable weight with many, more republican.'[43] Even Olson's grammar of 1898 maintained the capitals, and it was not until Flom's edition of *Synnøve* in 1905 that a school textbook followed the Norwegian example. The orthography of a newspaper like *Decorah-Posten* around 1900 was not essentially different from that of Norwegian newspapers of 1870, in spite of the changes which had been creeping in over there during the last decade of the century. It was a spelling that was Danish in all essentials.

Around 1900, however, the changes in Norwegian orthography could no longer be ignored. New forms had been quietly adopted in Norwegian schoolbooks, and a radical change was being prepared by a committee appointed by the ministry of Church and Education; persistent agitation by Knud Knudsen and his followers among the Norwegian authors had finally led to tangible results. The first major attempt to explain and justify this situation to AmN readers was made by a young clergyman, recently immigrated from Norway, S. Sondresen, in a pamphlet published in 1902: *Norsk Sprog i dets udviklingsstadier historisk fremstillet.*[44] His starting point for a historical sketch of Norwegian was the apparently 'planless confusion' that existed in current orthography. His purpose, which he carried out in admirable and entirely sound fashion, was to show that while it might be confusing, it was not without reason. He showed that 'the Danish written language has lost its authority' in Norway; he explained in some detail why this was so; and he concluded that thanks to the language struggle, the written Norwegian of his day was far more Norwegian than it had been and that there was some hope that in time the two present-day languages would unite in a single language. This point of view was one that was shared by leading teachers of Norwegian, such as P. J. Eikeland, and even some editors, such as Kristian Prestgard. Eikeland, then head of the Norwegian Department at St. Olaf College, published his grammar of Norwegian in 1908 with the new spelling which had become official in Norway in 1907. This example was followed by all the authors of college and high school textbooks as late as 1925, some years after the still newer spelling of 1917 had been decreed.[45]

Teachers of Norwegian generally welcomed the spelling of 1907 because it simplified the task of instruction. No longer was it necessary to teach students that in words like *kake, tute,* or *pipe* the spoken *k*'s, *t*'s, and *p*'s were to be written *k, t, p* initially but *g, d, b* medially. Since the teachers dealt primarily with youngsters, whose previous Norwegian spelling habits, if any, were not too deeply ingrained, they were less troubled by the spelling change than were the editors, whose customers were older readers, mostly immigrated from Norway before the spelling had been seriously tampered with. Because of their active interest in contemporary

Norwegian developments, the teachers were also more clearly aware of the reasons for the change and its cultural implications. Several articles in the literary magazine *Symra* for 1911 were written in the new spelling, one of them being by Professor Knut Gjerset of Luther College. In 1912 a contribution by Professor Ole E. Rølvaag to *Jul i Vesterheimen* was published in the new spelling, the first in that publication. Editor Kristian Prestgard wrote in his periodical *Symra* for 1911: 'It is only a question of time when the press — which oddly enough always comes last in these matters — gradually shall begin to reform its language. Certain Norwegian journalists have predicted that if the Landsmaal is introduced in Norway, Norwegian papers in America will have to take their Norwegian news from Danish newspapers. Such a situation already exists in part, not because of the "introduction" of Landsmaal, but because of the reforms in spelling of the Norwegian Rigsmaal. But such a situation is untenable.'[46] This proved to be a more than optimistic view of the situation.

The question of the press and the new spelling was raised once more by Prestgard in *Symra*, two years after the first time, and now in a more definitive form. An editorial in the 1913 volume was entitled, 'Our Press and the Riksmaal.' Prestgard was himself strongly in favor of the linguistic development in Norway, coming as he did of mountain stock and being imbued with the ideas of the folk high school. In his article in *Symra* he could express himself freely in favor of the new spelling; he asserted that it was an example of 'national-cultural reconstruction.' He then raised the question, 'What will the press do about it? For the time being there is probably no pressing need of doing anything. The overwhelming mass of the readers of the Norwegian-American press still are most at home with the language form which they find in their newspapers and which they have known from their childhood.' But he went on to say that he expected a pressure for the new spelling to come from the young people who were learning Norwegian in the schools and from new immigrants from Norway. He wished the papers to begin gradually introducing the new spelling, for example in the news from Norway, where it would not require any extra labor to introduce it.

He showed his own will to adopt the new by using it himself

and introducing it into *Symra* during the years from 1912-1914. He asked Eikeland to write an article for *Symra* on the use of the new spelling in the schools. Eikeland's reply and the succeeding correspondence is enlightening in this connection.[47] Eikeland agreed to write the article when he could find the time, but expressed his annoyance with the attitude of the press in these matters. 'Among the many and great hindrances which the teaching of Norwegian in this country has had to battle with in the last 20-30 years, the press is one of the very worst... The schools have tried to keep up with movements in Norway, but the press has carried on in the same rut... The large newspapers have been the worst, and Skandinaven the *very* worst... Now it appears that the press begins to feel that a change must take place, but now it is not easy. Now a great leap will be needed. If they had followed along gradually, they would not even have noticed the change.'[48] Eikeland accordingly disagreed with Prestgard's statement that nothing much needed to be done. He was himself a member of a committee appointed by the leading N-A publishing houses on the problem of orthography. By two to one this committee voted to adopt the new, but an effort of Eikeland on behalf of the committee to influence the publishers of the larger secular papers came to naught. An annual meeting of publishers held in Minneapolis on September 25, 1913, turned thumbs down on the professor. He wrote to Prestgard: 'The press meeting took all the wind out of my sails. Nice, pleasant gentlemen all of them. But the purse weighs more heavily than all the arguments in the world.'[49] The only report appearing in the press about the meeting was terse enough: 'Most of the expressions of opinion agreed that in view of the great confusion which the problem of orthography is causing in Norway, we in this country would do well to be cautious about reforms.'[50]

Eikeland did not give up. The article he had promised to write for *Symra* became a full-length plea to the press and the public for the adoption of the new spelling.[51] Its provocative title 'Retskrivning og vrangskrivning' foreshadowed its theme, that a bad orthography ('vrangskrivning') is a hindrance to cultural advance. He explained why it had been necessary for the N-A schools to keep in touch with Norwegian changes. It would seem to be obvious that when they taught their pupils Norwegian, it should be the Norwegian of their own time, and neither AmN nor older DN. But if the press refused to follow this lead, the younger generation would simply be unable to read it. It was his conviction that keeping up with Norwegian changes would help to maintain the use of Norwegian longer, for 'the linguistic contact with the mother country is the most important source of nourishment and rejuvenation for Norwegian in America.'[52] In the press Eikeland's plea fell on deaf ears, but within the church he was more successful. His officially appointed committee decided that the publishing houses of the churches should adopt the new spelling. The results were evident, not merely in the new textbooks previously mentioned, but also in the periodicals that reached a wider audience. In 1916 *Jul i Vesterheimen*, a Christmas annual, changed over, and in 1917 *Lutheraneren*, the official church magazine. Thus arose the paradoxical situation that the writings of the church, at least on the adult level, appeared in a less conservative dress than those of the secular press.[53] The only major newspaper in the Middle West to change was *Minneapolis Tidende*, which chose to change to 1907 spelling in 1934, just a few months before it collapsed.[54]

The church publications had no sooner decided to adopt the new DN spelling than the reformers in Norway succeeded in voting a second major change. The spelling of 1917 was an even more radical break with the accustomed word images of DN than was that of 1907. Its major changes of *å* for *aa* and doubled consonants in final position after short vowels (e.g. takk for tak, hopp for hop) created many obstacles to easy reading by those accustomed to the oldest DN. Even in Norway this spelling met with determined resistance, especially from conservative newspapers which hoped for a time that it might be rescinded. The lag in this country was correspondingly greater than it had been in 1907. Again the academic and literary response preceded that of the larger commercial publications. Organs representing more recently immigrated groups, such as the literary magazine *Norden* in Chicago, appeared between 1928 and 1933 in the new spelling. The first textbook in the new spelling was this writer's mimeographed edition of *Beginning Norwegian*, published in 1934. *Jul i Vesterheimen* changed in 1935. When *Lutheraneren* changed editors in 1939, it also changed orthography. In view of the fact that the chief secular organs,

Decorah-Posten and *Skandinaven,* were still appearing in the old DN spelling, this was indeed a radical step to take in the church organ which more and more was being read only by the oldest generation in the church. Rev. Herman Jorgensen, the new editor, a native Norwegian in close touch with the old homeland, not only adopted the new spelling, but also went over from Gothic to Latin type, thus at one blow changing completely the appearance of his journal.[55] The change in type font was in part dictated by considerations of expense.[56]

But a flood of protests forced the editor to defend the reform in an open letter to his readers.[57] With regard to the new type font, he pointed out that most of those who wished to keep the old type seemed to have no difficulty in reading American newspapers in Latin type. As for the spelling, he pointed out that very few subscribers appeared to realize that *Lutheraneren* had already changed from the oldest DN in 1917. Yet at that time the protests had been even more vehement than now. This showed that it was quite possible to learn a new spelling, if people really wanted to. The usual argument was that there was no use in learning the new spellings, since Norwegian was being maintained for the older generation anyway and the language would die with them. This argument the editor brushed aside with an appeal to the oldsters not to look selfishly at the matter, but to yield in the hope that the younger generation might be more likely to read a paper in the newer spelling which they were learning in college. He also emphasized the possibility of keeping a more vital contact with current developments in the religious literature of the homeland. Later issues of the magazine showed no retreat on the part of the editor; now and then he printed letters from subscribers approving the change.[58]

Some readers cancelled their subscriptions, and informants with whom the writer has spoken about the matter generally disapproved of it. But the actual loss of subscribers from 1939 to 1940 was not catastrophic, and it is hard to say whether it was due to the spelling change or to the natural loss to which a Norwegian press organ of this kind was subject. The circulation of *Lutheraneren* had been almost static from 1932 to 1939, though with slight fluctuations up and down; in the former year it was 9,919, in the latter 9,921. It reached a peak in 1937 of 10,631 and fell in 1938 and 1939; the fall in 1940 to 9,089 was larger than in the preceding years, but not surprising in view of the declining use of Norwegian in the churches during this period. A further one-third decline in subscribers from 1940 to 1947 was also not surprising under the circumstances.[59]

In 1938 confusion was compounded by the appearance of another Norwegian spelling reform, the third in this generation. Its purpose was to push the language a step farther in the direction of a unified spelling based on folk speech. The changes were of two kinds, orthographic and linguistic. The purely orthographic ones included the pronouns deg, meg, seg (formerly dig, mig, sig), hva 'what' (hvad), ble 'became' (blev), kunne 'could' (kunde), skulle 'should' (skulde), opp 'up' (op), and the diphthong øy for øi in all words. The linguistic ones included popular or dialectal word forms such as etter 'after' (efter), fram 'forward' (frem), hage 'garden' (have), and grammatical forms such as the ending -a in kua 'the cow', husa 'the houses', kasta 'threw'.[60] This writer's textbook *Reading Norwegian* (1940) was ready just in time to be changed into the new spelling, in accord with a decision made by the teachers of Norwegian. This and the writer's *Spoken Norwegian* (1946) are so far the only textbooks in the new spelling. Otherwise the spelling did not have much American influence until the end of the Second World War, when papers in the new spelling again became available from Norway. The church publication *Jul i Vesterheimen* went over to it in 1945, but not the magazine *Lutheraneren*. *Nordisk Tidende* in Brooklyn began experimenting with it near the end of the war, and gradually adopted it after Liberation (May 7, 1945). All the smaller local papers went over to it during these years, though very few of them were capable of maintaining a consistent orthography. A study of sample numbers of these papers appearing during 1950 showed that the following were more or less consistently being printed in the newest spelling: *Duluth Skandinav* (Duluth, Minnesota), *Minneapolis Posten* (Minneapolis, Minnesota), *Normanden* (Fargo, North Dakota), *Norrøna* (Winnipeg, Manitoba), *Norsk Nytt* (New Westminster, British Columbia), *Viking* (Chicago, Illinois), *Visergutten* (Fargo, North Dakota), *Washington Posten* (Seattle, Washington). These were all weeklies with a purely local following and usually badly proofread; the two Fargo papers used *aa* for *å* and were slightly more conservative in their spelling. In taking the new spelling, however, they regularly adopted only the orthographic changes, not the linguistic ones.

One reason for the rather widespread adoption of the latest spelling in these papers was that a large portion of their Norway news came from the news service of the Norwegian Embassy or from the Norwegian press. They could not afford to hire compositors with such skill in Norwegian that they could edit copy from one spelling into another. Hence there were often wide discrepancies between such news stories and the editorial and local columns. The reading public as well as the editors of these papers consisted largely of immigrants who left Norway after the spelling reforms began, and therefore were psychologically prepared for anything in this line. The few monthlies which still appeared in 1950 varied greatly in the policies adopted by their editors but were generally more conservative than the weeklies: *Folkebladet* (Minneapolis, Minn.) 1907 spelling, *For Gammel og Ung* (Wittenberg, Wis.) old DN, *Lutheraneren* (Minneapolis, Minn.) 1917, *Norsk Ungdom* (Chicago, Ill.) 1907 or 1917, *Sangerhilsen* (Minneapolis, Minn.) mixed, and *Sons of Norway* (Minneapolis, Minn.) 1938.

But the most representative organ of the older AmN generation, particularly in the rural Middle and Far West, *Decorah-Posten*, still held out against the forces of orthographic disruption. Its circulation was greater than that of all the others added together, and it could afford to maintain a staff of compositors who assured it of a consistent orthography. Yet even its subscribers were not getting the pure DN spelling of the pre-1907 era, though few of them appeared to realize it. At any rate they wrote to the editor and thanked him for maintaining the same spelling as the paper had always had. But in 1939 editor Prestgard quietly and without fanfare introduced a mild spelling reform. During the first three months of the year it gradually spread from the editorials to the news columns and finally to the readers' letters. Shortened word forms were adopted, of the type far, mor, ha, gi, ta, bli, la; preterites in -et and -dde took the place of older -ede; -t was dropped after -ig in adjectives and adverbs; av and hadde replaced af and havde; barn, barna was written for børn, børnene. These were all 1907 changes; but the paper stopped short of those major changes which would have materially altered the appearance of the printed page, such as eliminating the gothic type-face, the capitalization of nouns, or the Danish voiced consonants (*b d g* after vowels). The publishers have been willing to make one change, the elimination of the gothic type-face; but as late as 1949 a poll of subscribers showed 43.3 % who wished to retain it.[61] The moral appears to be that if subscribers are asked for their opinion, they will vote for the status quo; but if they are faced with a fait accompli, they will accept that also provided it is sufficiently disguised. This occurred in the summer of 1952 when *Decorah-Posten* gave up the gothic type without further ado and apparently without protest from its subscribers.

5. *The Men of Letters.*

The rise of an original literature in the Norwegian language followed close upon the establishment of cultural institutions among the immigrants. Once the conditions had been provided for the existence of professional writers through the rise of a strong press, church, and school, it was inevitable that the urge should come to write books. Before the Civil War the only books published were guides to prospective emigrants, which usually appeared in Norway, or reprints of religious manuals, the earliest being Pontoppidan's·*Sandhed til Gudfrygtighed* in 1842.[62]

The year 1874 was a significant turning point in the literary development of the group. In that year appeared the first novel of immigrant life, *Alf Brage*, by a schoolteacher and editor, N. S. Hassel. In English came R. B. Anderson's *America not Discovered by Columbus* and H. H. Boyesen's novel *Gunnar*. Down to this time, as a critic in the newspaper *Fædrelandet og Emigranten* wrote in 1872, 'our countrymen in America have chiefly been busied with the material concerns of life, and have not ventured outside the sphere of the farm and the workshop except for some ministers, and a few editors, doctors, and lawyers.'[63] Now things were to be different; a collection of 'esthetic' books was added to the Luther College library, at about the same time as the first Norwegian collection was established at the University of Wisconsin.[64] The newspapers began reprinting current Norwegian literature and reviews of newly published books.[65] In 1876 there was even a mature discussion of 'Norwegian-American Literature: Obstacles and conditions for its future existence and beneficial development,' written by Bernt Askevold, an editor of *Decorah-Posten* and the author of one of the earliest AmN novels.[66]

Altogether, the eleven years from 1874-1885 saw the first appearance in full-length book form of ten original authors: N. S. Hassel 1874, H. H. Boyesen 1874, R. B. Anderson 1874, Bernt Askevold 1876, Tellef Grundysen 1877, Ulrikka Bruun 1877, Andreas Wright 1881, O. A. Buslett 1882, H. A. Foss 1884, Kr. Janson 1885.[67] Most of these authors were endowed with modest talents, but they established a tradition which was carried to greater perfection by later writers. There is no intention of here surveying N-A literature. Some of its chief names in the years that followed include Waldemar Ager (1869-1941), editor, novelist, short-story writer, and humorist; Peer Strømme (1856-1921), minister, editor, novelist, and globe-trotting lecturer; Simon Johnson (1874-), prohibitionist, editor, poet, and novelist; Johannes B. Wist (1864-1923), editor, novelist, and humorous essayist; Julius E. Baumann (1870-1923), poet; Kristian Prestgard (1865-1946), editor and essayist; Ole E. Rølvaag (1876-1931), professor and novelist.[68] But it will be necessary to make some comments on their linguistic practices.

Since most of the practitioners of literature were also, or even primarily, journalists, and appealed to the same circle of readers as did the newspapers, we may expect that the framework of their language would be much the same as that of the newspapers. There were would-be authors whose language was hopelessly untalented, shot through with helpless anglicisms and stylistic boners. Norwegians whose ears were sensitively attuned to the stylistic niceties of their native tongue sensed in most AmN writers, even the best, a quality of stiffness or perhaps of self-conscious awkwardness. The pervasive influence of English made for a heavier Norwegian style because of its more complex sentence structure and its heavier burden of latinisms. While native Norwegian was moving towards an ever more vigorous and expressive homeliness, emigrant Norwegian tended to let English influence reinforce the elaborateness of an already conservative tradition. ⌐

⌐Writers themselves complained more than once of the inadequacy which they felt in the instrument of their art.⌐ In the passage quoted from Sigurd Folkestad at the head of this chapter we hear the voice of one who tried for many years to write Norwegian verse in America. He wrote further: 'You sit here with your little flower garden of Norwegian words which you have labored to preserve during your transplantation to a strange land, where the soil is tropically luxuriant in its growth of weeds. Little by little you see the weeds spreading their matting over all your flowers in spite of all your care. Far, far away from the language source in the old country you keep listening to words inside yourself and ask: Do I rightly remember what this one means, do I rightly remember how that one sounds? I never hear it from other lips than my own. You go out into the settlement and talk with people. Oh yes, they talk Norwegian. A mixture of riksmaal, landsmaal, dialects from North Cape to the Naze, and of English words which have made their home in Norwegian speech in this flat farmland, where mountains are not to be seen, where the thrush does not sing, and the lark does not trill, where the spring is strangely quiet, where life is lived in the earth and on the earth, but in a certain sense not under the skies, where song is born.'[69] A similar plaint was voiced by the novelist Simon Johnson in commenting on the achievement of Norwegian immigrant authors who succeeded in creating a literature in spite of their 'spoiled' Norwegian, which by many critics was regarded as 'only a sorry hash of the many Norwegian dialects, studded with mutilated English words and phrases.'[70]

Other writers disagreed vigorously with this opinion. N. N. Rønning insisted that the lack of a literary language in daily use was less significant than the shortcomings of the writers themselves in making use of the language which they did have.[71] O. E. Rølvaag agreed with Rønning: 'Language has very little to do with the question. The linguistic cause is surely the least significant. If we don't know Norwegian riksmaal, we probably know a Norwegian dialect. If we can't manage either one, perhaps we know Iowa Norwegian, or English; and a literature can be created in any one of these languages.'[72] This view is certainly a sound one, and goes directly to the kernel of the matter. In many cases it was precisely the fear of the immigrant author of drawing squarely and honestly on the speech of his environment which prevented him from producing anything but a pale Dano-Norwegian imitation. Possibly the best illustration of this thesis is the achievement of parochial schoolmaster Thor Helgeson in his two volumes *Fra Indianernes Lande*. He published other writings, in which he never got beyond the schoolmaster's prosy style. But in these books he committed to paper the living tales of his community, anecdotes gathered during his pedagogical perambulations. Because he told them in the 'Wisconsin-Norwegian' which was the vulgate of his community, they stand today as authentic gems of immigrant narrative.

Waldemar Ager was another who never hesitated to use the more or less mutilated speech of his environment as a part of his artistic reproduction of that environment. His characters express themselves freely in appropriate English terms wherever these are authentic, whether they refer to *greenhorns* and *saloons*, or to *picnics* and *smart yankees*. In his novel *Paa Veien til Smeltepotten* (On the Way to the Melting Pot) of 1917 he was particularly liberal in his use of anglicisms to satirize the easy assimilation of his countrymen. The very title of the book is an anglicism, a loanshift compound modelled on English 'melting pot'; Ager knew perfectly well that the correct Norwegian term was *smeltedigel* (it occurs in the title of an article he wrote during these years). In defence of his own practice he wrote (in the controversy described above): 'The language dress we use is no gala suit; it may well be rough and ready, but it covers the necessities...'[73] Ager may well have felt touchy about this problem, for his own training in writing was extremely sketchy. He had immigrated from Norway at the age of 17 and only gradually drifted into a career of writing. He showed a talent for vivid narrative, and his lively choice of words made him a favorite author. An interesting comparison could be made between his earlier and later writings; this writer has the impression that by dint of practice and unswerving determination he made great strides forward, from an awkward, undistinguished style to a personal and effective mode of expression. But he never shook off the characteristically AmN flavor of his language, and was severely criticised by unfriendly observers for his many anglicisms. It is easy enough to pick them out even from those of his later books that were published in Norway, which had presumably been weeded by publishers' editors. Here are two specimens from *Gamlelandets Sønner* (Oslo, 1926): her var mange av de saarede latt tilbake (E left behind) 251; alle syntes ængstelige for at (E anxious to) træffe hverandre og høre om hvad hver enkelt hadde oplevd 219. But it should be emphasized that these were not offensive to readers who had lived in America as long as Ager himself and had allowed their sense of Norwegian style to drift in the same direction.

Ole E. Rølvaag, master of AmN novelists, had the advantage over Ager and Helgeson in having literary training and a more vital contact with the language of contemporary Norwegian literature. He was more successful in keeping unconscious Americanisms out of his writing, even though he certainly did not escape them. That he was aware of the problem is clear from his handling of the theme in his first book, *Amerika-Breve* (1912). This purported to be letters written home by an immigrant during his first few years in America. Rølvaag's 'newcomer' was at first baffled by the Norwegian his Americanized kinsmen used, but before he fully realized it, English words like *excitement, harvest, farm, prairie, shanty, all right*, and even *common denominator* flowed off his pen even when he wrote to his kin in Norway. The moral of this gradual adaptation was not lost on Rølvaag himself, who frequently let his characters use the technical terms of the new culture. But at the same time he managed that which few other immigrant authors achieved and no one in the same degree as he, namely the creation of a personal style. His Dano-Norwegian drew from the resources of his own childhood dialect and from the breadth of his adult reading; even where it differed from the Norwegian of Norway, it did so in a way that reflected a sense of artistic fitness.

Chapter 8.

THE WRITING OF DIALECT AND NEW NORSE.

Dæi hæva truga deg i Bla og Bøker
at lese støt det stive danske Maal....
D'æ kji rart, at Bonden hev blit domme,
For han sko lese de, han ei forstaar.

(They've always forced you in their books and papers
To stumble through the stiff, old Danish tongue...
No wonder that the country folks grow stupid
When they must read a language they don't
understand.)

Tarjei Midbø, a North Dakota schoolteacher (1875)[1]

In the mid-nineteenth century a quiet, studious bachelor named Ivar Aasen threw a fiery brand of linguistic revolt to the Norwegian people. Though the revolt involved more ink than blood, it aroused a stormy cultural controversy which has featured Norwegian life ever since. In this chapter we shall study the response of the emigrated Norwegians to this new force which set in almost contemporaneously with their own departure. Offhand one might expect that Aasen's appeal on behalf of the Norwegian country dialects would have found a warm response among them. They were nearly all speakers of dialect and many of them were the proud possessors of those dialects which Aasen admired as 'good', because they had retained much of the old Norwegian quality.

1. *Linguistic Revolt in Norway.*

Ivar Aasen (1813-96) showed great courage and acute linguistic insight in raising the standard of revolt against the entrenched language of church and state on behalf of Norwegian folk speech.

His purpose was to introduce a new written language based on the more conservative dialects, with constant reference to the written language of medieval Norway. He argued that the standard written language of Norway was really Danish, introduced during Norway's union with Denmark from 1380 to 1814, and that it behooved a free country to have its own language. He pointed out the many advantages that would result for the major part of the nation, which still spoke dialects descended from Old Norse, in greater ease of learning to read and less humiliation in their contact with the educated classes. Aasen was himself a farmer's son, born in humble circumstances, and his movement was compounded in equal parts of patriotism and class feeling. He wished to dignify the native speech by making it an instrument of writing and culture. He created the norm single-handedly and called it Landsmaal (National or Country Language); nowadays it is also referred to as Nynorsk (here rendered as 'New Norse').[2] The language against which he agitated was generally called Bogsproget 'the book language' in his day; other terms have been Dansk-Norsk 'Dano-Norwegian' (which we use here when it is needed to make a distinction), Riksmål, and Bokmål. The issue he raised has not yet been solved, though today some look hopefully forward to a gradual amalgamation of the two.

Aasen's agitation on behalf of the country folk and their linguistic birthright began well after multitudes of them had started to leave Norway. Aasen's first grammar of the Norwegian dialects was published in 1848, his specimens of a constructed norm for writing them in 1853.[3] The instruments for writing it successfully were not generally available until the publication of his second grammar in 1864 and his dictionary in 1873.[4] Only one major literary figure entered the fold up to 1866, namely Aasmund Olafsen Vinje, a great lyric poet and wit. But in that year the movement suddenly gained momentum, when *Vestmannalaget*, a society for its promotion, was organized in Bergen, and one of its most literate members, Kristofer Janson, published his first book *Fraa Bygdom* (From the Countryside). In 1867 seven books appeared in the new language, in 1868 eleven, and in the latter year a second society came into the field, *Det norske Samlaget*, in Oslo. So the movement was well launched, with the two societies acting as sponsors of a publication program and as cells of agitation; a considerable flurry of interest was aroused among the reading public.

2. *New Norse among the Emigrants.*

Even before there was any expression of interest in the question by the emigrants themselves, two noted Norwegian writers who were agitating against the movement made casual reference to their attitude. The historian Peter Andreas Munch, who became Aasen's most dangerous opponent in the public discussion of New Norse, remarked as early as 1853 that the Norwegian colonists in Wisconsin apparently preferred the written Danish to their own dialects. 'They fill the holes in their vocabulary from English, never from the national Norwegian.'[5] Aasen had claimed that oppression was the cause of their use of Danish orthography; but now, wrote Munch, in their new home abroad 'there is nothing that prevents these colonists from using their folk speech as a written language.' This argument was something less than honest, since Munch must have known perfectly well that most of the emigrants before 1853 had not been reached by the new movement and that lifelong habits of writing are not easily overthrown.

Henrik Ibsen gave the argument a new twist in his play *Peer Gynt* (1867), when he let his hero interview a representative of the language movement in the madhouse at Cairo. Huhu has been held to be modeled on both Aasmund Vinje and Kristofer Janson; when he complains to Peer that his people have not valued his efforts to resurrect 'our own true forest language' and to maintain 'the people's right to gibber,' Peer reminds him that far to the west 'there's a tribe of orang-outangs in Morocco, which has neither interpreter nor national bard.' Since 'their language sounds Malabarish,' he advises Huhu to emigrate and serve these people. Huhu seizes the idea eagerly and cries, 'The East has rejected its singer; the West has orang-outangs!' This satirical reference to the emigrants reminds us that Vinje at one time thought of emigrating, and that Kristofer Janson actually did do so a few years later. But as we shall see, the response of the emigrants was even less enthusiastic than that of the folks at home.

The first echoes of the new movement appear to have reached American shores in 1872, when the emigrated professor-author Hjalmar Hjorth Boyesen published an article on 'Kristofer Janson and the Reform of the Norwegian Language' in the *North American Review*.[6] In the same year we find scattered references in the Norwegian language press also; the keynote is struck by a Minneapolis man who had written to a newspaper in Norway warning *Maalstrævere* (language agitators) against coming to America, and classing them with drunkards, fools, and sleepwalkers as 'undesirable citizens.'[7] A writer in the conservative Norwegian-American paper *Fædrelandet og Emigranten* (LaCrosse, Wis.) added that if any one should attempt to transplant this idea on American soil, he would agree 'that such people have nothing to do here, and that their efforts would be without purpose (et Stræv foruden Maal).'

Yet in the same paper at least two correspondents quite unselfconsciously quoted from poems by Ivar Aasen in the new language.[8] Similarly in the more liberal paper *Skandinaven og Amerika* (Chicago) where a verse by Aasen is cited on May 24 and two poems by Vinje on August 14, the latter on the occasion of the unveiling of his bust.[9] At an Old Settlers' Celebration at Rock Prairie a young instructor at the University of Wisconsin, Rasmus B. Anderson, spoke at length about the life and writings of Vinje and recited his poem *Vaaren* (Spring); a report of the speech was published in *Skandinaven og Amerika*.[10] There was no denying the appeal of this simple, earthy poetry to the country folk. That fall a recent arrival from Norway, Bernt Askevold, later to be known as a novelist and clergyman, wrote a series of essays on Norway in which he included an enthusiastic appreciation of the New Norse writers and the movement they represented.[11] Following Vinje, he emphasized the 'Germanic' and 'Scandinavian' value of the movement, since in his belief the elimination of 'foreign' elements in the language would lead to a closer approximation between Norwegian, Swedish, and Danish.

The movement was beginning to stimulate various subscribers to write more or less dialectally tinged epistles to the newspapers. In 1874 a correspondent to *Skandinaven* explicitly said: 'This time I shall write you some words in our Norsk-norsk language for a change; in other words, on this next-to-the-last day of the year

I shall play Maalstrævare (language agitator).'[12] But the editors were not pleased. They decided to clamp a stern lid on any such tendencies. On February 10 Svein Nilsson, the editor, wrote: 'Concerning articles written in Landsmaal it must be said that they bring difficulties for the paper, without, as far any one can see, bringing any advantage that cannot be attained in the customary language. In all likelihood 90 out of 100 of the readers of the weekly are farmers, who have the pleasure every day of hearing and speaking their country dialect, and we therefore regard it as superfluous to 'mock' them in the newspaper, so much the more since we see from their letters that they are all accustomed to the written language. Even in Norway the Maalstræv must be regarded as a poetic dream, a labor contrary to the stream of civilization, and here, where our next generation chiefly will use the English language, it must remain even more impossible to gain any practical advantage from it. The paper therefore wishes, as far as possible, to be spared this kind of articles.'[13]

The result of this editorial pronunciamento was to touch off the first full-scale linguistic debate in the N-A press and thereby lead to the first book-length publication on and in the new language, which had surely not been the editor's intention.

3. *The First Debate.*

It is a striking fact that this debate on the virtues of New Norse seems to have been also the first debate in the press on any purely cultural topic. Aside from personal and economic discussions, the only topics that had been extensively debated up to this time had been religious and political. Conditions were now favorable for a widening of cultural horizons. In Wisconsin a generation had passed since the first pioneer days, and new waves of immigrants were bringing ideas from contemporary Norway for which there was leisure and an awakening appetite. In 1870 the famous violinist Ole Bull had taken up his residence in Madison and made Rasmus B. Anderson, the newly-appointed instructor at the University, his protegé. A course in Norwegian, the first at any American school, was offered that year at the University of Wisconsin. In 1872 Ole Bull, an enthusiastic patron of everything Norwegian, including the New Norse movement, gave a concert to benefit the Norwegian library at the University and took the young instructor with him to Norway to buy the books.[14] In 1873 he took Anderson to Norway again, this time to promote the raising of a monument for Leif Ericson, discoverer of America. On these trips Anderson met Ivar Aasen, and his enthusiasm was awakened for the writings and aims of the new movement; he may also have been stimulated by his contact with Bjørnson, who at this period was still sympathetic to the movement.

The debate was launched by a farmer-schoolteacher, Peter P. Iverslie, living at Iola in Waupaca County, who had immigrated in 1847, just three years old. He had studied at Luther College from 1862 to 1864.[15] Iverslie agreed with the editor that it would be 'impossible to gain any practical value from the use of this language in our country.'[16] But he objected to the view that it was a mere dream and 'contrary to the stream of civilization.' He believed that the true purposes of civilization would actually be promoted, since it is 'the only right thing for a people to use its own language.' He could see nothing impossible in a change of written language, when it meant a return to the true language of the people. 'When the country people give up their own language, they have given up themselves.' The teaching of religion in a foreign language meant that it was less well understood and assimilated by the children. He quoted poems by Vinje and Janson to show the excellence of New Norse, and he adopted an argument by Vinje to the effect that New Norse would lead to closer cultural understanding between the Scandinavian countries.

This enthusiastic appeal brought two other contributors into the field, one pro and one anti, both anonymous. C. K. (from Kroghville, Wisconsin) denied that the standard book language was the cause of rural ignorance in Norway, held it to be a 'pretty and easily understood language,' and maintained that what was needed was to teach the country people to talk it so that they might give up their local variations of speech. In any case he could not see that it mattered whether it was Danish or Norwegian, any more than it was humiliating to Americans that their language should be English.[17] To this O. M. (of Galveston, Texas) rejoined that it would be tyrannical to 'force the Norwegian farmer to talk it when he owns and loves his own language, the Landsmaal.'[18] At this point editor Nilsson entered the discussion again. He recognized the noble purposes of the Maalstrævere in wishing to reduce or eliminate the cleavage between the officeholders and the farming classes. But while he approved a gradual Norwegianizing of the standard language, in the manner of Wergeland and Bjørnson, he denied the possibility of regaining a language once lost or of taking a dialect as a written language. 'It is not easy to find good reasons to prove that the present book language is not Norwegian as well as Danish, just as English is an American as well as an English language.'[19]

Once launched, the debate spun on for a year and a half, with Iverslie and O. M. upholding the affirmative, C. K. and others the negative. The arguments advanced were those that are familiar to readers of the similar discussion going on in Norway at the time and were no doubt secured from the same arsenals. The advocates underline the national and educational advantages, the opponents the expense and inconvenience of change, the value of tradition and Dano-Norwegian continuity, and the impossibility of adopting an 'artificial' language. We shall especially concern ourselves with the arguments that involve the relation of the immigrants to the new movement. Some were worried that a change-over in the language would make newer Norwegian books incomprehensible to the emigrants and thus break the contact with the mother country. To this O. M. pointed out that one reason for discussing the problem was to keep informed on changes in the homeland so that contact might be maintained; in any case the change would not come very soon, and would certainly cause them less trouble than the common AmN use of English words in their Norwegian was causing their cousins at home.[20] One forthright contributor asserted that 'it would be damaging to the Norwegian press in this country, indeed to this very newspaper; for if these lines were written in Landsmaal, no Dane could read them, and probably less than 20 per cent of the Norwegian readers could understand them.' If the language should be adopted in this newspaper, he went on to say, the editor could stop his subscription at once.[21] This kind of talk was only too well understood by the editor, who reassured the subscriber that no such intention was harbored by the present management; although four fifths of the subscribers were farmers, they had as much trouble as the editor himself in reading the Landsmaal.[22] One interesting evidence of support for the language was the poem by a Telemark schoolteacher in North Dakota cited at the head of this chapter.

⌐The majority of commentators were clearly on the side of the editor, one even going so far as to declare the project 'useless, foolish, and impossible.'[23] When Iverslie carried his arguments over into the newspaper *Norden,* the editor of that paper (Halvard Hande) declared that he did not intend to open the columns of his paper 'to any extended discussion of the language question, since this would seem to be rather fruitless over here.'[24] One contributor to *Skandinaven* sarcastically asked O. M. why he did not write in the language he advocated; to which O. M. replied that he had to use the language of the paper in which he was writing, but that he had no hesitation about calling it Danish. Most Norwegians, he declared, have a different mother tongue from the one they write, and they have 'hearts that are quite as fine and noble as those of the enemies of the Language Cause (Maalsagen).'[25] Perhaps underlying the whole discussion was a groping to find the reason for the lack of a cultural life among the emigrated Norwegians.⌐ Iverslie and the other advocates of New Norse maintained that an important contributory cause was the linguistic obstacle.[26] To this one caustic critic replied that 'among the emigrated country people the adventures of Norway's master thief Gjest Baardsen are far more beloved than anything produced in the *bondevenlig* (friendly to the farmer) literature in Landsmaal.'[27] This remained one of the chief issues throughout the discussion. O. M. maintained that 'the language struggle is closely connected with the cultural advancement and popular enlightenment of recent years; this is why the aristocrats are so strongly opposed to it'.[28] To this B. J. replied that there was no more enlightenment in the regions where Landsmaal was strong than elsewhere, and that the children were getting their enlightenment in the Dano-Norwegian anyway. He refused to believe that any change in language form would prevent the aristocrats from ruling.[29]

4. *Anderson and Janson.*

By a curious twist of irony it was neither Aasen nor Vinje who were to receive the first full-length introduction to a Norwegian audience in America, but the relatively second-rate author Kristofer Janson. In contrast to the others he was not himself a country lad, but a product of the urban culture of Bergen. His warm-hearted enthusiasm for nationality and rural culture led him into the folk school and the New Norse movement. Boyesen, in his previously cited article, introduced him to Americans as 'an author...possessed of poetic genius of a sufficiently high order to attract even those to whom the form of his writings was rather a discouragement than a recommendation.'[30] Poems of his began seeping into the columns of AmN papers in 1875, and his first story was reprinted by Rasmus B. Anderson as a part of the first and only book published in America entirely devoted to the cause of the Landsmaal.[31] Its title, *Den norske Maalsag* (The Norwegian Language Cause), suggested its scope. Anderson wrote it in 1874; it was published in the early half of 1875 by the John Anderson Publishing Company, publishers also of *Skandinaven*.[32] The second part of the book consisted of Janson's *Han Per og ho Bergit*, originally published in Bergen in 1866 as the first story in *Fraa Bygdom*. The first part was an essay on the backgrounds and development of the New Norse movement, with quotations from Aasen and Vinje in support of the cause. The book was dedicated to P. P. Iverslie, 'who has embraced with such love and skill the cause of Norwegian history and language and particularly its so-called "Language Cause".' In the preface Anderson attributed the initial impulse to writing the book to Iverslie and the debate raised by his advocacy of Landsmaal. But we learn from his autobiography that his own awakening came earlier, on his visits to Norway in 1872 and 1873, when he met Ivar Aasen himself. 'I visited him several times in his bachelor quarters and saw him in his slippers and long study gown smoking his meerschaum with a stem reaching to the floor. He was one of the most venerable men that I have ever met. I had become fond of the "Landsmaal" before I ever met Aasen, but after talking with him I became its advocate.'[33] Anderson sent the book to Janson, whom he had not yet met, and

Janson's acknowledgment appeared in *Skandinaven:* 'I rejoice to
see that the cause to which I have devoted my labors is not shut
in amid the mountains here, but that it accompanies the emigrants
into the foreign land, and that over there it finds such warm-
hearted and well-informed advocates as yourself and the man you
mention on the first page.'[34]

Well might Janson be pleased. The young instructor, shortly
to be made the first Professor of Scandinavian Languages in an
American university, had unequivocally come out in favor of the
new language. Not only did he accept entirely the New Norsemen's view of Norwegian linguistic history ('After Norway's union
with Denmark...Danish was placed in the high seat and the Norwegian language became its slave'), but he proudly proclaimed
his own membership in *Det norske Samlaget* and wished its supporters luck in their struggle 'to give Norway back a language that can
unite high and low and carry the best thoughts of the country
into the heart of the lowliest.'[35] He opened with a poem by Kristofer
Janson in praise of the Norwegian language, and described Janson
as 'the highly gifted poet.' He spoke of the two groups of language
reformers, the Dano-Norwegian and the New Norse, who both were
working for 'an independent language for the Norwegian people.'
He believed that the two movements would some day meet in their
courses, and that they were both historically justified. But his
real enthusiasm was reserved for the Landsmaal, and he wrote the
book to 'awaken interest among the Norwegians on this side of
the ocean for the beautiful and gifted literature which Norway's
language reformers have produced.'[36] Their books 'are written in
the language which sounded from your mother's lips when you sat
as a child on her lap'; they are 'Norwegian in thought, Norwegian
in form, Norwegian to the bottom of their hearts.' From personal
experience he spoke of the difficulties involved in learning the
catechism in Danish, a 'dead language' in Norway; and he cited
examples of words which 'do not speak to the heart of the common
man's children in Norway.'[37] He deplored the class distinction
between the educated with their Danish and the people with their
dialects (his own mother and father came from the two sides of the
fence, respectively). He believed that the hope of the future lay
in the activity of the folk high schools and the cause of the new

language which these generally supported. He refuted some of the arguments generally advanced against it, that Danish had an established position in Norway, and that the new language lacked terms for cultural advances.

⌈But what about the immigrants? He did not at all wish to urge their participation in the movement. 'There can be no question of reforming the Norwegian language here in America.'⌉His own chief language was, and must remain, English, as it must be 'for us, who are American citizens.'⌊But he wanted the immigrants to enjoy the fruits of Norwegian cultural endeavor, to pluck the 'thousands of glorious flowers, with which we can beautify and enrich our life and our work here in the Far West.'⌋Among these not the least were those produced in the New Norse language by such men as Janson, Vinje, and Ivar Aasen. It might even be well if some of the books used here in instructing Norwegian children in their religion might be rendered into their own language. 'Learn then, dear reader, to love this beautiful Landsmaal, which is not a bleating of goats, but a language with a ring like the steel that is brought forth from the grave mounds of the North.'[38]

The book was reviewed by anonymous reviewers in two separate issues of *Skandinaven* with great enthusiasm. One made the reservation that there were statements in it he would disagree with, but 'we are agreed on the main question.' 'I like the book well, and it does honor to its author, as do his previously published books.'[39] The other reviewer quoted extensively from the book, and added that 'the language question is such an important phenomenon in the recent literature and cultural life of Norway that one cannot be well informed about Norwegian literature without familiarity with it.' He found the book a 'truly worthy addition to the beginning Norwegian-American literature.'[40] In spite of these energetic puffs, the book sold slowly; and the author never again returned to the subject with anything like the enthusiasm of this early effort.

At least in the columns of *Skandinaven* no correspondent arose to challenge Anderson's glowing account of the movement. His reputation as nationally known Advocatus Norvegiæ was just being established by the publication of *America Not Discovered by Columbus* in 1874 and *Norse Mythology* in 1875.[41] As professor of

Scandinavian Languages by 1875, the protegé of Ole Bull and friend of Bjørnstjerne Bjørnson, he was becoming a formidable authority among the Norwegians of the Middle West. He had secured for *Skandinaven og Amerika* a series of correspondences from the author Bjørnson in 1873. A visitor from Norway in 1875 reported that Anderson advocated the coming over to America of Norwegian authors to maintain the spiritual contact between the homeland and the emigrants.[42] We need not, therefore, be surprised to discover that in 1876 *Skandinaven* could announce as its correspondent from Norway none other than the 'famous Norwegian author, poet, and folk high school teacher,' Kristofer Janson. At the same time they could comfort their readers by the assurance that for the benefit of all those who 'have not yet been able to get familiar with Landsmaal, Janson will write his letters not in Norsk-norsk, but in the usual Norwegian or Danish which is used in this newspaper.'[43] Janson's letters appeared irregularly in Skandinaven during 1876, but none of them dealt with the language problem.[44] He spoke freely about political and social problems, and at some length about the purposes of the folk high school. In one letter he uttered a sigh for the freedom of expression which he believed to exist in America. In private correspondence Anderson kept urging him to come to the United States on a lecture tour. In 1879 he was able to announce that Janson was coming under his management and would be available for lectures in either language, the Book Language or Landsmaal.[45] [Janson abstained from linguistic agitation during his visit and was, in Anderson's words, 'received and entertained as one of Norway's distinguished sons, and his visit did much to promote an interest in Norwegiandom on this side of the Atlantic.'[46] This first lecture tour led eventually to Janson's return to America, and his residence here for a twelve-year period (1881-93). But it cannot be seen that it led to any increase of public interest in the Landsmaal movement, for Janson's books published in the United States were all in Dano-Norwegian.[47] As Anderson had insisted, the movement was not a live issue among the immigrants; it could at best hope for an academic, cultural interest as one of the vital aspects of the 'cultural springtide' which Janson declared to be characteristic of the 70's in Norway. This release of cultural energies found its first response among the emigrants in a language discussion which was one expression of an awakening interest in problems of general culture among Norwegians in America.

5. *The Second Renaissance.*

The continued development of the New Norse movement, whether in Norway or America, did not entirely correspond to the expectations of the early enthusiasts of the 70's. Janson, as we have seen, emigrated and devoted his talents to other causes. While the movement acquired a major writer in Arne Garborg, he was overshadowed by the tremendous burst of Dano-Norwegian literary activity by Bjørnson, Ibsen, Lie, Kielland, and others. In this country whatever literary interest could be awakened was concentrated about these, with relatively less attention to the writers of dialect or New Norse. If New Norse books were reprinted in this country, it was in Dano-Norwegian translation, e.g. Jens Tvedt's *Hamnagrø* which appeared as *Hamnajenten*[48] or Kristofer Janson's *Han og Ho*, which appeared as *Han og Hun.*[49] Academic interest was shown in occasional learned articles, such as that of Wm. H. Carpenter on 'The Language of the Recent Norwegian Writers' in the *Atlantic Monthly* for 1890.[50] Anderson's successor as Professor of Scandinavian Languages, Julius E. Olson, had followed in his footsteps as an admirer of New Norse authors, as we see from an early review of Janson's *Fraa Dansketidi* (From the Danish Period) in which he enthusiastically declared that the Dano-Norwegian language was dead.[51] But the authors he taught in his courses at the University of Wisconsin were all Dano-Norwegian. Not until 1900 did he attempt to give a course in Norwegian Dialect Writers, described as 'selections from Aasen, Vinje, Garborg, Sivle, and a study of the language reform movement.'[52] But he got only two students, and the course was never again given. Yet his speech of 1899 on Norwegian literature to the assembled journalists of the Dano-Norwegian press in America seemed like an introduction to the renewed interest in the language which was to be characteristic of the early years of the twentieth century: 'We must not overlook the battle of the Landsmaal men, their attacks on the Danish quality of Norway's language, and their persistent efforts to build up their country. There is Springtide in the New Norse literature. Perhaps here we have something more suitable for our country people than Ibsen's and Bjørnson's modern dramas.'[53]

Since the eighties a new wave of immigration had begun to inundate the Norwegian communities. Free land was disappearing, and many of the young immigrants found better opportunities in the rapidly expanding cities of the Middle West. Among these were some who had been trained in folk high schools or in the teachers' training schools where New Norse sympathizers had acquired a strong position. They were members of a new rural youth, more self-conscious in their adherence to the folk culture, more assertive of their dialects and their national enthusiasm than most of the older immigrants. Among these we discover an entirely new ambition: to introduce the New Norse language among their countrymen in America. No one, however fond of the language, had entertained any such visions previous to 1900. In Norway the movement had gradually won the hearts of men and women willing to work and sacrifice for its advancement. A succession of laws passed by the victorious liberal party had established a firm status for the language. In 1885 it achieved official equality with Dano-Norwegian; in 1892 local school boards were given the option of determining in which language they wished their children to be taught; in 1896 the secondary schools were required to teach it. This is the movement we now see reflected among Norwegians in America.

A conspicuous fact about the new period is that the discussion no longer centers in Illinois and Wisconsin. The centers of cultural activity have moved farther west, to Iowa, Minnesota, and North Dakota.

In 1900 appeared what looked like a first bridgehead of the New Norse movement in America. This was a small monthly magazine entitled *Norroena*, with the proud subtitle of 'Det fyrste blad paa norskt maal i Vesterheimen.' (The first periodical in the Norwegian language in the Western World). In these words the editor and publisher, Peer Storeygard, flung down a challenge to all earlier publications in America which had considered themselves Norwegian, but which he now described as Danish. He opened the first issue with a poem called *Fyrestev*, a title borrowed from Aasen, in which, like another Noah, he declared that he was sending out a dove with the message of victory. He gathered around him a small but hopeful group of contributors, for the most part younger immigrants touched by the New Norse movement in the homeland. For Storeygard this one-man enterprise was pure idealism, and he poured into it not only his enthusiasm for the New Norse movement, but also for other ventures such as his belief in a 'solar biology' i. e. astrology.[54] In one issue he defined his purpose as 'a quest for the genuine, the true, an effort to know one's self and be one's self...'[55] Storeygard was born in one of the remotest Norwegian mountain valleys, Heidal in Gudbrandsdal, where old customs and a conservative dialect still held sway. In 1885 he emigrated with his parents, only fourteen years old, having a sketchy common school education and some skill in woodcarving and rosepainting.[56] As a printer's apprentice and later a normal school student he managed to satisfy an appetite for reading, but he earned his living in a country store at Walnut Grove, Minnesota, and devoted only his spare time to intellectual pursuits. After his wife's death he moved to Fargo, North Dakota, and for some years he operated a book store there.

In his first issue Storeygard wrote that he intended to follow the usual NN form, but actually varied rather widely from it: 'I skrivemáten er me tenkt pá fylgje den algjengne Landsmál-forme so nære som moglegt, men auk bygdemál kan brukast nár det skrivst noko-so-nær etter mállogi.'[57] He included an attack on Bjørnson's remarks on the NN: 'Du skulde ikkje fara med slikt tull du Bjørnson, som er so vidt uti ári komen.' Among his Norwegian-American contributors were Rev. L. P. Thorkveen, Dr. M. O. Teigen, Olav Refsdal, I. H. Kofoed, K. K. Rudie, Ola J. Rise, Dr. R. Leland, and Samuel Garborg. In his last issue he commented on the enterprise as one that took more time than he could spare. But he was not discouraged and felt that he had contributed, if only slightly, to the victories won in Norway.

It was apparent from the first issue that he had allied himself with the *Norske Samlaget* in Oslo and its representative in the United States, I. H. Kofoed, a parochial school teacher. A two-page ad by *Samlaget* welcomed the publication and presented a program for extending the movement across the sea: 'We know that there are among our countrymen enough of those who make information from the homeland available out there. But we have imagined that such information would be even more welcome, if it not only brought a message from home, but also presented it in the language of the old homeland, the only one that Norwegians, no matter where they are, can recognize as their true mother tongue, which they can feel at home in. ... Here we think that we may expect a great help from our countrymen in America in various ways. Just as we know that their help has been most valuable in awakening the sense of freedom in our people, so we believe that their example would be one of the most powerful aids in advancing the cause of the Norwegian Language, which we regard now as the greatest cause of the future in our country.'[58] In this hope they were certainly disappointed, for *Norroena* lasted only two years in its first phase. It was neither qualitatively comparable to other publications, nor did it do anything to make its appearance familiar to readers whose allegiance was primarily to the conventional Dano-Norwegian. The editor indulged his personal fancies for such peculiarities as the use of Old Norse á instead of aa (or å), and even the obsolete letters ð and œ.

In 1914 he made another attempt, after his removal to Fargo, and issued volumes 3 and 4 of the magazine, now called *Norrøna* and using the customary orthography of New Norse. These two years were more valuable than the first, with a wider circle of contributors, and the backing of an interested group in Fargo. The year before, a statue of Ivar Aasen had been unveiled on June 7, the centennial of his birth; and a society for the promotion of his movement had been formed, called Normannalaget.[59] Its purpose, declared the editor, was to 'protect our heritage in this country, and help to keep in touch with the advances and development in the fatherland, so that at last we can get back to ourselves and become natural people instead of apes.' In a letter to the writer, Storeygard has summed up his philosophy of nationality and language: 'Language is the soul of a nation. To lose your language is to lose your soul. The language is the nation, and no race or nation can stand erect under denationalization without suffering spiritual and physical degeneration.'[60] 'My dream was that Norwegian, Swedish, Danish, and Icelandic should agree upon a common orthography on Old Norse basis.' It becomes apparent that this independent character was a mystic believer in the importance of the Word and its influence on the world: to prevent world dominion he wished each nation to develop its own language and its own culture. This exaggerated faith in the word is probably characteristic of many followers of the movement, though few profess it as freely as Storeygard.

6. *Jon Norstog.*

No sooner had *Norroena* the first expired, than another short-lived effort arose to take its place. This was *Dølen* (The Dalesman), issued at Joice, Iowa, for a few months of 1902, by a recent comer to America, who was to become the living embodiment of the movement among the emigrants. Jon Norstog's title was that of his physical and spiritual kinsman, Vinje, and his ambition was to become for the emigrants what Vinje had been in the homeland. Born in Telemark in 1877, with teacher training at Notodden and in Oslo, he had published one book in Norway, a poem called *Yggdrasil* (1902). The reviews are said to have been so disappointing that he abandoned Norway and never saw it again. But in America he sought to carry on the movement he had been initiated into in Norway, and with a persistence and an originality that lacks its match among Norwegians in this country (unless it be Thorstein Veblen) he proceeded to carve out an existence according to his own head. He made himself independent of printers and publishers by typesetting, printing, binding, and selling his own books; his editions were small masterpieces of bookmaking. For some years he tried to make a living as a journalist, participating in the editing of a periodical called *Eidsvold*, as well as such North Dakota newspapers as *Normanden* and *Minot-Posten*.

In 1910, however, he deserted the haunts of men entirely, and homesteaded in the extreme western part of North Dakota, on the prairie land of McKenzie County. A nearby town, Watford City, came to be the place of publication of most of the books which he continued to turn out at amazingly short intervals. For his books were not such as spared the reader any effort. Most of them were dramatic poems in five acts on such weighty themes as Cain, Moses, Joshua, Israel, Joseph, King Saul, and King David. He seemed to have made it his goal to exhaust the Bible; his was an Old Testament spirit, a literal and fervent believer, who issued the same kind of warnings to his Norwegian countrymen in America as had the Hebrew prophets to theirs.

Unfortunately for the effectiveness of his message, his forbidding language made it almost inaccessible to most of his countrymen. He revelled in the vocabulary of his native Telemark, perhaps one of the richest of all the rural dialects and one of the most conservative. He piled epithet upon epithet, and ran the entire gamut from pious and humble worship to a barrage of fishwife's abuse for those phenomena and personalities of which he disapproved. As a writer he lacked the capacity for organization and restraint which marks the great artist. But in his shorter lyrics there are many passages of great beauty, worthy of a better fate than to be forgotten along with the great mass of his undisciplined lines. This is not the place to discuss the literary accomplishments of this 'poet in exile'; he has bewildered many a critic who tackled the 'problem Jon Norstog.'[61] We are here interested in the man as an instance of how a writer could create original compositions in New Norse even in America, but only at the expense of completely disregarding his potential audience. A few of his books were written in Dano-Norwegian, but most of them showed a deliberate and exasperating scorn for the reading public. As a cause, the New Norse movement has always attracted fighters, for the odds have been terrific and the rewards small.

When Norstog died in 1942, he had published 22 volumes, poems, stories, and dramas, all but two or three in NN. This was not only more than any NN writer in America, for there was no one to rival him; it was more than any Norwegian writer whatever in this country. In addition he had written innumerable articles in the AmN press, many of them on political topics. As a poet he had no followers and few readers, but he was a colorful and unforgetable figure. In the words of Agnes M. Wergeland: 'Here the Landsmaal makes an author even more lonely than he would otherwise have been.'[62]

While Norstog was not the only writer of NN among the emigrants, the others seem little more than writers of occasional verse when compared with his single-minded devotion. Poems by Ola J. Rise, Knut Martin Teigen, and Erik Arnesen Travaas appeared at various times in the new language.[63] Collections were published by Johannes Olavson Sæter: *Naar samvitet vaknar* (Minneapolis, n.d. [ab. 1927]), a narrative poem, and *Telelaget, Salmar og Songar* (Minneapolis, n.d.). A delicate, but genuine talent was shown by the emigrated school teacher, Signe Mydland Steinarson, whose poems were contributed to various papers, particularly *Skandinaven*.[64]

7. Progress and Rebuffs.

Some of the new journals in Dano-Norwegian that came into being after 1900 showed a more friendly attitude to New Norse, even though none of them went in for the language with the whole-hearted devotion of a Storeygard or Norstog. The years from the turn of the century to America's entry into World War I were years of cultural flowering among the Norwegian immigrants. New authors and new journals sprang up like mushrooms, and many of these had grown up in an atmosphere of good will to the New Norse language. Even an older writer like Peer Strømme included one of the major works of Arne Garborg in the first issue of his periodical *Vor Tid* (1904-07). This was the religious prose-poem *Den burtkomne Faderen* (The Lost Father); the editor had considered whether he ought to have translated it into Dano-Norwegian, but decided that 'you just couldn't offer Norwegian people a title like "Den fortabte Fader."'[65] 'Garborg handles the Landsmaal with such mastery that even one who otherwise might find it hard to feel at home in this language will be able to read him with ease.' In later reprinting Sivle's story *Berre ein hund* (Only a Dog), however, he did not follow this principle. Among his and Storeygard's contributors was one of the most ardent young supporters of the cause, Ola J. Rise, from Oppdal, Norway. Rise has since told of his experiences, including particularly a literary evening in the society *Fram* in Minneapolis on June 19, 1902, when the program was entirely devoted to the cause of New Norse.[66] On that occasion a speech was given by one Doctor R. Leland in which the speaker maintained that the best Norwegian literature then being written was in New Norse. This speech was later printed and spread abroad as propaganda for the movement; it included the following reference to immigrant conditions: 'I do not see why we cannot be New Norsemen in America if we want to be so in Norway. ...If a schoolmaster in Norway can teach the young folks better in Landsmaal than in Danish, why cannot a Norwegian schoolmaster do the same here? If a minister in Norway can preach more understandably, more heartfelt, and more touchingly in Landsmaal than in Danish, why can he not do the same in this country as long as he pretends to be preaching Norwegian to Norwegians?'[67]

To a new periodical called *Kvartalskrift* Ola J. Rise contributed a passionate defence of the cause, in which he wanted the newly formed society *Det norske Selskab i Amerika* (The Norwegian Society in America) to include this among its aims.[68] How will the situation be, he asked, if New Norse becomes the language of Norway; would it not be well to prepare the young people for this transition, so that there may not be a complete cleavage between them and the homeland?[69] But Rise's views were not accepted by the majority of the members, and sharp opposition was registered in later articles in the same periodical by the author O. A. Buslett and Dr. Anders Daae.[70] Another of Storeygard's contributors was the older writer Knut M. Teigen, whose collection of poems *Vesterlandske Digte* appeared in 1905; a number of these were either in dialect or New Norse, and several expressed strong admiration for the movement. To Arne Garborg he wrote: 'He most clearly showed me that the country language is delicate as the flute's tones, sharp as steel.'[71]

The year 1905 was a high point in patriotic endeavor among emigrated Norwegians, since it was the year of separation from Sweden, when fears and hopes ran high. In that year was launched a literary annual called *Symra*, edited by the editors of *Decorah-Posten*, Kristian Prestgard and Johannes B. Wist, especially the former. Prestgard came from the same remote valley as Storeygard and had attended folk high schools both in Norway and Denmark before emigration.[72] The title of his periodical was that of

Aasen's famous collection of poems from 1863, and its contents, while mostly in Dano-Norwegian, were strongly tinged by his sympathies for the New Norse movement. He had secured contributions from five well-known New Norse writers and had himself written an article on a sixth, the poet Per Sivle. Throughout the years of its duration (to 1914) there were occasional articles in New Norse and still more about the great folk renaissance of Norway, with which the editors were in full sympathy.

From the same town as *Symra* came a quarterly publication by students at Luther College called *Ervingen* (1908-13), another Aasen title. Here, too, the language was predominantly Dano-Norwegian, but the first issue opened with a poem by Aasen and a long article by S. Sondresen on the linguistic situation in Norway. Its linguistic policy seems to be expressed in an article of 1910 entitled 'The Language Controversy in Norway': 'Let us keep the Dano-Norwegian; for in it the new Norway has grown up. But let us also love and cultivate the Landsmaal; for it is the language of our hearts. To the Norwegian people the language controversy is a serious struggle. We Norwegians on this side of the ocean should not feel unconcerned about such an important matter (hjertesag).'[73] A third publication launched during these years (1909-14), also bearing a patriotic name, *Eidsvold* (the home of the Norwegian constitution), was even more directly associated with the movement. Although its prevailing language was DN, one of its two editors was the leading New Norse writer in America, the previously discussed Jon Norstog. The first issue included a NN poem, two reviews of NN books, and a NN survey of the 'Norwegian linguistic renaissance during the last century' by a well-known writer in Norway. This man, A. M. St. Arctander, expressed his opinion concerning the emigrants as follows: 'I do not doubt that if we at home had honored our Norwegian folk language more highly, our kinfolk in America would have clung more firmly to the old and the best in their national character (folkesvipen sin)...'[74] A fourth publication of wide significance was the Christmas annual called *Jul i Vesterheimen*, published from 1911 to the present by Augsburg Publishing House in Minneapolis. The editor, A. M. Sundheim, was· from Valdres and a strong sympathizer of the New Norse movement. Again the prevailing language was DN, but repeatedly leavened by stories or poems in NN, e. g. one by Jens Tvedt in the issue for 1913.

It would be easy to multiply the expressions favorable to the NN movement in the publications of this period. But we should be giving a misleading picture if we imagined for a moment that this was a majority opinion. When Ludvig Lima collected 250 poems by Norwegian writers in America in an anthology of AmN poems, only one of them was in NN (as it happened, by a brother of Arne Garborg).[75] When the Norwegian newspaper *Aftenposten* in 1909 sent out a questionnaire to all the leading men among the emigrants, including presidents of church synods and colleges, teachers, editors, etc., the answers were almost unanimously opposed to New Norse. The questions asked were: (1) What influence would the introduction of NN in Norway have on church, school, and press in America? (2) Would pastors use it? (3) Would Norwegian schools teach it? (4) Would the press use it? (5) Would it cause the advancement or retardation of the use of Norwegian in the United States? The consensus of the answers was that Norwegian institutions in this country had a hard enough time maintaining one kind of Norwegian, let alone trying a new one. Two or three expressed a fondness for NN poetry, but all agreed that the introduction of NN in Norway would mean the end of contact between emigrants and homeland.[76] This was, of course, the answer the conservative Norwegian newspaper wanted, and it was used in the agitation over there.

A prominent NN author who visited the Norwegian areas in America during these years and entertained them with his stories, Hans Seland, made some interesting comments on the attitude of the people who came to hear him. 'They understand Landsmaal very well when they hear it. I heard less complaints about my language there than at home, I think, ...but they thought, or imagined, that it was so difficult to *read*. ..They have no use for the Landsmaal, but then they have very few chances to get acquainted with it. Nevertheless the language cause has a few warm friends over there, and every once in a while they have a discussion in their papers. ...But it is understandable that their 'riksmaal' (national language), English, must catch up with them very soon.'[77]

·Another Norwegian visitor who was ardently favorable to the

New Norse cause, the writer Hulda Garborg, was more optimistic after a lecture tour among the immigrants in 1913. She wrote to a Norwegian paper that she heard 'Landsmaal' spoken on every hand among the immigrants and advised the Norwegian parliament to send over a Landsmaal speaker who should 'teach people over here that Landsmaal is their own language, developed and refined into a language of culture, the only language in the world which speaks to their hearts and fully can release their thoughts and feelings.'[78] Her letter awakened the fury of *Skandinaven's* editor, who pointedly commented that they had been entertaining the 'author Hulda Garborg and not the language agitator.' 'We get along just fine with the "language of culture" which we have. The language controversy in Norway has no direct practical interest for our people in this country... If the Landsmaal should supplant the Rigsmaal as the current language in Norway, one of the strongest bonds between the mother country and our people here would break...'[79] This position was typical of the journalists in the larger papers. An important exception was the previously mentioned Kristian Prestgard, who repeatedly tried to explain to his readers that the creation of Landsmaal was a step in the process of 'moving home' which Norwegians found necessary after living in a foreign culture for several centuries of their history. But even he had to admit that 'this rapid development of the language has been an inconvenience for us who work in the Norwegian language in America.'[80] In another article he declared, 'We are too busy keeping alive the language form which after all has become ours to think about transferring the Norwegian language controversy to America. That would be suicide.'[81]

The general distaste for New Norse has been abundantly confirmed by the writer's experiences among Norwegian immigrants. Aside from a few enthusiasts, the prevailing attitude among the emigrants was one of dislike and suspicion of the new language. A typical remark was that of an informant from Tinn, who complained that 'eg kann ikkje få noko ut av detta landssprokje — det e ikkje Tinn!' (I can't get anything out of this 'country language' — it's not Tinn dialect). Books written in New Norse were looked upon with annoyance, and some even included the changes in spelling of the Dano-Norwegian under their blanket condemnation of the New Norse language: it was all 'Landsmaal' to them. The one informant interviewed for this investigation who favored the language resented the fact that its spelling norm had changed since he left Norway: he wanted either Landsmaal or Riksmaal, 'inkje noko mitt imyllo' (nothing in between). It appears to be a general rule that the immigrant resents changes in his old homeland which deviate from the pattern which he carried away at his departure.

8. *Dialect Writing.*

Before 1870 the samples of dialect in the immigrant press were a mere trickle beside the broad stream of Dano-Norwegian. None at all appeared in the first newspaper, *Nordlyset*, from 1847 to 1850. But in 1853 *Emigranten* opened its columns to a poem in an East Norwegian dialect, primarily because its subject matter was of direct interest to the readers. This was N. R. Østgaard's *Øster-dølen hemkømmen fraa Amerika* (The East-daler's Return from America), a narrative poem by a well-known folk writer, published in Norway the same year.[82] The tradition of such dialect verse dated back at least to 1647 and included in its roster such distinguished names as Edvard Storm, Henrik Wergeland, and Tormod Knudsen (Borgegjorde), so that it involved no real threat to the established position of the written language.[83] Even so, the experiment was apparently not repeated in *Emigranten*. The only organ that directly represented a dialect group in this early period was the periodical *Wossingen*, a short-lived (1857-59) publication by a group of emigrants from Voss who lived at Leland, Illinois. Even here the dominant linguistic form was Dano-Norwegian, though dialect expressions can be detected in the letters published.[84] One literary composition in dialect appeared, a dialogue entitled *Et frieri i Hardanger* (A Wooing in Hardanger), which had been published two years earlier in Norway.[85] A few riddles from Aasen's *Prøver* complete the list of materials in dialect even in this out-and-out representative of a dialect-speaking group. None of these materials were original; the only attempt to use dialect by an original writer was found in the humorous epistles of one Terje Terjesen Terjeland, which appeared irregularly in *Emigranten* between 1857 and 1861. The name was obviously a pseudonym, and the contents were mostly of a satirical nature; the dialect was supposed to be from Kristiansand, but it was more distinguished by its excessive mixture of English words.[86]

There seems to be a definite connection between the New Norse movement and the upsurge of dialect writing after 1870. The references to the new movement in the papers and the full-scale debate of 1874 called attention to the dialects also, and encouraged some to try writing their own dialects. The influence is traceable in the mode of spelling dialect words, for which Aasen developed new rules, and in direct references, e. g. a writer of Valdres dialect who refers to the fact that 'in Norway they have started to print books in our dialect; this I like well, and wish them luck in their enterprise.'[87] A note of apology for the use of dialect was found occasionally, but may not be entirely sincere. A writer in *Fædre-landet og Emigranten* who discoursed on tobacco raising in what is apparently Telemark dialect declared that 'it would be easier for both of us if we could write English, but we'll have to make out as best we can with our country language (Bondespraakje kons)... We live a long way from the highway, so you mustn't be surprised if we are weak in the book language.'[88] Similarly a Trønder correspondent declared: 'I am no writer and must there-fore use the country language.'[89] One of the purposes of the New Norse movement was to free the country people from this kind of inhibitions with regard to their native tongue. A student at Luther College with sympathy for the movement declared in a speech of 1878 that the prejudice against the rural dialects was a major cause of the transition to English among immigrants in the cities.[90] The New Norse writer Kristofer Janson made much of this point in his book on his countrymen, written after his first visit among them. 'From home he [the Norwegian farmer] is ac-customed to regard his dialect as vulgar and coarse and therefore is ashamed not to be able to express himself in city language. So he finds it better to make his way into the new as quickly as pos-sible and forget that he was not always a Yankee.'[91]

Now and then the papers admitted dialect poems to their columns, and these appear to have constituted a genuine tempta-tion to the many versifiers who thrived among the immigrants.[92]

One Dr. J. C. Dundas who was a frequent contributor tried his hand also at dialect poems from his native Nordland.[93] The most interesting of these writers was Syver S. Holland, schoolteacher, farmer, and storekeeper at Hollandale, Wisconsin, who flourished in the 70's.[94] Some time between 1873 and 1878 he composed a poem in dialect which was destined to become one of the most widely known songs of Norwegians in America. In twenty stanzas of vigorous verse in the manner of Aasen and with definite reminiscences of his orthography, Holland praised the success of the Norwegian immigrant in overcoming the many obstacles of pioneering and humorously referred to his difficulties with the English language. Although Holland was born in Etne in Sunnhordland, a southwestern community in Norway, his dialect form was so near to Aasen's norm that other dialect speakers who memorized his poem and wrote it down in later years unconsciously adapted it to their own dialect.[95] Even closer to New Norse was an anonymous dialect poem which presented a debate between an earlier and a more recent immigrant on the respective merits of America and Norway. Here the form was that of the *stev*, or occasional lyric, of the Norwegian countryside. The poet touched skillfully on some of the most serious problems of immigrant adjustment.[96]

Between 1877 and 1879 the newspaper *Skandinaven* became the forum of a regular exchange of witticisms in dialect. The instigator was a man signing himself Erik i Kroke (Eric in the Corner); he addressed himself to 'Valdres people who subscribe to *Skandinaven*'. In what appears to be excellent dialect he made his contribution to a discussion then going on in the columns of the AmN press. The pastors of the Norwegian Synod were making serious efforts to establish a parochial day school among their parishioners, while the editors of *Skandinaven* upheld the point of view that the American public schools were quite adequate and should be preferred.[97] It is quite possible that the exchanges in Valdres dialect were all written by one person, though there were three different signatures. The writers all pretended to be great admirers of the pastoral group, but succeeded in casting a severely satiric light on their purposes. The point made was that the Synod pastors were opposed to education and enlightenment for the common man. One of the writers implied a definite satisfaction that

Skandinaven permitted simple-minded people to write against the pastors.[98] In these well-written satires the dialect became a vehicle of the common man's point of view against that of the 'official' class. A reference to the dialect itself occurred in one contribution, where a writer expressed appreciation at seeing 'a couple of pieces in our old and vigorous mother tongue — it has a good ring and wakens thoughts of days gone by.'[99]

Apparently *Skandinaven's* editor did not share this feeling, for in 1881 he clamped down on dialect contributions. 'It should be remarked that readers have frequently complained because articles written in some local dialect have been accepted in *Skandinaven*. "We do not understand them," say these dissatisfied writers, and for this reason we believe that it will be best to make less use of this kind of reading matter in the future.'[100]

Pride in dialect seems to have been confined in this period to the dialects of Valdres, Telemark, Hallingdal, and Sogn, which were among the dialects most highly regarded by Aasen and drawn upon by him for his Landsmaal. It is reported from 1875 that a member of the Moscow Reading Society (Iowa County, Wisconsin) spoke in Sogn dialect at a 17th of May celebration and said: 'I am a full-blooded Sogning and intend to talk the language I learned from my mother and have used all my life.'[101] A whole speech in this dialect was printed in the paper *Normannen* (Stoughton, Wis.) in 1892.[102] In that year appeared also what is apparently the only AmN book written entirely in dialect, a story of folk life in Dane County, Wisconsin, entitled *Dei møttes ve Utica* (They met at Utica) by S. H. Severson.[103] The merchant-author, who immigrated at the age of 2 and spent his life in the Koshkonong area except for a gold-digging expedition to Colorado in his youth, made no bones about his aversion to Landsmaal. The language he used was 'pure Telemarking', mixed with English in the conversations, 'as the common people talk it in the settlements.' 'I have not attempted any language-making of my own, nor have I tried to make a Landsmaal by jumbling together words and expressions from many more or less different dialects, as is the case with most Norwegian authors who write in the so-called Landsmaal.' His purpose in using dialect was to 'give the readers reality and not imagination'; he avoided using the Dano-Norwegian written language because 'the topic with which the story dealt seemed especially suited to dialect, which should therefore serve to increase the interest of the book.'[104] Unhappily for the author, the book was so inferior a product that even the dialect did not save it from a well-deserved oblivion.

9. *Dialects in the Bygdelag Movement.*

It was evident from the developments after 1900 that the dialects held a position among the emigrants which the NN written language could never rival. The NN movement was perhaps on too literary a plane to become anything more than the plaything of a relatively small coterie. The *bygdelag* movement, on the other hand, was indigenously AmN, and it gave more elbow room for the dialects than any attained in the earlier periods of immigration. The origin and meaning of the term *bygdelag* has been exhaustively and adequately treated by Professor A. A. Veblen in *The Valdris Book*.[105] The term was adopted in 1906 to describe 'a society composed of natives of some particular settlement or group of settlements in Norway and of their descendants in this country.' According to Veblen, who was one of the prime movers in this development, the word was first used by Dr. Herman Fjelde of Fargo, North Dakota, in a newspaper article of December 21, 1906. At that time only one such organization existed, the Valdris Samband, but this society did not use the term 'lag' in its title. The first one that did was the Telelag, organized early in 1907 in Fargo, N.D.; it was followed the same year by the Hallinglag, organized at Walcott, N.D. The infectious response to this development was the formation within three years of 15 more such groups, and by 1919 of a total of 38. Many of them are still in existence, and continue to serve the fundamental purpose of cultivating 'auld lang syne' by annual or semi-annual get-togethers of old friends and neighbors. Many of them also organized a program of publication, which came to serve as an important source of historical information about the 'grass roots' of Norwegian emigration.[106]

An important stimulus to this movement was the idea conceived by Rasmus B. Anderson of a series of articles in his newspaper *Amerika* extolling the accomplishments of each dialect group among the emigrants. A Valdres group had then already begun meeting informally in Minneapolis (since 1899) and plans were under way for the creation of a formal organization in 1902. But in the summer of 1901 Anderson invited a number of representatives of various dialect groups to write essays about the prominent men each had brought forth in this country. This feature turned out to be enormously popular, and some of the writers seized the occasion to use the local dialects. The first who did so was the Sogning representative, the young Wisconsin-born scholar George T. Flom, who declared: 'Naar eg skal skriva om Sogningadn, saa er det sjølsagt, at eg lyt bruka deira eige Maal'. (When I'm going to write about the Sognings, it is a matter of course that I have to use their own language.) The other dialects represented, with more or less extended quotations or original compositions, were: Valdres, Halling, Trønder, Rogaland, Land, Setesdal, Hordaland, and Østerdalen. A representative from Lier, in Eastern Norway, expressed regret that he 'has no melodious (klangfuld) dialect to make use of.' 'As far as dialect is concerned, we shall have to "take the back seat".' In his part of Norway, he said, 'people are so lazy that they don't bother to speak with accent or force, they just move their mouths and let the words run out without regard to meaning and content...'[107] Another representative of an Eastern lowland dialect (Biri and environs) believed that his dialect, as a compromise between the others, would eventually 'displace these melodious and beautiful, but too difficult dialects, such as the Voss, Sogn, and Hardanger dialect.'[108] He had spoken to Sognings who talked like East Norwegians, but never the opposite. He regarded such unity as desirable: 'but it is a matter of course that we cannot all at once jump into the written language, for then many of us would stumble; but a fusion of our dialects must be what we first unite upon.' The essays were later collected and made into a book, which was sold widely among Norwegians; the title was *Bygdejævning*, or 'community rivalry', a term invented by Anderson himself.[109]

The very terms *bygdelag, bygdejævning, samband,* etc. were drawn from a strictly native, NN or dialectal linguistic sphere rather than

DN. They struck the keynote, and formed the introduction to an interesting development in the use of dialect which we shall now proceed to trace in some detail.⌉

⌈We have already seen that the pioneers in the bygdelag movement were the people from Valdres.[110] Even earlier we had occasion to note the frequent use of this dialect in the public press. In Norway this tradition went back at least to 1850, when a Valdres schoolmaster, Anders Evensen Vang, published a volume of folktales in the local dialect. This book was reprinted in America by A. A. Veblen, together with a later volume of Vang's, in 1930.[111] The Valdres people had emigrated in great numbers, had a highly developed local patriotism, and spoke a dialect closely resembling the Aasen form of New Norse. Yet they did not warm up particularly to the written New Norse norm.⌉Veblen reported that at the organizational meeting in 1902 a representative of the *Norske Samlag* appeared, taking it for granted 'that a society such as the Valdris Samband would naturally give active support to his particular propaganda.' But he was received with a certain coolness, though Veblen claims he was given 'such courtesy as the circumstances permitted,' and he never again troubled the society with his presence.

⌈But the Valdres dialect was taken in use with the greatest of gusto.⌉The tone was set by the original article by Thomas Lajord proposing a get-together of Valdres people in 1899; poems read and speeches given at the meetings, and even the constitution of the organization effected in 1902 were in dialect.[112] This policy was carried on into the early volumes of *Valdris Helsing* (1903-10), edited by Veblen. We see, however, that by the third volume he was having to caution his contributors: 'Be careful about using dialect, except as samples of pure, genuine folk language. Write ordinary Norwegian [meaning DN], or if you prefer, English.'[113] In 1909 he regretfully noted: 'Comparatively few of our members and subscribers can read the dialect without difficulty, and we have often been told that Valdris Helsing contains too much material in Valdris dialect. But we have to bring samples of our dialect, especially when really good, old anecdotes are to be told, or someone has some specially characteristic or amusing notions, which are naturally expressed in the old folk speech.'[114]

The highest proportion of dialect materials was found in the remarkable periodical of the Telemarkings, the *Telesoga*, which was edited throughout its existence (March 1909-1924) by Torkel Oftelie.[115] There were DN articles in many issues, but the greater proportion of the contents was written by the editor himself in a modified Telemark dialect. His linguistic policy was stated in the first issue: 'The language in *Telesoga* is Telemark dialect. The orthography is slightly adjusted in the direction of Landsmaal... It was voted that *Telesoga* should be written in Telemark dialect or in Landsmaal; but the two are so nearly the same, that people who read *Telesoga* will say it is New Norse or Landsmaal.'[116] As is apparent from this statement, the editor's attitude to New Norse was a good deal more friendly than that of the Valdres group. He was, in fact, associated with the movement, a friend and collaborator of Peer Storeygard in the second appearance of *Norrøna*.

As far as the writer has been able to discover from the incomplete files available to him, no other Lag has gone in extensively for the writing of dialect. The groups representing East Norwegian lowland dialects are conspicuous by their failure to include any dialect or NN material: *Kongsberglaget*, *Vikværingen* (Kristianialaget), *Modum-Eikerlaget*, *Østerdalslaget* (only 1 volume available), *Sigdalslaget*, *Smaalenslaget*, *Totenlaget*. The same is true of the materials available from *Nerstrandslaget* (near Stavanger), *Selbulaget*, and *Sunnfjordsoga* (only one issue seen). But most of the mountain and fjord groups include considerable samples of dialect and even some New Norse: *Gudbrandsdalslaget* (speech in dialect 1915, pp. 19-22), *Hallingen* (a great deal of material, both in prose and poetry), *Mjøsenlaget* (very occasional dialect and NN), *Naumdøla* (some letters in NN from Norway), *Nord-Norge* (dialect poems and anecdotes), *Nordfjordlaget* (articles and poems in NN), *Numedalslaget* (dialect speech 1915, anecdotes 1917 etc. as well as many articles and poems in NN), *Opdalslaget* (dialect anecdotes, poems), *Romsdalslaget* (reprinted dialect sample 1917), *Saude og Nesherringer i Amerika* (dialect stories, NN poem), *Søndmørelaget* (a good deal of NN), *Trønderlaget* (dialect poems, occasional articles in NN), *Vossingen* (articles and poems in NN and dialect).

The editors of these publications were nearly all trained in DN only, and it is not surprising that they should prefer to edit them in that language. On the other hand, they were in close contact with personalities in the local home communities, from whom they often solicited contributions. ⌐A typical comment on the situation is that of Knut Rene, in an article on 'The Language of *Vossingen.*'[117] He commented on the fact that some of his readers might be troubled by the alternation of DN, NN, and Voss dialect in his journal. The predominant form had been DN because 'most people probably read this best, and the editor is most used to writing it.' But in Voss they now used nothing but NN, so that all greetings and newspapers came in this language; these he printed unchanged. Besides, he believed it to be the future language of Norway, and no dialect in Norway was closer to it than that of Voss. 'Here in America we need, to be sure, no controversy over the language of Norway, but it may be expected that necessary consideration will be taken when the subject is discussed. The DN language is used here almost exclusively, because it was in use from the beginning, and it is always a struggle to exchange something familiar; besides, it seems enough to have one language conflict [referring to the controversy between English and Norwegian]. But it must be admitted that NN also has its justification and is preferred by many. After all, it is quite possible to learn to read both languages and even Swedish with a little effort.'

⌐The meetings and publications of the Lags stimulated great quantities of dialect verse,⌐much of which can be perused in the publications. Some reprints of dialect verse from Norway were also made, e. g. Torkel Oftelie's *Tiriltunga* (old 'stev' from Telemark; Fargo, N.D., 1907); John and Hallvor Lie's *Hugaljo* (Telemark dialect, orig. pub. 1874, Minneapolis, 1913); Oddmund Urheim, *Nokre visor* (Ullensvang, Hardanger dialect, dedicated to the Hardangerlag; Story City, Iowa, 1914). On the other hand, such older dialect speakers as Knud Henderson and O. S. Sneve included only one or two dialect poems each in their collections of verse.[118] The latter, indeed, appears to have opposed the use of dialect or NN, for in a poem called *Sprogforvirring* (Linguistic confusion) he suggested to Norwegians who are tired of their 'Babel's confusion', that they can come to Amerika to hear 'the language that Ibsen wrote, a language well worth hearing.'[119] A prolific dialect poet of the period was Reier K. Ulen, who was born at Flå in Hallingdal in 1849 and immigrated to Spring Grove, Minnesota, in 1856. His earliest preserved dialect poem, however, is from a homecoming festival at Spring Grove in 1907. Contributions of his in prose and verse appeared in the newspaper *Amerika* and elsewhere after this time, especially in connection with the meetings of Hallinglaget. But the majority of his poems were in DN.[120]

10. *The Dialects in Literature and Scholarship.*

A few writers made use of the dialects in an objective way, when characterizing speakers of dialect. Only a few of the more important instances will be mentioned here. Certainly the most popular dialect-speaking characters were the figures of the only AmN comic strip, *Ola og Per.* They were the creation of a farmer-artist, P. J. Rosendahl, living near Spring Grove, Minnesota; the strip was printed in *Decorah-Posten* beginning Jan. 9, 1920 and ran for several years. The two title characters spoke distinct dialects, Ola some kind of EN lowland speech (possibly Hadeland), Per some kind of Midland mountain dialect (possibly Hallingdal). There was also a character named Lars who spoke DN. Their speech was authentic enough, being also liberally sprinkled with English expressions. The same was true of the tales from early settlement life contained in Thor Helgeson's *Fra Indianernes Lande.*[121] As noted in our last chapter, this old schoolmaster was probably the most successful raconteur among the emigrants, and he admirably carried through the principle announced on one of his title pages of reproducing the stories told him 'as much as possible in the storytellers' own manner of narrative and expression.' Another outstanding portrayer of Norwegian settlement life by means of dialect was Martin Midttun, whose sketches from a Sogning settlement in Buffalo County, Wisconsin, ran in *Decorah-Posten* from September 11, 1936 to January 29, 1937, under the title of *Sogninga-Saga.*[122] Most authors translated the speeches of their characters into DN; one of the few who made artistic use of the dialect was Ole E. Rølvaag, whose characters in the series initiated by *Giants in the Earth* spoke progressively a more and more marked Nordland dialect.[123]

The popular interest awakened in Norway and to some extent among Norwegian emigrants by the great linguistic controversies was reflected in a small but useful body of scholarly and informative studies. In 1898 Gisle Bothne wrote a detailed and objective discussion on 'The language of Modern Norway' for the PMLA.[124] In 1902 S. Sondresen published a small pamphlet in Norwegian, entitled *Norsk sprog i dets udviklingsstadier historisk fremstillet*.[125] This represented the views of the latest scholarship at the time it was written, and was remarkably balanced in its tone; it expressed the hope that 'from the union and fusion of these two languages a uniform Norwegian language will in time be formed.' The widely read American magazine *Review of Reviews* carried two articles, a panegyric of the movement by Mabel Leland in 1904 ('We can only account for the indifference and even antagonism, which prevails in certain quarters toward the movement by the inherent contempt felt on the part of the privileged classes for the peasant...') and a more non-committal, anonymous account in 1907.[126] Readers of PMLA were kept up-to-date by a well-written, understanding article of Calvin Thomas's in 1910.[127] The newly founded *Publications of the Society for Advancement of Scandinavian Study* included an article 'On the Forms of the "Landsmaal" in Norway' (1.165-75) in 1914 by Ingebrigt Lillehei, who was working on the topic for a doctoral dissertation. Another article by the same author on 'Landsmaal and the Language Movement in Norway' (JEGP 13.60-87) in the same year was more a pæan in praise of the movement than an objective evaluation. He wrote: 'We who prefer Landsmaal look upon the cultured speech of our Norwegian capital as provincial Danish...' (75). Of Knud Knudsen he said: 'This man devoted his whole life to the cause of three voiceless consonants.' (76). In 1917 the Society for Advancement of Scandinavian Study published a grammar of Landsmaal by Stanley Fowler Wright in which he cautiously remarked that Lm. 'merits recognition in that it is a praiseworthy, even if somewhat misguided, attempt to express Norse nationality in a peculiarly distinctive form...' Two years later came an article on '"Maalstræv" in Norway' by A. Hobek.[128] An article on Landsmaal and Riksmaal by Ottar Tinglum appeared in *American Journal of Sociology* in 1929 (34.686-92). The present writer completed a thesis for the

Ph. D. at the University of Illinois in 1931, on the topic, *The Early History of the New Norse Movement*, a chapter of which appeared in PMLA in the same year (48.558-97) under the title 'The Linguistic Development of Ivar Aasen's New Norse.' The chief scientific studies of Norwegian dialect have been made by Koshkonong-born George T. Flom, who has published the following major studies of his childhood dialect of Sogn: *A Grammar of the Sogn Dialect of Norwegian: Noun, Adjective, Numerals and Pronouns* (DNotes 3.25-54, 1905); *The Phonology of the Dialect of Aurland*, (Sogn, Norway) (Univ. of Ill. SIL I, Number 1); *The Morphology of the Dialect of Aurland* (Univ. of Ill. SIL XXIX, Number 4).[129]

11. *Summary*.

Throughout the history of writing among Norwegian emigrants in America, their underlying dialectal speech has on occasion been allowed to emerge. At first only as an occasional whim, later under direct stimulus from the New Norse movement in Norway, contributors attempted to use their dialects both in verse and prose. Writers from the regions of the old folk culture in the mountain and fjord valleys showed a distinct pride in this use of dialect, but for the most part the use of dialect was humorously tinged. Any extensive use of dialect was regularly opposed by editors, who were reminded through the complaints of readers that dialects were hard to read, even by those who spoke them. The reason for this was the lack of childhood training in reading dialect and a consequent unfamiliarity with the word images, which impeded rapid and satisfying reading. The dialects had their heyday within the bygdelags, old-home organizations founded since 1900, but only a few of these encouraged the inclusion of dialect material in their publications.

The New Norse movement, which aimed at and succeeded in establishing a new norm of Norwegian writing in opposition to the Dano-Norwegian, came too late to affect more than a tiny proportion of the emigrants during their impressionable years. The interest in it remained at all times a relatively limited, literary concern, which flourished during the two periods of greatest cultural activity among the emigrants, the 70's and the early 1900's. The enthusiasm shown during the 70's, of which Anderson's *Den norske Maalsag* is the chief product, was part of the romantically-tinged view of Norway which cultural leaders of the period entertained and promoted. In the 1900's sporadic efforts were made to introduce the new language among the emigrants. Magazines were published, books, articles, and poems were written, and one figure of genuine literary interest, Jon Norstog, devoted his life to the cause. But most cultural leaders of the immigrants were agreed that however interesting and beautiful the cause might be, the emigrants would be lucky if they succeeded in maintaining for a time the use of one written Norwegian without saddling themselves with the burden of two. An argument was frequently advanced by its advocates that Norwegians would be less eager to give up their language in favor of English if they felt prouder of their spoken dialects and had a written language that was their very own, instead of Danish. To the impartial observer other factors would seem to have been more significant in promoting assimilation than this one; actually, most ordinary immigrants who had not been indoctrinated by the New Norse movement felt a deep, almost religious respect for the written language of Norway. Even though it was not a language they would speak, except in meeting strangers or speaking of solemn matters, it did not occur to them to reject it as un-national. Nor does it seem that the Norwegian dialects were objectively more different from written DN than Swedish or Danish dialects from written Swedish or Danish, or many German dialects from High German.

Growing familiarity with NN might indeed have led speakers from many parts of Norway to feel it as a better norm for their writing than the old DN, but an opportunity for acquiring such familiarity did not exist for most emigrants. Their first reaction was that the new writing was neither their own dialect nor the traditional written language; it was and remained an unfamiliar and therefore repugnant hybrid. Even the growing sympathy for it expressed by many leaders after 1900 and the scientific attention devoted to it by a few serious students of language were insufficient to shake the basic conviction of the emigrants that the DN language they had learned to read in childhood was Norwegian and that any attempt by the homeland to change it was in the nature of heresy. A movement which aimed at increasing the countryman's love of his own language and causing him to cultivate it in writing thus had rather the effect among the emigrants of tending to alienate them from the homeland. The influence in this direction was not large, but it was a perceptible element in the criticism levelled against the homeland by many emigrants.

Chapter 9.

NAMES IN A NEW WORLD.

He that hath an ill name is half hanged.
John Heywood (1546).

The name disgraces no one who does not disgrace himself.
Norwegian Proverb.

Norwegians came from a country with an inexhaustible wealth of names, whether we think of the names applied to people, animals, or places. Place names alone have been estimated at five million in number, a guess based on an average of 100 names for each of Norway's 50,000 farmsteads.[1] In one remote mountain valley, where the situation has actually been investigated, a scholar found some 300 place names on each farm.[2] The very sparseness with which the population is distributed over Norway's jagged surface has promoted a tradition of many names. The farm was not merely a group of houses surrounded by fields, as are many American farms. It comprised also patches of woodland, mountain pasture, lakes and marshes, often at some distance from the tiny area of cultivation on the valley floor.[3] Villages were few and unimportant; the characteristic pattern of living was on far-flung farmsteads, each one like an island in the surrounding landscape. At the time of immigration a slowly changing social life had not altered the fact that the primary unit of Norwegian life was the independent farm, the allodial estate of the yeoman family. Around this farm clustered the names of the family and the domestic animals who lived upon it. Ancient ways of naming still survived which had long been given up in the cities.[4]

The Norwegian rural immigrant thus had a good deal to unlearn in making his adjustment to American patterns of nomenclature. In this chapter we shall follow his progress in each of the more important phases of namegiving. Names are often fraught with emotional overtones which influence men's lives, perhaps unduly. In any case they are keys to such important social institutions as the family and the neighborhood; as surnames they even persist beyond the life of the language from which they came. Wherever there are American descendants of Norwegian immigrants, Norwegian names will carry on, though inevitably disguised and maltreated. They will make up a part of that new element in American nomenclature which sets it distinctly off from the British, as pointed out by H. L. Mencken in his *American Language.*[5]

1. *The Problem of Surnames.*

The first naming problem that faced the bewildered immigrant was the necessity of choosing a definite surname by which he could be identified for business purposes. It was not that he lacked a surname, but rather that his rural surname customs were entirely different from those of the new country.[6] If anything, he was embarrassed by the wealth of choices that were open to him. In America he was expected to limit himself to a single surname which he would then transmit to all his descendants. This was a custom which had become general in Europe after the Renaissance, but before that time it had mostly been limited to kings and noblemen. It had filtered into Norway in the 17th Century, but remained the almost exclusive privilege of the urban population even as late as the 19th.[7]

In the Norwegian countryside an older custom prevailed, which had once been universal in large parts of the western world. Beyond his given name, a man was identified primarily by telling whose son he was. If anything more were needed, one could state the name of the farm where he lived. These practices define the two types of surnames that were actually in use: (1) *patronymics*, and (2) *farm names.* The patronymic consisted of the father's name followed by -*son* (usually spelled -*sen*) or -*datter*. If a man were named

Halvor Knutsen, his children would not be surnamed Knutsen, but Halvorsen and Halvorsdatter, according to their sex. The surnames were formed anew in each generation. Iceland is the only part of the Scandinavian area where this viking custom still flourishes undiminished.

In 19th century rural Norway it had become customary, at least in writing, to add the name of the farm as a second surname. A man thus had three names, a *given name*, a *patronymic*, and a *farm name*. We find most of the immigrants so recorded by their Norwegian pastors in the early church books: Torsten Olsen Bjaadland, Amund Andersen Hodnefjeld, etc. But not one of these was a family surname. For even though a family might indeed have lived so long on the same farm that the name by custom attached itself to all its members, the name did not belong to the family but to the farm. The name was a part of the neighborhood landscape, which served to identify the locality. It did not change with the shifting generations; some names can with certainty be traced back to the Early Iron Age B. C.[8] Anyone who moved from the farm automatically lost the right to use its name; and if he moved to a new one, he would soon be known by the new name.

But this kind of loose attachment to one's surname was entirely out of keeping with the practices of American society. The immigrant had to settle down to one of his several surnames, one which he would some day pass on to his children. Early handbooks published for his benefit even pointed out this necessity to him.[9]

A certain precedent for dealing with the situation had been established in Norway before emigration. Country folk who migrated to the cities had for some time been forced to follow urban customs of naming. A famous example is the poet Vinje (1818-1870), who wrote his name A. Olsen down to the time when he was appointed school teacher in the town of Mandal at the age of 26. Soon after this, he abandoned the name in favor of his farm name Vinje (written Winje at first) to avoid confusion with all the other Olsens. His writings appeared under the name A. O. Vinje, which he expanded in private letters as Aasmund Olafsen Vinje.[10] There was still a certain stigma of rusticity about the farm names in mid-nineteenth century Norway, which stimulated some to disguise them to look like Danish or German names. Just as Vinje wrote

Winje, so the first users of the west Norwegian farm name Verkland wrote it Wergeland. A simple name like Vik 'bay' came to be written in a multitude of ways, e. g. Vig, Viig, Wieg, Wiigh; Tveit 'grassy plot' turned up as Tvedt, Bakke 'hill' as either Backe or Bache. Many of these distortions are reflected in the forms of emigrant surnames.[11]

Most emigrated Norwegians were therefore not in a position to feel a very strong attachment to their surnames. Only the relatively small percentage of early immigrants who belonged to upper-class urban families brought with them well-established family names. These included many foreign names, belonging to families who had immigrated to Norway from Denmark or Germany at an earlier period, and who now participated in a new emigration as leaders in church or school. Such names as Preus, Brandt, and Stub carried a considerable prestige; no member of these families would have dreamed of adapting the spelling to American speech habits. But the average rural Norwegians had no such feeling about their sur-names; they had to make a choice among the several possible sur-names and then a decision on how the one chosen should be written. We shall now see how these decisions were generally arrived at.[12]

2. *Surnames from Patronymics.*

The importance of the choice is vividly illustrated in a scene from Rølvaag's pioneer novel, *Giants in the Earth*.[13] The chief characters of the book were known among their Norwegian fellow settlers as Per Hansa and Hans Olsa, dialectal forms of Peder Hansen and Hans Olsen. But one day a neighbor raises the question of 'what names Hans Olsa and Per Hansa intended to adopt when they took out the title deeds to their land.' The two are dumbfounded, and Per Hansa answers with some irritation that 'he couldn't understand why the name Peder Hansen would not be good enough even for the United States Constitution.' The question becomes the subject of a lively discussion in the two fam-ilies; Hans Olsa's wife speaks up and resolutely declares that 'if she had her choice she would rather be called Mrs. Vaag, from their place name in Norway, than Mrs. Olsen.' But they find Per

Hansa's farm name Skarvholmen too clumsy and settle upon Holm instead. 'After that day, each of the two families in question had a pair of surnames. Among themselves they always used the old names, but among strangers they were Vaag and Holm — though Hans Olsa invariably wrote it with a "W" instead of a "V".

In this scene Rølvaag concentrated in a single family council a number of decisions which were more commonly spread over a series of years. But the general tenor of it is essentially faithful to the development among the immigrants. The immediate use of the farm name was rather unusual, however, among the earlier generations of pioneers. Of the nine who took out the first deeds in the Koshkonong settlement in 1840 only one used a farm name (Gunnul Vindeg); the rest used patronymics.[14] But the use of one name within the group and another to outsiders was typical enough. The editor of the first AmN newspaper, *Nordlyset*, complained in 1848 that he had trouble reaching his subscribers because their 'real Norwegian names and the ones they use here often disagree.'[15] Such discrepancies might become quite startling, as in the case of the early Illinois settler Mons Knudsen Aadland, who was 'generally known among Yankees under the name of Monsen.'[16] An outstanding instance is the pathfinder of Norwegian immigration himself, the famous Cleng Peerson; this name inscribed on his Texas tombstone was a far cry from the name given him at birth: Klein Pedersen Hesthammer.[17]

Any one who studies the tombstones in such early Norwegian-American settlements as the Fox River settlement in Illinois or Muskego in Wisconsin will find that the surnames are predominantly patronymics. Throughout the history of the Norwegian group in Amerca the names in -son (or -sen) have played a very important role. They have been so common that most Americans have conceived of them as the typical Norwegian (and Scandinavian) surnames. The reasons are obvious: names in -son are relatively easy to spell and pronounce and can easily be adapted to an established pattern in English naming. Before the settlement of America such names as Anderson, Johnson, Nelson, and Thompson were well known in British usage, and they were as if made for Scandinavian immigrants. Their existence in Britain may even ultimately be due to the viking invasions.[18] In Norway the migrants from country to city adopted their patronymics as family names in great numbers, and this practice was easily extended to America.] There was something humble and undistinguished about the son-names; they passed muster without further comment in American society. Only a slight spelling adaptation was required: in Norway the ending had usually been -sen, which was generally changed in America to -son. The Norwegian could have no objection to this change, for many knew that the Norwegian form had once been -son also, and that some families in Norway were making an effort to revive this older form.

The only serious problem that could arise if one decided to take the patronymic was the question of whose patronymic should become the family surname. Within one family there were as many patronymics as there were generations. If Lars Olson came to America with his son John and his grandson Lars, there was the possibility of choosing any one of three patronymics, Olson, Larson, or Johnson, as permanent surname. The studies of Marjorie Kimmerle in the naming practices of two Wisconsin settlements suggest that the first American generation usually settled the problem and did so on the basis of whose patronymic was the most widely known. A son whose father had become well-known kept his father's name, while a father whose son became well-known might even adopt his son's.[19] But within the group the use of the correct patronymic might continue throughout a full generation, as we see from the church records. It was not until the late 70's that the records of the Springdale congregation in southern Wisconsin show the definite passing of -son and -datter as patronymics and the occurrence of -son for both boys and girls as permanent surnames.[20]

In spite of the popular impression that son-names are typically Scandinavian, it does not appear that they managed to maintain a majority among the Norwegian immigrants. Miss Kimmerle's study of two congregations in southern Wisconsin shows that the farm name was chosen by respectively 70 and 67 % of the family heads in the first generation. A list of 93 Norwegian families living in the Blair, Wisconsin, neighborhood included only 11 patronymics.[21] Only 30 % of the student body in the predominantly Norwegian-descended St. Olaf College bore patronymic surnames in 1949.[22]

The typical development appears in a family studied by Miss Kimmerle, where an unusually rich documentation was available. Consider the case of Halvor Anundsen Bjaaen, who arrived in the Koshkonong settlement in the early 1840's. The Reverend J. W. C. Dietrichson entered his name in the church books in this triple-barrelled form. But in the census of 1850 he appeared with the single surname Anderson, a distortion of the patronymic which continued to appear in his papers down to 1882. Halvor himself adopted Anundson as a business name, and in a multitude of misspellings this is the form that appears in most of his dealings with the American world from 1850 to about 1870. Documents involving other immigrant Norwegians often use both names. But from 1858 there was also frequent use of the name Bjaaen alone, and shortly after 1870 this name began to dominate. In spite of an absolutely inspired miscellany of spellings the name grows in intensity of usage; after 1878 a spelling of the farm name which looks as if it had started out as a misspelling becomes the accepted family name: Bjoin. This was the spelling adopted by the son and after 1890 promoted by the whole family.[23]

Even though it is likely that the farm names have a clear majority over the patronymics, it is quite understandable that the latter should seem more typical to non-Scandinavians. The patronymics are recognizable as a type and are reinforced by their even higher prevalence among Danes and Swedes. Individual names such as Olson or Larson are far more frequent than any single place name. The place names have no common cast which identifies them as Norwegian, in spite of such rather frequent suffixes as -stad, -land, -berg, -rud, and -dahl. By the time the place names have been accommodated to American speech and spelling only a specialist can recognize them for what they are.

3. *Surnames from Place Names.*

The turn in favor of farm names seems to have set in during the 1870's. The first generation, which had been disposed to encourage the patronymics as the easiest way out, discovered that there was a serious disadvantage in these names. The stock of given names

on which they were based was so small that in a community consisting almost entirely of Norwegians the patronymic surnames
failed to identify the families. Informants have emphasized the
confusion caused by excessive numbers of identical family names.
A glance at the Koshkonong records will reveal the magnitude of
the problem. In a group of 312 individual men appearing in the
records no less than 54 bore the patronymic Olsen! Of these nearly
all were recorded with this name alone in at least one of the census
records from 1850 to 1870. It was not possible to follow more than
33 of these down to the present time; of these only one is known
to be using Olsen as a family name. In one small neighborhood
there were six Olsens, of whom three bore the given name Aslak,
and every one had a son named Ole.[24] This is proof enough that
informants have told the truth in pointing to the confusion of
patronymics as the leading motive in the adoption of farm names
as family surnames. As a descendant of the Halvor Bjaaen mentioned above told the writer, 'the school teachers wanted us to be
Andersons, and the same for the Drotnings across the road; but
our letters got so mixed up that we went back to the names Bjaaen
and Drotning.'[25]

But this practical stimulus was reinforced by an ideal consideration which was widely proclaimed by leaders of the immigrant
group. The farm names, it was held, had a native Norwegian
quality which should recommend them for patriotic reasons alone.
The 70's saw a minor movement in this direction, the keynote being
struck in 1877 when a writer in the newspaper *Skandinaven* im-
plored Norwegians not to show disrespect for their own nationality
by rejecting the place names as 'countrified or old-fashioned.'
'Such a place name will always, no matter how long the world
stands, point back to our nationality, just as the runic inscriptions
point back to the hoary past.'[26] Among the leaders who advocated
this restoration of the more characteristically Norwegian names was
Professor Rasmus B. Anderson, then teaching at the University
of Wisconsin. At an old settlers' picnic on the fourth of July, 1878,
at Rock Prairie, Wisconsin, Anderson spoke on this subject, and
a resolution was passed supporting the adoption of farm names as
family names.[27] In his autobiography Anderson speaks of this
campaign and how it led him to advise the budding Norwegian

author Knud Pedersen to adopt the place name Hamsun.[28] Exhortations to this effect appeared frequently in the Norwegian-language press, and reinforced as they were by the obvious advantages of the farm names as family names, they seem to have had some effect.

The trend was reinforced by other considerations. A similar tendency in Norway, where the national movement included an emphasis on the farm names as a patriotic treasure, is apparent in the fact that later immigrants more frequently had adopted their farm names as surnames even before immigration. The prestige of the upper-class names in Norway led to an extensive desire on the part of rural families to have fixed names also. A further advantage of the farm names was their correspondence to a certain class of English family names. The use of place names as family names was a characteristic English procedure, as appears from such names as Cleveland, Washington, Berkeley, or Oglethorpe. These, too, were in many cases of Scandinavian origin, and had a certain likeness to those which were brought over from Norway in modern times. In spite of many strange combinations of sound there were thus less psychological obstacles to the adoption of a Norwegian farm name than e.g. to many types of East European surnames.[29]

The farm name by its very distinctiveness could awaken and maintain a fierceness of family pride which the more colorless patronymic rarely attained. Many must have felt as did informant Jacob Roalkvam, who was asked if many Norwegians had changed their names in his community. 'They changed my name, but I have never changed it. They call me J. K., but I still write it Jacob. In olden times they couldn't pronounce such names as Roalkvam. Then there were many who said to me: why don't you call yourself Thompson? Then I said: there are plenty of Thompsons around here, but too few Roalkvams! I wouldn't change anything, just to make it easier for Englishmen and Irishmen to pronounce it.'[30]

Even when the decision to take a farm name was made, it was not always a foregone conclusion as to which name should be chosen. A family might often have more than one name available. This was true if the family had lived on more than one farm, even if they had not owned all or any of them. It often happened that day laborers who had never owned a farm chose the name of a farm where they had worked for some time. The institution of the croft, a small subsidiary farm rented for life, also led to many 'improper' choices. The crofters often found the name of the croft unwieldy or humble; they preferred to take the name of the 'big farm'. Just as in Norway, it sometimes occurred that names of larger groupings than the individual farms were chosen, up to the name of a whole valley or community. The family name Bang in the Springdale area of Wisconsin is derived from a neighborhood in the parish of the same name (spelled Bagn in Norway). The family name Lerdahl is derived from the parish name of Lærdal in Sogn. The reasons for such choices might vary widely, as shown in Miss Kimmerle's article on Norwegian surnames.[31] But they are deeply rooted in the social connotations of the names, as well as in their acceptability in the American world.

A striking aspect of the choices made was that many families made more than one choice, so that to American eyes they appeared to be divided into as many clans as there were names. Brothers who settled in different communities might not have been in touch at the time the decision was made. But even if they were, they sometimes chose to go their own ways. The influences that led to the final decision were miscellaneous and sporadic: an American school teacher or neighbor, a more or less well-informed friend or relative. A decision made by the first immigrant of a family might be respected, as when the name Gulbransen in one family was abandoned in favor of Gilbertson because the latter had been adopted by an uncle who had immigrated in the late 60's.[32] A Civil War soldier named Jørgen Olsen Wrolstad wrote from Camp Randall at Madison, Wisconsin, to his wife: 'I have arranged everything about your bounty [i.e.pension], and your name is written Asberg Olsen [for Asbjørg Olsen], so I guess you had better write it the same way.'[33] A single individual might exert great influence on others to anglicize their names in various ways, as pointed out for a Vernon County community by H. R. Holand.[34]

There are numerous stories concerning the legal tangles which arose from this peculiar Norwegian habit of developing more than one family name. Prestgard tells with some amusement of one Anders Gulbrandsen Haug, who filed for land as Andrew Gilbertson, but took out his insurance under the name of A. G. Hill (a translation of Haug).[35] We need not wonder that his heirs had difficulties in probating his estate. A subscribers' letter to *Decorah-Posten* by a woman who immigrated in 1887 reveals that her older brothers and sisters adopted the name of their mother's birthplace, the younger ones that of their father's; her husband's name was Jacobsen, while that of his brothers and sisters was Myhre. The family of A. J. Opstedal illustrates an extreme case of four brothers with three different names. Until around 1900 the family had used Johnson, the father's patronymic; but at that time two of the brothers decided to take up the farm name. Each one anglicized it in his own way, so that the four brothers henceforth bore the names of Johnson, Opstedal, and Opdahl!

The habit of transforming place names into family surnames was deeply ingrained among the immigrants, and in a few cases it even persisted so as to include place names established in this country after immigration. One story to illustrate this usage is that of Gullik Knudsen Laugen, an early settler of the Rock Prairie region in southern Wisconsin. He settled near a spring and called his farm Springen 'the spring'. But from that time on his family was known as Springen.[36] Gulbrand Landru emigrated from Norway and bought a farm near Stoughton, Wisconsin, which had been owned by a man named Moen. Before long, people started calling him Moen, too, and the name stuck; his permanent name was Gilbert Moen.[37] A man from Hallingdal named Hølje Skattom went by the name Olsen at first; but after he moved on a farm previously owned by Jon Grovom, the neighbors started calling him Hølje Grovom.[38] Better still: Nils Nilsen from the farm Klægstad in Modum, Norway, got work at Stillwater, Minnesota, in the sawmill of an American named McCusick. He also worked in McCusick's stable. In due time he came to be called Nils McCusick![39] While these stories are sporadic, they are just frequent enough to show the transfer of the place name habit to America, and the casual way in which many Norwegians were willing to treat their surnames.

4. *Accommodating the Surnames to English.*

Most Norwegian surnames have been changed in some detail to accommodate their use in English.[40] The changes are similar to those which all foreign names have undergone in America, ever since the Hubers and the Zimmermans became Hoovers and Carpenters. There were three practical possibilities: (1) the Norwegian name could be kept unchanged; (2) it could be revised in spelling; or (3) it could be eliminated in favor of an English name. In practice these alternatives might overlap, since the orthographic revision could make a name coincide with a previously existing English name. Each possibility involves more than one alternative; the following classification should provide for most changes:

(1) Retention of the Norwegian name.

(a) With partial persistence of Norwegian pronunciation habits. This occurs within communities that are still partly Norwegian-speaking; though individual families can make their wishes felt even elsewhere. Thus in the list of names from Blair, Wisconsin, referred to above, the following examples occur: Nyen [niən] contrasting with Myhre [maiər], Bratland [bratlənd] contrasting with Granlund [grænlənd], Fagernes [fagernəs] contrasting with Hagestad [hægestəd]. A statistical study undertaken in the village of Deerfield, Wisconsin, by Miss Kimmerle showed an interesting confusion of pronunciations, reflecting the process of transition. The spellings suggested pronunciations contrary to American habits to a large percentage of the informants in such names as Hatlebak [hatləbak] (80 %), Braaten [brɔtən] (89 %), Herreid [hɛraid] (82 %), Solberg [solbərg] (100 %), Bjornstad [bj-] (92 %), Nesthus [nestəs] (98 %). But the prevailing tendency was toward the next group.

(b) With anglicized spelling pronunciations. These have radically altered the sound of the names, so that a native Norwegian would scarcely recognize them in hearing them pronounced. The following list will give some idea of the transformations; examples come from Blair: Skyrud [shirü] > [skairud]; Berg [bærj] > [bərg]; Thorsgaard [toːshgar] > [thɔrzgard].

(2) Revision of the Norwegian name.

(a) Respelling with an eye to suggesting the original pronunciation. This seems evident when such a name as Seim is changed

to Sime, Ris to Reese, Lie to Lee, Strøm to Strum; but it is hard
to tell whether some of these may not have been intended as English
names. An example from Koshkonong is Cherrie for Kjærret
[tçærrə]; from a list collected in various places by Olaf Huseby
come the following: Aas > Oace; Braaten > Brawthen; Fitjar >
Fitcha; Gjersjø > Jarshaw; Hove > Hovey; Rye > Rhea; Sørkjil
> Surchel; Sjøli > Shirley; Skjeldrud > Sheldrew; Sollid > Soley;
Skau > Scow; Tømmerland > Tamerlane. The number of such
names is quite small.

(b) Elimination of unfamiliar letter combinations. It is obvious
that Norwegian characters like æ and ø had to go, usually becoming
a or *e* and *o* respectively; *aa* (also written *å*) usually had to go.
Examples from Blair are: Ødegaard > Odegard, Rønning > Ren-
ning, Løkken > Lokken, Mørk > Mork, Bøe > Boe, Sørlie >
Sorlie; from Koshkonong: Hæve > Havey, Lægreid > Legreid,
Næperud > Neperud. But it was also common to eliminate such
combinations as *kv, sv, tv* in favor of *qu, sw,* and *tw:* Kvamen >
Quammen, Lekve > Leque, Kverne > Quarne, Sveger > Sweger,
Tvedt > Tweet. Even *v* alone was sometimes eliminated, though
it caused no difficulties of pronunciation: Vedvik > Wedvick. In
some cases older DN spelling used *w* for *v* in such names, and this
may be the source of the spelling. The digraphs gj [j], kj [ç], sj [sh]
could be kept and given a spelling pronunciation; but they were
often eliminated, e.g. Kjerret > Cherrie, Kjetilson > Chilson,
Gjerde > Jerdee, Gjerrejord > Jargo, Skjerve > Sherry. Kn- was
usually kept, but pronounced [n]; such spellings as Newtson (from
Knutsen) are not unknown, however.

(c) Abbreviation. Compounds were common among the Norwegian farm names, frequently consisting of one or more modifying
elements preceding a base. The immigrants generally took only
one of these, sometimes the modifier, but usually the base. The compounds very often lacked prestige, many of these being the names
of crofts and mountain chalets.[41] Examples are: Tællhaugen 'pine
hill' > Hauge, Bergslien 'mountain slope' > Lien, Buaasdalen
'Buaas valley' > Buaas, Halsteinsgaardbakken 'Halstein's farm
hill' > Bakken, Magnusholmen 'Magnus' island' > Magnus, Nore-
strand 'Nore shore' > Strand.[42] A rather common practice was to
shorten the patronymic by dropping the -son and sometimes adding

an -s, e.g. Jakobsen > Jacobs, Anderson > Andrews, Albertson > Alberts, Botolvson > Botolfs, Eivindson > Evans, Haakonsen > Hawkins, Henrikson > Hendrix, Sivertsen > Seavers, Sondreson > Sanders.[43] Bjørn Olsen Hustvedt of Koshkonong chose to use his father's patronymic Stefansen; but on the advice of a Yankee neighbor he shortened it to Stephens.[44] In many cases these names coincided with English names already occurring and therefore overlap with the next classification.

(3) Substitution of English names.

(a) By meaning: translation was not a common practice among the Norwegians, although a good many of the farm names were transparent enough. Perhaps a sense of absurdity held some back who might otherwise have been tempted. In Koshkonong Miss Kimmerle found only one example: Langhaug > Longhill; none occurs in the list from Blair. In the previously cited list of 317 names collected by Olaf Huseby the absurdities predominate; yet these are the only examples he was able to collect in several years of travelling among the immigrants: Askeland > Ashland, Bjedla > Bell, Bakkedal > Hillsdale, Brarik > Goodrich, Bjørkehaugen > Birchill, Flatmark > Plainfield, Gedde > Pike, Grinaker > Branchfield, Grønfjell > Greenfield, Haugen > Hill, Korsbakken > Crosshill, Knappen > Button, Lysaker > Lightfield, Lofthus > Upstairs, Nygaard > Newton, Nyhus > Newhall, Norskog > Norwood, Pladsen > Place, Rossevatn > Rosenwater, Røvang > Redwing, Rismyr > Rice, Sjonarhaug > Hill, Skogen > Wood, Steinnes > Stone, Skau > Forest, Østerhus > Easthouse. As will be seen, several of these also fit into the next category, in which no meaning is involved, but only sound.

(b) By sound: a similar-sounding (or looking) English name was adopted. The examples here are quite numerous, and include some of the previously cited names. It is often hard to say just how similar a name has to be to fall under this category. When Kleveland becomes Cleveland, the step is so small and inevitable that this might almost be regarded as a mere respelling of the Norwegian name. Among the patronymics it is striking that such a name as

Thompson does not exist in Norway, but is very common among the immigrants. It has absorbed practically all patronymics beginning with Th- (pronounced t in Norwegian), such as Thorstensen, Thorsen, Thomassen, Thorkelson etc. The name Anderson has picked up contributions from Anundsen, Amundsen etc. Nelson is non-existent in Norway, but has attracted to it many a Nilsen, Nielsen, or Nilssen; the non-Norwegian Gilbertson has absorbed the many Gulbransens. Johnson has drawn from Johansen and Johnsen. Among the farm names it would be possible to multiply examples: Aarsvoll > Oswald, Berg > Burke, Bakken > Bacon, Bjerkeli > Berkeley, Brua > Brown, Botolvson > Butler, Borgetun > Barton, Dønnem > Dunham, Fjeld > Field, Hoel > Hall, Kjenshus > Campus, etc. Transformations into non-English names may also occur, as when Vanvik > Van Wick or Øygaren > O'Gordon.

(c) By neither sound nor meaning: a completely unrelated name is adopted. This is not particularly common, but examples are available: Ilstad > Stone, Rauberg > Edwards, Rye > O'Leary, etc.[45] It is reported from Mt. Morris, Wisconsin, that a Sogning by the name of Jens Hundere permitted it to be changed to James Jarvis.[46] The author of this report uses it as a text on which to preach a sermon about 'the lack of independent spirit which characterizes people in this settlement with regard to their names.' He praises one Nils Nilsen as one of the few who were not subject to this 'ridiculous' practice: when it was suggested that he should change it to Nels Nelson 'because the illustrious American tongue could not pronounce it,' he stuck to his guns and insisted 'that his name should be respected.'

This theme has been hammered at by all leading Norwegians in America; in spite of it, a great deal of change has gone on. The practical difficulties were crucial, so that some change had to be made; the sense of family name tradition was weak. Yet it is surprising how many names can still be recognized as Norwegian, at least by those who are familiar with their characteristics, even after the sea-change through which most of them have passed. Patronymics can usually only be described as Scandinavian, when they are not also English; but the farm names are characteristic of Norwegian practice as contrasted with that of other Scandinavian peoples.[47]

5. *Given Names.*

⌈The immigrants who were thrown into contact with Americans quickly discovered that Norwegian *given names* also were a source of linguistic embarrassment. A man's surname was primarily a problem of writing; but his given name was the handle by which most of his associates knew him. His fellow workers were quick to find American substitutes for monickers which they were unwilling or unable to imitate. As we have seen with the surnames, there were many sounds and sound combinations which were unfamiliar; but even when the sounds were simple enough, as in Hans or Lars, American names, such as Henry or Louis, were substituted, if only for the sake of greater familiarity. In a group where a knowledge of foreign languages is absent and the general level of education is low, a foreign name meets resistance merely because it is new and unfamiliar. The speakers may even feel uncertain concerning the sex of such a name, e.g. Norwegian Sigurd (m.) vs. Sigrid (f.). Such names hardly feel like names at all to the speaker who has never heard them before. Since most immigrants were not in a position to resist the pressures of their environment, at least not in the cities, they tended to accept the names given them by their associates. But again the double standard might prevail: an American name at work, a Norwegian name at home.⌉

⌈The one thing that an immigrant could count on having left of his given name was the initial.⌉ In the above-mentioned list of anglicized names collected by Olaf Huseby only 41 of 317 or 13 % have changed initials; at least half of these consist in an elimination of the unpopular letter k, e.g. by changing Karl to Charlie. In America the initial itself can function as a given name, especially when there are two of them; and immigrants have often found escape from their native names by resorting to initials. Thus Torbjørn Aslaksen Aasmoen would be quite passably anglicized under the name of T. A. Osmun. The retention of the initial when adopting a new name is so common that it deserves a name: we shall call it 'alliterative naming.' This may be defined as the substitution of an American name for a Norwegian one with the same initial letter (Æ and Ø count as a and o, while K counts as C). It is the normal procedure of anglicizing names. In many cases there is of course a greater similarity and even cognate relationship between the names, as when Harald changes to Harold or Johannes to John. But this is only incidental and applies to relatively few names, mostly those which derive from Biblical or common Germanic sources. But most people were not aware of the origin of their names and gladly exchanged the Old Norse Haakon for the Frankish Henry, or the Latin Lars (from Laurentius) for the French (from Germanic) Louis. Tom became the least common denominator of such names as Trond and Torsten, Torleif and Torvald.

The list of name changes compiled by Olaf Huseby will serve as an excellent illustration of the choices forced upon the immigrants. The numbers show how many instances of each occur in the list, when there is more than one:

Aage	Albert	Fridtjof	Fred
Aasmund	Osmon 2	Gjert	Julian
Anders	Andrew 17, Albert	Gregor	George
Arne	Orin 2	Gudbrand	Gilbert 10
Arnfinn	Arnold	Gudmund	Gilbert
Arve	Harvey	Gulleik	Goodlet
Asbjørn	Oscar	Gunnar	Gilbert 2, Gust,
Aslak	Isaac 2		Hiram
Atle	Adolph	Gunnbjørn	Gilbert
Augun	August	Gunnleik	George
Bernt	Ben 2	Gustav	Gust, Gus
Bjørn	Burrie, Burnt	Haakon	Henry 2, Harry 3
Botolf	Butler	Haldor	Hiram
Brynhild	Betzy	Hallstein	Halfstone
Brynjulv	Brown 2, Bronje	Halvor	Henry 2, Harry 2,
Egil	Edward		Howard, Hall,
Einar	Elmer, Eddie		Oliver
Eivind	Edward 2, Edwin,	Hans	Henry 2
	Elmer	Harald	Henry
Elias	Ellis	Herman	Hiram
Endre	Elmer	Ingeborg	Betzy
Enok	Ed	Ingebrigt	Elmer
Erik	Erick 3, Edward	Ivar	Ira, Ives, Edgar
Erling	Earl, Elmer	Jacob	Jack 3

Jens	James 7, John 4	Orm	Oliver
Johan	John	Ove	Owe
Johannes	John 9	Per	Pete 10
Jørgen	George 2	Rasmus	Roy, Ross
Karen	Carrie	Rønnaug	Rawley
Kari	Carrie	Signe	Sadie
Karl	Charlie 5	Sigurd	Simon 2, Sam 2
Kjetil	Charlie 2	Steinar	Stanley
Knut	Charlie, Newt 2,	Svein	Simon, Sam
	Knute	Tjøstolv	Chester
Kolbjørn	Cameron	Tobias	Tom
Lars	Lewis 5, Lawrence	Tor	Theodore 2, Tom
Leif	Lyman	Tore	Tom
Maren	Mary	Torfinn	Tom
Mikkel	Milo, Mike, McCall	Torgeir	Tom
Mons	Morris	Torkel	Tom
Narve	Norvey	Torleiv	Tom, Tole
Nils	Nick, Nels	Tormod	Tom
Oddvar	Oscar	Thorvald	Tom
Olav	Oliver 4, Oscar	Trond	Tom
Oline	Olive	Vetle	Victor

⌈The immigrant's children went through some of the same experiences in the public school as the adult did in the workshop.⌋ An immigrant girl tells about herself and her sisters in a community of the early 1850's: 'As soon as we entered the English school, we had to have new names. Our friend, whose name began with N, was called Nellie. The Americans found Norwegian names difficult to pronounce and made no effort to do so. They simply gave them names which began with the same letters or sounds as their baptismal names. The innocent newcomers thought it was splendid to get such strange names, and in this way a bad habit was established. Knut and Kittil were changed to Charley, Halvor to Harvey, Helge to Henry, Ingeborg to Belle, Berit and Birgit to Betsy, Tor, Trond, Torsten, and Tollev to Tom, Guri and Guro to Julia, Siri and Sigrid to Sarah, etc.'[48] ⌈Of course the name changes were not always even alliterative,⌋ as the change of Ingeborg to Belle shows. The writer Joran Birkeland reports that in her Montana girlhood her Norwegian name of Jørunn, especially in her mother's Norwegian pronunciation, seemed so offensive that she refused to be known as anything but Lulu.[49] The children were, of course, even more sensitive than adults to anything that smacked of ridicule, and when their fellows told them a name was funny because it was different, they too thought it funny and avoided it. Informants have repeatedly told the writer about given names which they themselves have changed; their Norwegian parents saddled them with names which they found it desirable to exchange. A Mt. Horeb, Wisconsin, family of four children were baptized Kari (1866), Synneva (1871), Lasse (1875), and Bernhard (1890); as adults they were always known as Carrie, Susie, Louis, and Ben.

Those parents who lived within a N-A community sought to maintain Norwegian customs in this as in other respects. One of the devices whereby tradition of family descent had been maintained in Norway was the custom of repeating names within the family. The original practice had been to repeat only the names of the dead, on the theory that their souls accompanied the names. But this had been generally formalized in the custom of repeating the names of the grandparents, so that the first son was named after the father's father, the first daughter after the mother's mother, etc. This fitted well with the patronymic custom, so that one farm might show an alternation of Halvor Bjørnsen and Bjørn Halvorsen man after man for generations. An examination of N-A church records shows that this custom was generally honored by the first generation of immigrants. But as the younger generations began to show increased resistance to Norwegian names, the custom had to be modified. Then it was that the practice of alliterative naming turned out to be handy. Instead of the repetition of the name we get a symbolic alliterative repetition. As one informant said: 'They were going to call me Rasmus after my grandfather; but the name was so weird and old-fashioned that they decided to trim it up and called me Robert instead.'[50]

Some sample genealogies from informants will illustrate the practice. The informant's name has been italicised.

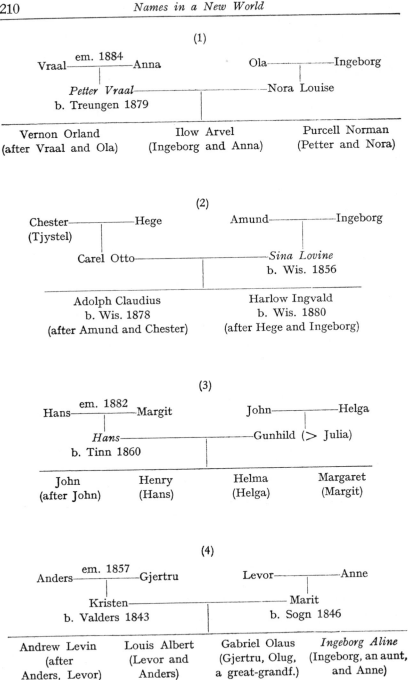

(1)

Vraal——em. 1884——Anna   Ola————————Ingeborg

Petter Vraal————————————————Nora Louise
b. Treungen 1879

Vernon Orland	Ilow Arvel	Purcell Norman
(after Vraal and Ola)	(Ingeborg and Anna)	(Petter and Nora)

(2)

Chester————————Hege   Amund————————Ingeborg
(Tjystel)

Carel Otto————————————————·Sina Lovine
b. Wis. 1856

Adolph Claudius	Harlow Ingvald
b. Wis. 1878	b. Wis. 1880
(after Amund and Chester)	(after Hege and Ingeborg)

(3)

Hans——em. 1882——Margit   John————————Helga

Hans————————————————Gunhild (> Julia)
b. Tinn 1860

John	Henry	Helma	Margaret
(after John)	(Hans)	(Helga)	(Margit)

(4)

Anders——em. 1857——Gjertru   Levor————————Anne

Kristen————————————————Marit
b. Valders 1843   b. Sogn 1846

Andrew Levin	Louis Albert	Gabriel Olaus	*Ingeborg Aline*
(after	(Levor and	(Gjertru, Olug,	(Ingeborg, an aunt,
Anders, Levor)	Anders)	a great-grandf.)	and Anne)

Not all the children have been included in these examples. Later children usually had to be content with being named after various aunts and uncles, or even great-grandparents, as in the fourth family.

The samples given in the previous paragraph will suggest [certain facts about the development of naming practices among the children of the immigrants. Not only do the names grow more American, but the American practice of giving two names instead of one gradually creeps in. Norwegian rural practice was to give only a single baptismal name; the further identification was taken care of by the patronymic. With the transition of patronymic to family surname or its disappearance in favor of a farm name, the second given name naturally comes in to fill the gap.] An examination of the Blue Mounds, Wisconsin, church records from 1868 to 1899 shows that this development came earlier for girls than for boys, reflecting either the greater social sensitivity of women or else the earlier disappearance of the -datter patronymic than the -son.

	One given name				Two given names			
	Boys		Girls		Boys		Girls	
		%		%		%		%
1868-70 ...	33	85	13	46	6	15	15	54
1871-75 ...	39	72	20	45	15	28	23	55
1876-80 ...	30	73	9	22.5	11	27	31	76.5
1881-85 ...	24	44	6	12	31	56	45	88
1886-90 ...	16	32	11	23	33	68	36	77
1891-95 ...	10	28	4	12	26	72	29	88
1896-99 ...	3	11	3	12.5	24	89	21	87.5

At the beginning of the period most boys and about half the girls were given only one name; by 1900 nearly all boys and girls were given two. The Koshkonong church records for 1856-61 show that the development there was similar, but somewhat ahead of the Blue Mounds congregation. Here the proportion for boys was 71.5% with one name, while for girls it was exactly 50 %.

The kind of names given in these congregations shows a similar development. In the early records we find almost entirely Norwegian names: Thorbjørn, Ingebret, Johannes, Kittel, Elling, Nils,

Hans, Jørgen, Mons, Anders, Christian, Erik, Helge, Gunder, Lars, Ole, Albert, Sivert, Alfred, Gunder, Sem, Thore, Iver, Hellik, Torkel, Helge, Reier. This list is drawn from the 1856 baptisms in Koshkonong congregation; while the names are not all Norwegian in origin, their general use in Norway has identified them with Norwegian life. In the same year the forms Henry (for Norwegian Henrik) and Andrew (for Norwegian Anders) appear; these were common cognate substitutions. In addition we find Augustinus and Nicolaus, taken from ecclesiastical tradition. Those who gave their boys two names called them Niels Gunsteen, Anders Christian, Ole Andreas, Niels Martin, Halvor Charles, Carl Martin, Johan Emil, Claus Benjamin, John Olaus, Harald Olaus, Johan Eliseus, Ole Johan, Peter Gustav, John Edvan, Jørgen Andreas, Henry Olav, Elias Augustinus. While most of these names are also in use in Norway, they suggest at once a somewhat more urbanized background, with less of the genuinely Norwegian folk culture. The girls were called Guro, Else, Tolline, Kirstine, Britta, Marte, Sigrid, Ingeborg, Oline, Gjertrud, Elevine, Kari, Augusta, Gjertine, Marit, Oline, Josephine, Christine, Maria, Lucy, and Synneva. Practically all of these were in use in Norway, and some of them are peculiar to the country. The girls who were given two names received the following tabs: Ingeborg Aline, Anna Gertine, Marta Helena, Anne Marie, Marta Marie, Kjerstine Berntine, Aslaug Eline, Berte Margrete, Kirstine Andrea, Ingeborg Dorthea, Inger Marie, Mari Aslaug, Caroline Margret, Elen Andrea, Eli Kirstine, Inga Monsine, Olive Amalia Elise, Margret Gurine, Marte Mathea, Marte Gurine, Marie Elise Fredrikka (pastor's daughter), Karen Oline. It is evident that the girls were getting names which were regarded as rather more elegant than the old-fashioned country names given the boys; the rash of names in -ine and -a would suggest this conclusion.

⌐A process of selection was clearly going on as the years rolled by, favoring the names that were common to Norwegian and American tradition, such as Albert, Carl, John, Martin, Andrew (N Anders), Clara, Anne Sophie, Marie etc. But it is not long before purely American names begin to bob up.⌐They come first to the girls: Betsy and Julia are early favorites, the former replacing Norwegian varieties of the same name, while the latter takes the place of almost any Norwegian name beginning in G, e. g. Gro,

Guri, Gunhild, etc. Before long extra fancy names are turning up, such as Kolora Peterine, Cordelia Onora, Bethilda Rowena. These are from the Blue Mounds records before 1880. Later examples of the same are: Veva Genet, Thoma Albina, Benoia Amanda, Bella Gelina, Stella Signora; all of Norwegian parents, be it noted. After 1880 the English names are predominant, both among girls and boys. In the year 1886 the girl's names given were: Cora Grace, Thea Berthine, Clara Oline, Inger Betsine, Alma Theoline, Berthe Maline, Elma Rosine, Milia Othilia, Betsey Serine. Some of the early boy's names with an American cast were Tom, Gilbert, Milo, Clarence, George, Otis, Elmer, Melvin, and Raymond. But Norwegian names like Oluf, Nils, Knut, and Halvor continued to appear now and then. Fancy boy's names were less common: Amel, Odeen, Almar. American heroes were commemorated occasionally: James Garfield, Benjamin Franklin. The names given to boys in 1886 will illustrate the mixture: Melvin, Olaus, Anton, Ole Selmer, Knudt Almar, Oliver Josef Bennet, John Almon, Johan Thorvald, Samuel Almer, Theodore Elmer, Albert Olaus, Stener Alfred, George Alfred.

The three stages here indicated in the study of church records from two southern Wisconsin congregations appear to be typical of the development in all rural settlements. The first settlers were country people who gave their children honest, homely country names drawn from the ancient Norse tradition as well as the early church. Under the influence of their pastors and the American environment they gradually dropped these in favor of somewhat more elegant names, after the fashion of urban Norwegians and Americans. In the last phase their feeling for Norwegian names weakened and they deliberately adopted purely American names, some of them rather on the gaudy side.

In later years an occasional reversal is found, whereby younger descendants deliberately seek out Norwegian names to mark their descent. Favorite names for this purpose have been Karen, Rolf, Ingrid, Kirsten, Thor, or Olaf. But a study of a representative group of young people of Norwegian background such as the students at St. Olaf College shows an infinitesimal number of Norwegian given names. At least 65 per cent of the student body in 1949-50 must have been of Norwegian descent, since 1047 of the

1630 students bore recognizably Norwegian surnames.[51] But of these only 92 or 8.8 % bore given names that were in any way distinctively Norwegian; of these 18 were family names used as second given names, while it seems probable that the 37 remaining second names were not actually used by the students. Only 45 or less than one in twenty had Norwegian first names; some of these were merely repetitions from the father's name, a custom not found in Norway. It is of some interest to note which Norwegian names were popular enough to be given more than once by the mothers of future St. Olaf students about 1930: Olaf and Solveig tie with 5 each, followed by Erling 3, Sonja 3, and 2 each for Thorleif, Lars, Sigurd, Roald, Ingolf, Knute, Iver, Oline, Gudrun, and Borghild. The name Norman is not Norwegian, but its popularity (13) is undoubtedly due to its reminiscent sound.

6. *Nicknames.*

Nicknames are an important part of the give-and-take of every-day living. The Norwegian dialects were rich in terms applied to people who were marked out in one way or another, either for some peculiarity in their appearance or some incident in their past. The color of these terms was closely tied to the life of the Norwegian language, so that very little of it could be passed on after the language change. Some of them were more or less humorous or abusive, like the word Vindgustæ 'the gust of wind' applied to an empty talker, or Tinta 'the medicine bottle' to a woman who prac-ticed healing with herbs (6P1; 5Q1). Other informants called the latter woman, who flourished in Koshkonong in the early days, simply Dokterkjerringa 'the old doctor woman' (4K1; 4L4; 5H4). A farmer who practiced bloodletting was popularly referred to as Doctor Knutsen in the Spring Prairie settlement (6P1). A Scotch woman who peddled candy in the Koshkonong area acquired the uncomplimentary by-name of Kænditufsa 'the candy wretch' (4L4).

Most of the nicknames, however, were used as identifiers to supp-lement the given name. If a man hailed from some particular *place*, different from that of the majority, this might be made a part of his name. In the Blue Mounds region a man whose real name was Thomas i Husi (i. e. Huset) was more generally known as Tåmmås Nordmann 'north-man', because he was from Sogn; in Valdres and Telemark people from Sogn were often called 'nordmenn' (5L1). In the Scandinavia area a Swede named Johan Peter Peterson was always known as Petter Svenske 'Swede'.[52] *Occupational* names were almost in the nature of nicknames, since they were not a part of the family surname tradition in Norway: Anders Snekker 'carpenter', Hølje Skomager 'shoemaker'.[53] A man near Mt. Horeb was called Smea-Per 'blacksmith Per'; while one Helge Mathiesen in the Winchester settlement was referred to as Hølje Tavane 'tavern' because he operated a tavern or hotel.[54] A man who was called Preste-Jon 'John the Pastor' was certainly not a pastor, however; but he probably carried on lay preaching.[55] A beggar woman who made the rounds of one settlement was known as Raffel-Kirsti 'waffle Kirsti'; perhaps she was especially fond of waffles (14C1). A man who had worked as a ful'er (one who shrinks wool) in Norway did not appreciate being cal'ed Tøvare-Knut in th's country, nor in having the term transferred to his family, since the word also means 'one who speaks nonsense' (4P1).

A man's *appearance* was naturally a welcome basis for nicknames, e.g. Svarte-Ivar 'Black Ivar' who was so-called on account of his black hair (15P3). Stor-Østen 'Big Østen' may have gotten his name because of his size, or merely because there were two by the same name in his family; the former is more probable, since he was known as Big-Ole among Americans.[56] Even more provocative of mirth was some *episode* which clung to a man's name. A man from Sogn named Per was observed admiring himself in the mirror because of a silk vest he had just bought. This led to the nickname Pene-Per 'pretty Per'; a stanza was made up about his sons:

> Pene-Per Ola og Pene-Per Las,
> Pene-Per Peder og Pene-Per Klas (5Q1).

In Kenyon, Minnesota, a dramatic episode in which one Halvor Johnson was called Halvor Fanden 'the devil' by an opponent led to his being known by this presumably unflattering term ever after.[57] Such terms as Bir-Erik and Whisky-Nils, reported by informants, speak their own language (5L3). No explanation is available of the nickname given to one immigrant: Halvor Eksæmpel 'example'; but it may be suspected that it was not because of any exemplary conduct (4L4).

7. *The Names of Animals.*

A naming tradition which was actively carried over from rural Norway to rural America was the giving of cow names. This contrasts interestingly with the practice relating to oxen and horses. As far as the writer's information goes, the latter were always given English names. The oxen were the first draft animals; they were bought from Americans and answered to names given by the latter. A common practice was to name them alliteratively, e.g. Buck and Bright, Dick and Dime.[58] Horse names were also English, almost without exception; informants have agreed that Norwegian names like Blakken 'the dun' and Brunen 'the bay' were never used. Typical names were Jack, Sally, Bill, Charley, Nip and Tuck, Frank, Prince, Dolly, Fanny, Kate, Belle, Lady, King, Nellie, Queen, etc. The first teams were bought from Americans, already trained; they were cared for by the men and used in operations which brought them into contact with Americans. But the cows were the special province of the women; they were often bought as calves and raised on the farm. Their care was a purely internal operation of the farm, and the women exercised their prerogative which they had carried over from Norway of giving them names, often in conference with the children.[59] These names show a great variety, going back as they did to an age-old tradition of cow naming. It is the opinion of one student of the subject that they were originally simply female names, but as of today the great majority are specifically descriptive of bovine qualities and cannot possibly be applied to women.[60]

The meanings of the traditional Norwegian cow names are often obscured by the fact that many of the elements have lost their original sense and have become standardized parts of cow names. As with human names, certain elements can be varied from name to name without thought of the original meaning. Thus the elements -*gås* 'goose', -*lin* 'white as linen', -*rei* 'the bearer', -*ros* 'rosy' are often used as the basis for new cow names without thought of the etymologies, which are themselves somewhat doubtful.[61] Barring these traditional elements, we may say that [the names identify the cows by reference to the following qualities: real or hypothetical ownership, coloring, beauty, horns, tail, size, disposition, and occasionally other characteristics.] The names were usually given while they were still calves, which accounts for the many endearing terms. Sometimes they combined more than one of the descriptive qualities as in Emros 'a rosy cow belonging to or named after Emma' (4H1). Then there are some which are simply girls' names, like the horse names given above; we cannot always tell whether these were intended to suggest ownership or merely were given for someone in the family. The following list includes most of the names collected from AmN informants; the explanations given are those of the informants themselves: (1) *Real or hypothetical ownership:* Dolin (from Dora), Betten (from Bertha), Karos (from Karl), Teoros (from Teodor), Liaros (from people named Li), Annros (from Anna); girls' names: Æli, Gjertrud, Sigrid, Astrid, Åse-Berit (after an old woman known to the family), Dafne, Runnur; Smebykua 'bought from Smeby', Moenkyri 'bought from Moens', Danska 'bought from a Dane', etc. (2) *Coloring,* the favorite means of identifying them: Flekkeros 'spotty', Jærteros 'with a heart-shaped rosy spot', Blåros 'with blue spots', Brunros 'red with a white stripe down the back', Blomros 'white with small spots all over', Brandros 'brindled', Kvitsi 'white-sides', Rødlin 'red and white', Salgås 'with a white saddle on the back', Lykkebot 'lucky patch', Skauta 'with a white head', Stjerna 'star', Plomma 'plum-red', Spreglo 'red and white patches', Bliss 'with white patch on forehead', Gulldropla 'with gold specks', Duk 'white as table cloth'. (3) *Beauty:* Fagerål 'with a pretty stripe down the back', Venegull 'pretty gold', Skjønnbot 'with a pretty patch', Finros 'fine, rosy', Fagerros 'beautiful, rosy', Deili 'lovely', Venaste 'most beautiful', Fagerlin 'lovely, white'. (4) *Horns:* Brykoll 'hornless cow belonging to Bry family', Svartekoll 'black hornless', Honnbrote 'broken-horn', Hønnkjælken 'horns protruding to the side', Køllekua 'hornless cow'. (5) *Tail:* Stubberova, Stubberompa, Stuttrompa 'short tail'. (6) *Size:* Litago 'little, good', Storigo 'big, good', Langfram 'long in front', Lita 'little'. (7) *Disposition:* Bliros

'kind, rosy', Litago 'little, good', Lykkros 'lucky, rosy', Blirei 'kind',
Sømmeli 'proper', Sinto 'the angry cow'. (8) *Miscellaneous:* Mollik
'like its mother', Droppelny 'white with black spots who had calved
a second time', Stjerneprud 'star-proud' (with star on head),
Roseneng 'meadow of roses', Julgås 'born at Christmas time', Vår-
fru 'born in spring', Jævrei 'of excellent quality', Gullterna 'the
golden maid', Ringei 'ringed'?, Rosebadn 'rosy child', Spækk 'fat',
Luse-Kari 'lousy Kari', Dritræva 'defecatory'.

As these examples have shown, most of the names are compounds. Certain elements are fairly constant in their reapparance
as second elements; those which appear in several names are:-*bot*
'patch', *-fru* 'lady', *-gås* 'goose', *-koll* 'hornless', *-ku* 'cow', *-lin*
'linen', *-rei* 'bearer'?, *-ros* 'rosy', *-rova* 'tail', *-si* 'side'. The most
popular of these is *-ros;* it is used in 32 different names, some of
them given by several different informants. Next comes *-lin* with
12, *-gås* and *-si* with 8 each. But the most popular single name is
Litago, given by 12 informants, followed by Lukkros 9 and Dagros
8. Altogether the material collected contains 104 compound names
and 47 simplexes, a small but representative sampling of the names
actually used. Most of the important types found in Norway are
represented; but the material does not permit a further analysis
by districts, beyond noting that the types in *-gås* are limited to
speakers from Northern and Eastern Norway, those in *-rei* to Telemark, Litago to Eastern Norway, Telemark, and Valdres, Storigo
to Valdres, Stjerna to the East and North. But these may be purely
accidental distributions.

Not all of the names used were Norwegian. Informants have
also given a liberal sprinkling of American names, though one gets
the impression that these were late and relatively few. Most of
them were girls' names, of the diminutive or caressing type suggested by such examples as Jessie, Lily Belle, Daisy, Fern, Lulu, Lou,
Fanny, Susie etc. In a small number of cases they were descriptive
like the Norwegian names, but seldom compound: Boots, Dots,
Whitey, Reindeer, Milrose, Brindle, Star, One-eye, Snowball,
Blackie, Spotty. The American names seem to represent the decline
of the naming tradition, for all informants are agreed that names
of any kind are rare in the herds of today. When asked about the
disappearance of Norwegian names, they have given various dates,

clustering around the period from 1900 to 1910, though many have no doubt continued the practice much later. Nearly all informants who were born before 1900 and some who were born after that date were able to give the cow names which had been used on their farms.

A prime factor in the disappearance of Norwegian names, aside from the general Americanization, was the growth of industrial dairying and the accompanying change in barn management. The growth of cheese and butter factories from 1880 onward led to the taking over of farm chores by the men and to a standardization of breeds which wiped out the distinctions in appearance on which many of the old names had been based.[62] The cow was no longer in the immediate care of the women and not in the same sense a member of the family; she was just as a number in the herd. Some typical comments by informants are: 'When I was a boy we had 65 head and all had names; now we have 20 and some don't have any' (24A1); 'all my cows have names, but only on paper — they are Dutch names like Peterje' (4Q2); 'we tend to drop the names now, because the cows are so much alike, all called by number' (5L3); 'before the [cheese] factories came, the women took care of the cows; but after that people got so very busy' (5H3); 'we gave the cows names because the children enjoyed it, but we quit when they grew up' (5C1).

8. *The Farm and its Parts.*

Once the settlers had oriented themselves on the new farms, they would naturally feel a need of applying names to its various *parts*. We have already seen how rich the naming could be on a Norwegian farm. But here the contrast between farming conditions in Norway and America becomes especially striking. Where the Norwegian farm was a complex and far-flung entity, running possibly from seashore to mountain-top, with innumerable hillocks and groves, bits of field and pasture, the American farm was a relatively simple and compact enterprise. Names were applied only as they were needed, and there was no lengthy tradition to preserve the memories of past needs. Farms consisted of little more than geometrically divided fields surrounding a small clump of farm buildings; there might be a single grove, or some brushwood, a marsh or bluff or creek, but rarely more than one. For identification the simple definite article was sufficient: grova 'the grove', brusken 'the brush', slua 'the slough', krikken 'the creek'.

The fields did need distinguishing, however, and the means used for this purpose included function, location, characteristic traits, and historical circumstances. Most commonly the *function* described was the crop raised in the field:

havrefila 'the oat field'	potetfila 'the potato patch'
kveitefila 'the wheat field'	tobakkfila 'the tobacco field'
kønnfila 'the corn field'	grønfila 'the grain field'

A field used for pasturage was referred to as habnefil 'grazing field'. Many informants reported no other way of identifying fields. Location was another favorite method, the simplest type being purely directional: norfila 'the north field', søfila 'the south field' etc. But most commonly the word *field* would be used with a descriptive phrase such as the following:

bak reilrådtrækken 'behind the RR track'	oppå heia 'up on the hill'
bortover mot Klomstaen 'over toward the Klomsta farm'	norme krikkjen 'north by the creek'
bortve gamle krimeri 'over by the old creamery'	på øvre batomen 'on the upper bottom(s)'
utpå tangen 'on the point'	på Hokkelsberblåffå 'on Huckleberry bluff'
vestom blåffa 'west of the bluff'	oppi Havredalen 'up in Oats Valley'

Compounds could also be used in this way, but less commonly:

skogfila 'the field in the woods'	ræilrodfili 'the field by the RR'
mittfila 'the middle field'	batomfila 'the bottom field'
skulusfila 'the schoolhouse field'	batemlæinne 'the bottom land'

A farmer with fields in adjacent townships referred to them as Mandovifili and Neipelsfili, from the names of the townships Mondovi and Naples.

The most obvious *characteristic traits* chosen for identification were those of size and shape:

langafili 'the long field' storfila 'the big field'
vetlafili 'the little field' ækern 'the acre'

Various traits of the landscape have been selected in the following names, some of which may not be field names, though they have been given as such:

vassdalen 'the water valley' vasshola 'the water hole'
stæistykkji 'the stone patch' sluestykkji 'the slough patch'
hæiestykkji 'the hill patch' horisonten 'the horizon'
hukkibakk 'bend-your-back' (a steep field)

The *historical circumstance* which was most often selected was that of original purchase or cultivation:

Foksrøverhola (bought from Fox River Valley Land Co.)

Grovefilæ, Groveførtien (bought from Andres Grove)

Våstykkji (grubbed by a man named Vå, who had a grubbing machine)

Danskefilæ 'the Danish field' (bought from a Dane)

Knutførtien (bought from a man named Knut)

Skrefilæ (bought from Knut Skred)

Pålfili (from Paul Syftestad)

Hålefilæ (bought from Samuel Håle)

Kalsdalen (from a man named Kal)

Norbefili (owned by family named Norbe)

Kampefili (owned by Kampen)

Skuleførtien (the school forty, originally set aside for schools, then sold)

Banklanne (once owned by the bank)

The following names refer to the breaking of the soil in pioneer days:

Nybrekken 'the new breaking' Likkjbrækken 'the little breaking'
Brekkinga (the last piece of land that was plowed) Storbrækken 'the large breaking'

Various circumstances are suggested in the following names:

Gammelhusbakken 'old house hill' (first houses built on it)

Ullteigbakken 'Ullteig hill' (possibly people by this name had lived there)

Annastykkjy 'Anna's patch'

Slåfila (people named Slå used to live there)

Lågåton (a pasture, inf. thinks some one so named used to live there)

Gråbenpastere 'the wolf pasture' (wolves had been seen there?)

Kvinneru (reason not known by inf. but may be some one who had lived there)

Seuablåffe 'the sheep bluff' (sheep had been pastured there?)

From a farm in Koshkonong it was reported that three springs were distinguished by the names of their finders:

Borjildasprinjen 'Borghild's spring'

Botolsprinjen 'Botolf's spring'

Brumbårsprinjen 'Brumborg's spring' (4P1).

The characteristic feature of the names used on the farms was that they were primarily used by the family and invented for its convenience. The removal of the family, or even the change of generations, with a gradual transition to English, would naturally lead to radical changes in this nomenclature.

9. *Neighborhood.*

The same would often be true of the names of larger features of the landscape and of social groupings, which we shall here call *neighborhood* names. The farms themselves were neighborhood features, and their names were means of identifying the activities of the neighborhood. In the early settlements there is a good deal of evidence to show that the farms were spoken of very much as farms were mentioned in Norway. Names which were borne by the first owners clung to the farms in popular speech much longer

than did the owners. When J. N. Luraas bought land in Dane
County in the earliest days, it is reported that he called his farm
Luraas after the ancestral farm in Telemark.[63] Informant O. B.
Stephens used the Norwegian manner of speaking whenever he
mentioned the old farms of Koshkonong: de va ein mura ovn på
Kjerre 'there was a brick fireplace at Kjerre' (4L4).[64] We have already seen how this usage sometimes led to the acquisition of a new
surname by succeeding owners of a farm. It seems slightly more
Americanized when some informants adopt a compound expression
and speak of Rekvefarmen 'the Reque farm' (4P1). Another common
usage is the term 'place', which often crept into AmN speech, as
in heimeplassen 'the home place'.

[Not only the farms, but also the natural features of the neighborhood had Norwegian names during the purely Norwegian phase
of these communities. Many names were of course taken over from
the established American practice, but there was still abundant
room for Norwegian neighborhood names. A bluff in the Perry
area was called Furehotten 'the pine knoll'; one in the Blair area
was known as Runnhæuven 'the round hill'; while one near Mondovi
was called Seksækerheuen 'the six acre hill'. A curious development is the one reported from Minnesota, where a settler named a
hill Svarthammar after a similar eminence in Valdres; this was
translated into English as Blackhammer, which is now the regular
form among Norwegians as well as Americans. According to Holand,
a Norwegian humorous appellation Blaasenberg 'windy cliff' is
the basis of the name Blossomburg in Door County.[65] In Koshkonong a hill was known as Blissehæugen from an American named
Chauncey Bliss on whose farm it lay (4L4). A sawmill near Iola
owned by an American named John Weeks was regularly known
as Vikamylla.[66] Schoolhouses were named according to the nearest
farm family, e.g. Tyvannskulhuse 'the Tyvann school house' in
Perry (5G1).

The most interesting development of nomenclature is that
which characterizes the communities in the hilly areas of southern
and western Wisconsin. Nowhere else does one get so strong a
sense of community feeling expressed in the names; the valleys
and ridges seem to have invited names with a Norwegian sound.
In the Perry-Daleyville area of SW Dane County, the socalled

Blue Mounds Settlement, informants have pointed out Støyle-dalen, Ellingdalen, and Robbdalen, the last named after an Irish-man whose name was Rob (5L3). Other names are Tveitandalen ('de va så mykjy Tveitanar'), Oladalen, Jentedalen, Nilsedalen, Bitsedalen (from Bates), and Valdersdalen.[67] The last name was coined in conscious opposition to the name Vestmannsbatomen 'the Westman Bottom', a name applied by the Valdres people to the Telemarkings (5L1). The term 'bottom' for the flat land in a valley was much used in such names, e.g. Lunsbatomen and Saga-batomen from the same area, the latter being due to the existence of a sawmill (5Q1). For the most part these names were based on the surnames of some prominent family in the region.

More examples can be found by consulting Cassidy's study of the Dane County place names.[68]

Similar conditions obtain in the other hilly areas, such as Coon Valley and Blair. A map showing the Norwegian names of Coon Valley may be found in Holand's book.[69] These have been con-firmed and expanded by local informants; most of the side valleys to the main watercourse are named for some early settling family, e.g. Ullteigdalen (11C4). Among the exceptions are Springdalen 'spring valley', Bohimidalen 'Bohemian valley', and Malassidalen 'molasses valley', the latter because molasses was produced there. The upper part of the valley is regularly known as Skogdalen 'forest valley' among the Norwegian speakers, and the name is even said to appear as the heading of a co'umn in the Westby papers, though the regular American word is Timber Coulee. In Western Wisconsin the usual American and occasional Norwegian word is the French *coulee*, but the regular Norwegian word is *dal;* in southern Wisconsin the American word is *valley*, which occasio-nally appears in Norwegian also. The names that do not appear on Holand's map are the names of the ridges, for which the Norwegian word *rygg* is used. The main ridges to the north and south are called Norryggen and Søryggen; some of the others are Lauvaasryggen, Jorderyggen, Tyskeryggen 'German ridge' (also known as Von Ruden-ryggen, from a German family many of whose members were quite thoroughly Norwegianized) (11C1-4). A similar name from the Sogn settlement farther south in Town of Utica shows that they also used the form: Helgesenryggen (12Q1). South of Spring Grove,

Minnesota, runs Vaterloryggen, a Norwegianized form of Waterloo Ridge.

In the Blair area a similarly contoured landscape led to a multiplicity of names for each valley. Among those named by informants are: Skutledalen, Vossedalen, Trompdalen, Salvedalen, Teppendalen, Frænskrikk (i.e. French Creek), and Leikslua (i. e. Lake's Slough, known in English as Lake's Coulee).[70] These names figure regularly in the local columns of the Blair newspaper, somewhat disguised as 'coulees'. A section near Bristol in Dane County was called Ronane 'the underbrush' by some of the early settlers from Sogn.[71] Some of the Norwegian names were more or less humorous and temporary, such as Vasslausprærien 'waterless prairie', a name reported for Highland Prairie in Fillmore County, Minnesota, or Griserumpen 'pig's tail', a long, winding ridge in the same neighborhood.[72] Near Harmony, Minnesota, a stretch of road was known as Hurrakroken 'hurrah corner' because drunken drivers returning from town made the road unsafe with their joyous antics.[73]

The names which referred to specific valleys and ridges tended to define a loosely organized neighborhood, less extensive than the 'settlement' as a whole. A word sometimes applied to such a neighborhood was the Norwegian word *bygd*, a rural community of somewhat greater extent over there. One speaker referred to inviting heile bygda 'the whole neighborhood' for a wedding (5H2). Another spoke of hær burti bygdi burtme kyrkja 'over here in the neighborhood by the church.' (4L4). A third said that her family va dai ainaste i haile bygdæ 'were the only ones in the whole neighborhood' who said 'papa' to their father instead of 'far' (4P1). Another, and more correctly Norwegian term is *grend* 'neighborhood', used by an informant in Coon Prairie who spoke of Gategreinna and Sjærvegreinna for the neighborhoods of two well-known families, Gaten and Skjerve (10C1). The writer Thor Helgeson uses both terms together in speaking of Vogslandgrænden, eller den bygden, som har faat navnet Tørtop 'the Vogsland neighborhood, or the community called Tørtop'.[74]

Even some of the small urban communities that grew up among the Wisconsin settlers bore informally Norwegian names among the immigrants: McFarland was known as bortpå dipoen 'over at the depot', Mt. Horeb was called stånji 'the pole' from a flagpole which preceded the town, Waupaca was called falle 'the falls', Norway Grove was known simply as grovi 'the grove', while Kosh- konong was made more familiar by being called Kaskeland instead of Kaskenang, the usual Norwegian pronunciation; the substitution of -*land* associated it with Norwegian names containing this element.[75]

10. *Settlements and churches.*

⌐The settlement names proper, which were applied to the larger groupings of Norwegian settlers, have in general tended to become identical with the names of the Lutheran congregations. Many of these were given at first as names of larger areas or features of landscape, accepted from American sources by the immigrants, and then used as names of congregations.⌐This is the case of the name Koshkonong, which was at first the name of a lake and of a creek flowing into it; the Norwegians who settled along the creek accepted it as the name of their congregation, and today its only current signification is that which associates it with these congregations. An area such as Liberty Prairie, which was separated at an early period by the founding of the Liberty Prairie church, came to be regarded as distinct from Koshkonong, although the Norwegian settlement area is continuous. The name Muskego, which became well-known as an early focal point in Norwegian settlement, was at first the name of a lake near which the first immigrants settled. But when the land proved to be unhealthy and they moved, the name Muskego accompanied them to the new place further south. The area known as Rock Prairie in southern Wisconsin included a Norwegian settlement; but within ten years of its settlement, the Norwegian congregation deliberately tried to eliminate this designation in favor of the church name of Luther Valley. A notice to this effect was inserted in the paper *Nordlyset*, but without too much result.[76]

An analysis of the names given to the 6-7000 congregations foun- ded since 1843 by Norwegian Lutherans in America, as these are listed in Dr. O. M. Norlie's compilation, shows that a very large number of Norwegian place names have been perpetuated in Ameri- can congregations. Even so they are few compared with the total number; the overwhelming mass of such names are simply the local place names where the churches have been located, as in the case of Koshkonong above. Another large group consists of those which bear religious designations, such as Trinity, Bethel, Nazareth, St. John, and the like. Closely related to these are the considerable number which bear names from Norwegian (or other Scandinavian) religious personalities, especially St. Olaf and the religious reformer Hans Nilsen Hauge; with these may be mentioned Pontoppidan, author of the commonly used explanation of the Catechism, and St. Ansgar, the apostle of the Danes.

A proportion which may be estimated at possibly 10 per cent bear names that can be traced directly back to Norwegian localities. The earliest were Gjerpen and Valders in Manitowoc County, Wisconsin, founded in 1850 by emigrants from these regions. Other early examples are Holden (Waushara Co., Wis., 1853), Stavanger (Fayette Co., Iowa, 1854), Elstad (Fillmore Co., Minnesota, 1854), Holden (Goodhue Co., Minnesota, 1856), Arendahl (Fillmore Co., Minnesota, 1857), and Christiania (Dakota Co., Minnesota, 1857). While we may assume that some of these names were due to a preponderance of settlers from the region named, this does not necessarily follow. Oral tradition in Waushara Co. reports that the name Holden was proposed by a man from this Telemark community, an early settler, and accepted even though there were only two other families from this community.[77] The explanation was that most speakers did not recognize the community name in its official spelling, but were reminded of their own community name of Holt, and therefore voted for it under false pretenses. A number of the city names used e. g. Christiania 1857, Bergen 1860, were probably not the homes of the immigrants, but possibly their ports of embarkation. Whatever the occasion, most Norwegian parishes have probably received a namesake at some time or other in AmN parishes. In addition a number of farm names which were not parish names in Norway appear to have been applied, such as the Elstad listed above; or Fjeldberg (Story Co., Iowa, 1856), Hoel (Clayton Co., Iowa, 1869), Bagstevold (Ottertail Co., Minnesota, 1875). The latter are probably the names of families on whose land the churches were located.

[A very small group of congregational names consists of those which do not refer to any particular Norwegian community, but suggest the nationality in a general way. The two congregations organized at Muskego in 1843 as the first in America were of this kind: North Cape and Norway. In 1870 came Nora in Pope County, Minnesota, followed by Norunga (Douglas County, Minnesota, 1871), Tordenskjold (after a famous Norwegian naval hero; Ottertail Co., Minn., 1871), Norman (Cass Co., N.D., 1872), etc. Even such pagan symbols as Odin (Martin Co., Minn., 1873), Viking (Richland Co., N.D., 1907), and Valhalla (Alberta, 1916), were not overlooked!

11. *Official Place Names.*

The number of official names on American maps which reflect Norwegian influence is much smaller than the proportionate number of settlers in the states affected. No one could possibly assess the extent and importance of the Norwegian settlers from the place names they have left behind of a civil and administrative nature, as has been done for the Scandinavian invaders of England in the viking period. This has been the subject of frequent comment among patriotic Norwegians, who have resented the willingness of their early settlers to accept the American names given their communities.[78] One need only rehearse the names of the towns and counties especially associated with Norwegian settlement to realize the truth of this contention: they consist of Indian names like Muskego, Koshkonong, and Decorah, French names like La Crosse and Eau Claire, English names like Stoughton, Coon Valley, and Spring Grove. The Norwegians were of course linguistically handicapped, being often met by the inability and unwillingness of Americans to tolerate their unfamiliar sound combinations. Seldom were they ready to take over political power on their first arrival, since more pressing problems of survival came first, and their participation in political life had to await their linguistic competence. Besides, many of the official names of legal subdivisions were fixed on the map by English-speaking surveyors, land-speculators, and legislators, even before the arrival of the first settlers. The charge made by Norwegian-American critics that the early settlers were reprehensibly lax in not insisting on Norwegian names is probably exaggerated, in view of the fact that it has been shown statistically that in Minnesota there are about twice as many place names of Norwegian origin as of Swedish, in spite of the greater number of the latter. But it is true that in comparison with the Icelanders of North Dakota and Manitoba the Norwegians make a poor showing.[79]

Nevertheless there is a scattering of Norwegian names on the American map. Unfortunately no complete list has ever been made; Swanson's compilation is only for Minnesota, and not entirely complete even for that state.[80] The Wisconsin names of post offices and townships of which the writer is aware are as follows: (1) Post offices: Haugen, Hollandale, Holmen, Klevenville, Larsen, Nelson, Nelsonville, Northland, Rosholt, Scandinavia, Starks (?), Strum, Valders, Westby; (2) Townships: Norway (Racine Co.), Christiana (Dane Co.), Scandinavia (Waupaca Co.), Christiana (Vernon Co.), Bergen (Vernon Co.), Nelson (Buffalo Co.), Drammen (Eau Claire Co.), Dovre (Barron Co.), Vinland (Winnebago Co.)[81] The list could undoubtedly be extended by an examination of detailed maps showing lake names and minor crossroads. In Dane County alone one could mention Daleyville, Klevenville, Little Norway, Nora, and Norway Grove.[82] As it stands, it compares favorably with the number of German names in Wisconsin, considering the much greater size of the German population. In the more recently settled states of the Dakotas we find proportionately a few more post office names. South Dakota: Baltic (see below), Ellingson, Herreid, Hetland, Lake Norden, Moenville, Rosholt, Sorum, Veblen; and one county name: Haakon. North Dakota: Arnegard, Berg, Bergen, Breien, Burnstad, Dahlen, Egeland, Hamar, Heimdal, Hofflund, Kongsberg, Larson, Lundsvalley, Nanson, Nelson, Skaar, Temvik, Vang, Voss, Wolseth; and possibly the two counties of Benson and Nelson. In Minnesota Norman County was given its name by a Norwegian immigrant, according to tradition; the name suggests *nordmann*, the Norwegian word for a Norwegian.[83]

The characteristic features of this name-giving are, in the first place, that it is extremely sporadic, and clearly not the result of any systematic plan on the part of the Norwegian group as a whole. This is explained by the obvious fact that at the time when the names were fixed there was no cohesion whatever among the Norwegian settlements, and no such thing as a Norwegian group; there were only Norwegian settlers. The majority of the post office names, and the same is true of the lake names listed from Minnesota in Swanson's study, are the names of individuals of Norwegian ancestry who happened to live at or near the places so named and whose names have thus been perpetuated for local reasons only. This is true, for instance, of Westby, which was named after a merchant who established the first store on the site that later became a town.[84] The town of Peterson in Fillmore County, M nnesota, was founded by one Peter Peterson.[85] Of more 'national' significance was the deliberate application of placenames from Norway. This generally took the form of using the name of a community from which many of the local residents hailed. A village named Bratsberg was established in Fillmore County, Minnesota; the name was suggested by the owner of the property because most of the Norwegians came from this district, more generally known under the name of Telemark.[86] Among the names listed above only a few come under this head: Valders, Dovre, Voss are the only certain ones. It will be noticed that a certain number of Norwegian cities are found on the list; but in view of the predominently rural origin of the immigrants, it is not likely that these were given for the same reason. In general they probably represent in a higher degree the desire to commemorate the nationality in general. This was certainly the case when the name Christiana was given to a township in Dane County by its first settler about 1842. According to the historian Svein Nilsson, 'he wished to commemorate Norway's capital; but as he was not particularly skilled in spelling, he unfortunately came to write Christiana instead of Christiania....'[87]

This error is typical of the uncertainty of the Norwegians in their relation to the American world and its official forms. They would gladly have asserted themselves, but often did not know how best to do it. Stories which are related among them elaborate this point, e.g. the tale of Baltic, S.D. The original post office was named St. Olaf, but this was abandoned for religious reasons in favor of Sverdrup; when the railroad came in the late 60's, the station agent was asked to settle the dispute on the condition that he would find something Norwegian. His ideas of geography were apparently vague enough to find Baltic appropriate; so Baltic it became. Shortly after this it was decided that the district name Meraker should be perpetuated; but it was felt to be too difficult for Americans, and was translated into Morefield.[88] A similar tragicomedy took place when the Town of Scandinavia in Waupaca County, Wisconsin, was named, according to the story of an early settler.[89] The town was organized entirely by Norwegian settlers, who felt it necessary, however, to call in a Swedish lawyer who happened to live nearby to help them with the legal details. At the first town meeting in 1854 the oldest resident, Hans Jacob Eliasson Oksom from Eidanger, proposed that it should be called Oksom after his home in Norway. This was rejected, and then another from Eidanger proposed it should be called after their home community, abbreviated to Danger in their folk speech. The Swedish lawyer wrote it down and looked hard at it: 'No, devil take me if you can use that name! In English Town of Danger would be the dangerous town.' In the end they were able to agree only on the highly neutral term Scandinavia, out of consideration for a few Danish families which had moved into the town.

Successful action in fixing Norwegian names to the map required the talents and leadership of individuals who could overcome the many conflicting ideas of the group, and who regarded the issue as important. In Ottertail County, Minnesota, a number of names such as St. Olaf, Tordenskjold, Sverdrup, Nidaros and the like testify to the initiative of one man, Ole Jørgens.[90] Yet even he is said to have met criticism and opposition in his efforts. Such names as Nora, Normanna, or Normania all testify to a consciously nationalistic attempt to commemorate the group. These are terms reminiscent of the effusive national poetry of the romantic period. This is not necessarily true of names including the word Norway or Norwegian; these may in some instances have been applied by American neighbors, and they occur in places where no Norwegians have settled, e.g. in South Carolina. These are what Swanson called 'Yankee labels'. Norway Grove in Dane County may be such a name, though it came to be accepted by the Norwegians as the name of their congregation. In Benton County, Minnesota, however, the village of Norway got its name because a local citizen gave the railroad company five acres on condition that the station should be called Norway.[91]

[It is thus apparent that the prevailing official nomenclature in the immigrant communities as elsewhere in the country is that which was given by the English-speaking element, or accepted by it from the preceding Indian, French, or Spanish inhabitants. Those who came later have only been able to inject an occasional name into this framework, enough to remind the connoisseur of their presence, but not enough to alter the pattern in any conspicuous way. No talk about an 'American Danelaw' should be allowed to obscure this main fact. The vikings of our day did not come as rulers but as citizens. They lived an in-group life of their own as long as they could, but in their outward behavior they conformed to all that America could possibly have expected of them.]

Chapter 10.

THE STRUGGLE OVER NORWEGIAN

> Now the question no longer is: how shall **we**
> learn English so that we may take part in the social
> life of America and partake of her benefits; the big
> question is: how can we preserve the language of
> our ancestors here, in a strange environment, and
> pass on to our descendants the treasures which **it**
> contains?
>
> *Thrond Bothne, Professor*
> *at Luther College (1898)*[1]

Throughout the history of the AmN community, the relation
of English and Norwegian involved an element of controversy.
Known as *Sprogspørsmaalet*, or the Language Question, this controversy raged more or less openly within family, neighborhood,
and social institutions wherever N immigrants settled in sufficient
numbers to create a self-contained group. We cannot hope to do
more than sketch the profile of this struggle in the confines of this
and the following chapter. Some of the more spectacular episodes
will be told, but with the understanding that these are only the
public expression of a private tension that had its root in the steady
pressure exerted on the immigrant by the dominant American
environment. The public discussion was protracted and often bitter,
with vigorous agitators on both sides; but the basic trend was
probably not greatly affected by it. The heart of the matter was
the situation within the family; this was the primary battleground.
But the individual family was supported in its linguistic usage by
other families, who together constituted a neighborhood. Social
institutions grew up which organized the teaching and indoctri-
nation of the language, above all the Church. We shall consider the

role of each of these social groupings in the language struggle — home, neighborhood, and institutions — and then sketch some of the major developments in the campaign which the immigrant fought so gallantly but vainly for the sake of maintaining the language of his ancestors.

1. *The Family and the Neighborhood.*

⌈Within the family the maintenance of a foreign language depends on the desire of the parents to carry it on, the authority of the parents over their children, and the degree of pressure from outside. Parents emigrating from Norway as adults usually had little desire to adopt English as the family language. All the lore that it is natural for parents to transmit to their children had come to them in N and was available to them only in that language. The nursery rhymes, the proverbs, the anecdotes, the family sayings, the prayers, the songs: all of these were woven into the very process of language learning in childhood. Even if the adult could learn them in a new language, they would have no flavor; and who was available in any case to teach them to him? Only in N could the immigrant father and mother function as such, and they vigorously resisted any attempt to lessen their socio-cultural role. By living in a N-speaking community they multiplied their chance of being able to carry it out, since their children were not then under any strong social pressure to use English. Wherever contact with English-speaking children was active, as in an urban community, the children brought with them home an active desire to speak English. Only by the establishment of iron-clad rules by which English was banned from the home could the parents resist this invasion. This counter-pressure by the parents had to be stronger than the social pressure of the environment toward English. If the social pattern in the community was favorable to English, the parents were placed in a difficult position. It now became a question of parental authority, with the children often sullen and rebellious and the parents torn between a determination to impose their own linguistic pattern and a desire to see their children content. American social patterns in general favored a weakening of parental authority, and so the rebellion against their linguistic pattern went hand in hand with a freeing of the children from their other social modes of behavior.⌋

⌈Wherever the parents were successful in asserting their authority over the children, some degree of bilingual competence followed. In country communities the children learned to understand, speak, and eventually read and write the language. Most of them became thoroughly bilingual, since the American public school prevented them from remaining N monolinguals. But within the family N was the sole means of communication, and the second, or America-born generation, acquired the same set of childhood memories and everyday lore that their parents had brought along from Norway. Many of this generation have felt a loyalty to the Norwegian tradition which was stronger than that of many first-generation immigrants. But whenever the point was reached that the community as such grew sufficiently Americanized so that the social pressure from the environment set up a strong internal resistance to the learning of the language by the children, we see that both city and country reacted very much alike. Instead of a full competence, the children acquired only a partial competence. Writing fell away first, then reading. The effort required to impose these skills became too great for the parents. Similarly, the children succeeded in limiting the sphere within which Norwegian was spoken. They spoke it only to one or a few older members of the family, usually a grandparent, while they spoke English to all others. If their position was exceptionally strong, they succeeded in evading the speaking entirely, even to their parents. This bilingual situation was highly typical, with parents speaking N and children answering in E. Eventually the parents might also succumb to the pressure exerted by this uncomfortable situation and go over to E themselves.⌉

The development here sketched is so typical that one encounters it again and again in discussing these matters with immigrant children. Both children and parents seem almost like pawns in a game which they do not themselves understand. The parents grumble because their children will not obey them and accuse the younger generation of turning their backs on the ideals of the past. The children complain at being made to learn a language which represents a 'foreign' outlook to them and is in no way associated with the glory of the goals held out to them by their surroundings.

Curiously enough, when they grow up and look back at their childhood years with adult eyes, they often blame their parents for not having taught them the language. By this time they have forgotten the bitter struggle they themselves put up against that teaching. They have come to realize some of the values that were lost in the shift, but only after it is too late.

A single family can, of course, carry on a linguistic tradition if its cohesion is sufficiently strong. Cultured families can be found where bilingualism is deliberately cultivated for the sake of maintaining contacts with the homeland. But most families cannot afford to carry on a bilingual tradition unless they are supported by the presence of other such families within the same neighborhood. Our discussion of the intra-family situation has shown that much depends on the strength of the external pressure. No family in a civilized society can live to itself alone, and if there is a whole neighborhood within which the immigrant language is maintained, the external pressure is in its favor or at least is less insistently unfavorable. The children who play together all come from N-speaking homes, and the few who do not are forced to learn their language instead of the converse. As late as 1918-20 school teachers have had to contend single-handed in some AmN communities with this immigrant-language pressure. Informants report with monotonous regularity that as children they spoke N except during the actual classroom instruction. The teacher often threatened them with punishments for speaking it in the schoolyard, but they returned to it with pleasure as soon as they were out of her surveillance.

In such cases the neighborhood becomes synonymous with those who speak the language; those who do not are outsiders, even if they live within the geographical radius. From Westby, Wisconsin, a story is told of a newcomer from Norway who wished to learn English and boarded in the home of the only Irishman in town, only to discover that Norwegian was spoken at the family table.[2] Under such circumstances the small villages which grew up as trading posts were themselves engulfed and became N-speaking centers. On Wednesdays and Saturdays farmers came in to buy and sell and be entertained. Even if they had ceased to speak N in the home because of the pressure from children or wives, they could here meet with others who spoke it and gain a real enjoyment in the immigrant tongue.

[Studies of communities where N has been preserved the longest show that at the grass-roots level the neighborhood spirit has played a powerful role.] John P. Johansen studied the use of the language in the N churches of South Dakota in 1935-6. He found that the use of N was strongest 'in the compact, early established settlements.' In those areas where the settlements were made before 1880, N was still used in 22.8 % of the services, while in the more scattered communities of the western part of the state it was used in only 4.4 %.[3] The same can be shown in Wisconsin. The areas where N has survived the longest in popular speech are not necessarily those areas where the number of persons born in Norway is largest nor those which were settled most recently. More Norwegian was probably spoken in Waupaca County with its 361 foreign-born Norwegians (in 1940) than in Racine with its 638 or Milwaukee with its 2,020. The Waupaca County settlements go back to the early 1850's, but they are still more Norwegian than the later settlements in the northern counties of the state, e.g. in Barron County. The same applies to larger areas: more Norwegian appears to be spoken in Wisconsin than in Washington, although the number of foreign-born Norwegians was 26,489 in the latter and only 23,211 in the former in 1940. Of course such factors as continued immigration have played an important role, since much of the recent immigration has gone to the same areas as the earlier and thereby reinforced the use of the language. But immigration which is dispersed in the cities or in marginal rural areas is more quickly anglicized than that which maintains its solid neighborhood core. In such areas people speak N simply because everybody else does, without reflecting much about it; for them it is not a cultural duty or a program of behavior. If you ask them why they do so, they can hardly give you any answer.]

2. *The Larger Institutions.*

[In due course the family and neighborhood situation was formalized by one or more institutions which provided tangible symbols around which the speakers of the language could rally. These institutions provided the terminology for a discussion of the use of the language on a community and nation-wide level. In the case of the Norwegians, as apparently among most immigrants, the Church is the primary institution which provides the immigrants with a justification for the use of the language. A map of the congregations of the Lutheran church, plus a few dissident churches, is practically a map of the organized use of Norwegian in America. As we have seen in chapter 6, the Church provided most of the instruction furnished in the reading and writing of N. Because of its essentially conservative nature, the Church acquired an institutional momentum which carried its insistence on Norwegian beyond the time when its younger members could appreciate the language. But eventually the rebellion against the immigrant language reared its head in the Church also. Faced with this problem, the church compromised its lesser goal for the sake of its larger one. To stay alive and carry on its spiritual message the Church had to yield and become first bilingual, then increasingly English. This did not take place without controversy, whether on the local, parish level or on the national, synodical level. The private grumblings of the family heads were here translated into a vigorous agitation for the retention of the traditional language, with its freight of cultural values, spiritual insights, and emotional overtones. The more or less passive resistance of the children now turned into an aggressive policy of Americanization, which not only tossed the language overboard, but with it a good many special practices of the Church which marked it out as an immigrant church in comparison with the older Anglo-Saxon churches. An instructive discussion of this development in the Swedish-American Church can be found in George Stephenson's *Religious Aspects of Swedish Immigration*, pp. 458-476. As might be expected, there are many points of similarity with the AmN development.

But the Church did not stand alone as a formal institution. The threat of cultural extinction which hovered over the group from the beginning was met by other forms of organization as well. Local, regional, and national societies have been organized in countless numbers.[4] While these had many purposes, most of them contained as one plank in their platforms the 'preservation of the Norwegian language.' The greater number of these have been urban, and belong to the period after 1900. Through the AmN press they have reached out and formed larger organizations and conducted agitation on a wider forum. They have been a secular counterpart to the Church in the work of reinforcing the family authority in favor of preserving the language. But in general they have been less effective than the Church in this part of their task, partly because they have seldom been able to include the whole family within their activities. A singing society has attracted the father, but not necessarily the son; a fraternal lodge has offered a type of program which did not always interest the children. American life has provided a multitude of seductions which competed successfully for the children's interest and attention, particularly in the cities and after World War I.

The most comprehensive in point of numbers is the Sons of Norway, whose backbone of support is provided by fraternal insurance. But its ability to attract young people to Norwegian-speaking programs has been very small, and this part of the program has very largely been abandoned in recent years. Next to it comes the Norwegian Singers' Association of America, whose singing carries on a male chorus tradition from Norway which has given many fine cultural values to American programs. The songs are still predominantly Norwegian, but the language of conversation within most choruses, at rehearsal and on festive occasions, is English. The so-called 'bygdelags', or home-valley societies, have retained more of the family-neighborhood speech tradition than other groups, but their membership is almost exclusively of the older generation. Their meetings are annual or semi-annual and more in the nature of old settlers' picnics than of effective, forward-looking organizations. Most of the societies are limited to the life of the Norwegian-speaking clientele, and will disappear with the disappearance of the language.

3. *Pioneer Days.*

The earliest N immigrants had no idea that their language would continue to be spoken for as long as has actually been the case. They were few in numbers and settled in scattered communities, and they did not anticipate the mass emigration that would follow

them for a century or more. Their first religious leader, Elling
Eielsen, walked from Illinois to New York just to have printed
an English translation of Luther's catechism.[5] The Norwegian
observer Johan R. Reiersen noted that most of the settlers in the
Illinois settlement at Fox River understood English and usually
attended the 'American churches in the vicinity.'[6] An immigrant
of 1845 expressed the opinion that the use of Norwegian would die
out 'in the second generation.'[7] Even the first immigrant newspaper, *Nordlyset*, made its appeal for readers in 1847 primarily
to those who had not yet learned enough English to become properly acquainted with American institutions.[8] Munch Ræder, the
Norwegian jurist who visited southern Wisconsin in 1847, looked
upon this development with some concern. The Norwegians, he
wrote, learned English with great ease, but they showed equal
facility 'in forgetting their own as soon as they cease to use it
every day.'[9] But Munch Ræder, who took the patriot's view of
the matter, saw before his eyes the rapidly forming settlements
of Wisconsin and realized that these would protect the Norwegians
'against influences foreign to themselves, because their relationship
to one another is stronger than their relationship to other races.'
This prediction was amply fulfilled in the century that followed,
for mass migration made it possible to reinforce the family urge
to retain Norwegian by the pressure of neighborhood practice and
the sanction of religious organization.[10]

Early immigrant pastors who might have been tempted to
commence preaching in English or to instruct the young in this
language were quickly encouraged to abandon such ideas. Instead,
the Norwegian language proved to be the *sine qua non* of successful
ecclesiastical organization among the immigrants. Preachers and
parishioners alike were relatively unskilled in the English language,
and there was obviously little attraction for them in English religious terminology. There were American faiths enough in the West
who would have been happy to attract the immigrants and who
did indeed succeed in siphoning off a good many in the early settlement days. By setting up a Norwegian Lutheran church the pastors
established the only conceivable counter-attraction which could
have gathered the immigrants into cohesive and permanent congregations. This was clearly expressed by a later observer, the

Reverend I. B. Torrison, who wrote: 'The Norwegian language was an instrument of union and a barrier against the sects.'[11] Here the immigrant who treasured the spiritual forms and values of his own childhood could carry on without a break the religious life which was the only one he had ever known and to him seemed the only one worth knowing. The Lutheran Church was not, like the Catholic, an international organization; in spite of common origin and many common features, its churches were national in organization and traditions. Even if there had been an effective American Lutheran church in the Middle West at this time, it is questionable whether the N immigrants would have patronized it. The university-trained religious leaders who organized the Norwegian Synod in 1853 were clearly aware of the value of Norwegian and expressed it through their concern for the establishment of Norwegian parochial schools.[12] Their work turned the tide of dispersion which had been conspicuous earlier. An unfriendly critic called it a 'pastoral Norwegianization': these ministers 'pride themselves on winning a great victory among the Norwegian Americans by uprooting a desire and zeal among them to let their children be trained in Americanism.'[13]

The critic, a Danish schoolmaster named Rasmus Sørensen, made himself the advocate of a program which later came to be espoused by the descendants of the same church fathers who then opposed it so vigorously. He roundly declared that it was the Christian duty of the Norwegian pastors to have the immigrants' children learn their religion and Christianity in English, 'the language of the country of their birth.'[14] Any other policy would be contrary to the best interests of the children, who might grow up as ignorant 'Norwegian Indians.' Sørensen was fearful of the possible transplantation to American soil of the pastoral overlordship found in many rural communities in Norway and looked with suspicion on the determination of the pastors to perpetuate the language. He and some others perceived that in the hands of the pastors the language was a potential instrument of power.

The church leaders did not allay this suspicion by their obvious leanings toward the German Missouri Synod, with whose doctrines and parochial school system they made themselves acquainted in 1857.[15] The uncompromising stand of that Church in its use of

the German language may also have stiffened the determination
of the Norwegian leaders in their stand on Norwegian. The president
of the Synod, A. C. Preus, made his position clear in his answer to
Sørensen's criticism, when he wrote that religion must be brought
to the child in 'the language of the heart.' 'To bring religious
instruction in English to those who daily hear and speak and think
in Norwegian is sheer humbug,' he concluded. In the following
year (1859) the assembled elergymen of the Norwegian Synod
took their stand on the question in these words: 'As long as most
of the members of our congregations do not yet have sufficient
familiarity with the English language, and as long as the Norwegian
language almost everywhere is the family language among us,
the language in which most naturally the daily prayer and family
devotions must be held, it is necessary that both our services and
our religious instruction shall take place in the Norwegian language.'[16] This was practically an echo of the words Preus had written
the year before, though he had then made a more definite prediction
for the future: 'When the English language supplants the Norwegian
in the home, our Norwegian speech will have lost its right to be
used in the church and in the religious school — but not before.'[17]

A year later Professor Laur. Larsen, then in St. Louis at the
seminary of the German Missouri Synod, reported that the organ
of that synod had printed the Norwegian declaration with approval.
He particularly emphasized that the declaration was not, as some
hinted, opposed to the use of English, but rather that it anticipated
its eventual adoption. 'To oppose it,' added Larsen, 'will always
be in vain, precisely because it is in the order of nature..' It was
necessary to teach the people English and to provide pastors and
teaching materials towards the time when English would become
the language of the church. But the main objective must be to
maintain the Lutheran faith and 'not be too quick to mimic everything American before we have tested whether it is better than
our own.'[18]

The Church had said its last word on this particular question
for a long time to come. We are not here concerned with the controversy that broke out when the leaders attempted to take the
logical next step, the establishment of a parochial school system
distinct from the American public school. As we have seen in an

earlier chapter, this attempt failed. In the meanwhile a policy was gradually taking shape in the secular field also. Early writers in *Nordlyset* had exhorted the Norwegians to keep alive their language, e.g. one Ole Marcusen who wrote in 1847: 'Above all, brother and sister, do not forget your mother tongue; for he who forgets his mother tongue is not far from forgetting his own self.'[19] The Norwegians were flattered in that year by the Wisconsin legislature which ordered 500 copies of the governor's speech to be printed in Norwegian. This took place over the protest of the representative from Walworth County who did not wish to 'encourage the immigrants to retain their old language by providing them with public documents in Norwegian or German.'[20] The editor of *Emigranten*, C. Fr. Solberg, arrived at a formulation of policy which foreshadows most of the cultural agitation for the language. Apparently apropos of the debate between Sørensen and Preus on the churchly situation, he declared: 'With regard to the amalgamation of the Norwegians with the Americans and the total exchange of the language with English, this is something that must take place gradually and will require several generations. We must not in every respect throw away the old Norwegian personality and at once adopt the new American one; there is much good in the Norwegian which should be transplanted in this country, and if the Americans have an influence in certain directions on our mode of thought and behavior, in others we should have an influence on theirs.'[21] This policy is vigorously supported by a subscriber in Chicago, who expresses the doctrines of a romantic nationalism when he writes, 'The language and literature of a people are an expression of the characteristic spirit and self-consciousness of a people... If one scorns the language and literature of one's ancestral land, then one also scorns the folk spirit that is expressed in it... But who benefits his new country most, the one who retains his national character and therefore preserves its good sides, or the one who throws it away?'[22]

This constructive position with regard to acculturation is one that has underlain most of the argumentation on behalf of retaining the immigrant language. Solberg pointed out in an *Emigranten* editorial that there were two extreme types of immigrants who did not accept this position of mediation between the cultures. On the

one hand there were those who praised America at the expense of
Norway, usually the ones from the most poverty-stricken layers
of Norwegian society; on the other there were those who did the
opposite, which included 'a small part of the more cultivated
Norwegians living here.'[23] The former might be expected to assimilate most rapidly, the latter most slowly. But the great mass of
the immigrants belonged to neither group; they accepted their
position as mediators, who spoke Norwegian as long as it seemed
useful to do so, but turned to English wherever Norwegian would
no longer reach. They did not take the uncompromising position
of the crab fisherman at Prince Rupert, British Columbia, who
refused to speak Norwegian to an AmN clergyman who interviewed
him. 'In Norway they speak Norwegian, in America English. I am
100 per cent American, therefore I speak English.'[24]

A later interpreter, the writer Waldemar Ager, described this
early period as one of 'fencing in' the group.[25] The purpose of the
leaders was to keep 'foreign' influences out, not only American
ones, but also many from Norway. It was his opinion that the shelter
thus provided gave the immigrants a chance to strike root in the
new country. These people were not trying to preserve a 'bridge'
back to their homeland; rather were they trying to secure 'something to keep themselves spiritually afloat.' Those parents who
taught their children Norwegian could tell about the homeland,
their family and their memories, help them with their lessons, and
in this way 'occupy a position such that the children naturally
would look up to them.' Those who proceeded to a rapid Americanization would place themselves in a position of inferiority to
their own children and inevitably lose their respect.

4. *The Inroads of English.*

As immigrants continued to pour in ever-increasing numbers
into the settlements of the Middle West, the church had its hands
full in attempting to provide them with services. The problems of
the day were largely organizational and doctrinal; as long as the
first generation constituted the bulk of its membership, the language
was no problem. A new secular press sprang up in the many centers

of settlement which provided a forum for the debates of the day.
These newspapers were naturally concerned in the retention of
reading skill in Norwegian. *Skandinaven,* then only five years old,
editorialized on the deplorable fact that 'many of the older settlers
read only English-language newspapers, while a good many of those
who have grown up in this country do not even understand Norwegian.'[26] The editor maintained that 'every Scandinavian who
has not been completely absorbed in American life (gaaet op i det
Amerikanske) should feel it as a necessity to keep in touch with
the political, social, and religious movements of the homeland.'
That the inroads of English on the younger generation were considerable even at this time appears from this quotation. Another
example from the same paper is a contribution by one who signs himself as 'born in America and educated in English'; nevertheless, he
says, he would like to 'keep up his mother tongue, but the opportunity for doing so is small.'[27] The writer must have grown up in
a community where the N settlers were not dominant, for his
statement contrasts sharply with a description of the situation
from about the same time: 'The fact that English is so to speak
a dead language in the large Norwegian settlements is an extremely
important matter, which must not be overlooked, since it puts the
greatest obstacles in the way of the school's advancement. When
the children begin their schooling, their vocabulary amounts only
to a few broken words, like stove'n, pail'n, fil'a [the field] etc.'[28]
The heart of the controversy between the Synod clergy and other
Norwegians in this period over the public school lay in the realization
of the former that the public school in English was bound to be
an opening wedge in the settlements for that language, as indeed
it proved to be. The compromise introduced by the young AmN
politician Knute Nelson in Wisconsin, of an hour's teaching of
Norwegian in the public school, satisfied no one.[29] Even such
whole-hearted advocates of the use of Norwegian as Professor
Rasmus B. Anderson could not stomach a parochial school through
which the Norwegians would be cut off from their fellow Americans.
In one eloquent passage he posed the issue very neatly: 'If the
Norwegian language cannot be preserved among us for two or three
generations without taking our children out of the common school,
very well; we will have to let the Norwegian language go. If the

Lutheran Church cannot make any progress among us unless we take our children out of the Common School, very well; let the Lutheran Church fall, and I will say, peace be with its dust.'[30] Fortunately for both church and language, no such drastic action was necessary.

[The acceptance of the public school by the Norwegians meant that other means had to be found for the preservation of their traditions. They resented equally any expression of nativism on the part of Americans which seemed to threaten their policy of gradual rather than sudden Americanization.] The Bennett Law (1889) in Wisconsin, which required a specified amount of English in all schools, seemed to some to constitute such a threat. This time Anderson joined those who wished to repeal it, on the argument that the English language needed no artificial support. 'The English language,' he wrote, 'is strong and aggressive; it makes its own way; it needs no artificial protection; it makes advances throughout the world; here in America it is not only the language of government and business, but also the language in which the various foreign nationalities communicate with each other, and the daily speech of practically all who grow up in this country. Nothing can stop the advance of this language; to use it as an excuse for persecutions is nonsense.'[31] State Senator John A. Johnson, who had been as ardent a supporter of the public school as Anderson, agreed fully; 'It is now almost impossible to find settlements where English is not spoken in every family — excepting for newcomers — and the use of the English language is constantly and rapidly increasing, while the use of foreign languages is decreasing in a surprisingly rapid degree.'[32] These testimonials give us valuable information concerning the trend in family speech during a period when the use of Norwegian was still a matter of course in all significantly large settlements. The Norwegian author Hans Seland, who visited the Norwegian communities around 1900, was surprised to discover how faithfully the Norwegians had preserved their dialects and the formal church language. But he also noted that the time was near when English would catch up with them, especially in the cities. 'The children who play in the streets soon grow accustomed to the language which the others use. And even if parents faithfully insist on Norwegian indoors, it does not do much good; they can ask in Norwegian, but the children will answer in English.'[33]

In a schematic presentation of AmN history made in 1925, O. M. Norlie dated the 'American period' as beginning in 1890, after a 'Norwegian period' 1825-60 and a 'Norwegian-American period' 1860-90.[34] 'In the American Period most of them speak English only...the Norwegian summer schools are dying, and Norwegian in the Sunday School and young people's society is of the past.' This was scarcely true at the beginning of the period which he calls 'American,' though it did become so by its end. The quarter century from 1890 to 1915 was a period when Norwegian activity was slowly dying out at the root, but nevertheless shot higher and finer blossoms than at any earlier period in its history. The flowering of social and cultural Norwegianism of these years gave to some people an illusion of permanence, but it bore the seeds of its own dissolution. Prosperity had come to the descendants of the immigrants, and their sons and daughters had gone to school. Institutions had attained a maturity which made possible the unfolding of intellectual and literary activity. Immigration rose to a new peak in the early years of the twentieth century. The immigrants who now came were better educated than the earlier ones, and were more able to take part in an urbanized culture. But the very fact of their urbanization, their comparative prosperity, and their education made it easier for them to enter American society on even terms. They still used Norwegian as their chief medium, but it was a Norwegian which no longer commanded the same simple loyalty as before. They also knew English, and their children did not learn Norwegian to the same extent as had the children of the early rural immigrants.

The first signs of institutional concern about the situation appear around 1890. A pastor of the Norwegian Synod wrote anonymously in the Synod's chief organ about the inevitability of the transition to English and the need for preaching and teaching in that language.[35] He admitted that while he was a student at the Seminary, he had not seen any need for preaching in English. But now he had had to catch up on his English, and demanded that the Synod provide English textbooks for the instruction of the young. He wished the children to learn Norwegian also as his own had done, but deplored that many children were growing up with an inability to speak freely in English on religious subjects. The historian Laurence M. Larson reports that at a church convention which he attended as a delegate in 1897 only one speaker had the temerity to speak in English, and faced general disapproval for so doing.[36] It does not appear that any sermons were being preached in English before 1900. But, in the words of a Synod pastor, 'English seems to lie in the air everywhere.'[37] This pastor did not believe that the church should insist on Norwegian, though he himself wished to keep it as long as possible: 'That would be to place the language above the kingdom of God.' The suggestions he made with regard to the transition were eminently sound and seem to have been followed: that English translations should be provided, so that the specifically Lutheran atmosphere would not be lost; and that congregations should not immediately change over to English, but should become bilingual and make the transition gradually.

Other expressions of opinion about this time tend in the same direction, e.g. John Dahle, who points out that English is the speech of most of the young people.[38] Andreas Wright (1835-1917), a pastor of the United Norwegian Lutheran Church, wrote in 1904 that 'our religious schools will still be conducted in Norwegian for some time, but the day is not distant when they must be held in English... You cannot force America to speak Norwegian, but it has forced us to try to talk English and to have our children brought up in it.'[39] An outspoken pastor of the younger generation in the Hauge Synod, Lars Harrisville (1889-1925), accused his colleagues of deliberately hindering the advancement of the church by insisting on the Norwegian language.[40] 'The pastor may ignore the English work. He may hold back the tide for a while. He may ridicule it. He may accuse the children and young people of being high-toned and foolish. But at the least opportunity the young people will go to some neighboring church where English is preached.' In the cities this is particularly true, he claimed, and he cried, 'when will the Norwegian, the Swedish, the German, and Danish Lutheran Synods awake out of their death-sleep?' He insisted that the Seminary must produce pastors who 'speak a pure English' and who could pronounce their 'th's, s's, and r's equally as well as a child in the Kindergarten.' Finally he predicted: 'The

English question is coming upon us as a mighty rushing tide. Let us be ready... The storm is coming. It will sweep the churches from shore to shore.'

5. *The Norwegian Counterattack.*

Whether the statement was made in a regretful or in an aggressive tone, the fact remained that younger church leaders were increasingly determined to promote the use of English. There was a sudden, almost panicky realization on the part of the lovers of Norwegian that the enemy was within the walls, determined not merely to demand a rightful place for English, but actually hostile to many of the values represented by the Norwegian language. This is certainly a part of the reason for the organization on a national scale during these years of secular societies dedicated to the preservation of various aspects of Norwegian culture. Singers led the way in organizing the first Norwegian secular association on a wider base. In 1891 The Northwestern Scandinavian Singers' Association was organized at Sioux Falls, S. Dak.; by 1910 it had become The Norwegian Singers' Association of America.[41] In 1900 was organized the so-called 'Supreme Lodge' of the Sons of Norway, a fraternity modelled on American lodges; by 1925 it had a membership of 21,000 in 250 lodges.[42] Its first stated purpose included 'to encourage and maintain an interest among its members in the Norwegian language to an extent that is not in conflict with the loyalty they owe the United States.'[43] In 1901-2 the Valdris Samband was organized as the first of the *bygdelags*, which came to be one of the most flourishing types of Norwegian organization. In the constitution of this society we read that one of its purposes is to gather and preserve everything that concerns the people, the communities, and the *language* of Valdres.[44]

But the really central organization in this movement was Det norske Selskab i Amerika, organized at Minneapolis on January 28, 1903. The preservation of the Norwegian language was the first plank in its platform, as appears from the statement of its purposes in its constitution: 'The purpose of the Society shall be to work for the preservation by the Norwegian people in America of a) their ancestral tongue, b) their historical memories and traditions, c) their interest in Norwegian literature, art, song, and music, and d) their national characteristics (folkelige Eiendommelighed) — to the extent that this can be reconciled with our obligations and position in American society.'[45] The leaders included many of the best-known pastors, professors, and writers among the immigrants; the organization was widely noticed in the press and won support from many sides. Many fine speeches were held at the annual meetings; but the membership always remained small, and its influence correspondingly limited. The activities which won most attention were the setting up of Norwegian monuments (chiefly of authors) in various centers, a 50-dollar annual prize for the best piece of AmN literature, and a medal for the winners of Norwegian declamatory contests.

The dreams entertained by the founders had been a good deal more ambitious. Professor Julius E. Olson wanted the society to publish editions of popular Norwegian classics which might reach a wide public, including the young people who ought to be given 'Norskhedens Stempel' (the stamp of Norwegianness). It was his opinion that Norwegian was an asset to the church: 'As soon as the Norse tongue is silenced, our people will discover the open doors in other churches and find it easier to leave the church of their fathers.'[46] Another early contributor declared that the practices then current in the church and school showed that bilingualism could be maintained; however difficult, it was not impossible.[47]

This came to be the chief theme of the publication sponsored by the society, the *Kvartalskrift*, which appeared from 1905 to 1922 under the constant editorship of the author and journalist Waldemar Ager.[48] In the first volume he rejected a view propounded by Johannes Wist that the chief function of the Society was to act as a bridge between the immigrants and the culture of Norway. Ager declared that it was more important to create something original, a literature and a culture that would have its own life.[49] But this could only occur, he felt, if the Norwegian language were maintained as the group medium. 'That a people give up their language is tantamount to cultural decay.'[50] 'History, I believe, will tell us that no nation can let its language decay and remain unpunished.'[51] He appealed repeatedly to parents to teach their children Norwegian as a means of preserving the cultural continuity of the Norwegian group. The idea that the immigrant's soul somehow found its most adequate expression in Norwegian and that this would remain true of his descendants if sufficient effort were made appears repeatedly in Ager's writings. He abhorred the idea of the 'melting pot'; in an article of 1916 he wrote ironically that the old Americans appear to take it for granted that the immigrants shall be happy to be melted down 'into something greater and better than they were before.' 'Out of the melting pot there is supposed to come a new man, a super-citizen, a superman with all the best features from the various races and none of the bad ones. But the so-called American does not himself wish to be assimilated with the foreigners; he does not wish either to assimilate or take up in himself the Russian, the Pole, or the Jew; but he wants these to be absorbed in each other.'[52] A series of articles by Ager entitled The Great Levelling (1917-21) showed that he valued cultural pluralism as an enrichment of the life of his new country.[53] But he had no faith in a cultural movement which was not borne by the native tongue: 'In reality it is the language — the Norwegian language — which is the bridge. When the language no longer carries, then there is no bridge.'[54]

In 1913 an interesting discussion of the problem was initiated by Kristian Prestgard, the editor of the literary periodical *Symra*. He asked two pastors with opposing points of view to present their opinions in his periodical. The 'Norwegian' point of view was represented by the Reverend Kr. Kvamme, who attacked rather bitterly the sense of shame which many Norwegian immigrants and their descendants felt over their language and culture. He gave examples, including expressions of scorn for 'everything that is Norwegian', the attempt to disguise Norwegian names and adopt English ones, the feeling of prestige attaching to 'American' ways of behavior both in secular and religious affairs, the criticism of Norwegian cultural trends in the homeland, reluctance to speak Norwegian in the presence of Americans. In his opinion the immigrants and their descendants were still 'more than three fourths Norwegian and only a tiny fraction American' and he described their striving to be something different as a 'Yankee fever', 'a kind of childhood disease, which they will get over sooner or later and then become healthy, normal people again.' He regarded this as a failure of personality, a loss of identity: 'One can lose some of one's identity, forget or partially forget what one is... lose one's way in a fog of "Americanism" such that one never again can find the way home to one's self.' The core of Kvamme's argument is the idea of a fixed national identity and the sacred duty of each individual to feel pride in this identity.[55]

The 'American' point of view was represented by the Reverend I. B. Torrison who argued that the characteristic quality of immigrants who had made America their permanent home was precisely that their national consciousness had changed. 'Their national consciousness is different from the one possessed by those who have not emigrated or who are here only temporarily and whose future lies in Norway.' This was either resented or not understood in Norway, and even many immigrants did not realize it until they met non-immigrant Norwegians or revisited Norway. Any work on behalf of Norwegian culture in this country had to take this factor of national feeling into account: the goal must not be to make Norwegians of the young people, but to stimulate their pride of ancestry and their assimilation of those elements in Norwegian culture which were of universal value. In practice the Norwegian language was no longer an instrument of union among the immigrants, but one of division. His final pointed remark concerned 'the relatively recent arrivals, and those who live among us as colonials': one reason that many of Norwegian descent shun Norwegian culture as 'foreign' is that these people 'let a good share of their Norwegian patriotism consist in scolding those who are at home in this country.'[56]

Both writers were agreed in deploring any inferiority complex which Norwegian-Americans might feel; they both favored a program of cultural self-assertion. But there was a genuine difference in their views of national personality which was typical in all such discussions. The 'Norwegian' point of view was maintained also by Professor O. E. Rølvaag in a fable called 'Hvitbjørn og graabjørn, et indiansk eventyr' (White Bears and Gray Bears, an Indian Fairytale).[57] The White or Polar Bears invade the country of the Gray Bears and settle among them; after a time the White Bears decide that they want to become gray, but in spite of everything they do, they still remain white, or at best a dirty or speckled gray. The biological simile here suggested, which Rølvaag also used elsewhere, implies the idea of an immutable national personality. The editor Luth. Jæger threw himself into the discussion with a strong attack on this idea, maintaining that the immigrants' children were being hampered in their whole-hearted devotion to America by the emphasis on the Norwegian language and 'foreign ideals.' The young people cannot 'divide themselves and be both Norwegian and American without harming their development as American men and women.' 'To be a good American does not require a denial of one's ancestors and the Norwegian heritage. But then we must also not sell our American birthright for a mess of Norwegian pottage.'[58] The writer P. P. Iverslie, who had grown up in this country, expressed violent disagreement with Jæger and instanced his own upbringing in both languages and cultures as an example of how it was not only possible but even desirable to maintain bilingualism. 'What a poverty-stricken half-life it would have been to know only the Anglo-American cultural life — and that with a Norwegian ancestry.' His basic contention, that 'those who know two or more languages have a wider horizon than those who know only one' has been a prominent and weighty argument in this debate.[59] It is repeated by the Reverend Hulteng in a contribution to the same discussion, contending that the young people should and could learn two languages because of the ancestral heritage whose values would be lost with the language. In his predictions for the future, however, Hulteng was probably the least realistic of the contributors; he did not want bilingual congregations, but advocated that those who wanted English in the church should form all-English congregations or even a distinct English synod. 'But that goal,' he wrote, 'still seems to be far in the future.'[60] The leading historian of the Church, the Reverend J. A. Bergh, wrote in 1914 that the Church must keep up with the language development; 'but most church work is still conducted in Norwegian, and this will no doubt continue for a long time.'[61]

The time of change proved to be less distant than Hulteng and Bergh had foreseen. The leaders of the church were not disposed to countenance any splitting up of congregations or synods into purely English and Norwegian parts. They preferred to keep parents and children together in the same organizations, instituting parallel services in the two languages so that both old and young might be satisfied. The Norwegian Lutheran Church was still split into a multitude of synods, and the problem of union was more important during these years than the problem of language. But on the local, congregational level the battle raged over a wide sector, for the language question was one that only the congregations had the power to settle. The president of the United Norwegian Lutheran Church, the Reverend T. H. Dahl, reported to the annual meeting in 1912 that the great need of the Synod was for ministers who could preach in English. 'Even parishes where the English language rarely or never has been used in the service demand English-speaking pastors when they change ministers... The time is past when our congregations were satisfied with broken English... It is an incontrovertible fact that our young people are growing more and more unfamiliar with our mother tongue.'[62] When Senator Knute Nelson of Minnesota visited Luther College in Decorah, he brought a message from President Theodore Roosevelt, advising the Norwegians 'not to cling too long to the Norwegian language as the language of the church. The result would be that the church would lose the young people. This had happened in his own church, the Dutch Reformed.'[63] The response of the church was evident in the statistics on the use of English in the official ministerial acts. By 1915 nearly one fourth of the sermons delivered in Norwegian Lutheran churches were in English: the percentage had risen from none in 1900 to 22 % in 1915.[64] Those ministrations which predominantly affected the young were even more anglicized: religious instruction in the Sunday school and confirmation training was 27 % English. The strategic positions were all held by the older generation, but the trend was clear, as is shown by the following table from O. M. Norlie, giving the percentage of English services:[65]

	1905	1910	1915
Sermons	.05	.13	.22
Confirmation	.18	.27	.27
Sunday School	.17	.21	.27

The three leading synods showed a slight difference in the rapidity with which the process was going, but hardly a significant one. In the year before their union, 1916, the sermons in Hauge's Synod were 17.2 % English, in the United Lutheran Church 21.6 %, and in the Norwegian Synod 25.7 %.[66]

6. *World War Hysteria.*

Then occurred a series of events which apparently shook the position of Norwegian more than all the previous agitation. In 1917 the three major synods were joined into a new, giant organization called The Norwegian Lutheran Church in America with a membership of 443,563 in 2,811 congregations, ministered to by 1,215 pastors.[67] In the same year the United States entered the First World War. Either of these events alone would probably have affected the use of Norwegian adversely; together they were catastrophic. Even so, they only intensified and hastened a development that was inevitable; but their dramatic effect was such as to make them seem responsible for it. The union of the synods raised in many leaders the vision of a future union among all American Lutherans, a vision to which the use of Norwegian was a distinct obstacle. The solution of the internal squabbles and jurisdictional rivalries left time for the church to consider its language problem as a whole. One of the first acts of the new church was to organize an English Conference, to which congregations 'whose official language is English' might belong.[68] This conference had a status equivalent to that of one of the eight geographical districts into which the church was divided, but congregations belonging to it were also members of the district organizations. At its first annual meeting in 1918, this conference, called the English Association, accepted applications for membership from 50 congregations.[69] In his first report the president, Rev. C. O. Solberg, pointed out that the Association might be only temporary, 'in order to help the widespread bi-lingual church in the difficult question of handling the language transition.' He recognized that the transition 'brings up problems of a spiritual type of congenial practice in ritual and outward forms, and many others.'

Except for the minutes of the English Association and some of the financial reports, the language of all church documents and of debate on the floor was still Norwegian in 1918. But in this very first annual meeting of the amalgamated Church there is a peculiar note of insistence on the importance of a rapid transition. The president's report declares that 'one of the most urgent matters before us at this meeting is unquestionably the socalled "English work".' He recommended the appointment of a committee to make proposals on the most effective means of meeting the threatened loss of younger members due to rival activity by non-Lutheran churches or even by English (i.e. English-speaking) Lutheran churches. But his most startling proposal was to abandon the name adopted in the previous year for the new church by omitting the word 'Norwegian' in its title and substituting some such name as 'The United Lutheran Synod.'[70] President H. G. Stub, himself an effective speaker of Norwegian, denied any possible charge of being uninterested in his Norwegian background and the preservation of Norwegian culture.[71] But he pleaded the unwillingness of congregations and individuals to join a synod designating itself as 'Norwegian'; he asserted that the Swedish Augustana Synod had abandoned the term 'Swedish' many years earlier and that the German Missouri Synod had abandoned the term 'German' in 1917.[72] He won strong support for his proposals, e.g. a testimonial from the District President of the North Dakota district to the effect that 'the last year has promoted the transition to English in a disturbing degree' and that the pastors must see to it that the needs of the young are not neglected.[73] The proposal to change the name was adopted by a vote of 533 to 61.[74] As it turned out, this preliminary constitutional change was not effected for many years; two years later, in 1920, the annual meeting refused to confirm the action and voted the word 'Norwegian' back by 577 to 296.[75]

It is clear that the 1918 meeting was under the influence of a wind of public opinion which did not grow naturally out of the situation within the Church. The change of name was so sudden that no one had even had time to think up a suitable new one. The President's report reveals quite clearly the source of pressure: 'Since our country entered the war, a great reversal has taken place in the direction of rapid Americanization.' A critic of the action taken at the meeting writes that 'the killing poison gas of the war spirit was strongly in evidence'. Those who tried to oppose the action were told that their opinions would lay them open to the suspicion of being disloyal.[76] At one of the meetings a circular from the office of Governor Harding of Iowa was read. The Governor had forbidden the public use of any foreign language in his state by a proclamation of May 23, 1918, and in his circular he interpreted the intention of this proclamation. He did not wish to forbid the use of foreign languages by those who did not understand English; but he did declare that their misuse 'is resulting in discord among our own patriotic people and in giving our enemies an opportunity to hinder the work of our Government during these critical times.'[77] A resolution was also adopted refusing admission to the Theological Seminary of students not mastering the English language, since they could no longer find parishes.[78]

The results of this concerted action on the part of ecclesiastical and secular leaders were not slow in appearing in the statistical reports of the Church. As can be seen from Table 6 (in the next chapter), the percentage of Norwegian services fell from 73.1 to 61.2 in 1918, or more than in any preceding or following year. About 9,000 Norwegian services were turned into English during this year alone. That this move was somewhat overhasty is shown by the fact that the percentage bounded back up to 65.7 and 62.8 during the following two years, bringing it more into line with the normal decrease. From 1918 to 1948 the fall in percentage of Norwegian services was almost predictably steady, constituting an annual drop averaging 2.3 %, which probably corresponds approximately to the death toll of the older generation. Against this background we see how violent the drop of 1918 was.

⌈A generation of monolinguals was clearly on the march. Their voice is heard most distinctly in the annual reports of the English Association within the Church.⌉The report of 1920 is especially insistent that 'English' interests be more actively represented in the high councils of the Church, that theological training in English be encouraged, and that evangelistic work among potential Lutherans be extended.[79] The report warns advocates of English not to be over-optimistic and cites figures to show how strong the position of Norwegian is and how weak many of the all-English congregations are. One section of the report has the interesting suggestion that a church using the English language has essentially different problems from one using Norwegian: it becomes a church which seeks to proselytize among all peoples and no longer enjoys the sheltered existence of a 'state' church. There is no doubt that the language had been the chief asset of the Church among the immigrants; but now it was, in the opinion of some, rapidly becoming a liability.

7. *The Last Rally.*

The supporters of Norwegian were taken by surprise in 1917-18, but the end of the War made it possible for them to counterattack. The Norwegian-language press re-echoed with appeals on behalf of the language and the Norwegian name. Waldemar Ager continued his campaign in the columns of *Kvartalskrift;* a bitter note crept into some of his articles, as in this passage from 1919: 'In order to kill whatever soul the immigrant may have brought with him, someone has hatched the plan of cutting him off as much as possible from outside cultural nourishment by forbidding him the use of the only language in which he can secure nourishment for his soul. It is a cultural blockade whereby his "foreign" soul is to be starved out, and the bidding that he must build himself a new soul is accompanied by an authorized plan for that soul all worked out for him by salaried government functionaries in Washington.'[80] But his old *Norske Selskab* no longer seemed to have much vitality left in it.

A new organization was felt to be necessary, and leading pastors, professors, and writers gathered again as they had done in 1903; this time they met in Eau Claire on October 19, 1919. They organized a society with the fitting name of *For Fædrearven* — 'for the ancestral heritage.' The constitution was not specific about preserving the language, but emphasized the cultural values: 'To awaken among the people of Norwegian stock in America a deeper appreciation of and love for the great values we have received from our fathers in history, language, religious and secular literature, art, and national characteristics...'[81] But whereas Ager had been the moving spirit of the old society, the man who surged to the front in the new one was Ole E. Rølvaag, professor at St. Olaf College and author; in the forefront among AmN cultural leaders, he still was not as well known outside his group as he soon after became. He was elected secretary and edited the publications of the society, the most important of which was a page headed *For Fædrearven* in the Canton, South Dakota, weekly *Visergutten* from Feb. 3, 1921 to June 15, 1922.[82] Many of his essays in this publication were reprinted in his book *Omkring Fædrearven* which appeared in 1922.[83]

Rølvaag's doctrines were the outgrowth, in the words of his biographers, of 'a social and cultural philosophy built upon years of experience and serious thinking.'[84] Rølvaag's direct contacts with the young people of the church in his classrooms gave his ideas a more authentic ring than those which were evolved by men associated only with the older generation. In his classes he also had a forum from which he could naturally expound his doctrines; he was in addition gifted with a personality and a talent of literary expression which won him followers among the younger generation. Rølvaag was an idealist, not amenable to the kind of practical but compromising reasoning which was fashionable in his day. He was also stubborn and outspoken, with a vein of quiet, earthy humor which gave his utterances force if not always tact. An extended discussion of the views he advanced may be found in his biography.[85] In brief, his advocacy was of a cultural pluralism for Americans, based on a devotion to the heritage of the fathers: a knowledge of Norwegian was an 'ethical duty' resting on every descendant of Norwegians. This 'duty' did not hamper but advance the best interests of America. The creative emphasis is clear in the words he used in a classroom lecture: 'I am well aware that many people today are seeking to blot out all racial traits in this country. To me such an act is tantamount to national suicide. If richness of personal color is desirable in the individual personality, why should the monotonous gray be desirable as a national idea?'[86] When Rølvaag resigned his position as secretary in 1922, the organization quietly collapsed. Its chief function had been to give an outlet for Rølvaag's energy at a time when the events of the war and its anti-foreign psychosis had seriously disturbed him. The discussion of the twenties was the richer for his contributions; and even if they did not alter the course of development, they were their own justification, if only for the stimulus they provided toward his writing of *Giants in the Earth*.

There was in the twenties a general feeling that an era had come to its close, in spite of everything Rølvaag and his fellow believers could advance. The number of living Norwegian immigrants had reached its peak in 1910 with 403,858 and declined in 1920 to 363,862. In 1924 the Congress passed the National Origins Act, which allotted to the Norwegian group an annual quota of immigrants amounting to only 2,377. Farsighted leaders could not help but see that this was the handwriting on the wall. An immigrant observer who had returned to Norway after twenty years of wide experience among his countrymen had written in 1913: 'As long as Norwegian emigration continues at the same undiminished pace as hitherto, the Norwegian language will survive in America, and just so long the Church and the Press will work side by side with the immigrants in retaining the language. But when immigration ceases..., it will not take a generation before the Norwegian language is a thing of the past in the N-A settlements.'[87] This feeling may have contributed to the enthusiasm with which the Norse-American Centennial was celebrated in 1925. The initiative came from the associated *bygdelags*, and the celebration was carried through by a committee representing all religious and secular organizations among the immigrants. The program and the exhibits at the Minnesota Fair Grounds included the finest that could be displayed by the group; it was an impressive demonstration of the passing of an era.

Chapter 11.

THE TRIUMPH OF ENGLISH.

> In these parts of our country the pioneer, no
> matter of what race, is fast disappearing. Often he
> is a tragic figure. History has left him behind —
> simply gone away from him. He may not even be
> able to converse intelligently with his own grand-
> children.
>
> *O. E. Rølvaag (1929)*.[1]

The generation from 1925 to the present has seen a further
weakening of the old language among the immigrants and their
children, but the victory of English is still not complete.

That it is inevitable in a not too distant future would seem to
be the natural conclusion to be drawn from the facts that will here
be presented. Parallels from history in all parts of the world could
be adduced to support this probability: the absorption of the Dutch
and the Swedes on the American east coast, the Danes and Norwegians in medieval England, the Goths in Italy, and the Vandals
in Spain. Many emigrated languages in America have disappeared,
but not, of course, all. French in Canada bids fair to survive.
Spanish in the American Southwest, French in Louisiana, and
German in Pennsylvania have shown a tough-minded resistance
to extinction which is even now meeting its most serious test.
Against these backgrounds one would like to know just where the
Norwegians stand. If they do give up their language, as now seems
probable, why do they do so? Have they retained it longer than
other comparable groups, say the Danes and Swedes, and if so,
why? Some speak of them as 'clannish', others say they are easily

assimilated. What kind of evidence can we bring forward that will mean more than one man's opinion? First we shall look at the available facts about the development since 1925, and then we shall make a stab at some interpretations.

1. *At the Grass Roots.*

The tide which was set in motion at the time of the first World War swept on through the twenties. By 1928 religious instruction of the young in Norwegian had practically ceased, as one can see by consulting Table 5. The Sunday school led the way, being an American idea and an urban institution in the first place. Confirmant instruction lagged behind, while the week-day school was the last to give up its Norwegian cast. As we have seen in Chapter 6, the week-day school derived directly from the public schools of Norway and thus was largely identified with the teaching of Norwegian, especially in the rural areas.

Table 5. *Percent of Religious Instruction in Norwegian (Norwegian Lutheran Church), 1917—1928.*

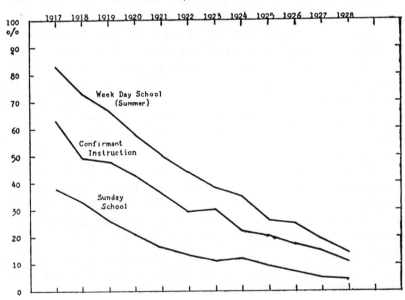

Table 6. *Number and Percentage of Norwegian Services in Norwegian Lutheran Church 1917—30.*

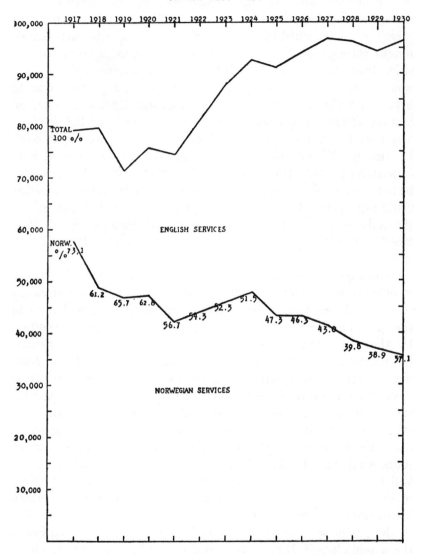

Divine services, being primarily for adults, naturally remained Norwegian longer than the religious instruction. In 1925 the number of English services exceeded the Norwegian for the first time, as appears in Table 6. By 1928 the all-Norwegian congregations numbered only ten per cent of the total with only five per cent of the membership. The all-English congregations were twice as numerous and four times as populous.[2] The decision in each congregation was reached by a vote of the members, with each change fought through by the younger members against a certain opposition from the older ones. While the precise course of this change was different in each congregation, the typical pattern was to begin with the introduction of an occasional English service, on Sunday afternoon or evening. Then would come parallel services, and a gradual fading out of the attendance at the Norwegian ones. In time the Norwegian services became the occasional ones, held at scattered intervals and inconvenient times. The change might be made suddenly, especially if a new pastor were called who either could not or would not preach in Norwegian. By 1928 one half of the calls received at the Luther Theological Seminary in St. Paul failed to mention the ability to talk Norwegian as a clerical qualification.[3]

The rapidity of the change was such as to strike the hearts of older church members with a genuine concern about the values that were being lost. Pastors whose whole training had been in the old language were placed in an exceedingly difficult position by the new demands that were being made on their language competence. As early as 1914 the Reverend J. A. Bergh had commented on the hyper-critical attitude of the younger generation toward the English of their elders: 'Our pastors are meeting with the unfortunate circumstance that their congregations are very critical with regard to their English, but are not at all particular about the Norwegian they speak. The situation is that they cannot judge what is good or bad Norwegian, having come from the various valleys of Norway each with its own dialect, while a great many of the young people in the congregation have attended American institutions of higher learning and have learned to criticise. Woe to the pastor who uses a word incorrectly or puts an intonation in the wrong place.'[4] More or less good-natured stories were in circulation about such errors, as we see from a collection of ministerial tales called *Fra Pioner-presternes Saga* (From the Saga of the Pioneer Pastors).[5] One pastor who intended to ask his congregation to remain standing until they were ready to pass out of the room

Table 7. *Number and Percentage of Norwegian Services in Norwegian Lutheran Church 1931—44.*

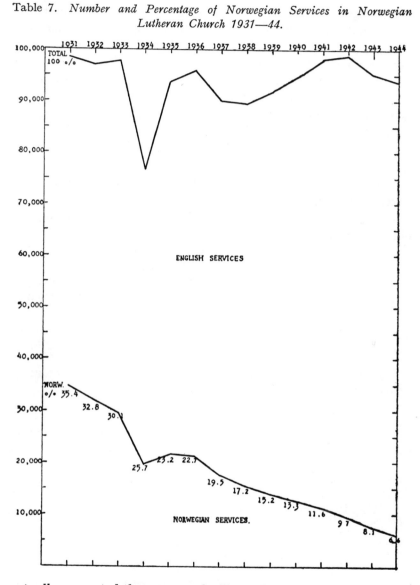

actually requested them to stand 'till we all pass away.' One member drily commented that this might take quite a while.

The bitterness engendered by this kind of criticism is revealed in a little novel by a pastor who felt resentful of the attitude of the younger generation: *Presten som ikke kunde brukes* (The Pastor who could not be used) by C. E. Nordberg.[6] The pastor 'who could not be used' is regarded as old-fashioned by some of the younger members in the congregation, and they intrigue to get rid of him in favor of a young 'hustler' who will organize lots of parties and entertainment for the younger set. A typical conversation is one between several church members concerning the language situation:

"It's not enough that he *knows* English," said John Asber; "he must be *perfect* in English."

"Then you don't care what kind of Norwegian he talks?" said Peter Hendrickson.

"Oh, any one who talks Norwegian in our time can only get old women to listen to him," said W. U. Nelson.

"We know that all the ministers have to know English nowadays," said Nils Olson, "but I think Norwegian will live a long time still, so that the ministers will have to know both Norwegian and English. These young ministers who know nothing but English

Table 8. *Norwegian Services in the Norwegian Lutheran Church (Evangelical Lutheran Church) 1930—48: Percentage of Total Services in Each District.*

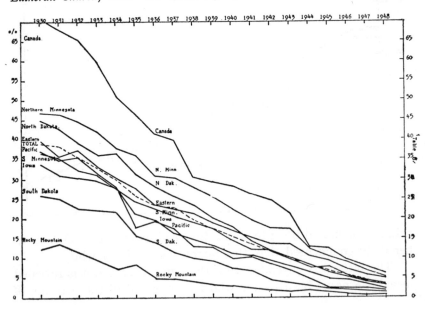

Table 9. *Norwegian Services in the Norwegian Lutheran Church 1930—48: Total Number in Each District (broken line on scale one-fifth of rest).*

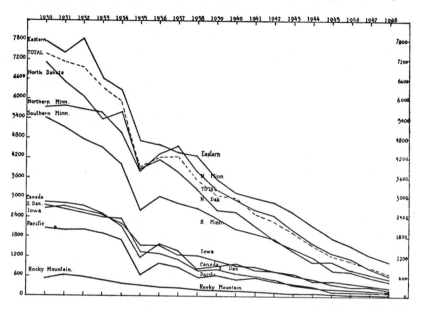

and can't talk even a fairly correct Norwegian will be just as badly off as those who can't speak perfect English."

It is obvious that the last speaker is the author's mouthpiece; Nordberg's book was written primarily to stem the tide.[7]

Resistance of this kind, as sketched in the preceding chapter, did succeed in delaying the disappearance of Norwegian in the church services for just about a full generation. Table 7 shows the steady decline between 1931 and 1944; the 6.6 % Norwegian services in the latter year was further reduced to 2.7 by 1949, leaving a total of only 2,677 services in that year. Rølvaag had predicted in 1922 that 'it is unthinkable that there will ever come a time in this country when Norwegian is not used as an instrument of culture and education by quite a large number of Americans of Norwegian descent.'[8] At least within the church there did not seem much likelihood in 1950 that his prediction would be verified.

Resistance to the change was much stronger in some regions than others. As noted earlier, Johansen found for South Dakota that the compact settlements in open country were most conservative.[9] In Tables 8 and 9 a graphic presentation has been attempted of the available information for each of the nine geographical districts into which the church was divided.[10]

As late as in 1930 there was still a wide variation between different districts. In Canada there were 70.6 % Norwegian services in 1930 compared to only 12.3 in the Rocky Mountain district. In the latter area the Norwegians were scattered and largely urban, while in Canada they lived in compact rural settlements in the prairie provinces. The farming areas of North Dakota and Northern Minnesota were also notably higher in their retention than South Dakota and Southern Minnesota. East coast and West coast show almost identical distributions, close to the national average. The so-called Eastern district included such midwestern states as Wisconsin and Illinois, but also urban communities like Chicago and Brooklyn. As the years passed, however, the difference between the districts was rapidly disappearing; Norwegian appeared to be approaching extinction at about the same time everywhere. In actual numbers, the Eastern district still held more services than the other districts; some of these were for the more recent arrivals in the New York metropolitan area, but others were for the oldest, relict areas in Wisconsin.

2. *The Wisconsin Scene.*

Wisconsin will here be considered in more detail as a typical example of old and compact settlement. The accompanying map (Plate 3) shows the situation in 1936, when there were still enough Norwegian services to make the distribution significant. At that time there were 4,613 Norwegian services in the Eastern District, which includes Wisconsin, or 23 % of all church services. The congregations have been distinguished into those having all Norwegian (3, or 1 %), more than half (47, or 14.8 %) less than half (170, or 53.6 %), and no Norwegian (97, or 30.6 %). The all-English congregations were divided between the urban centers and the scattered settlements. The less-than-half congregations were found everywhere, but were most typical of the southern and oldest

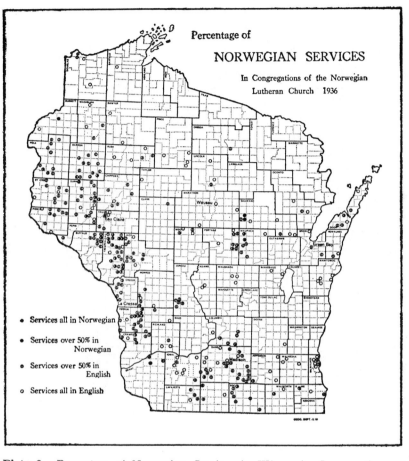

Plate 3. *Percentage of Norwegian Services in Wisconsin Congregations of the Norwegian Lutheran Church 1936.*

settlements. The only areas where more-than-half and all-Norwegian congregations were found in any quantity were in the north and west, especially in Waupaca, Vernon, and Trempealeau counties.

In order to bring this information up to date, the writer conducted a postcard poll in 1949 of the pastors serving congregations in Wisconsin belonging to the Evangelical Lutheran Church. Table 10 presents the results in percentages, while the accompanying

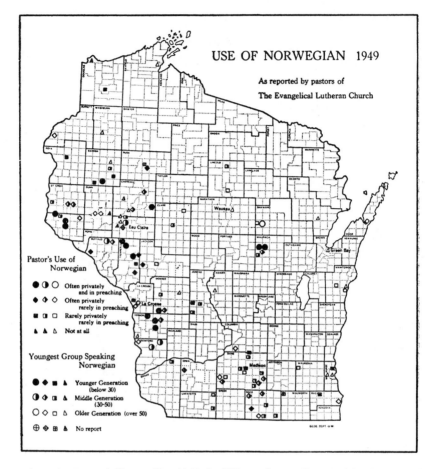

Plate 4. *Use of Norwegian 1949 in Wisconsin, as Reported by Pastors of The Evangelical Lutheran Church.*

map of Wisconsin (Plate 4) shows the geographical distribution of the frequency of Norwegian in daily use. The 120 pastors who answered (60 % of the total polled) were overwhelmingly American-born; only 12 claim to have studied in Norway. But their overall percentage of Norwegian blood amounted to 439 of 480 possible grandparents, or 91.5 %. About the same proportion, or 88.3 % had studied Norwegian in school, but less than half of them claimed any fluency in using the language. An exceptional pastor claimed to be 'eloquent' in Norwegian, but most of them confined themselves modestly to the label 'fair'. Those who knew the language found occasion to use it, at least privately; but only a sixth of the whole number used it for preaching. Their answers to a question on favorite occasions for speaking Norwegian might be summed up in the words: 'To the old and sick.' They mentioned communion and other special services, beside celebrations of Norwegian holidays and meetings of Norwegian societies. The median birth year of the last generation still speaking Norwegian was 1907, i.e. the age group reaching maturity shortly after World War I. The communities whose pastors reported continuing use of Norwegian were much the same as those revealed by the figures of 1936. The pastors were asked to guess on the percentage of non-Norwegians in their congregations; the median of 28 % seems reasonable. In some urban communities the figures run over 60 %, but this is hardly ever true in the rural areas. If these estimates are not grossly exaggerated, it appears that the membership of the church is a good deal more mixed than its leadership.

A further check on the situation in Wisconsin was made in personal interviews throughout various parts of the state. Younger people often expressed relief at the gradual disappearance of the language distinction, but most of those who had acquired a speaking knowledge of Norwegian found in its use a special enjoyment for which English had no precise substitute. A woman born in Waushara County, who could understand either language equally well, preferred Norwegian sermons. 'But as things are in this country,' she said, 'people marry into other nationalities, and the children don't get taught Norwegian so they can understand it. So I suppose it's best that it's losing out, but I'll be sorry to see it blocked out entirely.'[11] Many were impressed by the apparent inevitability of the change; in the words of a man in Juneau County: 'E synest de må gå den veien. Me æ i Amerika, engelsk æ landets språk, og de språke som verte brukt (I think it has to go that way. We're in America, English is the language of the land, and the language that is used).'[12]

In commenting on the process itself a number of informants pointed to the influence of the schools. A man in Waupaca County reported that when his son, born in 1935, was small, he spoke only

Table 10. *A Poll of 120 Wisconsin Pastors 1949.*
(Evangelical Lutheran Church).

1. *Ancestry*	All Norw.	More than $1/_2$	Half	Less than $1/_2$	No Norw.	Total
No.	101	6	8	1	4	120
%	84.2	5.0	6.8	0.8	3.2	100

2. *Knowledge of Norwegian*	*Speaking*	Fluent	Fair	None		
	No.	47	54	19		120
	%	39.2	45.0	15.8		100
	Reading					
	No.	58	39	21		118
	%	49.1	33.1	17.8		100
	Writing					
	No.	40	42	36		118
	%	33.9	35.6	30.5		100

3. *Where Norwegian Studied*	St. Olaf College	Luther College	Con-cordia	Luther Sem	Augs-burg	
No.	44	24	11	10	5	
%	34.6	18.9	8.7	7.9	3.9	
	Other church schools	Non-church schools	In Norway	(14 dupl., 3 tripl.)		
No.	15	6	12			127
%	11.8	4.7	9.5			100

4. *Use of Norwegian*	*In preaching*	Often	Rarely	Never		
	No.	19	41	59		119
	%	16.0	34.5	49.5		100
	In private					
	No.	52	47	21		120
	%	43.3	39.1	17.5		100

5. *Youngest Age Group Still Speaking Norwegian*	*Decade of birth*	1870—9	1880—9	1890—9	1900—9	
	No.	3	8	22	27	
	%	2.8	7.5	20.3	25.2	
		1910—9	1920—9	1930—9	1940—9	
		22	14	6	5	107
		20.6	13.1	5.6	4.7	100

Table 10. Continued.

6. *Percentage of non-Norwegians in Con-gregations*	*Per-centile*	0—10	11-20	21—30	31—40	
	No.	27	11	19	17	
	%	25.5	10.4	17.8	16.0	
		41—50	51-60	61—70	71 80	
	No.	13	9	2	6	
	%	12.3	8.5	1.9	5.7	
		81—90	91—100			
	No.	2	0			106
	%	1.9	0			100

Norwegian; after starting to school, 'så kjeinja 'n ratt åver, og nå snakker 'n så broken at de ser ut såm 'n glømmer dæ nårske språk aldeles (then he changed right over, and now he talks so broken that it looks like he'll forget the Norwegian language entirely).'[13] A man born in LaCrosse County in 1873 declared that 'vi brukte dæ norske mye tell barna voks opp, og da vet je itte håssen dæ ær, men dæ bi mæssom mindre tala no enn dæ brukte på å jæra (we used Norwegian a lot until the children grew up, and then I don't know how it is, but it's as if we talk it less now than we used to).'[14] A widow in Rock County described a typical situation when she said, 'Mæ 'n Alfred levde, så tala vi nårst støtt her, men ongene svara på ængelst (while Alfred was alive, we always talked Norwegian here; but the youngsters answered in English).'[15]

This cleavage of generations, at least after 1900, was apparent also when it came to defining the occasions for talking Norwegian. A man from Mt. Morris who was born in that year spoke only Norwegian in his childhood home, but when he and his brothers started going to school, they brought English with them into the home. As an adult, he said, he spoke Norwegian only to people 'who have just come over here or who have been living where they don't talk the American language all the time.' The young people, he said, talk Norwegian only as a joke — 'and if any one from Norway heard them, it would no doubt be a joke to them too, for they wouldn't understand it anyway.'[16] In a Rock County community a young man born in 1929 claimed to be the only one of his generation who could talk the language; he enjoyed using it with older people.[17] Many informants reported using the language to certain older members of the family, especially grandparents; in the words of a young man in Spring Grove, Minnesota, 'E må snakke nårsk te ho bestemor mi (I have to talk Norwegian to my grandmother).'[18] Children sometimes pointed out that their parents had had to use parental authority to secure this result: 'Når dai snakka ængelsk mæ bore, ville ikkje far svare (when they talked English at the table, father wouldn't answer).'[19] Even at meetings of societies devoted to Norwegian matters, such as Sons of Norway, the conversation might often lapse into English unless some determined individual reminded the members of their 'duty'. One uninhibited lady member of the Sons of Norway in a Wisconsin town said: 'De er noen såm bynner litt på engels, men så sier je de åt di je, nå får vi bruke de nårske, sier je åt dom. Ja, så blir de nårsk da, og så har dem moro ta me da vet du (some start talking a little English, but then I say to them, now we'd better use Norwegian, I say to them. Well, then they talk Norwegian, and then they make fun of me, you know).'[20]

In southern Wisconsin the informants were agreed that the first World War was a turning point in the use of Norwegian; in the words of a Koshkonong resident, 'so blai de raint bortvaska mæ nårsk' (then Norwegian was quite washed away.)[21] They tended to agree with the prediction of a Spring Grove, Minnesota, man made in 1942: 'I think it will only be this generation that keeps it up. Twenty-five years from now I think there will be awfully little left.'[22]

3. *Conflict in the Church.*

The policies of the church leaders could not remain unaffected by this grass roots movement in the local communities. Many of them even encouraged it in the hope of increasing membership after the elimination of the 'foreign' atmosphere. Strong competition was being offered in many communities by non-Lutheran churches and by English Lutheran congregations. But some leaders looked beyond the immediate problem of maintaining and expanding the membership of the church to an eventual amalgamation of the Norwegian Lutheran church with other Lutheran churches. To this end a rapid effacement of the national origins was imperative. In 1926 the problem of the church name came up once more, but this time the very president (now emeritus) who had introduced the original resolution of 1918 opposed a change and it was defeated. In 1928 it was again raised, and passed by a majority which was insufficient for constitutional change (508-302).[23] Advocates of the change pointed out that the growth of the church had been greatest in those areas where the use of Norwegian had been least, e.g. in the Rocky Mountain district.[24] Opponents insisted that most members of local churches were not seriously affected by the name of the synod, and that the word 'Norwegian' ought to remain as a reminder of the historical origin of the church. They also pointed out that the Norwegian church had shown greater gains during the twenties than other Lutheran synods which lacked the 'handicap' of a foreign name.[25]

In 1934 the change was again voted, by a majority of 486 to 321, on the plea that it was 'unwise to retain an official name the use of which is avoided in many public gatherings and the appearance of which on official publications tends to hinder their distribution.'[26] But when it was proposed to make the change final in 1936, a strong reversal of feeling occurred and it was voted down 208 to 628. A resolution was even passed to postpone the change until after the centennial of the church in 1943 (vote 358-320).[27] An appeal for funds was being made, and some feared that they might not flow quite so readily from the older members if the change were pressed. But at the first biennial meeting after the centennial the matter was again raised, and on May 31, 1944, the change was adopted by a vote of 766 to 269.[28] The Church Council which proposed it declared: 'We are satisfied that the desire for this change is not born of any wish to repudiate our Norwegian heritage.' On June 13, 1946 the change to the Evangelical Lutheran Church was made final by a vote of 1,256 to 402, which was better than the two-thirds majority required.[29] As a consolation to Norwegian sentiments a paragraph was inserted in the constitution to the effect that 'The Evangelical Lutheran Church was founded by the grace of God through the zeal and labors of the Norwegian pioneers in America.' Also, a Norwegian Conference was established 'to serve as a clearing house for contacts with church leaders and educational circles in Norway'; its purposes as set forth in the Annual Report were those of a caretaker for the last remnants of Norwegian interests in the Church.[30] A bare generation had passed since the establishment of an English Association in the Church, and now it was necessary to salvage the remains of Norwegian.

Services offered by the Church as a whole reflect strongly the trend here outlined. The language of official documents was changed from Norwegian to English in 1928. The English Association was dissolved as unnecessary in 1935.[31] By 1948 only two publications in Norwegian were issued by Augsburg Publishing House, the church publishing concern, viz., a calendar and a Christmas annual. The number of copies issued of the calendar was 6,500 compared to 18,000 of a corresponding English calendar, and 6,000 of the Christmas annual, compared to 160,000 of the English one. Two official church papers were still being published; their respective circulation over the years from 1921 to 1947 appears in the accompanying Table 11. At the time of the church union in 1917

Table 11. *Circulation of Official Church Papers of the Evangelical Lutheran Church 1921—47.*

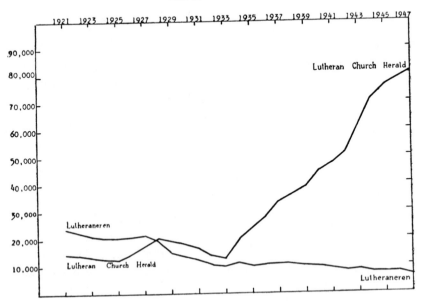

the Norwegian paper outsold the English by 3 to 1.[32] But the Norwegian one never recovered from the depression of 1929, while the English one soared to new heights during the 30's.[33]

4. *Secular Organs.*

The Church was not the only organization to feel the pressure of language change. The Sons of Norway, which was founded as a nationalistic organization, had to change the language of its chief organ to English in 1942, though it resisted pressure to change the name of the organization at the same time. In a defense of this move, the editor, Carl G. O. Hansen, wrote: 'If we insist on using the Norwegian language as our instrument, the contact with the great mass of our people will be lost. A uniting of our folk group and protection of the ancestral heritage is still among the chief tasks of Sons of Norway. Therefore we must make as much use of the language of this country as possible.' 'Paradoxical as it may sound, it can be maintained that a Norwegian activity in this country does not become any less Norwegian even if English

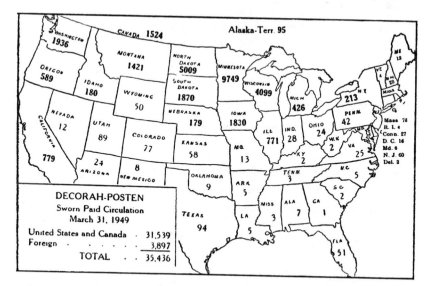

Plate 5. *Map Showing the Circulation of the Decorah-Posten by States on March 31, 1949.*

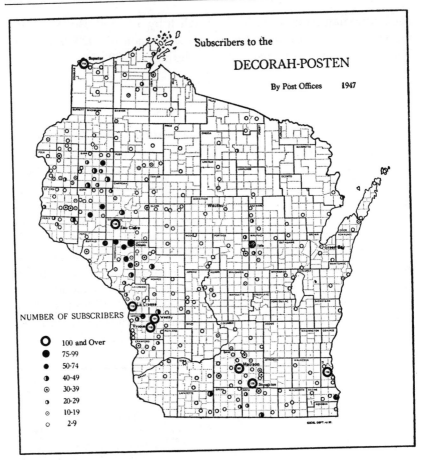

Plare 6. *Wisconsin Subscribers to the Decorah-Posten by Post Offices 1947.*

is given the place of honor; on the contrary, it can become far
more effective.'[34] Experience on the local lodge level, however,
makes it questionable whether the change to English has actually
made the organization much more acceptable to younger members.
It is held together today chiefly by the insurance feature; but the
active membership consists predominantly of those who understand
the Norwegian language.

The Norwegian-language press has had to face the same problem. At the beginning of the thirties there were three widely

circulated weeklies in the Middle West, *Decorah-Posten*, *Skandinaven*, and *Minneapolis Tidende*. By the end of the thirties only one was left. *Minneapolis Tidende* fell by the wayside in 1935, *Skandinaven* in 1941; their subscription lists were bought by *Decorah-Posten*, which carried on as the most widely circulated Norwegian-language paper in the country. Various newspapers have tried including English sections to interest the young people, or have turned entirely to English. But none of them could compete in reader appeal with the American press, and have had to give up. As long as there are people to read the original Norwegian, immigrant newspapers have something to give. But in English they appear to constitute an undesired limitation of scope.

The distribution of such a paper as *Decorah-Posten* is of interest because it identifies rather well the current attachment to the older brand of Norwegian culture. The accompanying map of the location of its subscribers (Plate 5) is almost a map of the midwestern Norwegian settlements. It must be remembered, however, that there are local organs in many of the larger urban centers which compete with it. *Nordisk Tidende* in Brooklyn commands the urban colony of the New York area, as well as a scattered countrywide clientele. Papers in Chicago, Minneapolis, Duluth, Fargo, Winnipeg, Seattle, and Vancouver draw off readers in these areas. A study of the location of *Decorah-Posten* readers in Wisconsin is also included because this is about the only secular Norwegian newspaper now being read in this state. The accompanying map of Wisconsin (Plate 6) shows that the western communities have the heaviest concentration of *Decorah-Posten* readers. The eastern and southern communities were formerly dominated by *Skandinaven* in Chicago, and many of its old subscribers probably fell away when it was sold to *Decorah-Posten*.

5. *The Tempo of Assimilation.*

The development here sketched has not been peculiar to the immigrants from Norway; a similar struggle has taken place within all of the immigrant language groups in the United States except the English. We cannot properly evaluate the significance of Norwegian behavior in this situation unless it is seen against the entire background of linguistic assimilation in the American nation. The facts on which an evaluation could be based are not yet available, and we are thrown back on popular opinion and such partial indices of behavior as we may be able to dredge up. To form an objective opinion about it is particularly difficult because of the emotions which are immediately stirred up if one suggests a comparison between different national groups. If a group is highly retentive of its language, this is seen by some as a sign of healthy pride in its heritage, while others look upon it as evidence either of sinister intent or of cultural backwardness. We have already cited expressions by Norwegian immigrant leaders implying that their countrymen were only too eager to throw their language away in favor of English; others could be cited in which they are berated for making efforts to preserve it.[35] Outside observers have expressed similarly contradictory opinions. Some have patted their Norwegian neighbors on the back for the ease with which they were assimilated, while others have accused them of being exceptionally 'clannish'.

This is essentially a sociological rather than a linguistic problem. Language is only one of the factors in the social configuration of the immigrant, though it is unique in being both a cause and a result of social differentiation. We cannot here take up the whole problem of immigrant acculturation, but confine ourselves to its linguistic aspects.[36] We may assume as obvious the fact that every national group arriving in the United States carried with it an in-group feeling of solidarity and a certain distrust of all other groups. We may also assume that no one learned English and began using it because they wanted to, but only because practical necessity forced them to. The strongest possible motive for language learning is the need of associating with the speakers of the language. Any facts we can find about linguistic retentiveness are thus in large measure bound to reflect the degree of social isolation of the group. Such social isolation can result from many factors; it can be self-imposed by a desire for religious separatism, by settling in a remote and inaccessible region, by unwillingness to acquire new social habits. It can be imposed from outside by the antagonism of other groups, or by their sense of superiority. If we know something about these factors, including the place and mode of settling, the social 'visibility' of the group, its religious forms, and the like, we may expect to find a high correlation between these and the linguistic retentiveness. Is there anything more involved? Does any group retain its language precisely because it is fond of that language, apart from the social factors mentioned above? Language did become something of a symbol in 19th century Europe, at least in some of the nations of relatively recent origin. But it seems doubtful whether we can assemble data which will be delicate enough to disentangle this factor from the others.

About the only large-scale data which can be offered as a basis for objective comparison between national groups are those presented by some of the recent censuses under the heading of 'mother tongue'.[37] In 1940 every twentieth American was asked to state the language spoken in his childhood home, other than English. Nothing was asked about the speaker's own competence or use of the language, so this is not quite the same as a census of bilinguals. But it does give us a rough index of the number and location of bilingual homes in the United States for each language brought in by European immigrants. The data are presented by states, by rural or urban residence, and by parents' place of birth.

Lowry Nelson has made an interesting attempt to discover from these data what he calls the *persistence* of each language in our culture.[38] As his chief index he has chosen the percentage of native Americans of native parentage who reported the language as their mother tongue. Thus he finds that of 658,220 Americans who reported Norwegian as their mother tongue, 232,820 were born abroad, 344,240 were born in the United States of foreign or mixed parentage, while 81,160 were born in the United States of native parents. The last figure is 12.3 % of the total for Norwegian, and so he calls this the index of persistence for that language. By calculating similar figures for other languages, he comes to the conclusion that Norwegian is three times as persistent as Swedish (4.1 %) and Danish (4.0 %). It is only about one-half as persistent as Dutch, however, with 22.9 %. The other languages more persistent than Norwegian are Spanish (38.6), French (36.7), and German (18.7). To explain these differences he proposes rural residence, religious separatism, and an indefinable factor of 'national and cultural consciousness'.

Unfortunately the index of persistence used by Nelson leads to some absurd results, such as proving that speakers of Greek, Russian, Yiddish, and Italian are the least persistent of all American groups. Even Danish is shown to be more persistent than these groups, which contradicts all experience. As Nelson himself realizes, this index is dependent in large part on the length of time a group has been in America; a group which has recently immigrated will have few third-generation members and hence a small index. Even when applied for comparison within the Scandinavian group it leads to inexact conclusions. This writer finds it contrary to his observation when Nelson concludes that Norwegian is three times as persistent as Swedish and Danish. Nelson has overlooked that Norwegians began arriving earlier in the 19th century and established compact settlements before the Swedes and the Danes arrived. Hence it is not surprising that they should have a larger third generation, and that this should be a relatively persistent group. As we shall see, this may not entirely account for the differential, but it does materially reduce it, and we should look around for a different approach. The comparison of Norwegian with Dutch does not hold either, since the figures given by Nelson are based on a misunderstanding of the word Dutch. It is clear that the Pennsylvania 'Dutch' have been included under Dutch, instead of under German where they belong. This writer strongly suspects that the same has happened in Ohio, where there are many Mennonite settlements who speak a 'Dutch' that is really German. It looks extremely suspicious that the persistence figures for Dutch in these states should be 88.5 and 65, while in the East North Central states, where nearly half the real Hollanders live, the persistence is only 18.2. Considerations like these have led the present writer to reject the index of persistence adopted by Nelson and to substitute for it a somewhat different one.

Nelson's figures tell us the proportion of third-generation bilinguals out of the whole number of foreign speakers. But what we really want to know is the proportion of foreign speakers in the third generation. As everyone realizes, this figure is unobtainable since the census does not keep track of the third generation immigrant. But we do have figures on the second generation; we know the total number and we know how many of these gave a foreign language as the language of their childhood home. By comparing these two figures we get an index of the extent to which immigrants continued to speak their language after the birth of their American children. This does not represent as long a tradition in this country as would corresponding figures for the third generation, but it does tell us something about the strength of the linguistic tradition among those who should have had the greatest interest in preserving it. Nelson gives some figures for the second generation in his Table 6, but rejects them as his main support because of certain discrepancies with his other data. In general, however, these figures agree better with the writer's experience; and the discrepancies for Dutch and French are easily explained. A breakdown of the second-generation figures for rural and urban population and for certain states is presented herewith in the following tables. In each case figures are given for the total number of second-generation immigrants and for the number of American-born foreign speakers; the ratio of the latter to the former is here called the *index of retention*. The census reports give the nationality of the immigrants in terms of the country from which they came, but their speech in terms of the language. Hence these figures can be derived only in those cases where the borders of the country and the language approximately coincide. For German an exception was made by including the figures for Austria and Switzerland; the non-German speakers in these countries were probably offset by German speakers from other European countries.

The data are presented in Tables 12—14. A study of the figures for Norway shows that the retention of the language is highest in North Dakota 66.8, followed by Minnesota 63.8, Wisconsin 62.0, Iowa 59.6, and South Dakota 58.9. All of these states are well above the national average of 52.0. The eastern and western states fall below the national average to 39.6 for Washington and 33.0 for New York; in these states, as in Michigan, the Norwegians are largely urban. The lowest figure is for Utah (16.7), where the Norwegians are mostly Mormons and hence not religiously distinct from the rest of the population. A study of the figures for urban—rural distribution shows that in every case the rural is more retentive than the urban, except in New York where there are practically no rural Norwegians. The difference is so constant that we

Table 12. *Mother Tongue of Second Generation Foreign White Stock for Selected Nationalities and States* (1940).

		Norway	Sweden	Denmark	Neth.	Germany	Austria	Poland	Finland	Italy
U. S.	Stock	662,600	856,320	305,640	261,320	3,998,840	781,340	1,912,380	167,080	2,971,200
	Language	344,240	374,040	95,460	103,240	2,435,700		1,428,820	118,460	2,080,680
	Retention	52.0	43.7	31.2	39.6	48.9*		74.8	70.7	70.2
Wisconsin	Stock	82,400	33,960	24,480	17,500	380,820	27,640	86,800	7,720	22,080
	Language	51,060	15,820	9,680	9,020	273,220		78,460	5,620	16,580
	Retention	62.0	46.7	39.5	51.6	64.3		90.3	73.0	75.2
Michigan	Stock	14,080	40,820	11,500	65,460	222,760	30,020	196,820	42,520	66,800
	Language	4,600	19,900	4,200	28,080	123,140		166,940	34,520	46,220
	Retention	32.7	48.8	36.5	42.9	46.9		84.9	81.1	69.2
Minnesota	Stock	176,940	161,960	29,560	13,020	224,660	16,360	28,640	34,100	10,860
	Language	112,620	89,280	11,080	6,160	160,780		23,660	27,840	6,900
	Retention	63.8	55.1	37.5	47.3	64.9		82.8	81.8	63.6
Iowa	Stock	35,720	34,060	27,880	24,940	183,140	4,320	2,280	160	5,500
	Language	21,220	14,460	12,640	13,480	119,180		1,220	100	3,460
	Retention	59.6	42.4	45.4	54.0	61.3		53.5	—	63.0

		1	2	3	4	5	6	7	8
S. Dakota	Stock	35,200	13,740	10,840	6,740	47,020** 1,800	1,540	1,880	540
	Language	19,580	6,240	4,440	3,120	48,660	780	1,700	220
	Retention	58.9	45.4	40.9	46.4	65.5	50.7	90.4	—
N. Dakota	Stock	75,260	16,200	5,440	1,180	34,680** 3,060	3,820	1,860	200
	Language	50,200	6,600	1,940	680	74,540	2,380	1,520	100
	Retention	66.8	40.7	35.7	57.6	80.5	60.6	81.7	—
Utah	Stock	3,000	9,100	14,400	2,660	7,160 980	160	460	3,680
	Language	500	2,180	3,320	600	2,920	60	120	2,300
	Retention	16.7	24.0	23.0	22.5	25.6	—	—	62.6
Washington	Stock	47,080	41,020	13,060	6,920	59,720 7,100	5,220	10,700	12,560
	Language	18,620	16,060	3,520	2,340	37,140	3,080	6,500	7,540
	Retention	39.6	39.1	26.9	33.9	50.3	57.8	60.7	60.0
New York	Stock	31,660	54,920	15,720	19,840	518,120 222,120	407,560	9,620	1,012,820
	Language	10,440	21,000	2,700	5,320	248,060	231,280	4,660	703,820
	Retention	33.0	38.3	17.2	26.8	32.6	57.2	48.5	69.4

* Swiss stock has everywhere been added to the German.
** South Dakota and North Dakota: the Russian stock must here be added to the German, after subtracting the number of actual Russian speakers. For South Dakota add 23,020 (24,180 — 1,160); for North Dakota add 53,660 (57,320 — 3,660).

Table 13. Mother Tongue of Second Generation Foreign White Stock for Urban and Rural Population in U. S. and Selected States (1940).

Region	Metric	Norway	Sweden	Denmark	Neth.	Germany	Austria	Poland	Finland	Italy
U.S. Urban	Stock	312,980	538,500	164,480	143,100	2,570,740	596,360	1,608,600	85,000	2,612,740
	Language	127,160	222,860	44,600	48,020	1,397,260		1,176,580	54,480	1,832,000
	Retention	40.7	41.4	27.1	33.6	42.6*		73.3	64.0	70.2
U.S. Rural Non-farm	Stock	134,660	148,360	64,380	48,120	651,360	125,680	186,000	35,140	283,100
	Language	72,080	63,100	19,120	18,320	412,380		151,420	24,420	193,300
	Retention	53.5	42.4	29.7	38.2	50.5		81.4	69.8	68.3
U. S. Rural	Stock	214,960	169,460	76,780	70,100	776,740	59,300	117,780	46,940	75,360
	Language	145,000	88,080	31,740	36,900	626,060		100,820	39,560	55,380
	Retention	67.5	52.5	41.3	52.6	70.7		85.6	84.3	73.6
Wis. Urban	Stock	30,600	14,680	12,820	8,520	214,080	17,040	60,980	2,460	18,260
	Language	14,900	6,260	5,100	3,480	145,120		53,600	1,460	13,800
	Retention	48.6	42.7	39.7	40.9	61.3		83.2	59.3	75.7
Wis. Rural Non-farm	Stock	17,980	6,920	4,860	2,840	63,640	4,200	7,740	1,480	2,440
	Language	11,500	3,020	1,620	1,700	46,220		7,200	1,180	1,820
	Retention	64.0	43.7	33.4	59.9	64.5		93.5	79.8	74.6
Wis. Rural	Stock	33,820	12,360	6,800	6,140	103,100	6,400	18,080	3,780	1,380
	Language	24,660	6,540	2,960	3,840	81,880		17,660	2,980	960
	Retention	72.9	52.9	43.5	62.6	70.7		97.8	79.8	69.6

Minn. Urban Stock	73,720	87,880	13,380	2,920	91,340	10,880	19,180	12,540	8,760	
Language	37,320	44,000	4,380	760	58,840		13,840	9,240	5,460	
Retention	50.7	50.2	32.7	26.0	55.7		72.3	73.6	62.4	
Minn. Rural Non-farm Stock	33,980	24,260	5,320	2,340	42,820	1,920	2,540	5,680	1,720	
Language	22,640	13,260	2,120	960	32,380		2,420	4,300	1,240	
Retention	66.8	54.6	39.2	41.0	70.7		95.3	75.8	72.2	
Minn. Rural Stock	69,240	49,820	10,860	7,760	90,500	3,560	6,920	15,880	380	
Language	52,660	32,020	4,580	4,440	69,560		7,400	14,300	200	
Retention	76.2	64.4	42.2	57.2	72.4		?	90.2	—	
N. Y. Urban Stock	27,700	44,380	12,160	12,380	433,180	207,960	365,220	7,500	952,440	
Language	9,620	17,260	2,000	2,440	210,780		196,580	3,500	664,760	
Retention	34.8	38.9	16.4	19.7	32.1		53.8	46.7	69.8	
N. Y. Rural Non-farm Stock	3,280	7,980	2,660	4,000	62,320	10,280	27,420	1,240	52,140	
Language	660	2,560	500	1,200	25,180		21,440	520	33,340	
Retention	20.1	32.1	18.8	30.0	33.4		78.3	41.9	63.8	
N. Y. Rural Stock	680	2,560	900	3,430	22,620	3,880	14,920	880	8,240	
Language	160	1,180	200	1,680	12,100		13,260	640	5,720	
Retention	—	46.2	—	49.0	42.5		88.9	—	69.6	

* Figures for Switzerland have everywhere been added to the German stock.

may consider this as a reliable index of the influence of rural settlement. It applies equally to other foreign groups excepting the Italians (of the ones here studied); in their case the overwhelming numbers of their urban settlements have permitted a social isolation in spite of the dispersing trend of urban life.

A comparison of Norwegians with other Scandinavians confirms their greater retentiveness, but reduces the difference to the ratio

Table 14. *Mother Tongue of Second Generation Foreign White Stock for all Nationalities not from the British Isles for U. S. and Selected States (1940).*

U. S.	Stock	19,134,400
	Language	10,976,540
	Retention	57.4
N. Y.	Stock	3,490,080
	Language	1,957,020
	Retention	55.3
Wisconsin	Stock	845,460
	Language	525,740
	Retention	62.5
Minnesota	Stock	847,220
	Language	501,980
	Retention	59.3
Washington	Stock	319,340
	Language	113,760
	Retention	35.6

5:4:3 for Norway, Sweden, and Denmark respectively. If we turn to the different states we find that this ratio holds approximately for the Midwestern states studied. But it does not hold at all for the other states, New York, Washington, Utah, and Michigan; in these the Swedish group is either the same as the Norwegian (Washington) or slightly more retentive. In Washington where both groups are recent and urban, they are almost exactly the same both in numbers and retentiveness; in the other states, where the Swedes are more numerous, they are also more retentive. The Danes, who are regularly fewer than the others in number, are also regularly less retentive. A further comparison of rural and urban shows that Norwegians are more rural in stock and that this almost wholly accounts for the difference in retentiveness. Throughout the country urban Norwegians are actually slightly less retentive: 40.7 to the Swedish 41.4 (the latter are considerably more numerous). In urban Minnesota, where the numbers are comparable, the index is almost exactly the same: 50.7 Norwegian vs. 50.2 Swedish. In urban New York the Swedes have something of an edge: 38.9 to the Norwegian 34.8 (they are again more numerous). It is true that the Norwegian rural stock is markedly more retentive than the Swedish rural stock, which largely accounts for the national difference. But this is due to the historical fact mentioned above that in all the midwestern states here included, the Norwegians came first and settled compactly in rural settlements to a much greater extent than the Swedes. The Swedes were more highly urbanized before emigration than the Norwegians; the Danish were more urbanized (and urbane) than either of the others.

A comparison with the other Germanic language groups shows figures that are not too different from those for Norwegian and Swedish. Dutch appears to lie at about the same level as Swedish, while German is more comparable to Norwegian. The fact that the figures rise sharply for the languages of more recent immigration from eastern and southern Europe probably reflects the greater difficulty of assimilation faced by these peoples. Anglo-Saxon Americans have been less willing to accept them; their languages are more remote from English; and the tremendous numbers in which especially the Poles and Italians have immigrated have made it possible for them to create self-contained groups even in the cities. But there is also the additional factor that the group as a whole is more recent and therefore has been less anglicized, so that the influence toward English is less strong within the group than among those who have lived longer in this country.

In Canada the problem is not quite the same as in the United States, but the development has been similar enough so that it is worth while to cast a glance across the border and see what their statistics report. In the census of 1931 Canadian census takers gathered data about foreign ancestry (which they called 'racial origin'), country of birth, mother tongue, religion, and wife's

Table 15. *Language spoken by Population 10 Years or Over by National Origin, Canada (1931).*

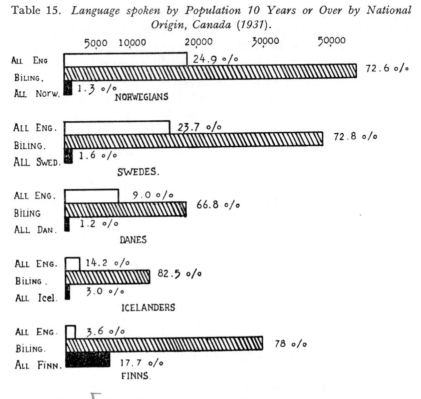

nationality.[39] The Norwegians and Swedes in Canada showed almost identical linguistic retentiveness: 46.8 for Norwegian, 46.9 for Swedish. The number of each stock and the percentage born in Canada were also very similar. But as in the United States the Danes, although more recent in their arrival, were also less retentive: only 28.1 used their mother tongue. An interesting contrast was formed by the Icelanders, who were numerous enough to appear in the statistics. Although 73.6 % were born in Canada, and the size of the stock was no larger than the Danish (12,684 to 12,776), the linguistic retentiveness was 76.2. Here there can be no doubt that a fierce pride of national culture has operated to keep alive the mother tongue. This difference is reflected also in the figures for monolinguals and bilinguals in the various groups, as presented in Table 15. The percentage which has given up the native language entirely is highest among the Danes (29.0), next-highest among the Norwegians (24.9) and Swedes (23.7), lowest among the Icelanders (14.2). This scale of assimilation is confirmed by the figures on marriage and religion. The percentage of males who have married girls of their own group (in which is here included other Scandinavians as well) runs as follows: Icelandic 61.8, Norwegian 56.8, Swedish 50.7, Danish 43.7. The percentage who still belong to the Lutheran church are: Icelandic 77.2, Norwegian 73.6, Swedish 62.3, Danish 55.4.

Figures for other stocks than the Scandinavian show a markedly higher retentiveness in Canada. The Germans run almost as high as the Icelanders in language (62.5) and higher in in-group marriage (72.5). The Poles are 72.6 linguistically retentive, marry 78.6 within their group, and retain their Catholicism to the extent of 85.4. The Italians are retentive to a percentage of 77.5 in language, 78.0 in marriage, and 93.4 in religion. The Finns top them all by being 87.0 retentive in language, 88.9 in marriage, and 88.3 in religion. The figures on bilingualism show only 3.6 % of the Finns who had given up their language in 1931, although 33.3 % of them were born in Canada.

It is not easy to draw any very significant conclusions from figures which include such large numbers and few factors as those for the United States and Canada. It appears that linguistic retentiveness is correlated with such factors as rural, i.e. isolated settlement; recency of arrival; size of group; religious separatism; social visibility. But exceptions occur to all of these factors to such an extent that it is not always easy to see just why a given nationality should be placed where it is in the scale. The consistent difference between Icelanders and Danes suggests that cultural differences existing before immigration must be taken into account. The scale within the Scandinavian countries corresponds roughly to one of urbanization: the Icelanders are less urban than the Norwegians etc. It also corresponds to one of national feeling, if such a factor can be compared: the Icelanders are more nationalistic than the Norwegians etc. Along the same line of reasoning one may say that Poles, Italians, and Finns are more rural and more nationalistic than the Scandinavians proper.

It is obvious that such conclusions would be more convincing and concrete if they were bolstered by studies of local communities where various ethnic groups could be directly compared. A few attempts have been made in this direction, but much remains to be done. A study by John and Ruth Useem of Norwegians in South Dakota and Iowa showed the usual marked distinction in linguistic retention between rural and urban residents; but in spite of much superficial acculturation, the Norwegians did not appear to them to be assimilated. Without having been inferior economically or socially, they still retained many of their traditional value patterns.[40] A comparative study of Norwegians, Welshmen, and Poles in the Wild Rose area of Minnesota by Douglas Marshall showed that 'the Norwegians are making a greater effort to retain their identity than any of the other groups.'[41] A doctoral analysis of the American, German, and Norwegian stock in certain areas of Wisconsin showed that the Germans conformed to a traditional pattern of living in a much higher degree than the more individualistic Norwegians.[42] Norwegians were found to be quick to adopt the agricultural folkways of the American stock. In spite of this, a poll of the agricultural agents in various areas of the state ranked the Norwegians above the Germans in 'clannishness'. But the Germans made a more determined effort to keep the boys on the farm. Studies by Peter A. Munch of the loyalty patterns of Norwegians in rural and small town areas of Wisconsin have also brought out very clearly the way in which these longsettled communities have maintained a close-knit social system in which kinship, religion, and common linguistic backgrounds have contributed to raise barriers between Norwegians and 'outsiders'.[43] But a study of certain Wisconsin Czech communities shows that the retention of language and other ingroup patterns was even higher than among the Norwegians.[44] The studies of Lester Seifert in Wisconsin German communities also seem to show a more determined effort to maintain the language than among Norwegians.

6. *Persisting Loyalties.*

The picture we have here given of a linguistic group in dissolution and rapid flight from its old traditions must not be allowed to obscure the fact that many individuals within the group show an interest, even an enthusiasm for the Norwegian language which persists well beyond the general extinction of practical use for the language. Such individuals do not show up in statistical tables, but they may often be quite conspicuous in the cultural life of their communities. Some of them volunteer for college and university classes in Norwegian even when their study has no apparent financial reward. Others seize opportunities to visit the ancestral land, urged by some obscure sense of loyalty, perhaps only a curiosity because of the narrative of some grandparent. Very seldom does this interest develop into a truly significant command of either Norwegian language or culture; at best it is a hobby or even just a dream. This, too, will eventually be dispersed, but in the meanwhile it represents a substantial enrichment of American life.

In large parts of America it is more or less taken for granted that each person has a particular national ancestry. It is a phenomenon scarcely understood in the solid South or other predominantnantly Anglo-Saxon communities that Americans can ask one another: 'What's your nationality?' Even if the answer is 'Norwegian', this does not connote anything more than ancestry. It does not suggest any form of disloyalty, only what might be called a sub-loyalty. This sub-loyalty is not to Norway, but to the other 'Norwegians' in America. The one who thus claims to be 'Norwegian' often cannot talk the language and knows even less about the country. But he has a vivid sense of belonging to a socioreligious group most of whose members are of the same stock.

Those few who have become sufficiently literate to find effective expression for this feeling have revealed some of the interesting facets of immigrant adjustment. Borghild Dahl, a Minneapolis writer, has told in her autobiography about the Norwegian stories which she heard in her childhood. 'I was only a very little girl,' she writes, 'when I began to wish for the day when I might visit this fairyland in the far North from which my parents had come.'[45] When she was studying at the University of Minnesota, her mother remarked, 'Why do you study so many languages and yet never think any more about the one that belongs to your own people?' Spurred by this remark, she took up the study of the Norwegian classics and 'found that I was doing much more than pleasing my mother by studying Norwegian literature at college.'[46]

Another writer, Joran Birkeland, tells about her childhood

sense of shame and inferiority at being Norwegian.[47] She did her utmost to escape from her background, the little town in Montana and the home where her immigrant parents had created her 'divided roots'. But when the occasion arrived to visit Norway after she had reached adulthood, she felt subtly and comfortably at home in the country, and a feeling welled up which came from deeply imbedded childhood memories she hardly even suspected she had harbored. Another such American-born wanderer who discovered an unexpected attachment to the Norwegian landscape is the poet and publicist Ted Olson. For him it was a childhood home in Wyoming which came back when he first saw Norway:

> Strange to have come so far
> And found a land not strange, a race
> Not alien, but familiar
> And intimate, and precious, and my own.
> Surely I must have known
> This gaunt and granite place
> Of wild green rivers, blue ice, and luminous night
> Since birth, and claim it now of my own right
> As heritage. This sinewy speech I know
> Although the words are new....[48]

Note: Abbreviations are explained in Appendix 2.

FOOTNOTES TO VOLUME I.

Chapter 1.

THE BILINGUAL'S DILEMMA.

[1] Cf. Marcus Lee Hansen, The Atlantic Migration, 1607-1860 (Cambridge, Massachusetts, 1941).

[2] Sixteenth Census of the United States: 1940. Population. Nativity and Parentage of the White Population. Mother Tongue, 2 (Washington 1943).

[3] Peter Kalm, Travels in North America, ed. A. B. Benson, 2.687-9 (New York, 1934).

[4] Lloyd Warner and Leo Srole, The Social Systems of American Ethnic Groups, 224 (New Haven, Connecticut, 1945).

[5] Lowry Nelson, Rural Sociology, 202 (New York, 1948).

[6] Hermann Paul, Prinzipien der Sprachgeschichte, 338 (2 auf., Halle, 1886): 'Die meiste Veranlassung zur Mischung ist gegeben, wo es Individuen gibt, die doppelsprachig sind, mehrere Sprachen neben einander sprechen oder mindestens eine andere neben ihrer Muttersprache verstehen.'

[7] Cf. Michael West, Bilingualism, 17 (Calcutta, 1926): '..the small language or dialect is the natural and most important distinguishing feature of the small group. ...Of all instruments for the intensification of group individuality, language is undoubtedly the most powerful.'

[8] Cf. L. Bloomfield, in Language, 25.1: 'This distinction (viz., between dialect and cultural borrowing) cannot always be carried out, since there is no absolute distinction to be made between dialect boundaries and language boundaries.'

[9] Hugo Schuchardt-Brevier (ed. Spitzer), 424.

[10] L. Ronjat, Le développement du langage observé chez un enfant bilingue (Paris, 1913). See Michael West, Bilingualism, 59, note 2 (Calcutta, 1926): 'Louis Ronjat uses either language with equal facility in ordinary conversation, but in technical matters he uses French, whereas for literary self-expression he turns to German.'

[11] Scribner's, 68.219-21 (1920).

[12] Cit. by O. Springer in JEGP 42.2 from Ellis, On Early English pronunciation, 652-3 (London, 1871).

[13] Gunnar J. Malmin, ed., America in the Forties, The Letters of Ole Munch Ræder, 33-35 (Minneapolis, 1929).

[14] See bibliography in the writer's article Problems of linguistic research among Scandinavian immigrants in America, Bulletin No. 34 of the American Council of Learned Societies (Washington, 1942).

[15] See bibliography in Otto Springer, The Study of the Pennsylvania German Dialect, in JEGP 42.1-39 (1943).

[16] See footnote 14 above.

[17] A bibliography of bilingual studies is in preparation, which will include full information about these contributions.

[18] The present study was foreshadowed by the writer's article, Language and Immigration in NASR 10.1-43 (1938), and his book, Norsk i Amerika (Oslo, 1939).

Chapter 2.

NORWEGIAN MIGRATION TO AMERICA.

[1] The chief authority on Norwegian immigration to the United States is the brilliant two-volume work by Dean Theodore C. Blegen, Norwegian Migration to America (Northfield, Minnesota, 1931, 1940). For additional studies of the Norwegian background of immigration see Arne Skaug, Norwegian Emigration, Its Fluctuations compared with Fluctuations in Migration from Other Countries since 1900 (stencilled volume); Ingrid Semmingsen, Veien mot Vest, 2 vol. (Oslo, 1941, 1950). An annual bibliography by Jacob Hodnefield has appeared since 1930 in the volumes of NASR.

[2] Knud Langeland, Nordmændene i Amerika, 122-3 (Chicago, 1888).

[3] For details see Karen Larsen, History of Norway, 431ff. (New York, 1948).

[4] Dølen, 14. January 1866.

[5] I. Ferenczi, International Migrations, 1.747ff. (New York, 1929).

[6] Reprinted in Anderson FC 70-5.

[7] The Norwegian statistics are gathered in Utvandringsstatistikk (Oslo, 1921), a publication of the Norwegian Statistical Bureau; see also I. Ferenczi, op. cit. The American statistics are from the Census of 1940.

[8] The estimate in the National Origins Act of 1924 (effective 1930) that Norwegian stock constituted 1.5 per cent of the population in 1920 is probably too low; this would make the actual number in 1940, 1,975,039. For other estimates see O. M. Norlie, HNPA 312.

[9] North American Review, 155.529 (1892).

[10] See Ørnulf Ødegaard, Emigration and Insanity (Copenhagen, 1932).

[11] Dr. J. S. Johnson in Valdris Helsing, 7.80 (1905).

[12] Information Please Almanac, 761 (1948).

[13] For details see Blegen NM 2.517ff.

[14] The fullest account of the N-A press is by Carl G. O. Hansen in Norsk-Amerikanernes Festskrift 1914 (Decorah, Iowa, 1914).

[15] See Theodore Jorgenson and Nora O. Solum, Ole Edvart Rölvaag, a Biography (New York, 1939). Surveys of N-A literature are found in Blankner, The History of the Scandinavian Literatures (New York, 1938), 74-84, and in Blegen NM 2.585ff.

[16] The publications of the NAHA include the series of N-A Studies and Records, as well as a considerable number of monographs, texts, and translations; those' published before 1938 will be found listed in the pamphlet A Review and a Challenge (Northfield, Minn., 1938).

[17] For sympathetic treatments of the language problem by students of immigration see esp. Leonard Covello in F. J. Brown and J. S. Roucek, Our Racial and National Minorities, 681-9 (New York, 1937); Everett V. Stonequist, The Marginal Man, 83-95 (New York, 1937); Theodore C. Blegen, NM 2.69-99.

Chapter 3.

THE LEARNING OF ENGLISH.

[1] By Syver Holland; see the writer's article in NASR, 15.1-19 (1944).

[2] See the excellent discussion in Blegen, NM 2.72-4.

[3] See Blegen, NM 1.255, for titles and quotations from some of the earliest manuals.

[4] Ole Rynning's Truthful Account of America, tr. and ed. by Theodore C. Blegen, 90 (Minneapolis, Minnesota, 1926).

[5] Blegen, NM 2.286.

[6] Nordlyset, 1.19 (December 30, 1847).

[7] Nordlyset, 1.34 (April 13, 1848).

[8] Friheds-Banneret, 1.20 (March 5, 1853).

[9] See L. M. Larson, Skandinaven, Professor Anderson, and the Yankee School, in The Changing West and Other Essays, 116-46 (Northfield, Minnesota, 1937).

[10] See Blegen, NM 2.73, for details.

[11] Niels Iverson Viche, 20. November 1842, in Rene HUV, 193.

[12] Janson, Hvad jeg har oplevet, 180 (Oslo, 1913).

[13] Friheds-Banneret, 1.13 (January 15, 1853).

[14] Friheds-Banneret, 1.20 (March 5, 1853).

[15] Symra (Decorah, Iowa), 10.151 (1914).

[16] Cf. Einar Haugen, Norwegians at the Indian Forts on the Missouri River During the Seventies, NASR 6.89-121 (1931).

[17] Helgeson FIL, 1.230.

[18] Helgeson FIL, 1.180.

[19] Helgeson FIL, 1.295.

[20] Informant 20F16.

[21] Joran Birkeland, Birchland, 13-15 (New York, 1939).

[22] Cf. Blegen NM, 2.100-130.

[23] Cf. J. M. Rohne, Norwegian-American Lutheranism up to 1872, 32-8 (New York, 1926).

[24] 12Q2.

[25] Cf. M. Kimmerle in AmSp, 1942, 160.

[26] 5L1.

[27] 11C2.

[28] 20P2 (letter).

[29] 9A2.

[30] 11C2.

[31] 17Q3.

[32] 20P2 (letter).

[33] 14C2.

[34] A Study of Norwegian Dialect in Minnesota, AmSp, 5.469-74 (1930).

[35] On the pronunciation 'ager' see L. Krueger in WMH, 29.333ff. (1946).

[36] See Davis and McDavid, 'Shivaree' AmSp, 24.249-55 (1949).

[37] Frederic G. Cassidy, Some New England Words in Wisconsin, Language, 17.324-39 (1941).

[38] Chicago, 1874; review by R. B. Anderson in Skand. 3 Nov. 1874/2/5.

[39] See Blegen NM, 1.255-6, 2.85; one guidebook not mentioned by Blegen is the useful and popular Udvandrerens Tolk (by A. T. Boyesen, according to Halvorsens's Norsk Forfatter-Lexikon), which first appeared in the 1860's and reached its ninth printing by 1888 (64 p.). As the author had spent some years in America in the late 50's, the sentences reflect conditions rather well, but certain turns of phrase and phonetic inaccuracies reveal his imperfect command of English.

[40] Louis Pio and Co., Chicago, 1879.

[41] Chicago, 1882. 8. thousand, Chicago, 1907.

[42] Chicago, 1882.

[43] Minneapolis, Minnesota, 1892.

[44] Martin Ulvestad, Engelsk-dansk-norsk Ordbog (Chicago, 1895); Svend Rosing, Engelsk-dansk Ordbog (4 ed., Copenhagen, 1874).

[45] Chicago, 1909. 4th ed., 1916.

[46] Johan Schrøder, Skandinaverne i de Forenede Stater og Canada, 132 (La Crosse, Wisconsin, 1867).

[47] Kort Udsigt over det Lutherske Kirkearbeide blandt Nordmændene i Amerika 828 (Chicago, 1898).

Chapter 4.

THE CONFUSION OF TONGUES.

[1] Gunnar J. Malmin, ed., America in the Forties, 33-5 (Minneapolis, 1929).

[2] Cf. examples in Blegen, NM 2.84; Rene, HUV 124-9; see discussion below.

[3] N. R. Østgaard in Blegen and Ruud, NESB 212.

[4] O. F. Duus, Frontier Parsonage, 28-9 (Ed. Blegen, Northfield, Minnesota, 1947).

[5] From the original ms., lent me by the kindness of Dr. Peter A. Munch.

[6] Skandinaverne i Amerika, 233-4 (La Crosse, Wisconsin, 1867).

[7] According to Halvorsen's Forfatter-Lexikon first printed in Aftenbladet 1860, No. 133-167; here cited from the 7. ed., Christiania, 1907.

[8] Op. cit., 80-81.

[9] Trangviksposten, Tredie Samling, 53 (Oslo, Norway).

[9a] Bjørnstjerne Bjørnson, Samlede Verker 6, 131-4 (Oslo, 1932).

[10] Peter Bendow, Det var dengang da, 157 (Oslo, 1935).

[11] H. J. S. Astrup, Blik paa amerikanske Forhold, 77 (Kristiania, 1893).

[12] Valdreser i Amerika, 66 (Minneapolis, 1922).

[13] Absalon Taranger, Inntrykk fra Amerika, 18 (Oslo, 1927).

[14] Thoralv Klaveness, Det norske Amerika, 114ff (Kristiania, 1904).

[15] Intime Forums 10-aars jubileumshefte, 19 (Brooklyn, N.Y.).

[16] S. Sondresen, Norsk-amerikanerne, 146 (Bergen, 1938).

[17] 25P3.

[18] 12R5.

[19] 11R1.

[20] 13N1.

[21] Amerika-breve fra P. A. Smevik til hans far og bror i Norge samlet ved Paal Mørck, 33-4 (Minneapolis, 1912).

[22] 4P1.

[23] 6Q3.

[24] 6Q1.

[25] 6Q3.

[26] 4P1.

[27] 4H1.

[28] Dialect Notes 2. 115-36 (1900).

[29] 4F2.

[30] 6P1.

[31] 4L1.

[32] 6Q3.

[33] 5H1.

[34] 6Q3, 8F1, 14D4, 4F1, 5H4 etc.

[35] 20P2 (letter); 8G1.

[36] 12R6.

[37] 12Q2.

[38] 14L1.

[39] 4Q3.

[40] 4P3.

[41] 5F1; 8L3; 8F1.

[42] 15P4.

[43] 6Q3.

[44] 15P4.

[45] 20Q2.
[46] 12R1.
[47] 8F1; also 4K1.
[48] 10C1.
[49] 6P4.
[50] 6P2.
[51] 9Q1.
[52] 15P1.
[53] 8C2.
[54] 8L3 (wife).
[55] 19A1.
[56] Anders Sylteviken in Numedalslagets aarbok Nr. 7 (1921). For other printed samples of AmN in the exaggerated style see J. Meiraak in Norroena, 2.26 (1901); Jan Barvaag, Ibid., 31; C. N. Remme, Brev til Guri Busterud fra Olava Kampen, Trondhjemsk-amerikansk, 273-5, Samband 1912; K. G. N(ilsen), Eksempel paa Amerika-Norsk, Østerdølslagets Aarbok 1925-6, 129.
[57] There are others which involve meanings not ordinarily heard in polite society; fit v., pool v., sheet n.
[58] 5E1.
[59] 20P2 (letter).
[60] 5E1.
[61] Brev fraa Gullik Uphaug, Valdris Helsing 13.45-6.
[62] 5E1.
[63] H. Meltzer, Til og fra Amerika (here cit. from Smaabilleder fra Livet, p. 347).
[64] 5E1.
[65] 5E1.
[66] 11C1; 3C1.
[67] 5L4; 11C4; 4H1; 6Q4.
[68] A. A. Veblen, Svall om sproget o rettskrivningen, Valdris Helsing 26.59-64 (1909).
[69] Einar Haugen, Language and Immigration, NASR 10.1-43 (1938).
[70] Northfield, Minnesota, 1940; pp. 69-99.

Chapter 5.

THE GREAT VOCABULARY SHIFT.

[1] Dialect Notes 2.115-19.
[2] Cf. E. Haugen, Language and Immigration, NASR 10.23 (1938).
[3] Cf. Aasen NO.
[4] Valdris Helsing No. 26, 59-64 (December, 1909).

⁵ On *parlor* and *living room* see Raven I. McDavid Jr. in Social Forces 25.171 (1946).

⁶ Valdris Helsing No. 26, 59-64. (December, 1909)

⁷ Cf. Blegen NM 2.175ff.

⁸ Blegen NM 2.190.

⁹ Ingeborg Hoff (Skjetvemålet 107, fn. 2) reports *norske* m. from Ytre Østfold, Aage Eifring from Hedmark (oral communication); the word does not appear in NRO or any dialect dictionary.

¹⁰ Cf. Pap P-AS 175, fn. 50.

¹¹ In NASR 10.33.

¹² In O. Springer, Study of PaGer Dialect, JEGP 42.20-1 (1943).

¹³ Dialect Notes 2.115-19.

Chapter 6.

THE TRADITION OF WRITING.

¹ NG² i.

² Cf. Torstein Høverstad, Norsk Skulesoga, 2v. (Oslo, 1918, 1930).

³ Statistiske Tabeller vedkommende Underviisningsvæsenets Tilstand i Norge ved Udgangen af Aaret 1840 (Christiania, 1843).

⁴ Beretning om Skolevæsenets Tilstand...for Aaret 1870 (Christiania 1873).

⁵ Beretning om Skolevæsenets Tilstand...for Aarene 1861-3 (Christiania 1866).

⁶ Op. cit., 120.

⁷ See accounts by Herman Ruge in Norsk Kulturhistorie 4.419-50 (Oslo, 1940); W. Keilhau, NFLH 9.259-67 (Oslo, 1931); E. Høygaard and Herman Ruge, Den norske skoles historie (Oslo, 1947).

⁸ Rohne NAL 131.

⁹ Emigranten 24 Dec. 1852.

¹⁰ NM 2.241-76; see also L. M. Larson CW 116 ff.

¹¹ Stephenson, Religious Aspects of Swedish Immigration, 410 (Minneapolis, Minn., 1932).

¹² Annual Report 1918, 515.

¹³ O. M. Norlie's School Calender 1824-1924 (Minneapolis 1924) includes biographies of many parochial school teachers; other references to the religious school may be found in Rohne NAL 71, 122, 130; Knut Takla, Det norske folk i de Forenede Stater 222-4 (Kristiania, 1913); S. Sondresen, Norsk-amerikanerne 100-4 (Oslo, 1938); Norlie HNPA 215-6; Holand CP 110-4; Holand CV 152-7; Knut Rene, Vossingen 5.1.13-14, 5.2.23-7 (1923); Osm. Aslakson, Symra 10.253-60 (1914).

¹⁴ Beretning om Skolevæsenets Tilstand 1869, 1870.

¹⁵ Sondresen NA 102.

16   Clara Jacobsen in Symra 9.120-37 (1913).
17   15P3; cf. Sondresen NA 103.
18   12R6.
19   Ager, Paa Veien til Smeltepotten 18 (Eau Claire, 1917).
20   Omkring Fædrearven 72 (Northfield, Minn., 1922).
21   D. G. Ristad in Fra pioner-presternes saga 181 (Decorah, 1931); other
     stories in this collection illustrate misunderstandings of the words
     svoger 'brother-in-law' (190) and *guder* 'gods' (142).
22   Here cited from R. Nygaard, Fra Dansk-norsk til Norsk Riksmål 32
     (Oslo, 1945).
23   Cf. esp. his essay Om Norskhed i vor Tale og Skrift in Lange's Norsk
     Tidsskrift for Videnskab og Litteratur 4.205-316 (Chra., 1850).
24   Cf. Peter Skautrup, Det danske Sprogs Historie 1.258 (Copenhagen, 1944).
25   Lange's NTVL 4.206.
26   Norske Huldre-Eventyr og Folkesagn, 3 ed., 146 (Chra., 1870); Skole-
     bladet 1900, 140.
27   Aftenposten 1892, No. 10; here cit. from Nygaard, op. cit., 68; cf. also
     Nygaard 36.
28   Maanedstidende for den norske Almueskole. 1ste Aargang (1861).
29   Op. cit., 58.
30   Op. cit., 74.
31   Op. cit., 120.
32   Op. cit., 179.
33   See Nygaard, op. cit., 22.
34   Forsøg til en videnskabelig dansk retskrivningslære (Copenhagen, 1826);
     cf. D. A. Seip, Norskhet i Sproget hos Wergeland og hans Samtid (Kra.,
     1914), 71.
35   Seip, op. cit., 74; Nygaard, op. cit., 74.
36   Nygaard, 36; Burgun 2.96.
37   A. Burgun, Le développement linguistique en Norvège 2.193 (Oslo, 1921).
38   Nygaard, 72.
39   A. C. Preus, Nogle Ord angaaende min ABC, Emigranten 26. August
     1857/2/5-6.
40   Copies of these books available in Luther College Library.
41   Decorah, Iowa, 1880-81.
42   Printed in Holand NSH 262-3.
43   Photographed for the writer by Peter A. Munch at the Norwegian-
     American Historical Museum in Decorah, Iowa.
44   Printed in Rene HUV 108, 124ff.; compared by the writer with the ori-
     ginals.
45   Einar Haugen, The Impact of English on American-Norwegian Letter
     Writing. Studies in Honor of Sturtevant 76-102 (University of Kansas,
     1952).
46   Cf. Aars, Retskrivnings-regler 1878, 8.
47   Hans Bergersen, Morsmålsoplæringen 51-121 (Oslo, 1935).

⁴⁸ Cf. Bjørset, Syd-Lesje og Nord-Dovre 11; Storm-Skulerud, Ordlister 57; Ross NB 1907, 43.

⁴⁹ Cf. Am. B. Larsen, Solørmaalets Lydlære 152; Hogstad, Elverum 35.

⁵⁰ For a more detailed treatment of this subject see the writer's article, The Impact of English on Norwegian-American Letter Writing (see fn. 45). Unfortuately en error in counting led to incorrect totals in the article for the number of lws.: on page 81 the number of distinct words should have been 229, the nouns 156, the stems 97, the derivatives 22, and the compounds 37, as will appear from the lists there given.

⁵¹ Quoted in full: (a) Inclost one Daller Bill $1.00 som betaling for Decorah Posten for 6 månt. Posten er von of de best blade i Amerika vot de siger er sant vi vilde blive glade om de vilde tage op merre Legislatur arbeide fra Minnesota. (b) der frend wil dere putte dise or ind in decoraposten om min fader. ei naa det er mange som naa him.

⁵² From the story Gamlinger in Lilje-Gunda og andre fortællinger (Oslo, 1919).

Chapter 7.

THE LITERARY LANGUAGE.

¹ Nordmands-Forbundet 18.219-27 (1925).

² Blegen NM 2.277-330.

³ Nordlyset 2.40 (23 Feb. 1850).

⁴ Nos. 6, 12, 18, 24.

⁵ Nordlyset 1.1 (29 July 1847).

⁶ For a general discussion of the contents of Nordlyset see the writer's article in Decorah-Posten 21 August 1947.

⁷ Nordlyset 1.1.

⁸ Nordlyset 1.23 (7 Jan. 1848).

⁹ Nordlyset 1.21.

¹⁰ Friheds-Banneret 1.1 (4 Oct. 1852).

¹¹ Emigranten 2.10 (20 May 1853).

¹² All examples in this section from Nordlyset.

¹³ Emigranten 2.9.

¹⁴ Ibid. 1.42.

¹⁵ Ibid. 2.13.2.1.

¹⁶ Ibid. 2.11.

¹⁷ Ibid. 2.10.

¹⁸ Ibid. 2.11.

¹⁹ L. K. Mørstad, D-P 7 Jan. 1930/3/6.

²⁰ D-P 9 Jan. 1900.

²¹ D-P 12 Jan. 1900/1/3.

²² D-P 18 March 1930.

[23] D-P 18 February 1930.
[24] D-P 11 Feb., 18 March 1930.
[25] D-P 24 Dec. 1929.
[26] O. Bogstad, 14 Jan. 1930; O-t., 28 Jan. 1930; E. Omdahl 24 Dec. 1929.
[27] D-P 11 Feb. 1930.
[28] Norsk-amerikansk Haandbog 25 (Chicago, 1879).
[29] Cf. the study of language usage in Nordisk Tidende advertisements for 1947 in Inga Wilhelmsen Allwood and others, The Norwegian-American Press and Nordisk Tidende (Mullsjö, Sweden, 1950).
[30] The only previous study of the Norwegian of the immigrant press is contained in George T. Flom's article, Um det norske målet i Amerika in Norsk Aarbok 1931, 113-24.
[31] No study of the teaching of Norwegian in the Lutheran colleges has been made; for some comments see Jorgenson and Solum, Ole Edvart Rölvaag, a Biography (New York, 1939).
[32] Einar Haugen, Wisconsin Pioneers in Scandinavian Studies, in WMH 34.28-39 (1950).
[33] Norsk-Amerikanernes Festskrift 1914, 334-5; see also George T. Flom, A History of Scandinavian Studies in American Universities (Iowa City, Iowa, 1907) and Esther C. Meixner, Scandinavian Studies in American Universities (Philadelphia, 1941).
[34] Cf. George T. Flom, Norwegian Language and Literature in American Universities NASR 2.78-103 (1927); for information on the present situation, see surveys by Hedin Bronner and Gösta Franzén in SS 19.239-60 (1947) and 23.173-98 (1951).
[35] Chicago, 1872. 202p.; cf. reviews in Skandinaven 26 June 1872/1/8; Fædrelandet og Emigranten 25 July 1872/2/8, 22 August 1872/4/6 (un-favorable), 29 August 1872/2/5.
[36] Chicago; Christiania, 1876.
[37] O. M. Peterson, A First Reader in Norwegian, 11 (Chicago, 1885).
[38] Chicago, 1898; J. Y. Sargent, Grammar of the Dano-Norwegian Language (Oxford, 1892); Peter Groth, Dano-Norwegian Grammar (New York, 1894).
[39] Chicago, 1905; 2. ed. 1912; 3. ed., Minneapolis, 1918.
[40] O. E. Rölvaag og P. J. Eikeland, Norsk Læsebok. (3 vols., Minneapolis, 1919-25); Jonas Lie, Lodsen og hans hustru, ed. w. introd., notes and vocab. by Nils Flaten (Minneapolis, Minn., 1924).
[41] Einar Haugen, Beginning Norwegian (New York, 1937).
[42] Einar Haugen, Reading Norwegian (New York, 1940); Spoken Norwegian (New York, 1946); see the writer's From Army Camp to Classroom, the Story of an Elementary Language Text, SS 23.138-51 (1951).
[43] Skand 12 May 1874/2/6.
[44] Decorah, Iowa, 1902.
[45] For a discussion of some major differences in the spelling see the writer's Spoken Norwegian 238 and Reading Norwegian 171.

[46] Symra 7.128 (1911).
[47] The letters were made available to me by Prestgard himself.
[48] Letter of July 8, 1913.
[49] Letter of Oct. 8, 1913.
[50] Minneapolis Tidende 2 Oct. 1913/5/5.
[51] Symra 10.19-26, 58-67 (1914).
[52] Op. cit., 60.
[53] See the Annual Report of 1917, pp. 379 and 600, for the recommendation of the Publishing Committee and the action of the Church meeting.
[54] Changed to Latin type, small caps, 1907 spelling on September 20, 1934.
[55] The change took place in the issue of 12 July 1939.
[56] Lutheraneren 39.587 (23 August 1939).
[57] Lutheraneren 39.549-50 (2 August 1939).
[58] Cf. Luth. 39.613 (30. August 1939), 39.843 (29 Nov. 1939).
[59] Figures from Annual Report 1948 of the Evangelical Lutheran Church (Minneapolis, Minn., 1948), p. 333.
[60] See Einar Haugen, Reading Norwegian, 171-2 (N.Y., 1940), for a more complete list.
[61] Private communication from the editorial staff.
[62] The only exception was Chr. Krug's Dyrlægebog, a veterinary handbook, of 1859; O. M. Norlie, HNPA 222.
[63] FoE 22 Aug. 1872/4/6-8.
[64] Norden 12 Nov. 1874/1/5.
[65] Cf. Lodsen og hans hustru by Jonas Lie in Norden from 15 Oct. 1874; anonymous reviews by R. B. Anderson appear in Skandinaven regularly during 1875.
[66] Budstikken, 14-21 Nov. 1876.
[67] For further details see this writer's Norsk i Amerika 98-116, Blegen NM 2.585-92.
[68] Jon Norstog will be considered in the next chapter; cf. the sketch of N-A literature by R. Beck in Bach, History of Scandinavian Literature 74-84 (N.Y., 1928); articles on special phases in NASR, see bibl. in A Review and a Challenge, 34-5 (Northfield, Minn., 1938).
[69] Nordmands-Forbundet 18.219-27 (1925).
[70] D-P 24 Feb. 1939.
[71] Familiens Magasin, Christmas Number, 1921.
[72] Omkring Fædrearven 115 (Northfield, Minn., 1922).
[73] D-P 18 March 1930.

Chapter 8.

THE WRITING OF DIALECT AND NEW NORSE.

1 Skandinaven 30 Mar. 1875/2/1.
2 See the writer's study of its early forms in PMLA 48.558-97 (1931); the best overall discussion of the language situation in Norway is Achille Burgun, Le développement linguistique en Norvège depuis 1814 (VSS H-F. Kl. 1917, No. 1; 1921, No. 5), Oslo 1919-21; on the early years see Vemund Skard, Frå Dølen til Fedraheimen (Oslo, 1949).
3 Prøver af det norske Landsmaal (Christiania, 1853).
4 Norsk Grammatik (Christiania, 1864); Norsk Ordbog (Christiania, 1873).
5 Morgenbladet No. 114, 115 (1853), repr. in Munch, Saml. Afh. 3.312, note 1.
6 115.379-401 (Boston, 1872).
7 Fædrelandet og Emigranten 28 March 72/1/5-8.
8 FoE 9 May 72/1/8; 26 Sep 72/1/7/.
9 Sk 24 May 73/2/3; 14 Aug 73/3/3-4.
10 SoA 10 July 73/2/1-3.
11 SoA 25 Oct 73/3/5, 27 Oct 73/3/3-4, 4 Nov 73.
12 Sk 27 Jan 74/3/6.
13 Sk 10 Feb 74/1/6.
14 Cf. Rasmus B. Anderson, The Story of My Life 104ff (Madison, Wis., 1913); Mortimer Smith, The Life of Ole Bull (New York, 1947).
15 For his biography see Bjork and Paulson in NASR 11.2-3 (1940).
16 Sk 17 Mar 74/2/4.
17 Sk 9 June 74/2/5.
18 Sk 16 June 74/2/4.
19 Sk 14 July 74/2/2.
20 Sk 16 June 74/2/4.
21 Sk 17 Nov 74/4/4-5.
22 Sk 24 Nov 1874/2/8.
23 B. J. in Sk 8 June 75/2/4-5. Other contributions not specifically cited elsewhere are: C. K. (anti) 25 Aug 74/2/7; Iverslie (pro) 22 Sep 74/2/6; George P. Sørensen (anti) 17 Nov 74/4/4; O. M. (pro) 24 Nov 74/2/8; 3 Aug 75/2/4; B. J. (anti) 7 Sep 75/2/3. A factual question about Ivar Aasen is correctly answered in Norden 11 Mar 75/2/4.
24 Norden 8 July 75/2/4; see also 2 Sep 75/2/3 and 14 Oct 75/3/4.
25 Sk 12 Oct 75/2/5; 26 Oct 75/2/4.
26 Cf. Iverslie in Sk 21 July 74/2/7-8; Anon. in Sk 28 Dec. 75/2/4-7.
27 Sk 1 Feb 76/2/5-7.
28 Sk 21 Sep. 75/2/3.
29 Sk 12 Oct 75/2/5.
30 See footnote 6 above.

[31] Janson poems in Sk 13 April 75 and Norden 25 Nov 75/3/6-7.
[32] Title page says 1874, but the first ad in Skandinaven was on 27 April 1875 and the review on 18 May says the book is published 'i disse Dager'.
[33] Life Story 249-50.
[34] Sk 6 July 75/1/4.
[35] Page 6.
[36] Page 41.
[37] Page 16.
[38] Page 50.
[39] P. T. in Sk 18 May 75.
[40] X. in Sk 4 May 75/4/3-4.
[41] For a complete list of his publications see the author's A Critique and a Bibliography of the Writings of Rasmus B. Anderson in WMH 20.255-69 (1937).
[42] Sk 16 Feb 75/2/1-2; Jørgen Gjerdrum.
[43] Sk 15 Feb 76/1/5.
[44] Sk 22 Feb, 6 June, 15 Aug, 14 Nov 1876.
[45] Sk 13 May 79/4/1.
[46] Life Story 299.
[47] In fact, Janson was never again to write anything of consequence in the New Norse language.
[48] Chicago, 1894.
[49] Cedar Rapids, Iowa, 1901.
[50] 66.117-21.
[51] Sk 10 Feb 78.
[52] Catalogue, University of Wisconsin.
[53] D-P 22 Sep 99.
[54] In later years he was devoted to such enterprises as a new calendar and a universal alphabet.
[55] Norroena 2.28.
[56] Biographical data partly from letter of Jan. 12, 1949, partly from article by Ingebrigt Sevre in Nynorsk Vekeblad 1948 (December), 16.
[57] 1.1.2/1 Jan. 1900.
[58] Norroena 1.6-7.
[59] Norrøna 3.2 (1914).
[60] Minneapolis, Minn., Nov. 12, 1948.
[61] Cf. Waldemar Ager, Problemet Jon Norstog, Reform 23 Oct — 27 Nov 1930.
[62] Symra 9.256 (1913).
[63] Travaas's poems were collected in Hjemve (Minneapolis, 1925).
[64] For a sketch of her life and poetry see Kristine Haugen, in Jul i Vesterheimen (1945), 14-20.
[65] Vor Tid 1.4.
[66] Maalmannsminne fraa Amerika, Ung-Norig 1923, 226-9.
[67] Reprinted in Ung-Norig 1923, 229-32.

[68] Norsk Maalbevægelse, Kvartalskrift 18-23 (1906).

[69] Other contributions by Rise, who later returned to Norway, are found in Kvartalskrift 3.7-12 (1907) and 4.2 (April, 1908); after his return he published a versified collection of stories from the prairies, *Snø* (Oppdal, 1929), in NN.

[70] 5.13-15 (Oct., 1909) and 5.6-21 (Apr., 1909).

[71] Vesterlandske Digte 208 (Minneapolis, 1905).

[72] See the appreciation of him in NASR 15.131-9 (1949) by Henriette K. Naeseth.

[73] Ervingen 4.3-4 (1911-12).

[74] Eidsvold 1.38 (1909).

[75] L. Lima, Norsk-amerikanske digte i udvalg (Mpls., Minn., 1903).

[76] Kvartalskrift 5.6-21 (April, 1909).

[77] Hans Seland, Um Amerika og Frendefolket i Vesterheimen 63-4 (Kristiania, 1904).

[78] Skand. 21 Aug. 1913.

[79] Skand. 21 Aug. 1913.

[80] Sprogrøret i Norge, D-P 9. April 1929.

[81] Sprogfred i Norge, D-P 13. Sept. 1929; cf. also D-P 10 Dec. 1929/8/1, 3 May 1929, 27 Aug. 1929.

[82] Emigranten No. 31, Oct. 21, 1853; reprinted and translated in Blegen-Ruud NESB 205-25.

[83] For a list of known dialect poems from the early period see D. A. Seip in SyS 1917, 178-86, 210-16; 1922, 79-96; 1928, 314-23; Ung-Norig nr. 2, 1921; Vestfoldminne II, 3-7; also J. A. Schneider in SyS 1902, 1-14, 97-111, 241-55; J. A. Schneider, Bygdemaalsdigteren Hans Hanson (Oslo, 1909); the poem from 1647 is printed in L. Hallager, Norsk ordsamling (Copenhagen, 1802).

[84] Cf. No. 12, 1858.

[85] Wossingen, No. 3 (1858); the author was Ole Utne, according to Anton Aure, Nynorsk Boklista 1.243 (Kristiania, 1916). A few riddles from Aasen's Prøver complete the list of materials in dialect even in this out-and-out representative of a dialect-speaking group.

[86] A letter written by another pseudonym in response to one of Terjeland's is translated by Arthur C. Paulson and Kenneth Bjork in NASR 10.76-106

[87] D-P 26 Sep 74/1/1-2.

[88] FoE 3 Oct 72/4/3.

[89] Sk 26 Dec 76/2/5.

[90] D-P 9 Oct 78.

[91] Amerikanske Forholde 108 (Copenhagen, 1881).

[92] Bonden i Bryllupsgaren in Norden 23 Sep 75/3/4; Jørund Telnes, Sterke-Nils in D-P 25 Sept 78/2/1 et seq.

[93] E. g. Sk 10 Aug 75/4/1; cf. also Underthun in Sk 23 Oct 77/2/4.

[94] Cf. Vaaren maa koma in Sk 20 Apr 75/2/1.

[95] For details see discussion by this writer in NASR 15.1-19 (1949).

[96] See text and translation by the writer in Jrnl. of Amer. Folk-lore 51.69-75 (1938).

[97] Cf. Blegen NM 2.241-76; he refers to these articles specifically on pages 273-4; see also Larson, CW, 144-6.

[98] Sk 29 May 77/2/8.

[99] Sk 7 Aug 77/2/7. The Valdres articles occurred in Sk 8 May 77/2/8, 29 May 77/2/8, 19 June 77/ Tillæg 2/4, 17 July 77/2/8, 7 Aug 77/2/7, 30 Oct 77/4/4, 9 July 78, 4 Feb. 79/2/6. There was oné article in a different dialect, prob. a Trønder in Sk 17 July 77/2/8.

[100] Sk 19 April 1881.

[101] Sk 15 June 75/2/7.

[102] Normannen 25 May 92.

[103] Stoughton, 1892.

[104] Page 7.

[105] Minneapolis, 1920, see esp. pp. 44-5, 61.

[106] See the brief sketch in Blegen NM 2.582-4.

[107] Bygdejævning 254.

[108] Bygdejævning 52-3.

[109] According to Bygdejævning V (Madison, Wis., 1903), the term was created from Mandejævning, a saga term, by substitution of bygd for mand.

[110] Valdres and Valders are alternative spellings; Valdris is a native of the region.

[111] Vang's Valdris-Rispo (Fullerton, Calif., 1930).

[112] See Veblen's Valdris Book, where they were printed in full.

[113] Valdris Samband 3.48 (1906).

[114] Valdris Helsing No. 26, 59-64 (1909).

[115] The last number in Luther College Library is No. 53 for March, 1924; an Aarbok for Telelage was published in 1926.

[116] Telesoga No. 1.61 (1909).

[117] Vossingen 9.1-5 (April, 1927).

[118] Knud Henderson (Løne), Digte om Hjemlige Tanker (Cambridge, Wis. 1928), 25 and 28; O. S. Sneve, Samlede Sange og Digte (Silvana, Wash., 1912), 340-1.

[119] Ibid. 320-2.

[120] Scrapbook made available to the writer by his widow and son George, in Decorah, Iowa, on July 26, 1940; Ulen died in 1925.

[121] 2 vols., Iola, Wis., n.d.

[122] Under the pseudonym of Lars-guten.

[123] I de dage — (Oslo, 1924) was the first volume; it was followed by Riket grundlægges (Oslo, 1925), Peder Seier (Oslo, 1928), and Den signede dag (Oslo, 1931).

[124] 13.350-64 (1898).

[125] Decorah, Iowa, 1902.

[126] 30.206-7 and 36.739-41.

[127] Recent Progress of the Landsmaal Movement in Norway, 25.367-78.

[128] 4.1-64 (1917); 5.297-304 (1919).

[129] Reviews, studies of place names, and bilingual studies are not here included; for a complete bibliography of his many contributions to Scandinavian and English philology see Scandinavian Studies Presented to George T. Flom by Colleagues and Friends (Univ. of Ill. SIL XXIX, Number 1, 1942), 16-31.

Chapter 9.

NAMES IN A NEW WORLD.

[1] Magnus Olsen, Hvad våre stedsnavn lærer oss, 6 (Oslo, 1934).

[2] Gustav Indrebø, Maal og Minne 1921, 113ff.

[3] See Peter A. Munch, Gard, The Norwegian Farm, in Rural Sociology 12.356-63 (1947).

[4] For a bibliography of Norwegian place-name studies, with a summary of the latest results, see Magnus Olsen, Stedsnavn, Oslo 1939 (Nordisk Kultur V).

[5] AL[4] 476 (N.Y., 1936). For the only previous survey of AmN naming see the writer's Norsk i Amerika 60-77 (Oslo, 1939).

[6] Important studies of immigrant Norwegian surname adjustments are those by Marjorie M. Kimmerle in NASR 12.1-32 (1941), AmSp 17.158-65 (1942), and University of Colorado Studies, Series B, 2.337-43 (1945). The writer has had access also to her unpublished Ph. D. thesis, entitled Norwegian Surnames of the Koshkonong and Springdale Congregations in Dane County, Wisconsin, (University of Wisconsin, 1938), prepared under his direction. The latter will be referred to in the following as Kimmerle Thesis.

[7] Cf. Pap in P-AS 126ff. on a similar situation in Portugal; Mencken AL 501 on the Jews; the only study of the Norwegian family name is the unsatisfactory C. D. Smidth, Vore Familjenavne (Kristiania, 1910); current legislation is summarized in C. S. Thomle, Norsk Navneret (Oslo, 1931).

[8] Cf. Magnus Olsen, Farms and Fanes of Ancient Norway, Oslo, 1926.

[9] O. M. Peterson, Fuldstændig norsk-amerikansk brev og formularbog (Chicago, 1877), 53.

[10] Cf. A. O. Vinje, Halvhundrad brev, ed. H. Koht (Oslo, 1915); Francis Bull, Norsk Litteratur-historie 4.130 (Oslo, 1937).

[11] Cf. Gustav Indrebø, Norsk Namneverk II ff. (Oslo, 1927).

[12] For similar problems among other immigrant groups see Roy W. Swanson, The Swedish Surname in America, AmSp 3.468-77 (1928); J.·I. Kolehmainen, Finnish Surnames in America, AmSp 14.33-38 (1939); Pap, P-AS 124-36, and of course Mencken AL, esp. Suppl. 2.

13 Ed. with an introduction by Vernon L. Parrington, 284-7 (N.Y., 1929).

14 Anderson FC 353-4.

15 Nordlyset 1.38.4.1 (11 May 1848).

16 Billed-Magazin 1.30 (1869).

17 Blegen NM 1.26n.

18 According to George F. Black, The Surnames of Scotland, xxiv-xxv (N.Y., 1946), alternating patronymics were in use in the Highlands as late as the 18th century, in the Shetlands even into the 20th.

19 Kimmerle thesis 97.

20 Kimmerle thesis 96.

21 List furnished by Dr. Odin Anderson.

22 St. Olaf College Catalog 1949-50.

23 Analysis by Kimmerle in thesis 130ff. based on 370 family papers now deposited in Wisconsin Historical Library.

24 Kimmerle thesis 99-100.

25 Interview Sep. 24, 1939, with Mrs. Henderson of Stoughton, Wis.

26 Skand. 20 Mar. 1877/2/6; see also 27 Feb. 77/2/5.

27 Clipping from Skandinaven in Julius Olson scrapbook No. 1, in possession of Wis. Hist. Soc.

28 Life Story 307: the account is denied by Hamsun, cf. Eidsvold Vol 1, No. 5, page 1 (Grand Forks, N.D., 1909).

29 Cf. Louis Adamic, What's Your Name? (New York, 1942); he comments on Norwegian names p. 51.

30 13N1.

31 A Study in Connotation, Univ. of Colorado Studies, Series B, 2.337-43 (1945).

32 Letter from A. N. Gilbertson, North Grafton, Mass., April 26, 1938.

33 Helgeson FIL 1.268.

34 Holand NSH 273-4.

35 Symra 10.90-1 (1914).

36 Billed-Magazin 1.171 (1869).

37 Reported to the writer by his widow.

38 Reported by Aslak Grimstad, a neighbor.

39 Holand NSH 325.

40 Cf. Mencken AL 474; his statement that 'changes (in Norwegian) have been fewer than among the Swedish names' is based on scant evidence and is probably not true; nor is the treatment of the subject on p. 492 adequate. See, however, his greatly improved treatment in AL Supplement 2.432-5 (1948).

41 See Kimmerle, A Study in Connotation, 340ff.

42 Kimmerle thesis 103.

43 Norrøna 3.91-4 (1914).

44 Information from his son O. B. Stephens.

45 Norrøna, loc. cit.

46 Holand, NSH 210-11.

[47] Cf. remarks by N-A writers on the subject in Knut Takla, Det norske folk i de forenede Stater, 291 (Kristiania, 1913); Olav Redal, En norsk bygds historie. Nordre Bottineau County, North Dakota, 11 (1917).

[48] Clara Jacobsen, in Symra 9.120-37 (1913).

[49] Joran Birkeland, Birchland, 84-5 (N.Y., 1939).

[50] 6Q3.

[51] St. Olaf College Bulletin, Vol. XLVI, No. 4 (April, 1950); all patronymics were counted as Norwegian.

[52] Thor Helgeson, FIL 1.153.

[53] Helgeson, FIL 1.145

[54] 5Q1; Holand, NSH 492.

[55] Helgeson, FIL 1.273.

[56] Helgeson, FIL 1.153.

[57] Holand, NSH 492.

[58] Fra pioner-presternes saga, 193 (Decorah, 1931); J. T. Odegard, Erindringer, 57 (Oslo, 1930); informant 4L4; the Norwegian names given by Per Hansa in Rølvaag's novel, Giants in the Earth, 264, Søren and Perkel, are unusual.

[59] The most important studies of Norwegian animal names are: Hallfrid Christiansen, En studie over nordnorske husdyrnavn, NTS 10.291-360 (1937); Helge Fonnum, Rektor Qvigstads samlinger av kunavn fra Troms og Nordland fylker, MM 1931, 72-98; Helge Fonnum, Gjeitenavn i Ål og Torpe, MM 1929, 81-92; Rektor J. Qvigstads samlinger av gjeitenavn fra Nordland og Troms fylker, MM 1929, 93-7; J. Byrkjeland, Norske kunavn, Tidsskrift for det norske landbruk 29.82-9 (1922).

[60] H. Christiansen, loc. cit., 297.

[61] Cf. discussion in Hallfrid Christiansen, 309, 317; Ivar Aasen, NO s.v. reid.

[62] Cf. B. H. Hibbard, The History of Agriculture in Dane County, Wisconsin, 180ff. (Madison, Wis., 1905).

[63] Billed-Magazin 2.114 (1870).

[64] Same informant: bortpå Kvåle, på Gjerrejord.

[65] NSH 243.

[66] Helgeson, FIL 1.153.

[67] 5L5; 5Q1; 5L1.

[68] Frederic G. Cassidy, The Place-Names of Dane County, Wisconsin (Pub. of Am. Dialect Soc., No 7, 1947), s.v. Drammen Valley, Holum's Creek, Jeglum Valley, etc.

[69] Holand, CV 13.

[70] 14D2; 15P3; see also Holand, NSH 284, 294.

[71] 6P1 on 6Q3.1.

[72] Holand, NSH 364.

[73] Holand, NSH 369.

[74] FIL 1.217.

[75] 4L4; Cassidy, op. cit. s.v. Staangji; Helgeson, FIL 1.27; 6Q3; 5L5; 4L1.

[76] Nordlyset 29 August 1847.

[77] Holand, NSH 209.

[78] Cf. Holand, NSH 467; Torkel Oftelie, Samband 3.600-4 (1912-3).

[79] Roy W. Swanson, Scandinavian Place-Names in the American Danelaw, Swedish-American Historical Bulletin 2.3.5-17 (1929); Oftelie, loc. cit.; cf. also Vilhelm Berger, Svenska namn på Amerikas karta, Namn och Bygd 26.61-102 (1938).

[80] I find the following post offices in the U. S. Postal Guide not included in his list; Brevik, Erdahl, Flom, Gonvick (?), Halstad, Ihlen, Inger (?), Dragnes, Melby, Melrude, Nielsville, Odin, Ronneby, Rustad, Skyberg, Steen, Thor, Ulen, Viking.

[81] Town of Lind in Waupaca Co. is named after the Swedish singer Jenny Lind; Helgeson FIL 1.23. Nelsonville was named for Jerome Nelson, an Englishman, acc. to letter from Malcolm Rosholt.

[82] See Cassidy, op. cit.

[83] Holand, NSH 533.

[84] Holand, NSH 271.

[85] Holand, NSH 370.

[86] Holand NSH 329.

[87] Billed-Magazin 1.388 (1869).

[88] Iver I. Øyen, Trønderlagets Aarbok 1926, 76-7.

[89] Reported by Thor Helgeson, FIL 1.34-5.

[90] T. Oftelie, Samband 3.600-04 (1912-13).

[91] Holand, NSH 469; there is no P. O. at this place today.

Chapter 10.

THE STRUGGLE OVER NORWEGIAN.

[1] Kort Udsigt over det lutherske Kirkearbeide blandt Nordmændene i Amerika 828 (Chicago, 1898).

[2] Rev. J. H. Holum told this story to the writer.

[3] Bulletin 313 of the S.D. State College of Agriculture and Mechanic Arts, Brookings, S. D., 56.

[4] Cf. discussion by Carl Hansen in Norsk-amerikanernes Festskrift, 266-91; he refers to some 650 societies, as of 1914.

[5] Blegen NM 2.136.

[6] Blegen NM 2.73.

[7] Blegen NM 2.74.

[8] Nordlyset 1.1.

[9] America in the Forties, 55; cit. by Blegen NM 2.84.

[10] Cf. Chapter 6.

[11] Symra 9.53 (1913).
[12] See the excellent discussion in Blegen NM 2.245ff.
[13] Rasmus Sørensen in Emigranten 1 Nov. 1858, here cit. from Paulson and Bjork in NASR 10.90.
[14] NASR 10.91.
[15] Blegen NM 2.248.
[16] Kirkelig Maanedstidende 4.156-7 (1859).
[17] NASR 10.98.
[18] Kirkelig Maanedstidende 5.50-1 (1860).
[19] Nordlyset 30 Dec. 1847.
[20] Nordlyset 28 Oct. 1847.
[21] Emigranten 15. Nov. 1858.
[22] Emigranten 18. April 1859; the signer, Rasmus Sørensen, is probably not the same as the schoolmaster mentioned above; the latter's home was in Waupaca County, Wisconsin.
[23] Emigranten 1 Febr. 1859/2/1.
[24] Fra Pioner-presternes Saga, 195 (Decorah, 1931).
[25] Norskhetsbevægelsen i Amerika, in Nordmands-Forbundet 18.211-19 (1925).
[26] Skand 20 Dec. 1871/1/1.
[27] Skand 27 Mar. 1872/3/3.
[28] Skand 27 Dec. 1876.
[29] Blegen NM 2.261; the law authorized instruction 'in any of the foreign languages, not to exceed one hour a day.'
[30] Skandinaven Oct. 17, 1876/2/4.
[31] D. M. Schøyen, Bennett-loven, 22-3 (Stoughton, Wis., 1890).
[32] A. Bredesen, Mod Bennett-Loven, Vidnesbyrd og Grunde (pamphlet printed ab. 1890, n.p.).
[33] Hans Seland, Um Amerika og Frendefolket i Vesterheimen, 64 (Kristiania, 1904).
[34] HNPA 95 (Minneapolis, 1925).
[35] Evangelisk Luthersk Kirketidende 36.277-80 (1892).
[36] The Log Book of a Young Immigrant, 249 (Northfield, Minnesota, 1939).
[37] Oluf Hanson Smeby, De krav som stilles til os med hensyn til brugen af det engelske sprog, især i arbeidet blandt ungdommen. Foredrag ved prestekonferansen i Red Wing, trykt efter konferansens beslutning. N.p., n.d. Smeby was born 1851 in Wisconsin.
[38] Norskdom, Vor Tid 1904, 49-53. Dahle was born 1875 in Iowa.
[39] Andreas Wright, Religionsskolen (Mpls., 1904). Wright immigrated in 1860.
[40] Festskrift udgivet i Anledning af Red Wing Seminariums Femogtyve Aars Jubilæum, 118 (Red Wing, Minn., 1904). Harrisville was born in Chicago.
[41] Nordmands-Forbundet 18.205 (1925).
[42] Norlie, HNPA 534.

43 Nordmands-Forbundet 18.305 (1925).
44 A. A. Veblen, The Valdris Book, 282 (Minneapolis, 1920).
45 Aarbog for Det Norske Selskab i Amerika 1903,4 (Minneapolis, Minn., 1904).
46 Aarbog 1903, 28.
47 Aarbog 1903, 84.
48 The last issue in the Luther College Library is called 17.-18. aarg., 1921-22.
49 Kvartalskrift 1.2-10 (No. 2, 1905).
50 Kvartalskrift 1.6 (1905).
51 Kvartalskrift 1.4.14-29 (1905).
52 Smeltedigelen, in Kvartalskrift 12.33-42 (1916); cf. also 12.108-13, 113-19.
53 Den store udjævning, in Kvartalskrift 13.73-89, 100-15 (1917); 16.9-16 (1920); 17-18.5-14 (1921-2).
54 Nordmands-Forbundet 18.211-19 (1925).
55 Symra 9.110-5 (1913). Kvamme was born in Norway in 1866, immigrated 1882.
56 Symra 9.49-54 (1913). Torrison was born 1859 in Wisconsin.
57 Symra 9.116-9 (1913).
58 Symra 9.170-3 (1913).
59 Symra 9.251-4 (1913).
60 Symra 9.193-5 (1913). Hulteng was born in Sweden 1860, immigrated 1887.
61 Den norsk lutherske Kirkes Historie i Amerika, 524 (Minneapolis, Minn., 1914).
62 Annual Report of Den forenede norsk lutherske kirke i Amerika, 1912, 55-56 (Minneapolis, 1912).
63 Cit. by I. B. Torrison in Symra 9.51 (1913).
64 O. M. Norlie, HNPA 357.
65 HNPA 357.
66 Annual Report 1931, 29.
67 Statistics in the annual report of 1918.
68 Annual report for 1917, 538.
69 Annual report for 1918, 425-30.
70 Annual report 1918, 20-21.
71 Stub was born 1849 in Wisconsin.
72 The Augustana Synod had never had the word 'Swedish' in its name.
73 Annual Report 1918, 392.
74 Annual Report 1918, 313.
75 Annual Report 1920, 247.
76 Navneforandringen, 5-6 (a pamphlet without date, signed by five pastors, printed in Decorah, probably about 1929).
77 Annual Report 1918, 307; cf. The Survey 40.394-5 (1918).
78 Annual Report 1918, 315.
79 Annual Report 1920, 369-74.
80 Kvartalskrift 15.44 (1919).

[81] Here cited in the translation of Jorgenson and Solum in Ole Edvart Rølvaag, A Biography, 294 (N.Y., 1939).
[82] Date checked for me by O. M. Hovde, librarian, Luther College.
[83] Northfield, Minn., 1922.
[84] Jorgenson and Solum, 294.
[85] Jorgenson and Solum, 291ff.
[86] Jorgenson and Solum, 298.
[87] Knut Takla, Det norske Folk i de Forenede Stater, 290 (Kra., 1913).

Chapter 11.

THE TRIUMPH OF ENGLISH.

[1] O. E. Rølvaag (1929).
[2] Philip S. Dybvig, Lutheran Church Herald 14.697-700 (1928).
[3] Dybvig, loc. cit.
[4] Den norsk lutherske Kirkes Historie i Amerika 523 (Minneapolis, Minn., 1914).
[5] Decorah, 1931; page 194.
[6] Minneapolis, Minn., 1922.
[7] Presten som ikke kunne brukes 17.
[8] Omkring Fædrearven 170 (Northfield, Minn.).
[9] Above, chapter 9.
[10] Data from the Annual Reports.
[11] 9Q1.
[12] 18H2.
[13] 8L4.
[14] 14F3.
[15] 2C1.
[16] 9G2.
[17] 2C2.
[18] 20F18; cf. also 14D10; 12Q4; 18C5; 8L8.
[19] 8M4.
[20] 10C12.
[21] 4Q2.
[22] 20C5.
[23] Annual report 1928, 186-7.
[24] Dybvig, loc. cit.
[25] Navneforandringen 14.
[26] Annual Report 1934, 16A and 304.
[27] Annual Report 1936, 33.
[28] Annual Report 1944, 35.

[29] Annual Report 1946, 394.

[30] Annual Report 1948, 448.

[31] Communication from A. J. Bergsaker, secretary of the Evangelical Lutheran Church, August 9, 1950.

[32] Annual Report 1918, 220: 33,500 to 10,300.

[33] Information chiefly from the annual reports, esp. 1948, 333, though the figures are somewhat discrepant with those obtained from other sources.

[34] Sønner af Norge, October 1942.

[35] For the latter cf. Andreas Ueland, Recollections of an Immigrant (New York, 1929); also his article 'A Minor Melting Pot' in Samband, March-June 1931.

[36] Evon Z. Vogt, Social Stratification in the Rural Middlewest: A structural analysis, Rural Soc. 12.364-75 (1947).

[37] Sixteenth Census of the United States, 1940: Population: Nativity and Parentage of the White Population, Mother Tongue. Washington, D. C.: Government Printing Office, 1943.

[38] Speaking of Tongues, AmJSoc 54.202-10.

[39] Seventh Census of Canada, 1931. 1.235; 1.1198. Ottawa, 1936.

[40] Minority-Group Pattern in Prairie Society, AmJSoc 50.377-85 (1945).

[41] Nationality and the Emerging Culture, Rural Sociology 13.40-7 (1948).

[42] Walter Lucius Slocum, Ethnic Stocks as Culture Types in Rural Wisconsin, Unpublished Ph. D. thesis, University of Wisconsin, 1940.

[43] Social Adjustment among Wisconsin Norwegians, AmSocRev 14.780-7 (1949).

[44] Glen Laird Taggart, Czechs of Wisconsin as a Culture Type. Unpublished Ph. D. thesis, University of Wisconsin, 1948.

[45] Borghild Dahl, I Wanted to See, 24 (New York, 1944).

[46] Ibid., 63-4.

[47] Joran Birkeland, Birchland, A Journey Home to Norway, 12-4 (New York, 1939).

[48] Ted Olson, Hawk's Way, 41 (New York, 1941).

THE NORWEGIAN
LANGUAGE IN
AMERICA

Vol. II.
THE AMERICAN DIALECTS
OF NORWEGIAN

Chapter 12.

METHODS OF INVESTIGATION.

> If a botanist wishes to study the growth and
> nature of a tree, does he go out into the woods or
> does he go to the botanical gardens? Just so the
> linguist, if he wishes to study the life of language,
> must not go to the masters of literature, but to the
> speech of the people. Any one who listens to the
> artless words that issue from their mouths will gain
> more enlightenment on the nature and develop-
> ment of language than from any study of written
> texts.
>
> *H. Morf (1888).*[1]

Earlier chapters have prepared us for the existence of a series
of spoken dialects of American Norwegian, carried over to the
immigrant communities and living for a longer or shorter period
on American soil. We have seen how cultured observers have spoken
their minds about these dialects, usually in an unfavorable vein.
But in order to derive reliable information about AmN speech, it
is necessary to leave our written sources and go out into the field
among the people who actually use these dialects. Such an investigation was undertaken by the present writer, and it will be the
purpose of this second volume to present its results. We shall begin
with a statement of the methods employed in carrying it out.

1. *The Basic Problem.*

The study of a bilingual community established within a fairly
recent period involves a problem which is not present in an older,
more homogeneous community. We cannot limit ourselves to the

intensive study of one or two informants with the reasonable assurance that these will be typical of the community as a whole. Neighbors may speak dialects separated by a thousand years of divergent development in the homeland. While Norwegian dialects are not strictly unintelligible to one another, there are often considerable obstacles to understanding.

The impact of the new environment will differ according to the basic structures of each dialect, and according to the kind of local influences to which each speaker has been subjected. So it becomes necessary to treat several different dialects within the same community, and the same dialect in several different communities. Only in this way may it be hoped to disentangle the factors involved in the bilingual process. But there are as many distinguishable dialects in Norway as there are parishes, and very few of them have been adequately described. In this country the Norwegians are dispersed over vast areas, and even their more cohesive settlements run well into the hundreds. In very few places has the language been spoken long enough to have become amalgamated into a new, homogeneous community form. For satisfactory sampling we thus need a broad selection of informants.

A further difficulty is the difference in degree of bilingualism within each community. Side by side live individuals, often within the same family, who speak no English, who speak it badly, and who speak it perfectly. Fortunately the English which serves as a model for their new speech is relatively uniform within the area being considered. But informants must be sought who exhibit each of the possible stages from one language to the other, from Norwegian to American monolingualism. For each informant we must find out how he stands in relation to the main linguistic current in his community. To what generation does he belong, and when did he have his determining linguistic experiences? We must be able to assess the significance of forms in terms of the degree of bilingualism shown by each informant.

These obstacles might seem insuperable if it were not for the techniques developed by modern investigators of dialect. The individual uninitiated in these techniques is often puzzled to know how one can decide whom to ask and what to ask, or what to listen for and record, or how to record what has been said. Informants have more than once exclaimed to the writer, 'But how can you write down the queer sounds that we make — there just aren't enough letters in the alphabet!' The basic elements in a successful field technique for linguistic investigations are (1) an adequate questionnaire, (2) thorough training in phonetic transcription, and (3) reliable sampling of the speech community. Perhaps one should add tact and a sympathetic approach, but these are not strictly technical in their nature and must be taken for granted. The thoughtful investigator always keeps in mind that his informants are not merely units in his statistics, but people like himself with value judgments and purposes that must be taken into account if he is to emerge with valid generalizations about them. It is not always possible to gain a full historical perspective of a community before going into it, but the more one can gather of the local background and atmosphere, the better one's linguistic judgments are likely to be.[2]

2. The Questionnaire as a Linguistic Tool.

Questionnaires as the chief tool of the dialect geographer have been popular ever since Georg Wenker in 1876 sent his list of forty sentences to all the school teachers of Germany and asked them to write them out in the forms of the local dialect.[3] The results of these first efforts by linguistically untrained men to write the local dialects were more impressive for their mass than their quality. But they did lead to the drawing of 1,646 maps of German dialects, now reposing in the archives at Marburg. An entirely different procedure was followed by the French scholar Jules Gilliéron when he made his plans for a corresponding French atlas. His questionnaire was more extensive and emphasized vocabulary rather than phonology and grammar; but most important was the fact that he sent a field worker out to make the records in person. Between 1896 and 1900 E. Edmont visited 639 French communities and interviewed one informant in each. The results appeared between 1902 and 1910 in the great *Atlas linguistique de la France*.[4]

In Norway Wenker's example was followed almost immediately by the brilliant phonetician Johan Storm, who began interesting himself in dialect studies in 1880 and sent out his first list of dialect words to the school teachers of Norway in February, 1882.[5] This little list of 300 words gave way to a much larger one which he printed in the same year.[6] The approximately 4,000 words included were here arranged to illustrate the history of Old Norwegian sounds in the dialects. In June, 1884, he prepared the final form of his list, which became the chief tool of Norwegian dialect investigators down to the present.[7] He intended this, he wrote, 'for those who wish to gain insight into one or more dialects in a short time and to contribute to their description.' There were only about 2,000 words in this list, so arranged as to illustrate the historical phonology and the morphology of the dialects. In the same year he published his dialect alphabet, which has become standard in Norwegian usage.[8] Storm's keen observations of dialect sounds have remained invaluable for all students of Norwegian. It may therefore surprise some readers that the writer did not adopt his questionnaire and his transcription for the study of AmN dialects. To explain this we shall have to look at the development of dialect study in the United States.

In the United States the methods of dialect geography were first applied in 1931, when the project of making a linguistic atlas of the United States was initiated by a large group of American scholars.[9] Under the direction of Hans Kurath, with Miles L. Hanley as associate director, field workers were sent out to 213 New England communities. In the course of two years they succeeded in interviewing 416 informants, using a questionnaire containing 814 words and phrases. The results have appeared in a series of three handsome volumes entitled the *Linguistic Atlas of New England*, published between 1939 and 1943, and in Hans Kurath's *A Word Geography of the Eastern United States*, published in 1949.[10] The work sheets, as the questionnaire was called, provided space to write not only the informant's response to the questions asked, but also any free remarks he might make during the interview. They were arranged according to natural topics of conversation, such as the weather, the dwelling, the farm, topography, domestic animals, etc.[11] The transcription used for recording was specially made for the purpose, but it was in general based on the alphabet of the International Phonetic Association.[12] In each community two informants were sought, one elderly and one middle-aged, one less and one more educated. Special effort was made to get natural responses from the informants, without direct suggestion. After interviews had been completed, phonograph recordings were made of the informants.

3. *The American-Norwegian Questionnaire.*

The many advances in technique of the Linguistic Atlas of New England made it inevitable that the general procedure of this enterprise should be adopted in the investigation of AmN. At first attempts were made to use Storm's lists and his transcription, but they were rather discouraging. For one thing they obviously did not include those words and phrases that most directly suggested the American scene, while they did include a great many that were irrelevant. For another they consisted very largely of similar-sounding words grouped together, without regard to meaning. Such a sequence as taka, baka, aka etc., with which the list abounds, tired the attention of the informant and tended to suggest incorrect answers. Besides, it was too long for the kind of wide-meshed investigation that was necessary if the enterprise were to be concluded in a reasonable time.

The primary purpose of a questionaire could not be to exhaust our knowledge of one dialect, but rather to provide comparable material from many dialects. For this purpose a questionaire arranged in principle, though not in content, like the NE atlas work sheets seemed best. In this way the interviews might (and did) become more like conversations, with a natural progression from topic to topic. The headings chosen for the questionnaire of AmN, with the number of questions asked under each, were as follows:

A Personal and family history (25)
B Home and family life (35)
C The human constitution (81)
D Household life (139)
E Buildings and grounds (85)
F Farming (117)

G Weather and Topography (43)
H Travel and communication (61)
I Business, trade, government (56)
J Social affairs and institutions (79)
K Human relationships (74)

The total number of 795 items included in the first version of the questionnaire were chosen after careful study of the materials available on AmN. Two considerations were paramount: there must be enough words for concepts that were normally expressed by Norwegian words so that one might gain a clear picture of the structure of the native dialect; and there must be enough words for concepts that were normally expressed by English words so that the impact of English could be measured. The items included in either category ought to be words that showed marked variation from dialect to dialect, or whose phonetic or grammatical treatment when borrowed into Norwegian showed marked variation. Fortunately it was not necessary to depend entirely on the writer's personal experiences with AmN speech. The very full lists of loanwords published by Professor George T. Flom from the Sogn dialect in the Koshkonong Settlement were carefully analyzed.[13] With the help of this list the writer was able to compile a corresponding list of words heard in his own childhood dialect of AmN. He also set a student from Blair, Wisconsin, Mr. Odin Anderson (14D3) to work with Professor Flom's list, which resulted in the most complete list yet made of such loanwords. The similarities and variations in these lists suggested some of the phonetic and grammatical problems that needed investigation. They also defined the nature of the oral material that might be expected in rural regions, particularly in Wisconsin, and the range of interests that could profitably be discussed with rural informants.

The first questionnaire, referred to here as Q36, was prepared in the form of 8 × 11 booklets of 35 pages, blank except for the numbered items listed at the left of each page. Two copies of each page were stapled together so that a carbon copy of each field record could be made. This was not merely for security, but in order to permit the arrangement of the material both by informants and by pages. The questions as finally chosen included three types of material: (1) general and cultural questions designed to bring out the informant's social and family background, and encourage him to speak in connected sentences about topics of interest to him; (2) expressions referring to objects nearly always described in Norwegian, such as parts of the body, days of the week, numbers, and the like; and (3) expressions known to be very generally drawn from English and illustrating most interestingly the adjustment to a new environment, such as barn, beer, hickory, river, car, railroad, field, and the like. The three types were not kept apart, but were mixed up within the sections outlined above. One innovation made on the method of the New England atlas was to provide pictures for as many as possible of the things asked about. A scrapbook was made from clippings found in magazines and mail-order catalogues. In this way much explanation was saved, and a certain assurance was had that the same thing was actually understood by each of the informants. The pictures also contributed to the hilarity of the occasion and often provided a welcome break in the questioning.

The problem of transcription was a troublesome one, but it too was solved along the lines of the Linguistic Atlas of New England. It was clear that the distinctions made by Johan Storm would all have to be noted, and possibly some others that he had not discovered. In dealing with a bilingual situation it was necessary to have symbols that provided for the often delicate distinctions between closely related sounds in two different languages. Storm's system is essentially based on Storm's own urban East Norwegian pronunciation; sounds that differ from this are given diacritic symbols, or they are printed in roman instead of italic letters. The use of italics seemed out of the question in a rapid field notation. The writer therefore devised an adaptation of the IPA aphabet which would combine maximum economy of effort with clarity of distinction. Using the values of his own Norwegian pronunciation as norms for the basic symbols, he then provided a series of shift signs like those of the New England atlas to mark values that lay farther forward, back, up, or down in tongue position. A detailed analysis of the symbols was prepared, with a symbol for symbol comparison with the norms of Johan Storm. This was submitted to Professor Hans Kurath, director of the New

England atlas, and discussed with him before its adoption. Other symbols were provided for marking the informants' responses as slow or uncertain, as having been suggested by the field worker, as having been corrected by the informant himself, etc.

4. *Field Work.*

With this equipment the writer took to the field in the summer of 1936 and completed twelve interviews as a test of his procedure. Most of these were made within fairly easy reach of Madison, Wisconsin, chiefly in the Koshkonong and Blue Mounds settlements. The problem of sampling was the most important one that faced him. How was he to find his informants and get them to tell him what he wanted to know? He found that his most valuable aids then and later were the pastors of the Norwegian Lutheran congregations, whose familiarity with the lives and accomplishments of their parishioners provided shortcuts into the communities studied. Even the younger pastors, who often did not themselves speak Norwegian, were well aware of who the more 'Norwegian' members of their congregation were. There was a tendency among such guides to steer the field worker to speakers of 'pure' dialect, which were not necessarily the best for this writer's purpose. He always stressed his desire to find people born in this country, and of as young a vintage as possible. His real triumphs were those occasions when he came across informants who were neither suspicious nor self-conscious about his inquiries, who entered into the spirit of his project, and spoke their dialect with fluency and precision. Most of the informants were not only patient, but in so far as they could spare the time, eager to participate. Some of them were veritable saga-men, persons of vivid memories and high narrative skill, who were happy to hold forth on the life of their community. The interviews could not be completed in one session, since they might last anywhere from ten to twelve hours. Occasionally it was not possible to complete the interview, either because the informant turned out to be inadequate, or because his time and patience gave way. But this was the exception; in most instances the informants were amused and flattered by the experience. Sometimes it became a family entertainment, in which an entire household participated and thereby widened the circle of investigation. Husbands and wives sometimes discovered that they had been talking different dialects for years without ever noticing it.

Even though the questionnaire was composed in English, the medium of discourse with informants was generally Norwegian. This was not strictly necessary, but usually operated to put the informants more at their ease. Since it was important that we get the informant's natural speech, the field worker made a point of using simple, unpretentious Norwegian. He did not attempt to speak the informant's dialect, which might have sounded like mocking, but avoided characteristically bookish forms and fell into dialect when it seemed appropriate. Some informants produced bookish forms at first, partly to show off, partly out of deference to the 'professor'. These attempts were gently discouraged, and with growing familiarity they disappeared except where they actually were a part of the informant's habitual speech. The writer's impression is that the field records generally represent quite accurately the state of rural AmN speech; though qualification must be made for the one point of loanwords. Comparisons made between responses to questions and the informants' free conversation show that they were reluctant to admit the use of English words. Some of them showed by their hesitations that they were trying to remember the Norwegian words for objects which they never ordinarily referred to by anything but English terms. The field worker's first concern was that his questions should be so framed as not to suggest answers. Anything that could be simply described or pictured was asked for in this way. He either pointed to the picture, or asked for it by circumlocutions: what is the first meal you eat in the morning — what is the month that follows June — what do you call the little room where food is kept — where do you get water? If unexpected synonyms were given, they too were recorded and the question was reframed to make sure that the word wanted was not just being overlooked. For expressions that could not be asked for in this way, English or literary Norwegian were used as a last resort: how do you say 'bashful' — 'I'll tell her a story' — 'now we're through'?

5. *Revision and Analysis.*

The informants interviewed the first summer represented a good cross-section of dialects and communities, and their responses were carefully studied to assess the value of the questionnaire itself. Some of the questions produced uniform replies among all the informants, varying only in unimportant details that were predictable from a general knowledge of Norwegian dialects. This was true of such words as 'husband', for which the response was always *mann*; 'bake' was always *baka*, 'healthy' always *frisk*, 'tired' always *trøytt*. Other questions had the opposite difficulty, of producing answers varying so widely as to show nothing of interest; the words for 'naughty', 'little by little', and 'broken' belonged to this group. Some questions proved to duplicate the information given in others; 'in the morning' was uniformly rendered with some form of *um morgonen*, but the same words and construction turned up in the phrases 'tomorrow' *i morgon* and 'in the evening' *um kvelden*. In all, 278 items were dropped, and 35 were added, which reduced the time required to complete interviews from 11 or 12 hours to about eight. This was the revised questionnaire referred to here as Q37, which was used from 1937 to 1942. The paging and numbering of the questions remained the same as in Q36.

Meanwhile the writer prepared forms that could be used for linguistic analysis of the materials gathered. Mimeographed sheets were made for each of the major phenomena to be investigated: stressed vowels, unstressed vowels, consonants, the morphology of nouns and adjectives, the morphology of verbs and pronouns. On each of these it was planned to enter illustrative words from the work sheets, thus bringing together as much information as possible that might bear on the linguistic structure. An index was prepared to the questionnaire itself, so that all items were readily available for study. Numerous analyses were actually made, and brought out many interesting facts. For one thing they showed the weaknesses to which the field worker is subject, weaknesses that have often enough been enlarged upon in phonetic literature.[14] They showed that shades of sound not used in the field worker's own dialect were not uniformly written, being now regarded as a variety of sound x and now as a variety of sound y, its next-door neighbors.

The writer adopted a procedure of making a rough analysis of each informant's sound system after the first session, and then checking back on doubtful items. This turned out to be a useful check on his hearing, and actually the first step towards a phonemic analysis of the dialect.

The analysis made of the materials derived from Q37 led in 1942 to a second revision of the questionnaire (here included as Appendix 3). The most radical change in this one was the introduction of two pages devoted entirely to grammatical forms. In many cases the analyses had shown that certain grammatical forms were lacking, and also that the labor of assembling the bare outline of the morphology of a dialect was needlessly great. A small number of words illustrating each category of morphological alternation were assembled on these sheets, which were then filled in by the field worker, who framed sentences to illustrate their use when asking for them. The results have proved very useful, even though certain less common forms cannot be relied upon. But such morphological uncertainty is rare, and can usually be detected without difficulty. These sheets permitted the dropping of a number of items that had been included chiefly for morphological reasons. Other items were added, until a total of 400 items remained, plus 23 biographical questions and about 100 items of grammar. This was the questionnaire used during the remainder of the investigation. The writer extended his operations to western Wisconsin in 1937, north central Wisconsin and eastern Minnesota in 1942.

6. *Completion of Field Work.*

Until 1947 the investigation was carried on single-handed by the writer, chiefly in time that could be spared from other and more pressing duties. Free time was available only in the summers of 1936, 1937, and 1942, plus the second semester of 1941-2, when he enjoyed grants from the University Research Committee and a Guggenheim Fellowship; to this should be added a semester in 1949 which was financed by the University of Wisconsin Committee on the study of American Civilization. In 1947-8 the same committee made available to him the competent services of Mr. Magne

Oftedal as a research associate. Mr. Oftedal had just completed his M. A. at the University of Oslo in Linguistics, with Norwegian dialects as his specialty. He took hold of the field work with skill and enthusiasm, and his notations are highly reliable. Interviews made by him are marked MO in the appendix on communities and informants. In analyzing his field records, the writer did not note any important variations in M.O.'s transcription practice from his own. M.O.'s field work permitted the filling in of records from communities in those Norwegian settlement areas which the writer had not had time to visit.

The making of recordings was an important aspect of our investigation at all its stages. The first piece of apparatus used was a portable recording set furnished by Professor Miles L. Hanley which he had used in New England. This made records on aluminum, and was later replaced by a Recordio outfit that recorded on acetate.[15] Difficulties were encountered in some areas where rural electrification had not yet penetrated, so that informants had to be transported out of their natural environment to some electrified point. Occasionally informants refused to be recorded, or suffered from "mike fright". But most of them have been recorded, some of them for as long as an hour and a half. The latest stage in recording was reached with the acquisition of a Soundscriber which was more portable and cheaper to operate than the earlier systems. This accompanied Mr. Oftedal on his excursions, which accounts for the greater extensiveness of his recordings. The archives thus built up include not only rural but also urban and even cultivated informants, some of whom have not been specially listed here. The archives are the largest in the country of recorded Norwegian speech, and should also prove of great interest for other purposes than the purely linguistic. The records have been indexed for loan words, unusual Norwegian terms, and cultural information. Many hours have been spent, both by the writer and Mr. Oftedal, transcribing the more interesting passages.

One method of using the recording apparatus was that which the writer adopted in Blair, Iola, and Spring Grove, of setting up the apparatus in a public place and inviting as many as wished to come in and have themselves recorded. He also did this at one meeting of the Vossalag, a society holding semi-annual meetings for people emigrated from Voss. The results are interesting for the cross-section they give, but difficult to analyze in view of the limited amount of information available about the background and speech of each informant. Of 260 informants interviewed 207 were recorded for a total of 3272 minutes, or 54 hours and 32 minutes. Of this about two hours was music, all the rest speech. The length of an individual recording ran all the way from a minute or two to an hour and a half, with the average at 15.8 minutes. A few general conversations were recorded, but rarely with much success. It was usually necessary to prime the informant by asking questions. But in a few cases the words flowed as readily as if they had been memorized.

7. *Analysis of the Informants.*

There is of course no theoretical limit to the amount of field work that could be done. There *is* the practical limit of personnel and time. The informants whose language has formed the immediate basis of the present study are listed in the appendix, with an account of the communities in which they live. Some idea of the work done and the value of the sampling made can perhaps be derived from a summary of the types of informants interviewed between 1936 and 1948. A total of 98 informants have been interviewed with some kind of word list. Of these 13 were subjected to Q36, 25 to Q37, 53 to Q42, and 7 to other lists, including Storm's. This group is referred to in this book as the *primary* informants. Another group of informants totalling 33 were made the object of briefer study, being either asked to answer questions in an abbreviated questionnaire or to record at some length. These are called *secondary* informants. The widest group of informants were the *occasional* informants, on whose language notes were taken or brief recordings of 10-15 minutes or less were made. Of these there were 129. Altogether, then, a total of 260 persons have been drawn into the investigation. Of these only 48 have come from outside the state of Wisconsin, including 10 primary, 6 secondary, and 32 occasional informants.

The accompanying map of Wisconsin (Plate 7) shows the com-

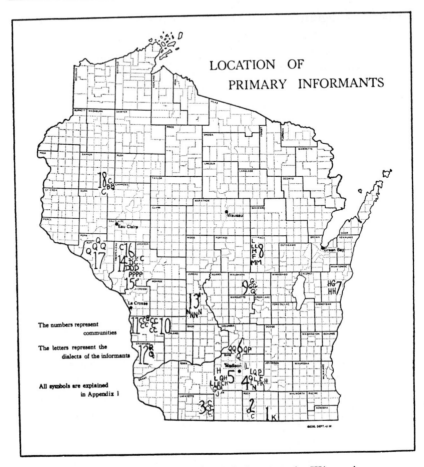

LOCATION OF
PRIMARY INFORMANTS

The numbers represent
communities

The letters represent the
dialects of the informants

All symbols are explained
in Appendix I

Plate 7. *Location of Primary Informants in Wisconsin.*

munities that were investigated in this state and the number of primary informants in each. Since the number of informants in other states is small, no map has been drawn of their location; the interested reader can turn to the appendix where they are listed. The informants have also been entered on a map of Norway (Plate 8) showing the distribution of their original dialects in that country. It will appear from this map that two regions are under-represented, namely the extreme south and the extreme north. These were areas which yielded little emigration to Wisconsin; their sea-coast

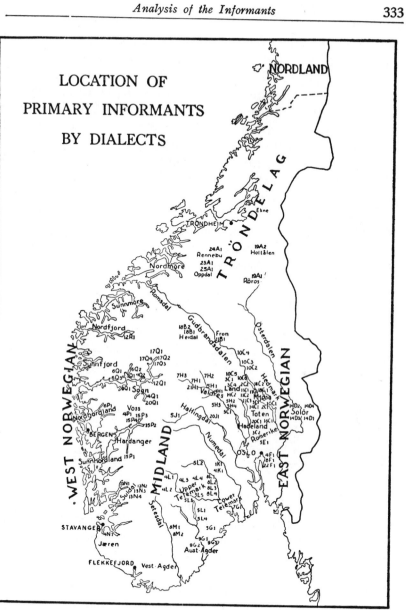

Plate 8. *Location of Primary Informants by Dialects in Norway.*

inhabitants generally found the American coasts more congenial. All the other major dialect areas of Norway are represented.

The informants included individuals born in Norway as well as many born in the United States. In classifying them, a distinction was made between those who immigrated before and after the age of 14, or whose parents immigrated before and after 14. Those who immigrated after their speech habits were formed are called 1A generation, those who came earlier the 1B generation. The latter are linguistically in much the same position as the 2A generation, whose parents immigrated after the age of 14, but who were themselves born in the United States. The 2B generation, the children of 1B's, are in much the same position as the third and succeeding generation, since their parents were subject to English influence in their childhood.

The informants are classified by generations in the following table:

Generation:

Type	1A	1B	2A	2B	2/3	3	3+	Un-known	Total
Primary ...	10	4	52	10	9	10	3	0	98
Secondary .	14	5	8	0	3	2	1	0	33
Occasional .	28	6	54	11	8	14	2	6	129
Total	52	15	114	21	20	26	6	6	260

This shows that the typical informant selected was the person born in the United States whose parents immigrated as adults. But the remaining 55 % were evenly distributed between those who had been here longer and those who had been here a shorter time.

The length of their American experience is shown in the following table, which gives the date of immigration for generations 1A and 1B, but the date of birth for the later generations:

Generation:

Date	1A	1B	2A	2B	2/3	3	3+	Un-known	Total
1850—59 ..		3	9	1					13
1860—69 ..	4	3	19	2					28
1870—79 ..	5	7	30	6	2	2			52
1880—89 ..	9	1	14	4	6	2			36
1890—99 ..	9		8	3	2	3	1	1	27
1900—09 ..	9		11	3	6	9			38
1910—19 ..	5		2	1	3	5	2		18
1920—29 ..			1			2	2		5
1930—39 ..						1	1		2
Unknown ..	11	1	20	1	1	2		5	41
Total	52	15	114	21	20	26	6	6	260

The median date of immigration for the 1A generation was 1891, with a spread from 1861 to 1915; for the 1B generation it was 1870, with a spread from 1851 to 1881. The median date of birth for the 2A generation was similar to the immigration date of the 1B, being 1875, with a spread from 1852 to 1900. The 2B generation was born between 1850 and 1912, with a median of 1883. The median birth dates of the later generations were 2/3 1898 (spread from 1873—1918), 3 1902 (spread from 1876—1930), 3 plus 1922 (from 1898—1930). While this distribution was not deliberately planned, it is believed that it represents fairly well the actual situation with regard to speakers of Norwegian.

The entire period of Norwegian settlement is represented (aside from the very earliest), the oldest informant having been born in 1850 and the last interview made in 1948. The 1880's were the peak period in Norwegian immigration, which corresponds well with the fact that 1885 is the median year of immigration for all first-generation informants and of birth for all American-born informants. Most of our informants thus had their first bilingual experiences in the years from 1885 to 1900, almost exactly a half century before they were interviewed for the present investigation. That their numbers should fall off after 1920 is only what we might expect in view of the gradual loss of Norwegian speaking after this time, as discussed in Chapter 11.

The use of questionnaires and of more or less random recording does not, of course, exhaust a subject of as great an extent in time and place as the present one. As a supplement must come the intensive analysis of particular localities and dialects with the help of natives. The most fruitful such aid was given the project by the previously mentioned Odin Anderson, who prepared a vocabulary of some 6000 Norwegian and English words from his native Solør dialect of Blair, Wisconsin.

Beyond this the writer had to depend on his own experience of American-Norwegian speech, as he has heard it in urban as well as rural communities from all parts of the Middle West, with occasional excursions to the East and Far West. In approaching informants he found that they often retained a sense of loyalty to the Norwegian tradition which made them proud of their language competence. Even if they did not interest themselves in the language as such, they were usually glad to speak of local lore and the tradition of their communities. Some took the interview as a kind of examination of their language ability. When the interview was over, they would ask, with a twinkle in their eyes, 'Well, did I pass?' In answer the writer can only say: they did.

Chapter 13.

DIALECTS IN DISPERSION.

When we stopped outside a gas station on the prairie in northern Minnesota, there was a bus outside the station. An older lady called into the bus in a dialect well known to me. It proved to be a lady from Karmøy in Ryfylke. She wrote to her grown children in her mother tongue, a dialect I also have spoken in my childhood.

Didrik Arup Seip (1932).[1]

Americans are often surprised to learn of the great diversity of dialects that are spoken in most European countries. Accustomed as we are over here to a relative uniformity of speech, we rarely realize that in Europe it is hardly possible for a native country-dweller to travel more than ten miles from his home without making himself conspicuous by his dialect. One AmN informant expressed it as his impression that in Norway, 'berre du krossa ein bekk, så va de eit anna språk' (every time you crossed a creek, there was a new language).[2] These differences reflect a period of centuries when most people stayed within their local communities and rarely had a chance to speak with strangers. Dialects are the result of isolation. But this isolation might be due to many factors — to natural barriers, such as forests, mountains, or large bodies of water, or to social barriers, such as administrative boundaries, feudal restrictions on travel, or class distinctions. One of the first effects of emigration was to wipe out the isolation and thereby to upset the delicate balance of dialect against dialect which was conditioned by the social geography of the old country. Speakers whose ancestors rarely had communicated in the course of a thousand years were suddenly thrown into close contact in an American community. It will be our purpose in this chapter to look at some of the outward effects of this development.[3]

1. *The Dialects of Norway.*

In central Europe the unit of social life and hence of the dialects was usually the village. But in Norway villages were rare and the typical pattern was one of separate farmsteads. The unit of uniform speech was the neighborhood or parish, within which the farmers enjoyed a fairly close solidarity of community life. A word in Norwegian for this unit is *bygd*, a term for which there is no precise equivalent in English. The *bygd* might be coextensive with the administrative township unit (the *herred*), with the religious parish unit (the *sogn*), or it might include several of these. But it always implies a measure of living together, of intermarriage and community of custom, which left its deposit in a substantial unity of speech. The outsider was the man who was 'betrayed by his speech'.

In the most exact meaning of the word 'dialect', one would have to say that there are as many dialects in Norway as there are such communities. If one chooses the *herred* or township as the handiest unit to count, there are 720 dialects; but since there are differences even within these, one might add the parishes and reach around a thousand. Of course, neighboring townships have many dialect traits in common, so that it is possible to reduce the number to a relatively small number of dialect groups. Perhaps the most significant grouping in relation to American emigration is that which refers to the larger 'folk' districts. Some of these are merely historical regions, having no present-day administrative standing; in some degree they go back to old tribal borders. Some of them correspond to the *fogderi* or sheriff's district, others to the *fylke* or county. Among them are such popular names as Sogn, Voss, Valdres, Nordfjord, Numedal, Gudbrandsdalen, Bamle, Hedmark, Toten, Romerike, and the like. It is usually impossible to specify any precise border where one of these leaves off and another begins, but the core areas are clear enough.

In the following dialect division the popular regions have been used as a basis, and these have then been grouped into larger areas. The dialects have been numbered from north to south in the east and from south to north in the west. This division into east and west is fundamental and corresponds to the north—south mountain range which divides the western fjords from the interior of Norway. But the mountain valleys which have here been called Midland have many traits common with the western dialects, and are in general among the most conservative in the country. The division here adopted is a practical one for the purposes of the present study; it makes finer distinctions in those regions which are well represented among our informants than in the rest.

EAST

   1) *Northern.*

A Nordland
  Trønder
  Nordmøre

   2) *Eastern.*

B Upper Gudbrandsdal
C Upland (region around Lake Mjøsa)
D Border Districts (Solør, Østerdal)
E Oslo Fjord
F General East Norwegian and Book Language
G Lower Telemark (Bamle etc.)

   3) *Midland.*

H Valdres
J Hallingdal
K Numedal
L Telemark

WEST

M Setesdal, Aust-Agder
N South-west (Vest-Agder, Rogaland)
P Hordaland (Voss, Hardanger)
Q Sogn
R North-west (Sunnfjord to Romsdal)

Such larger dialect groupings are more popular than scientific, but they do have a certain validity even after closer analysis of their characteristics. Much more precise are the areas delimited by specific dialect traits, but as a rule no two of these coincide entirely. Thus the two major traits used to distinguish East from West Norwegian follow similar but not identical paths. These are 1) the treatment of ON unstressed *a* after long syllables and 2) the treatment of *l* in certain (non-palatal) environments. WN has treated all *a*'s and *l*'s alike, while EN has changed some but not all the *a*'s to [ə] or dropped them and has changed some but not all *l*'s to a so-called 'thick' *l* which sounds a little like American *r* (but with a tongue flap). When such differences are drawn on a map, they are called isoglosses. They look like the lines left on a seacoast by the lapping of the sea, reflecting as they do the forces of social communication.[4]

2. *Transplantation to America.*

We have seen in Chapter 2 how the earliest emigration from Norway began in that southwestern corner of the country which juts out farthest into the North Sea. The emigrants aboard the Restaurationen in 1825 were all from Rogaland, the district around Stavanger. As the news of America spread from community to community, we can trace the wave of emigration northwards into the Hardanger fjord, then over the mountains to Voss in the north and Telemark in the east. In 1837 two leaders from the next valley to the north, Numedal, emigrated and two years later they led a large party of emigrants from their valley. Between 1840 and 1843 new conquests were made in Sogn on the west, in Lower Telemark in the east. Throughout the forties and fifties Telemark became the leading contributor of emigrants, but in the sixties it was surpassed by Sogn, Valdres, and Hallingdal.[5]

If we follow these early emigrants across the sea, we see that they tended to settle in this country in somewhat the same order. The emigrants from Rogaland populated the early settlements in northern Illinois.[6] But those who followed from the mountain regions of Voss, Telemark, Sogn, and Numedal did not choose to settle in this neighborhood. They pushed north into Wisconsin and became the dominant groups in the first settlement of the state. The speed of settlement was such that there was barely time for one group to occupy a large area before others came in.[7]

The settlement of Koshkonong in southern Wisconsin was typical of this mountaineer group. The church register of the Koshkonong congregation reports the place of origin of its earliest members. Of the 642 family heads listed, the largest single group or 236 (36.8 %) came from Upper Telemark.[8] Nearly all the *bygder* of this region were represented: Laardal 62, Kvitseid 44, Seljord 32, Tinn 20, Mo 19, Moland 16, Nissedal 9, Hjartdal 2. The second largest group were those from Sogn with 114 (17.5 %), followed by Voss 76 (11.8 %), Lower Telemark 69 (10.7 %), and Numedal 55 (8.6 %). Within the Koshkonong area these tended to form groupings of their own, but any kind of strict segregation was out of the question. There were, in addition, a good many who filtered in from other regions, e.g. Hallingdal 12, Valdres 10, Hardanger 17, Eastern Norway 33, etc.

By 1850 the Upland region around Lake Mjøsa was beginning to yield its share, followed by the valley of Gudbrandsdal to the north. Settlements like those of Coon Prairie in western Wisconsin and Scandinavia in eastern Wisconsin are dominated by these regions, though in quite different proportions. Lists of early settlers here are far from complete, but give interesting data concerning the dispersion of the dialect groups. The settlers of Coon Prairie from 1848 to 1869 show two major groups: 107 (38.9 %) from the Upland region (of whom 58 from Biri alone) and 65 (19.8 %) from the Rogaland region. The former were reinforced by a large contingent from adjacent Gudbrandsdalen (Lower 69, Upper 26).[9] As shown by the field studies of Peter A. Munch, these two groups of East and West Norwegians have remained distinct in many respects even down to the present time.[10] But there were also settlers from elsewhere: Upper Telemark 25, other Midland 5, Trønder 4, etc. In the Town of Scandinavia a similar list shows a considerable group from Gudbrandsdalen: Upper 16 (chiefly Ringebu) and Lower 58 (chiefly Gausdal), altogether 74 or 21.8 %. But instead of a dominant Upland contingent (here only 22), we have here a dominant East Norwegian

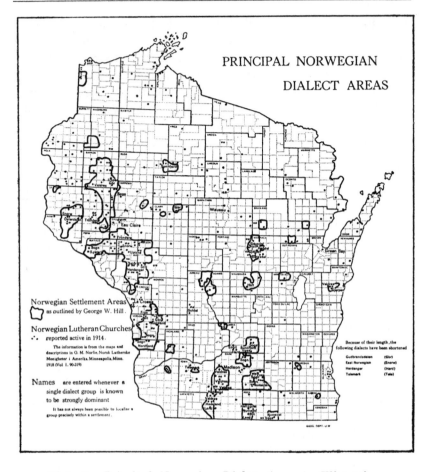

Plate 9. *Principal Norwegian Dialect Areas in Wisconsin.*

group from further south, altogether 148 or 43.7 %, mostly from
Gjerpen (35), Siljan (20), and Holt (28). Upper Telemark has a
group of 35, and among other Midland dialects are Setesdal with
22 and Valdres with the same number. West Norwegians were few
(21). This community was thus dominated by southern East Norwegian, with Gudbrandsdal and Setesdal as extremes.

Such settlements as these were typical of the larger areas of
Norwegian immigration. There were cores of certain dialect groups
which dominated the region, but always a large sprinkling of people

from other districts. Some settlements were 'purer', but they were generally smaller. The tendency was toward the resettling of old friends, neighbors, and relatives, but never one of deliberate planning for a whole community. Old loyalties persisted, but new ones began to replace them. The local pride of the old country was still felt, but was gradually replaced by the sense of belonging to a particular American community.

The settlements of Wisconsin fall into three well-defined groups, southern, northeastern, and western. These appear on the accompanying map (Plate 9), with designations of the dominant dialect groups in each. (1) In *southern* Wisconsin are found the 'mother' settlements which were organized between 1838 and 1845. As noted above, these are dominated by the mountaineer dialects of the West Norwegian fjords (Sogn, Voss) and the Midland valleys (Telemark, Numedal, Valdres). The only major exception is a strongly EN area in Wiota, chiefly from Land and Hadeland. (2) In *northeastern* Wisconsin there are several scattered settlements, settled from 1846 and well into the 1850's. Valdres and Telemark are well represented, but as we have seen from the discussion of the Scandinavia settlement, the valleys of Gudbrandsdalen and Setesdal have joined the procession, together with Lower Telemark and other eastern areas. (3) In *western* Wisconsin there is an almost continuous strip from Crawford to Washburn Counties where Norwegian settlement went on from 1848 to 1870 and later, as the frontier to the North Woods was pushed back. Here we find practically all the major dialects of Norway, but above all Gudbrandsdalen and the Upland regions. Border dialects like that of Solør from eastern Norway are strongly represented in Trempealeau County right next door to the Hardanger community of Beaver Creek. In Crawford and Buffalo Counties the prevailing dialect is that of Sogn, in the former tempered by that of Nordfjord.

No detailed study has been made of the dialect composition of the Norwegian settlement areas farther to the west. The only students of immigration who have given information on this point are Holand and Ulvestad.[11] Their hints could be expanded by a full study of the histories of each community and the records of the bygdelag organizations, if such a study were worth making. The northeastern corner of Iowa is said to contain large settlements

of immigrants from Hallingdalen (Allamakee and Clayton Cos.),
Land (Allamakee), Numedal and Hadeland (Clayton), Valdres,
Ringerike, Toten, Sigdal and Eggedal (all Winneshiek). South
and west of this area, esp. around Story City, the prevailing
dialects are said to be those of SW Norway, esp. Rogaland and Horda-
land. Hallingdalen is also strongly represented in Worth and
Mitchell Counties. In Chickasaw County there are people from
Lower Telemark at Turkey River, but from Sogn at Crane
Creek.

In the southern tier of Minnesota counties there are several
large settlements. In Houston County (Spring Grove) there are
many from Hallingdal and Hadeland, around Black Hammer
many from Sogn. In Fillmore County near Newburg and Preble
the settlers are from Rogaland, on Highland Prairie from Telemark
and Nannestad, east of Harmony from Toten, west of Rushford
from Numedal, north of Root River from Sogn, in York Twp.
from Setesdal. In Mower County the settlers north of Grand
Meadow are from Aurdal in Valdres, at Adams from Sogn, at Six
Miles Grove from Telemark. In Freeborn County there are many
from Sogn, from Ringerike, and from Hallingdal; it is said to
contain the 'most marked settlement of Hallings in America.'[12]
In Olmsted and Dodge Counties there are many from Hallingdal
and Sigdal, in Goodhue County near Kenyon from Hallingdal,
west of Zumbrota many from Land, further north many from Valdres, around the Rush River many from Østerdal. In Faribault
County many come from Sogn. In Western Minnesota the Jackson
County region has many from Southern Trøndelag and Northern
Østerdalen, west of Mankato many from upper Gudbrandsdalen,
in Kandiyohi County many from Biri south of Norway Lake, in
Burbank Twp. from Gausdal in Gudbrandsdalen, to the west some
from Valdres, east of New London a group from Nordland.

In South Dakota the eastern counties are strongly mixed, but
in the area between Yankton and Canton there are heavy concen-
trations of Trønders, which is also true in the area north of Sioux
Falls around Baltic and Brookings. For North Dakota the slight
information available suggests a wide spread of dialect groups.
On the West Coast the fishing regions of Norway are well represented, esp. Nordmøre, Sunnmøre, Trøndelag, and Nordland. On

the East Coast the southern and southwestern towns of the coastal region (Stavanger—Flekkefjord) are most frequently represented.

The details of this situation are neither very interesting nor particularly significant, except in so far as they show us how very much dispersed the individual dialects have been. They might try to limit themselves to one area, but could never succeed.

3. *Discovering the Dialects.*

For many Norwegians their arrival in America meant also their first acquaintance with the more remote dialects spoken in their homeland. They discovered that their own dialect could no longer be taken for granted as it had been in their native valley. Their origin in Norway tended to place them in a certain group in the eyes of others with whom they now came into contact. One conspicuous fact about each person was his dialect, and dialect differences became a common subject of conversation, particularly in the older generation. Most older informants have shown keen awareness of the dialect composition of their community. In some cases they have even been able to point out particular areas within the community which were prevailingly of one dialectal composition. A native of the Beaver Creek settlement described a ten-mile stretch along the road in which his own Hardanger was dominant. But just beyond his father's farm began a solid patch of 'Strilar', fishermen from the outer fjords, with whom the Hardanger group felt they had little in common.[13] In these descriptions the dialect names used are generally those of the larger regions, like Valdres, Telemark, or Hardanger; but there are also names which have special local meanings. In the Blue Mounds settlement there was a section called the Westman Bottom (vestmannsbatomen), because the Telemarkings lived there; the name 'westmen' was applied to them by the Valdres people. There was, in turn, a valley called Valdres Valley where the latter were especially strong.[14] In this settlement the term 'nordmenn' was applied to people from Sogn, because they came from 'north' of the mountains; one man was even nicknamed Thomas Northman, probably because there were so few from Sogn in this community (cf. Chap. 8). In the Iola settlement certain leading dialects were characterized, according to one informant, by their characteristic pronouns: there were the *oss*-people (from upper Gudbrandsdal; *oss* 'we'), the *kon*-people (from Telemark; *kon* 'we'), and the *e*-people (from Valdres; *e* 'I').[15] A similar division is reported from Coon Valley, where the upper part of the valley was inhabited by the *oss*-people and the lower part by the *vi*-people (from Biri and Lower Gudbrandsdal). Local names can be deceptive in some cases: in the Blair area there is a valley known as Voss Coulee (Vossakuli) in which there are no *vossings* whatever; the place got its name from a first settler who later departed.

The widening of linguistic horizon which thus came with immigration led to a keen interest in dialect forms on the part of many. Informants have repeatedly volunteered, usually with amusement, observations on the dialects around them. Most of these are statements about the use of particular words, but occasionally they tell about differences in phonology and grammar as well. These observations are highly sporadic and only partially accurate; marked differences between husbands' and wives' speech have often gone unobserved until the investigator's questions brought them out.

Although any Norwegian with a little patience can learn to understand all other Norwegian dialects, some who came into contact with new dialects lacked this patience, and occasional misunderstandings resulted. This is not surprising in the case of such remote and medieval dialects as that of Setesdal. A fluent speaker of this dialect living in Scandinavia, Wisconsin, assured the writer that he could always baffle other Norwegians with his dialect. But the most frequent misunderstandings were those between such major dialect groups as East and West Norwegian. In such cases it was nearly always the East Norwegians who failed to understand the West Norwegians, rather than the reverse. This is reported from the Blair-Beaver Creek area for Solør (EN) and Hardanger (WN) speakers.[16] The reason given is that the EN speakers are closer to the DN book language, which all have had to learn. A pastor raised on EN in Minnesota reported that his first meeting with Stavanger people in Illinois was quite mystifying to him and his wife.[17] An EN storekeeper in Spring Grove found it difficult to wait on Sognings.[18] Similar problems were reported from Iola, where Telemark (Heddal) and Gudbrandsdal (Gausdal) people met in one community, and from Blue Mounds, where Sogning and Valdris met.[19]

A Numedal woman said she had misunderstood a 'newcomer' from Stavanger, who said: 'Ska e ji grisane noko ta den stampen?' (Shall I give the pigs something from that tub?); in her dialect the word stamp meant 'potato masher'.[20] A favorite anecdote, told in several variants, was the one about a recent comer from Norway, who happened to be brought into contact with the speaker of a widely different dialect, and did not realize that it was Norwegian. From Coon Valley it is told in this way: 'There was a man from Flekkefjord who came in to visit a Norwegian family one day. There was an old Norwegian woman [probably from Biri] who listened to his talk. When he left, she said, 'Ja, e sku trast lære å tala engelsk e å hvis e ha en slik en i husi lengi.' (Well, I could learn English in a hurry too if I had a fellow like that in my house for a while!)[21] In Blue Mounds it was told about a Sogning who failed to understand a Valdres and said to him: 'Du lyt snakka norsk te meg, for e æ nett kome frå Norge.' (You'll have to talk Norwegian to me, for I've just come from Norway.)[22] In Spring Grove, Minnesota, it was told of a woman from Voss who had been listening to one from Singsås (Trøndelag); after the latter left, she said, 'Å nai, e vait e kunde snakke ængelsk så godt så ho!' (Oh my if only I could talk English the way she does!)[23]

4. *Dialect Humor.*

More common than actual misunderstanding, however, was the practice of more or less good-natured joshing of speakers with different dialects. A few informants have denied ever having heard such mocking, but for the most part it appears to have been a very common practice.[24] Many of the expressions used were carried over from Norway, where certain terms were fighting words. One of these was the name *Stril* for inhabitants of the WN coast, particularly the more poverty-stricken fishermen. One could anger a Stril by holding the heavy end of a whip against the buggy wheel, known as 'knocking on the boat', presumably to remind him of his humble origin.[25] In the Beaver Creek settlement, where Hardanger and Stril were neighbors, two girls got into a fight in the schoolyard. One abused the other by calling her a 'sildastril' (herring Stril); the other retorted with the term 'vossaskreppa' (Vossing bag).[26] In Blair the people from Solør were teased with a little rhyme:

> Solonger og geit
> er det verste je veit.

(Solør people and goats are the worst things I know).[27]

From a settlement in northern Iowa is reported a schoolchild incident in which the children of Røros parents mocked those of Voss families. 'We used to come home and cry because they made fun of our speech, and then mother said to us, "That's nothing you need cry about — just talk Norwegian the way you do here at home, for your speech won't shame you unless you shame yourself."'[28] This attitude seems to have been typical of the Voss emigrants; according to a Telemark informant from Koshkonong they had a tendency to be 'conceited'.[29] A healthy pride in their own dialect has certainly been characteristic of the Voss informants used in this investigation. There is a marked contrast here with their neighbors from Sogn, whose dialect does not sound too dif-different to outsiders. Yet the Sogn dialect has been the favorite butt of jokes in many N-A communities. Perhaps it is because its speakers are more numerous than others, at least of the more conspicuously 'different' dialects.[30] It is also connected with the fact that the communities of Sogn were largely fishing districts, in contrast to the more prosperous farming region of Voss. One of the most popular dialect readings among the immigrants was one entitled 'Sognekjerring' by the sisters Eleonora and Ethel Olson.[31] 'We always made fun of the Sognings,' declared a Solør speaker from Blair; 'we had to mock many of the Sognings,' said a man from Tinn, Telemark in the Blue Mounds settlement; 'we made fun of the Sognings, and they became Americans before we did because they were ashamed,' said a Gudbrandsdal speaker from Coon Valley.[32] This last remark was confirmed by a leading official in the national association of people from Sogn, who declared that his group were among the first to give up their Norwegian in favor of

English; one reason was that their dialect 'stuck out' and caused them trouble.[33]

An American-born woman who spoke a Gudbrandsdal dialect fluently stated that she hardly ever spoke Norwegian with her husband, who was born in Sogn: 'When he talks Sogning and I answer in Gudbrandsdal dialect, it don't hitch so good!' In the Blue Mounds settlement the only one who was said to be ashamed of her dialect was a Sogn woman, who preferred for this reason to speak English; and from Norway Grove it is reported of a Sogn man who said, 'Naor e ska snakka me ein mann [so eg ikkje kjenne], so like eg kje te snakka rått sogning!' (when I have to talk with a man [whom I don't know], I don't like to talk crude Sogning!)[34] We see in such episodes one of the most potent of assimilatory social forces at work, the effect of ridicule against all forms of nonconformity. In the N-A communities the conflict of dialects led in many cases to a complete abandonment of the Norwegian language. This was not limited to the Sognings, and it is comparable with a development reported from Gaelic Scotland, where speakers of different dialects often prefer to communicate in English.[35]

5. Dialectal Adjustments.

Intermarriage between Norwegians of different linguistic breeds could also lead to mutual adjustment and compromise between the dialects spoken. Such adjustment was usually a negative procedure, the avoidance of forms that were too strange and words that led to misunderstanding. Adults do not readily abandon their childhood speech, but some informants have maintained that this was what happened in the case of their own parents or other near relations. It may be mere coincidence, but the reports suggest that as a rule it was the husband who accommodated his speech to that of his wife.[36] Lest this be taken as a trend towards matriarchy, we might add that in most of these cases the community language has been that of the wife; the husband has simply moved into a differently speaking environment. Similarly in the case of the children of such 'mixed' marriages. Although we should expect that the mother's language would prevail, in view of her influence on the child's early development, we find that nearly as many children have claimed to follow their father as their mother.[37] Many of these children became dialectally ɔilingual, being able to switch over from one dialect to the other according to the situation. They have often reported differences between the speech of their parents. But the prevailing dialect of their own speech is not necessarily determined by their earliest influences. In most of the above cases they adopted as their own that dialect which was most generally used in the community, which often meant that dialect which was most like the DN. A typical expression of opinion is that of a very old woman who was born of a Swedish mother and a Norwegian father: 'Vi snakke svensk te vi kom te Kaskeland, da jore di nærr tå oss, da snakke vi som far.' (We talked Swedish until we got to Koshkonong; then they made fun of us and so we talked like father.)[38]

Some of the older informants complained that they were no longer able to speak their dialects purely. Even such an excellent informant as 20Q2 said regretfully: 'Da ha vorte miksa mæ så mange or so ikkje baint e sogning.' (It has gotten mixed with so many words that are not exactly Sogning.)[39] One from Gudbrandsdalen living in Coon Valley said: 'Vi snakke itt regeler frøning — dæ hopmiksa alt.' (We don't talk regular Fron — it's all mixed together.)[40] If this was true of the older generation, it is no wonder that the children might fail to acquire a pure strain of dialect in many cases. A Voss informant declared: 'Eg snakka ikkje rikti klart verken Voss eller Haring — eg miksa for mykje.' (I don't talk clearly either Voss or Hardanger — I mix too much.)[41] A Spring Grove speaker said that in his generation they did not speak much Halling, but that it was still heard in his father's generation.[42] From the Blue Mounds settlement we hear that it got so 'mest alle runt her so snakke dei vallers'; in the Telemark area of Koshkonong they would start talking Telemark; in Suldal settlement 'they talked Suldal no matter where they came from.'[43] A speaker from Coon Prairie declared that 'der ongan e vøkse opp samen, snakker dom alle likens' (where the children have grown up together, they all talk alike), a sentiment that is echoed by others.[44] A native of Koshkonong who spoke Voss dialect told of hearing the speech of hired men who came from EN: they said *ongar* where the Voss people said *bodn* 'children', *monn* for *kjeft* 'mouth', and *kona* for *kjering* 'wife', and the children were nothing loath to imitate them, in spite of admonitions from their parents.[44] A Valdres from Blue Mounds declared that when the Norwegians got together for weddings it was just like listening to the tower of Babel.[45]

A detailed account from a similar Iowa community shows the influences to which a child might be subjected: 'All of us children learned our parents' dialect first, so we talked in many different ways when we got together with people. It was not so easy for the one who had a different dialect from that which was spoken by the majority. For the most part it got so we talked the way the others talked. In the Highlandville school there were a few Voss children together with many Hallings, and so the Voss children talked Halling. For my part I learned the Voss dialect which my mother talked; my father was a Hardanger but did not speak it because he was educated as a school teacher. But some of our relatives from Hardanger who lived with us talked Hardanger, and so the young people made fun of us so we didn't use the special Hardanger forms like *kom hæga* 'come here' and *aukan* 'ours'. So now we children can't talk Hardanger dialect, which I regret, for I have learned to talk other dialects which were not my parents' speech.'[46] The feeling that it is necessary to talk as others do is expressed more than once: 'When I talk with anyone, I fix my mouth to suit the meal (så stiller je munnen ette matsekken).'[47]

It was inevitable that these social forces should have tended towards the development of generalized or central dialects in those settlements where many different dialects were spoken. This was especially true in such large settlements as Koshkonong, Iola, Coon Prairie, Coon Valley, and Spring Grove. It is common in these areas to hear the prevailing AmN dialect referred to as 'Westby dialect' or 'Spring Grove dialect'.[48] In Koshkonong informant 4F1 appears to be such a speaker, whose dialect cannot definitely be described as a variant of any one Norwegian dialect. It has the general traits of EN, but is certainly not his father's Halling dialect (nor his mother's WN Sogn). From Macintosh, Minnesota comes the report that there was a general mixture of dialects: Ringerike, Voss, Hallingdal, Trøndelag, Nordland. The informant himself was of Nordland and Østerdal ancestry, but learned to speak 'en oppblanda norsk dialekt som ikke hadde noen hjemmehørende på en plass eller en annen.' (A mixed up Norwegian dialect that did not belong either in one place or another). The analysis of his responses shows that he, too, was EN in type, with strong influence from the BL, to which he later went over entirely (as a pastor).[49] From the Coon area it is reported that 'du kunne ikke fortelja hår non tå dom var (fra) i gammellanne.' (You couldn't tell where any of them were from in the old country).[50] A common expression is that the dialects are 'oppblanda' or 'opp-miksa'.[51] The considerable number of informants who have had to be classified as 'East Norwegian' without any specification of dialect are evidence of this development, whereby many speakers have departed from their native speech in the general direction of the BL without of course attaining the norms of the latter. The so-called dialect mixture is thus not a true mixture, but rather a gradual elimination of conspicuous forms, while retaining in general the articulatory and grammatical basis of the underlying dialects.

Informants have often given specific information about forms that were remembered but no longer used, and now felt as obsolete. We shall list some of these here as examples of the kind of change that affects the dialects. They will be listed by dialect; it is evident that the 'older' dialects, such as Telemark, had more to rid themselves of in such a leveling as here took place. The 'older' form is listed first, followed by the 'newer' one:

(1) Trønder (24A1): søs'sjenbånn' — søs'kenba'rn 'cousin'; kva'r — vo'r 'where'; væ'kje — jæn'te 'girl'; gra'vel — begra'vels 'funeral'; tåƚ'ƚå — snak'ke 'talk'; sju'k — sy'k 'sick'.

(2) East Norwegian (several inf.): fir's — åt'ti 'eighty'; øy'kjån — hes'tan 'the horses'; vik'u — ve'ke 'week'; svep'o — svø'pe 'whip'; le' — grinn' 'gate'; skæp'pe — skå'pe 'the cupboard'; læp'per — låp'per 'fleas'.

(3) Valdres (5H1): hen'ne, hå'nå — ho' 'her' (dative); sno'di 'cozy, attractive' (eliminated); mob'bro — on'kel 'uncle'; mos'ter — tan'te 'aunt'.

(4) Halling (20J1): knød'ne — kne'a 'the knees'; ta'lika —

talær'ken 'plates'; jød'n — jønn' 'iron'; b*l*ei'e — la'ken 'sheet'; kå'r — hå'r 'where'.

(5) Numedal (4K1): jo'*l*ep'*l*e — pote't 'potato'; vo'n 'hope'.

(6) Telemark (several inf.): sen'gja — seng'a 'the bed'; hå'gån — ha'ven 'the garden'; svi'pu — svei'pa 'the whip'; mog'ne — sjæ're 'ripe'; ro'mi — røm'me 'cream'; jo'rep'li — po'tit 'potatoes'; ris'til — plo'gkni'v 'plow share'; ta'la — snak'ke 'talk'; nyk'la — nys'ta 'ball of yarn'; ok'kon — oss' 'us'; mjokk' — mel'k 'milk'; py'se — pøl'se 'sausage'; rø'e — snak'ke 'talk'; ho'vu — hug'gu 'head'; jo's — ly's 'light'; bå'e — beg'ge to' 'both'; svei'kall' 'bachelor'; kri'm — fårkjø'ling 'cold'; sjinn'fyd'de — sjinn'fell' 'sheepskin coverlet'; mø'keda'jen — on'sda'jen 'Wednesday'; læu'guda'jen — læu'da'jen 'Saturday'; skrad'dare — skred'dar 'tailor'; stop'pi — stol'pe 'post'; fai' — fa'r 'father'; møi' — mo'r 'mother'; tå'na — tå'a 'the toe'; stei'kje — stei'ke 'roast'; svår't — svar't 'black'; dyn'na — dø'ra 'the door'.

(7) Setesdal (8M1): kvai'ti — vai'te 'wheat'; hå'ft — hal't 'half'.

(8) Hardanger (15P4): vøt'teren — vin'teren 'the winter'.

(9) Voss (6P1): æk'kja — æn'ka 'widow'; gof'far — bes'tefa'r 'grandfather'; gom'mor — bes'temo'r 'grandmother'.

(10) Sogn (several inf.): be'l 'time'; vet'ter — vin'ter 'winter'; lar're — pri'm 'whey'; ek'kja — ein'ka 'widow'.

Some forms are mentioned by several informants, such as *snakke* for *tala*, *enke* for *ekkja*, *potet* for *jordeple*, *melk* for *mjokk*. The form *ekkja* was described as actually offensive by one Sogn informant: 'Me torde kje seia ekkja so ekkjune hoirde da' (We didn't dare say 'ekkja' so the widows heard it.)[52] The changes include phonetic, morphological, and lexical items, nearly always moving from a less to a more widely-used form, which often is that of urban DN.

6. *Dialect Attitudes.*

Only in the case of a few informants has it been possible to discover a strong sense of pride in the dialect. Such regions as Telemark and Voss, occasionally Gudbrandsdalen, the homes of folk poetry and greatly admired by the advocates of folk culture, show more sturdy independence with respect to their dialect than those regions that have not been so favored.[53] Many informants spontaneously expressed their feeling concerning the 'ugliness' of their own dialects. Sognings compared their own dialect unfavorably with that of Voss, while at least one Valdres compared his unfavorably with that of Sogn (and Voss).[54] A Sogn woman (6Q1) felt that her dialect sounded 'coarse' and had many more 'snodige or' (strange words) than the Valdres dialect which was more 'ette skriften' (according to the book). A speaker of Hadeland dialect in Spring Grove (20C5) preferred the Halling dialect, but another with Halling blood (20C2) found the dialect ugly. Gudbrandsdalen and upper EN informants in the Coon Area expressed dislike of the SWN Flekkefjord dialect (10C2), but some were just as free in calling their own dialect ugly (11C2): 'I never realized it was so homely a language.' Solør speakers commented on the 'broadness' of their own dialect, and tried to avoid some of its most conspicuous forms: 'Solungen snakker mie stikt' (The Solør speaker talks very ugly).[55]

But in spite of these feelings, most of them admit that they like to listen to their own dialect; as one informant put it, 'E synes da e no rikti stykt mange gånje, men me må no liva ijenom da likevel' (It sounds real ugly many times, but we have to live through it anyway).[56] An elderly Solør speaker declared, after speaking of the ugliness of his dialect: 'Je liker bæst å høre som der je kommer frå, je må tellstå de, så gammel je er' (I like best to hear the way they talk where I come from, I have to admit that, old as I am).[57] An illuminating instance of pride lost and recovered is the story told by a native of Koshkonong who was reared in the Numedal dialect, one of the Midland idioms. 'Once another woman and I were listening to two others who were talking the Numedal dialect. Then this woman said to me, "It's an ugly dialect (bygdemaal) these Numedalers have." She was half Telemarking this woman who said it. I didn't know what to answer her, so I just kept still. I was real ashamed. She didn't know that I was a Numedaler. But I've gotten over it now. I think my mother tongue is real fine, so I'm not ashamed any more (Je synes at morsmaale mit æ regti grust, saa je æ inkje skamfull meire).'[58] Here the change from the term *bygdemaal*, with a touch of contempt, to *morsmaal*, with a sense of pride, marks a new evaluation of her own background. She showed it in practice by writing long and valuable accounts of her early experiences, all in the dialect of her Numedal forebears.

The implied standard against which the local dialects are often judged is that of the written DN or of the corresponding spoken forms, particularly of urban dwellers in the eastern cities. From their pastors and other educated leaders they had learned that this was a more elegant form of Norwegian, and had in general accepted this judgment. A Telemark informant told of an episode in a carpenter shop in Kongsberg where he worked before emigration. His boss there told him that 'now you will have to learn to talk as we talk here' and get rid of that 'westland language,' i.e. the Telemark dialect.[59] His wife had a similar experience in this country, when she worked for a Norwegian-American pastor. The pastor's wife forbade her to speak Norwegian to the children, for they didn't want their children to learn her dialect; instead she had to speak English, even though she probably spoke it more badly than she did Norwegian.

Questions put to informants as to what kind of Norwegian they liked best frequently brought out responses showing that they had learned this lesson well. A sogning who had taken active part in church leadership declared, 'Skrift-språge ær dæ bæsta, naturligvis.' (The written language is the best, of course).[60] A telemarking of the same type declared, 'Byspråke dei kalla, de synes eg æ mest høvelikt å høre på.' (The city language, as they call it, I think is most suitable to listen to.)[61] A Coon Prairie woman declared that her own speech was only 'i simpel bygdemål — dæ lyes mye penere dette fænsi måle' (a homely country dialect — it sounds much nicer, this fancy language).[62] Two different men, one in Blair and one in Iola, made similar remarks about the speech of their wives, which they regarded as more elegant than their own. The first said of his wife that 'ho talar meir Kristjana-språk, som n far seier...meir ætte skreften, får je sea, den vægen som dæ æ skrivi....' (she talks more Christiania (Oslo) language as father says....more according to the writing, I would say, the way it's written....).[63] The second groped for his words in much the same way: 'Ho snakkar differnt norsk....ho snakkar rætti etter —

va vi ska si — etter bibeln (laughs) — eller etter boka vi sier da, ja, men dæ ha no jæ aldri kunt lært....' (she talks different Norwegian....she talks really according to — what shall we say — according to the Bible — or the book as we say, but I've never been able to learn that, you see.)[64]

A Sogning woman declared laughingly that when the preacher was listening, they made an effort to say *kona* instead of *kjering* 'wife'.[65] Some of the same reverence seems to have attached to the interviewer also, for many recordings and interviews have begun with the informants' best Sunday language, only to be gradually broken down into natural, effortless speech as their familiarity and ease increased.[66] The forms of their BL are generally pure spelling pronunciations: *etage* (pronounced with hard g instead of [sh] 12Q2), *fader* (for far 'father' 14D4), *koene* (for kyra 'the cows' 12Q6), revealing a complete lack of contact with the informal, 'cultured' pronunciation. The obvious practical advantage of a standard language as a means of common understanding was emphasized by an intelligent Suldal speaker: 'Ta for eksempel en lærdøl eller bergenser eller trånnjemmer å like ne te Kristiansann, så ær de svært vanskele for æin suldøl å forstå dei, å derfor så bejynner di å snakka ette skrifto, då kan han forstå di gott.' (Take for instance a man from Lærdal or Bergen or Trondhjem and all the way to Kristiansand, it's very hard for one from Suldal to understand them, and therefore they begin to talk according to the writing, and then he can understand them well.)[67]

The attitudes to the book language are ultimately traceable to class distinctions in the homeland between the educated upper class and the humbler country folk. Some informants have broken with the dialects and adopted book language, usually those who through training or ability have risen somewhat out of the ranks of the common people. Men who have had occasion to appear frequently in public, as lay preachers, church officials, or attorneys have usually departed from their dialects for good. Among such examples are informants 26P4 and 12R6, lay leaders in church work, 14F4, town clerk, 12F1, attorney, to mention only a few. A dialect basis was traceable in the speech of all these, but no amount of persuasion could bring them back to a dialectal form. In these men of prominence the book speech was no doubt expected by their community, but woe to one who tried to speak it without such justification. One Sogning declared that 'among the lay people they'd laugh at you if you tried to use book language — and say, "Kor store han e vorten pao da!" (How stuck-up he's gotten!).[68]

Stories were circulated about the affectation of certain people, particularly women, whose social ambitions misled them into refining their speech. One woman in Waterloo Ridge was said to change her speech as soon as an outsider came in: in commenting on the foggy weather, she might have been saying, 'Næi, va dæ itt skodda i dag!', and then quickly change over to, 'Dæ va så tykk en tåge.'[69] Another story is of a man from Ringebu in Gudbrandsdal who argued with another about the merits of their respective dialects, and clinched it by telling the other: 'Vi tålå mæir ætte boka vi hæll døkk jørre' (We talk more like the book than you do), but his own statement belied it by the broad dialect in which he said it.[70] A woman in Waterloo Ridge, Iowa, who stopped in at the parsonage, started her sentence in the finest book language, but wound up in the broadest terms, when she said: 'Nei, mange takk. Je har spist så meget je kan hlættes itt eta mer' (No, many thanks; I have eaten so much I just can't eat any more).[71] These anecdotes illustrate the general conclusion of many that it sounds 'på-tie' (affected) and 'domt' (stupid) to try to talk 'like the preacher'.[72] It implies that one is 'fin på det' (showing off), when one tries to ape the speech of the 'konsenert' or privileged class.[73] 'Knoting' is another term for adorning one's speech with fine phrases beyond one's station in life.[74] Some persons certainly suffered from this attitude, as Georgina Ritland Harris has reported for her mother, to whom it was a disappointment that the children used what she considered the less refined language instead of the one *she* spoke.[75] Others, particularly in urban centers, did like Halle Steensland, who on arriving in Chicago suddenly realized that no one was going to laugh at him any more for trying to talk better than his dialect, and so made use of the freedom of America to acquire his Dano-Norwegian speech.

7. *Significance of the Dialects.*

But for most speakers of AmN the feeling certainly prevailed that 'de e rart mæ dialektene — de e lettere å snakke slik enn etter skriften' (It's strange about the dialects — it is easier to talk this way than according to the book.)[76] This was their real language, which most of them clung to in spite of all criticism.[77] The use of dialects was more of a bond than a divisive factor in most cases, since it identified the speaker as an 'ordinary person', a 'regular fellow.'

In Norway dialect differences were sometimes associated with neighborly rivalries and enmities. In spite of diligent inquiry it has not been possible to find any important evidence that such differences were carried over into this country and associated with dialect differences. Most of the mocking has been good-natured, excepting only where other, more fundamental differences existed between the dialect groups. This was clearly the case in Beaver Creek where a Hardanger informant reported that the neighboring Strilar were 'rougher and tougher, and some again were bitterly pious — less friendly and likeable' than his own people.[78] 'Me e kje so Haringgane me, mæ dans te kvar kvell' (we're not like the Hardangers, with dancing every evening), they are reported to have said. The same kind of religious opposition existed between the more easy-going Hardanger people and the Sognings in the Lodi area, this time reported from the other side. The Sognings looked on the Hardangers as lost souls: 'Dai drakk å dai banna å dai raiste te kjerkao' (They drank and they swore and they went to church), while the others for their part regarded the Sognings as long-faced hypocrites. 'Ja,' declared a Sogning woman, 'da e so besynderleg me dai synodefolki — kven da e so prise presten dai salig!' (It's so strange with those Synod people — no matter who they are the minister declares them blessed!)[79] In the Coon Prairie area a church cleavage on dialectal lines took place many years ago; under the leadership of informant 10N1 most of the 'Flekkefjordings' seceded from the original congregation.[80] But in each of these cases we are dealing not primarily with dialectal differences, but with differences in psychology which affected the religious approach of these two groups. In general we are probably justified in taking the word of the venerable patriarch of Gays' Mills, Wisconsin, who said: 'I dæi daga så va dæ kji spørsmaol um ka bygd du va ifrao, berre du va norsk å æin go nabbo' (In those days no one asked what community you came from, just so you were Norwegian and a good neighbor).[81] A policeman in Blair, Wisconsin, who was asked whether there was any more misbehavior in one dialect group than in any other, laughingly replied, 'Å nei, når dei er fulle, så er dei alle like' (Oh no, when they're drunk, they're all alike.)[82] We may conclude that the dialects as such have not seriously divided the Norwegians, but have rather added spice, humor, and variety to an otherwise dull existence. Whatever weaknesses they might have as instruments of the highest culture, they are everywhere regarded as more fun than any other form of language.

It is commonly stated that colonial dialects are conservative, retaining many archaisms which have been lost in the motherland. While this has a certain kernel of truth, we have seen how every degree of dialect preservation, from the most faithful to a practically complete abandonment, can be found among the speakers of AmN, even within the group of informants specially selected for this study, nearly all of whom are rural and therefore conservative in their speech habits. It is not easy for outsiders to judge concerning the purity of a given local dialect, for a dialect that will strike an outside observer as highly authentic may yet be markedly changed in the ears of natives. Perhaps the best evidence is that which is frequently reported by returned emigrants and their children, who have had a chance to confront their own speech with that of the ancestral community. One such from Telemark related that 'når eg kom heim atte, ledde dei åt meg å sa at eg snakka gamalt førsdals' (when I went home again, they laughed at me and said that I talked old-fashioned Fyrisdal dialect).[83] A second-generation woman from Coon Valley reports: 'Da je kom te Biri, sa di at di hadde itte hørt så gammeldags biring' (When I got to Biri, they said they hadn't heard such old-fashioned Biri dialect).[84] But there was also the contrasting experience of J. A. Holvik, who visited the Nordfjord community of his ancestors and hopefully tried his dialect there only to have the natives declare that it was 'not genuine'.[85]

The informants who claimed superior authenticity for their American dialects explained the change in the homeland as being due to the influence of DN city language. This is true enough, but other factors are also involved. The AmN dialects have been subjected to many leveling influences, as we have seen, but even when these were in part the same as in Norway, they were of such different weight and applied under such different circumstances that we could not expect the results to be the same. In Norway the influences have been national and centralizing; in America they have been local and centrifugal. Native Norwegians listening to AmN speakers naturally notice those archaisms that have clung to their dialects, and fail to notice novations that they themselves have also adopted, unless these novations are in the direction of English, which is often the case. It is therefore exaggerated to say, as has often been said, that the Norwegian settlements in America are the best places to find Norwegian dialects spoken in their ancient purity. To the extent that it is true, it is true only for certain features in the dialects and for certain individuals, rarely if ever for whole communities. Within each settlement there is a conspicuous trend toward a new and American norm of N speech, which would not be identical with that of any N dialect. The second generation is more homogeneous in its speech than the first. But before the development toward a *lingua franca* is complete, the transition to English has interrupted a development that would in time have made the AmN world as happy a hunting-ground for the linguist as is Pennsylvania German. Before our eyes we see the pressures of social conformity at work in an effort to reestablish that linguistic unity which was disturbed for each N emigrant by the very fact of his emigration.

Chapter 14.

BILINGUALISM AND BORROWING.

> A language is so constructed that no matter
> what any speaker of it may desire to communicate,
> no matter how original or bizarre his idea or his
> fancy, the language is prepared to do his work. He
> will never need to create new forms or to force upon
> his language a new formal orientation — unless, poor
> man, he is haunted by the form-feeling of another
> language and is subtly driven to the unconscious
> distortion of the one speech-system on the analogy
> of the other.
>
> *Edward Sapir (1924).*[1]

The impact of American English on the Norwegian dialects
spoken by the immigrants was bound to be even greater than that
of other dialects or even of standard Norwegian. Relatively few
of the immigrants found it necessary or desirable to acquire any
other kind of Norwegian than that which they had learned at their
mother's knee. But most of them were forced by circumstance to
acquire enough English to meet the demands of the new culture
upon them. We have already discussed at some length the resulting
confusion of linguistic patterns, the attitudes of various observers
to this confusion, and some of the consequences in writing of this
situation. The time has come to study more closely the process of
interlingual influence, not from the point of view of the casual
observer, but against a background of present-day knowledge
concerning linguistic and social behavior in general.[2]

1. *The Meaning of Borrowing.*

We shall begin by abandoning forthwith the term popularly used about this process, which is based on the metaphor of 'mixture'. We used this in an earlier chapter, but only in deference to common usage among the N immigrants who generally say of a person that he 'mixes'. The AmG book entitled *Gemixte Pickles*, with its poems in an Americanized German, shows that the same metaphor is popular among the Germans.[3] Even an older generation of linguists used this term, as when Hermann Paul headed his chapter in the *Prinzipien der Sprachgeschichte* 'Sprachmischung'; this usage was also followed by e.g. Whitney and Schuchardt. As a description of the process it might seem to have a certain vividness that justifies its use, but on closer inspection it shows disadvantages which have apparently led later linguists, such as Sapir and Bloomfield, to abandon it. Even Paul had to warn against the misunderstanding that it was possible to mix languages 'ungefähr in gleicher Menge.'[4] The metaphor suggests that two languages can be put into a kind of cocktail shaker and then emerge as an entirely different concoction. Mixture implies the creation of an entirely new entity and the disappearance of both constituents, or a jumbling of a more or less haphazard nature. But speakers have not been observed to draw freely from two languages at once, aside from abnormal cases. They may switch rapidly from one to the other, but at any given moment they are speaking only one, even when they resort to the other for assistance. Speakers of e.g. AmN continue to speak a recognizably Norwegian language distinct from their English down to the time when they switch to the latter for good.[5]

Nor shall we use the term 'hybrid' in describing what has happened in AmN, for this term implies that some languages are not hybrid, but 'pure'. These are scarcely any more observable than a 'pure race' in ethnology. The term we shall use is *borrowing*, a technical term in general use among linguists. At first blush the word might seem almost as inept for the process we wish to study as 'mixture'. The metaphor implied is certainly absurd, since the borrowing takes place without the lender's consent or even awareness, and the borrower is under no obligation to repay the loan. It is more like a kind of stealing, though the owner is deprived of nothing and feels no urge to recover his goods. But actually it is an example of what anthropologists call *cultural diffusion*, the spread of an item of culture from people to people. Borrowing is linguistic diffusion, and can be unambiguously defined as *the attempt by a speaker to reproduce in one language patterns which he has learned in another.* Somewhere, somehow the speaker has learned a given linguistic item; he repeats it, but in a new context which happens to belong to a different language from the one in which he learned it.

This is something that has happened wherever there have been bilinguals. It is, in fact, unthinkable without the existence of bilinguals, and apparently inevitable where there is any considerable group of bilinguals. Borrowing has loomed large as a subject of discussion among linguists for a long time, and many theories have been built upon it. Yet there are relatively few who have made this field their primary concern, and we can hardly say that the basic laws of borrowing have been fully clarified. In order to provide a background for the AmN development, we shall include here a brief description of similar phenomena among other groups not too unlike the Norwegian immigrants. We shall choose four well-documented instances, including three quite different groups in the United States and one in Europe.

2. *A Quartet of Bilingual Situations.*

(1) As the type of an old-established, non-English dialect, we shall take Pennsylvania German; only Canadian (and Louisiana) French and Southwestern American Spanish are comparable. Shortly after the founding of Pennsylvania by William Penn, the Germans began to arrive. The first settlement was in 1683, the bulk of the settlers immigrated between 1720 and 1750, and by the time of the Revolution they constituted about one third of the population of the colony.[6] For two centuries these thrifty and industrious farmers have thus been settled fairly compactly and within one area. They date back to a time before the creation of an American nation, when the pressure from the English-speaking environment was relatively small. Their pride of ancestry,

their cultural and religious exclusiveness, and their economic strength have made them a little island in the American world. Only the persistent industrialization of this century has begun to make inroads on them, and it is a minor irony that just when signs are appearing of a breakdown in the use of PaG, it has become the object of linguistic attention as never before. Thanks to the initiative of Hans Kurath while director of the New England Dialect Atlas, we are better informed today about this language than any other non-English American speech.[7]

Among the several studies of PaG, there are some that deal primarily with the influence of English on this German dialect of the Rhine Palatinate. From these we learn that E has scarcely left any mark on its phonology or morphology, but has enriched its vocabulary by several hundred loanwords in common use.[8] These include many terms for objects first met with in America, such as bushel, college, cracker, county, pie, township, etc. But they also include many terms for which good German words were available, even in the rural dialects, e.g. *bockabuch* 'pocketbook', *fence-eck* 'fence corner'. For some terms there is vacillation between E and G words: *geld* beside 'money', *disch* beside 'table', and *schulmeeschter* beside 'teacher'.[9] As Learned noted as long ago as 1889, the use of English words, even in their native German, was stimulated by the need of transacting business with English-speaking tradesmen and dealing with representatives of the American government.[10]

The loans have generally been adapted to the sound system of PaG, but we have the testimony of J. W. Frey that earlier and later loans can be distinguished according to the extent of adaptation. Thus E $t > d$ in the early loan 'timothy', but remained t in later words.[11] They have been fitted into the native morphological patterns, such as gender and verb tenses, according to principles discussed in articles by Carroll E. Reed and Lester W. Seifert.[12] Some E material has been so thoroughly assimilated that new words have come into being like *uff-g'sobered* 'sobered up' and *Gekick* 'constant kicking (grumbling)'. Paul Schach has presented numerous examples of what he calls 'hybrid derivatives', like *becksel* 'small box', and 'hybrid compounds', like *wasserschpiket* 'water spigot' and *endschelfutkuche* 'angelfood cake'.[13]

Today, Schach informs us, 'nearly all PaGermans are bilingual.' The youngest generation understands the language, but many of them cannot (or pretend they cannot) speak it very fluently.' This is confirmed by Reed, of whose 42 informants 25 used English extensively.[14] The E spoken, however, is often phonetically inaccurate, with occasional German turns of phrase; but on the whole the younger generation speaks a good English.[15]

(2) As the type of a more recent immigration, we may study the situation among the Portuguese immigrants of Massachusetts. This has been described in a recent monograph by Leo Pap.[16] From this book we learn that the P were first drawn to this country by the whaling industry. In the first two-thirds of the 19th century it was common for Yankee whaling captains of New Bedford to replenish their crews by taking on men in the Azores. Many of these settled in New Bedford and nearby cities. After the middle of the century womenfolk and children began to follow the fishermen to New England, and by 1870 mass immigration set in. Whaling was by this time passé, and the attraction of New England lay in its textile mills. By 1900 'the bulk of the Portuguese were working in the New Bedford and Fall River factories.'[17] Many of them acquired small farms; it came to be said, 'If you want to see a potato grow, speak to it in Portuguese.'[18] Pap has shown how the immigrants formed cohesive groups, bound together by common linguistic and religious traditions, though split by many internal feuds. Some have wanted to perpetuate the national tradition, but the younger generation 'appear strongly Americanized in behavior and outlook.'[19] If they speak P at all, they do so imperfectly, while their E shows hardly a trace of P influence.

The P language spoken by the older generation, however, has undergone the same kind of large-scale borrowing from English as has PaG. Phonology and syntax have remained unaffected, except for occasional intonational changes and the introduction of E word order in certain phrases, e.g. *Portugues Recreativo Club* instead of *Club Recreativo Portugues*. Examples have also been noted of the use of intransitive verbs like *marchar* 'to march' in transitive connections as in English, e.g. Fagundes marched his men across.[20] Words for all kinds of cultural novelties were freely adopted: foods such as cake, pudding, sandwich; clothing such as slacks, sweater, overalls (*alverozes*); terms for housing such as building, cottage, bungalow, hall; amusements such as picnic, barbecue, clambake. In general, terms for politics, sports, diseases, law, school, means of communication, economic life were overwhelmingly American. P remained the terms for the human body and its functions, for family relations, and other phases of life in which the immigrants did not come into immediate contact with American speakers.

⌈Pap points out that in addition to the necessary, cultural loans there is a massive assortment of terms that are borrowed because they were associated with a new system of political and linguistic organization.⌉ 'Many words frequently heard impose themselves by the sheer force of repetition.'[21] Words like 'sure', 'O.K.', 'never mind' carry emotional connotations that could not easily be conveyed by similar Portuguese expressions. When they go so far as to borrow E words for potatoes, tomatoes, butter, and milk, he declares that it is nothing else than 'the plain impact of intimate linguistic contact in an advanced state.'

The loans made are incorporated into the language in two ways; either they are borrowed entire, or else they may influence native words. In some cases the resulting loans are homonymous with native words of totally different meaning, e.g. P *bordar* 'embroider' acquired also the meaning of E 'board'. Some loans are entirely adapted to P patterns, while others are relatively unadapted. In determining the assignment of gender forms, the most important influence is natural gender, then suffixes, and occasionally a synonymous native word. But there is great vacillation in gender, though nouns that are otherwise unadapted are generally masc., unless they refer to female beings. Morphological suffixes are sometimes added to loanwords, but not always.

AmP shows certain interesting peculiarities in its vocabulary loans. E 'spring' and 'fall' are borrowed; the year has only two seasons in Portugal. Of the twelve months only July is borrowed, due to the expression *fode julaia* 'Fourth of July'; Christmas is borrowed. A distinction is made between natural ice, for which P *gelo* is used, and artifical ice, for which E 'ice' is used.

(3) One group of peoples whose loanword problems have not been seriously considered until quite recently are the American

Indians. Yet here are peoples native to the Americas over a far longer period than the Spanish and English invaders. Socially they have been in an even more subordinate position than the most recent European immigrants. An interesting description is available of conditions among the Yaqui, a tribe in Arizona, whose villages were hispanicized by missionaries and political functionaries by the end of the 17th century.[22] Spicer shows how this kind of 'directed culture change' resulted in a one-sided borrowing from Spanish, with very few loan-translations or original inventions. Today 65 % of the domestic utensils, social organizations, and religious rituals are named in Spanish terms. Even their term for praying is part Spanish: *líosnóoka* from Sp *dios* 'God' and native *nóoka* 'speak'.

Here as elsewhere there are considerable differences in the extent of adaptation of individual words. Spicer believes that the most markedly modified words were introduced before 1800 when the Yaquis as a group were not widely familiar with Spanish. Since that time the tribe has become at least 50 % bilingual, and new Spanish words are admitted freely, without modification. Thus the word for 'stove' was borrowed from Sp *estufa* as *ehtúpa*, with a change of *f* to *p*; but in the recent *fonografo* the *f*'s are not changed. As for the extent of original creation, the author feels that 'it would seem possible to have invented descriptive terms which utilized Yaqui roots or to have applied the names for approximate equivalents,' but this was rarely done.

Among the Pima Indians the situation was somewhat different. George Herzog has shown that here a number of descriptive terms did come into being. They call raisins 'dry grapes', elephant 'wrinkled buttocks', and battery 'lightning box.' He attributes this activity to a period when the Indians were left pretty much to themselves after the departure of the Spanish and before closer contacts were established with the Americans. There are, of course, loanwords from the Spanish, and with the establishment of English schools and a growing bilingualism, English terms are slipping into their speech with an ease that 'reminds one of what happens to the native vocabulary of immigrants in this country.'[23]

(4) By way of comparison we may now turn away from the United States and study a European situation where the contact

between the two languages has been less intimate. In a recent monograph on E lws. in Modern Norwegian, Aasta Stene has surveyed the conditions of 'linguistic borrowing in the process.'[24] Through travellers and tourists, emigrants and sailors a lively traffic has been going on between Norway and the English-speaking world, particularly since the beginning of the eighteenth century. But in contrast with the situations described from the United States, most of the words have entered by way of writing. Schools have actively taught the language, giving at least a smattering to most people with a higher education. English and American books in the original and films with sound have been spreading it even more widely in recent years. The 'culture carriers' are Norwegians who have learned English as a foreign language.

The several hundred words that have come in through the activity of these bilinguals she sums up as 'representative of the age of the Industrial Revolution.'[25] They are words from the field of sports: team, outsider, fair play, halfback, knockout, golf, hickory, splitcane; travel, especially railroad engineering, road building, motoring and flying: sightseeing, globetrotter, trapper, and wild west; sailing and shipping: trawler, steward, skylight, deadweight; trade: boom, check, pool, trademark, bestseller. Highly characteristic are words for dress and fashions: plaid, tweed, pigskin, smart, up-to-date, sweater, make-up; food and drink: gin, sherry, cocktail, bar, bootlegger, beef, grill; cultural: film, essay, short-story, folklore, sketch; government and politics: home rule, boycott, strike, detective, gangster, revolver, boomerang; society: gang, mob, gentleman, slum, all right, OK, chummy, rough, square, bluff, flirt, bum, job, baby, drawback.

In their formal treatment of these words the N behave just as do other bilingual speakers. Some of the words they pronounce with some semblance of the English sounds, such as retaining the E diphthongs or the sound of *w*. This is especially true, says Miss Stene, of words which 'are felt by the N speaker to be distinctly alien, words that are mentally given in quotation marks.' In her word list she marks these with a special symbol, e.g. blizzard, speakeasy, darling, dreadnought, five o'clock tea. But even those that she does not so mark are by no means completely assimilated to the N pattern. Miss Stene has set up a list of synchronic criteria for detecting these, and excludes (as being no longer 'loanwords' in her definition) words which show none of these 'foreign' criteria.[27] Among monolinguals who adopt the new words, the model of pronunciation becomes either the spelling itself or the E pronunciation of N bilinguals. The greater influence of the spelling is apparent when one compares the pronunciation of lws. in American Norwegian: E 'bus' > N *buss*, AmN *båss*; E 'check' > N *sjekk*, AmN *kjekk*.

The morphology shows a similar range from partial to complete adaptation. While verbs are completely fitted into the pattern, adjectives often fail to get N suffixes for neuter and plural. Nouns like 'cocktail' get E rather than N plurals. Some compounds are adopted in full; some are partially translated, e.g. *grapefrukt* 'grapefruit', *filmstjerne* 'film star'; others are completely translated, e.g. *fotball* 'football'.

3. *The Direction of Linguistic Pressure.*

The similarity of what has happened in these four groups to the development of AmN will be clear without further discussion. In each case we have found a bilingual group that served as the vehicle of interlingual influence, and we may repeat with some assurance the dictum of Hermann Paul that such a group is indispensable to any large-scale borrowing.[28] If we ask for the reasons for borrowing, we may thus say that *the learning of another language is one essential condition.*

As we have seen in earlier chapters, the learning of English was a matter of social and economic advantage to the immigrant. But the very process of learning English was for most people an invitation to confusion. The immigrants were not carefully guided into the language by approved pedagogic method, with someone to point out for them the pitfalls of bilingualism. The language was learned in the market place, in situations where the immigrant was brought into contact with native speakers. It was picked up piecemeal, but effectively, and as a vital part of the process of acculturation. It was learned together with new technical procedures, new social customs, new attitudes of approval and disapproval. Whether he wished it or no, the immigrant was being initiated into one of the subtlest aspects of his environment, the invisible network of distinctions and congruences which the categories of the new language itself imposed on his universe of experience. This is what is ordinarily meant by 'learning to think' in a new language. But for every time he 'thought' in it, he was practically required to use patterns that differed from those of his native speech. Before he realized what was happening, he was beginning to substitute them for his native patterns.

Behind his learning of the language was a social pressure, and this social pressure exerted itself indirectly on his native language as well. This is clear if we consider the one-way nature of most interlingual influence. The German scholar Windisch formulated the relationship in a famous thesis of 1897: it is the language of the learner that is influenced, not the language he learns. English is hardly influenced at all by the immigrant languages, but these are all influenced by English; in Latin America the Indian languages acquire material from Spanish, but the Spanish shows very little influence from Indian.[29]

The reason for this is that the social pressure in such cases is all in one direction, because of the difference in prestige of the speakers of the two languages. One could almost set up an equation describing the strength and direction of such influence by counting the number of persons learning each language. Most Norwegian immigrants learned English, but very few Americans learned Norwegian. It is not merely a matter of numbers, however; the social prestige is what counts.

In any bilingual community we can distinguish various kinds of bilinguals, according to whether the second language was acquired in childhood (say before age 14) or in adulthood. If we wish to designate these varieties, we may call the native tongue A and the acquired tongue B, using capitals for full mastery, lower case letters for incomplete mastery. We will then be able to distinguish the following kinds of speakers in a typical immigrant community:

A — native monolinguals
Ab — adult bilinguals
AB — childhood bilinguals (who learned A first)

aB — childhood bilinguals (who lost their facility through lack of practice)

BA — childhood bilinguals (who learned B first; a rather rare case)

Ba — adult bilinguals (who acquired A as a second language)

B — monolinguals in the new language

A numerical and social analysis of the relative importance of these various groups should tell us much concerning the extent and direction of linguistic pressure within the community.

The fact is that for the individual language learner Windisch's formulation is not true. Those learners with whom we are most familiar in our foreign language classes or even adult immigrants do maltreat the language they learn. In their case there is bilateral influence between the languages. But the innovations they make in the language they learn do not spread to the native speakers of that language, while the innovations they make in their own language do spread. The immigrant learner is placed by the direction of linguistic pressure in a stream of influence where he is below the speakers of the other language, but above the speakers of his own. Any pollution he causes will flow downstream to his own countrymen. In more precise terms we may say that he is only an outsider within the group whose language he is learning; but within his own he may often gain prestige by his very knowledge of the other language, so that his novations have a chance of spreading. Such a situation must have existed in England at the time of the Norman dominance. We may even suspect that the true originators of that curious patchwork which is modern English were the servants of the Norman-French nobles. The grooms and the maids, whose native tongue was English, learned more or less bad French to converse with their masters. Large chunks of this French must have found their way into the English they spoke among themselves, and even to their Anglo-Saxon cousins and aunts. But when their masters gave up French, the English they learned and eventually made into the cultured tongue of the land was the speech they acquired in the nurseries from their own servants.

It is interesting to compare the pressure situations of the American immigrants acquiring English with those of the European intellectual. The English terms acquired by the AmN speakers were of general importance, involving crucial terms of American social and governmental life. But in Norway the terms were of rather special nature, being of greatest interest to only a limited section of the population. The immigrants were thrown into practical day-by-day contact with American life, while the Europeans were largely in indirect contact. The immigrant bilingual lacked social status, and his struggle to acquire it involved the need of accommodating within his language the entire structure of official and economic life in his new homeland. He was under strong pressure to acquire the new distinctions made by native speakers; any others that were provided for by his own language became superfluous and tended to be forgotten.

Most important for the immigrant was the fact that the new situations in which he learned his English were shared by a large number of other speakers of his own language. They were all in the same boat, drifting in the same direction. Without affectation or snobbishness they were speaking an Americanized tongue to each other before they were fully aware of what was happening to them. The needs of understanding and of social solidarity were most effortlessly met by a gradual infiltration of loans. These were not limited to actual cultural novelties or so-called 'necessary' words; the terms most characteristic of the new environment were often impressed on their minds by mere repetition in vivid situations. Their experience in the new language began to outstrip their experience in the old, and the discrepancy set up a pressure which led to linguistic change.

4. *The Selection of Loans.*

The force and direction of linguistic pressure also helps to determine the number and the kind of loans which one language makes from another. The lending language may carry prestige in one field and contribute words from this field without doing so in others. If there is some field of activity in which the speakers of the two languages have much contact, and in which one group is clearly superior to the other, this field is likely to be reflected in heavy borrowing by the inferior group. We shall see in a later chapter how this applies in the life of the Norwegian immigrant. Those fields, such as religion, where he isolated himself from his neighbors and felt no inferiority were fields in which he successfully resisted the invasion of technical terminology.

Linguistic purists, who often have been more at home with written documents than with the living language, have tended to deplore the admission of loans for any ideas which could already be expressed in the receiving language. The linguist Hugo Schuchardt regarded the use of French words in German as an expression of 'Affectation oder Raffinement', words which at the same time illustrated the practice he deplored.[30] A distinction was made by Eugen Kaufman between words adopted from other languages out of compulsion (lehnzwang), usefulness (lehnbedürfnis), and inclination (lehnneigung).[31] Such distinctions are the result of the observation already made above that borrowing always goes well beyond the actual 'needs' of a language. But in practice it is impossible to say just when a word is needed or not. At least we can say with some confidence that the speakers who use the borrowed word feel the need, or they would not use it. Who shall have the authority to decree that a given word is needed while another, equally popular, is not? It would be easy to show that in the final instance no foreign word is needed in any language, since every language, even English, can make up new ones at will, either by changing old ones (cf. Spam) or by combining them (cf. atom bomb).

The question of whether a word is 'necessary' (and therefore good) or 'unneccessary' (and therefore bad) is a value judgment rather than a scientific problem. It is based on a static conception of language, promoted in part by the way in which bilingual dictionaries are arranged. Students who have learned their second language by faithful use of the dictionary often think of the terms of two languages as being arranged in neat columns, one opposite the other. Bilingual speakers whose competence has been acquired in practical life situations are not so arranged, if we can judge by their behavior. They adopt new words which displace old words as well as new words which do not. Our knowledge of their learning situations does not suffice in every case to determine why they should do so. There was no strict need for Norwegian immigrants to adopt the English words for 'river', 'field', 'fence', 'barn', 'cousin', or 'pail'. They had adequate Norwegian words for all of these objects, and would certainly not have abandoned them even in America if they had not been placed under the strong linguistic pressure of English speech on their economic activities. Whatever the explanation may be in each individual case, the general trend is clear: the immigrant was forced to create an instrument of communication which would express the significant distinctions of American society in all those fields where he participated in the activities of that society. This was true even while he still spoke his native tongue, and hence the loans which he was forced to make.[32]

The cultured man, whose vocabulary is more extensive, and whose ability to form new expressions is more highly developed, will often be more successful in resisting loans than the average person, though he is also more exposed to certain kinds of loans because of his greater familiarity with foreign languages. Among the immigrants a characteristic expression of the common man's point of view appeared in a pioneer Norwegian newspaper in 1859. The writer was replying to a criticism of language 'mixture' which had appeared in a preceding issue: 'When, in our struggle to learn English, we happen to mix the two languages together, as might be natural enough under these circumstances, then comes *** and his like and makes capital fun of us for that.... When a man comes to this country without a penny, but with a family to support, there is usually no recourse but to go out among the Americans and seek work to earn one's livelihood.... That some who come here in response to a "call" and find a house and a farm in readiness for them, with an annual salary offered them, so they don't need to make their living among the Americans — that they don't "mix" the language does not earn them any great credit.'[33]

We see the results in the informants' frequent complaint that they are unable to recall the proper N word for some particular phenomenon. One American bilingual declared: 'Of course we have to mix — I can't possibly remember all the Norwegian words.'[34] Another, who did her utmost to give the N word whenever possible, finally sighed and said: 'Now and then I can't quite think of what it's called in Norwegian.'[35] A Norwegian bilingual from Blair was emphatic: 'Nobody talks N without mixing.'[36] One old Voss informant commented that he should probably have said 'town-kasserar' instead of 'town-treasurer', but 'somehow it doesn't fit so well to say that.'[37] 'They will all be more or less the same in mixing', declared his son-in-law, 'if they can't think of the word, they use the English.'[38] Or as another inf. said: 'For anything with which we were not immediately familiar we applied English.'[39] In speaking of corsets a Coon Valley lady explained: 'We called them corsets because we had to call them that at the store.'[40] When she recalled the N word for it a moment later — snøreliv — her sister commented that this word was 'konsjenert', i.e. upper-class, and therefore not natural to their speech. An American bilingual from Iowa noted that she grew up alongside Irish neighbors; as a consequence she never learned any N words for vegetables or spices. 'Den som trefte te å ha amerikanske å airis naboa, så måtte du apa ette så gått du kunne (If you happened to have American and Irish neighbors, you had to ape them as best you could).'

5. *The Learning Situations.*

The inability to recall the N word is of course part of the psychological mechanism that leads to the use of lws., and is itself due to the gradual shift in interests and attitudes which was described in chapter 5 as the 'great vocabulary shift.' When they have no Norwegian word for something, it may of course be due to the fact that they never knew it. Their experiences in Norway were often severely limited to their native locale, which was often pre-industrial in its culture. It might also be due to the fact that the word was purely passive in their vocabulary, a word heard by them in the usage of urban or educated people, but never used in their own daily conversation. The passage of years during which they never heard a custom referred to inevitably weakened the hold of many familiar words: spinning and weaving passed out of their lives, along with many of the food customs and social events they had known in the homeland. But over and beyond such purely cultural changes we must see the importance of *learning situations.* The number of new Norwegian words learned in contact with their fellow coun-trymen was not insignificant, but it was a static and conservative vocabulary, bearing reminiscences of the past. In English came to them all the excitement of a new and pulsing world which was being built around them. Many of their most novel and memorable experiences came in English, from the fourth of July celebrations to the political rallies, from the amazing machines that lightened their labor to the new media of mass entertainment. In such situ-ations they learned phrases that were not strictly necessary, but which contributed slangy bits of vividness to their speech, exclama-tions that brought back the gay informality of American social occasions. They learned easily to introduce their sentences with 'well —', to embellish them with 'by golly' and 'O. K.', and to describe people and things with the standard clichés of 'cute' and 'nice'. Cut off as they were from the sources of native renewal they might have found in the homeland, they sought some elements of dash and vividness in the new language. These did not necessarily displace the vivid phrases of the old dialects, many of which re-mained favorites as long as the dialects were spoken.

The learning situations had the further effect of giving to the English words a precision of meaning that was often lacking in corresponding N terms. The dominance of the Americans in those fields where the immigrant came into contact with them, and their mastery of the subtler distinctions of their own language forced him to regard them as experts whose usage he was bound to respect. It has often been observed that a potent source of linguistic renewal is the speech of specialists, whose terms are adopted by the less expert.[42] It is conspicuous in the usage of AmN informants that specialists in certain lines of work are more likely to use the E term than non-specialists. Most informants used N *brunn* in preference to E *well*, but not a well-digger, to whom the expression *drill a well* was the standard expression for his type of work. Carpenters are more likely to use E *nail* and *roof* than others, who often retain N *spiker* and *tak*. Those who raise peas for the canning factory are more likely to use *peas*, while those who raise them for home use are more likely to say *erter*. In each case these activities, by becoming economic rather than personal, led to a sharing of situ-ations with corresponding American experts.

Precision of reference was also promoted by the lws. in those cases where the number and meanings of terms do not agree in the two languages so that uncertainty can arise as to the meaning intended in a given situation. There are many words for hills in N, but the particular kind called 'bluff' in E is not distinguished. In a landscape where one wished to designate the bluff (or bluffs), it would be confusing to call it 'the hill' (bakken) unless it were the only one of its kind. Terms for streams of all kinds abound in N, but none of them fit exactly the distinction of *creek* from *river* which is characteristic of midwestern conditions. Since words are always used in particular situations, we see that the bilingual was often placed in situations where he wanted to make precisely the same distinctions as an American speaker. If a speaker of language A has three terms in a given range, and learns to speak a language B with four terms, he will discover a gap in his own language. But a speaker of language B who wants to talk like the speakers of language A will find himself with an *embarras de richesses* which makes him uncertain as to which of his terms to use. Such needs are of course entirely relative to the resources offered by the two languages. Until he learned English, the N did not feel the need of the American distinctions. But once he had learned the language, the need was there and could only be filled by the American term that had aroused it.

Possibly the most vivid illustrations of the effect of the learning situations on the use of native and borrowed words can be found in those cases where overlapping terms were both in use. Here we see very clearly that the dictionary meanings of words do not exhaust their effective meaning in actual speech. Only some such definition of meaning as that proposed by Bloomfield can begin to cope with the situation: 'the features of situation and action which are common to all utterances of a speech form.'[43] The situation in which the AmN bilingual heard the lws. was one which he shared with American speakers, and this situation became a part of its meaning. All informants knew that N *øl* and E *beer* referred to the same kind of drink; but they used *øl* in speaking of the homebrewed beer of early pioneer days, *beer* about the beer that was bought at the store. Similar distinctions have arisen in other languages under similar conditions: a classic instance is that of English *veal* and *beef* versus *calf* and *cow*. The bilingual servants of the Norman nobles came to make a distinction because they had to use the French words to their masters and the English words to the herders. A parallel instance from AmN is the use by at least one inf. of *høna* for the live chicken, *chicken* for the meat. Such distinctions are in many cases evanescent, since the situations get confused after the immigrants begin to speak E with each other and all partake of the same cultural patterns. A few examples of distinctions made between overlapping E and N words are the following:

E	N	
attic	loft	'The *loft* included the upstairs' 5L4.
barn	fjøs	'*Fjøs* was below, where the cow was' 11C2.
basement	kjellar	'*Kjellar* is in houses, *basement* in the barn' 5L4; more commonly *basement* refers to the church.
beer	øl	Several informants distinguish the home-made beer of the early period from the later kind that was purchased at stores: bir va stærkare dæ, dæ va dæ dei kjøpte 4F2; brygge øl men kjøpe bir 10C5 etc. (11B1 11C2 6Q4 8L3 10C3 10C2 10C1 12Q1 11C1 4L4); in telling about an early settler who brewed at home and started selling it, 4L4 alternated his use of the words.
brush	kvåst	The former for hair and paints, the latter only for painting 10C1.
bull	ukse	*Bull* used for breeding, *ukse* castrated and used as draft animals or meat (many inf.); fiksa dei når dei var små, så var dei ikkje bullar anna åksar 5G1 (cf. also 4F1 11C4 5L3 5H3 4P1 10C1).
ceiling	tak	'*Tak* is the roof' 6Q1; while 6Q3 identified them.
chicken	høna	'Always *chicken* when eating' 14C2.
country	land	'*Land* means farmland' 24A1.

E	N	
curtain	*gardina*	*Gardina* is the shade (dra ne gardina) 6Q1; 11C4.
feed	*for*	'*Feed* is grain; *for* is cornstalk, straw, hay' 4L1.
fork	*gaffel*	*Fork* in barn, *gaffel* in house 19A2; another inf. distinguished *fork* from N *greip*: the former had three tines, the latter five to six; 5H3.
garden	*hage*	Several agree that *garden* is a place for vegetables, *hage* a place for trees, equiv. to E orchard: the word *eplehage* 'apple orchard' was regularly used; 5L1 6P1 5C1 14D2 14C2 14D4.
handle	*handtak*	Stove *handle* but *handtak* on kettle 10C1: for the latter 10C2 uses *hanke*.
jug	*krukka*	'*Krukke* is open' 4F1.
meeting	*messe*	'Methodists, Baptists and lay preachers called it *midn* (*midding*)' 11C2.
moccassin	*ladd*	'*Maggis* were made of leather, mostly boughten; *ladder* were made for us by mother when children' 22F1.
mosquito	*myhank*	'*Miskit* small, *myhank* larger' 4L1.
rabbit	*hare*	*Rabbits* smaller 4Q2 5H3.
road	*veg*	Many informants agree that a *road* is a highway, while *veg* is a path or minor road; 'Han leve så langt ifrå råden, å så må eg kjøyre på denne vetle fillevegen hans' (quoted by 4Q2 from a visitor to his farm); *veg* also survives in phrases: 'han vi kje springe ut av væien når di kjørte ette råden' 5F1; cf. also 1D4 15P4 20J1 19A1 10C2.
strawberries	*jordber*	'*Strawberries* were domesticated, *jordber* grew wild' 4P1.
teacher	*lærar*	Frequently the former is used for the one in the English school, the latter in the Norwegian school.

E	N	
travel	*gå*	The former is often used in the sense of 'walk', displacing the latter; but one inf. distinguished them by using the former for a longer distance than the latter 14D4.
whip	*svippe*	'Når vi kjørde i bogge, hadde vi *svippe*, jort finere, i eitt; *hippe* var en stokk me snor i' 14D4.

6. *The Language Differential.*

So far we have tacitly assumed that the materials borrowed by one language group from another are to be accounted for exclusively by the relative socio-linguistic position of the speaker. But the example given above of the borrowing by AmP of the English word for 'ice' will show that this does not account for all the loans. To be sure, the fact that *ice* is borrowed for commercial ice, but not for natural ice shows that it is the contact with American business life that has brought about the borrowing. But AmN has the same contact, and yet has not borrowed English *ice*; the reason appears to be that in N the word *is* 'ice' is so similar to English *ice* that it is felt to be superfluous to borrow the English word. A simple equivalence is set up, so that N *is* corresponds exactly to E *ice* and is substituted for it whenever 'ice' is called for.

We may call this factor the *language differential*, by which is meant that some loans are facilitated by the degree of difference of the forms of the two languages. AmN would most certainly have had to have a word for maize, a type of grain which was unknown in Norway, except as a book term (*mais*). But instead of taking over the word *corn* from English, AmN substituted its own word *korn*, which was most often pronounced *konn* or *kodn* in the dialects. The tendency is clear, though it does not seem to be carried through with full regularity: *if a native word is similar in sound to a desired foreign word, it is often given the meanings of the foreign word*; if not, it is more common to borrow the foreign word. If possible, the foreign word is made to sound like some native word, at least in part. In AmP the words *overalls* and *overshoes* are borrowed as *alverozes* and *alvachus*, with substitution of the native prefix *al-* for the *o-* of the English words.[22]

As we see, this differential seems to affect rather the way in which words are borrowed (which will be discussed more fully in the next chapter) than the number of words borrowed. But it seems probable that the differential is also involved in the readiness with which influence may penetrate from language to language. If the adjustments required to adapt the material are sufficiently difficult, a resistance may be built up to the inclusion of such material in a language. Sapir expressed the opinion that 'the psychological attitude of the borrowing language itself towards linguistic material has much to do with its receptivity to foreign words.'[45] Some such force has been at work in modern Icelandic, which is entirely different from its kinsmen in the rest of Scandinavia in resisting the introduction of loanwords. But even here new words are constantly coming into being; the difference is primarily that they are generally built of native materials instead of being taken over lock, stock, and barrel. The fact that English loanwords have been taken into such utterly different languages as Japanese and Chinese shows that a great language differential is not in itself enough to neutralize the linguistic pressure of an expansive culture.

This conclusion would seem to be supported by the experience of immigrant languages in the United States. Their position is roughly comparable, since the same social pressure has been exerted on most of them by the American environment. Although they differ widely in structure, the result in terms of loanwords seems to be rather similar. It is too early to be dogmatic on this point, since we have not yet had enough detailed information on the various immigrant languages to make a satisfactory comparison. But it is clear from studying the material assembled by H. L. Mencken in the appendix to his *American Language* that all languages have adopted a roughly comparable vocabulary that is highly characteristic of the learning situations in which their speakers have been exposed to the English language.

The study of borrowing as a social phenomenon thus reduces itself to a study of the cultural relations between two language groups. Wherever bilinguals have arisen, the conditions have been satisfied for language influence; but a prestige differential was necessary to make this influence a strong one and to spread innovations from the bilingual group to the rest of the community. On the other hand, the prestige need not be attached to the language as a whole, and usually was not; different speakers might have different learning situations, so that some words could be acquired and others not; and the influence might very well be mutual between two languages if each had its own area of prestige.

Chapter 15.

THE PROCESS OF BORROWING.

> In hearing an unfamiliar foreign word.., we try
> to catch in it a complex of *our* phonological concep-
> tions, to decompose it into phonemes belonging to
> *our* mother tongue, and in conformity with *our* laws
> for the grouping of phonemes.
>
> *E. Polivanov (1931)*[1]

Since their borrowing from English is the most striking characteristic of the American-Norwegian dialects, it will be important
for us to analyze this process in more detail. As we saw in chapter
13, it goes on wherever bilingual speakers arise. It must therefore
in its origin be a process that takes place in each bilingual before
it is projected as group behavior. Each speaker of two languages
has to make his peace between the languages he masters, in one
way or another. Unfortunately we are unable to watch the mental
processes directly, and can only guess at them by observing their results and comparing these results with what the speakers themselves
report about their own mental experiences. Since most linguistic
behavior is implanted so early in life that it has become subconscious,
the remarks people make about it are generally inaccurate and cannot
be accepted as completely valid evidence. If we turn from the
individual speaker to the group within which he communicates,
we find that it is rarely possible to observe any given word on its
course from one language into another. Every loan must have been
made first by some individual, and then accepted and repeated
by many others; even this can have happened more than once.
All such limitations on our possibilities of observation must be
taken for granted. Yet it is possible to draw certain conclusions

from the loanwords observed in various languages, and it will be our purpose in this chapter to set up a terminology for discussing them. In the following chapters we shall then present the AmN material that supports our general conclusions.

1. *The Identification of Loans.*

We have seen in chapter 4 that speakers were not always sure whether some words were really Norwegian or English, even though they might be aware in a general way that they were borrowing from English. Some samples were there given of Norwegian words like *potet* 'potato' which some speakers thought were English; and of English words like *buttery* which some speakers thought were Norwegian. This sort of confusion is the best possible seedbed for borrowing. But what kind of criteria can the linguist apply to disentangle the confusion? Is it always possible even for him to be sure whether a given word or other linguistic feature is borrowed from another language?

The definition of borrowing given in the previous chapter was: the attempt by a speaker to reproduce in one language patterns which he has learned in another. This is a strictly historical definition, since it refers to a historical process and requires that the linguist prove for each borrowing that it first existed in language A and only after the first contact of A with B did it appear in language B; and that it could not have arisen independently in language B.

In studying AmN borrowings we must show then (a) that any given item was used in the English heard by the immigrants; (b) that it was not previously used in the Norwegian they knew; and (c) that they could not have made it up independently. Since we cannot actually observe the entry of borrowings, we must be content to make certain assumptions of high probability. One is that an immigrant language, under strong pressure from English, is not likely to have made up new linguistic items which parallel exactly the English forms except as an imitation of those English forms. We will thus arbitrarily regard any form which fulfills the other two conditions as not having been made up independently. Thus, if AmN uses a word *kornmjøl* to mean 'corn meal', ground maize, a word which in Norway meant only ground barley, it will be assumed that the new meaning is due to the English word. But when AmN uses a word *kubberulle* for an ox-cart with wooden wheels, there is no English word of similar structure or meaning, and it will be assumed that this was a creation of the immigrants, unless it is possible to prove that the word existed in Norway before emigration.

As might be expected, the chief problem is usually not to prove that a form existed in American English, but that it did not exist in the Norwegian of the emigrants. AmEng was relatively uniform, and the intense study of its variations has brought to light most of the expressions in question. But the Norwegian dialects were extremely diverse, as we have seen; and in spite of a long tradition of dialect study in Norway, there is still much that is not known about the speech forms of the rural communities. We cannot limit ourselves to the standard language, for our starting point is the actual speech of the emigrants at the time of emigration. Words that were well-known in the Norwegian cities may have been entirely foreign to the country people; while they had a vast vocabulary which was quite unknown in the cities. In any case, it is always harder to prove the non-existence of a form than its existence. Here are some types of problematic expressions.

(1) *Pre-immigration loans.* Some E loanwords penetrated into N speech before immigration through the channels of trade and shipping, in the nineteenth century through tourists also. N sailors had been in intimate contact with English speakers for a long time, and had picked up a considerable vocabulary of sailors' terms in their Norwegian.[2] Some immigrants may have learned their first Norwegianized English words on board the immigrant ships, not to mention the fact that there were many sailors among the immigrants. The English builders of Norway's first railroad in 1855 may be the ones who introduced the word *train* into the language. To this day many dialect speakers in Norway use this word in exactly the same form as do the AmN speakers: *et træn.* In cultivated N usage the word has been replaced by *tog*, modelled on German *Zug*.[3] A further complication is introduced by the fact that some immigrants returned to Norway and brought English words back to the homeland. The words *coat, courthouse, river, surveyor, table*

knife, and *ticket* are reported from Tinn, Telemark, as having been heard from returned 'Americans.'[4] For a number of words we can thus not exclude the possibility that even if they do come from English, they were not acquired in America.

(2) *International words.* A special problem is involved in those words that are so common to the west European languages that they have no special nationality. Such words as *cigar, district, section* were English, but they were also Norwegian at the time of immigration. They were spelled very much the same, though they were pronounced differently, and it was obvious to anyone that they were the same words. But it is often impossible to say whether they were known to the country people at the time of immigration. Some of them were probably a part of their passive vocabulary, acquired through reading, while others were entirely unknown. Since Norwegian dialect dictionaries have not usually included such words, there is no way of finding out whether they were known. The fact that they are often pronounced as Norwegian words does not prove that they were known in Norway, for they could acquire a spelling pronunciation over here also if they were first learned through the spelling. The words *alfalfa* and *timothy* must have been learned in America, since these plants were not generally known in Norway before emigration. Yet they are usually pronounced with Norwegian sounds. On the other hand, such words as *music, museum,* and *university* had their widely-known counterparts in Norwegian *musik, museum,* and *universitet.* Yet the AmN speakers usually pronounce these with American sounds, as if they were entirely new to them in this country.

(3) *Interlingual coincidences.* Some words are so similar in sound and meaning that it may be impossible to determine whether any transfer has taken place. The writer was challenged some years ago by the AmN writer Jon Norstog in a newspaper article for stating that *kru* as used by AmN speakers was from English *crew.* Norstog pointed out that he had known the word *kru* in his Telemark dialect since childhood and maintained that it had the same meaning as in English. Actually, its N dialect meaning is 'multitude, swarm', rather than a group of men working

together on a given job, as in the case of AmN *kru* and English *crew*. Two other objections occur: the N word is reported as neuter, while the AmN word is feminine; and the N word is of highly limited occurrence in the dialects, while the AmN word is universal, and is used in compounds such as *trøskarkru* 'thrashing crew', *seksjonskru* 'section crew' where its English origin is unmistakable. If such a word coincides in grammatical form with a Norwegian word of common usage, however, it seems most useful to regard it as a Norwegian word which has acquired a new meaning. This is true of *korn* 'corn', which has acquired all the meanings of AmE *corn* 'maize', but is usually pronounced with the sound and the forms of the N word in each dialect.

A difficult case is the word *travla* 'walk', which was widely used in AmN speech as the opposite of *kjøyra* 'ride'. No Norwegian word with this meaning has been recorded, though there is a *trava* 'trot' and a *travla* 'struggle, labor, slave.' It seems highly Norwegian in its sound, and one hesitates to derive it from E *travel*, since this is not recorded from Wisconsin in that meaning. It is hard to account for it as an independent creation, but this would be the only alternative if it were not that E *travel* is recorded in the meaning of 'walk' as a very widespread dialect usage in Great Britain.[5] A likely guess is therefore that from the English dialects this usage was brought to America and used in Wisconsin (though not yet recorded by dialect geographers), and there picked up by the N immigrants.

Another problem is exemplified in the word for 'cold', *kulde*. This is widely used for 'a cold spell' as well as 'an infection'; but the N word is nowhere recorded as having had the second meaning, and so it seems likely that this meaning is new and due to the influence of the E word. Yet some of the dialect terms, e.g. *kjøld*, are recorded as having had both meanings in Norway.[6] Only the fact that this usage is quite restricted entitles us to suppose that the change in meaning was an American development, and that it was due to the E word.

⌈It is not always possible to avoid arbitrary decisions in such cases as these, and it is quite possible that later evidence will change our classification. But for the great majority of cases the decision is not difficult.⌉

2. *The Role of Substitution.*

Every loan that is admitted to a language is an importation into that language; but as we have seen in some of the preceding examples, the importation may be only partial. It is not necessary nor even usual to take over a word with all its sounds, forms, and meanings intact. To do so would involve a complete shift of language, which most speakers avoid by substituting some of the habits of their own language. This is of course not a conscious matter; many speakers are simply unable to reproduce the forms of the other language in anything but an imperfect imitation. They may not even 'hear' that the other language is different from their own in some crucial respects. But such failure to 'hear' is a result of previous habits which interfere with the entrance of the new sounds to the brain.

Since we are unable to disentangle the psychological factors involved, we may adopt a purely linguistic point of view and say that we shall regard every loan as part importation and part substitution. If we know exactly how the model in the lending language was, we can compare it with the result in the borrowing language. Any likeness between them is an *importation*, while any difference between them is regarded as a *substitution* of native material. Substitution means that the imitation of the foreign model is less than perfect, but it also means that it has become more familiar to those who speak the native language.

This distinction between importation and substitution applies not only to a given loan as a whole but to its constituent patterns as well, since different parts of the pattern may be treated differently. An AmN speaker who tried to reproduce AmE *whip* [hwɪp] usually came out with *hyp'pe*. In so doing he imported the form as a whole; but he substituted the last syllable of *svepe*, his native word for 'whip', thereby making it a feminine noun with a particular set of endings in the definite and the plural. For the sound sequence [wɪ] he substituted the single sound *y* in his native language, and in order to keep the vowel short, he doubled the following *p* according to the rules of N prosody. Only the initial sound [h] remained the same; here we assume substitution, but there is no actual difference between the substitution and importation when the patterns of two languages are the same.

The term 'substitution' has been in use for some time among linguists in reference to the use of native sounds for the foreign ones in loans. The use of 'importation' as its complement was suggested by the writer in a study of the Analysis of Linguistic Borrowing published in *Language* in 1950.[7] Whenever the patterns of the model which it is desired to imitate are new to the borrowing language, speakers appear to make some such compromise as is exemplified in the preceding paragraph. An adjustment of habits takes place, whereby the speaker chooses one of his own patterns to stand for a similar one in the model. The results of this normally unconscious process indicate that while there are many apparently capricious choices, the overall tendency is not unreasonable. Without formulating it, the speakers are in a rough way carrying on an operation of linguistic comparison between the two languages. When a speaker of AmPort adopts the word *boarder* from English as *bordo*, he has clearly analyzed the English word into two parts, *board-* and *-er*. If he had not done so, his manner of treating other words ending in *-er* shows that the word would have become *borda*. The final *-o* is a Portuguese suffix of agency, which corresponds very well with the meaning of the E *-er*. In such a case he has imported the morpheme *board-*, but substituted his native *-o* for its suffix. This behavior is evidence of some kind of subtle reaction in his brain, by means of which he recognized a partial similarity of meaning and form within a complex morpheme. The linguist makes this procedure explicit by saying that the borrowed form shows partial morphemic substitution. In the same way he may speak of complete or partial phonemic substitution, or even of syntactic substitution.

Substitution and importation are thus to be regarded as mutually exclusive facets of linguistic reproduction, and their relationship determines our way of describing the results of borrowing.

3. *The Terminology of Borrowing.*

A well-established terminology is in existence for the description of borrowing. Three major types of borrowing are ordinarily distinguished, loanwords, loan translations, and semantic loans. *Loanword* is usually limited to those borrowings in which both the phonemic shape of a word and its meaning are imported. The AmE *shivaree* 'an uninvited serenade of newlyweds' does not correspond precisely sound-by-sound to the French word which it imitates (*charivari*), but it is close enough so that it is unmistakeably derived from it.[8] Whatever difference in sound there is can be accounted for as part of the phonemic substitution which is characteristic of most loanwords. But with many obvious loans there are significant deviations from this pattern. In a word like PaG *blaumepai* it is evident that AmE *plum pie* was the model. Before the speakers of PaG came into contact with Americans, they had no word for either pie or plum pie. But there is no way of explaining the form *blaum* as being directly imitated from *plum*; the sounds are too different, and there are no parallels in other words which would make it understandable. On the other hand, any one who knows PaG knows that there is a native German word *blaum* 'plum'. Once the PaG speakers had learned E *pie*, they could go on and make up a new native compound with their own *blaum* and the new word *pai*. Such words are sometimes called *hybrid loanwords*, because the material is partly native and partly foreign. In terms of our distinction between substitution and importation, we may say that they show importation of a compound word with substitution of one native morpheme.[9]

The type ordinarily called loan translations goes a step further. Here the only material that is imported is the overall pattern of the compound or derivative, with of course its meaning, but native morphemes have been entirely substituted for the foreign ones. The term 'translation' refers to this substitution, but the substitution is usually quite mechanical and is not a real translation. The French term *calque* 'copy' is a better description of the result. Among the examples ordinarily given of this type are the French *presqu'île*, German *Halbinsel*, modeled on Latin *paeninsula*; or German *Wolkenkratzer*, Fr. *gratteciel*, Sp. *rascacielos*, modeled on E *skyscraper*.[10] A closely similar process is that of the so-called *semantic loan*, where a word acquires a new meaning because of its semantic or phonetic similarity to some word in the other language. When AmPort speakers gave their native word *humoroso* the same meaning as AmE *humorous,* they were (probably unconsciously) extending the meaning rather far from that which it had had in Portugal, where it meant only 'capricious.' They were importing the AmE word *humorous,* but substituted the similar-sounding native form *humoroso* quite regardless of the meaning it had had before. This borrowing shows up only as a new meaning of a previously established word. When it is called a 'semantic loan', this refers to the fact that it is the only loan which is purely semantic. But it should not be overlooked that all the loans so far discussed are semantic.

Our discussion has brought out a distinction between the various types of borrowing which makes it possible to describe them a little more accurately. The loanword imports the phonemic shape of a foreign word, with more or less phonemic substitution. The hybrid loanword, however, substitutes a native morpheme for part of the foreign word. The loan translation imports the morphemic shape, but substitutes native morphemes for the whole word. The semantic loan does not even import a morphemic shape, but substitutes all native morphemes.

This permits us to distinguish two major types, according to the extent of substitution: loans which import part or all of the phonemic shape of the foreign word and loans which do not. The former will be called *loanwords* and the latter will be called *loanshifts.* The term 'loanshift' is adopted because the loan appears only as a shift of context on the part of a native word. The loanwords may then be divided into *pure loanwords* and *loanblends,* according to whether they are wholly or partially morphemic importations. The loanshifts may be divided into *extensions* and *creations* according to whether they consist of native terms in the same arrangement as before the loan was made or in a new arrangement. The extensions correspond to the semantic loans: their meanings have been extended. The creations correspond to the loan translations: they are new to the language.

Separate sections will be devoted to each of these types, and another to loans which fall outside this classification because they are not importations of meaning, but of structural features.[11]

4. *The Phonological Adaptation of the Loanword.*

The simplest and most common substitution is that which takes place when native sound sequences are used to imitate foreign ones. Complete substitution is characteristic of naive language learners and is heard as a 'foreign accent' by native speakers. However undesirable this may be when one is speaking a foreign language, it is normal when reproducing foreign materials in one's own. The results may be almost completely unrecognizable to the speakers of the model language, as when Spanish *virgen* is reproduced in Taos Indian as [m'ilxinạ] or English *spade* is introduced into AmPort as [shi'peiro].[12] In many cases the speakers are completely unaware that they have changed the foreign word, as in the story told by Polivanov of the Japanese student who asked his teacher whether *džurama* or *dorama* was the correct pronunciation of the European word *drama*. When the teacher answered that it was neither one, but 'drama', he nodded and said, 'Ah yes, then it's *dorama*.'[13]

Hermann Paul and many writers since him have described this process as one in which the speaker substitutes 'the most nearly related sounds' of his native tongue for those of the other language.[14] But neither the speaker himself nor the linguist who studies his behavior is always certain as to just what sound in his native tongue is most nearly related to the model. Only a complete analysis of the sound system and the sequences in which sounds appear could give us grounds for predicting which sounds speakers would be likely to substitute in each given case. When the Yaqui Indians reproduce Sp *estufa* as [ehtúpa], the [h] for [s] is a substitution that occurs only before [t] and [k], where [s] does not occur in their native language; elsewhere they have no trouble with [s]. Speakers have been trained to react to certain criteria in the stream of speech and to reproduce these in their own; but they are also trained to reproduce them only in a limited number of combinations and sequences. Loanword phonology is the attempt to recapture the process of analysis that results in phonemic substitution.

The problem of description is greatly complicated by the fact that the process of learning changes the learner's view of the language. The more he acquires of the new language the less necessary it is for him to interpret its habits in terms of the old language. So he gradually begins to import into his own language those habits of the other which he has mastered and which are not too incompatible with the previously established habits of the old. Linguists have generally assumed that a scale for the time of borrowing can be set up on the basis of phonological form. Early loans are assumed to be the more distorted words, while the late are more similar to their models. Thus Trager in his list of Spanish loans in Taos distinguishes between the 'oldest', the 'more recent', and the 'most recent' largely on the basis of differences in lw. phonology.[15]

In general the principle is sound, but we need to make certain reservations. First, there are some words that offer us no criteria, since they do not happen to contain the critical sounds. Second, the difference between the most and the least distorted is not so much one of *time* as of the *degree of bilingualism*. Bilingualism may come suddenly or slowly; it may persist over many generations, as among the PaG, and words may come in through various members of the community in several different forms. In AmN communities most lws. may appear in various forms, with more or less phonemic substitution; but some substitutions are so widespread that they can hardly have been borrowed recently. It is also possible for bilinguals to touch up the form of an older word and introduce a more 'correct' form if they happen to know it.

Since we cannot follow the fate of individual words and expressions from their earliest introduction, we can only guess at the factors that have influenced the form of any given word. We are entitled, however, to make certain assumptions. First, that *a bilingual speaker introduces a new lw. in a phonetic form as near that of the model language as he can.* Secondly, that *if he has occasion to repeat it, or if other speakers also take to using it, a further substitution of native elements will take place.* Thirdly, that *if monolinguals learn it, a total or practically total substitution will be made.* In the case of AmN we are dealing very largely with bilinguals, most of whom learned E in childhood. Their lws. are therefore likely to vary from a form wholly adapted to N phonology to one almost wholly unadapted.

We shall here reckon with certain characteristic stages, while realizing that these are not always chronological: (1) A *pre-bilingual* period, in which the loans are made by a relatively small group of bilinguals and spread widely among the monolingual majority; the words show (almost) complete native substitution, with great irregularity in the phonetic results. Some phonemes and phoneme sequences will cause the speakers to vacillate, so that they choose now one, now another of their own as substitutes. In AmN the rhyming words *road* and *load* are reproduced with different N phonemes as *råd* and *lod*. Such behavior may be called *erratic substitution*, and is comparable to the scattering of shots over the target by a novice marksman. (2) A period of *adult bilingualism*, when growing knowledge of E leads to a more *systematic substitution*, in which the same N phoneme is consistently employed for new E loans. This may often be accompanied by the use of familiar sounds in new positions where they were not found in the native tongue. Thus the initial *v* in E *very, vicious,* and other words of French origin must once have seemed strange to Englishmen who were used to pronouncing it only between vowels. In modern Czech *g* is found initially only in lws.; elsewhere it is only an allophone of *k*.[16] We shall call this process *phonemic redistribution,* since it affects the distribution of the phonemes. (3) A period of *childhood bilingualism,* in which the characteristic process is one of *phonemic importation,* i.e. completely new sound types are introduced. The Yaqui whose first-generation speakers had to substitute *p* for *f* in Spanish *estufa* 'stove', saying [ehtúpa], are by now sufficiently bilingual to produce [fonografo] 'phonograph' without difficulty. AmN speakers acquired E *whip* as *hyp'pe* in the first generation, but as *wipp'* in the second.

The loan is thus subject to continual interference from the model in the other language, a process which will here be called *reborrowing.* It is a commonplace among immigrant groups in America that younger and older speakers will use different forms of the same lws. The difference usually consists in the extent of phonological and morphological importation. Some other examples from AmN are the following:

	tavern	surveyor	Trempealeau	crackers	mocassin	lake
Older	ta'van	save'r	trom'lo	kræk'kis	mag'gis	le'k
Younger	tæ'vərn	sørvei'ər	trem'pəlo	kræ'kərs	ma'gəsin	lei'k

[The forms acquired will also be differently reproduced when speakers of different dialects attempt them.] This follows from our previous definitions of borrowing, but the situation becomes almost hopelessly confused when speakers of different dialects live together in the same community, as the case is among immigrants, and the form is passed from speaker to speaker, many of whom may be monolingual at the beginning. It has been possible in the case of AmN dialects to isolate a few instances that seem reasonably certain evidence for the transmission of lws. within the dialects. At least it is simpler to account for them as *interdialectal loans* than as directly derived from E models. They are listed in the following:

1 English model	2 Original borrowing	3 Transmitted form (interdialectally)
(1) E [dl] > WN [dl] > EN [ll]		
cradle (grain harvester)	krɪdl	krill
middling (coarse flour)	mɪddlɪng	milling
peddler	peddlar	pellar (one inf.)
(2) E [e] > EN [ei] > WN [ai]		
lake	leik	laik
pail	peil	pail
jail	jeil	jail
frame	freim	fraim
(3) E [o] > EN [å] > WN [ao]		
hoe	hå	hao
(4) E [ao] > EN [æu] { > Solør [əy] > Røros [ö] }		
flour	flæur	fləyr, flör
(5) E [ɔ] > EN [å] > Gbr. [öu]		
log	lågg	löugg

In each of the above cases the variations within the lw. forms correspond to different reflexes from the same Old Norw. originals, found in a considerable number of native words also. But other lws. with the same E phonemes have different forms, e.g. *mail* has not become [mail] in the dialects referred to above, but [meil].

A further source of interference with the process of borrowing is the influence of *spelling*. Spelling pronunciations may be suspected wherever the reproduction varies from normal in the direction of a pronunciation traditionally given to the letter in the borrowing language. In any literate community such influence is likely to be present in a number of words which have been brought to the community in writing. Among immigrants this is not true to any considerable extent, but at least in AmN there is a marked tendency to pronounce AmE [æ] as [a] and AmE [a] as [å], spelled respectively *a* and *o*.

	bran	alfalfa	saloon	
English model	[bræ′n]	[ælfæ′lfə]	[səlu′n]	
Oral reprod.	*bræ′n	*ælfæl′fa	*salu′n	
Spelling pron.	brann′	alfal′fa	salo′n	

	tavern	lot	gallon	battery
	[tæ′vərn]	[la′t]	[gæ′lən]	[bæ′t(ə)ri]
	tæ′vərn	latt′	*gæ′lən	bæ′tri
	ta`van	lått′	gal`lan	bat`təri
			gal`lon	

Such words as *lot* probably come from official documents, *bran* and *alfalfa* from grain sacks, *saloon* and *tavern* from signs, *gallon* and *battery* from advertisements. The striking part of it is that the spelling pronunciation does not usually affect the entire word, where a choice is possible, so that e.g. *gallon* may have an [a] in the second syllable, corresponding to the [ə] of the original. A comparison with the E lws. adopted in N, as reported by Aasta Stene, shows a much higher proportion of spelling pronunciations in the latter, e.g. *buss* 'bus' for AmN *båss*, *kut`te* 'cut' for AmN *kat`ta*, *hik`kori* 'hickory' for AmN *hek′ri* (or even *hik′rill*). As one AmN informant commented, when asked for the word for 'battery': 'They just give Norwegian sounds to the English letters'.

5. *The Morphological Adaptation of the Loanword.*

Since each loanword has to be incorporated into the utterances of a new language, it must receive some sort of morphological analysis in terms of the new language. The AmN speakers who adopted *barn* as *ba'ren* and understood the final *n* to be a Norwegian definite article were making such an analysis and proved it by creating a new form *bare* on the analogy of *haren* 'the rabbit' vs. *hare* 'rabbit'. From this kind of analysis to that which led to the rise of loanblends there is only a short step. In one sense every loanword which receives a new morphological suffix is also a loanblend; but the term is here restricted to those substitutions which involve non-inflectional morphemes.

It was, of course, possible to introduce a single word or phrase into a foreign context without adopting new morphological forms, just as with phonemes. The American who speaks of *indices* instead of *indexes* is doing just that. But for the most part speakers did not long maintain such niceties in AmN, the only form that acquired any general use being the plural *-s* for some words.

The first problem of the borrower was to pick the right grammatical class. In the case of such languages as E and N, where the structures are closely parallel, there was no problem at this level. E nouns were adopted as N nouns, and so forth. It is reported from Chiricahua, an Indian language, that the Spanish adjectives *loco* 'crazy' and *rico* 'rich' are borrowed as verbs.[17] Within the form classes which show inflectional endings there were problems for speakers of AmN also. N nouns are divided into three groups, traditionally called masculine, feminine, and neuter, each with different inflectional and syntactical characteristics. Since E had no corresponding division, E words must be assigned to one of these three classes on the basis of analogies which are often difficult to discover both for the speakers and the analyst. In most languages for which the phenomenon has been studied a clear tendency is seen to assign lws. to one particular gender unless specific analogies intervene to draw them into other classes. This is even more marked in the verbs, where practically every lw. falls into the first class of weak verbs. Such grammatical categories as definiteness, possession, and plurality correspond with sufficient closeness so that little more is involved than a substitution of N forms for E. Again, this would not be true in languages less closely related; the Yaqui have given many lws. a suffix *-um* with a singular sense though it is a plural in their own language.[18]

But even in the relation of E and N there are many cases of

erroneous analysis, based on special situations, so that e.g. E -*s* (plural) may be borrowed with its stem and treated as if it were singular. An example is *kars* 'car', plural *karser;* similarly in AmItalian *pinozzi* 'peanuts'. But the next step, correlated to a bilingual stage of learning, is to import the plural suffix for E lws. This becomes such a common thing that the N suffixed article may be added to it, producing a hybrid inflection -*s* + -*a* 'the', e.g. *kisa* 'the keys'. Adjectives and adverbs may also receive N suffixes, but to a much lesser extent. Here the E influence has frequently led to an importation of zero suffixes, i.e. the abandonment of inflection. Aasta Stene has pointed out that this is promoted by the fact that N also has zero suffixes in some positions.[19] The verbs, on the other hand, have invariably a complete N inflection, with practically no substitution from E. This phenomenon has been noted for several languages, and is sufficiently striking to merit some consideration.[20] Miss Stene stresses the opportunity available to nouns and adjectives of appearing in positions where inflection can be avoided, which is not possible for verbs. While this is true, it should not be overlooked that the function of verb inflections is somewhat different from that of the rest. Tense is a necessary feature of every N (and E) sentence in a way that plurality is not; verbs have no inflectional form with the kind of generalized function that the noun singular has. The noun singular not only refers to individuals of the species, but also to the species itself, and in many cases this is quite sufficient (e.g. rabbit as a lw. may refer either to a single rabbit or to rabbits in general). The adjective inflections are even more secondary, since they have no independent meaning but are dependent on the nouns which they modify. Thus the importation of the E lack of inflection is facilitated by the relative unimportance of the corresponding N inflections and we need not assume any deliberate 'avoidance of inflection,' at least by the unsophisticated speakers dealt with in this study.

In reproducing the forms of another language, speakers will frequently go farther in their adaptation than merely to substitute native sounds and inflections for the foreign ones. They may actually slip in part or all of a native morpheme for some part of the foreign, as in AmPort *alvachus* 'overshoes', *alvarozes* 'overalls', where the native prefix *al-* has been substituted for the E *o-*.[21] Such morphemic substitutions are not clearly discernible unless the phonetic results differ from those that derive from purely phonological substitution. Thus E *-er* is reproduced as AmN *-er* by phonemic substitution. But something else has clearly been at work when it occasionally appears as *-a*, e.g. in the word *kårna* 'corner'. Here it has been blended with the native N word, *hyrna,* just as we earlier noted that *whip* had been blended with *svepe* to produce *hyppe.* Similarly, when *farmer* turns up as *farmar;* in this case the agent suffix *-ar* has been substituted for the corresponding E *-er.* Since the suffix of *corner* is meaningless, we may call *kårna* a blended stem. But *farmar* is a blended derivative, parallel to the PaG words *bassig* 'bossy', *fonnig* 'funny', *tricksig* 'tricky'. In these cases the native *-ig* has been substituted for E *-y.*[22] Similar adjectives in AmN are hard to tell, since the N *-ig* is pronounced *-i* in most dialects and therefore phonemically equivalent to E *-y.*

Compounds constitute the largest class of loanblends in AmN. The two languages have parallel structures in compounding, so that compounds may be borrowed quite freely. Some are pure loanwords, being taken over as units with little, if any analysis, e.g. *wedh'ər-riport* 'weather report'. Whenever the nucleus alone is imported, the loanblend may be called 'nuclear'; otherwise it is 'marginal'. The examples in the preceding paragraph are all nuclear; the marginal loanblend is exemplified by PaG *bockabuch* from E *pocket* and G *buch.* If both parts have been substituted, the word is of course a loanshift. Some phrases which were not strictly compounds in English became so in AmN, e.g. *black walnut* > *blakkvalnot;* some speakers then developed a new word *blakkval* for the tree, a reasonable conclusion from the form of the compound.

Some words which have usually been considered loanblends are here regarded as independent creations in the second language. This is true whenever there is no E original on which the word can have been directly modelled.

6. *The Classification of Loanshifts.*

[We distinguished two major types of loanshift above, the extension and the creation.] The most detailed analysis of loanshifts so far made is that by Werner Betz in *Deutsch und Lateinisch*.[23] He calls the loanshift a *Lehnprägung*, the extension a *Lehnbedeutung*, and the creation a *Lehnbildung*. Some extensions involve the addition of meanings which appear to have no semantic connection with the earlier range of a given word. Thus *grosseria* which in Portugal meant 'a rude remark' is extended in AmPort to mean 'grocery'. Since the only basis for this identification is the similarity in sound, we shall distinguish this kind of extension as *homophonous*. A homophonous loanshift extension will be one in which the sound alone has given rise to the new meaning; in a dictionary the new meaning would presumably be listed as a separate lexical entry. Of course it is possible to disagree on this classification in practice, e.g. in AmPort *Crismas* 'Christmas'. It looks at first glance like an ordinary loanword. But the word existed in Port before immigration, so it is to be classed as a loanshift. Its meaning was 'oil of sacrament'; Pap, who has presented the example, considered it 'semantically related' to the English word.[24] But this writer is inclined to think that it is better classified as a homophonous extension, for they seem to have very little, aside from their ecclesiastical connection, in common. If, on the other hand, there is no similarity of sound, we may call the extension *synonymous*; i.e., the E and the N words have a partially identical range of meaning, which is made more similar by the importation of an E meaning into AmN. An example from AmPort will again illustrate this: as in AmN, the word for a 'cold spell' (*frio*) has added the sense of 'infection' under influence of E cold.[25] In most cases, however, both sound and meaning work together in creating the extension of meaning, and we may use the term *homologous* to describe this combination of the homophonous and the synonymous.

The principle of the loanshift extension may be compactly formulated as follows: whenever language A is subject to influence from language B, some of this influence will appear in the form of new contexts for those native words which remind speakers of foreign words. If there is a native word a_1 with meaning A_1 and another a_2 with meaning A_2, the word a_1 will often be used in meaning A_2 if there is a foreign word b which combines the meanings of a_1 and a_2, especially if a_1 resembles b in sound more than a_2 does. Thus P *livraria* meant 'bookstore, home library' before emigration, but from E 'library' it acquired the meaning of a public library also, for which the P had previously used *biblioteca*. This may be called a *semantic confusion*, since it obliterates a distinction previously existing in the language. There are also *semantic displacements*, where the meaning changes without colliding with any previous term because it describes a phenomenon in the new culture roughly similar to one in the old. Thus AmPort used the originally Spanish term *peso* for the American dollar.

The loanshift creation differs from the extension in showing importation of a foreign arrangement of morphemes, leading to a new word or phrase in the language. Thus E *corn crib* appears in AmN as *kornkrubba*, with complete native substitution; the words originally meant 'grain' and 'fodder-rack', but in AmN have to come mean a building for storing unshelled maize. When these are compounds, they are generally called loan translations. They have played a great role in the development of many languages, though perhaps no more than the loanwords and the loanshift extensions. Thus Gk. *sympátheia*, which in English was reproduced by importation, was reproduced by morpheme substitution in Lat. *compassiō*, G *Mitleid*, Dan. *Medlidenhed*, and Russ. *sobolěz-novanie*.[26] But the loanshift creation is not limited to compounds, for it may well include whole phrases. An example of such phrasal creation is the AmPort. *responder para tras* 'to talk back'.[27]

The popularity of such loanshifts as these in AmN makes it clear that the similarity of E and N is a definite factor in promoting linguistic confusion. It is tempting to pour new wine into the old bottles when the old bottles are scarcely distinguishable from the new. More precisely one may say: a partial overlapping of sound or meaning can be the starting point of a complete identification.

We may now sum up our classification of all loans in the following table, with one example given for each type from the AmN material.

A. LOANWORD (imports new morphemes, in part or whole)	1. Pure loanword (no morphemic substitution)	a. Unassimilated (no phonemic substitution)	*haɽˋdwæ'ɽ* 'hardware'
		b. Partly assimilated (some phonemic substitution)	*haɽˋdwærstȧ'ɽ* 'hardware store'
		c. Wholly assimilated (complete phonemic substitution)	*stȧ'ɽ* 'store'
	2. Loanblend (partial morphemic substitution; either nuclear or marginal, acc. to which part is imported)	a. Stem (meaningless suffix subst.)	*kȧɽˋna* 'corner'
		b. Derivative (meaningful suffix subst.)	*faɽˋmar* 'farmer'
		c. Compound (independent morpheme subst.)	*faɽˋmhu's* 'farm house' (marginal) *juˋlekar'd* 'Christmas card' (nuclear).
B. LOANSHIFT (substitutes native morphemes)	1. Creation (imports morpheme arrangement; may be derivative, compound, or phrase)	a. Literal (arrangement identical with that of model)	*plane* v. 'plan' *heimplassen* 'the home place' *vel av* 'well off'
		b. Approximate (arrangement different from that of model)	*hyrehjelp* 'hired help' (rare in AmN; cf. G *Vaterland* from patria, *Halbinsel* from paeninsula.)
	2. Extension (imports no arrangement; may be stem, derivative, compound, or phrase)	a. Homophonous (resembles model only phonetically)	*brand*, 'bran' (N 'fire') *fila* 'feel' (N 'file')

B. LOANSHIFT continued.

b. Homologous (resembles model phonetically and semantically)	*grøn* 'grain' (N 'cereal food') *lykkelig* 'lucky' (N 'happy') *god tid* 'good time' (N 'plenty of time')
c. Synonymous (resembles model only semantically)	(absent in AmN; cf. AmP *frio* 'cold'; *correr* 'run for office')

7. *Native Creations with Bilingual Stimulus.*

⌈Two kinds of native creations which are more or less directly connected with the bilingual or at least bicultural situation have been excluded from the above classification because they are not strictly cases of borrowing. These will here be called *induced* and *hybrid* creations.⌉

The induced creation, which corresponds to Betz's *Lehnschöpfung*, arises when the speakers of one language wish to have a word corresponding to some word in another language, but create a term which has no formal parallelism to the foreign word.[28] Betz gives the example of G *Umwelt* which was created to render F *milieu*. Indian languages under influence from English tend to follow this path in preference to borrowing.[29] Examples from the Pima Indians presented by George Herzog include such novel descriptive terms as 'having downward tassels' (oats), 'wrinkled buttocks' (elephants), 'dry grapes' (raisins), 'lightning box' (battery), etc.[30] Induced creations are extremely rare among the AmN, being limited largely to the word *kubberulla* 'oxcart' (cf. Chap. 18).

Loanword lists are also made to include a number of terms whose existence may ultimately be due to contact with a second culture and its language, but which are not strictly loans at all. These did not come into being as direct imitations of a foreign model, but were secondarily created within the borrowing language. An example is the Yaqui term *líosnóoka* 'pray', composed of the lw. *líos* 'God' (from Spanish *dios*) and the native *nóoka* 'speak'.[31] These are sometimes confused with loanblends, since they resemble these in being 'hybrid'. But seen in the light of the borrowing process as here defined, they cannot have come into being as imitations of a foreign model, for there is no Spanish word speak-to-God meaning 'pray'. A parallel form from AmN is *sjærbrukar* 'one who operates a farm for a share of the profits', a technical term much used in the tobacco-raising districts of Wisconsin. The first part is a lw. *sjær* (from AmE *share*), the second is a N *brukar* 'farmer, tenant'. The AmE *sharecropper* is not in use in these districts; a word *shareman* is sometimes heard in English. But neither of these can have suggested the AmN word; its origin must be sought in the N word *gardbrukar* 'farmer' (lit. farm-user), in which the lw. *sjær* was substituted for the native *gard*.

This kind of *reverse substitution*, in which lw. morphemes are filled into native models, is clearly different from the borrowings previously described and should be distinguished from them. PaG has an interesting series of terms of the type *Gekick* 'habitual kicking or objecting' (e.g. *Gekooks* 'coaxing', *Gepeddel* 'peddling', *Getschäbber* 'jabbering').[32] When classified without regard to the borrowing process, they appear as 'hybrids'; but their starting point is different from such loanblends as *blaumepai* 'plum pie' previously cited. These do not have a specific English model, for E has no words of this type, implying a habitual or even annoying activity. They appear to be secondary derivatives from the borrowed verbs (e. g. *kicken*), and are filled into the pattern of the native words of the type *Gejeemer* 'incessant moaning or lamenting'. The only criterion available for deciding whether a term belongs to this class of native creation is that no model exists in the other language. This may be difficult to ascertain without a rather complete knowledge of the language in question. A doubtful case is raised in the AmIt word *sciainatore* 'boot-black', apparently formed by substituting the lw. *sciainare* 'shine' in a native pattern of the type represented by *trovatore* 'troubadour'. But if, as the Italian scholar A. Menarini supposes, there is an AmE word *shiner* meaning 'boot-black', it could be a loanblend, in which the native *-tore* was simply substituted for AmE *-er*.[33] This writer has never heard or seen such a word (except in the sense of a black eye), the usual word being *boot-black*, but he recognizes that it does exist in the compound *shoe-shiner* (also and more commonly 'shoe-shine').

Since the type of creation here discussed needs a name to distinguish it from the kind of creation that consists entirely of native material, we might dub it *hybrid creation*, thus emphasizing its bilingual nature. But it must be recognized that it is not a part of the borrowing process; rather does it give evidence of an intimate fusion into the language of the borrowed material, since it has become productive in the new language. The number of hybrid creations seems to vary markedly according to circumstances. PaG appears to have great numbers of them, involving such highly productive suffixes as *-erei, -es, -sel, -keet, -meesig, -voll, -weis* and the verbal prefix *var-*.[34] AmN, on the other hand, has relatively few, which may be due to the comparative lack of productive affixes in Norwegian, but also to the briefer period of residence in America. Most hybrid creations are of the type in which lw. morphemes have been imported in the nucleus, while the marginal parts (the affixes) are native. The opposite kind, showing marginal importation, exemplified by E *talkative*, is not found at all in the AmN materials.

8. *Resistance to Borrowing.*

It has long been known that some kinds of linguistic items are more likely to be borrowed than others. In 1881 William Dwight Whitney set up a scale on which he ranged the various items according to the freedom with which they were borrowed.[35] Nouns showed least resistance to borrowing, then the other parts of speech in an ascending scale, then suffixes, then inflections, and finally sounds. He recognized that all of these could be borrowed, but maintained that inflections and sounds were rarely borrowed and then only as parts of vocabulary items. 'The exemption of "grammar" from mixture is no isolated fact; the grammatical apparatus merely resists intrusion most successfully, in virtue of its being the least material and the most formal part of language. In a scale of constantly increasing difficulty it occupies the extreme place'.

A similar view, apparently independent of Whitney's, was expressed in 1939 by Lucien Tesnière: 'La miscibilité d'une language est fonction inverse de sa systematisation.'[36]

In terms of linguistic habits this is equivalent to saying that those habits which are most frequent and therefore most firmly implanted are the least likely to be changed by the influence of a second language. Since the number of phonemes in any language is relatively small, and each one is repeated very frequently in speech, it is not likely that they will be changed unless the influence takes place at the learning stage in early childhood. Inflections are also well established at an early age, along with most of the productive suffixes. Since none of these items occur except as parts of utterances, they will only be borrowed when they constitute a part of words or phrases which are borrowed as a whole. We have seen earlier that substitution is most likely to occur in the case of phonemes and inflections, though there are instances of importation. We have also seen that derivatives and compounds could be borrowed in toto, but there are extremely few examples of suffixes which have become productive after borrowing. Native suffixes are easily applied to foreign stems, but not vice versa. This seems to reflect the fact that the native suffixes are part of the familiar language structure. Until the foreign suffixes have been introduced in a number of loanwords and thereby been incorporated into the language, they cannot be analyzed by the speakers and applied to new situations.

The relative ease with which the various parts of speech can be imported must also be seen in the light of the structural organization of the language. Every list of loanwords so far presented for languages with the usual west European structures shows a predominance of nouns over other parts of speech. The following statistics will give a rough index of the relationship in two immigrant languages, AmN and AmSw, which are typical of many others:

Percent of total loans:	Nouns	Verbs	Adj.	Adv.-Prep.	Interj.
AmN (author's word list)	75.5	18.4	3.4	1.2	1.4
AmN (Flom's Koshkonong list)	71.7	23.0	4.2	.8	.5
AmSw (Johnson's Chisago list) .	72.2	23.2	3.3	.4	.8

While articles and pronouns do not appear in these lists, loans do occur from these classes also, though none of these have become frequent enough to get established in the general speech. That pronouns can be acquired is shown by the example of English *they, their, them* imported from Scandinavian during the Middle Ages.

The fact that many nouns and verbs are borrowed, but few prepositions, interjections, pronouns, or conjunctions is quite simply correlated with the fact that the language has many of the former and few of the latter. The actual number needed of the latter is small, since they serve the structural purpose of indicating highly generalized relationships between the 'content' words. In some languages they do not appear as separate words at all, but are bound morphemes (inflections or suffixes). A list of uncompounded words in a Norwegian dialect investigated by the writer consisted of 917 words; of these 48.3 % were nouns, 24.6 verbs, 16.7 adjectives, 1.4 numerals, 4.8 adverbs, 2.3 pronouns, 1.2 prepositions, 0.4 conjunctions, 0.3 interjections, and 0.1 articles. The only important discrepancy here between the frequencies is the higher adjective and adverb count compared to the lower number of nouns. The process of borrowing in general favors those classes that are already large; masculine nouns are relatively more frequent among loanwords than in the native language, and the weak verbs likewise. So the nouns have become even more frequent in the loans than in the native language. The linguistic shift has not been one of changing the way in which things are said, but in changing the things that are talked about. Only incidentally has there been any change in linguistic structure. The more habitual and subconscious a feature of language is, the harder it will be to change.

If internal differences of this kind exist within a language, similar differences might exist between languages, in so far as these are structurally different. This has frequently been asserted, on the basis of the greater homogeneity of vocabulary of some languages than others. Typical is the treatment by Otakar Vočadlo, who set up what might be called a *scale of receptivity* among languages, dividing them into the major groups of 'homogeneous', 'amalgamate', and 'heterogeneous'.[37] Unfortunately Vočadlo excludes in his definition of 'receptivity' the words borrowed from other languages of the same stock, so that he regards e.g. Danish as a 'homogeneous' language. He is also more concerned with practical problems of linguistic purification, so that the basic question of whether structural or social forces are more important does not emerge too clearly. Kiparsky, in commenting on the paper, declared flatly that 'die Fähigkeit der sog. "homogenen" Sprachen, Entlehnungen aufzunehmen, hängt *nicht* von der linguistischen Struktur der Sprache, sondern von der politisch-sozialen Einstellung der Sprecher ab.'[38]

Perhaps one of the most hopeful fields for finding an answer to this question is the situation in the United States. Here a relatively homogeneous language and culture has exerted a similar pressure on a large number of different languages; much could be learned by comparing the borrowings of immigrant languages of different structures, and then by comparing these with the borrowings of Indian languages, whose structures are even more different than the immigrant languages among themselves. Most of the differences brought out by Vočadlo are not differences in actual borrowing, but in the relationship between importation and substitution, as here defined. Some languages import the whole morphemes, others substitute their own morphemes; but all are subject to borrowing if there is any social reason for doing so, i.e. the existence of a group of bilinguals with linguistic prestige.

9. *The Consequences of Borrowing.*

An interesting and much discussed question has been: what does borrowing do to a language? It seems to be clear from the preceding discussion that its chief effect is the obvious one of extending the vocabulary. But a strong and long-continued influence of one language upon another may result in such a large influx of vocabulary that the make-up of the language is greatly altered. Such an influence was exerted by the Scandinavian Vikings and even more overwhelmingly by the Norman French on English. The language may receive so many words belonging to certain structural types that those structural types are themselves incorporated in the language. We have seen tendencies in this direction in

AmN, especially in comparing the behavior of the first and second generation speakers of the language. Less effort is expended by the later speakers in adapting the loanwords to the structure of the language. But even so there is no widespread breakdown of the Norwegian parts of the language. Each dialect is still recognizably a form of that dialect, though sometimes with a levelling in the direction of a common type.

Wherever a language has categories which require that a choice be made when a new loanword is introduced, there is some likelihood that the categories will gradually be confused. One member of the category is usually favored at the expense of the others, as we have seen in the case of masculine nouns and weak verbs. Loanwords have been shown to be more unstable in their classification than native words.[39] The reason is that they often fail to show any criteria that make it possible for the speaker to classify them quickly into a given gender or plural class. In the long run this will create an increasing majority for the simplest category and a growing pressure to reduce the other words by analogy. The danger of destroying the morphological system of Icelandic has been one of the arguments advanced against loanword importation in that language. Morphemic substitution has been the remedy, whereby native materials were used to create the large number of loanshifts characteristic of that language.

In the phonology most loanwords do nothing more than fill up gaps in the native sound system. Thus when AmN acquired E *street*, pronouncing it *strit*, nothing new was added to the structure. The language already had words like *stri* 'stubborn' and *krit* 'chalk' with the same combinations of sound. But again a continued importation of loanwords sooner or later leads to a certain amount of reorientation. AmFinnish introduced the word *stove* as *touvi;* at this time there were no initial consonant clusters in the language. But at a later time the word *skeptikko* crept in, with an *s* in a position not previously tolerated.[40] This phonemic redistribution now makes it necessary to include the cluster *sk-* in a description of AmFinnish phonology. It is a further step when completely new sounds are imported. The only English phoneme which appears to enjoy its present status through foreign influence is the last sound of *rouge* [zh]. It occurs only in French loanwords; but its importation must have been facilitated by the fact that English already had the same sound in the complex phoneme [dzh], as in *edge, George*. Such sounds as the French nasal vowels or German *ch* are scarcely used by speakers of English except by people who have acquired at least a smattering of those languages. Aleutian Eskimo had no *p, b,* or *f* before its contact with Russian; in the earliest loanwords *k* was substituted for *p*, and *m* for *b*. Once the Aleutians mastered *p*, it was substituted for *f* until this sound also became familiar; Russian *furaška* 'cap' > *pura:sxix* among older speakers, *fura:skix* among younger ones.[41] Even here the sounds are made up of familiar movements of the vocal organs: the *p* combined certain features of *m* and *t*, the *f* certain features of *m* and *s*. It seems more startling that an *r* was also introduced at the same time, an *r* with the sound of a palatalized *z*.

In general all such new phonemes remain in a highly marginal position in the language structure. Many of them are limited to bilingual speakers, and the rest are limited to particular words and expressions. It is the common practice of linguists to skim off these 'foreign' parts of a language before making a description of the system of the language, in order to make it somewhat simpler to set up a consistent structure. But this willful simplification must not mislead us into thinking that such parts of the language are set off by speakers of the language themselves. In so far as they are able to pronounce them and have occasion to use them, all words are part of the language structure to the naive speakers. Those attempts which have been made so far to determine loanwords on a purely synchronic, descriptive basis have not been successful.[42] Most loanwords are not distinct from native words by any criterion that is applicable to a language at any given time. Some loanwords have retained certain aspects of their foreign model, but even the criteria that distinguish them will sometimes be shared by at least a few native words.

Loanwords that import features which differ from those of the native stock of words promote structural irregularity, but are not its only sources. Linguistic patterns are not rigid like mathematical formulas, but constitute extremely intricate and irregular shapes. Some parts of such patterns have a high frequency and are therefore more stable than others; but there is no absolute line between the more and the less frequent. No matter what their origin, patterns that are used frequently in a language will not sound 'queer' or 'foreign', and it would be hazardous indeed to try to say exactly where such a feeling might begin to appear. No one recognizes in *priest, due, law,* or *skirt* the fact that they are not native English words; the fact that other words may retain more of their foreign origin does not entitle us to set them up as separate systems within English. Bilingual speakers will tend to recognize such loans, and even tend to find them where there are none, but just cognate or coincidental similarities. But monolingual speakers will use them without any other sense of strangeness than that which somes from unfamiliarity of usage or difficulty of pronunciation.

Chapter 16.

THE PHONOLOGY OF LOANWORDS.

> Any one who would learn to speak a foreign
> language correctly must be trained to perform enti-
> rely new movements (bewegungsgefühle). Until he
> has acquired these, the speaker will always make
> use of the movements with which he produces his
> mother tongue. As a rule he will substitute the most
> nearly related of his native sounds for those of the
> foreign language.
>
> *Hermann Paul (1880)*[1]

The phonological adaptation of English loanwords by speakers
of AmN dialects requires them, as we have seen in Chapter 15,
to substitute many of their own sounds for those which they hear
in English. To begin with they master only their own sounds, and
must of necessity interpret what they hear in terms of the distinctions that are characteristic of their own language. We shall describe
the results of this adaptation by first presenting an account of
the N pattern, and then showing how each feature of the E pattern
was reproduced in AmN. In order to avoid excessive complexity,
a notation has been devised for the N forms which ignores minor
differences between dialects. With few exceptions, only those dialects have here been considered which have the most widespread
phonemic system of 9 vowels and 3 favorite diphthongs. Each dialect
offers its own problems, which will have to be treated elsewhere.

Within the phonology three subsystems can be distinguished
which permit us to break up the description into three major
sections: the prosody, the vocalism, and the consonantism. Within
each of these the relevant material is then presented, followed by
a summing up of the conclusions to be drawn concerning the various

substitutions that have been made. The approximate phonetic values of the symbols used are discussed in each section; but the reader is referred to Appendix 2, where all the symbols used are listed.

1. *Prosody.*

The successive phonemes of a language are continually modulated in speech by linguistically significant factors of timing. These will here be treated under the heads of stress, quantity, and tone. These factors are characteristically associated with the syllable as a whole rather than with the individual phonemes.[2] It is therefore possible to isolate them for discussion, even though they always appear as simultaneous components of the phonemes. Bloomfield called them 'secondary phonemes'; a more recent term has been 'suprasegmental phonemes'; the writer has suggested the use of the term 'prosodeme'. Each language has its own prosodic system, in which the various features are utilized in characteristic ways. English and Norwegian, being both Germanic languages, have fundamentally similar prosodies. The differences between them consist chiefly in the way in which the prosodemes are applied to specific words; there is also a major difference in the use of stress tone.

A. STRESS.

N stress patterns consist of an alternation of loud and soft syllables. Each utterance must have at least one loud syllable, and may have an indefinite number. The loud syllables are said to be *stressed*, the rest *unstressed*. Stress may appear in two significant varieties, *loud* (L) and *reduced* (R); loud will here be symbolized as ′ or ‵ (on the difference see the section on tone), reduced as ‚, placed after the vowel or consonant bearing the stress. Reduced occurs only after a loud stress and usually marks its syllable as being joined with the preceding loud in a single word. There is thus a significant difference between *høy′re mann′* 'the right man' and *høy′remann‚* 'member of the conservative party'; between *en kris'ten plik't* 'a Christian duty' and *en kris'tenplik't* 'a Christian's duty'. In each case a pattern of LL is contrasted with LR. Successive louds in one utterance will not be equal in strength, since additional emphatic stress (E) may be given some of them; but this does not concern us here.

Each word of more than one syllable has a significant placing of the stress; thus *po'sitiv* 'positive' contrasts with *positi'v* 'grind-organ'. In native Norwegian words the stress is on the first syllable; in many words borrowed from other languages the usage varies, so that some dialects accent later syllables than the first in imitation of usage in the language from which the word was borrowed. This is required in most forms of standard DN; but it is also practiced in many WN dialects.[3]

E stress patterns also consist of an alternation of loud and soft syllables. The general principle of substitution was that AmN speakers reproduced E loud with N loud and E soft with N soft, or in other words, that they substituted their own stress for that of E and placed it on the same syllables: E teacher > AmN *tit'kjer,* E finish > AmN *fin'nisja,* E settle > AmN *sett'la.* E has the same contrast between loud and reduced stress as N, as in a bla'ck bir'd and a bla'ckbir'd, so that reduced stress was also properly reproduced in AmN: E sep'ara'tor > AmN *sep'p(e)re'tar,* E chee'se fac'tory > AmN *kji'sfek'tri,* E bas'ket so'cial > AmN *bes'ketso'-sjel.*[4]

Reduced stress was often substituted for the second of two loud stresses; in this way E phrases were often reproduced as N compounds. E has many expressions with the stress pattern LL (sometimes called 'level' stress, though the second may often have emphatic stress), including subject-verb, adjective-noun, adverb-adjective, etc.[5] When these consisted of adjective-noun or noun-noun, they were usually reproduced as compounds in N, with the stress pattern LR. Examples are: the Bla'ck Riv'er roa'd > *blekk'røverrå'den;* East'er vaca'tion > *i'stervekei'sjen;* Leg'-horn roo'ster > *legg'hårnha'na;* sin'gletop' bug'gy > *sin'geltåpp-båg'gi;* tow'n treas'urer > *taon'tres'jer;* In'dian moc'casin > *in'dima'gus* (a flower); li'ght bugg'y > *lett'båg'gi* (a kind of buggy); sec'ond cous'in > *sek'kenkås'sen;* grav'eled roa'd > *græv'larå'd;* cov'ered wa'gon > *kåv'ravång'n;* I'rish sett'lement >

ei'rissetlamen't. Examples of phrases which were not turned into compounds by the use of pattern LR were: well off > *vell' a'v;* too bad > *tu' bæ'd;* no sirree > *nos'søri';* by golly > *ba'i ga'li;* around here > *ron't hæ'r;* all right > *å'l rei't.* Later borrowings tended to retain the E pattern without reduction of the second stress; about fifty examples have been noted, sometimes preceded by quotative hesitation, e. g. blackfoot blight, common sense, Canadian Pacific.

Unstressed syllables were sometimes given reduced stress even though they had none in English, if they fell into a pattern suggesting a N compound form. Examples are: E liniment > AmN *lin'nemen't;* breakfast > *brekk'fes't;* orchestra > *år'kes'tra;* settlement > *set'lamen't;* faucet (pron. fasset) > *fæ'sett';* bicycle > *bai'sik'kel.*

A displacement of stress occurred sometimes, in obedience to certain N rules of placement. (1) E words with stress on later syllables than the first were regularly reproduced with stress on the first in EN dialects. This followed the pattern of other loans in these dialects. Examples: alfal'fa > *al'falfa;* molas'ses > *mal'lasi;* guita'r > *get'tar;* cordee'n (accordion) > *kår'din;* shivaree' > *sjøv'ri;* appendici'tis > *pen'nesai'tis.* But in WN dialects stress on later syllables was usually retained, and sometimes even applied to new words, e.g. depot > *depo',* engine > *indjai'na,* gallon > *galo'n,* timothy > *timo'ti.* There was thus a possibility of such contrasts between dialects as surprise > *suprei's* and *sup'preis,* July > *jula'i* and *ju'lai.* Some E words show a similar vacillation, which was accordingly reproduced in AmN: gasoline > *gæseli'n* or *gæ'selin.* American bilinguals often retained the E placement, so that words like the following appeared with correct stress even in EN: cotillion > *kotil'jen,* quadrille > *kådrill',* election > *elek'sjen.* (2) Reduced stress was occasionally displaced by a rhythmic principle which operated also in native words, e.g. *lønn* 'pay' compounded with *på'legg'* 'raise' became *løn'spålegg'* (instead of *løn'spå'legg*). In the same way some AmN speakers compounded *påst* 'post' and *å'fis* 'office' into *pås'tåfi's; bar* 'barn' and *be'smæn't* into *ba'rbesmæn't.* The phrase 'black walnuts' was reproduced by some as a compound with substitution of N *netar* for nuts, plus a shift of reduced stress: *blak'valne'tar.*

B. TONE.

Each full stress in N is accompanied by one of two pitch contours, which has its significant nucleus within the stressed syllable, but extends over the succeeding syllables up to the next pause or stressed syllable. If no stress follows, the end of the contour is determined by the sentence tone. The phonetic nature of the two stress pitches varies greatly from dialect to dialect. Tone 1 is usually simpler in its movement than Tone 2, being either low with succeeding rise or (in some dialects) high with succeeding fall, while 2 may rise and fall within the same syllable and then rise once more in the rest of the contour. Tone 1 is here symbolized as ', Tone 2 as `, placed after the core of the stressed syllable. Their distribution within the lexicon is historically determined: Tone 1 is used in all monosyllables and those polysyllables that were monosyllables in ON; Tone 2 is used in those polysyllables that were polysyllables in ON. Words that have been borrowed since ON times have adopted one or the other of these tones according to various analogies, but have most often acquired Tone 1.[6]

In normal, unemphatic speech AmE uses a single high pitch to accompany each full stress. Up to the last stress in a phrase most other syllables are spoken on a middle pitch. After the last stress a continued high pitch means a question, a middle pitch means an incomplete statement, while a low pitch means a completed statement.[7] This is almost the exact inverse of the usual N intonation contour, though it agrees in part with those of SW Norway (around Stavanger) and northern Norway (Nordland). In reproducing E high pitch, AmN speakers used whatever pitch was characteristic of full stress in their dialect. The most striking deviation to American ears was the typical EN use of low pitch in the stressed syllable, with a succeeding contour which reminded an American of a question. The sentence contour was somewhat modified by E influence in the American-born bilinguals; but the pitch often remained 'sing-song' even in the English of these speakers.

In adapting the E stress to the N system, the speakers had to apply one of the two N pitch contours to each full stress. In so doing they were guided by the analogies of words already present in their vocabulary, but for some classes of words the analogies were weak and there was much vacillation.[8] Where consistent patterns can be found, they are usually correlated with inflectional forms.

All MONOSYLLABLES were spoken with Tone 1, as in N. Inflected monosyllables followed the rules for similar words in N. This meant that Tone 1 was applied to forms with suffixed definite articles, e. g. the pail > *pei'len;* the bluff > *blåf'fa;* the fences > *fen'sa.* Tone 2 was applied to words with plural suffixes and most other inflections, e. g. the pails > *pei'lan(e);* the bluffs > *blåf'fen;* coats > *ko'tar;* to cut > *kat'ta;* husked > *has'ka;* feeds > *fi'dar;* rough (pl.) > *råf'fe.* A few monosyllables were either interpreted as or associated with polysyllables, so that (in some dialects) they acquired Tone 2: barn > *ba'te* or *ba're,* jug > *jug'ga,* whip > *hyp'pa,* slough > *slu'a,* trap > *trep'pa.*

POLYSYLLABIC STEMS with stress on the first syllable show consistent use of tone only if they end in a suffix which is associated with a given tone in N. Verbs (with the suffix *-a*) regularly got Tone 2: harvest > *har'vista,* cultivate > *kål'teve'ta.* Words in *-el, -en,* or *-er* generally got Tone 1 when they were reproduced as *-el, -en,* ot *-er* in N, where many words having these endings go back to ON monosyllables, e.g. *fug'gel* 'bird', *vat'ten* 'water', *å'ker* 'field'. Examples in AmN are: *bai'sik'kel, busj'el, hen'del, kat'ten* (cotton), *kås'sen* (cousin), *gar'den* (garden), *æ'ger* (ague), *pas'ter* (pasture), *såp'per.* In some words, however, N suffixes with Tone 2 were substituted for these endings. Thus *-el* > *-ill* in *pik'ril* (pickerel), *skvæ'ril* (squirrel), *bæ'ril* (barrel), to which might be added *-y* > *-ill* in *hik'ril.* As a verb *-el* > *-la* in *set'la, tik'la, trav'la, trub'la.* Verbs in *-en* > *-na* as in *hep'na.* Nouns in *-er* > *-ar* (the suffix of agency) in words like *bæt'sjlar* (bachelor), *far'mar, ses'sar* (assessor). These were usually associated with a verb, but other nouns in *-er* received the suffix *-ert* with Tone 1: *dip'pert, guf'fert* (gopher), *låi'ert, rip'pert* (also *ri'par,* associated with *ri'pa* 'to reap'). Verbs in *-er* > *-ra* with Tone 2 in *fig'ra* (to figure). Other suffixes with Tone 2 are: *-ery* > *-eri,* e. g. granary > *grøn'ri,* grocery > *grås'seri,* factory > *fek't(e)ri;* *-ing* > *-ing,* e.g. hunting > *hun'ting,* farming > *far'ming,* middlings > *mil'ling;* *-ment* > *-ment,* e. g. basement > *be'smen't,* settlement

> *set'lamen't;* -y > -*i* (in adjectives), e. g. busy > *bis'si,* easy >
i'si. The syllable -et > -*et* is not a morpheme, but its association
with words of retracted accent in N appears to have induced Tone
2, e. g. in bucket > *båk'ket.*

Polysyllabic stems which did not end in a suffix that could be
associated with a N suffix were rather evenly divided between
Tone 1 and 2, without apparent attachment to either one. The
following had predominantly Tone 1: *æt(t)'ik, ba'tom, bren'di,
brekk'fes't, bis'nes, ken'di, sør'kis, sis'tern, klø'vis, ka'lidj* (college),
kok'ki(s), kæu'nti, fø'rnis, ai'len(d) (but *øy'lan'd,* with substitution),
pik'nik, plen'ti, pro'græm (but *pro'gramm'), sjat'tis, sei'lo, tør'ki(s),
vis'ki, jen'ki, al'kehå'l, rit'metikk', rei'dio, dif'fernt, ai'ris, ka'men*
(or *kåm'men), i'ven, sek'ken.* The following had predominantly
Tone 2: *ar'mi, en'ti, be'bi, båg'gi, bju'ro, den'tist, di'po, gre'vi, har'vist
jøs'tis, mår'git* (but *mår'gidsj), mju'sik, åf'fis, pa'pa, sjan'ti, ta'van,
væl'li, år'kes'tra, tim'moti, reg'g(e)ler.* It is tempting to regard the
use of Tone 2 as evidence of a greater assimilation to the native
pattern; this is the conclusion of Aasta Stene with regard to the
E lws. in DN.[9] But the evidence is not clearcut; the use of Tone
2 is generally more common in AmN than in the urbanized DN.

Polysyllabic stems with the accent on a later syllable than the
first always received Tone 2 if the accent had been moved back
to the first according to the rule given above, in the section on
stress. Otherwise they got Tone 1. This was in accord with a
regular procedure of the N dialects. Examples of Tone 1: elect
> *elek'ta,* garage > *gera'dj;* of Tone 2: alfalfa > *al'falfa,* pneu-
monia > *nu'monja* (but WN *numo'nja).* If the first syllable had
been apocopated, the word of course belonged to the tone class of
its suffix: amount > *mao'nta,* assess > *ses'sa.*

COMPOUNDS in N followed the general rule that the first element determined the tone of the whole compound. The rule is
apparently consistent in the case of polysyllabic first elements.
AmN examples are: *lar'mklok'ka, bråd'derinlå', ræ'telsnek', hyp'-
peltre'* (whippletree), *bar'bersjapp', bæ'rilkjin'na* (barrel churn),
grev'larå'd, mån'keren'sj. But monosyllabic first elements varied,
some (like *ku* 'cow') produced Tone 1 in compounds, while others
(like *bru* 'bridge') produced Tone 2. In AmN words the following
produced Tone 1: black > *blekk'-;* front > *från't-;* log > *lågg'-,*

while these produced Tone 2: bed > *bedd`-;* share > *sjæ`r-.*
Those which had a combining vowel, so that the first element became polysyllabic, always had Tone 2: cordwood > *kår`dave¹;*
fence post > *fen`sapås¹t.* Otherwise the compounds showed no
very definite pattern; the greater number had Tone 1. Examples:
bei`sbå¹l, kjæ´rmann¹* (chairman), *kji´sfek¹tri, fott´bå¹l; homm`stedd¹,
lå`su¹t* (lawsuit), *slapp`pei¹l, stå`rki¹par.

Some of the later loanwords of childhood bilinguals failed to
acquire the N tones, but retained E tone. This tendency to dis-
regard the N distinctions had not affected the native words of the
informants here examined. But in the case of a number of speakers,
the ends of the tonal contours which constituted the sentence into-
nations were markedly affected by English. No effort has here
been made to study this aspect systematically. But it was evident
that the sentence tone ending on a high note was often given up in
favor of the falling tone of English. This could sound to the ear
of a Norwegian as an approximation to certain kinds of west and
north Norwegian; the comment was made by Professor D. A. Seip
on visiting the U. S. A. in 1931 that AmN speakers generally sounded WN. Peter Groth wrote in 1897 that 'persons who have been
in America a long time. . . .acquire a foreign quality in their voices,
so that no matter how fluently they speak their native language,
one can still hear that it has become a foreign tongue to them.'[10]
Much of this is due to the sentence tone.[11]

C. QUANTITY.

Each stress in N is accompanied by syllabic length, sometimes
known as 'quantity'. Quantity does not, however, refer to the
length of the whole syllable, but to the nature of the phonemes
which constitute its core. The CORE of a syllable is defined as the
minimum residue without which it cannot be pronounced. A
stressed syllabic core must begin with a vowel, but can end with
either a vowel or a consonant. A vowel which can both begin and
end the core is called *long*, one which can only begin it is called
short. In slow speech the long vowels may average twice as long
as the short ones, but in rapid speech there is very little difference

of time.[12] In most N dialects there is for each long vowel a short vowel of similar, though usually relaxed quality. For this reason the long and the short vowels are here written with the same symbols, and their length is indicated by the placing of the stress mark. Whenever a vowel is immediately followed by a stress mark, it is long; if the stress mark is placed after one or more following consonants, the vowel is short, and the intervening consonants belong in the same syllabic core. In most N dialects a diphthong may serve as a core parallel to the long vowels; in some dialects there are also short diphthongs which require a following consonant. The consonants that follow the short vowel are sometimes called long also, and are often longer than others, especially in slow and distinct speech.[13] The contrast is maintained also under reduced stress, but in unstressed syllables all sounds are short.

The difference between the two kinds of stressed cores may be described as one of *contour:* a core ending in a vowel has *vocalic* contour, one ending in a consonant has *consonantal* contour. For convenience we shall symbolize a vocalic contour as VV, a consonantal one as VC. Examples of each are given below; the cores are italicized:

Followed	VV		VC
by	Long vowels	Diphthongs	Short vowels
0 cons.	ro' 'rest'	nei' 'no'	takk' 'thanks'
	ro'e 'to quiet'	nei'e 'to curtsy'	tak'ke 'to thank'
1 cons.	ro's 'praise'	ei'k 'oak'	tak't 'tact'
	ro'se 'to praise'	rei'se 'to travel'	sak'te 'slowly'
2 cons.	ro'st 'praised' pp.	rei'st 'travelled' pp.	tek'st 'text'
	ro'ste 'praised' pt.	rei'ste 'travelled' pt.	tek'sten 'the text'

The usual pattern for VV is one in which it is followed by no more than one consonant; in most dialects the second consonant must be an inflectional suffix.

In reproducing E sounds, speakers of AmN applied one of their two quantity contours to all stressed syllables. AmE lacks long consonants, but has a correlation between length and syllabic distribution which at some points resembles that of N. Certain vowels which usually average somewhat shorter than the rest can only occur before consonants, e.g. the syllabics of *pit, pet, put,* and *putt.* These have been shown by laboratory measurements to have average durations ranging from .16 to .25 sec.[14] This is a good deal longer than the N vowels with which they were regularly reproduced, but the contours are similar enough so that AmN speakers nearly always reproduced these vowels as shorts, with a syllabic contour of VC. Examples are: E trick > AmN *trikk'*; shed > *sjedd'*; bug > *bågg'*; bull > *bull'*. There are sporadic exceptions, e.g. visit > *vi`sita* or *vis`sita*; yes > *je's* or *jess'*; bedroom > *be`dromm*ˡ or *bedd`romm*ˡ. Some dialects do not permit the doubling of *v*, and accordingly have such forms as clevis > *klø'vis*; living > *le`ving*; river > *rø'ver*; shivaree > *sjø`vri*. But others have short vowels here. Before *r* VV is the rule in reproducing the vowels that can occur in this position in AmE: beer > *bi'r*; care > *kæ'r*; bar > *ba'r*; store > *stå'r*; squirrel > *skvø`ril*; sure > *sju'r*.

N short vowels were also substituted whenever the E vowels occurred before two consonants unless they were reproduced as diphthongs. Since *ng* [*η*] only occurred doubled in this position, it also belongs here. But clusters of *r* plus dental are in an uncertain position, since some dialects coalesce their own *r* with following dentals into a single retroflex sound. Dialects differ in their handling of these combinations, but the rule seems to be that *rn* and *rl* are short, *rd* is long, while *rs* and *rt* may be either. Examples of these various possibilities are: (a) VC before two consonants: beans > *bin's*, fills > *fil's*, rails > *rel's*, bent > *ben't*, tramp > *trem'p*, box > *bak's*(*t*), spokes > *spåk's*, tools > *tul's*; (b) VC before *ng:* pumpkin > *pan'ki*; yankee > *jen'ki*; shingle > *sjing'el*; (c) VC before *r* plus dental: cordeen (accordion) > *kår`din*; of course > *kårs'*; curtain > *kør'ten*; (d) VV before *r* plus dental: turn > *tø'rna*; parlor > *pa`rler* (or *par`ler*); chores > *kjå'rs*.

Those stressed E vowels which can occur in final position were all reproduced as VV. Examples are: gee > *jy'*; play > *plei`a*; pa > *pa'*; lawsuit > *lå`su*ˡ*t*; mow > *mo`a*; slough > *slu`a*; July > *ju`lai*; lawyer > *låi'ert*; allow > *lao`a*.

Those vowels which can occur both finally and before consonants in E, and which accordingly correspond structurally to the

N long vowels because they can constitute a complete core by themselves, fall into three groups. All of them average longer in AmE speech than the vowels discussed above; the same set of laboratory measurements found them averaging between .24 and .37 sec. when pronounced in isolated words. But they were differently reproduced according to their degree of diphthongization. Those that are (a) least dipththongal in English were frequently reproduced as shorts (VC); a slightly diphthongal group (b) was most often reproduced as longs (VV), while the markedly diphthongal group (c) was nearly always reproduced as longs. (a) In the position before single consonant the syllabics of cat [æ], cot [a], and caught [ɔ] were reproduced both long and short, with older speakers favoring the short, younger speakers the long. (b) The slightly diphthongal syllabics of beat [i], bait [e], boat [o], and boot [u] were sometimes reproduced as shorts, but more often as longs. (c) The diphthongal syllabics of bout [au], bite [ai], and boy [ɔi] were reproduced as longs almost without exception.

Examples of these substitutions are the following: [æ] > VV: add > *æ'da*, back > *bæ'ka*, bad > *bæ'd*, bass > *bæ's*, can > *kæ'na*, cash > *kæ'sj*, tavern > *ta'van*; [æ] > VC or VV: attic > *æ(t)'tik*; bach > *bæ(t)'tsja*; fasset (faucet) > *fæ(s)'set*; gasoline > *gæ(s)'seli'n*; molasses > *mala(s)'ses* (*ss* all from Vald. and Hedal); rabbit > *ra(b)'bit* (*bb* mostly EN); rattle (snake) > *ra(t)'tel* (*t* from 9 of 11 inf.); rattlesnake > *re(t)'telsne'k* (*tt* from 16 of 54 inf.); travel > *tra(v)'vla*; valley > *væ(l)'li* (*ll* 2 of 10 inf.); [æ] > VC: black > *blekk'*; jack > *jekk'*; map > *mapp'*.

[a] > VV: bottom > *ba'tom*; common > *ka'men* (also *kåm'men*); [a] > VC or VV: closet > *kla(s)'sett*; crop > *kra(p)p'* (*pp* from 46 of 53 inf.); moccassin > *ma(g)'gis*; watermelon > *va(t)'termel'len*; [a] > VC: block > *blakk'*; cob > *kabb'*; cotton > *kat'ten*; door knob > *dø'ranabb'*; job > *jabb'*; mop > *mapp'*; schoolmam > *sku'lemamm'*; schottische > *sjat'tis*; shock > *sjakk'*; shop > *sjapp'*; slop > *slapp'*.

[ɔ] > VV except in faucet > *få(s)'set*; office > *å(f)'fis*; across > *kråss'*; cross > *krås'sa*.

[i], [e], [o], [u] > VV (for examples see later sections of this chapter) except: depot > *dip'po* (7 of 59 inf.); keep > *kip'pa* (9 of 69); meeting > *mid'den* (11 of 24); reap > *rip'pa* (18 of 66);

reaper > *rip'par* (21 of 95); brake > *brekk'*; plate > *plett'* (5 of 63); railroad > *rell'rä'd;* stable > *steb'bel* (4 of 58); gopher > *gof'jert* (49 of 82); grocery > *gros'seri*; homestead > *ho(m)m'stedd'*; yoke > *jogg'* or *jokk'* (7 of 41); euchre > *juk'ker* (2 of 14); stoop > *stupp'* (2 of 37).

[ai], [ɔi], [au] > VV: pinery > *pai'nri;* joist > *jåi'st*; county > *kæu'nti* (sporad. *kon'ti*).

On the basis of the reproduction of E vowels by N speakers, we may divide them into four classes: the short, the semi-short, the semi-long, and the long. The short are [ɪ], [ɛ], [ʊ], [ʌ] (always VC); the semi-short are [æ], [a], [ɔ] (VC before CC; often VC before C; VV finally); the semi-long are [i], [e], [o], [u] (VC before CC; rarely VC before C; VV finally); the long are [ai], [au], [ɔi] (always VV). That this division is related to the syllabic situation in E will be clear; it appears that what the AmN speaker is reacting to is the syllabic contour and not the precise length of the vowels.[15] The earliest bilinguals reproduced the syllabic contour of AmE wherever possible, though with much vacillation for the intermediate (semi-short) vowels [æ], [ɔ], and [a], and with nearly complete elimination of longs before consonant clusters. Later bilinguals gradually introduced AmE longs before clusters and made all vowels long except the four unambiguously short ones.

2. *Vocalism.*

The vowels of N vary in quality from dialect to dialect, but the number of different phonemic systems is relatively small.[16] As stated above, the most common system is one with nine vowels and three favorite diphthongs. The symbols chosen to represent these units are in close agreement with standard N orthography (excepting for the last diphthong, which is spelled *au*): *i, y, u; e, ø, o; æ, a, å; ei, øy, æu*. Each symbol covers a considerable range of actual sounds, but no two will overlap in any one dialect. The sounds of WN are somewhat closer to E, having some of the diphthongal glides which are so characteristic of the latter language. In the Midland dialects the phonetic values are close to those of German, but in EN a vowel shift has taken place which has overrounded all the back vowels (*a, å, o, u*) and tended to make them sound like their next higher or fronter neighbor (*å, o, u, y*). In unstressed syllables many but not all dialects pronounce *e* with the value of [ə].[17]

The following phonetic chart indicates the approximate tongue position and lip rounding of the EN sounds, which are underlined. The AmE sounds have also been entered for the sake of comparison. The symbols for E are approximately those of John S. Kenyon in his American Pronunciation.[18] Tongue position is marked by the relative height and advancement on the chart; rounding is indicated by parentheses. Diphthongs are shown by means of arrows pointing the direction and approximate distance of tongue movement.

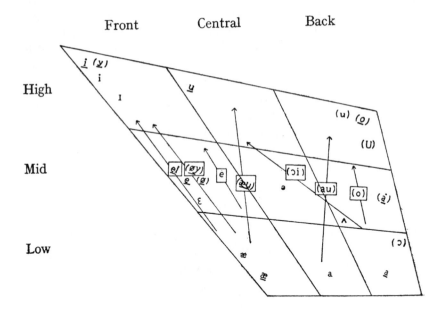

The two systems will perhaps be easier to compare if they are set up side by side in terms of their significant components. In AmE rounding is of minor importance, as we see from the relatively sluggish lip movements of speakers and the lack of front rounded vowels in the system. Tongue movement is the major factor.

In EN the position of the tongue appears to be less significant than the amount of rounding, since *i*, *y*, and *u* are all relatively far forward and are chiefly distinguished by their degrees of rounding.

English				Norwegian		
	Front	Central	Back	Spread	Round	Overround
High	i		u			
				High *i*	*y*	*u*
Lower high ...	ɪ		ʊ			
				Mid *e*	*ø*	*o*
Mid glide	e		o			
Mid	ɛ	ə	ʌ			
				Low *æ*	*a*	*å*
Low	æ	a	ɔ			
Low glide	ai	ɔi	au	Glide *ei*	*øy*	*æu*

The vowels of AmE will now be listed in the order of their appearance in the preceding table, reading from left to right across each row. The chief AmN substitutes will be given first, with examples, and then some of the exceptional or sporadic ones.

E [i] > AmN *i*. Examples: (a) Stressed: beat > *bi`ta;* ceiling > *si`ling;* cheese > *kji's;* easy > *i'si;* seed > *si'd;* beans > *bin's;* (b) Unstressed: buggy > *båg`gi;* country > *kon'tri;* turkey > *tør'ki.* Variants: (1) > AmN *e* in depot > *dep`po* (13 EN inf. of 88), possibly due to a variant AmE pron. with [ɛ]; unstressed in gravy > *gre`ve* (cf. N *greve* 'count'); army > *ar`me* (cf. N *arme* 'army'); shanty > *sjan`te* (cf. N *hytte* 'cabin'); monkey-wrench > *mon`keren's* (cf. the verb monkey > *mon`ke*). (2) > AmN *y* in gee (call to oxen) > *jy';* sporad. in depot > *dy`po;* reap > *ry`pa;* treat > *try`ta.* Labialization occurred near labial consonants; also in animal calls, cf. pig-pig > *py'g-py'g.*

E [u] > AmN *u*. Examples: deuce > *du's;* lose > *lu`sa;* music > *mju`sik;* slough > *slu`a;* stoop > *stu(p)p';* suit > *su't;* crew > *kru'.* Variants: > *o* sporadically in some words which more often have *u*, e.g. euchre > *jo'ker;* tools > *tol's;* two-step > *to'stepp[1]* (cf. N *to* 'two'); and in some less well attested words, such as boom, boost, cool, fool etc.; regularly in saloon > *sa`lon* (exc. 2 inf.). Since nearly all of these are words with double *o*, it seems likely that the pronunciation with *o* is due to the spelling.

E [ɪ] > AmN *i*. Examples: (a) Stressed: biscuit > *bis`kit*; disc > *dis'k*; picnic > *pik'nik*; (b) Unstressed: dentist > *den`-tist*; mortgage > *mår'git;* (c) Before r: beer > *bi'r*; gear > *gi'r*; steer > *sti'r*. Variants: (1) > AmN *e* in many words, often alternating with *i*, e. g. in arithmetic > *ret`metikk¹* (or *rit'*-); brick > *brekk'* (or *brikk'*); chinchbug > *sin'kjbågg¹* or *kjen'sbågg¹*; middlings > *mel`ling* or *mil`ling*. In restressed syllables we have both *e* and *i:* guitar > *get`tar* and *git`tar*. E [ɪ] is lower than N *i*, so that there is a general tendency to substitute *e* in many dialects; in a few EN and northern dialects there is no *i* in some positions, so that *e* is always substituted. (2) > AmN *y* in whip > *hyp`pa*; whippletree > *hyp'peltre¹*; occasionally also cistern > *sys'tern*; dipper > *dyp`per*; dish > *dyssj'*; crib > *krybb'*; dinner > *dyn'ner*; risk > *rys'k*; arithmetic > *ryt'metikk¹*. Labialization occurred in contact with labial consonants, including [r] and [sh]; in whip and whippletree, sporadically in whiskey, the [w] was reproduced as labialization only. (3) > AmN *ø* in river > *rø(v)'ver* (also -*i*-, -*e*-); shivaree > *sjø(v)`veri* (also -*e*-, -*i*-, -*y*-); occ. arithmetic > *røt'metikk¹*; risk > *røs'k*. (4) occ. > AmN *u* in whiskey > *hus'ki*; arithmetic > *rut'metikk¹*.

E [ʊ] (1) > AmN *u*. Examples: bull > *bull'*; bushel > *bus'sjel*; put > *put`ta*; before r regularly: bureau > *bju'ro*; cure > *ku'ra*; poor house > *pu'rhu¹s*. (2) > AmN *o*. Examples: bookcase > *bokk`-kei¹s*; broom > *bromm'*; cookie(s) > *kok'ki(s)*; football > *fott'bå¹l*. N *u* and *o* are both different from E [ʊ]; it is striking that all the above examples (except those before *r*) follow the spelling. This is not universal; some words not here included show variations from the rule, cf. rootbeer > *rutt'bir* (3 inf.), pulley > *pol'li*. Cognates with *o* may have influenced bookcase (N *bok*) and football (N *fot*). N *u* is rarely found before *kk* and *m*, being usually lowered to *o*. In some WN dialects there is a lowered [ʊ] which is the regular substitute for E [ʊ].

E [e] (1) > AmN *e*. Examples: basement > *be`smen¹t;* brake > *brekk';* cake > *ke'k;* case > *ke's;* freight > *fre't;* game > *ge'm;* grade > *gre'd;* rails > *rel's;* save > *se`va;* shade > *sje'd;* shave > *sje`va;* surveyor > *save'rar;* vacation > *veke'sjen*. This was the usual substitution. But at the same time there were cases of (2) > AmN *ei*. Examples: basin > *bei's(a);* change > *kjei῾nja* (*e* 4 inf.); frame > *frei'm;* jail > *jei'l;* lake > *lei'k;* painkiller > *pei'nkil῾lar.* This sound usually has a lower beginning and a shorter first element than the E [e] glide. Younger informants tended to import the E [e] with their loanwords: *be'bi.* (3) > AmN *æ.* Examples: acre > *æ'ker* (sometimes *ei* or *e*); ague > *æ'ger* (also *e*); make > *mæ῾ka* (also *ei* or *e*); stable > *stæ'bel* (also *e* or *ei*). The pre-immigration train > *træ'n* shows that this was an old substitution; it is limited to older words. The common pail > *pæ'l* is probably a loanshift, though it could also belong here. (4) > AmN *i* before two cons. in cradle > *krid'l* (> *krill*); grapes > *grip's* (also *e* and *ei*). These may have gone by way of WN *e*, which is high enough to sound like an *i* to EN speakers.

E [o] (1) > AmN *å.* Examples: hoe > *hå';* no > *nå';* road > *rå'd;* spokes > *spåk's;* stove > *stå'v.* N *å* is overrounded and gives an acoustic impression not unlike that of *o* in other languages; early speakers substituted it especially in final position. (2) > AmN *o.* Although the acoustic quality is quite different from E [o], many loans were taken over with this sound, possibly due to the spelling; often *o* and *å* varied. Examples: cloak > *klo'k;* close > *klo's;* coat > *ko't;* grove > *gro'v* (also *å*); mow > *mo῾a;* oatmeal > *o'tmil;* poker > *po'ker.* In some EN dialects younger informants imported E [o] in many loanwords.[19] (3) > AmN *u* sporad. in gopher > *guf'fert* (cf. N *kuf'fert* 'trunk'); yoke > *ju'g* (cf. N *ju῾ga* 'lie').

E [ε] > AmN *e.* Examples: ahead > *ehedd';* anyway > *en'-nivei;* bent > *ben't;* bet > *bet῾ta;* check > *kjekk';* fence > *fen's;* next > *nek'st;* second > *sek'ken;* pencil > *pen'sel.* In some dialects the *e* is quite low, approximating an *æ*.[20] Variants: (1) > AmN *i* often in wrench > *rin'sj,* sporad. in WN pronunciations of assessor, democrat, desk, pencil etc., where the short *i* is lowered; (2) > AmN *ei* in some dialects where *e* is diphthongized before dentals: fence > *fein's,* rent > *rein't,* (3) > AmN *ø* near labial consonants in clevis > *klø(v)'vis,* separator > *søp῾pere῾tar,* sporad. necktie > *nøkk'tai,* sheriff > *sjør'f.*

E [ə] > AmN *e.* Examples: creamery > *kri῾meri*; nickel > *nik'kel*; liniment > *lin῾nemen῾t*; election > *elek'sjen*; cousin

> *kås'sen*. Note that the AmN *e* is often phonetically [ə] also, though a little higher than the E one. Variants: (1) > AmN *i* in moccasin > *ma'gis* (also *u*), university > *ju`nivør|seti*, sporad. in ahead > *ihedd'*, at all > *itå'l*; (2) > AmN *a* in regular [rɛg'lə] > *reg'la* (also *e*), molasses > *mala'ses*, tavern > *ta`van*, surveyor > *save'r(ar)*, allow > *alao'a*, gallon > *gal`lan* (also *o*); (3) > AmN *o* in automobile > *å`tomobil* (also *e*), timothy > *tim`moti*, gallon > *ga(l)`lon*, bottom > *ba'tom*, kerosine > *ker`rosin*. Most of these variant forms are clearly due to the spelling, but a few of them are substitutions in positions where N rarely had *e*. E [ə] was often lost, esp. (a) initially, or (b) between consonants or diphthongs and *r* or *l:* (a) allow > *lao`a*; amount > *mao`nta*; arithmetic > *rit`metikk|*; assessor > *ses`sar*; alarm clock > *lar`mkluk|ka;* accordion > *kår'dien*; across > *kråss*; (b) trouble > *trub`la;* cover > *kåv`ra*; granary > *grø(n)`nri*; pinery > *pei`nri*; factory > *fek`tri;* figure > *fig`ra;* tickle > *tik`la;* regular > *reg`la;* separator > *sep`p(e)re|tar;* settle > *set`la;* battery > *bæ(t)`tri;* bother > *ba`dra;* garage > *gra'dj* (also *ge-, ga-*); squire > *skvæ'r;* style > *stai'l;* wire > *vai'r;* spoil > *spåi`la;* flour > *flæu'r;* towel > *tæu'l*. In some words E pronunciation in unstressed syllables varies from [ɪ] to [ə] and this is reflected in a vacillation between *i* and *e* in AmN.

E [ʌ] (1) > AmN *u*. Examples: grub > *grub`ba;* hunt > *hun`ta* (also *å* or *o*); jug > *jug`ga* (also *å*); rub > *rub`ba* (also *å*); trouble > *trub'bel*. (2) > AmN *o*. Examples: country > *kon'tri* (also *å* or *ø*); lumber > *lom'ber* (also *å* or *ø*); monkeywrench > *mon`keren|s* (also *å*); trunk > *tronk* (also *å*). (3) > AmN *å*. Examples: bluff > *blåff;* bug > *bågg;* buggy > *båg`gi* (also *ø*); bucket > *båk`ket* (also *ø*); bulb > *bålb* (also *ø*); buttery > *båt`tri* (also *ø*); bust > *bås`ta* (also *ø*); cover > *kåv`ver;* front > *frånt* (also *a, ø, o*); near one > *næ'rvånn|;* rough > *råff;* tough > *tåff;* tub > *tåbb* (also *ø*). (4) > AmN *å* in WN, *ø* in EN. Examples: brother-in-law > *bråd'derinlå|;* brush > *brøssj:* cousin > *kås'sen;* cultivate > *kål`teve|ta* (also *u*); judge > *jødj;* lunch > *lånsj* (also *a* or *o*); rug > *rågg* (also *a*); run > *røn`na;* stuck > *ståkk;* sucker (a fish) > *såk'ker;* supper > *såp'per;* truck > *trøkk*. (5) > AmN *ø*. Examples: (a) before r: circus > *sør'kis;* clerk > *klørk;* curtain > *kørt'en;* turkey > *tør'ki* etc.; (b) elsewhere: dust >

døst; justice > *jøs`tis* (also *u*); shut > *sjøt`ta* (also *a*). (6) > AmN
a. Cut > *kat`ta* (also *ø*); cutter > *kat`tar* (also *ø*); husk > *has`ka;*
pumpkin > *pan'ki* (also *å* and *o*). The AmN reproductions have
in common only that they are short and more or less labial; most
of them can be accounted for by the consonantal environment,
which has drawn the indefinite [ʌ] in one direction or another.
Labial environment favored *å*, dental environment *ø*. Spellings
influenced the pronunciations of *u* and *o*, the latter required before
mb and *nk* in many dial. Some cases of *u* have similar N analogues:
trub`la* (cf. *grub`la), *jug`ga* (cf. *mug`ga*), *grub`ba* and *rub`ba* (cf.
skrub`ba). The use of *a* is prob. the nearest phonetic equivalent,
and is characteristic of younger speakers. Some of the more
widespread loans show stable forms which must have passed from
one community to another, e.g. *jug`ga, trub`bel, kat`ta, has`ka,
pan'ki.* *Pan'ki* was reshaped in some WN dialects as *paon'ki;* in
the Iola area, however, an independent form, *pon'kis*, was in use.

E [æ] (1) > AmN *e* before clusters. Examples: aunty >
en`ti;* basket > *bes`ket (also *a*); camp > *kem`pa;* candy > *ken'di;*
chance > *kjen's;* draft > *drej't;* flax > *flek's;* pantry > *pen'tri;*
stanchion > *sten'sjen* (also *a*); tramp > *trem'p* (also *a*). Since *e*
included a number of lower sounds and there is no distinction of
e and *æ* when short, it was natural that AmN should not distinguish
between [ɛ] and [æ] in general. (2) > AmN *æ* before single consonants. Examples: (a) before *r:* barrel > *bæ`ril* (also *a*); care >
kæ'r; chairman > *kjæ'rmann¹;* fair > *fæ'r;* square dance >
skvæ'rdan¹s; upstairs > *upp`stæ¹rs;* (b) before other consonants:
add > *æ`da;* bass > *bæ's;* fanning mill > *fæ'ningmyl¹la* (also *e*
and *ei*); gravel > *græ'vel* (also *e*). Since N had a distinction of *e* and
æ before single consonant, there was more tendency to keep this
in AmN lws. (3) > AmN *a.* Examples: bran > *bran'(d);* gallon
> *gal`lon* (or *gal`lan*); map > *mapp'* (also *æ*); molasses > *mala'ses
{mal`lasi*); pasture > *pas'ter;* rabbit > *ra(b)'bit* (also *æ*); rattler
> *ra(t)'tel;* shanty > *sjan`te;* tavern > *ta'van;* travel > *trav`la,*
and sporad. in many of the above. In view of the widespread agreement of spelling and pronunciation in these words, we cannot
overlook the probability that spelling was the reason for the use
of *a* as a reproduction of [æ]. Variant: > AmN *ei* sporad. in back
> *bei`ka;* blanket > *blein`ket;* fanning mill > *fei`ningmyl¹la*

(4 inf.); tank > *teink;* yankee > *jein'ki.* Due to same causes as *ei* for E [ɛ].

E [a] (1) > AmN *a.* Examples: barn > *barn* (*ba'te, ba'ne, ba'na*); block > *blakk* (also *å*); bother > *ba'dra;* box > *baks(t);* carpet > *kar'pet;* closet > *kla'sett* (also *å*); cob > *kabb.* (2) > AmN *å.* Examples: substantial minorities use *å* in most of the words that are spelled with *o,* e. g. common > *kåm'men;* crop > *kråpp;* schottische > *sjåt'tis.* This can be due only to the spelling with *o,* which could be interpreted by Norwegian readers as *å;* British pronunciation would hardly be a factor. Variant: > AmN *æ* sporad. in farm (2 inf.) and yard (7 inf.), mostly Midland and WN dialects; in cob > *kæbb* 24A1, where the change is due to the absence of *a* before *bb* in the dialect.

E [ɔ] > AmN *å.* Examples: chores > *kjå'rs;* cord > *kår'd;* store > *stå'r;* across > *kråss';* chalk > *kjå'k* (also *a*); faucet > *få'sett*[1] (also *a*); lawn > *lå'n* (also *a*); overall > *å'verå'l* (also *a*). Before *r* the E [ɔ] is high enough so that it is regularly reproduced as *å* or even *o;* but elsewhere it is low and comes close to N *a,* which is quite far back. Variants: (1) > AmN *a* in haw > *ha* (call to oxen), and several words listed above; (2) > AmN *o* in board > *bor'da* (cf. N *bo'r* 'table'); horn > *ho'rna* (also *å*); court > *kort'* (cf. N. *kort* 'card'); porch > *por'tkj* (also *å*); sporad. elsewhere; (3) > AmN *æu* in automobile > *æu'tomobil* (spelling); log > *læugg* in certain Gbr. and Tr. dialects where no *o* occurs in this position.

E [ai] (1) > AmN *ei.* Examples: fine > *fein;* Irish(man) > *ei'ris;* license > *lei'sens;* pile > *pei'la;* ripe > *rei'p;* rising > *rei's;* silo > *sei'lo;* surprise > *sup'preis.* In most dialects this was the only available diphthong for rendering the E one. In some dialects this diphthong actually was [æi] or [ai], very near the E [ai]. (2) > AmN *ai.* Examples: appendicitis > *pen'nesai'tis;* bicycle > *bai'sik'kel;* dining room > *dai'ningromm*[1] (also *a*); fried cake > *frai'dke'k;* goodbye > *gudba'i;* July > *jula'i;* nice > *nai's;* pie > *pa'i;* style > *stai'l;* wire > *vai'r.* This diphthong occurred as *a'i* in N in the word *ma'i* 'May', and as *ai'* in some recent loanwords like *kai'* > 'quay'. It was regularly imported with the lws. by later bilinguals. Variant: > AmN *æ* in squire > *skvæ'r,* an early loan (cf. wire > *vai'r*).

E [ɔi] (1) > AmN *øy*. Examples: lawyer > *løy'er(t)*; joist > *jøys(t)*. Only a few of the oldest inf. used this substitution, though it is given as regular in Nils Flaten's Valdres word list from Goodhue Co., Minn.; it has also been heard by the writer in the words choice, joint, oyster, poison. (2) > AmN *âi*. Examples: join > *jâi`na;* spoil > *spâi`la* (also *ei*); toilet > *tâi`lett¹*. A few dialects had this diphthong as an equivalent of the *øy* in other dialects; but the sound was everywhere introduced with loanwords by younger bilinguals.

E [au] (1) > AmN *æu*. Examples: county > *kæu'nti;* crowd > *kræu'd;* flour > *flæu'r;* sound > *sæun`(d)a;* towel > *tæu'l;* town > *tæu'n;* township > *tæun'sjipp¹*; trout > *træu't*. Most inf. have the *ao* listed below in these words; only *flæu'r* is practically universal. In this word it has even been passed on into some dial. as a monophthong: *flø'r*. (2) AmN > *ao*. Examples: allow > *alao'a;* amount > *mao`nta*. Certain WN dialects have this diphthong; but most American bilinguals have imported it with the lws., even reimporting it in words which at first were pronounced as *æu*.

We may sum up this discussion of the substitutions of AmN for E sounds by listing the most common identifications as follows:

	Spread	Round	Overround
High	[ɪ, i] > *i*	[ɪ, i] > *y*	[ʊ, u] > *u*
Mid	[ɪ, ɛ, æ, e] > *e*	[ɪ, ɛ, ʌ] > *ø*	[ʊ, o, ʌ] > *o*
Low	[ɛ, æ, e] > *æ*	[a, ʌ] > *a*	[ʌ, ɔ, o] > *å*
Glides ...	[e, ai] > *ei* or *ai*	[ɔi] > *øy* or *âi*	[au] > *æu* or *ao*

The confusions shown here can be illustrated from our materials by the following word pairs:

rip v. > *rip`pa*	depot n. > *dy`po*	bull > *bull*
reap v. > *rip`pa*	dipper n. > *dyp`per*	tools > *tuls*
brick n. > *brekk*	river n. > *røv'ver*	trunk n. > *tronk*
brake n. > *brekk*	clevis n. > *kløv'vis*	cookies n. > *kok'kis*
trip n. > *trepp*	dust n. > *døst*	yoke n. > *jogg*
trap n. > *trepp*		

wrench n. > *rensj*	cut n. > *katt*	stuck a. > *ståkk*
ranch n. > *rensj*	cot n. > *katt*	stalk n. > *ståkk*
back v. > *bæ'ka*		spokes n. > *spåks*
acre n. > *æ'ker*		

pail n. > *peil*	joist n. > *jøys(t)*	flour n. > *flæur*
pile n. > *peil*	join v. > *jâi͡na*	amount v. > *maon'ta*

The reproductions show that N speakers were more sensitive to labialization than E speakers: they heard labial qualities of [ɪ], [i], [ɛ], and [ʌ] which were not distinctive in E because they were due to neighboring labial consonants. But they failed to hear tense-lax distinction of [i]-[ɪ] and [u]-[ʊ], though in some cases they rendered [ɪ] and [ʊ] with the lower sounds of *e* and *o*. At first they did not hear the diphthongal glide of [e] and [o], though they later substituted their own *ei* for the former. In contrast with N learners of British English they did not substitute their *æu* for the [o], but used it only for [au]. They could not distinguish [ɛ] and [æ], or [ɔ] and [o], and their reproduction of [ʌ] varied according to environment and spelling. The earliest learners of E identified their own three diphthongs with the E low glides, but soon began importing the E sounds instead. Growing bilingualism brought with it also a less haphazard reproduction of the E sounds. Where the N substitution made by the first generation seemed too far off, the second generation reborrowed the word in a more accurate phonetic form. This meant particularly the introduction of the E glides, not only the three low glides mentioned, but also E [e] and [o], as well as the introduction of [ʌ], [ɔ], and [æ].

The influence of spelling has been seen at several points. None appeared for [ai], [e], or [au]; and some sounds were nearly always spelled the same way in both languages, e.g. [ɪ], [ɛ], [o]. Only in the case of [æ] spelled *a*, [a] spelled *o*, [ɔ] spelled *a*, [u] and [ʊ] spelled *oo*, and [ʌ] spelled *u* did we find presumptive spelling influence. The fact that for many words alternative pronunciations existed, one phonetic and one orthographic, would seem to confirm this hypothesis.

3. *Consonantism.*

The phonetic differences of the consonants in various dialects are conspicuous, but the structural differences are not great. The symbols chosen are those of standard N orthography, even in cases where two symbols have to be written to represent one sound: *b, d, g; p, t, k; m, n, ng; l, r; j, kj; v, f; h; s, sj.* In addition, a flapped variety of *l* (similar to E [r]) is written as *ɫ;* this is characteristic of EN dialects. In SW Norway the *b, d, g* are partially unvoiced, while elsewhere they are voiced; but they are not confused with *p, t, k.* The *r* is tongue-trilled in most of the country, but uvular in some SW areas. The symbols *ng, kj,* and *sj* represent only single sounds in EN, but clusters or affricates in many WN dialects. Long postvocalic dentals are palatalized in the northern half of the country, while in EN the *r* plus dentals coalesce into single, retroflex sounds. In general, the N dentals are 'light', while the E are 'dark' in their resonance; the only exception is the retroflex *ɫ* of EN. The N *kj* is pronounced [ç] in EN, but has a preceding closure in many Midland and WN dialects.

A comparison of the two systems shows that they correspond quite well, except for the class of oral continuants, where N lacks voiced sibilants, interdental spirants, and a [w]. Substitutions will now be listed for each E phoneme. Examples for each position within the syllable will be given when they are available.

E [b] > AmN *b.* Examples: band > *bæ'nd;* beauty > *bju'ti;* black-berries > *blekk'beris;* breakfast > *brekk'fes'ᵗ;* cob > *kabb';* bulb > *bål'b;* barber > *bar'ber.*

E [d] > AmN *d.* Examples: dish > *dissj';* drill > *drill';* seed > *si'd;* Indian > *in'di;* garden > *gar'den.* The N is postdental, the E alveolar. After *l* and *n* the *d* is often lost: field > *fi'l;* sound > *sæu'n(d)a;* appendicitis > *pen'nesai'tis;* mind > *mai'n(d)a.* The E [d] is often absent in American folk pronunciation, and in many N dialects there can be no *d* in this position.

E [g] > AmN *g.* Examples: gear > *gi'r;* glue > *glu';* granary > *gre'neri;* bug > *bågg';* bargain > *bar'gen.*

E [p] > AmN *p.* Examples: pie > *pa'i;* pure > *pju'r;* play > *plei'a;* program > *pro'græm;* spear > *spi'ra;* map > *mapp';* camp > *kem'p;* carpet > *kar'pet.*

E [t] > AmN *t*. Examples: two-step > *tu'stepp¹*; træmp > *trem'p*; twine > *tvai'n*; suit > *su't*; attic > *æ(t)'tik*; draft > *drej't*; elect > *elek'ta*; cent > *sen't*; smart > *smar't*; dust > *døs't*. The N is postdental, the E alveolar. The N *t* is substituted for the E [t], even when the latter is voiced in certain medial positions, excepting in the word meeting > *mid'den*, where *d* has been substituted.²¹ Other sporadic substitutions for voiced [*t*] are: putty > *påd'di*; cutter > *kar'ter*; buttery > *bår'tri* (the last two only in a Gbr. dialect).

E [k] > N *k*. Examples: coat > *ko't*; cure > *ku'ra (kju'ra* 1 inf.); clevis > *klø'vis*; crowd > *kræud*; quilt > *kvil't*; picnic > *pik'nik*; sucker > *søk'ker*; sulky > *sal'ki*; tank > *ten'k*; husk > *has'ka*. In agreement with the practice of some dialects, a final *k* is affricated before palatal vowels: the attic > *et'tikjen* (15P1, 13N4); the arithmetic > *rip'pentikj¹en* (4L1). Variant: > *g* in moccasin > *ma'gis*; yoke > *jo'g (jugg)*. AmE [k] is occasionally voiced intervocalically.

E [m] > N *m*. Examples: mow > *mo'a*; music > *mju'sik*; cemetery > *sem'mete¹ri*; frame > *frei'm*; farm > *far'm*.

E [n] > N *n*. Examples: pneumonia > *nu'monja*; town > *tæu'n*; candy > *ken'di*; horn > *hor'na*; corner > *kår'na*. Postdental in N, alveolar in E.

E [ng] > N *ng*. Examples: get along > *get'telång¹*; pumpkin *pan'ki*. Sporad. lost in fanning mill > *fæ'nimyl¹la*.

E [v] > N *v*. Examples: valley > *væl'li*; surveyor > *save'r*; river > *rø(v)'ver*; stove > *stå'v*.

E [w] > N *v*. Examples: wire > *vai'r*; quilt > *kvil't*; squirrel > *skvæ'ril*. Variant: > labialization of *i* in whip > *hyp'pa*; whipple-tree > *hyp'peltre¹*.

E [l] > AmN *l*. Examples: leave > *li'va*; saloon > *sa'lon*; island > *ai'len(d)*; mail > *me'l*. N postdental, E alveolar; in dialects with palatalized *l*, these are substituted in the proper places: *bull'*, *drill'*, *svill'*, etc. In dialects with cacuminal *l* (*ļ*), this is occasionally substituted in some words, especially after non-dental consonants: blackberries > *błekk'beris*; blanket > *błen'ket*; bluff > *błåff'*; clean > *kłi'na*; flax > *fłek's*; flour > *fłæu'r*; plenty > *płen'ti*; plug > *pługg'*; regular > *reg'ła*. But it does not occur in all possible positions, and varies from dialect to dialect.

E [r] (1) > AmN *r*. Examples: rattler > *ra'tel;* Irish > *ei'ris;* bar > *ba'r;* brother-in-law > *bråd'derinlå¹;* quadrille > *kådrill';* frame > *frei'm;* grade > *gre'd*. This substitution is made regardless of the phonetic quality of the N *r* (lingual or uvular). (2) > AmN untrilled *r*. Examples: cordeen (accordion) > *kård῾in;* curtain > *kørt'en;* barn > *ba'rn;* parlor > *pa῾rler;* chores > *kjǟ'rs*. This occurs only in dialects where *r* has been amalgamated with following dentals. It is often hard to tell this sound from AmE [r]. (3) > AmN *ʆ*. Examples: barn > *ba῾ʆe;* poker > *po῾keʆ*. Only in dialects having this sound, and not in many words. (4) > AmN *ɽ*. The sound is very commonly imported in loanwords, especially in dialects having *ʆ* already, with which it is often confused.²² (5) > lost esp. before dentals. Examples: tavern > *ta῾van;* cars > *ka's;* saucer > *sa῾sa;* barn > *ba῾ne;* parlor > *pa῾lar;* chores > *kjo's;* crackers > *krek'kis*. Chiefly in WN dialects not having cacuminal *ʆ* or *r*.

E [dh] > AmN *d*. Examples: bother > *ba'der;* brother-in-law > *bråd'derinlå¹*.

E [z] > AmN *s*. Examples: zero > *se'ro;* peas > *pi's;* beans > *bin's;* chores > *kjǟ'rs;* fills > *fil's*.

E [zh] > AmN *sj*. Examples: rouge > *ru'sj* (1 inf.); treasurer > *tres'sjer*.

E [j] > AmN *j*. Examples: yankee > *jen'ki;* music > *mju῾sik*. In a few dialects it is an affricate, approximately *dj*, so that it is confused with the following sound.

E [dzh] (1) > AmN *j*. Examples: gee > *jy';* joist > *jøy's(t);* engine > *inn῾jai῾na*. The most common first-generation substitution esp. in EN. (2) > AmN *dj*. Examples: garage > *gara'dj;* college > *ka'lidj;* judge > *(d)jød'j*. Common in dialects having *dj* for *j;* elsewhere more frequent after than before vowels. (3) > AmN *t*. Example: mortgage > *mår῾git*. Common in this word only, probably an early loan. (4) > AmN *dsj*. Example: judge > *jød'sj*. (5) > AmN *ds*. Example: judge > *jød's* (rare).

E [f] > AmN *f*. Examples: fair > *fæ'r;* flax > *flek's;* freight > *fre't;* selfraker > *sel'f-*.

E [s] > AmN *s*. Examples: circus > *sør'kis;* screen > *skri'n;* slough > *slu῾e;* smart > *smar't;* rattlesnake > *ra'telsnei῾k;* spider > *spei῾dar;* spread > *spredd';* stoop > *stu'p;* street > *stri't;*

swill > *svill';* squire > *skvæ'r;* flax > *flek's;* chance > *kjen's;* grapes > *grip's;* horsepower > *hårs'pao¹er.* Variant: > AmN *sj* (often the same as *rs*). In dialects having retroflex *r*, *sj* occurs after *r* and before *l:* slough > *sjlu`a;* of course > *kårssj;* pencil > *pen'sjel;* boxelder > *bak'sjel.* By confusion with similar native forms, it is found in the common form husk > *hasj`ka* (cf. *harsk* 'rancid') and sporad. in clevis > *klø'vesj.*

E [sh] > AmN *sj.* Examples: shed > *sjedd';* dish > *dissj';* vacation > *veke'sjen;* corn shredder > *ko`rnsjed¹dar.* Variant: > AmN *s.* Examples: Irish > *ei'ris;* schottische > *sjat'tis;* sporadically in bushel > *bus'sel;* cash > *kæ's.*

E [th] > AmN *t.* Examples: timothy > *tim`moti;* arithmetic > *rit`metikk¹;* through > *tru'.* Sporadically labialized to *p* or *f* before m: *ryp`metikk¹.*

E [tsh] (1) > AmN *kj.* Examples: check > *kjekk';* cheese > *kji's.* The usual first-generation substitution. (2) > AmN *tkj.* Examples: chalk > *tkjå'k;* teach > *ti(t)`kja;* porch > *por'tkj.* This is a somewhat closer approximation to the E sound, which is often imported in those dialects where no such affricate exists. (3) > AmN *sj* or *s.* Examples: lunch > *lån'sj;* wrench > *ren's̓j, rin's;* chinchbug > *kjen'sbågg.* Only after *n;* not universal. (4) > AmN *ts.* Sporadically in bachelor > *bets`lar (bes`lar);* pitch > *pit's* (one inf.).

E [h] > AmN *h.* Examples: hickory > *hik`ril;* whip > *hyp`pa.* Often lost in second element of compounds, when reduced stress is lost. Examples: poor house > *pu'rus;* log house > *låg'gus;* leghorn > *leg'gårn.*

The substitutions of AmN for E consonants followed a fairly regular pattern. All the stops and nasals were reproduced by closely similar phonemes; of these only the dentals had a markedly different articulation in N from that of E. The labiodentals [v] and [f], the palatal semivowel [j], the unvoiced sibilants [s], [sh], and the laryngeal [h] were also reproduced by phonemes mostly indistinguishable in sound from the E. The affricates [tsh] and [dzh] were reproduced by the fricatives (in some dialects affricates) *kj* and *j*, though they were also imported into N by some speakers, the latter as *dj* or *dsj* (not unvoiced as in AmGer). The liquids *l* and *r* were rendered by the sounds that corresponded to these symbols in N, whatever their phonetic quality, which often was quite different from the E. The E sounds were often imported. Five phonemes could not be reproduced in N without identifying them with other phonemes: [w], [dh], [th], [z], and [zh]. They were identified with *v*, *d*, *t*, *s*, and *sj*. In contrast with the handling of the vowels, there were very few random substitutions.

As the examples given for each consonant show, the distribution of the consonants singly and in clusters corresponds quite closely between E and N. Both languages permit normally three consonants before or after a vowel, with *s* the only consonant that can stand as the third consonant preceding or following (except that *t*, and in N also *k*, can occur in this position in a few combinations). All consonants except *ng* can immediately precede vowels, and all except *j* and *h* can follow vowels. No consonants can precede *b*, *f*, *d*, *s*, *kj*, *sj*, *g*, or *h*, and only *s* can precede *p*, *m*, *t*, or *k*. Only the voiced continuants and nasals (excepting *m*, limited to *sm-*) can be rather freely preceded and followed by other consonants (e.g. *dv-*, *fn-*, *kl-*, *vr-*, *nj-*, *-mp*, *-vl*, *-nt*, *-lg*, *-rk*, *-ngd*). Most E clusters occur also in N, at least after the phoneme substitutions listed above have been made. The following E clusters do not occur in N words: *vj-*, *skj-*, *shr-*, *hj-*, *hw-*; *-lb*, *-ld*, *-mb*, *-ngg*, *-nd*, *-rd* (the preceding five occur in some dialects), *-ldzh*, *-ndzh*, *-rdzh*, *-ltsh*, *-ntsh*, *-rtsh*, *-lsh*, *-rsh*, *-mps*, *-nks*.

In importing words containing these and some other clusters, many speakers simplified them by omitting unfamiliar elements. Since different dialects had different clusters, these changes remained sporadic. Examples: gamble > *gem'la;* mumps > *moms;* tramp(s) > *trem's;* whip > *hyp'pa;* field > *fi'l* etc.; wrench > *ren'sj;* harvest > *har'vis* (2 inf.); locust > *lo'kus;* corn shredder > *ko`rnsjed'dar;* license > *lai'sen;* cure > *ku`ra* (also sporad. in cucumber, argue); mortgage > *mår'git* (or even *mår'gis*); shingle > *sjing'el* (no g). Some of these, as well as the following, may be due to folk pronunciations im AmE: joist > *jøy's;* surprise > *sup'preis;* surveyor > *save'r;* quadrille > *kådrill';* government > *guv'vament;* horsepower > *håss'pao¹er;* håndkerchief > *hen`kekjiff¹;* regular > *reg'la.* Very seldom were consonants added: box > *bak'st* (cf. N *bakst* 'baking'); sickle > *sir'kel* (cf. N *sir'kel* 'circle'); gallon > *gal'land* (in WN); tavern > *ta`vande;* bran > *bran'd* (cf. N *brand* 'fire').

Both clusters and phonemes were imported in positions where they resulted in phonemic redistributions. Among the imported clusters were: *dj* in judge > *djød'j;* *dsj* in silage > *sai'lidsj;* *tkj* in chalk > *tkjå'k;* *lb* in bulb > *bål'b* (one inf. > *bål'v*); *nd* in band > *bæ'nd;* *rd* in board > *bor'd;* *bl-, fl-, kl-, pl-* in some dialects which had only *bl-* etc. before. Among the single phonemes which occurred in new positions were: *g* in gear > *gi'r* (only in the call *giss* and in a few lws. in N); *f* after vowels in office > *å`fis* (also *åf'fis*); *d* after vowels in seed > *si'd* (no *d* in most dialects, except in lws. like *gud* 'God').

Actual phonemic importation was characteristic of second-generation speakers for some words and sounds. E [r] was the most common of these; after that came [w]. The interdentals were less common, being not always mastered even in E by bilinguals. Least common were the voiced sibilants, the last to be learned by AmN speakers. Typical was the treatment of E slippers: older loanform *slip'pers* (or *slippesj*), later *slip'pers* (with E [r] but voiceless [s]).

Chapter 17.

THE GRAMMAR OF LOANWORDS.

> Grammatically, the borrowed form is subject to
> the system of the borrowing language, both as to
> syntax and as to the indispensable inflections and
> the fully current, »living« constructions of compo-
> sition and word-formation.
>
> *L. Bloomfield (1933)*[1]

It was once thought that the categories of grammar were universal and that they reflected the categories of human thinking.
But the vast extension in recent times of our familiarity with different linguistic structures has shown that there is no category
which can be said to occur in all languages. Even such apparently
indispensable divisions as singular and plural, or present and past
can and often must be handled in other languages by lexical rather
than grammatical means. If we limit grammar to refer to recurrent
similarities between words which correspond to some aspect of
their meanings, we shall find that no two languages are exactly
alike in their grammar. Even if they have categories which are
of common historical origin and closely similar function, such as
the plural in E and N, we will soon discover that words which are
plural in one are singular in the other and vice versa. Scissors and
oats are plural in E, but singular in N; smallpox and money are
singular in E, but plural in N. Grammatical patterns change very
slowly, but they do change; and the structures that we know have
grown up more or less haphazardly over a very long time. They
submit to no logical analysis, but they tend to impose themselves
on our thinking by their insistent presence in our speech and writing.

We have seen in Chapter 15 how the borrowing language requires some degree of morphological adaptation of the new words. It is exceptional for a word to be imported in more than one form, so that e.g. a singular like 'phenomenon' may exist alongside a plural 'phenomena'. A single form is usually imported and is then given whatever endings the language requires to make it feel like a proper word and to express the categories which this particular language requires its words to express. In this chapter we shall take up the grammatical categories of N one by one and show how loanwords were adapted to them.

1. *Gender.*

The three Indo-European genders of masculine, feminine, and neuter are distingushed in all N speech except for certain urban dialects which have coalesced the first two. Older written DN, following Danish, had only two genders, common and neuter; but in speech this usage was adopted only in Bergen and upper-class urban circles. Gender may be regarded as a quality attributed to each noun which determines the choice among alternative forms of accompanying articles, adjectives, and pronouns of reference. It applies to all nouns, regardless of whether they can refer to male or female creatures, and often in direct disagreement with their natural sex. It is essential that new words be fitted into one of these categories so that some choice of accompanying modifiers can be made, and it is best that it be always the same for any given word so that there will be no hestitation. In addition to the form of modifiers, gender partly determines the form of plural and other inflections, though here the correlation is not perfect.

A similar categorizing of nouns into two or three form classes is found in most European languages. The fact that E has lost this distinction and that E nouns in being borrowed into other languages have to be reassigned to a gender has excited great interest among students of American immigrant languages. Lists of loanwords with their new genders have been published and various attempts have been made to determine the reasons of the speakers for assigning the words to one rather than another gender.[2] Some investigators have hoped to throw light on the origin of gender; but it seems more likely that this study can do no more than tell us something about the present-day function of gender in these languages. As with other theories concerning the operation of borrowing, we cannot check the mental processes of the speakers. Where several factors have operated, we have no good way of saying which one was the most important. We cannot rule out the possibility of coincidence unless we have a large number of instances and as few exceptions as possible. At best we are dealing with probabilities.

The explanations advanced so far have not made it possible to set up rules by which one could predict the gender of every noun. Most students have had a residue of forms which seemed to defy every rule, and one is tempted to say with C. B. Wilson that chance has been a considerable factor. Nevertheless it has been possible in each language to point to certain associations with forms in the native vocabulary which have led to many of the gender assignments. From the beginning it has been apparent that these associations could be based either on similarities of sound or meaning or on a combination of the two. Similarities of sound have included the so-called 'rhyme analogy', though they are seldom very exact in their rhyming; this is the explanation given by Haden and Joliat for the CanFr habit of making masculines in -*eur* out of E nouns in -*er*. Similarities of meaning have included the influence of natural gender, which appears to operate quite generally with names for living creatures. Some have tried to set up meaning classes, e.g. fruits, flowers, bodies of water, etc., which were supposed to have a predominant gender which would impose itself on loanwords belonging to the same groups. Others have sought out specific native words of similar meaning which might explain the assignment of certain genders. Aron assumed for a few words that homonyms might be given different genders in order to keep them distinct. Over and above these particular factors, it has been pointed out that most languages show a strong tendency to assign otherwise unattached nouns to a specific gender. In AmGer Aron found a 'feminine tendency'; in most other immigrant languages, e.g. Lithuanian, there is a clear masculine tendency. Aron thought the 'feminine tendency' in AmGer was due to the similarity of German *die* and E *the*. The masculine tendency of AmN was explained by Flom as due to the DN literary language.

As we present the data for AmN, the first fact that strikes us is the high degree of vacillation in the assignment of gender, even among nouns which were quite widespread and well-documented. Of the 317 noun stems included in a selected vocabulary 59, or 18.7 % of the total, show more than one gender. By an amusing coincidence this is also exactly the percentage of vacillation in E lws. in standard German, according to C. B. Wilson. This vacillation has been pointed out for other languages as well, e.g. by Stene in her study of E lws. in standard N. We may conclude that there are a good many words which offer the speaker no definite 'handle' by which to decide the proper gender. Such words appear most likely to be assigned to one gender, which may in this way become a habitual repository for new and unassimilated words. The extent to which this is true of AmN will be suggested by the following figures on the selected word list:

	Fixed		Vacillating				Potential totals	
	No.	%	m-f	m-n	f-n	m-f-n	No.	%
Masc. ...	227	88	17	21		19	284	72
Fem. ...	5	2	17		2	19	43	11
Neut. ...	26	10		21	2	19	68	17
Totals ..	258	100	17	21	2	19	317	100

Masculine accounts for more than seven times as many fixed genders as the other two added together; and the feminine can be applied to only one noun in nine, even counting those which get it sporadically. Flom's figures from the Sogn dialect at Koshkonong agree well with this distribution: m. 79 %, f. 7.7 %, n. 11 %. The somewhat stronger position of feminine in his count agrees with the general observation that f. is better represented in the Midland and WN dialects than in the EN. That his percentage of vacillation was only 2.3 % may be accounted for by the fact that he was dealing with only one dialect and one American community.

In accounting for this predominance, we shall first consider the numerical relationship of the genders in the native dialects. If we take the writings of Ivar Aasen as representative of the dialects, we find that the gender markers which clearly distinguish three genders (ein 'a', min 'my', sin 'his') had a frequency in running text of m. 49.3 %, f. 24 %, and n. 26.7 %. The lexical words beginning with B in his writings, excluding derivatives, were distributed m. 44.5 %, f. 23.4 %, and n. 32.1 %.[3] Flom's count of the words in certain dialects showed m. 52 %, f. 29 %, and n. 19 %. In general, these figures suggest that the masculine accounts for about one half of the words; but in AmN it has shot way up beyond this figure. Flom explained the discrepancy as deriving from the influence of the written DN, believing that some of the lws. found their way into circulation through the N-A press. This may have been true of some words; we have seen that their pronunciation has been partially influenced by the written word. But it does not seem likely as an explanation of the virtual disappearance of the feminine. The feminine showed no weakening in native words, but was in full use among all the speakers investigated. The real explanation seems rather to be that *a technique of borrowing had already been established before emigration,* whereby lws. were normally made masculine. In his grammar of 1864 Aasen complained that country people adopted words of French and Latin origin with erroneous gender; he declared that words with feminine suffixes like *-ion, -ur,* and *-tet* 'either vacillate between the two genders or fall into masculine.'[4] His explanation was that they were all taken in by way of DN where their 'common gender' suffix *-en* was identical with the dialect masculine. Haden has shown for French that the masculine was established in France as the gender of citation for anything whose gender had not yet been determined[5].

The relationship to DN is not precisely the same as that suggested by Flom, since it does not require the assumption that any given word came in through the printed page. It merely points to an old habit of the country people in accepting new words from socially superior sources: they took them with a gender which seemed identical with their own masculine. A reinforcement of this theory is the fact that the feminines and neuters are generally found among the early loans; where the same words were borrowed again later, they were sometimes given masc. gender. Among these were the early *hyppa* f. 'whip' and *tavan* n. 'hotel', later borrowed as *wipp* m. and *tævern* m. Unassimilated loans in citation forms by younger speakers were almost universally masculine. Just so in CanFr the word swing 'a plaything' > *swigne* f., a well adapted word, but in the meaning of 'allure' > *swing* m. Of course, the masculine tendency does not preclude masculine nouns from having received their genders by specific association, just as have the feminine and neuter nouns. But we cannot use masculine gender to prove such associations, unless we first show that they apply to the other genders as well. Too many writers have been inclined to assume that gender identity between two words also proved a gender association which was the cause of that identity.

The problem of gender association is closely related to that of the loanshift extension, which was discussed in Chapter 15 and will be more fully handled in the next chapter. Some writers have assumed that gender association could only take place between homologues (words of similar meaning); Flom dismissed the possibility that *fil* 'field' got its feminine from N *fil* 'file' and *skrin* 'screen' its neuter from N *skrin* 'chest'. 'To bring about analogy in gender some relationship in concept is assumed as necessary', he wrote.[6] But there is no other possible explanation for these words; N *åker* 'field' is m., and for 'screen' there was no N word. Whereever it occurs, the word *fil* is homophonous with N *fil*, lacking the [d] of the E word and in some dialects having an *i* that is different from the *i* usually substituted for E [i]. The writer has been able to find a number of other such words, which will be treated with the loanshifts, since they have become identical with N words, even to the extent of acquiring umlaut plurals, which no other lws. do: court > *kort* n. (N 'card'); note > *not* f., pl. *nøter* (N 'large fishing net'); (wagon) tongue > *tång* f., pl. *tenger* (N 'pliers'). This usage is widespread, if not universal; there are occasional identifications of gender like the following: deck (of cards) > *dekk* n. (N *dekk* 'deck of ship'); grove > *grov* f. (N *grov* 'brook, brook bed'); trap > *trapp* f. (N *trapp* 'staircase').

These examples prove that gender association can exist on a purely phonetic or mechanical level, the gender being associated with the sound of the word rather than its meaning. The present writer is inclined to this explanation even in the case of two AmN words whose gender is contrary to that of all homologues: (a) crew > *kru* f., which could have got its gender from rhyming words like *bru, tru, ku* etc. all feminine; (b) store > *står* n. (N *bu* f., *butikk* m.), which might have been influenced by such neuters as *hår, kår, lår, sår, skår* (exceptions are *tår* m., *vår* m.). In languages where certain endings are associated with specific genders, there are abundant examples of such purely phonetic assignment of gender. In AmLithuanian nouns ending in a vowel (party > *pari*) were all feminine; in CanFr nouns ending in a nasal (tongue > *tonne*) were feminine. The nearest to this in AmN was the assignment of some lws. to the masculine because they ended in -*n*, which was taken to be the definite article (see below). In one dialect having a feminine def. art. in -*o*, the word bureau > *bjuro*, was identified as a feminine, and a new indefinite form *bjura* created.

This kind of direct phonetic association is seen also in a number of suffixes which proved to be gender determiners. It was Aron's opinion that AmGer -*ing* was feminine because of the G suffix -*ung;* he included this under 'rhyme analogy'. Similarly in CanFr this suffix became feminine because of the Fr -*ine*, which was often substituted for it. Evidence for the same kind of association is found in AmN words ending in -*ri* from E -*ry:* battery, buttery, country, creamery, factory, granary, grocery, pantry, pinery, shivaree; all of these are neuter, as are words in N ending in -*ri*. The exceptions are hickory > *hikrill*, with a masc. suffix, and *cemetery*, a late loan. The suffix -*ing* is partly f. and partly m., corresponding to the usage of the various dialects.[7] Examples were ceiling f. (16 inf.) m. (10 inf.); farming f.m.; living f.; meeting f.m.; middling(s) m.; hunting m. The suffixes -er, -el, and -en were masculine whenever the N suffixes -*ar* or -*ert*, -*ill*, or the definite article were substituted for them: cutter > *kattar*, reaper > *rippert*, barrel > *bæril*, pumpkin > *panki(n)*. The suffix -*ment* was often n., as one would expect from the N situation; but it was not too well established in the N dialects and many used a m. in words like basement and liniment. Other word endings do not appear to have played any particular role as gender determiners.

In the case of the suffixes, however, it may be objected that we are really dealing with morphemes, and that the association therefore is based on a semantic rather than a phonetic similarity. This is partly true, and we should probably recognize such suffixal influence as a special case of the rule that the last morpheme in a word always determines its gender. But this did not apply until after the suffix had been recognized as associable with a native suffix; the association was therefore of the same nature as that which we find in the loanshifts. But it is quite apparent that such an association was not established unless the suffix was phonetically similar; and in the case of such a suffix as E -el > N -*ill* it is hard to see what semantic contact there is. In AmLith the final [-ər] of 'picture' led to the association with a native -*eris*, a suffix of agency, which inevitably made the word masculine. In AmN those words in -*er* that could be interpreted as words of agency acquired N -*ar*, while certain words acquired N -*ert;* but a few retained -*er*, among them cover > *kåvver* n., which seems to have gotten its gender from its homologue N *lokk*. Similarity of sound did thus not necessarily lead to gender association; but once the similarity had led to suffix substitution, the native suffix inevitably determined gender.

Recent students of PaG have made determined efforts to reestablish the validity of semantic similarity as a leading factor in gender association. Writers like Reed and Springer go so far as to question the 'feminine tendency' and especially the influence of the phonetic similarity of E the to PaG *die* in turning nouns feminine. In one sphere there can be no doubt about the influence of meaning, viz. in natural gender. AmN nouns which are feminine for no other reason than that they designate female beings are aunty > *ænti* and schoolmam > *skulemamma*. Conversely we may assume that such words as brother-in-law, bull, clerk, dentist, judge, squire, steer, tramp could hardly be anything but masculine so long as there is no suffix or phonetic restriction which forces them to be anything else. In AmLith a female bootlegger acquired a special suffix -*e* or -*ka* to designate sex; a teacher > *týčeris* became a *týčerka* if she was feminine. One reason for this was certainly the necessity of using a feminine pronoun of reference in speaking of female creatures; this automatically brought with it the feminine gender.

Natural gender does not apply to very many words, however, and it emphatically does not apply to the neuter gender, which is not the same as the absence of natural gender. The attempts that have been made to set up classes of words in meaning groups with the same gender have been unsuccessful. For the N dialects Aasen tried to correlate gender with every possible classification, but he found e.g. that of the words for fields and meadows 8 were f., 5 of other genders; words for hills included 9 m., 4 f., 3 n.[8] Such associations were too weak and contradictory to mean much to the speakers. The only really convincing type of correlation in the field of meaning is found when we can show that a given word has been semantically associated with another word. This is none too easy, and the writer feels that many of the associations alleged have been weak, since there was no way of either proving or disproving them.

The only satisfactory, though not always conclusive evidence is that furnished by the speakers themselves. Any lw. might have several different synonyms, according to the particular meanings emphasized. But unless the synonym was felt as a genuine substitute for the lw. by the speakers who used it, one could not rely on it as valid evidence. Gender is not associated with ideas, but with words; and unless the lw. somehow brought with it a sense of the context in which the native word was used, it could not acquire its gender from that native word. In order to bring to this difficult problem some evidence which had not been introduced before, the writer collected from his questionnaires all those instances where informants gave a N word instead of or beside the E loanword. These have been included in the selected loanword list in chapter 20. The occurrence of these as alternative responses to the loanwords at least guarantees that they might have been associated in the minds of the speakers and thus have had a chance to influence the gender of the loanwords.

Of the 317 nouns in the list 62 % or 197 had N homologues suggested by informants. Those that apparently had no homologues were all masculine, except for a few with the suffixes -ery and -ing and some which had close homophones in N. Among those with homologues there was greater vacillation of gender (23.2 % to 10 % among the rest) and relatively fewer masculines. Even so the masculines led all the rest; the fixed genders were 125 m., 4 f., and 21 n. Of the 46 which vacillated all could be m., and the other genders were about evenly divided. Those 135 lws. whose N homologue or homologues had only one gender were divided as follows: 95 or 70 % had the same gender as their homologue, while 40 or 30 % did not. If we break this figure down by genders, we find that no word with m. homologue became f. or n., excepting two with the suffix -ery. On the other hand 17 with f. homologues, 14 with n. homologues, and 6 with f. and n. homologues became m. Those 4 f. and 15 n. which remained all had N homologues; they included the feminines aunty (*tante, mosyst*), schoolmam (*lærerinna*), slough (*myr*), and whip (*svipa*), of which two had natural gender and one was a partial homophone. The neuters were rope (*reip*), team (*par*), town (*herred*), township (*herred*), train (*tog*), trick (*knep, puss*), grain (*korn, grjon*), yoke (*åk*), corner (*hyrna*), cover (*lokk*), bother (*plunder, bry*), trouble (*bry*), buttery (*spiskammers*), country (*land*), creamery (*meieri*), county (*amt*). Of these several are partial homophones, while others end in -*ry*. Of those which had more than one gender among their N homologues, all were m. except the neuters fence (*gjerde* n., *gard* m.), pasture (*beite* n., *hamnegang* m.), curtain (*umheng* n., *heng* n., *gardina* f.), and sign (*skilt* n., *plakat* m.). Of 23 nouns which had vacillating gender in AmN (not elsewhere discussed), 18 had one homologue of either f. or n., e.g. beer m. n. (*øl* n.), flour m. n. (*mjøl* n.), map m. n. (*kart* n.).

We are led to conclude from these data that figures showing a high percentage of homologues with identical genders may not be too significant. The reason for the 70 % agreement is mostly to be found in the masculine tendency, which is another word for the established technique of borrowing in N. The force of this tendency is not only apparent in the overall size of this group, but also in the fact that all 'changes' of gender were in the direction of masculine. Of those that resisted this change and retained the f. or n. of their homologue, a number were rather to be explained as getting their gender by homophony or natural gender. Several examples show that in case of conflict, the latter forces were stronger. It cannot be denied that, especially in the mountain dialects, a core of words remains whose genders were somehow associated with words of closely similar meaning. But the general rule is that *all nouns became masc. unless they were associated with a homophonous fem. or neut. morpheme or a female creature.* The number of exceptions to this rule would not run higher than a score of nouns in the entire corpus of material.

If any explanation is needed for this situation, it can probably be found in the casual way in which the loans were picked up. They were not, like the loans of learned men, adopted after due consideration and with full awareness of what native words they might be substituted for. Most of them were used precisely because the native word escaped the speaker or because he had never heard a native word for the idea in question. There is no reason to suppose that his subconscious should have whispered the gender of the native 'equivalent' to him when it failed to deliver the equivalent itself. But in adapting the loanword to its new context, he might easily be reminded of some native word of similar phonetic form which he could follow without qualms.

2. *The Inflection of Nouns.*

All N dialects distinguish plural and definite forms by means of suffixes added to the singular and indefinite forms. A large number of dialects distinguish within the definite class a subclass of datives which alternate with the nominatives according to syntactical function. There are also possessive forms, but these are mostly limited to the indefinite class and used as the first element in compounds. Loanwords showed dative and possessive forms to about the same extent as native words; there was some tendency toward loss of the former in AmN, but it was in full use in most dialects which had it in Norway.

The *plural* is distinguished from the singular by the following possible endings, as these were generalized by Aasen (dialect forms are added in parentheses):

	Masc.		Fem.		Neut.	
	Strong	Weak	Strong	Weak	Strong	Weak
Sing.	-0	-e	-0	-a(-e)	-0 or -e	-a
Plur.	1 -ar (-a, -er)	-ar (-a, -er)	1 -er (-e, -ir)	-or (-ur, -o,	-0 or -e	-o (-or etc.)
	2 -er (-e, -ir)		2 -ar (-a, -er)	-å, -er, -e)		
	3 -'er (-a, -ar, -, -e)		3 -'er (-a, -ar, -, -e)			

In AmN the lw. was almost universally given the most common plural ending of the gender to which it had been assigned, the 1st class of the strong forms given above. Examples of words from each gender follow: masc. pieces > *pisar;* creeks > *krikkar;* fem. bluffs > *blåffer;* neut. stores > *står;* teams > *tim.* Words ending in -el or -er lost their -e- in the plural: dippers > *diprar;* handles > *hendlar;* pencils > *penslar;* sickles > *siklar;* stables > *stæblar.* Only a handful of words received the respective weak declensions, and none the less numerous declensions 2 or 3. Examples of weak nouns are: barn > *bale* (bare, bane) m., plural *balar* etc.; garden > *garde* m. (4 inf. Suldal); slough > *slua* f., pl. *sluor;* whip > *hyppa* f., pl. *hyppor;* basin > *beisa* f., pl. *beisor;* corner > *kårna* n., pl. *kårno.*

Words of measure followed N rules in adding no plural suffixes. Thus five cents > *fem sent.* Words of this type were: cent, dollar, acre, cord, bushel, quart, yard. Other nouns which used a singular form where E would often use a plural were the uncountables beer, yeast, seed, bug, mosquito. A typical sentence would be: *miskitten er fæl* 'the mosquitoes are bad'.

The only inflectional form imported into AmN from E was the plural suffix -*s*. Pre-bilingual borrowers were not aware of its plural value, and took it as part of the stem, adding further endings as they saw fit. With other stems speakers used it for both singular and plural, while in the completely bilingual loans they established it as the common plural for loanwords. At no time has the writer heard it used with N words. The loans were typically of words heard most commonly in the plural. Similar loans made into DN before emigration were cokes > *koks*, drops > *drops*, cinders > *sinders*.[9]

The examples are here classified according to their use with various suffixes. (a) In a few cases N plural endings were added, showing complete loss of the plural function by the -*s*. This was generally true of cars > *kars*, plural *karsar;* in the Indianland region also pumpkin > *ponkis, ponkisar. Kars* was first used to designate 'the cars', an old word for a railroad train; later it was applied to automobiles. (b) Some words were used as singular or plural, vacillating between plural forms with or without suffix. Thus *kokkis* meant either 'cooky' or 'cookies', with an occasional plural *kokkisar* 'cookies'. Other examples: crackers > *krekkis;* slippers > *slippers;* tramps > *trems;* trucks > *tråks;* turkeys > *tørkis.* These are all masculine. (c) Some words may be either singular or plural, without plural suffix. In the definite plural form these always add the neuter suffix *-a* (*-i,* etc.); but since this is identical with the feminine singular, there is some confusion concerning their gender. Examples are: fills (shafts on a buggy) > *fils;* rails > *rels;* spokes > *spåks;* ties (on a railroad) > *tais.*[10] (d) Some words have predominantly plural meaning, but may in AmN still add the masculine singular definite suffix *-en* as well as the neuter plural *-a.* In some words a distinction is made, e.g. the beans > *binsen* 'the bean crop' (collectively) or *binsa* 'the beans' (individually). Other examples are: blackberries > *blekkberis,* chores > *kjårs,* dishes > *dissjis,* grapes > *grips,* peas > *pis,* tools > *tuls.* There is vacillation between singular and plural for such words as overall > *åveral* or *åverals,* pliers > *pleier* or *pleiers.* Uncertainty of analysis is revealed by the occasional appearance of erroneously subtracted forms, such as *pendik* from appendix. Sporadic examples of singulars in *-s* on words not included in the selected list were: dye > *dais;* pickle > *pikkels;* pill > *pils;* stamp > *stemps;* step > *steps;* tack > *tæks;* tomato > *tometos;* trustee > *trøstis.* (e) Among childhood bilinguals especially there was much adoption of forms with *-s* in their correct plural function. Some words rarely adopted N plurals at all, though there was much vacillation on this point. Examples of words with predominant use of *-s* were: bottom, brake, brick, bulb, crowd, game, gear, grade, rug, shed, tavern, trick. Words that vacillated between *-s* and *-ar* were deed, drill, block, rod, term, frame, yankee. The use of *-s* naturally increased as time went on.

Whether words were singular or plural, with E or N endings, they had to add the N *definite article* under appropriate circumstances. E *the* would not be acceptable, except in an occasional complete phrase such as *di først taim.* In the masc. and neut. singular, the form of the N definite suffix is practically nationwide. But it varies greatly for the other genders and numbers. The definite suffix always follows the singular and plural stem forms given above. Some typical dialect forms appear in this table:

	Masc.		Fem.		Neut	
	Strong	Weak	Strong	Weak	Strong	Weak
Sing. Def.	-en	-n	-a (-i, -e, -æ, -o, -å)	-a (-å, -o)	-e	-a (-e)
Plur. Def.	-n(e) (-na, -a)		-n(e) (-na)		-a (-i, -e, -æ, (-un) -o, -å)	-o

The predominant forms are the -n of the masculine singular, the -e of the neuter singular, the -a or other vowel of the feminine singular and the neuter plural, and the -ne or -n of the masculine and feminine plural. The dative suffixes are not included above.

The suffixed articles were used even on relatively unassimilated words, e.g. the weather report > *wedh'ərripɔr'ten*. They were even used with E plurals in -s; here the usual form of the article was neuter plural, at least when the meaning actually was plural. This hybrid declension had its exact parallel in AmSwed, as reported by Walter Johnson: pills > *pils*, the pills > *pilsen*, with the same suffix as neuter *barn* 'children', *barnen* 'the children'.[11] Examples from AmN were: peas > *pis*, the peas > *pi'sa;* beans > *bins*, the beans > *bin'sa;* with other dialectal endings: the spokes > *spåk'si;* the tools > *tul'sæ*. The explanation of this usage is the absence of plural suffix (from a N point of view). Only neuters form their indefinite plural without suffix; hence any plural which seems to have no suffix is provided with the neuter definite article. As we have seen earlier, the singular suffixes can also be used, but only in a singular sense, e.g. *kokkisen* 'the cooky', *relse* 'the rail', *fillsa* 'the fill' (limited to a few inf.). The use of *binsen* to mean 'the beans' is also singular from the N point of view, being a collective singular like *haren* 'the rabbit(s)'.

In a small group of quite common words, the older settlements show an interesting type of back formation, in which the final -n or -en was interpreted as a masculine definite article. This was especially tempting since there was a certain awkwardness in adding a second -en. Most speakers then used the same form for indefinite and definite. But in some communities new forms arose for the indefinite by subtraction of the final -en, and this new stem could then be declined as if it were a N word. The most widespread examples were barn, basin, Indian, moccasin, pumpkin, salt rising, and watermelon. Occasional instance were heard of cistern, garden, saloon, vacation, sabbaterian, and lantern. The usage is most understandable for such a word as barn, which was mostly spoken of in the definite form since there usually was only one on a farm: *gå ut i barn* 'go out in the barn'. In western and northeastern Wisconsin the word barn almost universally had indefinite forms without -*en: ba'le* in the dialects with cacuminal *l, ba're* in others; in WN dialects the forms *ba'ne* and *ba'na* reflected the same development. These truncated words had a complete set of inflectional forms: *ba'le, ba'len, ba'lar, ba'lan*. Several of them are collectives which in N were singular; 'the Indians' came to be *in'dien*, from which was formed the indefinite *in'di*, which was universal. The popular name for the northeastern Wisconsin settlements was *Indilandet*, with this form as its first element. Other collectives were moccasin > *ma'gis*, def. *ma'gisen*, plural *ma'gisar* (western Wisconsin and Spring Grove, Minnesota); pumpkin > *pan'ki*, def. *pan'kin*, plural *pan'kiar* (universal except in NE Wisconsin); watermelon > *va(t)'termøl'le*, with substitution of the N word for 'mill' (widespread); basin > *beis* or *bei'sa*, the latter showing an unexpected feminine suffix, probably due to contamination with N homophones; salt rising > *sal'trei'ls*, where the AmE pronounciation obviously was [-ən] rather than [-ɪng]. These words were all so thoroughly assimilated that they felt like N words and were sometimes thought of as such by unreflective speakers. As far as these studies have gone, such words as cotton, cousin, or curtain seem to have escaped this tendency entirely; and it does not occur at all in many communities.

3. *The Inflection of Adjectives.*

Adjectives are inflected in N for gender and number, agreeing with the noun which they modify. If they follow a limiting word (definite article, possessive adjective, demonstrative pronoun etc.) or precede a vocative, this is reduced in most dialects to a single 'weak' ending, usually -*e*. The other or 'strong' endings are as follows:

	Masc.		Fem.		Neut.	
	1	2	1	2	1	2
Singular	-0 (-'e)	-en	-0 (-'e)	-ˋa	-t	-ˋe
Plural	-ˋe	-ne	-ˋa (-ˋe)	-na (-ne)	-ˋe	-ne

In addition, there is a comparative, -*are* or -*re*, and a superlative -*ast* or -*st;* the superlative can add -*e* for weak or for plural. Adverbs derived from adjectives have the neuter singular form of the adjective.

Relatively few of the borrowed adjectives were inflected according to the above scheme. The following do not seem to have been inflected at all: all right, bad, close, different, plain, plenty, regular, second, stuck. These seem to have the same status as certain native N adjectives which are defective in their declension. The following could add -*e* (or -*a*), but according to N rules could not add a -*t:* next, busy, easy, smart. Examples of words which have been noted with the neuter -*t* are: common > *kaˊmen, kaˊ- ment;* ripe > *reip, reipt.* Both the -*t* and the -*e* have been noted with nice > *nais, naist, naiˋse;* rough > *råff, råft, råfˋfe;* tough > *tåff, tåft, tåfˋfe;* cheap > *kjipp, kjipt, kjipˋpe.* No examples of declension 2 (ending in -*en*) have been found. The comparative suffixes were freely applied; some examples are the following: easier > *iˋsiaˋre,* oddest > *aˋdest,* plainest > *pleiˋnaste.* No cases were found of adverbs ending in -*t,* but it seems likely that any adjective capable of taking the -*t* might be used in this way.

When compared with nouns and especially with verbs, the adjectives were significantly less responsive to N structural rules. As pointed out in Chapter 15, this may be associated with the secondary role which these inflections play. Since gender and number are already sufficiently indicated by the noun inflection, and the meaning of the adjective is in no way affected by its suffixes, there is less immediate urge for their use.

4. *The Inflection of Verbs.*

N verbs have two finite tense forms, the present and the preterite, which in general agree very closely in use with the corresponding E forms. The same is true of the auxiliary tenses, formed with *hava* 'have' or *vera* 'be' plus the perfect participle, and the modal constructions with *skal* 'shall', *vil* 'will', *må* 'must' etc. plus the infinitive. As in other Germanic languages there are special forms for the imperative, the present participle, and the present and preterite subjunctive; there are two broad form classes, usually known as 'strong' and 'weak'. In addition there is a passive mode ending in *-st* (*-s*). In N persons are nowhere distinguished, and only the more conservative dialects distinguish singular from plural. The following are typical forms of the *first weak conjugation*, which is the one nearly always applied to loanwords:

Inf. *-a* (-e, -0)	Pres. part. *-ande* (-ende)
Pres. *-ar* (-a, -er)	Passive pres. *-ast* (-est)
Pret. *-a* (-e)	Imperative -0
Perf. Part. *-a* (-e)	

An example is the verb *elska* 'love': *elskar, elska, elskande, elskast, elsk*. This conjugation is the most regular and contains the largest number of words. There is a *second weak conjugation* consisting of verbs whose stems end in consonants; these have *-er* in the present, *-te* in the preterite and *-t* in the perfect participle: *meina* 'have the opinion', *meiner, meinte, meint*. A *third weak conjugation* has stems ending in vowels, to which are added *-r*, *-dde*, and *-dd*: *tru* 'believe', *trur, trudde, trudd*.

Loan verbs were nearly always given the suffixes listed above, attached directly to the E stems. A sporadic exception was *belångste* 'belonged', where the E third person form 'belongs' was adopted as if it were a stem. Even verbs which have a change of stem form in E usually do not reflect this as a loanword. Thus 'catch', which in E has the preterite and p. p. 'caught', is regular as an AmN loanword: *ket'ja* 'catch', *ket'jar* 'catches', *ket'ja* 'caught', *har ket'ja* 'has caught'. Sample sentence: *dette æ fiste gången je ha vørti ketja* 'this is the first time I've been caught' (14D1). Verbs ending in -el or -er lose the suffix vowel, as in native N verbs: tickle > *tik'la*, happen > *hep'na*, cover > *kåv'ra*.

Traces of the second and third weak conjugations are found sporadically. The second conjugation is more widely used in WN dialects than in EN, and the following examples have mostly been collected among WN speakers: cared $>$ *kæ'rte,* cleared $>$ *kli'rte,* felt $>$ *fi'lte* (cf. DN *følte*), fenced $>$ *fen'ste,* homesteaded $>$ *ho'mstet'te,* kept $>$ *kif'te,* left $>$ *lift* (cf. N *lift* 'lived'), lost $>$ *lu'ste* (as p. p. also *låst* from E lost 9 inf.), made $>$ *mæk'te,* mixed $>$ *mikst,* piled $>$ *pei'lte,* reaped $>$ *ri'fte.* The change from *pt* to *ft* found in two of the above examples was in response to a similar alternation in some N dialects. The third conjugation was even more sparingly represented, the only common word discovered being E played $>$ *pleid'de;* other examples were hoed $>$ *håd'de,* shivareed $>$ *sjøv'rid'de.* In these cases the final vowel of the stem invited the new preterite forms.

The strong conjugation, with its many irregular forms, did not find any application among the lws. Sporadic cases were found: dug $>$ *dagg* and *dogg;* beat $>$ *beit* (pret. of *bita* 'bite'); these contrast with the usual *digga* and *bita.* In one dialect E show $>$ *sjå* 'see', with the past *såg,* as in the sentence: *han såg itt opp* 'he didn't show up'.

5. *Compounding.*

N compounds are formed in very much the same way as E. In both languages they consist of two juxtaposed elements, the first bearing loud stress, the second reduced stress. The practice of giving the first element a special combining form, as in E hogshead, is somewhat more common in N than in E. The suffix added to the first element is historically associated with certain words and represents an old possessive inflection. The forms found in present-day dialects are *-s, -a,* and *-e,* as in *livstid* 'lifetime', *solagla* 'sunset', *hestehår* 'horse hair'. The forms with vowels are more common in WN and Midland dialects than elsewhere.

Whenever N words entered into AmN compounds, they usually showed the same combining form as they would in corresponding native compounds. Examples are: section boss $>$ *sek'sjonsba's;* summer kitchen $>$ *såm'mårskjø'ken;* door knob $>$ *dø'ranabb';* grave digger $>$ *gra'vadig'gar;* wood shed $>$ *ve'asjedd';* calf bin $>$ *kæl'vebinn';* dish water $>$ *dis'kevat'n;* brush land $>$ *brus'ke-lan'd;* fork tine $>$ *for'ketin'd;* horse stable $>$ *hes'taste'bel;* ox team > *åk'sati'm;* pig pasture > *gri'sapas'ter;* pig pen > *gri'-sapenn';* chunk of wood > *ve'akjån'k;* fish pole > *fis'kapå'le;* wash tub > *vas'katåbb';* thrashing crew > *trøs'kakru';* wash basin > *vas'kabei's.*

It may be more surprising to find that in a few cases the same combining suffixes were added to E words when these entered into compounds as first elements: (1) -s: gallon jar > *gal'lanskruk'-ke;* handkerchief > *hæ'nkeskjiff';* traveling man > *trav'lingsmann';* (2) -a: rail fence > *rel'safen's;* fence post > *fen'sapås't;* cord wood > *kår'dave';* fence corner > *fen'sakro'k;* quilting party > *kvil'tapar'ti;* tool box > *tul'sabak's;* Mandt wagon > *man'ta-våg'n;* cake box > *ke'kabak's.* These were usually sporadic or limited to certain dialects. In each case the combining vowel here served the additional purpose of breaking up a difficult inter-vocalic cluster.

Most E compounds, however, were borrowed in their basic form, without change: brick yard > *brekk'jar'd;* cowboy > *kao'-båi'.* In a number of cases compounds were created in AmN from material that was not so in E. We have seen instances of this in the discussion of stress (Chapter 16), where phrases with level stress like second cousin were made into compounds like *sek'ken-kås'sen.* In a few cases the same happened with prepositional phrases, e.g. suit of clothes > *klæ'su't;* bundle of shingles > *sjing'elbun't;* ball of twine > *tvai'nnys'ta;* chunk of wood > *ve'akjån'k.*

6. *Syntax.*

N word order is similar to E, and offers no serious problems in the adaptation of lws. Each lw. was used in a N sentence in the position to which its word class entitled it. N has the same kind of prepositional and adverbial constructions as E, and the same order of modifiers before nouns. It was thus natural for AmN to import phrases consisting wholly or partly of E lws., more or less completely adapted.

Such loans could consist of complete utterances: *bai' ga'li, nås'søri', tu' bæ'd, ai' sjud sei'.* In such cases they followed E rules and were not adapted to N in any other way than the purely phonetic. But they could also consist of action-goal constructions, such as catch cold > *ket'ja kul'le;* or of verb-adverb combinations, such as dress up > *dres'sa opp¹*, tip over > *tip'pa å'ver*, beat out > *bi'ta u¹t;* or of adverbial combinations like well off > *vell' a'v,* hard up > *hart' op'pe;* or of preposition-noun constructions like on time > *på ti'd;* or of coordinate nouns, like fox and geese > *fak's n gi's.* In many cases these were partly translated. In no case did they bring new types of construction into N.

An interesting case of syntactic adaptation of a lw. phrase was the common importation of 'get along' in which the verb was separated from its adverb according to N usage: *dæm git'te vist itte lång' fæ'lt gått'* 'they don't seem to get along very well' (14D7). When such verb-adverb combinations were used as participial adjectives, they had to be reworked in N into a compound, e.g. *ne'lak¹ka i tron'kjen min* 'locked down in my trunk'; *han er svæ'rt ne'røn¹na* 'he is very much run down'; *rå'den er u'tvas¹ka* 'the road is washed out'.

In specific constructions E influence could result in a new word order which contradicted N usage for that particular phrase. Thus one commonly heard *over natten* for the N *natten over* 'over night', and *oppe her* for N *her oppe* 'up here', *runt her* for N *her omkring* 'around here'. Dates were often turned around from the N *12te mars* to the more E *mars den 12te*, especially in writing. In all such cases one word common to the two languages had a tendency to draw more with it, so that the entire phrase in which it was embedded might be more or less completely reproduced.

Chapter 18.

NATIVE FORMS FOR FOREIGN: LOANBLENDS AND LOANSHIFTS.

> Language is not an abstract construction of the
> learned, or of dictionary-makers, but is something
> arising out of the work, needs, ties, joys, affections,
> tastes, of long generations of humanity, and has its
> bases broad and low, close to the ground.
>
> *Walt Whitman (1885)*[1]

While the loanword is the most obvious deposit left upon a language through bilingual contact, it is by no means the only one. A more insidious transfer of patterns occurs when morphemes already existing in the borrowing language are used in new ways inspired by another tongue. A speaker familiar with a foreign expression which he finds occasion to use when speaking his own language may reproduce the expression entirely by means of native morphemes. It does not matter whether he does so deliberately, for the sake of enriching his language, or unconsciously, because he is unaware that the new expression really belongs in the other language. The deliberate use is illustrated by the so-called 'loan translations' of such puristic languages as German and Icelandic, as when *Fernsprecher* 'far-talker' was created to substitute for telephone or *goðafræði*' god-wisdom' for theology. A similar usage among less sophisticated speakers is the AmGer *Butterfliege* for E butterfly, reported from Wisconsin by Seifert, where each part was reproduced by a substitution of native morphemes. The more usual type of substitution in everyday speech, however, is that which occurs when a native morpheme is used in new contexts because of awareness by the speaker of some similar-sounding or -meaning foreign morpheme. AmG speakers generally use *gleichen* 'resemble' to mean 'like', because of the contact between the adjective *gleich* and AmE 'like'. Ukrainian speakers in America, having borrowed E streetcar, also change the usage of their native words for 'catch' and 'take', so that these words may be used in the phrases to 'take a streetcar' or 'catch a streetcar'.[2] AmPort speakers even go so far as to adopt an entire phrase like 'running for mayor' and render it as *correr para mayor*, which would certainly be entirely meaningless in Portugal. All such forms of foreign influence in which native morphemes have been used in ways suggesting foreign models will here be regarded as examples of the process called *morphemic substitution*. This was discussed in Chapter 15, where a scheme for classifying the various kinds of substitution was presented. This scheme will here be followed in presenting the materials of AmN morphemic substitution.

1. *Loanblend stems.*

A small number of loanwords have received a suffix which cannot be accounted for as a mere phonological substitution. In practically every case these appear to be the result of a contamination between the loanword and a native term of similar sound or meaning. The N analogue usually had a consonant in common with the E lw. which facilitated the transfer of the following gender suffix from the N to the E word. In this way a new stem was created; the suffix, being without meaning, does not make it a derivative noun.

The most widespread and certain examples of this blending were the following:

E corner > *kår'na* (under influence of N *hyrna* 'corner')
E jug > *jug'ga* (N *mugga* 'pitcher' and *krukka* 'jug')
E whip > *hyp'pa* (N *svepa* 'whip')
E shanty > *sjan'ta* (N *hytta* 'cottage')
E basin > *bei'sa* (N *ausa* 'dipper')

The following examples lack the common consonant, but appear to have arisen in the same way:

E trap > *trep'pa* (N *fella, glefsa* 'trap')

E hoe > *hå'a* (N *hakka* 'hoe')
E barn > *ba'le, ba're, ba'ne* (N *låve* 'barn')
E garden > *gar'de* in AmSuldal dialect only (N *hage* 'garden')

A confirmation of this analogy is the existence in one dialect of *ba'na*, corresponding to a form *laoa* 'barn' in that particular (Sogn) dialect.

The remaining examples have no homologues from which the influence could come, but homophones can be suggested:

E slough > *slu'a* (cf. N *lua* 'cap').
E shop > *sjap'pa* (cf. N *kappa* 'cape')

The use of *slu'va, slu'vu* 'slough' in one dialect corresponds to the forms *luva, luvu* for 'cap'. All the other words that show the same process are used only sporadically: E bluff > *blåf'fa;* saucer > *sa'sa;* bull > *bul'le* (cf. N *ukse*); cordeen > *kårdi'ne,* gallon > *gallo'ne,* overall > *o'verhål'se* (all three from one speaker, 8M3).

Some speakers reproduced E stanchion, not as *sten'sjen,* but as *sten'sjel,* thus apparently blending it with N *stengsel.* But this could be due to an AmE [stænshəl], reported by Seifert. The word bait was often reproduced as *bei'ta* f. and *bei'te* m. or n. But in this case the N dialects retained various forms of the word and we may actually be dealing with native N forms.

2. *Loanblend Derivatives.*

All the derivatives included here consist of borrowed stems with native suffixes. Such final syllables as -el, -en, or -er were most frequently reproduced by substitution of the corresponding N phonemes. But in some dialects and with some speakers other substitutions are found which show that some sort of equivalence of a morphemic nature was felt between the E suffix and a similar-sounding N suffix.

Suffix substitution took place in the following cases: (1) E -el > AmN *-il* (WN *-edl*), with masc. gender and Tone 2. Examples: barrel > *bæ'ril;* pickerel > *pik'ril;* squirrel > *skvæ'ril;* handle > *hæn'dedl;* pencil > *pen'sedl;* stable > *stæ'bedl;* satchel > *set'sjil* (14D1, 3). (2) E -er > AmN *-ar (-ari)*, with masc. gender and Tone 2. Examples: assessor > *ses'sar;* bachelor > *bet'slar;* cultivator > *kål'teve¹tar;* cutter > *kat'tar;* dresser > *dres'sar;* elevator > *el'levei¹tar;* farmer > *far'mar;* hunter > *hun'tar;* mower > *mo'(v)ar;* painkiller > *pei'nkil¹lar* (4Q2); peddler > *ped'lar;* poker (the implement) > *po'kar;* reaper > *ri(p)'par;* renter > *ren'tar;* seeder > *si'dar;* separator > *sep'p(e)re¹tar;* spider (frying pan) > *spei'dar;* storekeeper > *stå'rki(p)¹par;* teacher > *tit'kjar* (rarely); settler > *set'lar;* surveyor > *save'r(ar).* Most of these have also a verb in *-a* (as in the cases described by Miss Stene for DN), but not all.[3] (3) E -er > AmN *-ert*, with masc. gender and Tone 1. This suffix is found in native N in a number of foreign loans, e.g. *daggert* 'dagger', *kikkert* 'telescope', *rekkert* 'racket', etc.[4] Examples: dipper > *dip'pert;* gopher > *gu(f)'fert;* lawyer > *låi'ert;* reaper > *ri(p)'pert.* A few WN speakers have the form *-art: løy'art, dip'part.* (4) E -y > N *-ill*, with masc. gender and Tone 2. Example: hickory > *hik'ril.* This is widespread, but limited to the one word. (5) E -ish > AmN *-is*, with masc. gender and Tone 1. This case is difficult, since it is not clear that the N *-is* can be considered a morpheme; but it occurs as final syllable in a number of semi-foreign, slangy words, such as N *kompis* 'companion'; also in such loans as *kandis* 'rock sugar', *melis* 'powdered sugar', and *anis* 'anice'. Examples: Irish > *ei'ris;* schottische > *sjat'tis.* These two widespread forms seem to have joined the E [-əs] or [-ɪs] > *-is*, e.g. circus > *sør'kis;* justice > *jøs'tis;* clevis > *klø'vis* (2 inf. *-ers);* office > *å(f)'fis.*

Other N suffixes were so similar to E suffixes of parallel function that no perceptible substitution took place. Examples of these were: -ing, -ery, -ment, and possibly -et. That there nevertheless may have been substitution can be inferred from the fact that the words were assigned to the same gender and tone categories as the corresponding N words; see the discussion in Chapter 16.

3. *Substitution in Compounds.*

A total of 1086 different borrowed compounds were noted by the writer in the course of his investigation of the spoken dialects. Of these only a few appear in the selected word list as separate entries; many of the rest are given under the simplexes of which they are made up. Most of them consist of noun plus noun. But other types are also represented, for instance adjective-noun (*ʄrai'dke¹k, tu'stepp¹, ka'mensku¹le, blakk'valno¹t, blekk'bo¹r, ʄrån't-romm¹, pu'rhu¹s, sing'eltre¹*), verb-noun (*trøs`kakru¹, ʄis`kapå¹le, vas`katåbb¹, vas`kadissʄ¹*), preposition-noun (*å'verko¹t, upp`stæ¹rs*).

About one half of the compounds were so directly modelled on their E originals that they show nothing beyond phonological substitution. This includes such examples as oatmeal > *o'tmi¹l*, sidewalk > *sai'dvå¹k*, brother-in-law > *brød'derinlå¹*. Some of them are not particularly transparent in E, and it is not surprising that they should be imported as morphemic units: cockpit > *kakk'pitt¹*, crowbar > *kro'ba¹r*, grandstand > *græ'ndstæ¹nd*. These are obviously unanalyzed loanwords. Other all-English compounds, however, consist of parts which also occur as separate loanwords, crossroad > *kråss`rå¹d;* lawnmower > *lå`nmo¹var;* cake box > *ke`kbak¹s;* baseball > *bei'sbå¹l;* brick yard > *brekk'jar¹d;* drug store > *drøgg'stå¹r;* grub hoe > *grubb`hå¹;* storekeeper > *stå`rki(p)¹par;* surprise party > *sup`preispar¹li*.

It may also occur that a given speaker will use a compound containing a borrowed element which he does not use by itself. Thus cheese factory > *kji'sʄek¹tri*, but many still say N *ost* 'cheese'; horse power > *hårs'pao¹er*, but horse is still N *hest;* necktie > *nekk'tai¹*, but neck is N *hals;* cream separator > *krim'seppere¹tar*, but cream is N *rømme*. In such cases two developments were possible. Some speakers might start saying *kjis* and *krim*. Many loanwords may have made their way into the language in just such compounds. The other possibility was to substitute a more or less N form for one or both of the elements to make the compound as a whole feel more native.

Some compounds vacillated between forms with and without substitution. Examples were: bedspread > *bedd`spredd¹* or *bedd`spre¹* (N *spre*); codfish > *kadd'ʄisʄ¹* or *kadd'ʄis¹k* (N *ʄisk*); calf bin > *kæl`vebinn¹* vs. feed bin > *ʄi`dbing¹e* (N *binge*); freight train > *ʄre'ttre¹n* or *ʄrak'ttre¹n* (N *ʄrakt*). In these cases it required only a rather slight phonetic adjustment to make one element N. Where it was a question of actual translation to a word of quite different phonetic make-up, there seems to have been little inclination to substitute. Thus blackberry was not translated although N words for black and berry were in general use; it was borrowed as *blekk'ber'ris.*

Where substitution did take place to any great extent, it was nearly always in compounds where the elements were obviously analyzable as standing in a rather literal or concrete relationship to one another. Thus N *ve(d)* or *tre* was generally substituted for E wood whenever reference was being made to actual wood, e.g. wooden pail > *tre'pæ'l;* chunk of wood > *ve'akjån'k;* wood box > *ve'bak's;* cord wood > *kår'dve';* wood pail > *ve'pei'l;* wood shed > *ve'asjedd'* (but also *vodd'sjedd').* Wood remained in woodpecker > *vodd'pekk'er* and cottonwood > *kat'tenvodd'.* Similarly with the element man: a substitution of N *mann* took place whenever reference was being made to a person, e.g. chairman > *kjær'mann';* policeman > *pol'lismann'.* But not so in blackman (a card game) > *blækk'mæn* and pitman (part of a machine) > *pit'men.* E cow always > AmN *ku* in compounds where the bovine function was apparent, e.g. cowbarn > *ku'ba'le;* cow stable > *ku'ste'bel;* cow track > *ku'trekk';* cow yard > *ku'jar'd.* But no substitution was made in cowboy > *kao'båi'* or cow catcher > *kao'ket'sjar.* One informant distinguished between snowball, a flower > *sno'bå'l* and the ball of snow > *snø'bå'l* (N *snøball*).

Of the 1086 compounds mentioned, 566 or 51.2 % show some degree of morphemic substitution. Of these 200 have retained their E nucleus, 277 have retained their E marginal element (the first or modifying element), while 79 have become entirely N. Those with only one N element are loanblends, while those with two are loanshifts.

4. Loanblend Compounds.

The largest group (277) is that which shows only marginal importation. If this means anything at all, it suggests that the speakers feel an urge to identify the thing being spoken of with something in their previous experience. But the substitutes inserted in the nucleus are in nearly every case more or less homophonous, as the following examples will show: steamboat > *stim'bå'l* (N *båt*); barrel churn > *bæ'rilkin'na* (N *kinna*); alarm clock > *lar'mklok'ka* (N *klokka*); square dance > *skvæ'rdan's* (N *dans*); poor house > *pu'rhu's* (N *hus*); warehouse > *væ'rhu's;* frame house > *frei'mhu's;* log house > *lågg'hu's;* kerosine lamp > *ker'rosinlam'pe* (N *lampe*); shareman > *sjær'mann¹* (N *mann*); chairman > *kjær'mann';* fanning mill > *fæ'ningmyl'la* (N *mylla*); hickory nut > *hik'rilno't* (N *not*); black walnut > *blakk'valno't;* swill pail > *svill'pæ'l* (N *pæl*); slop pail > *slapp'pæ'l;* surprise party > *sup'preispar'ti* (N *parti*); fence post > *fens'pås't* (N *påst*); living room > *le'ving-romm¹* (N *romm*); bedroom > *be'dromm';* sitting room > *sit'-tingromm';* dining room > *dai'ningromm';* front room > *frånt'-romm';* common school > *ka'mensku'le* (N *skule*); whippletree > *hyp'peltre¹* (N *tre*); single tree > *sin'geltre';* lumber wagon > *lom'bervång'n* (N *vångn*); cordwood > *kår'dve¹* (N *ve*).

One of the very rare instances of a purely synonymous substitution is the form log cabin > *lågg'hyt'ta* (N *hytta* 'cabin'). On the other hand it can be matched by the purely homophonous substitution watermelon > *va'termyl'la* (N *mylla* 'mill'). The latter is quite widespread, and is shown to be more than just an erratic phonological substitution by the fact that it occurs in several dialectal forms, varying with the form of the word *mylla* to *mølle* and *mylna* or *mylda*. The AmE folk pronunciation 'watermillion' may have helped to suggest it; in any case the final -*n* was taken to be a definite article, though the result was feminine (since *mylla* 'mill' is feminine). A few words show vacillation between a substituted and a non-substituted form, e.g. pieplant > *pai'-plen'ta* or *pai'plan'ta* (N *plenta, planta*) and *pai'plæn't;* blackboard > *blekk'bo'r* (N *bor* 'board') and *blekk'bor'd*.

The 200 loanblends which show only nuclear importation (N modifier substituted) also involve the simplest kind of homophonous replacement. The following elements were never permitted to remain E, at least in the available material: bread (N *brø*), corn (N *korn*), door (N *dør*), fish (N *fisk*), grave (N *grav*), machine (N *maskina*), over (N *åver*), ox (N *ukse*), post (N *påst*), school (N *skule*), thrashing (N *trøska*), tobacco (N *tobakk*), up (N *upp*), wash (N *vaska*), wood (N *ve*). Examples of these are breadbox > *brø'bak's;* corn shredder > *ko'rnsjed'dar;* doorknob > *dø'ranabb';* fish pole > *fis'kapå'le;* graveyard > *gra'vjar'd;* machine shed > *masj'-*

*insjedd*¹; overcoat > *å'verko*¹*t*; ox yoke > *uk'seju*¹*g*; post office > *pås'tåfi*¹*s*; schoolmam > *sku'lemam*¹*ma*; thrashing crew > *trøs'kakru*¹; tobacco shed > *to'bakksjedd*¹; upstairs > *opp'stæ*¹*rs*; wash dish > *vas'kadissj*¹; woodshed > *ve'asjedd*¹.

The only element that appears regularly in N form without phonetic resemblance is pig > N *gris*, as in pig pen > *gri'sapenn*¹. Others vacillate between substitution and nonsubstitution, e.g. barber shop > *bal'bersjapp*¹ (N *balber*) and *bar'bersjapp*¹; lawsuit > *lå'vsu*¹*t* (N *låv*) and *lå'su*¹*t*; slop pail > *slabb'pæ*¹*l* (N *slabb*) and *slapp'pæ*¹*l*; homestead > *hei'mstedd*¹ (N *heim*) and *ho'mstedd*¹; dish water > *dis'kevat*¹*n* (N *disk*) and *dissj'vat*¹*n*; front porch > *framm'por*¹*tkj* (N *framm*) and *frånt'por*¹*tkj*; selfrake > *sjø'lrei*¹*k* (N *sjøl*) and *sel'frei*¹*k*. Certain elements were used in N form in some compounds, but in E in others, according to the principle of analysis suggested earlier. Examples are: black oak > *svar'tei*¹*k* vs. black walnut > *blakk'valno*¹*t*; cow barn > *ku'ba*¹*le* vs. cowboy > *kao'båi*¹; horse stable > *hes'tastæ*¹*bel* vs. horsepower > *hår's-pao*¹*er*; housekeeping > *hu'ski*¹*ping* vs. housewren > *hao'srenn*¹; icebox > *i'sbak*¹*s* vs. ice cream > *ai'skri*¹*m*.

5. *Loanshift Compounds.*

When substitution occurred in both elements simultaneously, the compound was entirely native in form, even though it might never have occurred in the language before. Within such compounds one should distinguish between those that had occurred, and were merely shifted in meaning, and those that were true innovations. Under our classification of loanshifts these have been called respectively *extensions* and *creations*. In the case of compounds it is not always possible to make this distinction, since the dictionaries do not list all the possible N compounds. In theory any two stems may be joined in compounds, which makes their number practically infinite.

The difficulty is illustrated by the apparently parallel terms *hy'reka*¹*r* 'hired man' and *hy'rejen*¹*ta* 'hired girl'. The first is an extension, since the word occurred in Norway, where it was used in the northern fishing districts about a man who worked for others instead of having an owner's share in a boat. But the regular word for a 'hired man' on farms was different, either *dreng* or *tenar*, while a girl was called *taus* or *tenestjenta*. *Hy'rejen'ta* is thus a creation, apparently made on the analogy of *hy'reka'r*, and probably among the immigrants, since it is not recorded in any N source.

Other creations, in which both elements have been substituted for E originals, are illustrated in the following list of what might be called also 'pseudo-Norwegian compounds': corn crib > *ko'rn-krub'ba* (N *korn* 'grain'; *krubba* 'fodder rack'); corn field > *ko'rnfi'l* (N *korn* 'grain; *fil* 'file'); court house > *kort'hu's* (N *kort* 'card'; *hus* 'house'); doorknob > *dø'ranabb'* (N *dør* 'door'; *nabb* 'peg'); corn plow > *ko'rnplo'g* (N *korn* 'grain'; *plog* 'plow'); small grain > *små'grø'n* (N *små* 'small'; *grøn* or *grjon* 'grain, esp. thrashed'); high school > *hø'gsku'le* (N *høg* 'high'; *skule* 'school'); school district > *sku'ledis'trikt* (N *skule* 'school'; *distrikt* 'district'); selfbinder > *sjø'lbin'dar* (N *sjøl* 'self'; *bindar* 'binder'). There was vacillation between citizen paper > *bor'gerpa'pir* (N *borger* 'citizen'; *papir* 'paper') and *sit'tisenpa'pir;* screwdriver > *skru'dri'var* (N *skru* 'screw'; *drivar* 'driver') and *skru'drai'var*. It will be noted that the above list includes a number of purely homophonous extensions; these will be discussed below.

6. *Loanshift Extensions.*

The influence of foreign models may do no more than alter the kind of situations in which a word is used, or in other words extend its meaning to more or less identity with that of a foreign word. As we have seen earlier, the point of contact which leads to an extension of meaning may be either a phonetic or a semantic similarity or both. It may be quite impossible to say which it is for any given case, but it is significant that in AmN there are more which can be shown to be purely phonetic than purely semantic; of course, the great majority are both.

The purely phonetic, or homophonous pairs, may from one point of view be regarded as mere coincidences.[5] The fact that E field has become identical in form with N *fil* 'file' may be spoken of as an adaptation of the E word to a phonetically similar N word.

But the substitution that here takes place is not purely phonetic, even though phonetic similarity is its starting point. The substitution is of the whole word for another word; that this is so appears from the identity of grammatical usage which usually accompanies this kind of change. Not only has field dropped its [-d] and in some dialects acquired a different i-vowel from most other words, but it has also acquired feminine gender and the corresponding plural forms. This is especially striking in the case of a word like note > *not* with its plural *nø'ter;* if it were not for this identification, its plural would have been *no'tar or no'ts.* Not all speakers or dialects make the following substitutions, but all of them are widespread.

Available examples of homophonous loanshift extensions in AmN; N equivalents given in parentheses were either literary or inexact:

E model	AmN substitute	Original N meaning	'Proper' N equivalent
block (city)	*blåkk'* f. (m.n.)	block of wood	(*kvartal* n.)
bran	*bran'd* m.	fire	*kli* n.
crop	*kråpp'* m.	body	*avling* f.
drag (harrow)	*dregg'* m.	small anchor	*harv* f.
field	*fi'l* f., pl. -*er*	file (also jack in card game)	*åker* m.
feel	*fi`la* v., pt. *fi`lte*	file	*føla* v.
court	*kort'* n.	card	*rett* m.
lake	*lei'k* m.	game	*sjø* m., *vatn* n.
note (financial)	*no't* f., pl. *nø'ter*	fishing net	(*veksel, skuldbrev*)
pail	*pei'l, pæ'l* m.	half pint	*bytta* f.
pen (enclosure)	*penn'* m.	pen (writing)	*gard* m.
pick	*pik`ka* v.	peck, tick	*plukka* v.
screen	*skri'n* n.	small chest	(*netting*)
spend	*spen`na* v., pt. *spente*	kick	*bruka, øyda, ødsla*
stalk (corn)	*ståkk'* m.	stick, log	*stylk* m.
swamp	*svam'p* m.	sponge	*myr* f.

E model	AmN substitute	Original N meaning	'Proper' N equivalent
tongue (on wagon)	*tång'* f., pl. *teng'er*	tongs, pliers	*stong* f.
track	*trekk'* m.	draft	*spor* n., *veg* m.
trust	*trøs'ta* v.	comfort	*lita på* v.

The largest number of loanshifts occurred in AmN between pairs of words which resembled one another both in sound and meaning. Whenever they had words which were homologous in both respects, it was only natural that the speakers should substitute their native words for whatever E terms were needed. It would have been absurd for the immigrants to borrow E mile when they already had a Norwegian *mil* which could be used. The fact that in Norway it had referred to a distance seven times greater made no difference in America, where they were concerned with American miles only. If they had to make a distinction, as when they spoke to recent immigrants or wrote to their relatives in Norway, they could simply prefix the word *engelsk* or *norsk*. The function of the word *mil* remained the same in the new as in the old culture, and its new value was an incidental aspect of the cultural displacement of the immigrants. This kind of change in meaning we have here called a semantic displacement, to distinguish it from the semantic confusion discussed below.

The examples of semantic displacement, arranged by fields of activity, are the following:

E model	AmN substitute	Original N meaning	New E meaning
(1) Terms of measure:			
forty	*fyr'ti* m.	40 (numeral)	40-acre plot
eighty	*åt'teti* m.	80 (numeral)	80-acre plot
quarter (section)	*kvart* m.	1/4 mile	160-acre plot
quart	*kvart* m.	1/4 barrel	1/4 gallon
section	*sek'sjon* m.	division	1 square mile
mile	*mil* m.	37,056 ft.	5,280 ft.
pound	*pund* n.	498 grams	453.6 grams
foot	*fot* m.	31.37 cm.	30.48 cm.

E model	AmN substitute	Original N meaning	New E meaning
(2) Monetary units:			
shilling	*sjil'ling* m.	ab. 1 cent	12.5 cents (common in pioneer times)
quarter	*kvar'ter* m. or *kvart* m.	1/4 barrel (or ell)	25 cents
dollar	*da'lar* m. (*daler, dale*)	ab. $ 1.20	$ 1.00
(3) Natural phenomena:			
brush	*brusk* m.	tuft of straws, small plants	uncleared woods and bushes
spring	*spring* m.	fountain, pump, tap	natural source of water
(4) Tools and machinery:			
shovel	*sjyf'fel* m.	hoe-like instrument of iron	broad-bladed implement for removing loose matter
fork	*fårk* m.	stick with forked end (in some dialects also for a fork)	instrument with tines, used in farming (often also for the implement used in eating)
binder	*bin'dar* m.	one who binds or knits	machine that cuts and binds grain
stanchion	*steng'sel* n. (some dialects)	bar, barrier	bar in cow stall
(5) Household utensils:			
dish	*disk* m. (some dialects)	wooden plate	container used at table
oven	*omn* m.	stove	part of stove in which baking is done
(6) Foods:			
corn	*korn* n.	grain, chiefly barley	maize, Indian corn

E model	AmN substitute	Original N meaning	New E meaning
grain	*grøn* n. (*grjon*)	grain, especially after thrashing	grains other than maize, esp. wheat, oats, barley etc.
corn meal	*ko`rnmjø'l* n.	barley flour	ground maize

(7) Working activities:

boss	*bas* m.	headman, esp. on a fishing boat	employer or superintendent of workmen
hired man	*hy`reka'r* m.	hired worker on boat	hired worker on farm
top	*tåp`pa* v.	place as top, form a top (on something)	remove top from tobacco plants (may also be N dialect)

Actual collision of meaning, such that we can speak of a semantic confusion, occurred in a number of cases where N words were extended to include the usages of E words of partially similar meaning and sound, to the exclusion of the N words previously used in those contexts. It would be possible to cull many more examples, but some of the more widespread ones have here been chosen:

E model	AmN substitute	Original N meaning (also in E)	New E meaning	'Proper' N equivalent
board	*bor(d)* n.	plank	official body	*styre* n.
credit	*kred`dit* m.	financial confidence	honor, commendation	*ære* f.
cold	*kul`de* m.	coldness	infection	*krim* m., *forkjøling* f.
paper	*pa`pir* n.	substance for writing on	newspaper	*avis* f., *blad* n.
party	*par`ti* n.	united group	social gathering	*gjestebod*, *lag* n.
place	*plass* n.	locale; tenant's farm	any farm	*gard* m.

E model	AmN substitute	Original N meaning (also in E)	New E meaning	'Proper' N equivalent
pole	*på'le* m.	pointed stake	slender piece of wood (e.g. telephone pole)	*stolpe* m., *stong* f.
way	*veg* m.	road	manner	*måte* m.
handy	*hen'dig* a.	capable	convenient	*lettvint*
lucky	*luk'keleg* a.	happy	fortunate	*heldig*
break	*brek'ka* v.	crack	plow up virgin soil; tame animals	*brjota; temja*
drive	*dri'va* v.	operate	guide animal or vehicle	*køyra*
tell	*fortel'ja* v.	narrate	discern (you can't tell)	*sjå; segja*
go	*gå* v.	move, walk	travel	*reisa, fara*
live	*le'va* v.	be alive	dwell	*bu*
mean	*mei'na* v.	have in mind	signify	*bety*
raise	*rei'sa* v.	erect, set in motion	rear	*dyrka, avla*
split	*split'ta* v.	disunite, disperse	cleave (wood)	*kløyva, hogga*
stick	*stik'ka* v.	thrust	cling to	*halda med*
stop	*ståp'pa* v.	come to a halt	stay, live (a short time)	*stogga*
well (interj.)	*vel*	good	hesitation, surprise	*nå, ja*

One would expect also to find some words which were confused purely because of semantic resemblance. In terms of our formula in Chapter 15, this would have meant that a_1 could acquire the additional meaning A_2 simply because it had meaning A_1 in common with b, without phonetic resemblance between a_1 and b. It does not seem possible to find any such examples in AmN, apparently because of the widespread phonetic resemblance between E and N. This is somewhat surprising in view of such expressions reported from other immigrant languages as AmPort, where Pap reports phrases like *correr para mayor* 'run for mayor' or *fazer sentido* 'make sense'. In AmN both of the verbs (as well as the nouns) were borrowed: *rønna for major* and *mæka sens*. From AmYiddish are reported *ausguken* 'look out' and *oprufen* 'call up'.[7] The former has not been heard in AmN by the writer; for the second he has heard *kalle upp*, where there is clear homophony. He has heard *sjå upp* for look up ('*sjå meg upp når du kjem te byen*'), and similar expressions do occur in writing, especially when writers of modest training have misused the dictionary, cf. the translator of American ads who produced the sentence *brolamper til salgs* when he meant home bridge lamps, not the large kind that stand on bridges. Purely synonymous extensions are reported from N children living a brief time in the United States, and they occur regularly in American classes in Norwegian. The following children's howlers are typical: *Tass laget meg skrike* 'Tass made me cry' (E make > N *lage*, instead of *fikk...til å* because of their common meaning of 'construct'); *du vet henne* 'you know her' (E know > N *vet*, instead of *kjenner*, because of their common meaning of 'know a fact').[8]

It appears to be a rule of spoken AmN that adults do not make this kind of error, but resort either to loanwords or to homophones. The similarity of phonological and morphemic structure makes this the easy way out. On the other hand, we must not overlook the fact that the examples given from the AmPort and AmYiddish are parts of phrases. It seems probable that only in more or less fixed phrases can this kind of substitution take place. Even in the examples given above one of the two members had a certain degree of phonetic resemblance, e.g. *mayor* in *correr para mayor*, *sentido* in *fazer sentido*, *aus* in *ausguken*, and *op* in *oprufen*.

7. *Phrasal Loanshifts.*

We have already seen in Chapter 17 that complete phrases may be borrowed with nothing but phonological substitution. But some phrases constitute patterns of such a characteristic and intimately joined meaning that they impose themselves as wholes and may then be subject to morphological substitution as well.

In a certain sense every loanshift extension occurs first as a part of some larger phrase and could therefore be regarded as a substitution within the phrase, much as we have regarded compounds with one or both elements translated as being more or less blended. It is not easy to decide the limits of such a phrase, and one's classification might be affected by differences of opinion on this point.

Phrases consisting of verb and adverb were freely borrowed in AmN, with substitution of the nearest N adverb. In most of these the verb was imported, e.g. clean up > *kli`na opp¹*, dish up > *dissj`a opp¹*, fix up > *fik`sa opp¹*, fence in > *fen`sa inn¹*, change over > *kjei`nja å¹ver*, pick out > *pik`ka u¹t*, played out > *u'tplei¹a*, locked down > *ne'lak¹ka*. Other E phrases adopted were: do up, dress up, feed up, fire up, gear up, get up, hold up, hook up, pick up, keep up, mix up, pry up, prove up, put up, soak up, sober up, map out, tip over, beat out, run down (malign). It seems probable that any such phrase would automatically be adopted as needed. When the N analogue was sufficiently similar, it might be substituted, as in wash out > *vas`ka u¹t* (the road), sell out > *sel`ja u¹t*, lay off (workers) > *legg`ja a¹v*, come out (well) > *kåmm`a u¹t*, lay down (a rule) > *legg`ja ne¹*, help out > *jel`pa u¹t*, hire out > *hy`ra u¹t*, show up > *sjå` opp¹*. A slightly variant situation existed in the case of the expression *opp'reist* used by one informant for E raised 'reared'. Here the N *oppdratt* or *oppvokset* may have been blended with the E word, with substitution of N *reisa* 'raise'.

Other combinations with partial or complete substitution were wash dishes > *vas`ka diss'jis;* well off > *vell' a'v;* hard up > *hart' op`pe;* on time > *på ti'd;* on the side > *på si`a;* on hand > *på hån'd;* all around > *all' run't*. Such phrases are formed continually. Some of them already existed in the language, but with a different meaning, as *legg`ja a¹v*, which in Norway meant to lay aside, as a habit or a piece of clothing; here it added the meaning of discharge from one's job, like AmE lay off. But for each loanshift extension there were many creations; or perhaps we should say that every phrasal creation resulted in extensions of meaning for the words that made it up.

8. *Immigrant Creations.*

As we have noted earlier (Chapter 15), the conditions of immigrant life were not conducive to the creation of new words, other than those which were more or less directly reproduced from E. There is a theoretical possibility that some of the creations described as loanshifts might also have been made up by the immigrants without a knowledge of English. But in view of their large number and obvious similarity to well-known English words, we are on the safe side in attributing their origin to direct imitation of English. After all of these have been eliminated, however, we are left with a small residue of forms which have no apparent E model and no known N existence. These are the only ones we may be reasonably assured were the result of creation by the immigrants as an adaptation to their new environment.

Hybrid creations are distinct from hybrid loans because they lack an E model and therefore show that the model must have been a N word. Into this N model has then been substituted an E element, thus reversing the usual process of substitution. This can scarcely have taken place before the E element was an integral part of the language, so that its substitution was no different from that suffixing or compounding procedure which is always taking place in the language. The simplest form of such creation was to make verbs from borrowed nouns; the following had no direct E models: *kjå'rsa* 'to do chores', from *kjå'rs* 'chores'; *skvæ'ra seg* 'get married by the squire', from *skvæ'r* 'squire' (justice of the peace); *bætsj'la* 'bach it, do one's own cooking' from *bætsj'lar* 'bachelor'; *ri'pla* 'reap', from *ri'pel* 'reaper'.

A number of hybrid creations were due to the suffix -*vis*, which occurred in such words as *hundrevis* 'by the hundreds', *dagevis* 'day after day'. In this pattern any E term of measure could also be substituted, creating new AmN terms like *bussj'elvi's* 'by the bushel', *jard'vi's* 'by the yard'. This might be symbolized as follows; N *hundrevis* + E bushel > AmN *bussj'elvi's*. Similarly when N *femøre* 'five-øre piece' + E cent > *fem'sen't* 'five-cent piece', and N *tiøre* + E cent > *ti'sen't* 'dime'. A small group of compounds go back to E prepositional phrases, as noted in Chapter 17; these may perhaps as well be regarded as hybrid creations, since they have as concurrent models N compounds. An example is *garnnysta* 'ball of yarn' + E twine > *tvai`nnys'ta* 'ball of twine'.

Two practically synonymous words which were much used among the immigrants to cast aspersion on those who were overly ready to anglicize themselves were *eng'elskspreng't* and *jen'ki- spreng't*. Among the N words which could have served as models for these terms are *bibelsprengt* 'Bible-minded', *blodsprengt* 'blood- shot', *gråsprengt* 'grizzled', *melkesprengt* 'distended with milk' (of udders), *sprenglærd* 'excessively learned', etc. The element *sprengt* means 'distended to the point of bursting', in this case referring to one's pride in being 'English' rather than Norwegian. Another char- acteristic immigrant word in Wisconsin was the word *sjæ`rbru'kar*, used of farmers who worked a crop, especially tobacco, in return for a share of the proceeds. The model cannot have been sharecropper, since this term was not used in Wisconsin; the only E term reported is shareman, which some AmN speakers have adopted as *sjæ'rmann'*.[9] As noted earlier, its origin must have been N *gardbrukar* 'farmer', with substitution of AmN *sjær* for the first element. Other com- pounds of similar origin are: N *våningshus* 'dwelling' + E living > AmN *lev'vingshu's;* N *murstein* 'brick' + E brick > AmN *brikk'- stei'n* (Brickstein is also AmGer); N *matbæta* 'bite of food' + E field > AmN *fi'lbæ'ta* 'bit of a field'.

Certain extensions of meaning may also be attributed exclusi- vely to the circumstances of immigrant life, without appeal to American models. The usual term for a recent arrival from Norway, a term used much as Americans might use 'greenhorn', was *ny`- kom'mar*. He was the butt of all jokes, the most bewildered and eager to become acclimatized. There is a N *nykommar*, but its meaning does not appear to have been specific previous to migra- tion. Nor does the E newcomer seem to be specific. But among the immigrants it was universal in this meaning, as illustrated in the title of O. E. Rølvaag's first published novel, *Nykommerbreve* 'A Newcomer's Letters', of 1906. When the immigrants referred to Norway, they often used the term *gammellandet* (or *gamlelandet*) 'the old country'. Without an investigation of its use in Norway, it would be impossible to say whether the use over there preceded its appearance in America. The earliest citation given in NRO is from 1930, but it occurred long before this in AmN; it is illustrated by the title of Waldemar Ager's novel *Gamlelandets Sønner* of 1926. It may actually stem back to the E expression 'the old country', which was common in many immigrant groups.

A Norwegian word which may have gained new meanings in AmN is *gra'vplass*[, which is cited in NRO only in reference to pagan burial mounds. It was used among the immigrants as a N equivalent of cemetery, whenever the cemetery was not a churchyard, or *kyrkjegard*. Since the secular cemetery was a cultural novelty to many immigrants, the extension may be regarded as a semantic displacement, induced by the cultural change. Another extension took place in connection with the word *bygdelag*, which in Norway meant 'rural community or region', a late parallel to the use of *lag* in the Danelaw. The use of the word *lag* to mean 'club' or 'society' was due to the rise of the New Norse movement which desired to avoid the DN word *forening*. The earliest societies of out-of-town people in Oslo used the word *forening* (*Den nordlandske Forening* 1862; *Lillehammerforeningen* 1877), but in 1883 *Telelaget* was formed, and after this time most such societies were 'lag'.[10] But there is no evidence that the common term *byg'dela'g* was used until after it had first been adopted in this sense among emigrant Norwegians. This was also the contention of A. A. Veblen, the father of the movement in America, who traced its first use to Dr. Herman Fjelde in 1906.[11] It was adopted after some discussion of possible alternatives, and it is today standard both in AmN and native N usage.

Besides these original AmN extensions, there are two words which came into being as native creations. The only one found in popular usage was *kub'berul'la*, an ox-cart with wheels made of whole wooden slabs. This homemade contraption did not exist in Norway and the name is not recorded in any Norwegian source. The nuclear element, *rulla* f., is a word for a small cart; the marginal element, *kubbe*, is a piece of a tree, used e.g. in *kubbestol* to describe a chair made from a whole piece of tree trunk. The compound *kub'berul'la* is thus an exact description of the object. The other word is found in more literary and self-conscious usage: *Vesterheimen*, referring to America and particularly the Norwegian settlements therein. The earliest written use of this term so far discovered is from 1874, in an article by Prof. Rasmus B. Anderson;

his contact with Icelanders and Icelandic usage at this time suggests that he adopted it from Icelandic *Vesturheimur*, a common term for the Icelandic settlements in America.[12] There are several instances of its use in the late 70's, and between 1880 and 1892 four newspapers with this title were started among Norwegians. Its best-known usage came with the publication from 1911 by the Norwegian-Lutheran Church of a Christmas annual called *Jul i Vesterheimen*.

The forms discussed in this chapter have exhibited various degrees of original creation on the part of the immigrants. While the great mass of their AmN innovations consisted of lws., there is a respectable body of words that show some effort to adapt native morphemes to new uses. The simplest instances are the loanblend stems like *hyppa* for whip and the derivatives like *guffert* for gopher. In compounds we have seen that substitution of native morphemes took place especially when the parts stood in a fairly obvious relation to one another and the N substitute resembled the E morpheme phonetically. Thus cowbarn and cordwood were partially 'translated' as *kubale* and *kårdve*, but cowboy and cottonwood were not. About one half of the compounds show some substitution; a few even have it in both parts, thereby giving rise to such pseudo-Norwegian compounds as *smågrøn* 'small grain'. Phonetic similarity also tempted many to extend the meanings of familiar words into new situations, sometimes in defiance of the previous meanings and sometimes as a natural displacement due to cultural changes. Phrases might similarly be borrowed either entire or with partial substitution. But the actual number of creations not modelled on American originals is small, though significant enough as expressions of highly characteristic immigrant attitudes and institutions.

Chapter 19.

SPECIMENS OF AMERICAN NORWEGIAN.

"The time has come," the Walrus said, "To talk
of many things: Of shoes — and ships — and sealing
wax —
Of cabbages — and kings —"

Lewis Carroll (1872)

No study of a language is complete without texts to illustrate
its living usage. The investigator should share some of his primary
source material with his readers, particularly when it has a cultural
as well as a linguistic interest. Texts permit the reader to make
up his own mind about the language and at the same time they
introduce him to the men and women who speak it and to the
culture they represent. The specimens of AmN that follow have been
selected from the writer's extensive archives of recordings and
notations. It is intended that they shall be at once *authentic,
representative,* and *culturally significant.*

All but one of the specimens were transcribed directly from
recordings made in the field; the exception (No. 31) was transcribed from word of mouth narration. All but two were spontane-
ous and unrehearsed; the exceptions (nos. 22 and 25) had been
written down in advance by informants with academic training in
a rough dialectal orthography of their own devising. Only those
speakers were included who spoke into the microphone without
marked self-consciousness, and in the same style of speech as they
were accustomed to use in everyday conversation. The occasional
'book forms' that will be found in the texts are partly due to the
general influence of BL on speech, partly to the recording situation.

But they are not numerous or disturbing, and they generally vanish as soon as the speakers warms to his subject.

Much of the authenticity which these specimens can claim will rest upon the accuracy of the transcription. The writer has made a sincere effort to render every shade of sound as accurately as the records permit. This is not always easy, for reasons which are partly mechanical and partly linguistic. None of the recordings made can be described as high-fidelity, and while they generally suffice to identify what is being said, they often resist all attempts to determine particular sounds. This is especially true of unstressed syllables and of voiceless consonants: for Norwegian it is not always possible to tell *s* from *sj*, *e* from *æ*, or *t* from *rt*. Repeated listening to a doubtful or evanescent sound will often lead to various interpretations. This is reflected in certain inconsistencies which the attentive reader will note. The *linguistic* problem is that of classifying the sound into relevant categories once they have been heard. Since it was not possible to make a phonemic analysis of each speaker's dialect, the best that could be done was to set up certain broad classes of sound for each dialect and adopt a consistent symbol for each. As far as possible, sounds that are perceptibly different will have different symbols if they occur in identical environments. The result is a spelling which follows rather closely that of standard Norwegian, though it is more consistently applied. With some attention it should be readable by the ordinary Norwegian native, and at the same time it should give the linguist the information he wants.

The general value assumed for each symbol is stated in Appendix 2. Thus *r* stands for a tongue-trilled *r* unless there is a statement to the contrary at the beginning of the selection; if *r* is uvular, or if it is untrilled before dentals (*l*, *s*, *t*, *d*, *n*), that information is provided under the head of *Pronunciation*. Since the vowel systems vary sharply in different parts of the country, they are described in general terms as EN, Midland, and WN. EN has shifted the values of the vowels *a*, *å*, *o*, *u*, and *y* so that they are rather different from the general European sounds; to a German ear each one sounds like the next in the series (and *y* like *i*). Midland is closest to the German system; while WN agrees in part with Midland, but shows more or less diphthongization of the old long vowels, especially, *i*, *y*, *u*, and *o*, which sound something like *ey*, *øy*, *uw*, and *ow*.

Stress and tone have been marked, with a distinction being made between loud reduced, and soft stress, and between tone one and two. The placing of the stress-tone mark is also significant, since it always follows immediately after a long vowel, but when the vowel is short, it follows the next consonant. Doubling of consonants is thus not linguistically significant except between vowels, where it represents a syllabic division: *hatt'* vs. *hat'ten*. Two or more consonant symbols which stand for only one sound get the accent mark after both symbols: *tt*, *sj*, *rs*, *ng* etc. (where these really are single sounds). Beyond the word stress there is a phrasal stress, whereby special emphasis is given to one, often the last, of the full stresses. This is not marked, but is suggested by the punctuation. Phrases which constitute intonational units are marked off by commas. Periods are used as a reading convenience when one or more phrases constitute a complete utterance or grammatical unit. Hesitations and abrupt shifts in construction are marked by dashes. A few minor stammerings have been eliminated, but in general the reproduction has been entirely faithful to the uncertainties and repetitiousness of most speakers.

Earlier specimens of AmN by the present writer were published in *Romerike, Studier og Samlinger* (Oslo, 1947); but those appearing in his *Norsk i Amerika* and *NASR* 10.39-43 were somewhat more normalized. None of these have been duplicated in the present volume, though two of the speakers in the latter group are here represented with different specimens. The only other published specimens of authentic AmN speech are those of Nils T. Flaten in *Maal og Minne* 1939, 30-50.

The present selections are intended to be representative of the various dialects and communities studied. They appear in the order of numbering of communities, as these are listed in Appendix 1 and on the map of informants (Plate 7). It was not possible to include all communities or dialects, but there is an even spread through the material. To show the variations within community or dialect, some were given more than one selection. Other things being equal, the writer confesses to having included those passages which were most interesting, either for their narrative skill or for their cultural value. Skillful narrators are the bearers of community tradition. The stories here told are typical of those one can hear among the immigrants and their descendants. They illustrate the wit and the wisdom of the community, and they come from those speakers who were most willing to open up and talk freely to the investigator. Most of the recordings were made after a completed interview, during which an air of mutual confidence had been established.

For readers without knowledge of Norwegian an interlinear translation has been provided. Those words in the N text which show E influence have been identified by a preceding star. Words spoken in an all-English pronunciation are enclosed between double quotation marks. E [r] is written *r* to distinguish it from the N *r*.

1. *A Koshkonong Viking.*

(Voss dialect from Koshkonong; inf. 4P1, recorded Feb. 3, 1938. Born on a farm near Deerfield, Wisconsin, in 1869, this woman was an unusually valuable informant, with a marked pride and interest in her dialect. Her father and mother came from Voss in 1841 and 1845. *Pronunciation:* WN vowels, with marked diphthongization of *i, y, u,* and *o;* unstressed *u* is a lowered high back vowel [ʊ]; unstressed *e* is a mid front [e]; *æ* is a raised low front vowel [ɛ]; *kj* is an affricate [tç]; *sj* is [shj]; *ng* is [ngg].)

(A) *Witchcraft.*

Han Gul`laik va bao`de so han trud`de pao tråll`kje'ringa å
Gulleik was such that he believed both in witches and other

an't. Å dao han sjøn`te attu han in`kje fekk' nåkk' smø'r tao
things. And when he realized he wasn't getting enough butter from

kjyd'na sina, so trud`de han attu na`bokå'no kunde ma`na
his cows, he thought that the neighbor woman could charm the

røm`men u't or kjyd'na hans, fy \*pas'tre dairans — ham`nagan'jen
cream out of his cows, for their pasture — 'hamnaganjen' [Norw.]

— va nett' yve ve'jen i frao dar na`bokå'na \*lev`de.
—was right across the road from where the neighbor woman lived.

So viss`te han rao'. Han to'k ai byr`sepi'pa å fyl`te dao i' da
Then he knew a remedy. He took a gun barrel and filled it with what

han kunde fin'na mæ tråll`kattespy'a,
he could find of 'troll cat spew' [a kind of fungus],

set`te ain svæ'ru kår'k i, å la` pi`po uppi ao'ren i smid`jo si,
put a big cork in it, and laid the barrel in the forge in his smithy,

bejyn'te te å blao`sa mæ bæl'jen so han fekk' ne go' å hai't. Å
began to blow with the bellows so he got it good and hot. And

dao' skulde dan' so sjyl`dig e', elde dan' so va tråll`kje'ring, dao'
then the one who is guilty, or the one who was the witch, would

skulde ho' lota kåma fram' naor pi`po ,byn`te te var`ma se. Men før
have to come out when the barrel began to get hot. But before

han visste o'r tao', so bykste pi`po pao gål've,
he knew what was happening, the barrel hopped out on the floor

å kår'ken for u't. Men Gul`laik skåd`de i gla'se
and the cork flew out. But Gulleik looked through the window

å sao'g pao na`bokå'no kåm' yve *fi'læ, å dao'
and saw the neighbor woman coming across the field, and then

hadde han bevi's nåkk' attu ho' va dan' so va misten'kt...
he had proof enough that she was the one he had suspected...

(B) *A Business Deal.*

Naor Gul`laik kjøpte lan'de tao Nils Jil`jaru's, so hadde Nil's
When Gulleik bought the land from Nils Gilderhus, Nils had

saott' — eg huk`sa ikkje kor' mange \*ei'ker mæ kvai`te. Å da
sown — I don't remember how many acres of wheat. And then

va dao' ak`korten attu — i da min`sta fårsto' Nil's da so', attu
the agreement was that — at least Nils understood it so, that

han' skulde fao kvai`ten, naor hæus'ten kåm. Nil's kjøpte
he would get the wheat when fall came. Nils then bought

seg dao' lan'd dar Lib'erti-præri-kjyr'kja stao'r, å flyt'te.
himself land where the Liberty Prairie church stands, and moved.

Å naor kvai'ten blai sje'ru, so bejyn'te Gul'laik å *krid'la, å had'de
And when the wheat was ripe, Gulleik began to cradle, and had

*kridla ne' næstan hai'la *fi'læ naor Nil's Jil'jaru's fækk ve'ta
cradled down almost the whole field when Nils Gilderhus heard

da. Å dao' vatt han' ræd'du, kan du ve'ta, ka skul'de han jæ'ra,
about it. And then he got scared, you know, what should he do,

han tor'de in'kje ta pao' han Gul'laik, fy han va' ain både sto'ru, stær'ku
he didn't dare to go after Gulleik, for he was both a big, strong

mann' mæ my'kje mo't. Å Nil's Jil'jaru's had'de ikkje
man and a courageous one. And Nils Gilderhus didn't have very

svæ'rt my'kje mo't. So rais'te han te bro'r sin, te han O'la Jiljaru's, å
much courage. So he went to his brother, to Ola Gilderhus, and

spo'rde itte rao'. Å so sa' han O'la, ja, e'g vai't ikkje
asked him for advice. And then Ola said, I don't know what

ka' me ska jæ'ra, fy han Gul'laik e' kje so lett' å ha' mæ. So rais'te
we should do, for Gulleik isn't so easy to deal with. Then they

dai te han Anders Li', te han bæs'tefa'r, å spor'de han' ka' dai
went to Anders Li, to grandfather, and asked him what they

skulde jæ'ra. Ja', eg vai't ikkje sa han, men eg ten'kje da bes'ta me
should do. Well, I don't know, he said, but I think the best we

kan jæ'ra e', me te'ku kve'r si våg'n å *ti'm, å så rai'sa me
can do is that we take a wagon and and a team apiece and go

bur't itte da e mør'kt, å så les'sa me pao' al't da me kunna fao', å
over after dark, and then we load on everything we can get, and

kjåi're da darifrao'. Å dai' so jo're. Itte da va mør'kt, så kåm'mu dai
drive it away. And they did so. After it got dark, they came

mæ tre' våg'na — *ti'm å tre' våg'na — å les'te
with three wagons — teams and three wagons — and loaded them

pao', å jo're ai'n *trepp', å teba'kers attu, å les'te pao', å
up, and they made one trip, and then back and loaded up, and

fekk rai`sa mæ da' å'g før mår`gån kåm', *å dao' hadde dai*
got away with that too before the morning came, and then they

rais't mæ mæs'ta al't sam'ma. *So dan' gån'jæ fækk' ikkje Gul`laik da*
had taken nearly all of it. So that time Gulleik didn't get things

so' so han vilde ha' da.
the way he wanted them.

2. Early Days in Koshkonong.

(Sogn dialect from Liberty Prairie; inf. 4Q2, recorded Nov.
28, 1936. Born in Sogndal in 1857 and immigrated in 1877, this
man farmed and kept a store; he was widely read and a good
story-teller. *Pronunciation:* WN vowels, with slight diphthongization; *æ* is raised low front; *kj, sj,* and *ng* are as in the preceding
speaker.)

(A) Divorce

Men da va no æi'n tin'g so va fårun'darle. Sjil'smis¹se va u`kjen¹t
But there was one thing that was strange. Divorce was unknown

i la'g mæ dæi når`ske \*pai`one¹ra, dæi når`ske fål'k. Får e
among the Norwegian pioneers, the Norwegian people. For I

huk`sa, e had`de en na`bo æg, han va' kje tao gu'ds bes`te båd'n.
remember I had a neighbor, who was not one of God's best children.

Han va *æin såg`ning, hadde våre spæ`lemann¹, å han hadde møs't
He was a Sogning, had been a fiddler, and he had lost

kå`nao si, han va nem`maste na`boen min, å so blæi han at'tejif¹te
his wife; he was my nearest neighbor, and then he got married

mæ æi æn`ka ne' ifrao Mekfal'lan, å ho' hadde væl sitt' bæ're
again to a widow down from McFarland, and she had seen better

da`ga spao'r eg. Han drakk' støtt' å' denne he'r. Å so'
days, I suppose. He drank constantly, too, this fellow. And

blæi han so' at han [vart] opphæf'ta mæ æi ån`når jæn`ta, å so maotte
then he got mixed up with another girl, and then he

han *jif'ta ho, å so væi't du han maotte jøy'ma o, å
had to marry her, and then you know he had to hide her, and

fao sjil'smis'se. Du kan se' ko fårun'darleg da va' dan gån'gen —
get a divorce. You can see how strange it was that time: on

sam'me da'gen so de kåm u't i a'visedn atte han hadde faott
the same day as it appeared in the papers that he had gotten

sjil'smis'se, so dræi'v dar to tri amerika'nera opp te mæ'g å spo'rde om
a divorce, two or three Americans came up to me and asked if

da — var da ver'kele san't, fy dæi hadde al'dri hæu'rt en når'sker
it — was it really true, for they had never heard that a Norwegian

hadde hatt sjil'smis'se.
had gotten a divorce.

(B) *Brewing beer.*

Du se'r, ø'le va bil'likt hæ'r dan gån'gen. Bøg'gen va bil'lige.
You see, beer was cheap here at that time. Barley was cheap.

Du kunde laga te' ditt æi'ge mal't. Kas'ta nåke sek'ke mæ bøgg' ne'
You could make your own malt. Throw some sacks of barley down

ti en *spren'g, elle i en *tæn'k, lidd'ja dar en trif 'fire da'ga,
in a spring, or in a tank, (let it) lie there for three or four days,

ta n åpp'atte te dess' at n bejyn'te å *hi'ta. Å so ha' n inn'på en beng', å
take it up again until it began to heat. Then put it in a bin and

rø'ra i dan, to'k umkring ni'e da'ga, so *sprao'ta n, å blæi
stir it; this took about nine days, then it would sprout and get

sø'te. So tur'ka dan — da væs'ta dæi va *up'pe hæ'rimo't va
sweet. Then dry — the worst they were up against here was

te tur'ka da. So tur'ka di da, di tur'ka da pao æin mao'te, maon'ge
to dry it. Then they dried it, they dried it in some way, many

hadde tur'kehus, to'k da pao møl'lao å *krek'ka da, å dao' va
had drying houses, took it to the mill and cracked it, and then it

da fær'dikt. Å la'ga te' æin *bæ'ridl mæ hal'm(ne'ti?), å nå'ke — hel'ste
was ready. To make a barrel of straw (?), and some — prefer-

si'derpås'ta ha di sun'de so blai un'de so at da sku
ably cedar posts broken up (?) which were put under it so it would

ræn'na. Å so hel'te di da pao' dar, å hel'te tao' da, so læin'je so atte
run. Then they poured it in there, and poured from it as long as

da va go'e sma'k pao da. Å so' kok'te di da, hadde hum'le pao da,
there was good taste in it. And then they boiled it, put on hops,

*å le't da — *fermen'ta gao' en dak's ti', å so' skaka da upp'.*
and let it — (let) the ferment go for a day, and then shook it up.

3. Folklore in Perry.

(Telemark dialect from Perry; inf. 5F1, recorded April 23, 1938. Born near Daleyville, Wisconsin, in 1855, this man spoke a dialect which was not the same as that of his ancestors who came from near Lillehammer in 1850. It was rather a kind of Telemark speech, prevalent in the Perry region. *Pronunciation:* Midland vowels; *ȯ* is a rounded central vowel between *ø* and *å; ei* approaches *æi;* short *e* approaches *æ; kj* is an affricate [tç]; *sj* is [shj]; *r* is untrilled before dentals.)

De va' no ein hei'l mas'se av dei gam'te såm kåm' i frå
There were a great many of the old people who came from

Når'ge såm hadde å'vertro'. De va' kje full't de sam'me
Norway who were superstitious. It wasn't quite the same beliefs

dei hadde al'le. De va fårsjel'li på fårsjel'lie kan'ter. Som'me så va
they all had. It was different in different parts. Some were mostly

no nis'sen så om å jø're, som'mestan¹ så va de no bær'jtröll¹, å så'
concerned about the »nisse«, some places it was the »trolls«; now

va de no de', å så' va de de'. On'derjor'diske kalla dei
it was this, and now it was that. 'Underground people' they

som'me av dei. De va'r som'me av dei såm var så il'le at
called some of them. Some people were so bad that

dei praktise'ra de hæ'r. De va ei ga'mal kjæ'ring hær bor'te. Om
they practiced it here. There was an old woman over here. On

ju῾leſ῾tan så måtte ho la῾ga eit sto′rt kårs′ av kju῾ru åver *stæ′bel-
Christmas eve she had to paint a huge cross of tar over the stable-

dø῾ra — *ba῾rndø῾ra — så at ikk῾je dei skulle kåm῾me. Å så
door — the barn door — so that they wouldn't come. And then

va dæ to′ gam῾te kjæ῾ringer såm lå′g i u῾greie om de′
there were two old women who were in disagreement over what

dei kalla tröll῾kat῾ten. Dei trud῾de bæg῾ge på det῾ta. Å så
they called the 'troll cat'. They both believed in it. And then

sa′ den ei῾ne då′ ser u, at den an῾dre hadde *trei῾na
one of them said, you see, that the other one had trained the

tröll῾kat῾ten så dæ′ at den sta′t mjöt῾ka uto ku῾ene hen῾nes, so at ikkje ho′
troll cat so that it stole milk out of her cows, so that she didn't

ſekk′ no. Å den′ tröll῾kat῾ten, den la῾ga dei, dei sam῾ta hå′r
get any. And this troll cat was something they made; they gathered

såm dei ha ſel′t u῾tor — kvinn῾ſåt῾ka, så vei′t du, når dei′ har
hair which they had shed — women, you know, when they have

my῾e hå′r, så sam῾ta dei hå′r å dei a′vskå῾rne neg′tan å
lots of hair, they gather hair and nails that have been cut off and

sa῾e nå slaks ſår῾mula′r dei had῾de ſår å ſå det῾ta jyl῾dikt då′
said some kind of formulas they had in order to make this effective

ser u.
you see.

4. *An Old-fashioned Wedding.*

(Valdres dialect from Springdale; inf. 5H4, recorded Nov. 21, 1936. Born in Springdale Twp., Dane Co., Wisconsin in 1862, this man was a fluent second-generation speaker. His father immigrated from Tinn in Telemark, his mother from Bagn in Valdres, about 1844. *Pronunciation:* Midland vowels; *ë* is an unstressed vowel which retains its mid front quality, not becoming [ə]; *kj* is an affricate [tç]; *sj* is [shj]; *r* is untrilled before dentals, unvoiced before other unvoiced consonants.)

Ja', e va' umtrent fjort`en å'r, da' va e mæ' på æit brøl`løp.
Well, I was about fourteen years old; then I was at a wedding.

E føl`de — fekk a`ka mæ na`boen. Fys't ræis`te dæi te
I went with — got a ride with the neighbors. First they went to

kjør`kja å vart vig`de. Så ræis`te dæi da'rifrå¹, å
church and got married. Then they went away from there and

te hu'se, å dæ fys`te me så'g da'r så var dæ — dæi kal`la
to the house, and the first thing we saw there was — they called

dæi sjæn`kara, æi'n sjænk`te *vis`ki å æi'n sjænk`te *bi'r. Så
them »pourers«, one poured whisky and one poured beer. Then

måt`te dæi drik`ke æit gla's *vis`ki å så' æit gla's *bi'r. Så'
they had to drink one glass of whisky and one glass of beer. Then

va de å — kåm' de noko kvinn`føl¹k mæ *ke'k.
they — there came some women with cake.

Så' va de in`kje så læng`e før elle de vart mid'dag. Å et`te mid'dag
Then it wasn't very long before the dinner. And after dinner

så va' de å prø`ve å ha' mo`ro på mang`e slaks vi's. [Hva de gjorde?]
they tried having fun in many different ways. [What they did?]

Å', sum`me tå dæi...drok'st, å sum`me *båk`sa *hætt'... væi't
Oh, some of them...wrestled, and some 'boxed hats'... don't

kji ko du kal`la de' på nårs'k — å sum`me håp`pa. Å
know what you call that in Norwegian — and some jumped. And

når kvæl'den kåm', så fækk dæi kvæl`sma¹t, å når dæi — et`ter
when evening came, they got supper, and when they — after

dæi hadde stel`t ifrå¹ sæg me ma'ten, så va' de te å dan`se.
they had finished up with the food, they started to dance.

Dæi dan`sa hæi`le nat`të. Å så had`de dæi a`en mo`ro att`vë.
They danced all night. And then they had other kinds of fun besides.

I det`të brøl`løpe såm e snak`ka om no' hadde dæi en spel'lemann¹.
In this wedding I'm telling about now they had a fiddler.

Han' va sæk's fo't — næi' han va sju' fo't å fi`re tomm`a hø'g, å
He was six feet — no, he was seven feet and four inches tall, and

bræi' å sto'r. Å så spel`te n mæ kjæi`va. De
broad and large. And then he played with his left hand. There

va' ikkje mang`ë såm kunna få' slikt må't i fe`la
weren't many who could make the fiddle sound the way

såm han'. [Hva han spilte?] Al`le slaks to`na, dan`seto'na. Dæ
he did. [What he played?] All kinds of tunes, dance tunes. There

va spring'dan¹s, å val's, å *sjat'tis, å ham'bår¹g,
was 'spring dance', and waltz, and schottische, and 'hamborg',

å *skwæ'rdan¹s, å sum`meti¹er dan`sa dæi hal`ling.
and square dance, and sometimes they danced the 'halling'.

I det`të brøl`løpe så *fik`sa dæi opp¹ dæi kal`la dæ æin *mju'l.
In this wedding they fixed up something they called a 'mule'.

Dæ va to' ka`ra såm jikk' kro`kete, å så kas`ta dæi æin "ro'b"
That was two men who walked stooped over, and then they threw

åver dæi, å så kåm' dæi lab`ban inn ijø'no hu'se
a robe over them, and then they came plodding through the house,

ser du, å skræ`mde mang`e såm ikk`je viss`te ko det`ta va' får noko.
you see, and frightened many who didn't know what this was.

Mang`e vart ræd`de. Men dæ va' no mes'te får mo`ro væit du. Å
Many were frightened. But it was mostly for fun you know. Oh,

e huk`sa no dæ' at da må`rån kåm', så va' dæ tæ`ta,
I remember that when morning came, the ground was frozen,

å mø måtte gå' hæi'matt umtrent to' *mi'l. Dæ' umtren't al't e
and we had to walk home about two miles. That's about all I

kan huk`se tå dæ'.
can remember of that.

5. *Immigration in the Fifties.*

(Telemark dialect from Perry; inf. 5L3, recorded Nov. 28, 1936.
Born in Perry Twp., Dane Co., Wisconsin in 1876, this man became
a law graduate of the University of Wisconsin. His father was

born in Kvitseid, Telemark, and immigrated with parents and grandparents in 1850. *Pronunciation:* Midland vowels; *ȯ* is a rounded mid-central vowel, between *ø* and *å;* unstressed *e* retains its front quality to some extent; *kj* is a palatal affricate [tç].)

Ein moʻrbroʻr te faʻr kåm' hit fys't, å så sen'te han pengʻar
An uncle of father came here first, and then he sent money

tebaʻkers te Nårʻge. Å såʻ kåm faʻr min å besʻtefaʻr min,
back to Norway. And then came my father and my grandfather,

å besʻtefaʻr te faʻr kåm. Di kåm' ifrå Kraʻgerø' å te Nu' Jåʻrk.
and father's grandfather. They came from Kragerø and to New York.

Å så kåm' di inn' ijæʻnem kanaʻlen i Nu' Jåʻrk, å te
And then they came in through the canal in New York and to the

innʻsjøʻane, kåm' te Milvåʻkiᵢ å når di kåm' te Milvåʻki
Great Lakes, came to Milwaukee, and when they came to Milwaukee,

så møtʻte di en mann' såm *leʻvde mæ Raʻkdeiʻl i Deiʻn Kaoʻnti. På den'
they met a man who lived by Rockdale in Dane County. At that

tiʻ va navʻne Klinʻten. Så fikk di kjøʻre mæ den' mann' då,
time the name was Clinton. Then they got a ride with that man,

ifrå Milvåʻki å opp te Klinʻten. Kjeʻring å ungʻan dei kjøʻrde
from Milwaukee and up to Clinton. Wife and youngsters rode

i vågʻni, å menʻnan fikk' heiʻle veʻgen, frå Milvåʻki
in the wagon, and the men walked the whole way from Milwaukee

te Deiʻn Kaoʻnti. De kåm' ei ganʻsje haʻr rægʻnskuʻr, å så
to Dane County. Quite a violent rainstorm came, and then they

stȯpʻpa dæi mæ e liʻti *lȯggʻhuʻs. De va ein *jænʻkifameʻli såm *levʻde
stopped by a little log house. A yankee family lived

dær. Å så hadde di — all maʻten di hadʻde vaʻr sm
there. And then they had — all the food they had was what

di tok mæʻ se frå Nårʻge, å de va mangʻe viʻkur,
they took with them from Norway, and that was many weeks,

å då di kåm' inn i dæ *jænʻkihuʻse då', så hadde *jænʻkikjeʻringi
and when they came into the yankee house, the yankee woman

*ba`ka *frai'dke¹k, å så fækk' di *frai'dke¹k å sø't mjøl'k mæ*
had baked friedcake, and they got friedcake and sweet milk with

rom`men i, å de sma`ka ek'stra gòtt' sa di. Å så
the cream on it, and that tasted extra good, they said. And then

bòu' di te beta'la før ma'ten, men di vil'le ikkje ta' noko
they offered to pay for the food, but they would not take anything

fø'r de.
for it.

Når di kåm' på kana'lbå¹ten i Nu'jårk, så had`de dei ein
When they got on the canal boat in New York, they had a

sto'r ne'ger de'r, sm ar`beidde på bå'ten, å han va fæ'lt
large negro there, who worked on the boat, and he was awfully

snill' mæ dissa emigran'tan. Han ga' di ma't, å han va snill'
kind to these emigrants. He gave them food and he was kind

på mang`e må`tar. Å ifrå den' ti', te fa'r dø', så
in many ways. And from that time until father died, he always

snak`ka han støtt' gått' — gòtt' om ne'gran.
spoke well about negroes.

*Å så når di kåm' hi't då, så lev`de dei i et *lògg'hu¹s, såm*
And when they came here then, they lived in a log house; it

ha bare eit' romm'. Å så va'r di ti' ell tåll' i al't. Å ei'
had only one room. And they were ten or twelve in all. And one

nått' då mæ bæs`tefa¹r te fa'r va sju'k, så va' dæ omtren't klòkka eitt'
night when father's grandfather was sick, it was about one o'clock

*um nåt'ti, å så va' dæ noko såm lyf'ta *hæn'deln på *stå'ven upp', å*
at night, something lifted the stove handle up and

slæp`te ne' på *stå'ven tri' gång`er. Å so' sa bæs`te-
dropped it down on the stove three times. And then said grand-

mo¹r, hør`de du de'? sa o. Å so' sva'ra en to` tri,
mother, »Did you hear that?« she said. And then two or three

sa ja', e hør`de de. Vei't de' va' de bety'r? sa o.
said, »Yes, I heard it.« »Do you know what that means«, she said.

Nei', sa dei. *Væll', sa o, om tri' da'gar så vil bæs'tefa'r
»No,« they said. »Well,« she said, »in three days grandfather will
døy'. Å han døyd'de inna tri' da'gar.
die.« And he did die within three days.

Fys't dei fløt'te upp te Pe'ri i at'ten hun'dre å fi're å
When they first moved up to Perry in eighteen hundred and
fæm'ti, å så va dæ *brus'k mæs't al'le sta'n veit du.
fifty four, there was brush just about everywhere, you know.
Å så reis'te fa'r på æng'els sku'le ein mòr'go. Å så'
And then father went to English school one morning. And then
blei kjy'en bur'te, å så sæn'te di besje' te fa'r te
the cows disappeared, and they sent a message to father that he
kåmma hei'm å væ'ra mæ å fin'ne kjy'en ijenn'. Å så sprang' n i
should come home and help find the cows. And then he ran in
*brus'ken hei'le da'gen, å til sis'ten fann' di kjy'en. Men fa'r
the brush all day, and at last they found the cows. But father
kåm al'dri teba'ke te sku'len mei'r. Han *spen'te bær're ein hall' da'g på
never went back to the school again. He spent just half a day at
æng'els sku'le i Ame'rika.
English school in America.

6. *The Boy Farmer.*

(Voss dialect from Spring Prairie; inf. 6P2, recorded Apr. 17,
1937. Born on a farm near Sun Prairie, Wisconsin, in 1854, this
man was a skillful story-teller, with great vitality for his age.
His father and mother immigrated from Voss in 1847. *Pronunciation:* same as for the speaker of selection 1, except that he uses
e for *u* in unstressed syllables.)

E mao fårtel'ja litt' um naor e liv'de pao *far'men. E vatt
I must tell a little about the time I lived on the farm. I was
fød'de pao den *far'men so n fa'r kjøp'te, å den' aig'de eg innte fy ait
born on the farm which father bought, and I owned it until a

ao'r si`an, å e kan hus`ka atte me hadde åk`sa — bruk`te åk`sa.
year ago, and I can remember that we had oxen — used oxen.

Å me dan fys`te \*ri'paren me kjøp`te, dao' va eg fem' ao'r gamm`adl,
And with the first reaper we bought — I was five years old then

å me se`la upp åk`sane li`kaso dai jo`re me hes`ta, å
— we harnessed up the oxen just as they did with horses, and

set`te dai fy \*ri'paren å \*ri`pa kvai`te å by'gg me åk`sa.
hitched them to the reaper and reaped wheat and barley with oxen.

Å li'k ai'ns me ti slao' håi', so kun`de me \*fik`sa dan *ripp'aren so atte
And the same with cutting hay, we could fix that reaper so that

me kunde slao' håi' so sto' up`pe, so so kløv'er å *timot'ti.
we could cut hay which stood up, such as clover and timothy.

Men ån`nåt håi' — min'dur håi' — da maotte me slao' me
But other kinds of hay — smaller hay — that we had to cut with

ljao'. Å æ'g ha slej`je ain hai'l de'l me håi' med ljao' — æg slo' kvar't
a scythe. And I have cut a lot of hay with a scythe — I cut every

ao'r — me had`de umtrin't ød`leve *æ'ker so me maot`te slao' me
year — we had about eleven acres which we had to cut with

ljao', æ'g å n fa'r. Han fa'r va gam`madle dao han kåm' he'r te',
a scythe, I and father. Father was old when he came over here,

han va ain sjæu' aot`te å før'ti ao'r, å æ'g måtte bejyn'da,
he was forty-seven or forty-eight years old, and I had to start,

æ va' kje sto're ka'r før æ måtte ta' ljao'dn, å fylja
I wasn't a very big fellow when I had to take the scythe and keep

et`te mæ' an. Naor æ va' ain tret`tan fjor'tan a'or,
up with him. When I was about thirteen or fourteen years old,

so kunde æ' slao' li`ka gått' so han'. Å æ li`ka te *dri`va — han kjøp`te
I could cut hay just as well as he. And I liked to drive — he bought

se no hæs`ta dao', å æ li`ka te *dri`va dai', so kunde æ je`ra da be`re
horses then, and I liked to drive them; then I could do that better

elde hann'. Men han ar`baidde han' å'g hai`le ti'æ so læn`je so han va
than he. But he worked, too, all the time as long as he was

go' te, å han' blai' to' å åt'teti å'r å ni`e må`na gam`madl.
able to, and he lived to be eighty-two years and nine months old.

Å mo'r mi ho' blai tre' å syt'ti å'r gå`mål. Dai bæd`dje
And my mother got to be seventy-three years old. Both of them

død`de pao \*far'men so dai kjøp`te naor dai kåm' te Ame'rika.
died on the farm which they bought when they came to America.

7. *A Lesson in Norwegian.*

(Voss dialect from Sun Prairie; inf. 6P3, recorded June 21, 1941. Born in Town of Burke, Dane County, Wisconsin, in 1907, this man was vigorously interested in his dialect and his Norwegian heritage; his father immigrated in 1897. *Pronunciation:* same as for speaker of selection 1).

Men dao', naor æg va aot`te ao'r gam`madlu, so byn`t e pao sku`len
But then, when I was eight years old, I started to go to school

hæ'r i Ame'rika, å da' va al't e kunna sai`a pao æn`guls va »yes and
here in America, and all that I could say in English was »yes and

no«. Men æg had`de ain go'u kamera't, na`bokamera't mæ' mæg, so
no«. But I had a good friend, a neighbor friend, with me, who

jækk' pao sku`len mæ' mæg, å han' va tål`daren min, å naor
went to school with me, and he was my interpreter, and when

dai snak`te æn`guls te mæg, so skåd`d æ pao kamera'ten min, å so
they talked English to me, I looked at my friend, and then he

fårtål'de han mæ'g da pao når'sk dao, ka va' da dai sa' te mæg.
told me in Norwegian what it was that they were saying to me.

Å du kan væ sik'ker pao' attu dai lo' ain hai'l de'l. Å nao'r æ kåm
And you can be sure that they laughed plenty. And when I got

hai'm dao, so va' kje da len`dji før æg bydd te' å så ville bæ`re jus`ka
home then, it wasn't long before I offered to start just chattering

æn`guls. Å so sa' o mo'r, nai Johan'nes, no mao' kje du
in English. And then mother said, »No, Johannes, now you mustn't

snakka æn'guls hai`ma, fy viss du snakka æn'guls te mæ'g, so vi'kj æg
talk English at home, for if you talk English to me, I won't

sva`ra dæg. Å æg trud`de kje ne mo'r æ'g, attu ho vil`de in`kje
answer you«. And I didn't believe mother, that she wouldn't

sva`ra mæg pao æn'guls viss e snak`ka te ne pao æn`guls. Men du kan
answer me in English if I talked to her in English. But you can

væ sik'ker pao', attu al't ho jo`re va nætt' te å ris`ta pao hå`ve sitt. Å e
be assured that all she did was just to shake her head. And I

*læu't snakka når'sk, å dan' væ'jen æ' da at æ *vai't ko' te å snakka*
had to talk Norwegian, and that is why I know how to talk

når'sk i da'g, tak`ka førel'dre mine fy da', fy da va
Norwegian today; (I can) thank my parents for that, for it was

dai' so lær`de mæg te å snak`ka dette hær go`e når`ske sprao'kje mitt.
they who taught me to speak this good Norwegian language of mine.

8. *The Parson and the Sexton.*

(Telemark dialect from Iola; inf. 8L3, recorded Nov. 23, 1942.
Born in Heddal, Telemark, in 1872, this man immigrated in 1893
and spent most of his time on a farm north of Iola, Wisconsin.
He preferred to speak Norwegian to English, and found little
occasion to use the latter language. *Pronunciation:* EN vowels;
r is untrilled before dentals (*l, n, s, t, d*); *kj* is [tç].)

To'r H., han var når's'k sko`telæ'rar — rel`ijonslæ'rar hær
Tor H. was a Norwegian schoolteacher — religious teacher here

i — å læng`e va'r æ — va'r æ i sæk's å sæk'sti å'r, å han hål't sko`te
for — how long was it — for sixty-six years, and he taught school

te no`en da`er før han dø`e. Dæ va'r en svæ'r sel`skapska`r
till a few days before he died. He was an extremely sociable fellow

å en fæ't skrø`nema`ker. Han kunne fårtet`a skrø`ner hei`le da'gen å
and a terrific storyteller. He could tell stories all day and

hei`le nat'ta. Å' ja', de' va væ't. Men e kan' ikkje gått' fårtet'a dem
all night. I should say so. But I can't very wery well tell them

upp'att, e ha glem`t bort my`e ta dem, mes`tede¹la ta dem.
now; I have forgotten many of them, most of them.

Han va klåk`kar hæ'r. Han va klåk`kar i mangfål'die å'r.
He was the sexton here. He was sexton for a great many years.

Så va' H. sli'k han lik`te e glas ø'l óu' han sum`tier,
Now H. was this way that he liked a glass of beer now and then,

å så' når n kóm' i gått' sel`ska¹p, så kan`sje sum`tier så ble de
and when he was in good company, he might sometimes take a

li`te gran'ne før my`e óu'. Så hadde præs'ten fått re`de på det`ta hæ'r ein
tiny drop too many. Then the pastor had heard about this

gong' at n hadde vö`ri i eit \*bi`rkala¹s å skulle je' n
once that he had been at a beer party and was going to give him

skrøf't. Men så kóm' n me de' på så ra'r ein må`te, han
a reprimand. But he came out with it in so strange a way. He

sa' de' atte, æ'g — æ drøm`te æ va i him`meri¹ke sa n, å dæ'r kóm æg
said, 'I dreamt that I was in heaven,' he said, 'and there I went

inn' i dæ' hu'se såm va te'låg¹å fø klåk`karæn sa n, å dæ'r
into the house that was prepared for sextons', he said, 'and there

hål't dæm no fæ'lt te hu's sa n. Di var slet'tes ikke sjik`kelege,
they were carrying on something awful. They weren't decent at all,

å di var hø`gmæ¹lte å di hadde drik`kanes *ståff' dær,
and they were loud-mouthed and they had stuff to drink there,

å di var slet'tes ikke sjik`kelige. Jas`så, sa H., jo're du de'. Ja e'g
and they weren't decent at all. 'Is that so,' said H. 'Well, I

óu' drøm`de sa n, at eg va i him`meri¹kje, å kóm inn' i dæ rom'me
also dreamt,' said he, 'that I was in heaven, and went into the room

såm atte va te'låg¹å fø præs`tæn. Men dæ'r fan's ikkje ein ei`naste
that was prepared for the pastors. But there I didn't find a single

præs't.
pastor.'

9. From Childhood to Courtship.

(Setesdal dialect from Waupaca County; inf. 8M2, recorded Sep. 15, 1942. Born near Scandinavia, Wisconsin, in 1884, this man had a remarkably detailed knowledge of his parents' dialect; they immigrated from Bygland in 1861. He farmed until 1924, when he moved to town. *Pronunciation:* WN vowels, with marked diphthongization, so that long *i* is [ei], *y* is [uy], and *u* is [eu]; *æi* approaches *ai;* *å* is low back, about like E *a* in *law;* *æ* is low front, about like E *a* in *hat; kj* is [tç].)

Eg va føtt′ i Våpæk′ka *Kao′nti, *Tao′n åv Far′mington, i å′rī
I was born in Waupaca County, Town of Farmington, in the year

at′ten hun`dre fi′r å fi′rs. Mi`ne fårel′dre va føtt′ i Når`ge,
eighteen hundred eighty-four. My parents were born in Norway

å kåm′ ti detti lan′di i at′ten hun`dre å æi′n å træss′. Dæ
and came to this country in eighteen hundred sixty one. They

ha′ æin li`ten gu′te so va fødd′ i Når`ge, men den′ dø`e på sjø′en.
had a little boy who was born in Norway, but it died on the sea.

Då dæ kåm′ ti det`ti lan′di, då \*set`la dæ på en *ho`msted¹de som e′
When they came to this country, they settled on a homestead

no *Tao′n åv Far′mington. På den`ne \*ho`msted¹den va dær el′leve
in what is now Town of Farmington. On this homestead eleven

bonn′ so va fød′de, å i′eg va den yng`sti. Då eg va gå`må¹le
children were born, and I was the youngest. When I was old

no′g te gå′ på sku`li, so djekk′ eg på sku`li borti et *ai′ris-setlamen¹t
enough to go to school, I went to school in an Irish settlement

som di kad`da Sjør′tn, å du væi′t kos dæ *ai′risan æ′ ti
which they called Sheridan, and you know how those Irish are

slå`ast. Å ja då′ jikk dæ fæl′t, ska e sæi′ dikkå. Ja
at fighting. Yes, then things were pretty tough, I tell you. Well,

då′ e had jen`je på sku`li di′er ti eg va′ en træt`ten å′r,
when I had gone to school there until I was about thirteen years,

så sæn`te dæ meg på en kjør`kjesku¹li som dæ kad`da *Akade´mien.
they sent me to a church school which they called »the Academy«.

Di'er jekk´ eg te eg var en syt`ten å'r, men så mått´ eg
There I went until I was about seventeen, but then I had to go

tiba´kers på *far´men å a`rbæi på *far´men. Å ja', då' ska eg sæi' deg
back to the farm and work on the farm. Then I'll tell you

mi a`rbæide om da`gan, å som` mi drakk´ å slos't om
we worked in the daytime, but oh how we drank and fought at

net´tan. Får du væi't sæ`tesdø¹lingan, dæi' hev sto`re stæi`na å
night. For the Setesdøls, you know, they have huge rocks and

kjæm`peka¹ra!
powerful men!

Då eg blæi' u't i kju`geårsal`deren, då fo'r eg mæ åsså ræi`se på fri`eri.
When I got into my twenties, I started to go a-courting.

Så fann´ eg meg æi rek`tik fi'ne djen`te uppi æin li`ten by'e som dæ
I found a really fine-looking girl up in a little town they

kad`dar Skana´vi, å fai'r henni han va' en *stå¹rki´pari. Men du
call Scandinavia, and her father was a store-keeper. But you

væi't dæ læi`aste som va', va' at ho ha to' små' sys´ta, å når e'
know the worst of it was that she had two little sisters, and when I

kåm på fri`eri, so vil`le ikkje des`si små`djen¹tun led`dje sek. Å du
went courting, these little girls wouldn't go to bed. And you

væi't koss de æ', då ti'eke du mæ' deg noko *kæn´di liksåm
know how it is; then you take with you some candy as a kind

ti låk`kema¹te, å så vil dæi' sitje up`pi å iete *kæn´di. Men så
of bribe, and then they want to sit up and eat the candy. But then

tæn`kt eg mæ meg sjø'le, e sill finne på' æi`kårt. Så sa' eg de mæ' dæ
I thought to myself, 'I'll figure out something.' So I said to them

at, dæn' såm fys´te kan avklæ' seg ska få fæm' *sæn't. Ja
that the one who first could undress would get five cents. Then

så bejyn´te dæ te ri`v av sekå klæ`in så at nap`pan fæu'k. Mæn
they started tearing off their clothes so the buttons flew. But

då' ska eg sæi' deg at gam`la tok ja't å' meg, jår at
then I tell you the old lady gave me the dickens for making the

små`djen`tun ræi'v sun'de klæ`in si. Mæn djæn`ta jækk' eg li'k
little girls tear their clothes to pieces. But I got the girl just the

væ'l. So' blæi' mi djip`te i å'ri nit`ten hun`dre å
same. Then we were married in the year nineteen hundred and

tret`ten op`pi en li`ten by'e såm dæ kad`dar Hå'kens. Då mi
thirteen up in a little town which they call Hawkins. When we

ha' no blitt jip`te, å mi ha hatt' kvels-ma'te, so kjæ'm *hor`naran. Å
were well married, and had had supper, the 'horners' came. Oh,

ja dæ slo' på sa`gi å dæ ring`la bjød`du å dæ skæu't.
they hammered on saws and they rang bells and they shot off guns.

Ja så mått' eg u't åsså dji'ev dæ noko pæ`ning, så at dæ kunn få kjøp't
So I had to go out and give them some money so they could buy

seg noko ø'l.
some beer.

10. *Homesteading in Wisconsin.*

(Hedmark dialect from Coon Prairie; inf. 10C1, recorded Nov. 2, 1942. Born in Stange, Hedmark, in 1860, this man immigrated with his parents in 1867; he spoke rapidly, sometimes stumbling over his words. *Pronunciation:* EN vowels (overrounded *å, o, u*); *r* untrilled before dentals; *ll, nn, dd* slightly palatalized after short vowels).

*Væ'l, de' ska je nå jårtet'ja dæ på den' må'ten, de va'r den`ne hær're
Well, I'll tell you about it in this way: it was this here forty

jørt'i *æ'kern såm n *pa' — såm n ja'r *ho`msted'de da veit du. Så
forty acres which pa — which father homesteaded you see. Then

kjøf'te n da', de va en *plass' såm var tett' me' øss såm vart u'tsål't.
he bought — it was a place that was near by us which was sold.

Så sto` de att' nå gam`le hu'ser, sæ`rsjil't et sto'rt pe'nt
There were some old houses left there, especially a nice, large

*gre`neri. Så kjøf`t n fa`r de', å så fløf`te n detta de`r bort på denne hærre
granary. Then father bought it and moved it over on this here

*klei`men såm n to`g opp, mæs`som inn i sjøf`ve *brus`ken få je
claim that he took up, right in the midst of the brush, as you might

kal`le de. Den' \*ve`gen byg`d n opp de', å fækk' de nåk`så — de vart li`te
call it. That way he built it up, and got it quite — it was small,

men vi gred`de de da. Å se`a vi vart' litt' sto`re da, så —
but we got along all right. And after we got a little bigger then —

by`nte vi å \*grub`be veit du å, *kli`re, å \*grub`be, å bren`te.
we started to grub, you see, and cleared and grubbed and burned.

Te slut`ten så vart' de så em fækk ei' ku', å så' vart' de så de vart to'
At last it got so they had a cow, and then it got so there were two

ku`er å — Men je' va' itte mæ' så fæt't my`e he`me je, på den'
cows, and — But I wasn't along so very much at home, for the

må`ten atte da je vart ni', åt`te på de ni`ende å`re
reason that when I got to be nine, eight going on my ninth year,

så, kåm' de ei`n ta na`boa å vil`le je skulle kåm`ma bort te hæn`nom å
one of the neighbors came and wanted me to come over to him and

va`ra de`r, så skulle je få' ma't å klæ`er, å go`e klæ`er skull je få', men
stay there; then I would get food and clothes, good clothes, but

itt`nå an`na før — få' ma't å klæ`er. De`r vart' je i tre'
nothing else for — get food and clothes. There I stayed for three

å`r, unta`gen je va`r så nem`me de' at je flæu`g hem`att å byt`te
years, except that I was close enough so that I ran home to change,

veit du, klæ`er å, vas`ken å, tæll de' at je hadde gått'
you know, clothes and my wash, until I had gone to the minister

før præs`ten.
for confirmation.

Da' va`r vi he`me, to' tre' ta øss' brø`rn, å jo`rde me`re
Then we stayed at home, two or three of us brothers, and did

grub`bing. Så' jo`rde vi dom`ning da, får å få \*kli`re ta dær,
more grubbing. Then we had a work bee, and got it all cleared off,

å *bræk'ke dæ, kjæm' je hæu'. Å klun'dre klun'dre klun'dre den'
and broke the soil, I remember. And putter, putter, putter that

*væ'gen, tæll de' att vi — så' kjøf'te vi et par kæt'ver ta ei'n ta
way, until we — then we bought a couple of calves from one of

di an'dre na'boa op'på dær ne'åver, inn åt Blækk' River rå'den såm vi
the other neighbors up there by the Black River road where we

nå' gå'r, å a'vte opp dom' tæll dem vart' litt' åver
go nowadays, and raised them until they got a little more than

to' å'r, så by'nte vi å *bræk'ke dom. Da vi fækk' dem
two years old. Then we started to break them. When we got

i tre' å'rs al'dern så vart' dem sto're nåkk¹. Da by'nte
them to the age of three they were big enough. Then we started

vi å kjø're, je' å e'n a'en bro'r min. I frå' je va' en
to drive them, I and another brother of mine. So from the time

sæk'sen å'r tæll je vart' en søt'ten, at'ten, å opp' tæll nit'ten
I was sixteen until I was seventeen, eighteen, and up to nineteen

å'r va' je he'me da, å jøf'te desse an'dre brø'rn min
years, I stayed at home and helped these other brothers of mine

å *kli're *å klire, å va bo'rte bæ're noen støn'ner i mel'lom den'na ti'a.
to clear and clear, and was away only for short periods in this time.

Så' ætter de', så vei't du je to'k ittno får min ei'en de'l,
Then after that, you see I didn't take anything for my own part,

rei'ste u't te Min'neso'ta, ar'bedde de'r ei'n såm'mar. Å høu'st å
I went out to Minnesota, worked there a summer. And fall and

vå'r, da je va' i nit'ten å at'ten å opp' te kju'geårs
spring, when I was nineteen, eighteen, and up to twenty years of

al'dern, så to'k je på¹ svæ're *grub'bejab'ber, lang't noløu'sti hær, ve
age, I took big grubbing jobs, far up northeast of here, by

Norr'wå'k di kaller.
Norwalk as they call it.

11. A Fisherman and a Frog.

(EN dialect from Coon Prairie; inf. 10C2, recorded Nov. 2, 1942. Born near Westby, Wisconsin, in 1874, this man was a lively, interested informant who had many stories to tell. His father immigrated from Øyer in Gudbrandsdalen in 1857 and his mother from Gol, Hallingdal, as a child. *Pronunciation:* EN vowels; *r* is untrilled before dentals; long dentals are not palatalized).

Dæ va'r ei'n gong' vi va'r dær, han Ole Jan'sen å dåk'ter Ræk've,
Once we were there, Ole Johnson, and Doctor Reque,

Eijil Ei'jilsen. Vi va'r i Mina'kva å fis'ke, dæ va'r en ann' gong dæ',
Eiel Eielson. We were at Minocqua fishing, that was another time,

å så skul vi — dæ va' omtræn't klokka — dæ va' om fø'remiddan klokka
and then we were — it was about — it was in the forenoon around

ti' øl'løv, vi skulle u't å fis'ke om æt'temid'dan. Så
ten or eleven, and we were going out fishing in the afternoon. Then

skulle vi finna frås'k te *bei'te, å e' å n Ei'jil hel't på å *hun'ta
we had to find frogs for bait, and I and Eiel were busy hunting

frås'k u'te runt *ka'tijen dær, å n Ræk've han' va kåkk', han' dræiv
for frogs around the cottage there, and Reque was cook, he was

å kåk'ke. Han Ole Jan'sen han' bar inn vat'ten å ve'. Han tør'de
busy cooking. Ole Johnson carried in water and wood. He didn't

itte å ta' frås'k, han va rædd' frås'ken, han O'len, han tør'de itte
dare to hunt frogs, he was afraid of the frogs, Ole was, he didn't

å ta' ti frås'ken. Så kom' n O'le fårbi' me' opp
dare to handle the frogs. Then Ole walked past me on his way up

te *kat'tijen, så sa'n atte, dæ ligg' en frås'k u'tafår hu'se sa
to the cottage, and he said, 'There's a frog outside the house', he

n, e la' hat'ten min å'ver n e' sa n, du kan ta' n du sa n.
said, 'I laid my hat over it,' he said, 'you can take it', he said.

Ja e to'k frås'ken, å så jikk' e inn' åt Ræk've, så sa' e
Well, I took the frog, and then I went in to Reque, and I said,

nå' ska vi ha' litt mo'ro mæ O'le. Fan't e en *kå'ṛd, å så
'Now we'll have some fun with Ole'. I found a cord and then I

batt' e frå — leg'gen på frås'ken i ban'ne, å så batt' e de fas't i ban'ne
tied the fro — the leg of the frog to the band, I tied it to the hat-

på hat'ten, å så jikk' je u't å la' n dær hat'ten ha li'je, så
band and then I went out and laid it where the hat had been lying,

lå'g frås'ken un'ner hat'ten. Å han Ei'jil kom itt — han O'le kom itte
so that the frog lay under the hat. And Eiel didn't — Ole didn't

mei'r i hæu'g hat'ten å, vi' hadde mid'dan å, to'k åss ei go' stunn'
remember the hat, and we had our dinner. It took a good while

fø'r vi sku rei'se på fis'king, så sku vi nå u't å
before we got ready to leave for the fishing, we were going out

fis'ke al'le sam'men. Så had'de e fårtær't di an'dre detta hæ'r atte,
fishing all of us. Then I had told the others about this, that the

frås'ken lå'g unner hat'ten hass O'le. Å da vi jikk' ut al'le sam'men, så
frog lay under Ole's hat. And when we all went out, Ole said, 'I've

sa' n O'le, ja e' må ha' hat'ten min sa n. Så ftæu'g n sta sku ta' hat'ten
got to have my hat,' he said. He hurried over to pick up his hat,

sin n O'le, å to'k hat'ten ifrå bak'ken å, sku sæt'ta n på
and picked it up from the ground, and was going to put it on his

hug'gue. Han fækk' n oppi an'sikte, så dang'la frås'ken i an'sikte
head. When he got it as far as his face, the frog dangled right in

på n. O'le kas'ta både hat'ten å al't sam'men, han tøṛ'de itte å — *Væ'l,
his face. Ole tossed away the hat and all, he didn't dare to — Well,

vi hadde my' mo'ro mæ n Ole Jan'sen. Han æ'r dø' nå'. Men han
we had a lot of fun with Ole Johnson. He's dead now. But he

hadde my' mo'ro mæ fis'ke, han lik'te å fis'ke.
had a lot of fun fishing, he enjoyed fishing.

12. *A German Boy among the Norwegians.*

(Lower Gudbrandsdal dialect from Coon Prairie; inf. 10C14, recorded Oct. 31, 1942. Born near Westby, Wisconsin, in 1894, this man had farmed all his life; he was of German ancestry, but learned Norwegian in his boyhood, as explained in this selection. *Pronunciation:* EN vowels, but his *å* is low back, about like E *a* in *law; ll* is palatalized; his *ł* is identical with his E *r.*)

*Væll', da vi' var små', så måt`te vi tał`a tys'k, å da
Well, when we were small we had to talk German, and when

vi vok`s upp da ma så måt`te vi læ`re \*eng'lisj å — å når vi byn`te
we grew up, we had to learn English, and — and when we started

å gå på sku`łe da ma, så måt`te vi lære nårs'k. Vi *le`vet i et nårs'k
to go to school, we had to learn Norwegian. We lived in a Norwegian

*sæt`telmen¹t å ung`a såm jikk' på sku`ełn (skulen) så kun`ne m itt
settlement, and the children who went to the school didn't know

anna nårs'k. Å da' måt`te vi læ`re nårs'k,
anything but Norwegian. So then we had to learn Norwegian,

hell så ha' itt vi kunna tał`a ve om. (Var det andre tyske
or else we couldn't have talked to them. (Were there other German

familier?) *Væll', dæ va' ei'n fa`meli tæll', on`keln min lev`de i
families?) Well, there was one other family; my uncle lived in

såm'må des`trik¹te dær. Da e jikk' på sku`ełn, så va ung`an hass'
the same district there. When I went to school, his children were

vak`sin dom, så dom jikk' itte på sku`łe dom. (Hva syntes foreldrene dine
grown, so they didn't go to our school. (How did your parents like

om at du lærte norsk?) Ja', dm lik`te de. Dm sin`nes
it that you learned Norwegian?) Oh, they liked it. They thought

de va gått' får ung`an å læ`re å tał`a fårsjel'lige spro'k.
it was good for the children to learn to talk different languages.

13. *A Student Rebellion at Luther College.*

(Book language with dialect traits from Jæren as spoken at
Coon ·Prairie; inf. 10N1, recorded Nov. 4, 1942. Born in Sokndal
in 1849, this man immigrated with his parents in 1857 and became
one of the earliest students at Luther College after its establishment in 1861. But he returned to farming and became a community
leader in the Coon Prairie region. For Anderson's own account
of the following episode see *Life Story,* 47ff. *Pronunciation:* WN
vowels, with very slight diphthongization; *r* is uvular; *kj* is [tç].)

Dæ var streng`e reg'ler i den' ti'. Får eksem'pel, vi va
There were strict rules at that time. For instance, we were

fårbutt' te gå te by'en fåru'ten lå'v. Om vi træng`te å kjø`pe
forbidden to go to town without permission. If we needed to buy

lite grann', så måt`te vi spør`re om lå'v eller skri`ve våre nav`ne på en
something, we had to ask for permission or write our names on a

tav`le får å kåmme te by'en. Å så va der
bulletin board to be allowed to go to town. And then there were

my`e an`dre re'gler såm sy`ntes væ`re kansje nåk'så streng`e. Vi måtte
many other rules which seemed to be quite strict. We had to

sa`ge vår e`gen ve' når vi bren`te — vi hadde ba`re åv'n den' ti' i Lu'ter
saw our own wood — we had nothing but stoves that time at Luther

Ka¹ledsj byg`ning — å sa`ge å hug`ge vå'r ve', å så' var vi på'lakt
College — saw and chop our wood, and then we were required

å så sa`ge å hug`ge ve' får læ`rerne... Når dær sku
to saw and chop wood for the teachers... When there was going

være præs`tekonferen¹s så blei dær no`en av ele'vene u'dvalt te å pusse
to be a pastoral conference, some of the pupils were chosen to shine

sko'ene deres. Å Rasmus An'dersen han va e'n av dei' så sy`ntes
their shoes. And Rasmus Anderson was one of those who thought

det`te jekk' får vitt'. Dæ va' kje fri'he¹d nåkk'.
this went too far. There was not enough freedom.

Så' fikk han' i stann' en slak's — en slaks *straí'k, å så fekk' han
So he organized a kind of strike, and he got

no'en å skrí've — han skreí'v opp' fårsjel'lige ting' så vi ville
someone to write — he wrote up various things which we wanted

være fri', å så fårsjel'lige ting' så vi fårlang'te vi ville ha'. Vi
to be free from, and various things which we demanded. We

ville ha' me'r ret'tighe\der å me'r fri'he\d. Så va' dæ kje
wanted to have more rights and more freedom. Now it was not

me'ningen at den'ne he'r — den'ne så vi hadde skreve on'ne, skulle opp'
the intention that this — this that we had signed should come up

får dæ førs'te, dær sku en komite' gå opp' te profes'sor
to begin with, a committee was supposed to go up to Professor

La'rsen å så fårtel'le va vi' fårlang'te, å prø've å få' dette uden å
Larsen and tell him what we asked for, to try to get it without

tving'e sei ijen'nem... Å så' va der en ong' præs'tesønn[1], han'
forcing it through. And then there was a young minister's son, he

ville ås'så skrive on'ner, men Rasmus An'dersen han ville ikkje ha' hans
wanted to sign it too, but Rasmus Anderson wouldn't have his

on'nerskrif\t. Han sa', du e får ong' te å skrí've, han va ba're træt'ten
signature. He said, you are too young to sign, he was only thirteen

å'r gammel. Å så' blei der præs'tekonferen\s, da vi' hålt jus't på'
years old. And then the pastoral conference met, just while we

me det'te hæ'r ve *Lu'ther Kal'ledsj. Så' jekk' han' te fa'r sin
were busy with this at Luther College. Then he went to his father

å fårtel'te om det'te...
and told about this...

Å så' blei Rasmus An'dersen kalt fram' får præs'te-
And then Rasmus Anderson was called before the pastoral

konferen\sen. Så fårtel'te Rasmus And'ersen sel'v da han fårtel'te mei
conference. This is how Rasmus Anderson himself told it to me

nå' sis't e ta'lte mæ an. Da han ble kal't fræm',
now the last time I talked with him. When he was called before

så sa'd præs`terne, he`le præs`tekonferen¦sen di sa'd
them, the ministers sat, the whole pastoral conference, they sat

li'ksåm i en hall`sir¦kel, dæ'r på \*hå'len. Å så' sæt`te profes'sor La`rsen
in a kind of semi-circle there in the hall. And then Professor Larsen

en sto'l mitt' i' dæ'r, å så sei`e an te profes'sor An'dersen
placed a chair right in the middle, and told Professor Anderson

at han sku sæt`te sei dæ'r. Ja', så blei' dær stil't, ing`en
that he should sit down there. Well, then there was a silence; no one

sa' no te han (so) sa'd dær. Så sei`e Rasmus An'dersen,
said anything to him (who) sat there. Then Rasmus Anderson said.

ær dæ jei' så ska være få`rmann¦ får den`ne fårsam'ling? Da' vak`na
'Am I supposed to be the chairman of this gathering?' Then Professor

natu'rlivi¦s profes'sor La`rsen. Han var no ås'så his`sig. Ær du
Larsen woke up of course. He was quite angry too. 'Are you

u`fårskam¦met ås'så sa an.
impertinent too,' he said.

Ja' så blei' dæ te dæ' at di had`de fårhø're å'ver han då.
Well, so they got started on a cross-examination of him.

Å Ras'mus An'dersen vil`le ikkje je' inn', han va' no stri' å sti'v.
And Rasmus Anderson wouldn't give in; he was pretty stubborn.

Ja', så blei dæ bestæm't så' at han sku vi`sast u¦t, å så blei dær e'n
Well, so it was decided that he would be expelled, and then one

av profes'sorne såm ette Si'vers, han skulle al'tså ta
of the professors whose name was Sievers, he was supposed to take

An'dersen opp' te væ`relse sitt, så han sku få pak`ke *tron'ken sin. Å så
Anderson up to his room, so that he could pack his trunk. And so

fekk' han dæ', å så va' dæ kvæl'len. Å då han hadde fått
he got that done, and then evening had come. When he had gotten

pak`ket *tron'ken, så sa' di di sku ta *tron'ken ne' om
his trunk packed, they said they would take the trunk down in the

mår`nen, men han' sku u't me dæ sam`me. Å så' — så', ja', je sto'
morning, but he had to leave at once. And then — well I stood

å så' på då profes'sor Si'vers, han kom dri`vande mæ an,
there and saw it when Professor Sievers came dragging with him,

ja`ga an fø`re seg, e sto' å så' på dæ, han kåm
chased him in front of him; I stood there looking at it as he came

dri`vande ne' mæ' an ne' trap'pen dæ'ran, å dre'v han
dragging him along down the steps there, and drove him

ne', å sa', gå' fo'rt, gå' fo'rt, sku sjy`ve på' an,
ahead, and said, 'Walk fast, walk fast!' And he shoved him so

han sku gå'. An'dersen va' ikkje i sli'ge has't, men
that he should hurry. Anderson wasn't in quite such a hurry, but

han sjy`vde på', å han sku gå' — han sku' kje ståp'pe, å snak`ke te
he kept shoving so he would go — he mustn't stop and talk to

noen. Å så' blei han ja'kt ne', ne'åver trap'pen u't,
anyone. And then he was chased down, down the stairs and out;

Si'vers fulte et`ter han¹, han ble ja'gd såm en hunn'.
Sievers followed him, he was chased like a dog.

Så stop`te an då', då an kåm' u`tenfår *kå'ledsjen, så'g
Then he stopped when he got outside the college, and looked

teba'ke. Nå', sa Si'vers, gå' sa n, gå' sa n. Så
back. 'Well,' said Sievers, 'go away,' he said, 'go away'. Then

måt`te an ne', å så u't. Då nes`te mid'dag, då' hadd eg æ'ren
he had to go down and away. Next day at noon I had an errand

te by'en. Då' kåm' e å så'g Rasmus An'dersen, å så' kåm an u't
to town. Then I went to see Rasmus Anderson, and he came out

a hotel'le, å så snak`te te' me å ba' je sku ta mæ' en li`ten
of the hotel, and talked to me and asked me to take along a little

*no't te ei`n a klas`sekamera¹tene, Ju`ve. Men an va' kje så mo`tig da'.
note to one of the classmates, Juve. But he wasn't so brave then.

Da' bejyn`te tå`rene å tril`le litt ne' a kjin'nan på an, han hadde
Then the tears began rolling a little down his cheeks; he had had

fått' betæn'kt seg. Men så måt`te an avste'.
a chance to think it over. But then he had to leave.

14. *In the Good Old Days.*

(Upper Gudbrandsdal dialect from Coon Valley; inf. 11B1, recorded Aug. 22, 1942. Born in Coon Valley, Wisconsin, in 1870, this woman was still an active user of her parental dialect. Her parents immigrated from North Fron in 1855 and 1866, respectively. *Pronunciation:* EN vowels; short vowels occur before short consonants, even under stress; post-stress *e* is mid-front; *ll* and *nn* are often preceded by an *i*-glide and are themselves slightly palatalized in this case; *r* is untrilled before dentals; *s* before *l* and after *r* is [sh].)

Ja de va' da æn Kres`tafer å Ain`ne Ba`kli'en va i fys`te
Well, it was when Kristofer and Anne Baglien were in the first

hu'se dem ha' ette dem va kom`me her, e vei't itte hå ti'
house they had after they had come here, I don't know what time

de va. Å så kom' n Knu't Rul`lainn å sånn' hass', dem ha vor`e
it was. And then Knut Rulland and his son came; they had been

på *præ'rien æll nåinn' sta'n å så fått' nogo mjø't — nogo *flæu'r
up on the prairie or somewhere and gotten some meal (Norw. flour)

— æll å' de va, å da dem kom' di't, så va
— some flour — or whatever it was, and when they got there,

dem in`ne der, å så va' de nåk`så lang't åt Rul`lainn deinn'
they came in; it was quite far to (the) Rulland (farm) at that

tia, læing'er hæll de e nå', så dem *ha`ta å gå'. Å så sa n dæ' n
time, farther than it is now, so they hated to leave. And then

Knu't Rul`lainn, at viss du' vil hæille mjøt'k no sa n, så ska e'
Knut Rulland said, "If you will supply the milk, I'll supply the

hæille mjø't, så ko`ke vi græu't å så æ't vi tesa'men. Å ho
flour; then we'll cook porridge and then we'll eat together." And

bæs`tmo'r Bak`lien va så gła' ho kunn jær`a detta dæ'r, å så sa n
grandmother Baglien was so happy she could do that; but then

dæ' n Øs`ten sånn' hass Knu't, at næi sli'k som du' e' lel fa'r, sa n,
Østen, Knut's son, said, "How can you be like that, father, say

se'a sli'k sa n. Men når o bæs'tmo'r fårte'lde de
anything like that," he said. But when grandmother told about

*se'a, så sa' o o va' så' gla' sa o, får de va' itte my'y *flæu'r*
it later, she said she was so happy, for there wasn't much flour

deinn' tia te græu't. Så' ha dem græu't å mjæl'k å så
those days for making porridge. So they had porridge and milk,

e't dem ail'le tesa'men.
and they all ate together.

Deinn' tia måtte dem, når dem skull mål'å, så måtte dem
In those days, when they wanted to grind their flour, they had

reise li'ke te Preri du Sji'n. Nåinn' va' de såm
to go all the way to Prairie du Chien. There were some who were

*ræi'ste, å så kom' dem opp på *præ'rien, å da dem kom' di't, så vart*
going there, and then they got up on the prairie, and when they

dem inn'sno'ga, å kuin'ne itte komm' att,
they got there, they were snowed in, and couldn't get back again,

kuin'ne itte få' u'tatt las'se før te om vå'ren, kjør'de me
couldn't get their loads out again before spring; they drove with

uk'sæ, å når dem sku ræi'se åt Læk'råss, så måtte dem ræi'se um
oxen, and when they were going to Lacrosse, they had to go by

*Præ'ria æll um Væst'by, hæll *oppe dæ'r nåinn *plass', kuin'ne*
Prairie (du Chien) or by Westby, or up there somewhere; they

itte ræise um da'len, dæ va itte vai'g dæ'r ne
couldn't travel through the valley, for there wasn't any road down

jenom deinn' tia. Dæ va mang'e mi'l læing'er æll d e nå'.
through there at that time. It was many miles farther than it is now.

(Julebukk?) Å ja', dem jø'r de' en'da sumestess.
(Christmas mummery?) Oh yes, they still do that some places.

De bruk'te på væra mo'di mor'osamt de' fø'r i ti'n, får de va ba're
It used to be great fun in the old days, for there were only the

ung'dom'men i nab'ola'ge. Men nå' sia de vart *åt'emobi'ler,
young people of the neighborhood. But now since the automobiles

så kjem' dem *frå lang't å'v såm du it'te kjein'ne dem om dem
came, people come from far away whom you don't know even if they

tæ' tå se mas'kuinn, da æ' de itte nå mor'o mæi'r, får dæ' at dæ æ'
take off their masks; then it isn't any fun any more, because it's

så fræm'muint. Men deinn' tia de va be're ung'dom'men
so strange. But in those days when it was only the young people

i nab'oskap'e, så va de mo'di mor'osamt å jet'a på vemm' dem va', får
in the neighborhood, it was great fun to guess who they were, for

vi kjen'de dem så gått'...
we knew them so well...

Dem bruk'te på å ko'ke *mal'asi, de va' vel *mei'pel, *lønn'-
They used to cook molasses; I guess it was maple, maple

malas'i. Dem ha' nå sto're pæin'no, sto're lang'e pæin'no, dem va' vel
molasses. They had some big pans, big, long pans, they were some

en sæk's fo't lang'e, ten'kje e. Dem ha' dem burti — liksom en da't
six feet long, I think. They had them over — in a kind of valley

burti her. Å deinn' ti va de bjøinn' her. Å bjøinn'
over here. And that time there were bears here. And the bears

kom' ne¹ om nat'ta å så e't opp *mal'asien, li'ke så gått'
came down at night and ate up the molasses; they liked so well

dæ' som e søitt'. Ja de ver'kele sainn't de, får de va æn bæs't-
all kinds of sweet things. Yes, that's really true, for it was grand-

fa'r Ba'klin såm kok'te *mal'asien. Deinn' da'ṭen kail'le dem
father Baglien who cooked the molasses. That valley they call

*Mal'asida'ṭen te den da'g i da'g.
Molasses valley to this very day.

15. *Amusements in Coon Valley.*

(Biri dialect from Coon Valley; inf. 11C1, recorded Aug. 20, 1942. Born in that community in 1869, this man was well acquainted with the life of the valley and spoke its dialect without effort. His mother came from Biri in 1850, his father from Hol, Hallingdal, in 1849. *Pronunciation:* EN vowels, except that his *å* is low back, about like E *a* in *law; r* is untrilled before dentals; *ll* and *nn* are palatalized, also *tt* after front vowels; *s* before *l* and after *r* is [sh].)

Hæ'r i *set'lamæn'te så var æ svæ'rt te um'gang, ak'kerat li'k ei'ns
In this settlement there was lots of social life, just

såm all' di an'dre nårs'ke *set'lamæn'ter, æt'ter dæ' atte ong'dommen
as in all the other Norwegian settlements, after the young people

vart vøk'sin tæ'. Å da ha' dem nå no *pik'niker da ma om såm'marn, å
grew up. They used to have picnics in the summer; and (parties)

je'neste i ju'ḷ. I åt'tiå'rom så va' dem no svæ'r te å ha'
generally at Christmas. In the eighties it was common to have

denna ju'ḷemo'roa da, å da — mo'ro se de bæs'te dem kun'ne da,
this Christmas fun, and they amused themselves as best they could,

in'ne i hu'som, så lang't såm rom'me jikk' a'n, bå'de mæ å så mo'ro
inside the houses, as far as the room made it possible, both with

se mæ kjæ'ringa mæ sta'va, å u't å gå' på brann'vak't å,
playing 'old lady with the stick', and 'fireman's watch', and

sjæ'ra sjæ'ra ha'ver å, væ'va væ'va vøm'møt å — Å sit'tanes
'cutting the oats', and 'weaving the woolen cloth' — And of sitting

mo'ro så va' de å så prø've å pas'se på ring'en såm jikk' i
games there was one in which you tried to watch a ring that passed

fra ei' hann tæ einn a'enn, å ei'nn sto' nå i ring'a
from one hand to another, while some one stood inside the circle

å skull' nå prø've å få fatt' i denn' ring'en.
and was supposed to try to get hold of that ring.

Å', ei' ti' så va' de sto're brøl'leper hæ'r i da'la.
Oh, at one time there used to be big weddings in the valley.
Dæ vart' nå me'r å me'r å'vlak't dæ i sei'nere å'rom. (Hvordan bad de
That was given up more and more in later years. (How did they
*til bryllup?) *Væ'l, jen'este bruk'te (dem) vel på de*
invite guests to the wedding?) Well, usually they did it in the
nårs'ke vi'se da væ, at dem had'de en — bo'ar — bjo'ar å så jikk'
Norwegian way, I guess, that they had an — 'inviter' — who went
han' runn't å så ba' hann da åt brøl'lep. (Begravelser?) Begra'velsa
around and invited people to the wedding. (Funerals?) Funerals
va dæ nes'ten slik't da' å', at dem skulle gå' runn't å
were almost always this way too, that they had to go around and
be'a, å så skull' em nå kåm'ma te hu'se
invite people, and then they were supposed to come to the house
att, å så få' en ma'tbe'ta a ma æt'tepå. Men dæ va' nå ei'nn ting' va' nå i
again and get a bite to eat afterwards. But one thing here in
Kon Val'le hær, e visst al'ler tå' at dæ va' no slik't såm no sto're drek'-
Coon Valley was that I never heard of such big drinking parties
*kela'g ætter begra'velsen sm dm ha' i som'me *plas'ser.*
after funerals as they had in some places.

16. *The Newcomer's Distress.*

(Romsdal dialect from Coon Valley; inf. 11R1, recorded Aug.
21, 1942. Born in Erisfjord, Romsdalen, this woman emigrated
at the age of 18 and settled among speakers with a markedly different dialect, which contributed to the feeling of estrangement
described below. *Pronunciation:* EN vowels; her *å* is high, approaching *o;* *ll, nn, dd, tt* are palatalized, exc. *tt* and *dd* after *a;*
r is untrilled before dentals; *l* is unvoiced and palatalized before
t; r is unvoiced before *k.*)

Å', de føs̄'te e kåm' hit, so va' de no al't nytt' å ra'rt,
Oh, when I first came here, everything was new and strange,

får e had'de itte vore u't tu byg'den, a'ent enn e ha vo're te
for I hadn't been outside our valley, except that I had been to

by'en æi'n å a'en gonn'ja. Mæn når e kåm' hi't te Amæ'rika, so va' de
town a few times. But when I came here to America, everything

al't nytt', e måtte te' å le're opp'att all' ting'. Æi'n ting' va
was new, I had to learn everything all over again. One thing was

nå de', at de va mør'ke ne't. E kåm' åt on'kel å tan'te mine,
this that the nights were dark. I came to my uncle and aunt,

å når klåk'ka va en åt'te om kvæ'lln, so sa' o, nå'
and when it was about eight o'clock in the evening, she said, "Now

får vi finne i lam'pa å tænne i denn'. Lam'pa, sa e', e
we'll have to find the lamp and light it." "The lamp," said I, I

trud'de de' at e hadde ræis't på en plass' so sku være ly'sar å be'er
thought I had gone to a place which would be brighter and better

ænn Når'ge, å når e kåm' hit, so va de sann'deli mør'kare. De
than Norway, and when I came here, it was actually darker. It

vart be'kmørt¹ når de vart kvæ'lln. Det'te kunn e mæs'som all'der
got pitch dark when evening came. I could never really

kåmme å'ver, før de'r me oss' so sjæi'n so'la te klåk'ka va ha'l
get over this, for at home with us the sun shone until half past

el'lev om kvæ'lln, å litt' skom'ring — sjy'mt mett
ten in the evening, with a little twilight — darkening in the middle

på nat'ten. Men her' va de be'kende mørt', ja de va te' å mæ' må'n-
of the night. But here it was pitch dark; there was even moon-

sjinn¹ mett' på som'marn hæ'r. Å' e kun'ne itte kåmme å'ver
light right in the middle of summer here. Oh, I couldn't get over

det'ta fys̄'te som'marn.
that the first summer.

Å so en a'en teng' va *skri'ndø'rinn. E'n tå føs̄'te
And then another thing was the screen doors. One of the first

kvæl`lå e va' hær, so skull e gå u't ette vat'ten, å når e snud`de
evenings I was here, I was going out for some water, and when I

me att, so fækk e sjå' et dy'r so hing' mot lam`pen, mæ
turned back, I saw an animal hanging against the light, with its

rom`pa ne' å al`le fi`re fø'ten u't. E sat`te ti ett skre'k å slæp`te
tail down and all four feet out. I let out a scream and dropped

vass`byt'ta. Hann on'keln minn, hann' lo'. De va' itt no a'ent ænn en
the water pail. My uncle, he laughed. It wasn't anything but

katt' so hadde krabba oppå'ver *skri`ndø'ra, men e' kunn all'der
a cat which had crawled up the screen door, but I could never

tæn`kje på et slik't dy'r imot lam`pa om kvæ'lln. Ja',
imagine such an animal against the lamp in the evening. Yes,

ænn fa'r skrei'v åt mæ, spo`re me om e træf's. *Nå', e træf's nok
father wrote to me, asked me if I was happy. No, I certainly was

itte e'. Mæn tru'r du e' ville fårtæ'l hånå de'? Næi' da, de'
not happy. But do you think I would tell him so? Oh no, he

skull n it`te *vøl'i åver.
wasn't going to have to worry about that.

17. *Old-time Neighborliness.*

(Sogn dialect from Crawford County; inf. 12Q2, recorded Nov. 6, 1942. Born in Årdal, Sogn, in 1855, this man immigrated 18 months old with his parents. He became a community and church leader in the Gays Mills area; his dialect shows occasional book forms. *Pronunciation:* WN vowels, with very slight diphthongization; *kj* is [tç]; *sj* is [shj]; his *æi* approaches *ai*.)

Jel`psåmhe'ten va so' atte dær'som æi'n nab`bo hadde håi' u`te
Their neighborliness was such that if one neighbor had hay out

å da sao`g ut te reg'n, so to'k den an`dre nab`boen
in the field and it looked like rain, the other neighbor would take

uk'sadn sine å våg'ni, å ræis'te å jål'te nab'boen te jao' inn håi'e før
his oxen and go to help his neighbor get the hay in before

reg'ne kåm'. Å dær'som atte æi'n nab'bo hadde bru'k får nåke da'lar,
it rained. And if a neighbor needed a few dollars,

å han spur'de nab'boen om han had'de dæi, å han had'de dæi,
and he asked his neighbor if he had them, and he did have them,

so va dæ ja' — in'kje nåken *no't å ing'en ting' — men dæ va ing'en
the answer was yes — no note or anything — but no one ever

såm møs'te æin *sen't i dæi' da'ga. Dæ va jin't å le'va i dæi' da'ga.
lost a cent in those days. It was fine to be alive in those days.

Nab'boadn prøv'de ikkje te hågga æu'gudn or kåra're, å prø'va
Your neighbors didn't try to claw each others' eyes out and try

pao ad'le mao'ta te jao' i jrao' de dæ vet'la du hadde lak't opp',
in every way to take away from you what little you had laid up,

men dæi va jålp'såm å dæ sao'g ut te' atte dæi va li'kaso my'kje
but they were helpful and it looked as if they were just as much

*in'teres'ta i nab'boen so dæi va' i se sjå'l.
interested in their neighbors as they were in themselves.

Dæn vet'le jårsam'lingen i Kå'par Krikk' hadde ju'lajæstabo'
The little congregation in Copper Creek had Christmas parties

kår æi'naste ju'l. I dæi' daga so bruk'te dæi te bryd'dja te ju'l.
every Christmas. In those days they used to brew beer for Christmas.

Dæi had'de æin mann' so va inn'jløtt'. Han va' ijrao Had'lingda'l,
There was a man who had moved in. He was from Hallingdal in

Når'ge. Han va snik'kar, å han' jore bryd'jekjæ'ral, å so
Norway. He was a carpenter and he made brewing vessels and

kjøp'te me kå'parkje'l so va kåm'men ijrao Når'ge.
then we bought a copper kettle which had come from Norway.

Å so bryd'ja me ø'l. Å dæ va dæn æi'naste ti'i atte me sao'g lite
And then we brewed beer. And the only time we saw a little

suk'ker, so va' dæ ju'lehel'gi. Men kå' smaott'
sugar was at Christmas time. But no matter how skimpy

dæ va' ao're tiene, so lev'de me gått' i ju'li.
things were at other times, we lived well at Christmas.

Men i dæi' da'ga so va' de kje spur'smao'l um kå byg'd du
But in those days it was not a question of what community you

va' ifrao, ber're du va nårs'k å æin go' nab'bo. So'læis
came from, just so you were Norwegian and a good neighbor. It

so blæi e ve'l kjen'd me man'ge norfjo'ringa,
so happened that I got well acquainted with many from Nordfjord,

ise'r æin norfjo'ring so *lev'de pao væ'gen imødlo dæ'r so e' lev'de
especially one Nordfjord man who lived by the road between my

å en *plass' dæi kadla Fæ'rivill¹. Han va æin svær't
farm and a place they called Ferryville. He was an extremely

ven'nese'l mann', å dæi fys'te nor'fjo'ringa so
friendly and hospitable man, and the first Nordfjord people who

kåm'... so kad'la dæi gam'le An'ders Mål'drem on'kel. Æi'n da'g e kåm
came here... called old Anders Moldrem "uncle". One day I came...

...opp' te hu'sdø'ri åt Mål'drem, kåm' han' å vilde u't. So
up to Moldrem's house door, he came and was going out. Then

sa' an, gao inn' å sett de ne' sa n, e kjem at'te tras't. Ja',
he said, "Walk in and sit down," he said, "I'll be right back." Well,

han syn'te me inn i dæ' so me kadla pao æin'gelsk — "liv'ing roo'm." Å
he showed me into what we call in English, the "living room." And

e sæt'te me ne', dæ'r håi'rde e to' kvinn'fål'k prat'te uti kjø'ke.
I sat down, and there I heard two women talking out in the kitchen.

E hadde vå're so u'får sik'tig at e hadde tas'ka li'te mæ æi
I had been so careless that I had played around a little with a

no'rfjorjæn'ta. Å e fann' ut atte dæ' so dæi prat'te um
Nordfjord girl. And I found out that this was precisely what

va net'tupp dæ'. Den æi'ne sa' te den an'dre: Dæi sæi'e dæ
they were talking about. The one said to the other: "They say the

e gått' upp i rø'k mæ n Tås'ten Sæi'm å o An'na. Å
affair between Tosten Sime and Anna has gone up in smoke." Then

so svar`te den an`dre, å' jæu', kan`sje ho An'na æ li`ke se'l,
the other one answered: "Oh well, maybe Anna is just as well

han æ' kje an't æl æin lu`sesåg¹ning alli'kave'l!
off, for he's nothing but a lousy Sogning anyway!'"

18. Concerning Wells and Divining Rods.

(Nordfjord dialect from Crawford County; inf. 12R3, recorded Nov. 1, 1942. Born near Ferryville, Wisconsin, about 1890, this man was the son of an immigrant from Nordfjord. *Pronunciation:* WN vowels; his *ai* approaches *æi; j* is here written after *l* and *n* to mark a strong palatalization at the end of these consonants; *kj* is [tç]; *sj* is [shj]; *ng* is [ngg].)

*[Æ] va fød'de i Viskån'sin, *ne`e hær på Båk'krikkridd¹jene.*
[I] was born in Wisconsin, down here on Buck Creek Ridge. My

Fa'r min va An'ders, å mo'r mi va Ma'ri. Mo'r mi hon dø`e on'ge
father was Anders, and my mother was Mari. My mother died young;

hon, hon va' kje mai'r ell ått' å før'ti nå hon dø`e, femm' å træ`dve
she wasn't more than forty-eight when she died, thirty-five

å'r sia. Å fa'r min han dø`e ått' å fe'mti. Dai' va
years ago. And my father died fifty-eight years old. They were

små' når dai kåm å'ver, fa'r min va kje mai' ell fi`re
little when they came across; my father wasn't more than four

å'r når han kåm å'ver. Å mo'r mi va fårfæ'rdele ong' å'
years when he came. And my mother was extremely young

når hon kåm å'ver, hon va ber`re ai li`tor småjent'e. Vi prat`te ain hai'l
when she came across, she was only a little girl. We talked a

de'l når'sk hai`me. Æ jekk' — dæ va' kje fårfæ'rdele my`kje
lot of Norwegian at home. I went — there wasn't very much school

*å gå' på sku`le hæ'r — på når'skesku¹len. *Væ'l, du sje'r æ*
I could go to here — to the Norwegian school. Well, you see I

va den æl'ste tå gu'tene å fa'r min va i ton'ge sku'lde, å
was the oldest of the boys, and my father had a heavy debt, and

så kunn' kje han hy're [jelp] å e' læut vere hai'me å jel'pe ne.
and so he couldn't hire [help] and I had to stay home and help him.

Når æ bejyn'da å *dri've *ti'm i *fi'la, så va æg sæk's å'r ga'malj.
When I started to drive teams in the field, I was six years old.

Æ huk'sa fa'r — æ kann' kje huk'se, dæt'ta va i *fi'la, fa'r min
I remember father — I can't remember, this was in the field, father

fårta'lde mæ æ' va sæk's å'r å *ti'me var sju',
told me that when I was six years old and the team was seven,

han' dræi'v *si'daren, å så skulle æ'g *drive *ti'm på hår'va,
he drove the seeder and I was to drive the team with the harrow,

å så va' dæ ain bak'ke so vi jikk run't. Å så va han' på ai'
and then there was a hill which we went around. And he was on

si'e å såd'de, å så va æ' på hi' sie å hår'va.
one side of the hill sowing, while I was on the other harrowing.

Å så tik'te han dæ var så læn'je før han så'g noko te'
And then he thought it got to be such a long time since he had seen

mæ, å så rais'te han *kråss' *fi'la å kåm bur't te' mæ, å
me, and so he went across the field and came over to me and

dæ'r lå'g æ ba'k i hår'va å så'v. Æ hadde sætt' mæ ne' å kvi'le, å
there I lay behind the harrow asleep. I had sat down to rest, and

så' hadd æ såm'na, å *ti'me dæ sto' dær. Dæ' kan æ kje huk'se
then I had fallen asleep, and the team stood there. I can't remember

æg.
that.

Så va æ hai'me te æ va træ'dve å'r ga'malje å arbæd'de,
Then I was at home until I was thirty years old and worked;

så læut æg u't før mæ siø'l. Da va' dæ æ bejyn'da på *dril'je-
then I had to get out for myself. Then I started with the drilling

masji'na, *dril'ja *væll' — bryn'ja. Dæ kje my'kje
machine, drilling wells — "brynja" (Norw. word.) There isn't much

å fårtel'je om dæ'. Ak'kurat no' hell e på' å *dril'ja oppe hæ'r eit li`te
to tell about that. Right now I am drilling up here a little

styk`kje oppe. No' ær æ ne`re to' hun`dre å fæm' å før'ti fo't, å
ways off. Now I am down two hundred and forty-five feet, and

så blai æ *ståkk'. Dæ'r stå'r æ no'. (Bruker du ønskekvist?)
then I got stuck. There I stand now. (Do you use the divining

*Nå', dæ *arbai'e ikkje dæ hæ'r, dæ æ' ikkje noko gang'n i hæ'r på
rod?) No, that doesn't work here, there's no use in it here on the

Rid`jene — \*nå'. Æ viss`te ikkje no`ko um' dæ før el dæ va hæ'r får
Ridge — no. I didn't know anything about it before a

nåk`re å'r si`a nepå Rid'jen nere hæ'r, æ skulle dril'je
few years ago down here on the Ridge, when I was going to drill

åt en mann', Tås`ten Sai'm, dai kal`te n føre. Å så kå'm han' opp'
for a man, Tosten Sime they called him. And then he came up

når æ flut`te masji'na å ville sy`ne me kar æg skulle
when I moved the machine and wanted to show me where I should

set`je \*wæl'len. So kå'm han' å so en slækt`ninjen hass mæ kvær' sin
place the well. Then came he and a relative of his with a stick each.

kvi'st. Å so bjyn`na dai å gå ron't i tu'ne dær so dai trud`de
And so they started to walk around in the yard where they thought

dai ville ha' brun'jen dril`ja, å æ'g hadde ikkje sett' noko
they wanted to have the well drilled, and I hadn't seen anything

slek't før'ut. Så sæt`te dai... ne' på kne'nå, å så
like that before. Then they set... down on their knees, and then

jikk' dai run't i tu'ne å utå`ver å kå'm på ain plass', å dæ'r
they walked around in the yard until they got to a spot, and there

skulle æ sætt' na, dæ'r *arbæd'de kvis'ten. Æ kåm ne' i —
I was supposed to put it, there the twig worked. I got down into

"mud" å å`pninga å al't sli'kt, dæ' va dæ kvis'ten arbæd'de på!
mud and openings and all kinds of things like that, and that's
what made the twig work!

19. The Jew who Spoke Norwegian.

(Suldal dialect from Elroy; inf. 13N1, recorded Nov. 28, 1947. Born in Suldal, Norway, in 1890, this man immigrated in 1908 and made his home near Elroy, Wisconsin. *Pronunciation:* WN vowels, but without perceptible diphthongization of long vowels; short *a* is more front than long *a; æu* is [əu]; *kj* is [tç]; *sj* is [shj].)

Eg sko de'ran ne' på æin li῾ten fårret'ning ne' te Ma'desen, å sko
I was going down to Madison on some business, and was going

ar῾bæia får æit *nør῾serikam⎮peni å sælja *nør῾seri, å så' va
to work for a nursery company and sell nursery [goods]. Then

eg inn' på *Fø'rst *Næ'sjenel *bæ῾nkbil⎮dinjen der dæi hadde *å῾fisen
I went into the First National bank building where they had their

sin, å fækk' al't i år'den de'r. Så hadd eg en῾då æin to'-
office, and arranged everything there. Then I still had two or

tri ti῾mar at'te, føre *tri'ne jækk', så e konne kåma teba'rs. Så
three hours before the train left, which would take me back. Then

tom῾la e meg åpp' te *kapito'le då' å sko sjå' sto῾regub⎮badne. De va
I wandered up to the Capitol to look at the big shots. It was

hel'ste guvernø'ren e vil῾le sjå', men han' va῾ kje in῾ne, så e fann῾kje
really the governor I wanted to see, but he wasn't in, so I didn't

te han'. Så *hæ῾pna de så' at e kåm inn' på *å'fisen te
find him. Then it happened that I went into the office of the

sta'ts kasse'raren då'. Så va der æi'n som spo῾re om eg ville sjå'
State Treasurer. Someone there asked me if I wanted to see

Levai'ten, kasse'raren, å de sa' eg eg had῾de kje någe å sjå'
Levitan, the treasurer, and I said I didn't have anything to see

han' får, men e sko' no li῾ka å sjå' kos an såg u't, å han' va'
him for, but I would like to see what he looked like, and he was

så næ῾re han hæu're de, å han kåm u't å snak῾te mæ æi'n gång'
so close that he heard me, and he came out and talked right away

å va fæ'lt fø`rekåm'mandes. Så spo`r an nå ka de va' eg vil`le. Å så sa`
and was extra polite. Then he asked what I wanted. I said that

eg, de va` kje nå`enting¹ eg vil`le nettåp, men eg hadde hæurt je`te di hadde
I didn't really want anything, but I had heard tell, they said

fårtal't meg åppi El`råi at an konne snakka når`sk, å så hadd eg hæu'rt
in Elroy that he could talk Norwegian, and I had heard that

at an sku vara jø`de, sa eg, å sko finna u't om de va san't. Å så
he was a Jew, I said, and I wondered if this was true. Then he

sa' an mæ æi'n gång', næi', når`sk kan je ikk`je snak`ka, men je kan
said right away, "No, I can't talk Norwegian, but I can

snak`ka såg`nemao'le. Å itte den' ti'o så snak`t eg mæ an æit hæi'lt
talk Sogning." After that I talked quite a while with him,

bø'l då, å an snakte både eng'elsk å når`sk, å natu'rligvi's dæ
and he talked both English and Norwegian, and of course, it

va' såg`namå'le, får dæ' hadd an vær`kele læ'rt... Dæ va u'tanem
was Sogning dialect, for that he had really learned... Outside

Ma'desen æin de'l såg`ningar, å de'r hadd an vå're mø`kje
Madison there were some Sognings, and there he had gone a great

me krå'm, klæ'r å slik't nåke, å så' hadd an
deal with peddler's wares, clothes, and the like, and then he had

*ståp`pa isjå når`skar omtren't sta`dikt å dær, så an snak`te tæm`mele
stayed with Norwegians nearly all the time so that he talked

gått' såg`namå'le.
Sogning pretty well.

20. Weddings and Funerals.

(Suldal dialect from Elroy; inf. 13N4, recorded Jan. 2, 1948.
Born in Juneau Co., Wisconsin, in 1918, this man is the son of the
speaker of the preceding selection. His mother was born in Wisconsin, of Suldal parents. *Pronunciation:* same as preceding,
except that some of his loanwords have E sounds.)

*U't på it'temidda'jen så har di sto're *såp'per då', å kan'sje*
Later in the afternoon they have a big supper then, and perhaps

*ad'le så æ — å liksåm fa'r å mo'r å on'klar å *æ'ntiar å*
all who are — like father and mother and uncles and aunts and

slik't kje'me då' å e'te mæ di, jav'nast i hæi'men åt bru'rå.
such come then and eat with them, usually in the bride's home.

Nå me' blæi jif'te så hadde me' de i kjør'kjå, å kjør'kjå
When we were married we had it in the church, and the church

va jud'le å mang'e utfø're, så konn' kje kåma inn'. Å så
was full and many were outside, who couldn't get in. And then

*it'tepå då', så va me neri *beis'menten på kjør'kjå, me hadde*
afterwards, we were down in the basement of the church, we had

*litt *lån'sj dæ'r, å sa't ron't å tok — *pit'sjer. Då'*
a little lunch there, and sat around and took — pictures. Then

*jekk me hæi'm te hæi'men åt kjæ'rinjå mi, å dær o'pna me *åpp ad'le*
we went home to my wife's home, and there we opened up all

gå'vene våre, å då' — mo'r å fa'r hin'nas å mo'r å fa'r mi[n]
our presents, and then — her mother and father and my mother

å søs'ter å brø'dne te beg'ge av åss va' dær. Nå bro'r min
and both our sisters and brothers were there. When my brother

blæi jif'te så va de bær're nak'le åv åss i kjør'kjå... æ'g åsså
was married, there were only a few of us in the church... I and

kjæ'rinjå hans å søs'ter hin'nas va ad'le så va i — "se'rmoni"
his wife and her sister were all who were in the — ceremony

el ka du vil kad'la de — mo'r å fa'r hin'nas å mo'r å fa'r te
or what you want to call it — her mother and father and my

*bro'r min va' dær, å då' *jekk me ne'*
brother's mother and father were there, and then we went down

*te *Ri'dsberg åsså tok di *pit'sjer åv bru'rfål'kjå. Å*
to Reedsburg and they took a picture of the bridal couple. And

*då' kåm me teba'rste te hæi'men åt kjæ'rinjå ans å hadde sto're *såp'per*
then we came back to his wife's home and had a big supper there.

dæ'r. Å de sål'stn måŋg'e plar jæ'ra de, bær're at
And that's how many are accustomed to do it, only that

som'me har dan's ittepå *såp'peren då', åsså kje'me me gå'vene
some have a dance after the supper, and come with the gifts after

it'te dan'sen.
the dance.

(På begravelse:) Å jav'naste di ha'r hann' så e dø' på —
(At funerals): Oh, usually they take the one who is dead to —

"funeral parlors" då', åsså ha'r di litt bønn' dær, åsså te'ke
funeral parlors then, and have a little prayer there, and then

di — bær're får dæi næ'rsjyl'daste — åsså då te'ke
they take — only for the nearest of kin — and then they take

di — *ba'din åpp te æi kjør'kja, præs'ten æ dæ'r, å han' *jir'
the — body up to the church, the pastor is there, and he gives

— ta'len å sæie litt' um man'nen — jav'naste nå an
— the speech and says a little about the man — usually when he

va fød'de, å ko'r å kos'dan de va' nå an dø' å — å litt' um
was born, and where and how he died — and a little about his

fami'lien ans, koss maŋg'e så an *liva at'te, åsså då' —jav'naste—sæi'e
family, how many he left behind, and then — usually — he says

an litt' te dæi' så æ at'te, koss di ska le'va, å skak'kje ta' de
a little to those who are left, how they should live, and (that they)

så ha'rt å — kje'me te å kåma tesa'men atte jædna.
shouldn't take it too hard and — that they will meet again, usually.

Å så då' itte dæ' så te'ke di hann' så æ dø', å ad'le går
And then after that they take the one who is dead, and all walk

ron't kjis'tå å se'r på han. Så *klo'sa di åpp¹ kjis'tå
around the casket and look at him. Then they close up the casket

å teke de u't te — te *hør'sen, å då' går di u't i
and take it out to — to the hearse, and then they go out into the

*gra'vjar'den, å jav'naste præs'ten sæi'e litt', nak'le o'r
graveyard, and usually the minister says a little, a few words

dæ'r, æi li`tå bø'n, å då' le'te di kjis`tå ne' i, å då'
there, a short prayer, and then they lower the coffin, and then

æ de al't ø`versta'. Å itte fål'kjå æ fa'rne frå', så \*kåv`ra di åpp'
it's all over. And after the people have left, they cover up the

kjis`tå.
coffin.

21. *Norwegian Foods.*

(EN dialect from Hixton; inf. 14C1, recorded Feb. 18, 1948.
Born between Hixton and Pigeon Falls, Wisconsin, in 1878, this
woman had lived in Beloit since her marriage in 1898. Her father
immigrated from Vestre Toten ab. 1860, her mother from Valdres
in 1851; but her speech is strongly affected by DN and English.
Pronunciation: EN vowels; *r* before dentals is untrilled; *s* before
l and after *r* is [sh]; she occasionally uses Eng. *l.*)

Ja'a, vi bruk`te nes`ten bestan'di når'sk ma't. (Hva slags?)
Ye-es, we nearly always used Norwegian food. (What kind?)

*Vell', får — får *brekk'fest' så hadde vi nes`ten bestan'dikt — kok't
Well, for — for breakfast we nearly always had — boiled

ha`vre — ja dem — je tru'r — kal`te dæi dæ ha`vregrøu't? Ja',
oats — well they — I think — did they call it "oatmeal"? Yes,

å *tos't å, brø' å, sli`ke ting'. Å får mid'dag så had`de vi
and toast and bread and such things. And for dinner we had —

— fa'r bruk`te å li`ke nårs'k kjøtt`sup'pe veit du, me po`tet
— father used to like Norwegian meat soup you know, with potatoes

å gu`rut å fårsjel'lige ting' slik't i. Å dæ' had`de vi
and carrots and different things like that in it. And we had that

my`e, å få`rekå'l veit du, dæ' va ein ting' dæi bruk`te
a lot, and mutton stew, you know, that was something they used

å li`ke. Å åf'te får \*brekk'fes't så hadde vi panne`ka`ke, så vi kal`te
to like. And often for breakfast we had pancakes, as we called

dæ. Om vin'tern så *bokk'vitpanneka¹ke, å vi had`de støtt' veit du,
them. In winter buckwheat pancakes, and we always had

hei`meba¹ka brø' å — får kvæl's hadde vi åf`te
homemade bread, you know, and — for supper we often had

læf`se å flatt'brø å sli`ke ting'. Dæ' bruk`te n fa'r å li`ke
"lefse" and "flatbread" and such things. Father used to like

etter n vart æl'dre å hadde dår`lie ten'ner, så vil`de n — ja
that after he got older and had poor teeth; then he wanted —

han kal`te dæ søll', han hadde flatt'brø væit du opp'brø¹ti
he called it "søll", he had "flatbread", you know, broken up in

— *kai'n ev — væit du — flø`te, ja ell ru`memjøt¹k såm vi' kal`te de,
— kind of — you know — cream, or "rumemjølk" as we called it,

ru`memjøt¹k. De' lik`te han, an'ti de', hel'ler vilde n ha' va
"rumemjølk." He liked that, either that, or else he wanted some-

an kal`te vass`grøu¹t, "that's kind of like our cereal, you see".
thing he called "vassgrøut", that's kind of like our cereal, you see.

Han lik`te dæ'. Men vi' an'der lik`te mjøt`kegrøu¹t væit du, mjøt`ke-
He liked that. But we others liked "mjølkegrøut", you know, milk

grøu¹t mæ — ka`nil å suk'ker på, bro'nt suk'ker å ka`nil,
porridge with — cinnamon and sugar on it, brown sugar and cinna-

å sli`ke ting'. Å vi' hadde nes`ten bestan'di ru`me
mon and things like that. And we nearly always had sour cream

på bo'le væit du... ru`me å brø'. Men' så va de åf`te mo'r
on the table, you know, cream and bread. But then it often hap-

væit du, it`te hadde ti`er å ba`ka brø' så
pened, you know, that mother didn't have time to bake bread so

åf`te, får ho ba`ka brø' hæi`le ti'a, så kok`te o grøu¹t væit du,
often, for she baked bread all the time, you know, and then she

mjøt`kegrøu¹t før åss'. Men fa'r vilde hel'ler ha vass`-
made milk porridge for us. But father would rather have water

grøu¹t, så bruk`te o å ko`ke dæ' væit du, så ho kunde
porridge, and so she used to cook that, you know, so she could

*ha' de ifrå æin kvæll', *væll', ifrå æin da'g te æin a'en væit du,*
have it from one evening, well, from one day to another, you know,

han' vilde lik'så sna'rt ha kall' vass'grøu't han'. Å så
he would just as soon have cold porridge. And then they

had`de dom no'e såm dm kal'te tet'temjøł'k — *"you know what*
had something that they called "tettemjølk" — you know what

that is?"... vi bruk'te nes'ten bestan'di å ha' de hæi'me.
that is?... we nearly always used to have that at home.

22. Easter Vacation.

(Solør dialect from Blair; inf. 14D3, recorded May 21, 1935.
Born in 1914 on a farm near Blair, Wisconsin, this man was a
student at the time of the recording. This specimen was composed
in advance and read into the microphone, in connection with an
investigation he was making of his own dialect. An immediately
following section of the same specimen is included in the writer's
Norsk i Amerika 120. His father and mother were born in America;
only one of his grandparents came from Solør. His dialect is
authentic Solør as spoken in the community, though with marked
variations from that of his uncles and his neighbors. *Pronunciation:*
EN vowels; *u* is similar to DN *y*, which is absent in his dialect;
s before *l* and after *r* is [sh]; *o* is identical with his E *u*, which is
used in some lws.; *r* is untrilled before dentals; *kj* is identical with
E *ch*, *sj* (and *rs*) with [sh], and *ł* with [ṛ].)

*Je teng'te at je kunne fertæł'je om *i'stervekei'sjen min lis'så gått'*
I thought I might tell about my easter vacation, just as well

*som nåe an't. Je var *løk'keli å få sjyss' me *an'der-*
as anything else. I was lucky enough to get a ride with the under-

*tei'kern ifrå Blæ'r, som var nè afør på ein *Bi'vermø'te. De var gan'ske*
taker from Blair who was down for a Beaver meeting. It was quite

*fi'nt ve'r på væ'gen opp', å på ei'n *płass' ståp'te vi å hadde*
fine weather on the way up, and at one place we stopped and had

ein *hæ'mbør'ger å eit gla's *bi'r. På sis'ten kom' vi tæl Blæ'r. Dæn
a hamburger and a glass of beer. At last we got to Blair. That

bi'en e'r så stil'le å ro'li da ein er van't tæl ein stø're bi'.
town is so quiet and peaceful when one is used to a larger town.

Men de e'r itte så værs't å kåmme hem'mat li'kavæ'l̄. *Far'men
But it's not too bad to get home again just the same. The farm

lig'ger fi're *mi'l ifrå Blæ'r. Da de va'r så fi'nt ve'r, dro'g je i væ'gen
lies four miles from Blair. As it was such fine weather, I started

å *trav'le. Gra'se hadde bin't å grøn'nes, å je så'g mang'e
off walking. The grass had started to turn green, and I saw many

slaks vå'rfug'ler som *ra'bins å *blo'bø'rds. Da je var hæ'l-
kinds of spring birds like robins and bluebirds. When I was half

væ'gas, kom na'bon vår kjø'rnes me *ka'rsen. Sål'lesen fekk je
way, our neighbor came driving in his car. In this way I got a

a'ka li'ke hemm'. Så sna'rt som hunn'n fekk se' mæ så
ride all the way home. As soon as the dog caught sight of me, he

seik'te n. Han trud'de visst je va fræ'men. Men da' han
barked. He must have thought I was a stranger. But when he

kom nem'mere, kjin't n mæ at'te å visk'te i rom'pa. Så gått' de
came closer, he recognized me and wagged his tail. How good it

va'r å kåm'me hem'matt ei stunn'. Je va'r så lei' denna kjå'ken
was to get home again for a while. I was so tired of this slaving

på *jo'nivø'rsitin he'le ti'a.
away at the University all the time.

23. *The Man who Got Lynched.*

(Solør dialect from Blair; inf. 14D4, recorded Sep. 3, 1942.
Born near Blair, Wisconsin, in 1880, this man was an unusually
valuable informant; his stories of the community and his skill
as an old-time fiddler were equally entertaining. His father and
mother both immigrated from Våler in 1871. *Pronunciation:* EN

vowels; *u* similar to N *y*, which is missing in this dialect; *r* is untrilled before dentals; *s* before *l* and after *r* is [sh]; palatalized are *nn*, *ll*, and after front vowels *dd* and *tt*.)

Dæ va'r ein na'bo je får se'a hæ'r såm vart hæng't,
There was a neighbor I'll have to call him, who was hanged here,

en fæm'ti å'r sea, je tru'r dæ ein fæm'ti å'r sea i hæus't. Å
some fifty years ago; I think it was fifty years ago this fall. And

hann' va'r mo'di slæmm'. Na'boa var rædd' n da, al'le sam'man,
he was plenty bad. The neighbors were afraid of him, all of them,

dem var rædd' n fær an — va rædd' n skulle jæ'ra nå gæ'li.
they were afraid of him — were afraid he would do something bad.

Å så skul'le dem sta skræ'me n da tur — (Hva
And then they were going over to frighten him out of the — (What

hadde han gjort?) Å', hann' hadde — hann' hadde vø'ri på sla'veri fø'r
had he done?) Oh, he had — he had been in jail before,

*åv kårs', å så hadde n — hann sål'te *grubb' denn' tia tæll bi'en
of course, and then he had — he sold grub at that time to the city

hær, dem sål'te *grubb' — (Hva mener du med det?) *Grubb',
here; they sold grub — (What do you mean by that?) Grub,

dæ' var dæ' dem *grub'be opp dæ', istel'lefær ve' da veit du, bren'ne
that was what they grubbed up, instead of wood, you know, burn

*ka'kugrubb¹ vi kal'te. *Ka'kugrub'ben denn' va brønn' —
"cake grub" as we used to call it. "Cake grub" was burned —

er i lann' som bir brøn'nin ne', å brøn'nin å'ver å å'ver, så bi'r dæ
is soil that is burned down, and burned over and over, until it

en *ka'kugrubb¹ brei' som dette hæ'r, å da' måtte dom
becomes a "cake grub" as broad as this, and then they had to

høug'ge opp denn' fær å fin'na ro'ta mitt' unner *ka'kugrub'ben. Da
chop it up to find the root right under the "cake grub". Then they

to'g dm des'sa *pi'sa n høugg' opp dær, å så sål'te dem de på
took these pieces which he chopped up there and sold them to the

stå'ra da' veit du, å som'mestan¹ kunne dæ væra en sto'r grubb'
stores then, you see, and some places there could be a big grub,

å' veit du me'. Å dæ'r viss'te dem itte o'te tå' fær ell dæ høll'
too, you know. And there all of a sudden a store in Blair just

*på å ble's opp i *stå'r ni Blæ'r hær, som an hadde bå'rå inni mæ en*
about blew up because he had bored into it with an

na'var å så hatt' i kru't. Å så ha n sli'ji ti en tapp'
auger and put in gunpowder. And then he had put in a plug

*dær, å så rætt' som dæ va'r dem var inn'på *stå'ri, så ble's *stå'ven*
there, and right while they were in the store, the stove blew into

*i hun'dre fil'ler, å døm un'tres på' å dæ va'r, dæ *æks'plo'de dæ'*
a hundred shreds, and they wondered what it could be that exploded

*i *stå'ven. Å da bin'ne dem å sjå' åver *grubb'pai'len som*
in the stove. And then they began to look over the grub pile which

*lå'g u'te da. Da fann' em to' *grub'ber tæll' dær nå som*
was lying outside. Then they found two more grubs there which

var tæll'la'ga å sku blå's opp mæ. Å den'na man'nen va'r mo'di
were prepared for exploding. Oh, that man was plenty bad, he

slæmm', han var fæ'lt lei'.
was awful mean.

*Så va'r dæ *kjæ'rmann hær i *tao'ne hær, hann skulle — hann'*
Then the chairman of our town here, he was going to — he

va'r mæ hann' å', åsså skull m gå' di't engong' da, å så skræm' n hær
was along too, and they were going to go there once and scare him

*i frå', i frå' dette la — *køn'tri hær. Så jikk' dm ditt', han*
away, away from this la — country here. So they went there, he

*lev'de ni en da't, neri *slu'e el ni en da't. Så sto' dæ*
lived down in a valley, down in a slough or a valley. There was

i sto'rt tre' bein't ne'a dæ gam'le hu'se hass dær. Å da' jikk'
a big tree right down below his old house there. And they went

dem i dø'ra å så spo'rde dem n om n ville gå' ifrå' hær, æl'les så
to the door and asked him if he would go away, otherwise they

skull m ta' fatt' på n. Nei' sa n, je gå'r itte hær i frå'
would grab hold of him. "No," said he, "I won't leave this place,"

sa n, je har vø`ri på sla`veri sa n, je har gått` ut — ut dæ'
he said, "I have been to prison," he said, "I have gone out what

je har — kjen`t ut dæ' je har — straf`fa fær dæ' je har jort'
I have — served out what I have — punished for what I have done,"

sa n. *Væ'l, vil' du itte rei`se sa dem, så tæ'ger vi dæ
he said. "Well, if you won't leave," they said, "we'll take you

u't, å så sæt'ter vi på' dæ i rei'p. Så jikk' dem bei'nt inn i sæng'a,
out and we'll put a rope on you." Then they went right into his bed

å to'g n bei'nt tu sæng'en om nat'ta, å så ba'r dm
and took him right out of his bed at night, and then they carried

n u't å sæt'te på i sto'rt — i rei'p da, å så kas`te dem
him out and put on him a big — a rope, and then they tossed

rei'pe å'ver en grei'n som stakk` ut på tre'e, å så
the rope over a branch which stuck out on the tree, and then

to'g dem i væ'gen å så bin`ne å dra' n i ve're, dro'g n i ve're å så slæf`te
they started to pull him up, hauled him up and dropped

dem n ne', å så spo`rde dem n om n ville gå' da'. Nei', han
him down, and then they asked him if he would go then. No, he

vil`le itte gå' sa n, han vil`le itte gå'. Så dro'g dem n
wouldn't leave, he said, he wouldn't leave. Then they pulled him

opp' att ijænn', å slæf`te n ne' att. Kjæ`ringa sto' å glåm`ne på. Å
up again and let him down again. His wife was looking on. And

da spo`rde dem n på nitt' om n ville gå'. Nei', han vil`le itte
then they asked him again if he would leave. No, he wouldn't

gå', dærifrå'. Da dræi'v m på' a dro'g å dro'g tæll dæ —
go away from there. Then they kept hauling and hauling until —

tæll slut'ten så vart' n hæng`en i ve'ri dæu' da.
until at last he hung there dead.

 Å je va'r dær ei stønn' et`terpå, så ha m dri`gi rei'pe så dæ
 And I was there a while later, and then they had pulled the rope

var ei ju'p sku're i kvis'ten dæ'r som rei'pe ha
so that there was a deep incision in the branch where the rope had

*slai'da att' å fram' da, ju'p sku're i kvis'ten. Da' va'r
slid back and forth, a deep incision in the branch. Then there

dæ to' ifrå Blæ'r hær som sprang' ne' å så mæl'te dem da. Døm'
were two from Blair here who ran down and reported them. They

slapp fri', men di an'dre læut bet'tala hun'dre, je tru'r
were not punished, but the others had to pay a hundred, I think

dæ var hun'dre å nit'ten el kju'gu *da'la væ'r, å en fæmm'
it was a hundred and nineteen or twenty dollars each, and five

el sæk's tå dem som kom' på sla'veri, dom va'r dær i fæmm' å'r, på
or six of them went to prison, they were there for five years, in

sla'veri.
prison.

(*Men hva syntes folk om dette?*) *Å', døm fækk' i gått'*
(But what did people think of this?) Oh, they got a good

o'l hæ'r run't, dem vart red'de fål'k runnom
reputation, people around here, they were scared of people from

Blæ'r hær. Fær je' å bro'r min res'te ut i Min'nesota å ar'beidde
Blair. For I and my brother went out to Minnesota and worked

på en *bækk'jar'd. Dæt'ta var da ful kan'sje træ'dve å'r et'terpå. Men
in a brickyard. This must have been thirty years later. But then

da spo'rde dem om vi va'r i frå Blæ'r, Vis'kånsen. Ja' sa vi,
then they asked if we were from Blair, Wisconsin. "Yes," said we,

vi e'r dæ'. Dæ må væ'ra mi'e *råf'fe fål'k dæ'r run't
"we are." "There must be a lot of rough people around there,"

sa n. Ja de kann' vel hen'ne de ha vø'ri fø'r sa je, men je
he said. "Well, maybe there have been before," said I, "but I

ha' itte viss't om noe slek't ak'kerat nå' sa je. *Væ'l,
haven't heard about anything like that right now," I said. "Well,

dem hæng'ne en mann' — to'g en mann' bæi'nt u't tu sæng'a å så
they hanged a man — took a man right out of his bed and

hæng'ne dem n sa n. Ja, dem jo'te dæ' sa je, men ma'ann
hanged him," he said. "Yes, they did so," said I, "but the man

va stig'gene lei' sa je, de brann' opp en *ba'te som em *klei'ma
was awful mean," said I, a barn burned up which they claimed

han' hadde jort' da veit du, en ba'te, som brann' opp mæ
he had set fire to, you know, a barn which burned up while the

ku'en låg brein't i hæ't dær. Så *klei'me dem hann' hadde jort'
cows were burned to death in it. Then they claimed he had done

de' da veit du. Han va'r færfær'dele slæmm', denn' Han's Ja'kop.
that, you know. He was terribly bad, that Hans Jacob.

24. *The Backgrounds of an Emigration.*

(Hardanger dialect from Beaver Creek; inf. 15P1, recorded
September 6, 1942. Born in Odda, Hardanger, in 1866, this man
immigrated in 1887 and farmed in the Beaver Creek settlement
until he retired to Blair, Wisconsin. *Pronunciation:* WN vowels,
slightly diphthongized; his *æi* vacillates from *ei* to *ai;* the words
dæ, dæn, dær vacillate to *da, dan, dar; ng* is [ngg], *kj* is [tç], and
sj is [shj]; *r* is a uvular scrape.)

Ja ja, så ble' dæ så lang't då ser du, atte når æ kåm' i konfir-
Well, then the time came, you see, that I reached the age of

masjo'nsal'deren, at æg sku gå' te præst'en, så' måtte æg *trav'la
confirmation, and had to go to the minister; then I had to walk

to' når'ske mi'l, da bli fjor'ten æn'gelske mi'l dæ', så æ måtte gå'
two Norwegian miles, that's fourteen English miles, so I had to

på sji', å så på sjæi'sar ø'ver vad'ne. Å så blæi æ konfirme'rt då'
use skis, and then skates, over the lake. And then I was confirmed,

ser du, æg hadde gått' får præs'ten i æit å'rs ti', så blæi æ konfirme'rt
you see, after I had gone to the minister for a year, I was confirmed

i at'ten hun'dra å æi'n å åt'teti, dæ va' i *julai', men æ kann' ikkje
in eighteen hundred eighty one, it was in July, but I can't exactly

sæia ak'kurat da'toen, å så' va æg u't å a'rbæide iblant fål'k då', får
say the date, and then I was out working among people then, for

fa'r var æin fat'tig mann'. Han hadde æin sto're gå'r, men op'pe i
father was a poor man. He had a big farm, but up in the moun-

fjed'le væit du, så va' dær ikkje my'e å *mæ'ka dæ'r — eller få'
tains, you know, there wasn't much to be made there — or to get

dæ'r, uta dæ han hadde kræt'tur, ku'er, so me mjel'ka oppi
there, except that he had cattle, cows, which we milked up in

fjed'le, oppå stø'len so di kad'la.
the mountains, at the "støl" or mountain dairy as they called it.

Dæ gå'r *å'l rai't? Ja ja, når æg va' då konfirme'rte då', så hadde æg
This is going all right? Well, when I got confirmed, I had

æi'n så va goss'var min, so di kad'la på — i Ha'rdanger, han
a man who was my godfather, as they call it — in Hardanger, he

va goss'var min å kjæ'rinjæ han's, ho var god'mor mi, å de'r va
was my godfather, and his wife, she was my godmother, and there

æg fys'te som'maren æg va u'te å a'rbæide. Då' var æg fjo'rten
I stayed the first summer I was out working. Then I was fourteen

å'r gam'mal, å då' fekk æg åt'ta kro'ner får dæ', dæ' blæi' omtræn't
years old, and I got eight "kroner" for it, that would be about

to' da'lar hæi'le som'maren. E' detta gått' nåkk? Ja ja, så
two dollars for the whole summer. Is this good enough? Well,

ba'lte æg, å va u'te å vå hæi'ma i sjå fa'r å *mæ'ka
I struggled along, was away and at home with father and made

— me va sju' sjys'jæn væit du, dæ sku my'e te' oppi
— we were seven brothers and sisters, you know, it took a lot up

fjed'le dæ', fyr klæ' å all'ting. Ja når
in the mountains there, for clothes and everything. Well, when

æ blæi' så gam'mal då' at æg hadde fått' såpas'sa ve't at æg tæn'kte æ
I got old enough so that I had enough sense to realize that I had

måtte u't å *mæ'ka *le'ven min inkvanstass — æ sku' kje
to get out and make my living somewhere — I shouldn't have

sakt *mæ`ka, men dæ få'r no ve' så, så tæn`kte æg då' at æg borde
said "make", but that can't be helped, then I thought that I ought

ræi`sa te Ame'rika. Å så had`de æg jæn`to mi då' veit du, kjæ`rinjæ mi
to go to America. And then I had my girl, you know, my wife

hæ'r, å då va' me fårlå'va. Æ va' kje anna ein gu`tunj¹e på ty`ve
here, and we were engaged. I wasn't anything but a kid of twenty

å'r, å ho' va to' å ty`ve å'r, å så had`de me in`jen væ'rdens ting', å så
years and she was twenty-two, and we had nothing at all, and then

sa' ho', me ræi`se te Ame'rika, me'. Å så ræis`te me bæd`dje to'.
she said, "We'll go to America". And so we left, both of us.

Me fækk *tik`ket ifrå Li' Illinåi's... å så' når me ræis`te ifrå
We got a ticket from Lee, Illinois... and then when we left my

hæi'me mitt i Hardan'ger, dæ' var den æi'n å ty`vende ap`ril at`ten
home in Hardanger, it was the twenty-first of April, eighteen

hun`dra å sju' å åt'teti. Å så kå'm me te Stavan'ger, dæ'
hundred and eighty seven. And then we got to Stavanger, that

va'r den fi'r å ty`vende ap`ril, å så kåm' me te Ham'bårg i
was the twenty-fourth of April, and then we got to Hamburg in

Tys'land — la me no sjå' — ja eg kan' ikkje sæi`a dæ — men dæ'r-
Germany — now let me see — well, I can't say it — but from

ifrå ræis`te me te Brem'en, Brem'en i Tys'land, å dæ'r va' me
there we travelled to Bremen, Bremen in Germany, and there we

i fi`ra da'r. Bå'ten sku kje gå' nettop ak'kurat såm me' var.
were for four days. The boat wasn't going to leave right away.

Så kåm' me te Bremerham'n, å så' sku me op`pi —
So we went to Bremerhaven, and then we were going up — on

ombo'r i den sto`re bå'ten så jekk' yve Atlan'terha've væit du,
board the big boat that went across the Atlantic Ocean, you know,

å så va' n så lang't utpå fjo'ren så han kun`ne ikkje gå opp' te
and it was so far out in the fjord that it couldn't come close to

lan'de, før dæ va' får grun't. Dæ va' kje vat'ten nåkk', so
the land, for it was too shallow. There wasn't enough water, so

me måtte ta' noko små' bå'tar, u't te den sto're bå'ten sku
we had take some small boats, out to the big boat that was going

ta' åss øver Atlan'terha've, å den' va' så hø'g atte me måtte
to take us over the Atlantic Ocean, and it was so tall that we had

ha' noko sti'ja te gå' opp', op'på den sto're bå'ten å kåmma inn'.
to have some ladders to go up, up in the big boat to get in.

Å nå'r me hadde læss't opp, så va me at'ten hundra main'nisje
When we had finished loading, we were eighteen hundred people

ombo'r. Å så' va me nit'ten dø'ger i Atlan'terha've. Å så
on board. Then we were nineteen days in the Atlantic Ocean. And

kåm' me te Bal'timo'r dan nit'tende ma'i, dan nit'tende ma'i, at'ten
we got to Baltimore on May nineteenth, May nineteenth, eighteen

hun'dra å sy'v å åt'teti. Å så lå'g me ombo'r i dam'pen
hundred and eighty seven. Then we slept on board the steamer

nat'tæ, å så *jekk' me te Sjika'go *nek'ste da'jen, å så kom' me te Li',
that night, and left for Chicago next day, and we got to Lee,

Illinåi's den e'n å ty'vende ma'i, dæ va ein søn'dag på it'temid'dajen,
Illinois, on the twenty-first of May; it was a Sunday afternoon,

å då' sto me på *pla'tfår'mæ dæ'r, å då va' me så fat'tige me kun'ne
and there we stood on the platform, and we were so poor we couldn't

ikkje snak'ka, å så va me sjyl'dige sy'v å åt'teti *da'lar!
talk, and besides we were eighty-seven dollars in debt!

25. Conflicting Attitudes.

(Hardanger dialect from Beaver Creek; inf. 15P3, recorded Nov. 28, 1936. Born in Jackson County, Wisconsin, in 1878, this man graduated from the engineering course at the University of Wisconsin and came to hold a position of high responsibility in the state administration. His father immigrated from Ulvik, Hardanger, in 1854. This specimen was prepared in advance.

Pronunciation: like that of the preceding speaker, except that his *r* is tongue-trilled.)

Eg va fødd' i at'ten hun'drede ått' å syt'ti þao en *far'm,
I was born in eighteen hundred and seventy eight on a farm,

so me sæi`e, lig'gande i ves'tre de'len tao "Jackson County, Wis-
as we say, which lies in the western part of Jackson County, Wis-

consin." Pao den'na kan'ten æ dar æit set'lamen't, so me sæi`e, omtren't
consin. In this district there is a settlement, as we say, about

fem`tan *mi'l lang' å nes'tan *så bræi', dar so ad'le fål'k æ
fifteen miles long and almost as broad, where all the people are

når`ske. Net'top i da' na`bola'g so far'men vao'r lao'g i, va' dar
Norwegian. Right in the neighborhood where our farm lay, there

æin nåk`re fame'liar, so me kal'te fy sø`ringar, men som`me sa'
were a few families whom we called "southerners", but some said

atte dæi va stri`lar. Litt læn'gre æu'st va dar flæi're
that they were "strils". A little farther east there were many from

gul`bransdø'lingar, men te ves'ten \*før au`tta *mi'l va ad'la sa' [man]
Gudbrandsdal, but west of us for eight miles everyone was

i frao Hardan'ger, man`dje tao dæi kjen`ningar å slæk` tningar i frao
from Hardanger, many of them acquaintances and relatives from

Når'ge. Han fa'r kom' te Kasj`kenang, so når`skarane kal'te får
Norway. Father came to Koshkonong, which the Norwegians called

Kas`keland, i at'ten hun`drede fi'r å fæm'ti, fæm`tan ao'r ga`mal,
"Kaskeland," in eighteen hundred and fifty four, fifteen years old,

mæ fåræl'drena å æi'n bro'r. Da'r lev`de dæi æin fi`ra
with his parents and one brother. There they lived for four

helde fem' ao'r, å dao' ræi`ste dæi no'r te "Jackson County" å
or five years, and then they moved north to Jackson County and

kjøp`te nytt' lan'd i frao sta'ten...
bought new land from the state....

Eg va ba`re tre' ao'r gam`mal naor me ræis'te ifrao far'men å flut`te
I was only three years old when we left the farm and moved

te by'en, men e'g va bestan'dig ho'ga te kåma u't pao far'men ijenn,
to town, but I was always eager to get out on the farm again,

å jo're da bestan'dikt naor eg kun'de. Å eg va' dar naor eg var't
and did so every time I could. And I was there when I got to be

æin gan'sje sto'r gu't å ar'bæidde om som'rane å li'te grann om vin'teren.
quite a big boy and worked in the summers and a little in the winter.

Da'r va æin æk'te gam'mal når'ske *plass', da'r so dæi hadde når'ske
It was a genuine old Norwegian place, where they had Norwegian

sjik'kar. Å me fekk kjen'nast man'ge fål'k frao man'ge
customs. And we got acquainted with many people from many

fårsje'lige de'lar tao Når'ge. Net'tup run't da'r so me' *lev'de
different parts of Norway. Right around there where we lived

va dar flæi're sø'ringar, å dæi' va bestan'dig så —
there were several "southerners", and they were always such —

sli'ke go'e kjirk'efål'k. Ha'ringane va ikkje
such good church people. The Hardanger people were not like

so'læis, dæi vilde bestan'dikt ha li'tegrann¹ mo'ro um einan'.
that; they always wanted to have a little fun with each other.

Eg huk'sar æi'n tao dæi gam'le sø'ringane so kal'tes får I'var
I remember one of the old "southerners" whose name was Ivar

Dom'marsne¹s. Æi'n vao'r byg'de han æit nytt' hu's, å
Dommersnes. One spring he built himself a new house, and the

sjik'ken va' at me sku innvi'a hu'se mæ æin dan's. Da
custom was that we should have a housewarming dance. There

va æin tre' eller fi'ra gu'tar — brø'r, so va gan'sje bra' spe'lemenn¹,
were three or four boys — brothers, who were quite good fiddlers,

å dæi ræiste upp' te denne her gam'le Dom'marsne¹sen, å spo're han
and they went up to this old man Dommersnes, and asked him

om dæi kunne fao lå'v te å ha dan's i hu'se hans. Men
if they could have permission to have a dance in his house. But

det'ta lik'te ikkje han'. Han sao'g pao dæi æi stun'd, å dao' svar'de
he didn't like this. He looked at them a while, and then he answered:

han: Næi', sa han, me æ' kje so ha`ringgane me', dan's te
"No," he said, "we're not like the Hardanger people, with dancing
kva'r kvæl'd!
every evening !"

26. The First Automobile.

(EN dialect from New Auburn; inf. 18C1, recorded August 28,
1942. Born in Town of Sand Creek, Dunn County, Wisconsin, in
1900, this man grew up in a farming community where much Norwegian was spoken. Both his parents were born in Wisconsin,
and the only date of immigration he knew was that of his father's
father, 1857. His mother's parents came from Biri and Ringsaker,
but his dialect seems to correspond approximately to that of
Hedmark. *Pronunciation:* EN vowels, but his *å* is low back,
about like E *a* in *law; r* is untrilled before dentals.)

Denne hæ'r far'men såm je nå' le'ver på æ'r — de ær far'men til,
This farm I'm living on now is — it is the farm of,

*væ'l, min bæ`stefa'rs bro'r, sku je si'. Den var al'tså
well, my grandfather's brother, I should call him. It was his

*ho`msted'den has'ses. Han \*ho`msted'de dæ'r på såm'må ti'a såm
homestead, that is. He homesteaded there at the same time as

bæ`stefåræl'dra \*ho`msted'de litt' læng'er ne' hær. Å
(my) grandparents homesteaded a little farther down here. And

far'men e'r itte så sto'r, men vi ha'r nå litt plan`ting, å litt grønn',
the farm isn't so large, but we have a little planting, a little grain,

å litt hei', å mjæl`ke en tåll' træt'ten ku`er å —
and a little hay, and (we) milk twelve or thirteen cows and —

så vi rus`ker nå på' litt. (Hva slags grøn?) \*Væ'l, vi \*rei`ser
well we get along all right. (What kind of grain?) Well, we raise

før de mæs`te bær're ha`vre, litt' bigg' som`me sta'n. (Hva gjør dere
mostly just oats, a little barley some places. (What do you do

med havren?) *Væ'l, vi bru`ker de tell \*fi'd te ku`ene, før de mæs`te.
with the oats?) Well, we use it to feed the cows, for the most part.

*Å så *rei'ser vi litt pot'tit, litt' te sæl'je å litt'*
And then we raise a little potatoes, a little for sale and a little

før åss sjø't, å "string beans, snap beans." Je ha'r ingen
for ourselves, and string beans, snap beans. I don't have any

*i å'r, men je ha'r hatt *opp tæll' i å'r. (Har det vært stor*
this year, but I have had up to this year. (Has there been a great

*forandring i farmingen?) *Væ'l, *je's, a'tsjel'li føsjell'. En'da så*
change in farming?) Well, yes, quite å bit of change. Even so

*huk'ser itte je' så læng'e, *å kårs' de by'ne å bi' no'en*
I don't remember so far back; of course, it's getting to be some

*å'r nu'. Je' kan nå se' føsjell', sto'r føsjell' på *rå'da*
years now. I can see a difference, a great difference in the roads

*run't i dette hæ'r *kon'tri, je hu'ser fis'te *a'tomobil'en je så'g.*
around in this country; I remember the first automobile I saw.

*Vi *liv'de ak'kerat næ're hæ'r da', omtræn'tli e *mi'l hæ'rifrå, hall' *mi'l*
We lived right close to here then, about a mile away, half a mile

*hæ'rifrå, å je sprang' al'ler så lang't før åsså få se' den *ka'rn vættu,*
away, and I ran ever so far to see that car, you know,

*å de' va hø'gju't ak'kerat såm en *båg'gi, en gam'meldaks *båg'gi.*
and it was high-wheeled just like a buggy, an old-fashioned buggy.

Kom' dom borti en bak'ke, så måt'te dom til' å sjy've, å som'me så
If they got to a hill, they had to start shoving, and some couldn't

*kom' dom no itte opp' fårut'ta å ha' i *hæs'teti'm på'. Å*
even get up without having a horseteam hitched to them. And

*da' snak'ke dem på' mæ di lå'gju'te *ka'ta bin't å kåm'ma*
then they talked about these low-wheeled cars when they started

u't atte, ja dæt'ta bi' nå fæ'lt te grei'er, bort'jennom dessa hæ'r ju'pe
to come, that this will be an awful business, in these deep

*rat'sa sier em, såm *vång'ntræk'ken hadde gått', såm va'r en*
ruts, they said, which the wagon tracks had made, which were a

fo't å en hall' jup't. Men dæ ha ræt'ta se tæll'.
foot and a half deep. But that has all been straightened out.

27. Language and Courtship.

(Trønder dialect, with EN influence, from Waterloo Ridge; inf. 19A2, recorded Nov. 15, 1942. Born in Waterloo Twp., Allamakee Co., Iowa, in 1894, this man was a third-generation American on his mother's side; his father was born in Holtålen, a community in South Trøndelag. *Pronunciation:* EN vowels; *r* untrilled before dentals; *s* before *l* and after *r* is [sh]; *nn, nt, dd, tt* are palatalized.)

De va en gam'meł tys'k nab'bo, e snak'ka mæ n iłjo'ł.
There was an old German neighbor, I talked with him last year.

Å så had`de n små`jen'tan åt så'en sin dær. Så byn't e å spo'rde n e' —
He had his son's little girls there. Then I started to ask him —

e snak'ka når'sk me n — å dem het'te, om dæ æ
I talked Norwegian to him — what their names were, if it was

Ing'ebø'r ell dæ æ Sig'ri å slik't bortette. Så sa' n dæ', at ja', de hæ'r æ
Ingeborg or Sigrid and the like. Then he said, "Yes, this is

Sig'ri å hæ'r æ Be'ret å hæ'r æ Kirs'ti sa n. Å små'-
Sigrid and this is Beret and this is Kirsti," he said. And the little

jæn'tan dæm sto bæ're å gaf'te, dæm viss'te itte hå
girls stood there with their mouths open; they didn't know what

bæs'tefa'r deres snak'ka om vet du, når an snak'ka
their grandfather was talking about, you know, when he talked

nårs'k. Så byn't en å fårtæł'de om mang'e å'r sea, da
Norwegian. Then he started to tell about many years ago, when

n dre'v å trøs'ka borti Pæ'r Hæn'driksabak'ken vi kal'la dæ, dær
he thrashed in the Per Hendrickson hill, as we call it, and the

*sti'men'djin to` ut før n neå'ver bak'ken. Å så rul'la n un'der
steam engine started down the hill. And then he rolled under

å fikk' — e'ne ju'le jikk` åver fo'ten hass, hæll åver læg'gen va' dæ nå.
it and got — one wheel went over his foot, or rather his leg.

Men så va' dæ e søkk' i bak'ken så at n it'te vart
But there was a depression in the ground so that he didn't get

*fårdær'va, men han les'som *skin`na fo'ten hass litt'. Å så had`de n*
damaged, but he sort of skinned his foot a little. And then he had

*nå *al'kehå¹l mæ' såm n smor`de på¹. Å så vett' du*
some alcohol with him which he rubbed on it. And then you

*når *trøs`karkru¹e fann' den *al'kehå¹len, så byn't dm å*
know when the thrashing crew found this alcohol, they started to

drakk' tå n, litt' no' å litt' da', så nå m kom'
drink from it, å little now and a little then, so that when they got

opp tæ Si'vert Vi'ken å sku trøs`ke, så had`de n itt nå
up to Sivert Viken and were going to thrash, he didn't have any

ål'kehå¹l al'te. Å når — Mæ`ret Vi'ken va' dæ o het`te — kom`
alcohol left. And when — Marit Viken was her name — came

u¹t å så spor`de a ka dæ va' såm fel'te n, n jikk' å hin`ka å hal'ta
out and asked what was wrong with him, he went around limping,

ser u, å så sa' n dæ' at å', sa in`djain to` ut før me ne`åver Pæ'r
you see, he said, "Oh, the engine got loose from me down the Per

Hæn'driksabak¹ken sa n. Å så spor`de a, ha'r du itte nå å ha`
Hendrickson hill," he said. Then she asked him, "Don't you have

på a, sa a. Jo' sa n, e ha'r nå å ha` på.
anything to put on it," she said. "Yes," he said, "I have something

Ja men kje`re kje`re jart`andes da, sa a, ha'r du itt nå
to put on." "But oh dear, dear," she said, "don't you have any-

*å ha` på a? Så sa n, jo', e had`de en *gal'lon mæ *al'kehå¹l, men*
thing to put on?" Then he said, "Yes, I had a gallon of alcohol,

dm ha drøk`ke opp dæ fø'r mæi. Å dæ' va en tys'ker, å han'
but they've drunk it up for me." And that was a German, and he

snak`ke så gått' nårs'k såm nånn' tå åss...
talked just as good Norwegian as any of us...

Dem gam`le nårs`keran dem snak`ka om da m jikk' på
The old Norwegians have told about how they used to go a-

fri`eri så va' dem litt' me'r fø'r se ell dem æ' no'. Dem bruk'te å så ha
courting a little more boldly than they do now. They used to have

en sta`ga ser u, å kli`ve opp i gla'sa. Å dæ
a ladder, you see, and climb up through the windows. And there

va' en tot`ri tå m fikk na`ra e'n te å kli`ve opp i
were two or three who got one fellow fooled into climbing up the

sta`gan å krab`be inn. Så to' m sta`gan un`na, så mått n
ladder and crawl in. Then they took the ladder away, so he had

hæi`se se neå`ver væg`gen, æll'er så mått n gå` ne trap`pa.
to hoist himself down the wall, or else he had to go down the stairs.

Da' va dæ my'y tå ti'a at gam`lingan vak`na opp å kom' å
Then it often happened that the old folks woke up and came and

ja`ga n å'. Dæ va nå e'n som vart pæn`na (?) dæn *vei'en.
chased him away. There was one who got panned (?) that way.

Han va' opp' å så`g um jen`tan, å så va' dæ no skur`ka
He was up visiting the girls, and then there were some rascals

som ha kom`mi å ti' sta`gan hass vet du, å så kom' n itt
who had come and taken his ladder, you know, and so he couldn't

u't att. Sku gå` ut att da, så hadde m vø`ri inn' i trap`pa
get out again. When he was leaving, they had been in the stairway

å sætt` opp en he'l sma`ta mæ blæk`kan¦na å græi`er vet du. Når
and set up å whole raft of tin cans and things, you know. When

n trød`de på tåp`pen tå ste'ge, så res`te he'le stel`lasi
he stepped on the top of the step, the whole shebang tumbled

neå`ver så de ram`ta å slo' bok`ta i my'y tå dæ. (Holdt de
down with a big crash and made dents in much of it. (Did they

lenge på med den skikken?) *Nå', dæm had`de no slut`ta den' ti
keep up this custom a long time?) No, they had quit by the time

e' bynte å frid`de. E bruk`te nå al`dri å kli'iv staga e', men e
I started to court. I never used to climb around on ladders, but I

vart' no jif't langt om længe e' å'.
finally got married just the same.

28. Anecdotes from Spring Grove.

(EN dialect from Spring Grove, Minnesota; inf. 20C2 [selections B and C] and 20F9 [selection A]. The speaker of selection A was born in 1898; her father was born on the ocean in 1854 of a Halling family, while her mother was born in Oslo [then Christiania] in 1859. The speaker of B and C was born in 1900 of mixed EN ancestors: her father's parents came from Hallingdal and Hadeland, her mother's parents from Sigdal and Hadeland. These spirited informants were recorded without their knowledge, but subsequently they approved the recordings. *Pronunciation:* EN vowels, but with some substitution of AmE qualities, esp. for *a*, *å*, and *o;* *l* is often like E [l]; untrilled *r* (before dentals) and *t* are like E [r].)

A. Dialect Attitudes.

Når n pap'pa va ba're en små'gutt¹ å mam'ma va ei små'jen'te,
When papa was just a little boy and mama was a little girl,

så had'de nå n pap'pa la'ga nå hø'nehu's han, såm n had'de nå hø'ner i.
papa had made some chicken coops, which he had some chickens in.

Å så had'de n nå snik'ke'rt des'sa der sjø'l. Så sku' n nå lik'såm te
And he had carpentered these himself. So he made as if to brag

skri'te litt' han da, at n si'ns n hadde jort' go' *jabb' dær.
a little about this, that he thought he had done a good job there.

Å så sa'n dæ' atte, si'ns du ikke dæ' atte, des'sa de'r æ kjæk'ke, sa n
And then he said, "Don't you think that those are nice," he said

te o mam'ma, dm var no ba're ong'ar beg'ge to'. Å' sa o, dæt'ta
to mama, they were only kids both of them. "Oh," said she, "this

kan du fårtæl'ja bøn'ner å ik'ke bi'ens føl'k sa o. Ho pra'ta så
you can tell to farmers and not to city people." She talked so

fi'nt ho, å så han pap'pa pra'ta me'r hal'ling han'. Mam'ma pra'ta
elegantly, while papa talked more Halling dialect. Mama talked

mæs'som så fi'nt ho, å han dre'v å skrit'te tå dæt'ta hø'nehu'se da,
so sort of elegantly, and he kept bragging about this chicken coop,

så trud`de ikke ho på' detta dæ'r va' så svæ'rt ho — får ho var
but she didn't think it amounted to so very much — for she was

bi'ens føť k ho, kom' ifrå bi'en, ifrå Kres'tiana ho...
city folk, came from the city, from Christiania...

B. *A Courting Episode.*

Han si`ntes dæ bi`nte å bli' får mi`e støy' \*opp`ste¹rs,
He thought there was getting to be too much racket upstairs,

han bes`tefa¹r En`dru, veit du. Så — å pakk' dekkan ne'
grandfather Enderud, you know. Then — "oh, get out of here

nå' sa n. Å pakk' dekkan ne' nå', ifrå *opp`ste¹rsen veit du.
now," he said. "Oh get out of here," from the upstairs, you know.

Å så sa' n, dæ va'r æin tro`njæm¹mer, å' ja', nå e bli fæ`tig så
Then one fellow said, he was a Trondheimer, "Oh sure, I'll be

kjem' e no. Jad`den, du ska' no visst få se' du ska kåm`ma før du
coming when I'm ready." "By golly, I'll see that you come before

bli fæ`tig. Å han bes`tefa¹r had`de slikt jim`mit han' ser u. Å'
you're ready." Grandfather had such a temper, you see. And

den`na der stak`kars kro'ken kåm' neå`ver trap'pa hug`ustu¹p, å sprang'
that poor fellow came down the stairs headfirst, and he jumped

ut'åver å rul`la åver kæť van å ku`inn såm lå'g uti
down and rolled over the calves and cows which were lying in

*ba`rnjar¹de, å han vart' al`deles fårskræm't,
the barn yard, and he was completely frightened out of his wits;

han bes`tefa¹r la't n fårstå' at n men`te *bis'nes...
grandfather let him understand that he meant business.

C. *The Enderud Waltz.*

Bes`tefa¹r En`dru, han kåm' hi't når an va' væl ein træt'ten
Grandfather Enderud came here when he was about thirteen

å'r. Ho mam'ma fårte'lte om bes'tefar Ben'sen, de va
years old. Mama told about grandfather Benson, his name was

En'dru, å så *kjei'nja n nå nam'ne sitt te Ben'sen nå n kåm'
Enderud, and then he changed his name to Benson when he came

hæ'r te Amer'ika... Han bruk'te å så *en'tertei'ne... føt'ka hæ'r i
here to America... He used to entertain... people here in

Ame'rika me å spil'le Har'dangerfe'le — fi'olin sin. Han var ud-
America by playing Hardanger fiddle — his violin. He was extre-

mær'ket go' te å spil'le. Han bruk'te å spil'le på al'le brøl'loper, i al'le
mely good at playing. He used to play for all weddings, at all the

*ba'rndan'sen såm va', i al'le brøl'loper så spil'te han
barn dances there were; at all the weddings he used to play the

fe'le. Så bruk'te han å ha' e'n såm spil'te *kår'din mæ
fiddle. Then he used to have one who played the accordion with

se. Å dæ' va så go' *mu'sik. Når de va' no,
him. And that was such good music. Whenever anything was

så va'r e n Em'bret En'dru såm skulle væ're spil'lemann'.
going on, it was always Embret Enderud who had to be the fiddler.

Å han' kun'ne spil'le Har'dangerfe'le. Å e huk'sa når
He really could play the Hardanger fiddle. And I remember when

e va li'ten, så bruk'te e ha' n te å spil'le åt me, å e dan'sa att'
I was little, I used to have him play for me, and I danced back

å fram' på gøt've å trud'de e kun'ne dan'se. Å En'dru-
and forth on the floor and thought I could dance. The Enderud

val'sen ha' vørti nem'nt etter han', å den' æ'r nam'njit'in *all' å'ver
waltz has been named after him, and it's famous all over

*run't hær... Den' gå'r tril'lene run't, å al'le så kjen'ner dem te
around here... It whirls around like a top, and everybody knows

den En'druval'sen ska e si' dei.
that Enderud waltz, I'll tell you.

29. Goblins and Witchcraft.

(Sogn dialect from Blackhammer; inf. 20Q1, recorded Nov. 12, 1942. Born in Blackhammer Twp. near Spring Grove, Minnesota, this man is a third generation American, whose grandfather came from Aurland, Sogn, in 1849; though his mother was born in Sweden, she now speaks predominantly Sogn dialect. *Pronunciation:* WN vowels, with strong diphthongization of the long vowels, so that e.g. the long *i* is identical with E [e] in a word like *bait;* *a* is central; *kj* is [tç]; *sj* is [shj]; *ng* is [ngg].)

Å' ja', fa'r *bruk'te pra'ta my'kje um des'sa nis'sedn å trål'li
Oh yes, father used to talk a lot about "nisser" and "trolls"

å al't det'ta he'r. Me bruk'te spør'ja n man'ge *ti'e, naor me kåm'
and all that. We used to ask him many times, when we went

neri *ba'rn å skulle ji' hes'tadn ma't vait
down in the barn and were going to give the horses feed, you

du, elle me skulle skra'pa dai å *fiksa dai upp' lite grann'.
know, or we were going to curry them and fix them up a little.

Så vai't du man'ge *ti'e ma'ne pao hes'tadn va nes'ten
Then, you know, many times the horses' manes were nearly woven

isa'menvot'te, å så' spo'rde me' kållai'sen da' hadde se. Å så sa' n
together, and we asked how that happened. And then he said

atte da va nis'sen såm hadde jor't detta he'r, han hadde flet'ta ma'ne
that it was the "nisse" who had done this; he had braided the

pao hes'tadn. Å so vai't du da va flet'ta i sa'men
horses' manes. And then, you know, they were braided together

gan'sje gått', å so vil'de me' ta kni'ven vait du, å sje'ra da opp'.
pretty tightly, and we wanted to take our knives and cut them open.

Å so sa' n, nai', di mao tuk'ka da ifrao' inan' mæ fin'gradn
But then he said, "No, you have to separate it with your fingers,"

sa n, fy bru'ka de kni'ven å så sje'ra da sa n, so rai'se nis'sen
he said, "for if you use your knives to cut it," he said, "the 'nisse'

i frao' åss å te'ke ma'ten i frao' dessa hes'tadn,
will go away from us and take the food away from these horses

å så ji'r da te noke an'dre, fy an li`ka ikkje da' at du bruka
and give it to some others, for he doesn't like it that you use the

kni'ven pao ma'ne aot hes'tadn...
knives on the horses' manes..."

Da va' ain når`ske so \*lev`de i ain da'l æu`stom åss', dai
There was a Norwegian who lived in a valley east of us which

kad`la da Å`gesenda'len. Å dan gam`la kje`ringi pao dan' plas'sen
they called Ågesen valley. And the old woman on that place they

*klei`ma dai had`de lite tråll`kun|st i' se. Naor ho slep`te kry`tyri
claimed had some witchcraft ability. When she let the cattle

ut i *fi'li um hæu'sten sa dai, so had`de o ain kjepp' å so rai`ste ho
out on the fields in the fall, they say she had a stick, and she went

bor't å so dro'g o han' ette *kånn`filkan|ten å so
over and dragged it along the edge of the corn field, and then

sa' dai da' at kry`tyri jikk al'dri *kråss' da'r so o hadde
they said that the cattle would never go across where she had

*dræ`ga dan' kjep'pen. Å so vai't du da va na`boen hinna,
dragged that stick. Then, you know, there was her neighbor,

e hok`sa nam'ne, men han ån'keln min, han Klin'genber|g, han bruk'te
I don't remember the name, but my uncle Klingenberg used to

å snak`ka my`kje om han', å da va ai' gong' han had`de ain hes't som
talk a great deal about him. One time he had a horse which had

hadde våre bor't i *vai'erfen|se å så skå`re se so styk't fårdær'va, at han
gotten into the wire fence and cut himself so very badly that he

hel`t pao å hadde blødd` i hæ|l. Å så kas`ta han se pao
was bleeding to death. And then he jumped on the back of

ain hes`tarygg| han, å så rai' han ne' da'r å skulle fao' denna he'r
a horse, and rode down there and was going to get this

man'nen te å kåmma opp' å *kju`ra denne hes'ten so han ik`kje skulle
man to come up and cure this horse so he wouldn't

blø' i hel. Å so sa'n atte, e ha'r ikkje nå`ke op`pe da'r å jæ`ra,
bleed to death. Then he said, "I haven't anything to do up there;

du kan raisa hai'matte no' sa n, fy no' ha blo'e
you can go home again now," he said, "for now the blood has

ståp`pa pao hes'ten, så e' ha' kje nåk`e oppe da'r å je`ra.
stopped on the horse, so I haven't anything to do up there."

Å naor han' kom hai'matte så hadde blo'e ståp`pa pao hes'ten,
And when he got home again, the blood had stopped on the horse,

*klei`ma n, å hes'ten vart *å'l ṛai't.
he claimed, and the horse was all right.

30. *Beliefs about the Fairy Folk.*

(Sogn dialect from Blackhammer; inf. 20Q2, recorded Nov. 10, 1942. Born in Aurland, Sogn, in 1859, this old woman was remarkably clear and informative about the early days of settlement as well as the beliefs carried over from Norway; she had immigrated in 1870 and had kept her dialect unusually pure. *Pronunciation:* same as preceding speaker.)

E vai't ikkje mai'ra om' da, anna det`ta he'r so han gam`le bes`tefa'r
I don't know any more about it, except what old grandfather

sa', atte da skulde kåm`ma ain hul`dreka'r mæ ain kvi'te hes't
said, that there had come a "huldre" man with a white horse

å vilde by`ta uti ain svar't. Pao Ot`terne`s hadde dai
who wanted to trade it for a black one. At Otternes they had

ain svar't, å den`na he'r han kom' mæ ain kvi't hes't å vilde
a black one, and this man came with a white horse and wanted

by`ta. Å so vil`de ikkje Ot`terne`s by`ta, å so' skulde
to trade. And then Otternes didn't want to trade, and then the

hul`drekal`len ha sak't da' atte dar skulde al`dri tri`vast svar'te
"huldre" man was supposed to have said that black horses would

hes't pao Ot`terne`s maira. Å han gam`le mo'r — bestefa'r na, bes`tefa'r
never again thrive at Otternes. And her old grandfather,

*te *mis'sis Røl'vå¹g, da va' no han' so fårtal'de da, han va'*
Mrs. Rølvaag's grandfather, he was the one who told it, he came

darifrao vait du, han sa' da' atte, da had'de ikkje vå¹re
from there, you know, he said that there had never again been a

svar'te hes't da'r sai'nare sa n. Men da va' vel nok' av atte
black horse there later, he said. But that was probably because

dai in'kje turde setja pao' ain svar'te hes't kansje. (Visste han
they didn't dare to breed a black horse, maybe. (Did he know

*hvor lenge siden dette hendte?) *Nå', da' e lain'je se¹ao, da*
how long ago this had happened?) No, it's a long time ago, it

va' visst fy're han's ti', så atte da æ' så lain'je se¹ao vait du.
must have been before his time, so that it's very long ago, you know.

(Vil du fortelle litt om din mors tro om
(Will you tell something about your mother's belief concerning

kokende vatn?) Ja', da' kan e. Da va forsjel'likt vait
boiling water?) Yes, I can do that. It was different then, you

du, naor me' ko'kte no po'tet, so va' da no fø'r i ti',
know: when we boiled potatoes, as it used to be in former times,

so va' da my'kje atte dai ko'kte dai mæ rå'se pao', å so'
it was quite common to boil them with their skins on, and then

jikk dai ut' å slo' van'ne, had'la van'ne tao' dai vait du, pao mar'kji.
they went out and poured the water off them, on the ground.

Å so sa' o da' atte, da' skulle me ikkje jæ'ra. So vil'de no me'
And then she said that we shouldn't do that. Then we wanted

ve'ta kofår' me ikk'je skulle jæ'ra da vait du, å lo' aot dætta hær me'.
to know why we shouldn't do it, you know, and we laughed at this.

Ja', de fao'r no jæ'ra so de vi', de' sa o, men e' ha no vårte få'r da e'g
"Well, you can do as you please," she said, "but as for me,"

sa o, at eg in'kje ska jæ'ra da å in'kje ha eg jor't da hel'ler
she said, "I'm not going to do it, and I haven't done it either,"

sa o. Han ska' kje slao ko'kande vat'ten pao djo'ri, får
she said. "One shouldn't pour boiling water on the ground, for

dao bren`ne han dai' so æ innun'de sa o. Da' skulde væra
then one burns those who are underneath," she said. That was

hul`drefål`k da vait du, so va innun'de.
supposed to be the "huldre" people, you know, who were underneath.

31. *A Snowstorm on the Prairie.*

(Trønder dialect from Irene; inf. 23A4, taken down by the writer in 1930. Born in Oppdal in 1851, this man immigrated in 1873 and homesteaded near Irene, South Dakota, shortly afterwards. Some DN forms are mixed into his speech. *Pronunciation:* EN vowels; *ö* is a low-front unround vowel, similar to AmE *u* in *cut;* *ll, nn, n* (before consonants) are palatalized, also *tt* and *dd* after front vowels, including *u;* *l* before *t* is palatalized and unvoiced; *r* before dentals is untrilled; *s* before *l* and after *r* is [sh]; a special feature is the frequent splitting of single vowels into two.)

E ska fårtæ't dåkk um denn' gång'inn e næs'sen mes`ta li've får
I'll tell you about the time I almost lost my life for the sake

kaf'fen sin skull'. Dæ va snø`vinn¹tern i ått' å åt'teti. Dæ
of some coffee. It was the snow winter of eighty-eight. There

va en *ped`lar såm \*le'evd tett att`mæ åss, minn hann' ha' itt att' nå
was a peddler who lived close by us, but he didn't have any more

me'r kaf'fe. Vi ha' te', men dæ' va' itt vi' nå å`vte på'. Så
coffee left. We had tea, but we weren't much for that. Then

va' dæ en da'g e hel't på å stå`ka mæ nå ve'fang¹ i ga'ra.  Så sa' o Æ`li,
one day I was busy with some wood in the yard. Then Eli said,

dæ va' itt væ'æst væ'r i da'g. Så sjøn't e ka såm sto` på¹.
"The weather isn't too bad today." I realized then what was up.

Ho vess`te dæ va kaf'fe å få' på Mai'fi¹l, tri' å en hal'v
She knew there was coffee to be had at Mayfield, three and a half

*mi'l dær'ifrå. Så kas`ta e me på ryg'ginn på en ø'k å sett` i vei¹.
miles away. Then I jumped on the back of a horse and started off.

E va no kledd' bær're allminn'dele, e ha` på en kort' *sjinn`ko¹t, å
I was dressed just ordinary, — I had a short leather coat on, and

*så' ett benn' såm e ha' ronnt li've. Da e kom' utpå *sku`l-*
then a band around my waist. When I got out on the school

*seksjo¹on umtrent tri' kvart' *mi'l frå åss, så`g e en kvi't vægg'*
section about three quarters of a mile from us, I saw a white wall

**ehædd'. Å så tvi'lt e på' at dæ va snø`står¹m i an`mars, å så*
ahead. Then I suspected that a snowstorm was coming, and I

snudd` e um¹ å *start`a i rett'ning av he'em så gått' e kun`na.
turned around and started in the direction of home as best I could.

Minn så va' dæ så my'y snø', at e re' me fas¹t i snø'a, å
But there was so much snow that I got stuck in the snow and

e mått a'v å le' hæs'ten. Å da va' dæ så stinn't e kunn næs'ten
had to get off and lead the horse. And it was so thick that I could

itt se' hann'da får'ran me, å e to' rett'ninga så
hardly see my hand in front of me, and I took the direction as

væ'l e kun`na. Men e sjø'ønt e kunn' itt, får ø'kinn slo' se bær`re onn`da
well as I could. But I realized I couldn't, for the horse shied away

venn'da. Så tænk't e dæ va bæ'æst e ga' me sjæ`bnen i våll',
from the wind. Then I thought it would be best to accept my fate,

får e tæ'ænkt at va' dæ no så' besjik'ka at e skull kåm`må fram att,
for I thought that if it was so determined that I should get back,

så kom' e no fram'. Å dæ' jo'or så my'y at e strak'st kom' på ett
I would get back. And that made it so that right away I found

**pas'ter. Dæ va bær're en *pås't um å får`rå, el'les ha e*
a pasture. It was just a question of a single post, or else I would

all'der sett dak'sens ly's ijenn'. Å de' va år`sa¹k at ø'kinn
never have seen daylight again. And the reason was that the horse

*slo se onn`da væ're, å så föf't e dæ *fæn'se. E sjø'ønt*
shied away from the wind; and then I followed the fence. I rea-

*dæ måtte væ're *Li'pas¹tre eller Mon`kvåll¹.*
lized it must be the Lee pasture or Munkvold.

Så fann' e *ste`blann, å e kunn kåm`må inn i *ste`blann, men
Then I found the stables, and I could get into the stables, but

e kunn' itt få ø'kinn in`ni. E fækk ga'ang ø'øln
I couldn't get the horse in. I got a chance to walk some body

ti me, men de va væ'æst får ø'kinn. Å så fårsøk't e to' gång'
heat into myself, but it was worse for the horse. I tried twice

å fi'inn hu'se, minn kunn' itt finn' dæ. Å da' va' dæ så stritt'
to find the house, but couldn't find it. The weather was so terrific

e mått gå' ba`klæng¦s får å kåm`må att, e va rædd' får å *lu`se
that I had to walk backwards to get back; I was afraid of losing

*ste`blann. Ann'der gång'inn tænk't e dæ va bes't å ven`te te
the stables. The second time I thought it was best to wait until

dem komm op`pi å jo'or *kjå'rsen, får e tænk't no sek'kert dem villa
they came up and did the chores, for I thought surely they would

kåm`må. Da dæm itt' kom', tænk't e e mått fårsø'øk en gång' te',
come. When they didn't come, I thought I had to try once more,

får e li`ka itt å \*lu`se ø'kinn, e ha nyss' kjøf't n. Da
for I didn't like to lose the horse; I had just bought him. When

e klæm't i væi¹ att, va dæ um' dæ e ha rul`la åver æi snø`fånn¹, å da
I started off again, I almost rolled over a snowbank, and then I

fekk e sjå' hu'sa, dæm va' itt læng'er bort' inn å'ver
caught sight of the houses; they weren't farther away than over

*port'ja hær.
this porch.

Da e kom` inn¹, spo'r e um e kunn få' nånn' te å gå` mæ me å
When I got in, I asked if I could get someone to go with me and

få' inn ø'kinn. Tru'r du vi finn' oppi *ste'beln,
get the horse in. "Do you think we can find our way to the stable,"

sa n Han's Li'. Hann ha vörre u't to' gång' å skull jår`ra *kjå'rs,
said Hans Lee. He had been out twice trying to do the chores,

minn han vil`la itt gå op`pi får al't såm va op`pi dær. Å
but he wouldn't go up there for all that was in the barn. They

dæm ha fått' to' ny`bær¹re kjy' um nat'ta. Å så spo'r n
had two cows that had just calved that night. And then he asked

me um e trudd' e kunn finn` att *ste'beln. Ja e ha' no
me if I thought I could find the stable again. "Sure, I've had plenty

prak`tise¹rt såp'pas sa e. Men så litt' n me'r på se sjø'ł inn på me',
of practice," I said. But then he relied more on himself than on me,

å så sett' n i væi'. Vi jekk mess' av ste'beln, så kom' vi åt en brenn`-
and so he started off. We missed the stable, and got to a hay

höistakk¹ såm sto' oppi ga'ra. Dær sto' de æi *sjøf'fel, å så *start`a vi
stack up in the yard. There stood a shovel, and so we started off

på ny' ku'ł, å fann' *ste`blann å fekk jort' *kjå'rsa.
anew, and found the stables and did the chores.

Chapter 20.

A SELECTED VOCABULARY OF ENGLISH LOANS

Ord ? Som Verden saa foragter ? . . . . . .
Fremad dog, I usle Rader!
Hær af ord!

Henrik Wergeland (1842)

An important part of the source material collected for the present investigation consists of the E lws. in AmN which have been noted from the speech of the writer's informants. The total number of such words in the writer's material runs well over 3,000, but many of these occur very rarely and would offer little of interest to the reader. In the following list only about ten percent of that total has been included. The criterion of inclusion has been that a word should have been noted at least fifteen times or have some special feature of interest. Most of the notations were made as responses to items in the questionnaire, but a wide sampling has also been made of the recordings and free conversations. Wherever convenient, examples of their use in context have been included.

The following information is presented for each word listed: (1) The *English model,* with its part of speech (n. 'noun' etc.), one or more meanings actually borrowed, and the number of informants from whom a borrowing of this word has been noted; the definitions are not exhaustive, being intended merely to identify the meanings. (2) The *Norwegian equivalents* of the loanword, preceded by the letter N, wherever these were actually given by informants in response to inquiries concerning the word they themselves used (no special effort to elicit such equivalents was made); if no such N word was given, the letter N is followed by

'no equiv.'; this does not mean that no equivalent exists in the
N language, and wherever the writer found that some obvious
equivalent was probably known to the immigrants, he has added
this in parentheses; the equivalents are given in a normalized
spelling, not necessarily reflecting the exact pronunciation of the
informants. (3) The *English pronunciation(s)* of the word most
likely to have been heard by the immigrants, here given in brackets
preceded by the letter E; this is written in a phonetic alphabet
described in Appendix 2. (4) The *AmN pronunciation(s)* of the
loanword, immediately following the English pronunciation and
an arrow > which should be read 'is reproduced by AmN informants as'; the phonetic alphabet used is described in Appendix 2;
ignoring minor differences between dialects, an attempt has
here been made to represent all significant variations in a simple,
readable alphabet; the first pronunciation given is the most common one among the writer's informants, and will be used by all
who are not specifically indicated as pronouncing it otherwise;
the other pronunciations are usually identified by the number of
informants using them (when no special dialect or community
trends could be observed) or by the code number of the informants
(when they were few in number); the use of either figures or code
numbers means that a given form is limited to those informants.
(5) The *grammatical forms* of the lw., immediately after the first
pronunciation (n. 'neuter' etc.); unless stated to the contrary,
they apply to all the other varieties of pronunciation also; the
abbreviations used will be obvious, except perhaps that —
means 'no ending' (zero suffix); the grammatical forms are normalized, in a way agreeing approximately with Aasen's NN forms,
so that e.g. -*a* in verbs stands for the infinitive or preterite, regardless of the precise forms used in particular dialects; -*ar* in nouns
refers to the first class of masculine nouns, even when some dialects
have -*er* or -*a* for this class; -*en* includes the pronunciation -*n*
after dentals. (6) The *compounds* noted by this writer into which
the lw. enters, here preceded by Cpd; a preceding hyphen means
that the lw. precedes the stem given, a following hyphen that it
follows; the stem is given in the language in which it usually appears
in the lw. compound, with an English equivalent in parentheses
whenever the first form is N; the spelling of the stems is normalized,

not phonetic; some *derivatives* are also given in the same way, preceded by the letters Der. (7) Illustrations of *contexts* in which the lws. have been used by the writer's informants, preceded by the letters Quot; these are usually as brief as possible, and are identified by the informant's code number (for further information on them see Appendix 1); the contexts are in the same broad phonetic notation as the lw. pronunciations and the specimens of Chapter 19.

It should be mentioned that this list was reduced in size after its original preparation, so that some of the statistics given in chapter 17 do not apply to the present, but to the original list, which included all words occurring in five or more notations, and was about twice as large.

accordion n. musical instrument 79. N *dragspel* n. 1K1 24A1 22F1; *beljespel* n. 8L3 7H2; *trekkspel* n. 4N1 4K1. E (1) [kɔrdi'n] > kår'di'n m. (n. 7 So. Nfj. Tel.); kå'ŗdi'n 5; kårdi'n 8 (mostly So. Vo. Set.); kårdi'ne f. 8M1 8M2; kår'ding 4L4 (quot.) 5H4; E (2) [əkɔr'dien] > kår'dien m. 12; ækåŗ'dien m. 7. Quot: Dæm bruk'te itte kå'ŗdi'n 14D14; vi kal'ler dæ kå'ŗdi'n runt he'r (itte dra'gspæll') 14D9.

acre n. land measure (43,560 sq. ft. or 4,047 m.²) 115. N no equiv. (but cf. *mål* n.). E [e'kər] > æ'ker m. (n. So. Vo. Nfj.), pl. —; e'ker 5; a'ker 3C3. Quot: hun'dra å tju'e æ'ker 6P2; ti' æ'ker mæ pot'te't 5F1; fi're ei'ker mæ tob'bak 10C14; kor man'ge e'ker 4P1; så kjøp'te me åt'ti æ'ker sko'glann' 5H7.

ague n. a malarial fever 29. N no equiv. E [e'gər] > e'ger m. (found in def. only, e'geren); æ'ger 7. Cpd: tobacco-, whisky- 8M1. Quot: de va fø'r eg hadde hatt æ'gern. On this disease and its AmE pronunciation see Lillian Krueger in WMH 29.333 (1946): 'He ain't sick, he's only got the ager.'

alarm clock n. clock that rouses sleepers 64. N *vekkjarklokka* 8; *ringeklokka* 10C6 18C2ι24A1 22F1; *vekkjar* 12Q1. First part E [əla'rm-] > lar'm- 22 (with ŗ 8); elar'm- 14 (with ŗ 12); alar'm- 12 (with ŗ 1); lar'm- 16C1 18B1; al'larm- 14C1. Second part always N.

all right a. safe, sound, satisfactory, OK 17. N (*bra, godt, riktig, rett*). E [ɔ'l rai't] > å'l rai't 9 (with ŗ 3); å'l rei't 5; å'ŗait 20F2; al't rett' 6Q1; al't rek'ti 4H1. Quot: Han kåm' no å'l rai't

20F9; de' ville hø've å'l rai't 5H4; lan'de va å'l rai't nåk 11B4; dæ gå'r å'l rai't 15P1; leg'gen hass va al't rett' 6Q1; si'a blei han al't rek'ti ijenn' 4H1.

arithmetic n. a school subject 49. N *rekning* f. 9. E [ərıth'mətɪk] > rit'metikk¹ 18 (with ɾ 13); rit'me- 11 (with ɾ 1); erith'me-3; ɾith'me- 2; ret'me- 2; ret'me- 2; erip'ne- 4L3; rep'me- 11C1; eɾet'me- 3C1; rup'me- 1K1; ɾøt'me- 18B2; rip'me- 3; rip'pentik 4L1 (quot); rif'me- 5C1; ryf'me- 6P1. Quot: Å', de va ɾi'ding å ɾit'metik får de mes'te 8L7; ɾit'metikk¹, dæ' va je svæ'rt kɫe'n ti 10C12.

assessor n. official who assesses property for tax purposes 88. N no equiv. (*likningsmann* m.). E [əsɛs'ər] > N ses'sar m.; ses'ser 13; sæs'ser 9; sæs'sar 4; æses'seɾ 7; asses'sar 4N1; æs'sæsser 7G1; sis'sar 11B1; sais'sar 15P4; sessa'r 8M1 8M2.

at all adv. (esp. in the phrase not at all) in the least 15. N no equiv. (*slett ikkje*). E [ətɔ'l] > etå'l 6; ætå'l 5; itå'l 4. Quot: Eg hør'te kje et'te henne e tåll' 4P3; ong'an kan ikke ta'ɫe nɔrs'k etå'l 5L2; du ha'r inkje nå vett' etå'l du far 11C1; eg ha'r kje noko imo't dæ eng'elska ætå'l 13N5; dom far'me itt itå'l 18C3; je va' ikke in'teræste i sko'ɫen ætå'l 20C5; ing'en gram'matikk ætå'l 24A1.

attic n. garret 65. N *loft* n. 10; *trev* n. 4L4; *høgd* f. 5H1; *raust* n. 5H3; *lem* m. 4P1 12R1; *rotalem* m. 13N3; *uppstugu* f. 8L3. E [æ'tɪk] > æ'tik m.; æt'tik 12; at'tik 13N4; æ'tæk 14D2; e'tik 11B1. Quot: i e'tika (dat.) 11B1; et'tiken — al'lesam'men fårstå'r de' 11C1.

aunty n. mother's or father's sister 51. N *faster, fasyst, moster, mosyst, tante,* all f. E [æ'nti] > æn'ti f., pl. -ar; æ'nti 10; en'ti 6 (esp. So. Vo. Nfj.); æ'nti or æn'ti 5; æn'te 2C2 21H1 5N1; æ'nte 3C3 4F3. Quot: Æ'g æ æn'tia te Missis Kva'me 12R5; ho va grei'tæn¹ti mi 10C1; ån'klar å æn'tiar 15P4.

automobile n. a vehicle 62. N *bil* m. 14C1. E (1) [ɔ'təməbi¹l] or (2) [ɔ'təməbi'l] > å'tomobi¹l m., pl. -ar; a'to- 7; a'te- 5; at'to-14D3; o'te- 11C4; å'te- 10C2; åt'te- 3; au'to- 7H1; æu'to- 4Q1; æu'te- 14D2 18B2; other var.: accent 1 by 3 inf.; accent on -mo-4 inf.; accent on -bil 8 inf.; -bill 7G1 7H2 2C1; o'tmilbåi¹lar 4P1 (hum. quot.). Quot: itte våg'nidn å båg'giadn, så kåm å'tomo¹-biladn 4Q3; han hadde hæs't før de va å'temobi¹l 10C2.

baby n. infant 32. N *unge* m. 22; *barn* n. 9. E [be'bi] > bei'bi m., pl. -ar 20; be'bi 14; bei'bi 2. Cpd. -sister. Quot: Han hadde net'top sak't da mæ bei'bien sin... han skulde slep'pa ar'baia dan bei'bien, vait du 20Q2; en bei'bisøs¹ter såm dø'de 5L1.

bach v. keep house alone, of men, usually in phrase to bach it 34. N no equiv. E [bæ'tsh] > bæ'tsja, pt. -a 8; bæt'sja 6; bæ'tkja 15P4; also the new formation from bachelor: bæ'tsjla 10; bæt'sjla 8; bæ'tsla 13N1; bæt'sla 9G3 22F1 12R1; bæ'sla 13N2; bæs'la 8L3; bæ'tkjla 19A2. Quot: Han har bæt'sja de i fem' å kju'ge å'r 4L4; je' å gam'mern dre'v å bæt'sjle 10C1.

bachelor n. (1) unmarried man; (2) man who does his own housekeeping (cf. Question column in D-P 9 Oct. 1947) 41. N *ungkar* m. 14 (EN and Gbr.); *laus(a)kar* m. 12 (esp. WN); *peparsvein* m. 10; *sveinkall* 4 (Set. Tel.). E [bæ'tshlər] > bæt'sjler m. 9 (-ŗ 14C1); bæ'tsjler 8 (-ŗ 3); bæ'tsjler 4; bæ'tsjlar 3; bæt'sjler 3; bæt'sjlar 3; bæ'tkjelar 8L4; bæt'slar 12R1 17Q2; bæt'sler 22F1; bæ'tsler 9G3; bæ'tslar 4L2 13N1; bæs'lar 8L3; bæsj'ler 14D4; bæ'sjlar 26A1; bæ'sjler 14D1 13N2.

back v. go backward, often in phrase back up, back out 35. N no equiv. E [bæ'k] > bæ'ka v., pt. -a; bei'ka 4P1 5H3. Quot: Bæ'k opp al't du kann' 23A2; to tre da'ga et'ter så bæka ho u't 6Q4.

bad a., adv. not good, chiefly in certain phrases, esp. feel bad etc. 11. N (*dåleg, slemt, for gale*). E [bæ'd] > bæd. Quot: Ho fi'la så bæ'd 20C1; han fi'lte bæ'd 14D2; i en bæ'd fik's 14D15; dæ ha kje vå're nett' so bæd' 12R1; kjei'nsbåg¹gen blei så bæ'd atte dei måtte slut'te 5G1.

bait n. lure for fish 46. N *agn* n. 14; *agnmakk, -mark* m. 4; *makk* m. 5; *mark* m. 11B1; *metan* 18C1; note that 'bait' is a N word also, occurring as *beit* m. (VAgder), *beite* m. (Ma. Ned.), *beita* f., and that there is a *beite* n. 'pasture'. E [be't] > beit or bet m. 15 (f. 3, Spr. Gr. and Wat. Ridge; n. 15 Blair—Solør, Wautoma—Holt, Heddal etc.); beite m. 2 Set. (f. 5 EN; n. 4 Coon V. -Koshk.); bett n. 18C1; bitt 1K1. The form bet (for beit) has 15 inf. Cpd: fiskar- 4; agn- 5L5 (also in Ross NO). Quot: Så kom' n oppåt Mår'ris å ville ha' nå bei'te 10C2.

ball n. round body 17. N *ball* m. 8F1 8L7 1K1 8L2 9G2. E [bɔ'l] > bå'l m.; båll' 8G1 20F5. Cpd: base-, basket-, snow-, foot-, foul-, barbed wire-, kitten-, volley-; -bat, -bearing, -game, -park, -playing. Quot: Da pleid'de vi bå'l 10C12; vi spel'te bå'l 10C13.

band n. orchestra containing brasses 13. N no equiv. E [bæ'n(d)] > bæ'nd m. (n. 2), pl. -ar 6; bæn'd 4; bæ'n 3. Cpd: -music. Quot: Så spe'la eg i bæ'nd 26P3; så jåi'na eg bæ'n 20F13; så ha'r di bæ'ndar dæ'r te plei'a før seg 13N4.

barber shop n. place for cutting hair 82. N no equiv. E [ba'rbersha'p] > bar'bersjapp' n. (also f. and m., cf. shop); bar'bersjapp'; bal'bersjapp'; etc. (the first form is prob. E, the two latter are N substitutions); -sjap'pa, -sjap'pe f. 6 (Tel. and Set.).

barn n. farm building 112. N *låve* m. 7H3 (*løa* f., *fjøs* n.). E [ba'rn] > ba'ṛn m., pl. -ar (general); ba'rn 4Q2 20Q2 17Q3 17Q4; ba'rne 6P4 3C1; ba're 10 (Utica Sogning and Nfj; Tele; Suldal); ba*t*e (all EN speakers in Western Wis. and Indianland, also 3C2 4K1); bane (most WN speakers in Western Wis. and Indianland, also 4P1 4P2 6P1 5J2); bana ł. 6Q1 6Q3; ban 9Q1; bar 21H1. Cpd: cow-, hay-, horse-, livery-, log-; -basement, -dans (dance), -dør (door), -golv (floor), -tak (roof), -vegg (wall), -yard. Quot: gå' åt ba'*t*a 11B2; vi had'de itte ba'*t*i 4K1; en ba'*t*e bræn't opp 14D4; u't i ba'nao 6Q3; ny' brunn' i ba'nen 15P5.

barrel n. cylindrical vessel 66. N *tønne* f. 3; *kagge* m. 9Q1. E [bæ'rəl] > bæ'ril m., pl. -ar 22; bæ'rel 17; bæ'rel 5; ba'ril 7 (esp. Wiota, Spr. Gr., Wat. Ridge); ba'rel 6 (esp. Mt. Morris); bæ'ridl 4Q2; bæ'redl 12Q1 17Q2; bæ'ril 4K2; bær'ril 25A1. Cpd: -kinne (churn). Quot: ein li'ten bæ'ril 14C1; tre fi're bæ'reler mæ bi'r å så vis'ki 12R5.

baseball n. a game 29. N no equiv. E [be'sbɔ'l] > bei'sbå'l m.; -ball' 4N1 9G1 9G3; be's- 5H4 8M2; bess'- 8M1. Cpd: -game. Quot: Vi plei'de bei'sbå'l 10C4; spe'la bess'ba'l 8M1.

basement n. underground story, esp. in a church 66. N no equiv (cf. *kjeller* m.). E [be'smənt] > bei'smen't m. n. (m. 38, n. 28); bei's-; be's-; be's-; bes'se- 14D2; bei'se- 22F1; be'semen't 8M2 4N1. Cpd: barn-, concrete-, stein-. Quot: ne'r i be'smen'ten 13N5; eg ha våre mæ' å byk't bei'smen'te 15P1.

basin n. circular tin or porcelain container without handle 34. N *fat* n. 8L1 10C3. E [be'sən] > bei'se, -a f. 13; bei'se m. 5; bei's f. 10, m. 2, n. 2; bei'sen m. 3C4 14D1. Cpd: brød-, blikk-, vaska-. Quot: ei gam'mal bei'se — blekk'kåpp 5G1.

basket n. flexible, wooden receptacle 66. N *korg* f. 22. E [bæs'-kət] > bæs'ket⌐ m., pl. -ar or -s 17; bas'ket⌐ 16 (esp. WN); also bes'-, bæ's-, bas'-, -ke't, -ket, -kit. Cpd: bushel-, lunch-; -ball, -party, -social. Quot: Dæi hadde kår'ga eller bes'kets så me kad'la he'r i Ame'rika å vilde sel'ja 12Q2.

basket social n. occasion for auctioning food baskets 24. N no equiv. E [bæ'skətso'shəl or -so'shebl] > bæs'ketso'sjel m. 8, bæs'ketso'sjebl m. 12, pl. -s; bæs'ketpa'rti 4. For forms of basket see above.

battery n. electric storage apparatus 52. N *batteri* (not known at time of emigration). E [bæ'tri] or [bæ'*t*əri] > bæ'tri n., pl. -r or -s 21; bæt'ri 7; bæ'teri 6; bat'ri 6; ba'tri 17Q1; bat'teri 4; ba'teri 18B1; bateri' 17Q4; bæ'tri̞ 5.

beans n. a legume 87. N *bønner* 9G2. E [bi'nz] > bin's m., def. -a (-i, -o, -e) or -en 45; bi'ns 42. Cpd. snap-, soy-, string-. Quot: Den'ne ti'a så pik'ker em bin's 18C4.

bedroom n. sleeping room 85. N *sengkammers* 11C1 7G1; *kammers* 5Q1; *soverom* 8L3; *sengerom* 11C2 10C5 17P1 4H1 (may be an AmN creation). E [bɛd'ru'm] > bedd'romm⌐ n., pl. —; bedd'-; be'd-; be'd-; bæ'd- etc.; bedro'mi 8M2. Cpd: -slippers.

bedspread n. top cover 74. N *åklæ* n. 11C1; *tæpen* n. 11C2; *sengespre* n. 8L3. E [bɛd'sprɛd⌐] > bedd'spredd⌐ n. m. (n. 58, m. 13); seng'espredd⌐ 8; bedd'- 24; bedd'spre⌐ 14D2; for forms of bedd- see **bedroom**.

beer n. a beverage 73. N *øl* n. (generally claimed to refer to homebrew). E [bɪ'r] > bi'r m. n. (m. 60, n. 13, of whom 6 Sogn. Cpd: root-; -hane (cock), -kagge (keg), -parlor. Quot: Ho mo'r la'ga bæ're ø'l hell den bi'ren mø kjø'pe 5H4; dæ va dei' såm kjøp'te bi'r i kag'gar 5L1; dar æ styr'kje å kraf't å hel'sebo't i bi're 6Q3.

bent n. section between two beams in shed or barn 25. N *høy-brot* 7H2. E [bɛn't] > ben't m. n. (m. 19, n. 6), pl. — or -s. Cpd: høy- (hay). Quot: oppi høy'ben'te 5H2. Not known in Minnesota, but common in So. and W. Wis.

binder n. machine for cutting and binding grain 20. N no equiv. Reproduced by morpheme substitution as bin'dar m.; bit'tar 6Q1 12Q7. Cpd: grain-, sjøl- (self). Quot: Vi hadde bin'dar på den' ti 4P4; bru'ke bin'nern 8C5.

black walnut n. nut of Juglans nigra 7 (all from Blue Mds. and Spr. Grove). N no equiv. E [blæ'k wal'nət] > blak'valne'tar

5G1 5L1 5L5; bɫak′val- 20C1 19A2 19A1; bɫak′vaɫ- 20J1. Cpd: -tre (shortened to blak′valtre¹ 5L1). Quot: Han hæu′g ne et blak′valtre¹ 5L1.

blackboard n. writing board in school 68. N *tavla* f. 12 (some use it only for a slate). E [blæ′kbɔr¹d] > blækk′bo¹r n. (with morpheme substitution of N *bor* or *boɫ* n. for the second part) 51; blæ′kbå̱r¹d, blækk′bå̱r¹d, blæ′kbɔr¹d m. 16; with all forms: blækk′- 45; blæ′k- 19; bɫækk′- 4.

blanket n. loosely woven bedcovering 94. N *tjeld* 4L1 4L4; *kvitel* 6P1 5Q1 6Q2. E [blæ′ngkət] > blæng′ket¹ m., pl. -ar; bɫang′- ket¹ 13 (all EN); bleng′-, bɫæng′-, bɫæng′- etc.; -kit, -ket etc.; bleing′kit 6Q3; bɫeing′ket 14D4. Cpd: ull- (wool), kjøpe- (boughten).

block n. section between intersecting streets 77. N no equiv (cf. DN *kvartal* n.; *blokk* f. m. n. 'block of wood'). E [bla′k] > blakk′ m. f. n. (m. 30, f. 9, n. 6), pl. —, -ar, -s; blåkk′ f. m. n. (f. 11, mostly from Indianland, m. 2, n. 2), pl. —; bla′k m. 15, pl. -s; in EN dial. bɫakk′ and bɫåkk′ can take the place of blakk′ and blåkk′; blak′s m. 15P1. Quot: en pa′r bɫåk¹ka 8G1.

bluff n. steep hill 61. N *haug* m. 3C4; *bakke* m. 18B1 18B2; *berg-knaus* 3C1. E [blʌf′] > blåff′ or bɫåff′ f. m. n. (f. in W. Wis. and E. Minn.; m. in S. and N.E. Wis.; n. in Suldal), pl. -er; blaff′ 3C3; blåf′fe m. 8M1 8M2; blåf′fa, blåf′fe f. 15P4 12Q1 12R1. Cpd: -kant (edge). Der: -ete (-y). Quot: Vi jikk′ oppi bɫåf′fa 14F2; hø′ge bɫåf′fer 11C2; åver nek′ste bɫåf′fa 20E1.

bookcase n. shelves for books 23. N *bokhylla* f., *bokskåp* n. (most inf., about evenly divided). E [bʊk′ke¹s] > bok′kei¹s m. 9; bok¹kei¹s 7; bo′kkei¹s 5; bo′kkei¹s 5L3; bo′gakei¹s 4N1.

bother v. annoy, worry 17. N no equiv. (cf. *bry*, *umaka*). E [ba′dhər] > ba′dra, pt. —. Quot: Han dre′v å ba¹dre mei 14D18; dæ ba¹drar tå¹le my′ 8L8; ba¹dra tå mis¹kiten 4Q2; du ba¹dra kje me′g 5L5; mine kreature badrer ekke dine sjaks 20Q2 (in letter).

bottom n. low-lying land near river 15. N no equiv. E [ba′ɫəm] > ba′tom m., pl. -s; bat′tom 5L1; ba¹tem 3C3; ba′tem 3C4. Cpd: -land. Quot: Ba′tomen ne ve krik′ken 5E1; ne på ba′tomen her 11C6; da vi kåm′ neri ba′tomen 5C1; på ø′vre ba′tomen 14D2.

box n. rectangular container 100. N *kasse* f. 11B2 5F1; *kista* f. 15P2; *bidna* f. 17Q3. E [ba′ks] > bak′s m. (f. 1K1 15P6 4P1), pl. -ar; bak'st m. 18 (all EN, but quite sporadic); båk's 4P1 6P1; bak'se 6Q4 6Q3; bas'k 14C2. Cpd: brød- (bread), cake-, cigar-, corn-, dubbel- (double), is- (ice), jury-, mail-, fyrstikk- (match), miter-, avis- (newspaper), tobakk- (tobacco), tool-, vogn- (wagon), ved- (wood); -car, -elder, -social. Quot: Ein run'de bak's me hø'l i 4Q2; lak't seg i bak'sen å lå'g å så'v 5F1; bak'st is val'lers, in general we say bak's 5L1; tok sæm'pels u't or kva'r bak's 4P3; bak'sain å kas'suin 11B2.

brake n. device for stopping movement 73. N no equiv. (cf. *bremse* f.). E [bre′k] > brækk′ m. n. f. (m. 55, n. 7, f. 5 So. Set.), pl. -s; brekk′ 12 (mostly EN); brikk′ 17Q2 15P1 20Q1; brei′k 17; bre′k 5; bre′k 6; brei′k 5; bræ′k 10C6. Inf. 14D3 distinguishes between a breik on an auto and a brækk on a wagon. Cpd: emergency- ; -mann (man).

bran n. ground husk of grain 87. N *kli* n. 8L3 4Q2 5L2 (who identifies *kli* rather with 'middlings' q.v.). E [bræ′n] > brann′ m. (n. 8M1 8M2); bran′d (in dial. with final -*nd*); bra′n 14D1 14D2 14D3 14D4; bræ′n 1K1 18B2; bræ′n 4F3 24A1. Cf. N *brand* m. 'fire'. Cpd: -røre (mixture).

breadbox n. box for keeping bread 89. N *brødbidne* 17Q3; *brødkopp* 5L2. E [brɛd′ba′ks] > brø′bak′s m. (for varying forms of box see that word); brø′rbak′s 16C1.

break v. (1) plow up virgin soil; (2) tame animals 18. N no equiv. (cf. *brjota; temja*). N *brekka* is always substituted for the E, pt. *brekte*. Quot: (1) Naor han va a′tjan ao′r, så bejyn′te han te å bræk′ka lan′d 4P1; åss måtte brækk′ ti′ æ′ker 25A1; e va′ mæ å bræk′te grubb′lann 19A1; dei brek′te opp præ′rien 4L4; han bræk′te mi′e lann′ mæ døm 14D4; upp′brækt lann′ 18B2; (2) Vi had′de dæm (oksekalvene) te dæm vart litt′ åver to′ år′, så bejyn′te vi å bræk′ke dæm 10C1; men se′a så bræk′te n i oks′tim tæll′ da 14D4.

breakfast n. morning meal 106. N *bisk* m. 13 (So. Vo. Vald. Tel.); *dugurd* m. (Vald. Tel.). E [brɛk′fəst] > brekk′fes′t m., pl. -ar; brækk′fæs′t (in dialects with open short æ); brækk′fest (less common than others); brækk- 3C2 15P3. Quot: Så fik′se e brekk′fest 11B5; la′ga te bræk′fæst 4H1.

brick n. burned clay block 91. N *murstein* m. 18B1; *tegelstein* m. 3C1 18C1. E [brɪk′] > (1) brikk′ m. (n. 15P3 9G2 8L4); brekk′;

brækk' 14D2 19A2 14D4 24A1; brikk' 11; (2) with substitution in N *murstein* or *tegelstein*: brikk'stei¦n m. 30 (in all comm., said to be old-fashioned); the same term occurs in AmGer from Ger *backstein*, acc. to Meyer AmSp Dec. 1926. Cpd: -cheese, -hus (house), -yard. Quot: å bræn'ne brekk' 20F6; et brekk'steinhu¦s 20F6 10C14.

broom n. implement for sweeping 19. N *lime* m.; *sopelime* m.; *sodel* 15P4 15P3; *sovel* 15P1; *sopil* (several inf. from So. and Vo.); *sopling* 7H1 7H3 12R1 12Q1 (the N words are given more frequently than the E). E [brʊm'] or [bru'm] > bromm' m. 13 (with ꭉ 1) bro'm 3; bru'm 4Q1; bru'm 7H2; bråmm' 17Q3.

brother-in-law n. male relative by marriage 25. N *svoger* m. 5; *måg* 15P4; *systermann* m. 6Q2; *svigerbror* m. 7 (an AmN creation?). E [brʌdh'ərinlɔ¦'] > bråd'derinlå¦ m;. form of word is extremely uncertain, with no general pattern: ꭉ generally for r; å varies to ø, ə, ʌ; dh is retained by some; cf. brød'derlå¦ 8M4. Quot: Min bro'r å min brød'derlå¦ 8M4; han er brʌdh'ərinlå¦en min 12Q4.

brush n. thicket, dense growth. N *brusk* m. universally used in this sense, prob. a loanshift ('tuft of straws or small plants; wisp, faggot' Aasen NO from Bergen diocese, Gbr. Tel.); bræus'k 15P2 6P1 4P1 15P4 20Q1; bru'sk 12Q1. Cpd: -land, -thicket, -haug (pile); hassel- (hazel), små- (small), under-. Der: bruske v. clear brush 14D3 14F3. Quot: ryd'de vekk brus'ken 5L1; borti brus'ken 10C11; kip't brus'ken ne're 18C1.

brush n. implement 27. N *kost* m. (preferred by most inf. to the E word); *kvost* m. 5 (Gbr. Vald.); *boste* m., *bæuste*, *bøste* many inf. (esp. Tel. Vald.). E [brʌsh'] > brøssj' m., pl. -ar; bråssj' (esp. WN); brʌssj'; brås'k 13N4 (def. brås'sjen); brus'k m. 4N1. Cpd: hår- (hair).

buggy n. vehicle 95. N no equiv. E [bʌg'i] > båg'gi m., pl. -ar; bog'gi, bøg'gi (esp. Tel.); båg'gë (esp. Midland dial.); båg'gi 6Q4 4Q3 7G1 6P1. Cpd: covered-, lett- (light), single-top-, topp- (top). Quot: i fys'te båg'gien 6P1; red'de får båg'gien 6Q4.

bulb n. glass around electric lamp 21. N no equiv. E [bʌl'b] > bål'b m., pl. -s; bøl'b 11C1 4K2; bal'b 14D1 14D3; bal'v 14D2. Cpd: light- (also lys-). Quot: Vi har små' bål'bs 26P4.

bull n. uncastrated male bovine 36. N *stut* m. 15P1 9G2;

ukse m. (used only of the draft animal in AmN). E [bʊl'] > bull' m., pl. -ar; boll' 4N1 6Q3 13N1; bul'le 14D3; bu'l 14C2. Cpd: -kalv (calf), -dog, -head, -hjul (wheel). Quot: Når dei fik'sa dei når dei var små', så va'r dei ikkje bul'lar anna åk'sar 5G1.

bureau n. chest of drawers 48. N *kommode* m. many inf.; *dragkista* f. 8. E [bjʊ'ro] > (1) bju'ro m. (f. 22F1, n. 8M2), pl. -ar; bju'ro; bju'ṛo; bju'ṛo; (2) bju'*t*u m. 3C2 3C1 18C1 8F1 (f. 20J1 3C4); bju'ru m. 4F1; (3) bju'ra f., def. bju'ro 4N1 13N1 13N4; bu'rau 20Q1; bju'rå 20Q1; byr'rå 10C6.

bushel n. unit of dry measure 91. N no equiv. E [bush'əl] > bus'sjel m., pl. —; bu'sjel 15P4 15P1; bus'sel 16 (esp. from -sl-dialects); bus'sjel 4N1. Cpd: halv- (half); -basket. Quot: en bus'sjel mæ pot'teter 8B2; 1,930 bus'sjel mæ grø'n 14D21; fem' å tju'ge sen't bus'sjelen 5F1.

business n. affairs, trade 21. N no equiv. (cf. *forretning*). E [bɪz'nəs] > bis'nes m. (n. 21H1); bis'nis 4; bis'nes 14D11 14D3. Cpd: insurance-, lumber-; -college, -mann (man), -møte (meeting). Quot: Dæ hadde jen'ge sjei's me bis'nesen 4L4; n ten'ne itte sin ei'en bis'nes såm n skul'le 14F2; han me'nte bis'nes 20C2.

buttery n. pantry 98. N *spiskammers* n. 7G1 11C1 10C5; some inf. believed buttery was N (14D1 5L2 5H4 7H3). E [bʌt'ri] > båt'ri n.; bòt'ri, bøt'ri, båt'ri (rare); båt'ṛi 4; båṛt'ri 20J1 18C2 14C1; båṛt'i 11B1.

cake n. sweet baked food in loaf or layer form 26. N no equiv. E [ke'k] > N ke'k m., pl. -ar; kei'k 5. Cpd: angelfood-, blod- (blood), brura- (bridal), devil's food-, fried-, johnny-, molasses-, pan-, små- (small); -box. Quot: et styk'ke mæ ke'k 5L3; ke'k så dæi kad'la he'r i Ame'rika 12Q2.

candy n. confection 40. N *godter* 5L4. E [kæ'ndi] > kæn'di m.; ken'di (about half the inf.). Cpd: chocolate-, horehound-, stick-. Quot: du ti'eke mæ' de kæn'di te låkkema'te 8M2.

car n. (1) railroad carriage; (2) automobile 61. N *bil* m. 11C4 8M2 (a recent word). E [ka'r] > ka'ṛ m., pl. -ar 29; ka'r 4L2 6Q2; ka'rs 10 (chiefly WN); ka'sj (ka'rs as pron. in EN) 19; ka's 12Q1. Cpd: baggage-, box-, freight-, hand-, stock-. Quot: han kjøf't se ein ka'ṛ 11B6; vi ræis'te i tre' ka'rsa 8M4; sto're, svæ're ka'ra 14D21; du sku ki'pe ka'rsen din i kontroll' 14D19; han ble dre'pen tå ein ka'ṛ 5L2; di lå'gju'*t*a ka'*t*a 18C1.

care n. in phrase 'take care of' 16. N *vare* 12R4. E [kæ′r] >
kæ′r̥; kæ′r (only WN). Der: -laus (-less). Quot: Ta kæ′r̥ tå pås′ten
10C13; mø må ta kæ′r̥ tå krø′tere 5H4; je tar kæ′r̥ tå før′nissen
20C1; såm tok kæ′r ao han 25P1.

care v. be concerned 43. N *bry seg* 20J1 and others. E [kæ′r]
> kæ*l*a or kær̥a v., pt. — (-te 12R1 6Q5 17Q4 17Q1 4N1; -d 18C1);
kæra (most Midland and WN inf.). Quot: E tenk′te ikkje du kæ′ra
så my′kje 4L4; en små′gu′t såm itte kæ′*l*e åkke hi′t ell di′t 10C1;
e kæ′r̥e itt så my får′ n 11C4; no kæ′ra eg ikkje, eg gå′r te kvenn′
da e′ 12R5.

carpet n. rug 56. N *matta* f., *golvmatta* f. (many inf.). E
[kar′pət] > kar′pet m., pl. -ar; kar′pet; kar̥′pet; kar′pët′ or
-pit′; ka′pit 4L1 (quot). Cpd: fille- (rag). Quot: Så bruk′te
di å væ′ve kar′pet 4F2; kar′pet so du spi′kra ne′ 6Q1; kar̥′pet e′
når dæ kåv′ra hei′le ro′me 5L4; hai′melaga kar′pet 6P1.

cash n. money on hand 33. N *kontant* m. preferred by most
inf. E [kæ′sh] > kæ′sj m.; kæ′s 12R1 12Q1 8M1. Cpd: -account,
-crop, -money, -register, -rent.

catch v. capture 41. N no equiv. (*fanga, taka* etc.). E [kɛt′sh]
> ket′sja v., pt. — 22; ket′kja 19. Cpd: -colt. Der: ket′sjar
(catcher). Quot: Det′te æ fis′te gång′en je ha vørti ket′kja 14D1;
ket′kja n mæ sam′ma n va′ på fæn′se 4P4; så′ vart n ket′kje tå
sa′ga 10C7; han ket′kja kjyl′d 12R1; dem ket′sje (pt.) dep′te′*l*i
(diphtheria) 14F2.

ceiling n. overhead interior lining of room 26. N *himling* f.
26 (m. 3); *tak* n. 28; *lem* m. 12R1 4Q2 4P1 9Q1; *rot* f. 8M1. E
[si′lɪŋ] > si′ling f. m. (f. 16, m. 10).

cent n. 1/100 of a dollar 71. N no equiv. E [sɛn′t] > sen′t m.
pl. — (after numbers), occ. -ar; sæn′t 12; sein′t 3C1 3C4. Cpd: fem-
(five). Quot: De bli ti′ sen′t pun′de 4Q2; før′rekju′ge sæn′t 11R1.

chance n. opportunity, risk 22. N *anledning* m. 20C5; (cf.
høve n., *tilfelle* n.). E [tshæ′ns] > kjæn′s m., pl. -er; kjen′s; tsjæn′s
tsjen′s; kjan′s. Quot: Kjen′s mæ na′bojen′tene 12Q4; kjen′s
te å få gått′ *l*ann′ 4L4; når du ik′kje ei′de en par′t i sku′tene, så
hadde du ing′en kjæn′s 4F4; så fækk′ je itte kjæn′sen 14C2.

change v. (1) alter; (2) exchange money 46. (1) N no equiv (cf.
brigda, byta, skifta); (2) *veksla* (many inf.). E [tshe′ndzh] >
kjei′nja v., pt. —; kjei′ndja; tsjei′ndja; kjen′sa 21H1 25A1 14D2

24A1. Quot: Dem ha kjen'sa nam'ne 25A1; no ha dai kjei'nja rå'den 20Q1; han kjei'nja mai'n sin 8L8; så bejyn'te vind'en å kjei'nja 17P1; di måtte kjei'nja på nav'ne 13N1; så bli dæ jen'ne om'kjein¦ja 3C2; kjei'nja ratt' å'ver 8L4.

chinchbug n. insect destructive to wheat 42. N *kveitefluga* 4P1. E (1) [tshɪn'tshbʌg¦] > kjen'sbågg¦ m.; kjin's-; kjæn's-; kjei'ns- 5G1 8L4 14D4; tsjin'tsj-, tsjin's-, tsjin'sj- etc.; (2) [sɪn'tshbʌg¦] > sin'tkjbågg¦ 10C2 10C3 17Q4 8M1. Quot: Så va' dæ kjei'nsbågg¦ eit å'r 14D4; kjei'nsbåg¦gen blei så bæ'd atte dei måtte slut'te (with the raising of wheat) 5G1.

chores n. pl. care of farm animals 73. N (kvelds-, fjøs-) *stell* n. many inf.; *stull* n. mostly Tel.; *styr* n.; *studdre* 8M1; *sjodn* f. 4P1. E [tshɔ'rz] > kjå'rs m., def. -en; kjå'ṛs; kjo'rs 4; tsjå'rs etc.; kjå's 15P1 4L1 4N1; kjo's 8M2 12R1 12Q1. Der: kjå'rsa v. do the chores 12; kjo'sa 14D4; kjå'ra 13N1; kjo'rsa 7H2 12R1. Quot: jo'ṛde all tsjå'ṛsen 10C13; har kjå'rsen å jæ'ra 17P1.

circus n. an entertainment 54. N *sirkus* 8L3. E [sər'kɪs] > sør'kis m., pl. -ar; søṛ'kis 18; sør'kus 14D1 22F1 25A1; sør'kis 13N3 3C2.

clean v. free from dirt 52. N *pynta* 3; *renska* 9G1 (not equiv.). E [kli'n] > kli'na v., pt. — or -te (the latter WN: 8M1 12Q1 15P4 17Q2 17Q4 6Q2 13N1 3C3); kḷi'na 11B1 7H2 9G3. Cpd: hus- (-ing), vacuum- (-er). Quot: kli'ne opp ba'ten 14D2; kḷi'ne ba'ṭinn 11B1; kli'n ut ba'nen 8M1; kli'ne hu's (many inf.).

clerk n. assistant in a store 87. N *betjent* 7H2. E [klər'k] > klør'k m., pl. -ar 62; kløṛ'k; kler'k 25. Cpd: clothing-, county-, skule- (school), town-.

clevis n. U-shaped metal piece for attaching to a drawbar 81. N *klave* 4L4 (not equiv.). E [klɛv'ɪs] > klø'vis m., pl. -ar; klø'vis 4; kḷø'vis (all EN dialects having kḷ in *kløver*); kløv'vis 7; klev'vis 8F1; kḷø'ver 4K1 8L1; klå'vis 7H2; klø'vesj 14D1 14D3; kḷø'vers 8L4; kle'vis 5. Cpd: plog- (plow).

closet n. small room for clothing 94. N *klækammers* n. 7G1 4L4; *klærom* n. 6P1; *klæskåp* n. 6Q3. E [kla'zət] > kla'set¦ m. n. (m. 85, n. 7); klå'set¦ 17; kla'set 13; klå'set 3; -set, -sit many inf.; kḷa'set 4; kḷå'sett¦ 10C6; -ss- 5. Cpd: klæ- (clothes).

cold n. infection 96. N *krim* m. 6 (Vald. Tel. and 4Q2); *forkjøling* f. 9 (Tel. Suld. Hard. and 4Q2); *forkjølelse* m. 6. Most inf.

have given one of the N words for 'cold' (in the sense of 'coolness'); these are most likely all loanshifts, except *kjøld: kulde* m. 51 (EN Midl. Tr.); *kalde* m. 14D1 11B1; *kale* m. 14D2 14D4 14D6; *kule* m. 4P1 6P1 15P4; *kjøl* m. 7; *kjøld* f. 15 (all So. Nfj. plus 2C2 3C4). These often appear in phrases modelled on E catch cold: ket'kja kul'le; han a tikj'i kal'de 25A1.

common school n. public school 34. N *folkeskule* 14C1 25P3. E [ka′mǝnsku'l] > ka′men- 7 (second half is always N *skule* m.); ka'men- 7; kåm'men- 8; kåm′men 6; kam′men- 3; kå′men- 2. Quot: Almin′dele kam′ensku'ɫe 4H1; jekk' ut kåm′mensku'ɫen; kåm nå nes′ten ijø′no almin′dele kåm′mensku'len so mi kad'la dæ i dæi′ da'ga 6Q3.

cooky n. a small cake 90. N *bakels* m. 7H2. E [kʊk′i] > kok′ki m., pl. -s; kok′kis m., pl. — or -ar (more common than the preceding); kuk′ki (chiefly So.). Cpd: sirup-. Quot: Ho mo′r ba'ka kok′kis 20Q1; me'ka kok′kis 13N5.

cord wood n. sawed wood for fuel 55. N *famnved* m. 12R5. E [kɔr′dwʊd'] > (1) kår'dve' m. (second half is N *ve* 'wood'); (2) kår'dave' m. So. Hard.; kår'deve' Hall. Land Vald. Hedd. Toten; also kåṛ'd-, kåṛ'de-, kår'- 14C2, kå'ṛ- 16C1. Cpd: -pile. Quot: splitt'a kår'dve' 5L1.

corn n. maize. Always reproduced by the N word *korn* 'grain', excepting for a very occasional kåṛn. Cpds: pop-, seed-; -beef, -binder, -box, -brød (bread), -country, -crib, -fed, -field, -husker, -husking, -meal, -picker, -planter, -planting, -plog (plow), -shock, -shredder, -stalk. Quot: Dæ va kåd'n å kvæi'te 4P2; plan'te kønn′ 5G1; dri've å has'ka kåd'n 15P6.

corncrib n. structure for storing unshelled maize 89. N no equiv. A loanshift cpd. in which the first part is N *korn* (see preceding word), second part is usually N *krubba* f. 'fodder rack'. A few inf. have E [krɪb′] > krybb′ m. (4 Iola inf. and 1K1 14D2). Quot: Omtren′t so sto′r so ai kånn'kryb'ba 4P1.

cornmeal n. coarsely ground corn 79. N no equiv. E [kɔr′nmi'l] is reproduced by morphemic substitution as ko'rnmjø'l, with the forms appropriate to each dialect, except > kå'ṛn- 4N1 4F2 5F1; -mi'l 14D1 2C2. Cpd: -flour. Quot: Hal'vde'len kvei'temjø'l å hal'vede'len kår′nmjø'l 5F1; en kopp′ mæ ko'rnmjø'ɫ 18C5; mjø'l — da va kje kvi′t flæu′r, mjø'l va bruk′t um mid'lingen åfta 4P1.

corn shredder n. machine for shredding corn 30. N no equiv. E [-shrɛdˈər] or [-shedˈər] > -sjredˈdar m., pl. -s 10; -sjredˈdeɾ 9; -sjɾedˈder 5; -sjedˈdar 4 (all from Blair); -sredˈdar 4N1; -skredˈdar 1K1.

corner n. intersection of roads or property lines 56. N *hynne* n. f. 4K1; *jørne* n. 6; *kro* f. 6P2 4L1. E [kɔrˈnər] > kåˈɾne n., pl. — 25 (EN); kårˈna n., def. -a 20 (WN Tel. Gbr.); kårˈna n., def. -ae 11 (WN Tel. Gbr.); kårˈne f., def. -a 6; kårˈna f., def. -ao 6Q1 6Q3; kåˈɾna m., def. -n 5H1 5H3; kåˈɾneɾ m. 4; kåˈɾner m. 7G1 7H1 7H2 (n.). Cpd: fence-, street-, woodbox-; -post, -stone. Quot: Oppå kåˈɾna hær ve Maont Hoˈreb 4K2; baˈkom kåˈɾne 14D4; i samˈma kårˈne på samˈma gamˈle huˈse 15P4; i noˈrvæsˈtre kårˈna 20P2.

corset n. female garment 64. N *snøreliv* n. 9; *korsett* n. 5N1; *strypeband* n. 7H3. E [kɔrˈsət] > kårˈsettˡ m. 13; kårsˈet 9; kåɾˈset 27; kåˈrsettˡ 14; kårsˈlettˡ 8L1.

country n. (1) rural neighborhood; (2) nation 65. N *land* n. 19. E [kʌnˈtri] > konˈtri n., def. — or -e, pl. — or -ar 21; konˈtri 3; kønˈtri 7 (Sol. Gbr.); kønˈtri 2; kånˈtri 12 (WN Tel.); kånˈtri 12; kʌnˈtɾi 5; kuntriˈi 8M1. Cpd: korn-, farm-, farming-, pinery-; -skule (school). Quot: De va e uˈhelsi kånˈtri 14F2 (ref. to Koshkonong); i fråˈ dette kønˈtri hæˈr 14D4 (the Blair region); hæˈr i disˈse kønˈtrie 11B6; i kånˈtrie runˈt 12Q4; skuˈ*l*en i konˈtri 20F13; e vilˈt konˈtri 10C14; ditˈti skulle vaˈra ett frittˈ konˈtri 3C2.

county n. division of a state 85. N. no equiv. (cf. *amt* n.). E [kauˈn*t*i] > kaoˈnti n., pl. — or -s; kæuˈnti 12 (older form); konˈti 18C2; kønˈti 8L1. Cpd: -attorney, -board, -clerk, -judge, -office, -paper, -seat, -superintendent. Quot: kåmˈmå på kaoˈntie (on relief) 25A1; en skrækˈkeli mængˈde fålˈk ifrå fiˈre kaoˈnti 5F1.

court n. legal institution 54. N *rett* m. 18B1 5L1. E [kɔˈrt] > N *kort* n. ˈcardˈ; only 5 make it m. (4 Solør and 5Q1). Cpd: circuit-, supreme-; -hus (house), -street. Quot: so skulˈ me no haˈ ain traiˈel dao, å so [setˈte me] korˈte daˈr 6P2.

cousin n. uncle or aunt's son or daughter 43. N *syskenbarn* n. given by most inf., but E word used freely in conv. E [kʌzˈən] > kåsˈsen m., pl. -s, def. pl. -sa 19; køsˈsen 10; køsˈsen 12R5 25A1; kosˈsin 4H1; kusˈsen 4P1; kasˈsen 14C2; kasˈten 9G3. Cpd:

fyrste- (first), second-. Quot: E har en kås'sen i Når'ge såm e yng're ell e'g 4Q2; døt'te åt køs'sen mi 12R5; je hadde skre'vet te en køs'sen a mei 26P4; kås'sinsa doms 5E1.

cracker n. thin, crisp biscuit 81. N no equiv. E [kræ'kər] > (1) kræ'ker m., pl. -s 21 (15 r̥); kræ'ker; kræk'ker̥; (2) kræ'kers m., pl. — or -ar 31 (17 r̥); kræk'kers 7; (3) kræ'kis m., pl. — or -ar 10; krek'kis 6, krek'ki 4N1 (WN informants); kræ'kar 6P2 4P1 (quot); krek'kerte 8M2. Cpd: fire-, graham-, nut-, soda-, sweet-. Quot: So va dan kræ'karen so tur're 6P2; kji's å kræ'ker̥s 4Q2.

cradle n. scythe with attached wooden frame 55. N no equiv. E [kre'dəl] > krid'del (krid'l) m. all WN inf. (exc. 15P2 15P3 15P4); krill' (most inf.). Quot: E batt' ette krill' æu e' 11B2; e huk'sar den ti' di brukte krill' 5L1; små'grø'ne de slo di ne' mæ en krill' 4K1.

cradle v. cut grain with a cradle 11. N no equiv. E [kre'dəl] > krid'la v., pt. —; kril'le. Quot: Oss kril'la runt fi'lin 11B2; fa'r min kril'le fæm' æ'ker på en da'g 14D4; så byn'te Gul'laik å krid'la 4P1; kril'la dæ mæ hån'd 12R6; kril'le gr̥e'ne mæ en krill' 8F1.

creek n. small stream 90. N *bekk* m. 3C1 7H2. E [krɪk'] > krikk' m., pl. -ar; krekk' 11 (EN, chiefly Solør). Quot: So'*l*onga sæie bækk' dæm i stæl'le fær krækk' 14D7; fis'ke i krik'kjen 4L4; fis'k i krik'kåm 5F1; bai'nt ne i krik'kjen 4P1; ba'tomen ne ve krik'ken 5E1; en krikk' eller en e*l*'v 11C2.

crew n. group engaged for particular job 72. N no equiv. (cf. *mannskap*). E [kru'] > kru' n. f.m. (n. 34 in Indianland, Mt. Morris, Suldal, Dovre, Wiota, Waterloo Ridge; f. 34 in Coon Prairie and Coon Valley, Lyster, Spring Grove, and Valdres inf.; m. 4 scattered). Cf. N *kru* n.f. swarm, multitude (Aasen: Nordhordland; Ross: Hardanger, Lister). Cpd: section-, trøskar- (thrashing). Quot: sto'rt kru' 8L7; dæ an'dre kru'e 8B2; jaga dan'sekry'e ut 4P1.

crop n. produce 56. N *avling* f. 43 (of whom 12 also give 'crop'); *grøe* f. 4L1 4P1 5G1 8M2. E [kra'p] > (1) krapp' m., pl. -ar 29; kr̥app' 9; kr̥a'p 10; (2) kråpp' m., pl. -ar 8. Cpd: eple- (apple), cash-, second-. Quot: En svæ'r kr̥a'p mæ hei' 14D21 (a moment later: bæ're a'v*l*ing); re'sa go'e kråp'pa 5H7; mo'di go'e kr̥ap'per 14D4 (also krap's); får å få' inn kr̥ap'pen den såm'mårn 14D4.

cultivator n. farm implement 78. N no equiv. (but many give *kornplog* m. from E corn plow). E [kʌl'təve'tər] > kål'tevei'ter m.; kål'te- 32; kål'ti- 8; køl'ti- 10; kul'ti- 5; kol'ti- 24A1; -kal'ti-5H1; kol'te- 16C; kål'le- 14D2; -vei'ter 30 (EN Midl.); -vei'teɽ 7 (EN); -vei'tar 14 (WN and 14D3); -ve'ter 4; kålteve'ter 8M2; kåltivet'ter 8M1. Cpd: sulky-. Quot: Fys'te kål'tive'tarn me hadde 4P2.

curtain n. fabric hung around windows 65. N *gardina* f. many inf.; *umheng* n. 4K1 4L4 5L2; *heng* n. 17P1. E [kər'tn] > køɽ'ten n., pl. -s or —; kør'ten 12.

cut v. sever 29. N *skjera* v. in general use; 'cut' is primarily used with crops. E [kʌt'] > kat'ta v., pt. —; køt'ta 21H 11C1 (has also heard kørt'e). Cpd: -out, -worm. Quot: Eg ha kat'ta kåd'n 15P4; kat'ta smao'grø'ne 6P1; kat'ta gra's 14D2; dom kat'ter itte i år' 10C1; rai'p te å kat'te 4F1; sto å kat'ta ban'd 5L1; å den' kat'ta di opp å søɽ'va 13N5; O'*t*a vart fårdær'vakat'ta i en mo'var 25A1; når in'kon kattar upp' 4L3 (i. e. plays pranks).

cutter n. small, one-seated sleigh 48. N no equiv. E [kʌt'ər] > kat'tar m., pl. -ar 14; kat'ter 9; kat'ter 10; kat'tar 4L3; kart'er 5 (all Coon V. and Pr.); kut'ter 4 (all from Iola); køt'ter 19A2 7G1; køt'təɽ 19A1 3C2 3C3. Quot: Dæi kjø'ɽde te kjær'ka på ju'*t*eda'gen me kat'ter 5E1; han had'de så fi'n kart'er 11B5.

depot n. railroad station 88. N *stasjon* m. 13. E [di'po] > di'po m.f.n. (m. 77, f. 4, n. 7, 1 m.f., 1 m.n.), pl. -ar 39; di'po 16; dip'po 7; dy'po 10C2; dipo' 8M2; dep'po 13; de'po 5; depo' 12R5; de'po 5H1; de'på 2C1. Quot: Ein an'jen depo' 12R5.

deuce n. twospot in cards 23. N (*hjarter*)*to* m. 8; *toar* 15P3. E [du's] > du's m. Cpd: hjerter- (hearts).

dig v. turn over earth 67. N *grava* 25 (of whom 13 also give 'dig'). E [dɪg'] > dig'ga v., pt. — (dagg' 9G2; dogg' 3C3; dig'de 14C1). Der: digger; in cpds. like gold-, grave-. Quot: Man'nen dig'ga ron't i kjis'ta 4L4; dom kunne dig'ge brøn'ner 20E1; om høs'ten dig'ga n ti' æ'ker me pot'tet oppå kå'rna hær 5F1; ein go'feɽt va så lei' te dig'ge upp kòn'ne 5G1.

dining room n. room for eating 34. N no equiv. (cf. *spiserom* 7G1). E [dai'ningru'm] > dai'ningromm' n. (the second part is N); da'ning- 4Q1. Quot: u't i dai'ningrom'me 6P1.

dipper n. container with handle for dipping liquids 51. N *ausa*

f. 7. E [dɪp'ər] > (1) dip'per m., pl. -rar 18; dip'per 11; dip'par 4N1; dyp'per 2; dyp'per 2; (2) dip'pert m., pl. -er 10; dyp'pert 3; dyp'part 15P4.

dish n. open, shallow container 19. N no equiv. (cf. *fat* n., *skål* f.). E [dɪsh'] > dissj' m.; dis'k Set. Tel. So. Suld. Vald. (cf. *disk* m. 'wooden plate' Tel. etc.); diss' 3 Vald. Cpd: sauce-, vaska- (wash); -pan, -vatn (water). Quot: Dis'kevatn å an'na såm de ik'kje va fi'd i 4L4.

dishes n. pl. tableware 39. N *koppar* 8M2. E [dɪsh'əz] > dis'sjis m., def. -en; dis'sjes 4F2 18C2 18B2; dys'sjys 11C4; dys'-sjes 18B2. Quot: Dem vas'ka dis'sjis 18B3; jæt'pe dom mæ dis'-sjisen 14D22.

dollar n. 100 cents 42. N *dalar* m., an old-fashioned N monetary unit, abolished in 1875, worth about $1.20, took over the value of the Am. dollar. Forms: da'lar So. Vo. Hard.; da'lar 4; da'ler Tel. Vald.; da'ler 2; da'*l*e EN Gbr. Tr.; da'le Hard.; dal'lar 6Q3; dal'ler 4Q2; da'li 8M2. Quot: træd've tu'sen da'*l*e 14D11; ain da'lar kva'r....ait pa'r da'la pao kva'r 6P2.

dresser n. dressing table, bureau 29. N *kommode* m. most inf.; *dragkista* f. 8; cf. bureau. E [drɛs'ər] > dres'ser m., pl. -s or -ar 21 (with one or both ṛ 13); dres'sar 7; dressa'ri 8M1.

dust n. fine earth 65. N *støv* n. 13; *dust* m. 3; *duft* f. 4; *gyft* f. 2; *gøyva* f. 18B1 18B2; *dumba* f. 4; *føykja* f. 4K1; *gøyv* m. 4L4; *ryk* n. 15P1. E [dʌs't) > døs't f.m.n. (f. 33, m. 15, n. 2C1 1K1). Cpd: sag- (saw); -mop, -pan, -rag. Der: -er, -ut (-y). Quot: Set'tle døs'ta 5H6.

engine n. machine 67. N no equiv. E (1) [ɪn'dzhain] > (A) in'(d)jain m. (f. 7H1 7H2) 24; in'(d)jein 10; in'(d)jain 5; en'(d)jain 5; en'djøyn 4L4; in'djåin 11B1; in'(d)jøyn 18B2 18C2; in'jørn 18B2 (quot); (B) in'(d)jaina f. 6; in'dzhaine 4L3; en'djåina 15P4 6P1; indjai'na 6Q1; in'djaine 12R1; indzhai'ne 8M1 8M2; en'-dzhaina f. 6Q5; in'djena 4Q2. (2) [ɛn'dzhɪn] > end'jin m. 3; in'djen 3; en'djin 2. Cpd: automatic-, gasoline-, steam-. Quot: Sti'm-en'djin to' ut før n neå'ver bak'ken 19A2.

factory n. building for manufacturing 48. N *fabrikk* m. 15 (n. 9G1). E [fæ'kt(ə)ri] > fek't(e)ri n. 21; fæk't(e)ri 17; fæ'ktri 12; fekteri' 4N1 7G1 18B2. Cpd: cheese-, mjølk- (milk), pea-. Quot: Så rei'se vi på fek'trie 5C1; de såm me' få'r på fæk'trie 4H1.

fair n. exhibition 85. N no equiv. E [fæ'rʲ] > fæ'r̩ m.f. (m. 51, f. 34); fæ'r 29 (cf. N *ferd* f., pron. fæ'r in WN, fæ'l or fæ'r̩ in EN). Cpd: state-; -ground. Quot: på fæ'ren 14D22; sa små' fæ'ra 14D1.

fanning mill n. machine for cleaning grain 53. N no equiv. E [fæ'nɪngmɪlʲ] > fæ'ningmylʲla f. (second part always N); fæ'- ning- 21; fæ'ning- 8; fen'ning- 8 (mostly EN); feiʹning- 4 (Holt Valdres); fæ'ni- 14C2 14D3 20Q1; fæʹne- 5 (all WN); fan'ning- 10C1; fæiʹne- 13N3; feiʹn- 8L1 8L4.

faucet n. tap, cock 51. N *kran(e)* m. 37; *(bir-)hane* m. 4. E (1) [fæ'sət] > fæʹsettʲ m., pl. -ar; fæʹset, fæ'set, fæ'sit 20; (2) [fa'sət] > faʹsettʲ, fasʹsettʲ, fa'set, faʹsit 15; (3) [fɔ'sət] > fåʹsettʲ, fåsʹsettʲ, få'set 16.

feed n. food, esp. grain, given to farm animals 33. N *for* n. (several use the N word ab. hay, straw, cornstalks, the E word ab. grain only). E [fi'd] > fi'd m. Cpd: heste- (horse), krøter- (cattle); -binge (bin), -loft. Quot: go' fi'd te vin'tern åt krø'tera 14D12; bru'ka byd'dje te fi'd 4L4; vi bru'ker dæ tell fi'd 18C1; fi'den vart så ry'r 11B2.

feed v. give food to 24. N *gjeva* 17Q2. E [fi'd] > fi'da v., pt. —. Quot: Vi fi'da me hånn' 4K2; dei' kan du fi'da upp sjø'l 14L1; fi'de ti'me 14F3; fi'de da sai'lidsj 8M1; fi'de krøt'tera fi'd 18C3; fi'da ku'a frå ba'kein'n 11C1.

feel v. have sensation 43. N *føla* v., pt. -*te* 16 (8 gave both words); an urban word, requiring the refl. *seg* when speaking of bodily states. E [fi'l] > fi'la v., pt. -te 27, — 12 (incl. all Tel. and Tr.), both pt. 5. Quot: E fi'la då'le 24A1; nå' ær je sæk'sti å'r å je fi'ler lik'så gått' såm da je var to' å tju'gu å'r 14D13; nå me fi'la te de 5L2 (when we felt like it); han Bø'r̩t fi'lte visst gått' 14D7 (was drunk); hæ'r burti byg'di burtme kjyr'kja sa dei 'han fi'lar no' 4L4 (is moderately drunk).

fence n. enclosure 64. N no equiv. (cf. *gjerde* n., *gard* m., *ut-gard* m., *skigard* m.). E [fɛn's] > fen's n. (f. 1K1, m. 14C2); fæn's 22; fein's 10C5; fen'ts 15P3. Cpd: rail-, wire-; -krok (corner), -line, -post, -stretcher. Quot: Bor'ti æit fen's 6P1; fek'sa fæn'se 4L4; ja no ha e kasta djævelen bort i fensakroken 20P2 (letter).

fence post n. post holding up fence 47. N *gjerdestolpe* m. 4L2; *stolpe* m. 7H3. E [fɛn'spoʲst] > (1) fen'spåsʲt m. 10; (2) fen'sepåsʲt

m. 31; (3) fen'sapås¦t 5 (So. Suld. Hard.). Second part always N.

field n. piece of land for pasture or tillage 94. N *åker* m. 4; (cf. *mark* f.). E [fi'ld] > fi'l f., pl. -er (always identical in form with N *fil* f. 'file'); fi'ld, fi'l 12Q7. Cpd: grøn- (grain), korn- (corn), kløver- (clover), harvest-, havre-(oat), kveite- (wheat); -arbeid (work). Quot: Lang't utpå fi'la 20C3; ar'be uti fi'la 4H1; i fi'læ 15P3; utpå fi'låm 11C1; ar'beidde fi'line 4L4; å set'ter dei ut i a'keren eller fi'lda såm vi sei'er 12Q7; fi'la va så u'tma¦gra 5H7.

fills n. pl. shafts of a carriage, thills 38. N *skåk* f. 6; *tindla* f. 12Q1. E [fɪl'z] > fil's n.f.m. (n. 22, f. 11, m. 3, m.f. 1, m.n. 1), pl. —; fill' 2C2 17Q4; fyll' 3C2.

fine n. penalty 42. N *mult* f. 13. E [fai'n] > fai'n m.f.n. (m. 32, f. 3, n. 3, m.n. 1, m.f. 2, n.? 1); fæi'n 17Q3 13N2 9G1 8M2; fei'n 4L2. Quot: Beta'le litt fai'n 14L2.

fine v. impose a fine 23. N no equiv. (cf. *multera*). E [fai'n] > fai'na v., pt. —; fæi'na 11B1 20F18; fei'na 5G1. Quot: So fai'na eg dai ain da'lar kva'r 6P2; han vart fai'ne 2C2.

fish pole n. pole used for fishing 44. N *fiskestong* f. (or *stong* f.) 25; *fiskesprett(e)* n.f. 5 (all EN, mostly Upl.); *fisketroa* f. 5 (Hard. So. Vo.). E [fɪsh'po¦l] > fis'kepå¦le m., in which both parts are N substitutions (-på¦le 26, of whom 9 -*t*-); -po¦l 12; -på¦l 6 (incl. all from Valders, Wis.; 4 have *t*).

fix v. (1) repair, order; (2) prepare, arrange; (3) dispose of, settle; cf. fix up, well fixed etc. 34. N no equiv. (cf. *gjera i stand, stella, avgjera*). E [fɪk's] > fik'sa, pt. —. Quot: (1) So kun'de me fik'sa dan rip'paren 6P2; fækk fiks' opp atte 10C1; flin'k til å fik'se al'le ting's 14F2; fik'sa fæn'se 4L4; fik'sa opp tob'baks-plan¦ta 6P1; byn'te å fik'se på detta lan'ne 5F1; fek's opp hu'se 19A3; åffer fik'ser du itte rå'den vår 14D13; (2) dæi fik'sa upp mæi'r ell almin'deli te ju'*t* 5H4; fik'sa te sæng' åt n 8L5; så fik'sa dei te' rutt'bir 5L5; dom fik'sa lu'tefis¦ken sjøl've 4F1; fik'se tæll te ju'*t* 10C1; fik'se te ma'ten 18B3; så hadde mi fik'sa opp ain kå'r sin såkk' 20Q1; så fik'se e brekk'fes¦t 11B5; (3) me sku fik'sa han me' 6P2; dæ va in'jin a'en såm va så væ'l fik'sa 4L4.

flour n. finely ground meal, esp. of wheat 104. N *mjøl* n. 6 (used by older people about coarser meal 4P1 5L3). E [flau'ər] > flæu'r m. (n. 4, only altern.); flao'r 5. Cpd: coarse-, graham-, rug- (rye); -byra (bin), -mylla (mill), -sifter. Quot: Ain må'le mæ flæo'r 6P2; mjø'l va kje kvi't flæo'r 4P1; de va' itte my'e flæu'r den' tia 11B1.

fork n. implement (1) for farm work, (2) for eating 35. N (1) *greip* n. 11B1; *gryp* n. 11C4; (2) *gaffel* m. many inf., esp. EN. E [fɔr'k] > N *fork* m. 'stick with forked end' Vald. Hall. Used by all inf. for the farm implement; by most WN and some EN inf. for the eating implement. Cpd: høy- (hay), gjødsel- (manure), møkk- (manure), pitch-, potet- (potato), strå- (straw); -tind (tine). Quot: En får'k å dig'ge pote'tene mæ 8F1.

forty n. piece of land 40 acres large 15. N no equiv. E [fɔr'*ti*] > N *fyrti* m., the numeral for 40. Only in Indianland is the E word often retained (as generally in that community with the numerals): to få'rtis av lann' 8C4; ei få'ṛtileng'd 8L. Quot: en før'ti me lann' 12Q4; di'd pao før'tien 4P1; fjort'en ført'ia 20F6; så ein ført'i te' 5H7; dan vet'la fyr'tien 20Q2.

frame house n. house with frame construction 33. N no equiv. E [fre'm hau's] > frei'mhu's n. (second part always N); frei'm- 13 (2 ṛ); fre'm- 13N1; fremm'- 5H3; frei'mus 4Q1. Quot: frei'm-hu's å lågg'hu's 11C2; al'le frei'mhu's 19A1.

front porch n. porch before front entrance 26. N *veranda* 8L3. E [frʌn't pɔr'tsh] > från'tpår'tsj m. 12; frånt- is also frånt-, frant-, front-. The other inf. substitute N words for one or both parts: från'ttramm' m. 13N3 20J1; framm'pår'tsj m. 9; framm'-tramm' m. 8M1; framm'stu'p m. 12Q1 6Q1. For forms of **porch** see that word.

front room n. parlor 27. N *stova* f. etc. (see **parlor**). E [frʌn't ru'm] > från'tromm' n. 12 (second part N); also front-, frunt-, frønt-, frant- with tone 1 or 2.

gallon n. four quarts 62. N no equiv. E [gæ'lən] > gal'lon m., pl. — or -ar 22; ga'lon 16; gal'lan 12 (Rock Pr., Wiota, Blue Mds. and Coon Pr.); galo'n 6; ga'lan n. 9Q1; ga'lant 6P1; gal'lion 9Q1 (quot.); galo'ne f. 8M1; gal'lon 8F1; gal'len 9G3. Cpd: -krukke (jar). Quot: tju'ge sen't gal'lonen 5H4; ein fem'gallonkag'ge 5H4; e had'de en gal'lon mæ al'kehå'l 19A2.

game n. pastime 51. N no equiv. (cf. *leik* m.). E [ge'm] > gei'm m., pl. -s or -ar (-s 18, -ar 22) 29; ge'm 22. Cpd: ball-, base-ball-. Quot: ein li'ten gei'm 4L4; så plei'de dom gei'mer 14F3;

dem had'de fårsjæl'lige ge'ms 2C3; gei'ms å e'venty'r 4P1; sto'
i dø'ra å ba'sa gei'men 10C13.

garden n. cultivated plot 53. N *hage* m. 16; 17 give both words,
and some make a distinction of *hage* 'orchard' vs. *garden* 'flower
and vegetable plot'. E [gar'dn] > gar'den m. most inf.; gaṛ'den
20; gar'den 7 (mostly So.); gar'de m. 4 (all Suldal); gar'din 1K1.
Cpd: blomster- (flower); -stoff (stuff). Quot: han gå'r i gar'den 19A3.

gee interj. command to oxen to turn right 21. N no equiv.
E [dzhi'] > dji' (dzhi') interj. 11; djy' (dzhy') 6; jy' 4. Quot: når du
ska tø'rne te høg're, så si'er du jy' 10C2; te høg're sa vi djy' 10C1;
ha' å dji' 10C3.

get along v. succeed, agree, make progress 14. N no equiv. (cf.
klara seg, greia seg). E (1) [geťʾəlɔng'] > get'te lång' v., pt. get'ta;
(2) [gɪtʾ-] > git'te lång' 4. Quot: dom kun'ne væl itte get'te lång'
14D11; dei kan' ikkje get'te lång' 5L3; dæm git'te vist itte lång'
fæ'ťt gått' 14D7; da get'ta ho lång' ganske gått' 20Q1; je gette
lång' nåkså gått' på al'le sku'ťer 20J1; å get'te lång' så vitt'
dom kunne læ'va 10C8.

good-by interj. farewell 27. N *farvel, du får leva så vel*, etc.
(many inf.). E [gudba'i] > gudba'i interj. 15; guba'i 8; godbai'
3; gubæi' 8M2.

gopher n. an American ground squirrel 82. N *rindemus* f. 7H2
(?); (cf. *vond* m.). E [go'fər] > gof'fert m., pl. -ar 22; guf'fert 19;
go'fer 11 (mostly WN; 5 r); gof'feṛ 7; gu'fert 4; guf'fer 17Q4;
go'fot 17Q2.

grain n. cereal seeds 75. N no equiv. (cf. *korn* n.). E [gre'n] >
(1) gre'n n. 10; grei'n 4P1 8B3 (nearly all inf. located in Koshkonong and Indianland communities); (2) N *grjon* n. 'food prepared
from grain; a kernel of grain', with forms in dialects (acc. to Aasen);
P *grjon*, BL *gron*, HJR *grjøn*, D *gryn*. Acc. to A. Eifring *grøn*
means 'grain' in Hedmark; see also Hoff, Skjetvemålet 143; also
Romerike. AmN forms are: usually grø'n, but also gro'n 5L2
11B1, grjø'n 7H2, grønn 5G1 9Q1 11E1 22F1. Cpd: små- (small),
vinter- (winter); -binge (bin), -avling (crop), -elevator, -field,
-harvest, -hus (house), -stakk (stack). Quot: te å har'veste grø'ne
5L1; litt' grø'n 18C1; vi by'ner mæ å sjæ're grø'ne 5E1.

granary n. storehouse for thrashed grain 92. N *bu* f. 7G1;
kveitehus n. 4L3 4P1 5L3 15P2 and *grønhus* n. 8 (mostly Coon V.

and P.) appear to be AmN creations; the closest building in Norway would be the *låve* m. (cf. *grønlåve* Hedmark). E [gre'n(ə)ri, græ'n(ə)ri] > (1) gre'nri, gre'neri, grei'neri n. 14; gren'ri 14; grin'-neri 4L1 5L3; gren'dri 4N1; grin'dri 1K1 (forms with e or i are chiefly found in S. and E. Wis.); (2) grø'nri, grø'neri n. 20; grøn'ri, grøn'neri 32; gry'nri 7H1 7H2; gryn'neri 8M1; grunri'i 8M2; grøn'dri 6Q2 8L4 12Q1. Quot: stab'bur bruk't te grønn'ri 5F1; bruk'te de te grø'neri 4L4.

grapes n. pl. fruit of the genus Vitis 26. N *druer* 9; *vindruer* 8. E [gre'ps] > grei'ps 15; grei'ps 3; grip's 11; grip's 3; grep's 9; grep's 2; gre'ps 2. Quot: dei la'ga te vi'n tå grep's 5H4.

gravel road n. road surfaced with gravel 56. N *grusveg* 3C1 8M1. E [græ'vəl ro'd] > græ'velrå'd m., pl. -ar (10 inf. substituted N *veg* m. for the second part); græ'vel- 17, græ'vel- 5, græ'vel- 11, græv'vel- 13, græv'vel- 2, græv'la- 6, græ'vla- 2. For forms of **road** see that word.

graveyard n. burial ground 43. N *kyrkjegard* m. and *gravplass* m. share with graveyard approx. the same number of inf.; the first is limited to a burial ground by a church. E [gre'vjar'd] > gra'vjar'd m. The first part is N *grav* m.; for the second see the word **yard** (-djard 8M2; -jærd 15P3). Quot: oppme gra'vjar'den 8G1; begrø'vin på Konval'le gra'vjar'd 11C1; no kvitt' såm hel't på upp' å ne' i gra'vjar'den 5L3.

gravy n. dressing of fat and meat juices 101. N *saus* m. 4; *dubbe* 5L2 (? duppe, cf. Aasen). E [gre'vi] > (1) gre'vi m. 30 (3 r); grei'vi 21 (4 r); græ'vi 2; (2) gre've m. 38 (4 r, 2 ei); identical in form with N *greve* m. 'count'. Other forms: grei'vi 4K1; gre'vi 4F1 12Q1; gre've 4Q2.

grocery n. a store; (in plural) goods sold at a grocery 36. N no equiv. E [gro'səri] > (1) gro'seri n., pl. -s or -ar 14; gro'seri 4F1; gros'seri 4; (2) gräs'seri n. 9; grå'seri 8. Cpd: -store. Quot: al'le sta' dær di hadde grå'seris 4L4; dom bruk'te nå på å gå te O Klæ'r ætter grå'serier 18C4.

grove n. small wood 34. N *lund* m. 14C1; *skoglund* m. 7H2 8L3. E [gro'v] > gro'v m.f. (m. 15, f. 14); grå'v f.m. (f. 6Q3 4P1 12Q1; m. 7G1 7H1). Cf. N *grov* f. 'brook, brook bed'; *gråv* f. 'grave'. Quot: neri gro'va 11B1; uppi gro'ven 5H7.

handle n. part of an implement 68. N *handtak* n., *hav* n., *hank* m., *hald* n., *hivil* m. E [hæ′ndəl] > hæn′del m., pl. -dlar 34; hen′del 25; hæ′ndel 5; hæn′dedl 5 (all WN); hen′nel 4N1; hæin′nel 3C4; han′del 7G1. Cpd: pumpe- (pump), stove-, øks- (ax); -bar. Quot: å så lå′g de ein hen′del på stå′ven 5L3; nå'kån så lang′ hen′del 5H4.

happen v. occur 19. N (cf. *henda, skje; slumpa til, råka til*). E [hæ′pən] > hæp'na v., pt. — 17; hæ′pna 8L2; hep'na 20J1. Quot: no'ko såm hadde hep'na 20J1; da hæn skrei′v var no'e som hæp'na 8G1; dom si'er dæ hæp'ner 20C1; je′ hæp'na te å vara præs′ident i dæ′ nå′ 2C2; je hæp'ne te kåm'me inn 14D15; de kunne hæp'na me had'de litt 13N1; i Nør′je va de jam′t de rå'ka de hæp'na 5L2; e hæp'na itte te å gå′ 14D4.

harvest n. gathering of crops 67. N *slått* m. 4 (not strictly equiv., refers to haying rather than harvest; the right equiv. is *skurd* m. or *skurdonn* f.). E [har′vəst] > har'vis't m.; har'ves't 13; har'vest 3; har′vest 3; har'vis 5 (chiefly Coon V.); harves′ten 8M2. Cpd: grøn- (grain); -redskap (equipment), -field. Der: -er. Quot: i slått′ å har'vist 5F1; i har'ves'ten 4F2; så kåm′mer har'vis'ten 14D14.

harvest v. gather crops 41. N *hausta* v. 5. E [har′vəst] > har'vis'ta v., pt. — 28; ha'rves'te 4; har'veste 2; har'ves'te 4; har'vese're 14D1; har'vise're 5L4 (quot. from 5H7), har'viste′ra 14D21. Quot: har'ves'te — te å høu'ste inn 12R1; te å har'ves'te grø′ne 5L1; når da kjem′ te har'vis'ting 6P4; såd'de å ikkje har'- vis'ta 20F15.

haw interj. command to oxen to turn left 21. N no equiv. E [hɔ′] > *ha′* 19; *hå′* 3C1 9Q1. Quot: ska du tø′rne te væn′stre, så si'er du ha′ 10C2.

hickory n. tree of the genus Carya 79. N no equiv. E [hɪk′(ə)ri] > (1) hek'ri m. 16; hek'ri 4; hek'ṛi 1; hik'(e)ri 13; hik'(e)ri 5; hik'(e)ṛi 8; hek'kori 14D2; hik'ræ 15P1; (2) hik'ril m. 12; hek'ril 6; hek'ril 5. Cpd: -not (nut), -stikke (stick), -tre (tree). Quot: ain sto′re hek'ri å ja'ga på åk'san 4P2.

hoe n. implement 56. N no equiv. (cf. *grev* n., *hakka* f.). E [hɔ′] > (1) hå′ m. most inf. (f. 1K1 7H1 7H2 7H3 14D2); (2) hao′ 6P1 4P1 15P4; (3) hå'e f. 14D4 14C2 14D5. Cf. N *hå* m. shark; *hå* f. aftermath. Cpd: grub-. Quot: e to′ grubb'hå'en på ak′sla 11B6.

homestead n. land acquired by pioneer and occupied by him as his home 27. N no equiv. E [ho'mstɛdⁱ] > ho'mstedd¹ m.n. (m. 12, n. 6), pl. -s 19; ho'mstedd¹ 4; homm'stedd¹ 4; with partial substitution: hæi'mstedd¹ 14N4 1K1; ho'mste¹ 9Q1 8L1 23A3; ho'msta¹ 2C4 (cf. N _heimstad_ 'home'). Cpd: -land. Quot: eg tok ho'mstedd¹ i Monta¹na 14Q1; fa'r tok ho'mstedd¹ 22F1.

horn v. serenade with horns (cf. **shivaree** and see McDavid in _Social Forces_ 25.170); this word is limited to Koshk., Wautoma, and Indianland communities 13. N no equiv. E [hɔr'n] > ho'rna v., pt. — 7; hå'rna 6. Cpd. -crowd. Der: -er; -ing. Quot: så' kåm ho'rnarar 4L4; kåm'mer å ho'ṛner dem 4K1; di hå'rna di 4F2; en ho'rnarkrøu¹d 8L4.

hunting n. chasing game 41. N _jakt_ m. 4; _skytteri_ n. 4H1. E [hʌn'tɪng] > hun'ting m. 21 (EN-Midl.); hån'ting 13 (WN); høn'- ting 5; hon'ting 2. Cpd: deer-, duck-; -ground, -tid (time). Quot: på fis'king men it'te fæ'rt mi'e på høn'ting 14C2.

husk v. remove husk (of ear of corn) 94. N no equiv. E [hʌs'k] > (1) has'ka v., pt. —; høs'ka 7G1; (2) hars'ka v., pt. — 21 (mostly EN, in communities 2, 5, 8, 10, 11, 14, 15, 16, 18, 22); hærs'ka 4 (9G2 10C6 13N2 13N3). Der: -er; -ing. Quot: has'ka da jo're me mæ hån'd 6P4; has'ka kåd'n 5Q1; kåd'ne dæ has'ka dæi i stæ'- beln 4P2; e ha dre've å has'ka 20F16; has'ke på fi'la 11C6.

Indian n. aboriginal American 55. N _indianer_ m. 11 (as an alternative). E [ɪn'diən] > in'di m., pl. ¹-ar; def. sing. in'dien = Indians, the Indians. Cpd: -doktor (doctor), -mocassin (a flower), -følgje (party), -stig (path), -squaw. Quot: da va so full't av in'di so dai rais'te to' å to' 20Q2; flæi're in'diar 4Q3; in'di å slang'er 14F4; [da fo'r] so mykje in'dia fårbi' 6Q4.

insurance n. contract for reimbursement of loss 72. N _assurans_ m. 5L1 11C2 10C12 (cf. _forsikring_ m.). E [ɪnshu'rəns] > (1) inn'- sju'ṛens m. 19; innsju'ṛens 15; inn'sjurens 2; innsju'rens 5; (2) inn'sjuring f. 15; innsju'ring 2; (3) inn'sju¹rings m.f. 8; innsju'- rings 7. Cpd: township-; -business. Quot: itte en sæn't inn'sju¹- rings 14D11.

Irish a. and n. native of Ireland and immediate descendants 75. N _irlendar_ 4L2. E [ai'rɪsh] > (1) ei'ris m., pl. -ar 31; ai'ris 22; e'ris 3C4 10C 14D3 14D5; i'ris 3C1; (2) ai'risj 9; ei'risj 8. Cpd: -kjerring (woman), -kona (woman), -settlement. Quot: vi hadde ai'risa te na'boa 20F10; ei'risa dem ville deng'e opp nårs'-kan 11C1; han sen'de itte ai gam'mal ai'risjko'na 6Q3; ei ei'ris-kjær'ring 5L1.

island n. land surrounded by water 40. N *øy* f. many inf.; *holme* m. a few. E [ai'lənd] > (1) ai'len m. 20; ai'lend 5 (n. 2); (2) øy'lan'd n. 12 (all from Holt, Wiota, Heddal, Gbr., Tr.); ei'lann' 9G1 9Q1 16C1. *Øyland* n. is a N word. Quot: på æin ai'lend 20Q2; e ha' den tan'ken at da dem kjem' ne'afør Cha'seburg si'e dem ai'len 11C1.

jack n. knave in cards 32. N *knekt* m. 13; *jil* f. 5 (So. Tel. Vo.). E [dzhæ'k] > djæ'k m. 9; jæ'k 3; djekk' 7; jekk' 4; djækk' 2; jækk' 6. Cpd: kløver- (clubs) etc.; cf. lumber-, pump-, screw- (another kind of jack).

job n. employment 21. N (cf. *arbei* n., *annplei* n.). E [dzha'b] > jabb' m., pl. -ar; jåbb' 20Q2. Cpd: kyrkja- (church), police-, små- (small). Quot: fækk' ingen jabb' 14D15; en let'tare jabb' 8L8; fys'te jab'ben e had'de 12Q4; en sted'di jabb' 8B2; en tåff' jabb' å kåm'må inn 20C1; fæ'rt te jabb' 20J2; ain stø'dige jabb' 12R1.

judge n. magistrate 69. N *dommar* m. 10. E [dzhʌdzh] > djød'j m.; jød'j etc. (j- init. 13, never final; dj- init. and final 29; dsj or dzh 28; ø 47; å 11; ʌ 9; a 2); jød's 4 (Valders Wautoma); djuy's 8M2. Cpd: county-.

jug n. earthenware vessel with handle and narrow neck 61. N *krukka* f. 50 (often as alternative); *mugga* f. 16C1 (not equiv.). E [dzhʌg'] > (1) jug'ge, jug'ga f. 24; jåg'ge 8; jog'ge 4 (Solør); jöug'ge 4 (Gbr.); (2) jågg' m. 10; jögg' 5; jugg' 4; jogg' 1; jʌgg' 1. A number of inf. have dj- or dzh-, esp. WN. Cpd: alcohol-, molasses-, whisky-.

July n. seventh month 84. N *juli* 10 (have heard but do not use). E [dzhula'ɪ] > jula'i (init. dj- esp. WN); ju'lai 8 (esp. EN); jul'lai 14C1 14C2. Quot: dju'li sau'nda nett' so kris'mes 6Q1; pres'ten bru'ka på å si' ju'li 11C4; mam'ma sa ju'li 18B1; [vi hålt på me] grub'bing li'ke tell omtrein't den fjer'de jul'lai 14D4; i djula'i mao'ne 6P2.

justice n. magistrate 20. N no equiv. E [dzhʌs'tɪs] > djøs'tis m. 13; jøs'tis 3; jus'tis 7H2 8L4 26A1 25A1. Cpd: supreme-. Quot: han va jøs'tis 14F2; jus'tis av pi's 25A1.

keep v. maintain; preserve; subscribe to; continue (with 'on'); maintain pace (with 'up') ab. 75. N *halda* v. many inf. E [ki′p] > ki′pa v. 60; kip′pa 9 (EN); pt. — 41, -p′te 11, -f′te 11 (pt. in -t- chiefly So. dial, esp. Lyster, Wiota, Coon, Blair). Der: -er, e.g. in bok- (book), hus- (house), store-, time-. Quot: han bruʹka å kiʹpe ein hesʹt 4K2; kiʹpe huʹs får gutʹtane 5E1; å kipʹpe n åt griʹsan 8C5; dei skulle kipʹt dæ nårsʹke gåʹen 12R1; kokʹkisen æ haʹ*l* å kiʹpe 11B1; den kiʹpa se når ein settʹ den i kjelʹlern 10C3; dæ kiʹpa se no deʹ 19A1; de er mangʹe såm kipʹper Decoʹrah-Posʹten 14D2; kårsʹ vi kiʹper itte nå nårsʹk papʹper 14D21; kipa aʹn me dæ 13N4; kiʹpe opp mæ staiʹlsi 12Q4.

kerosene lamp n. lamp burning kerosene 17. N no equiv. E [kærʹəsiʹn læʹmp] > (1) kæʹresinlamʹpe m. 10; kæʹro- 4; keresiʹn- 4P1; kerosiʹn- 6P1; (2) kaʹrosin- 4K2 4F2. Quot: hadde æin keresiʹnlamʹpe 4P1.

lake n. water surrounded by land 92. N *innsjø* m. 3C1 (cf. *vatn* n., *sjø* m.). E [leʹk] > N leiʹk m., pl. -ar; laiʹk 12; leʹk 9; in most dial. identical with N *leik* m. 'game' (not 5Q1 11B1 12R1 15P4 18B1 20Q1); 4Q1 uses leiʹk with proper names, laiʹk otherwise. Cpd: -trout.   Quot: denne her leʹken 4F3; på stiʹmbåʹtadn på leʹkadne 13N1; [e] va ne på leiʹkjen 8M1.

lawn mower n. machine for cutting grass 84. N no equiv. E [lɔʹnmoʹər] > (1) låʹnmoʹeɽ m., pl. -s 27; laʹn- 18B1 18B2; låʹn- 9Q1 10C6; laʹn- 8L1; låʹnmoʹer 19; laʹn- 9G3; læʹn- 14D2; låʹn- 13N3; låʹnmoʹar 16 (Midl. WN); låʹn- 5L3 25A1; låʹnmouʹari 8M2; (2) låʹnmoʹver m. 8; låʹnmoʹvar 4 (all Tr.); låʹnmoʹvar 14D1.

lawsuit n. court case 58. N *sak* f. 21 (often as alternative). E [lɔʹsuʹt] > (1) låʹsuʹt m. 21; låʹsuʹt 18; laʹsut 7G1 9G3; (2) låʹvsuʹt m. (f. 7H2 21H1) 14; *låv* f. is a N substitution. Quot: [dei] hadde stoʹre låʹsuʹt 4Q2.

lawyer n. barrister 80. N *prokurator* m. 23; *sakførar* 8. E [lɔʹjər] > (1) låiʹeɽ m. 40 (13 r); låʹjeɽ (7 r); låiʹer 5; låʹjar 4P1; løyʹer 5; løyʹar 15P1; (2) låiʹert m., pl. -ar 5L3 4Q1 17Q2 22F1; løyʹert 5L1 11B4.

leave v. (1) depart from; (2) allow to remain 19. N (cf. *ganga, reisa frå; lata vera*). E [liʹv] > liʹva, pt. — (pp. lifʹt 4N2 23A4). Quot: (1) spellemannen...spelʹte frå dei liʹva heiʹmen å te dei kåmʹ te kjerʹka 5H3; ein minuʹt frå e liʹva gålʹve 4P1; han (nissen) vil'la kje li've dei 13N5; da præs'ten li've hær 19A1; (2) han kun'ne ikkje li've den on'ge kjer'ringa å des'sa ong'an alde'les alei'ne 5F1; eg måt'te å sei' li've altsa'men 14L1; li've att ann'bo 11C1; koss mån'ge så an liva at'te 13N4.

license n. official permit 100. N no equiv. E [lai'səns] > (1) lai'sens m.n. (m. 31, n. 5 mostly WN), pl. — or -ar 50; lei'sens 2; (2) lai'sen m.n. (m. 26, n. 3 mostly WN), pl. — or -ar 40; lei'sen 8. Cpd: hunda- (dog), gifta- (marriage).

log n. felled tree 31. N no equiv. (cf. *stokk* m., *tømmer* n.). E [lɔ'g] > lågg' m., -en coll., -ar pl. (-s 4L4); lògg' 4L4 5L1; læugg' 19A1 18B1. Cpd: tamarack-; -barn, -cabin (also -hytte and -stova), -camp, -kyrkja (church), -shanty, -hus (house), -stable, -stubb (stump), -vegg (wall). Der: -a, -ing. Quot: lôg'gar som va split'ta i to' 5L1; tæl'ja di di'gre lag'gå 14D4; lakt mår'ter millom låg'gane 4P1; vi bod'de i et lågg'hu's 22F1; alle hu'sene va lågg' 11C2; (da va) ar'bett tå lågg' 15P1; så håg'de dai lågg' 20Q2.

lumber n. sawed timber 81. N *bord* n. 9Q1; *timber* n. 6Q2. E [lʌm'bər] > lom'ber m. (n. 5H2 2C2 3C4); lom'beṛ 15 (EN Gbr. Vald.); låm'ber 7 (So. Hard.); lòm'ber 4F1 4L4; lʌm'beṛ 5H1 7H3; löm'beṛ 11C1; lom'boḷ 11B1 18B1; lom'bur 4P1. Cpd: -business, -camp, -jack, -mølle (mill), -vogn (wagon), -yard. Quot: å pæi'le lom'ber 8F1; [de va] go'e lom'ber i dæi' da'ga 4P2.

lunch n. light meal 35. N no equiv. E [lʌn'tsh] > lån'(t)sj m. 11; lån'(t)kj 3; lan'(t)sj 6; lan'(t)kj 4; løn'(t)sj 4; løn's 17Q1 17Q3 17Q4; lan's 9G3; lon's 4N1; lon'k 6P1 4P1 (quot.). Cpd: midnight-; -basket. Quot: en li'ten lån'sj 17P1.

mail n. things posted 42. N *post* m. most inf. (many give both). E [me'l] > mei'l m. 24; me'l 17; mæ'l 3C2. Cpd: air-; -box, -mann (man).

make v. earn; prepare, fashion; undertake; cause, compel; amount to 58. N *tena* v. many inf.; *laga til; gjera; få til*, etc. E [me'k] > mæ'ka v., pt. — (-te 12R1); meka 14 (esp. Suldal, Heddal, Holt, Valdres); meika 4. Der: -ar (dressmaker, cheese-maker). Quot: vi mæ'ka søt'ti da'le 8C2; æg mæ'ka ikkje my'kje på far'men 15P1; vi mæ'kar go'e peing' 14D9; dæm mæ'ka lev'-vinga mæ 8L; kårs' du kan mæ'ke li'ving 5P1; såm me me'ka kok'kis 13N5; mei'ka na kḷub'ben 1K1; æin so mæ'ka æin tripp' te Når'ge 17Q; de mæ'kar køn'ne væk'se fort' 3C2; han ha mæ'ka me ban'ge 11B6; men de me'kar kje nå'ken fårsje'l 13N4; viss lu'tefis'ken bli gått' upp'løy'ste, vil han mæ'ka sek's-sju' pun'd 4Q2.

map n. representation of a surface 53. N *kart* n. 4. E [mæ'p] > (1) mapp' n. m. (n. 32, m. 8L1 8L2 17Q1), pl. —; mæpp' 9Q1; ma'p 15P4 3C1 3C4 14C2; (2) mæ'p m. n. (m. 12, incl. all younger Solør; n. 4), pl. -ar; (3) map'pa f. 4N1. Cpd: road-.

meeting n. religious service, esp. of a Low Church type (cf. quotations, and Rohne NAL 79) 30. N *messe* f. (chiefly EN), *preik* f. (chiefly WN), *gudstjeneste* m. BL. E (1) [mi'tən] > mid'den m. 13; mi'den 11; mi'd 14D3 14D4; (2) [mi'tɪŋ] > mi'ting 18B1 18C2; mit'ting 5L1 (quot.); mid'ding 23A2. Cpd: business-, camp-; -hus (house). Quot: var de mid'den, så va'r de ikke lut'-tersk 4L4; mid'den va hæugi'aner 4L4; hæugia'nerne sa mit'ting 5L1; Ma'rit Ra'num brukte å si' mi'ting, høṛ'de te Hau'ges kjer'ke, hadde læ'ṛt de i Mar'tinville, lev'de i la'g me amerika'nera 5H3; han jikk' på mid'den' støtt' 19A2; mi vil rai'se ao' pao mit'ten 6P1 (humorous quot.).

middlings n. coarsely ground wheat with bran 80. N no equiv. E [mɪd'lɪŋgz] > (1) mid'ling m. (f. 4Q1) 34; med'ling 6; midlin'ge 8M2; (2) mil'ling m. 30; mel'ling 10. Stem 1 is WN, 2 is EN; -e-predominates in Blue M., Blair, Lyster, Spr. Gr. Cpd: -brø (bread). Quot: flæu'r å mid'ling 6P1; litt mid'ling 12Q2.

mix v. blend, confuse 31. N *blanda* v. 5L1. E [mɪk's] > mik'sa v., pt. — (pp. -t 12Q4 19A1 20F5 20Q1); mek'sa 8 (Tr. and Solør). Der: -er, -ing, -ture. Quot: han mik'sa te nå med'isin 11C1; mik'sa opp mæ vann' 5H3; mik'st kat'ten (cotton) å ull' 12Q4; dæ trub'la me at e mik'sa da upp (the language) 12Q1; dæ opp'-mek'sa fæ'rt 14D4; e mik'sa får my'kje 4P4; dæ va mik'st — Å'len, Hol'tå'len 19A1; mik'st nårs'k 20F5; da ha vår'te mik'sa 20Q2; almin'deli mik'st far'ming 20Q1.

moccasin n. shoe of soft leather 41. N no equiv. E [ma'kəsən] > (1) ma'kesen m., pl. -s 4; ma'kesen 3; ma'kesin 14C1; ma'kesin 7H1 13N2; må'kesin 10C2; ma'kesjinn' 7H3; (2) ma'gesen m. 8L2 17Q1; ma'gesin 9G3; ma'gesin 16C1; ma'gasin 10C1 (pl. -er); må'gesin 17Q3 17Q4; magasi'n 4L2 (pl. -er); (3) ma'gis m., pl. -ar 7; mag'gis 8; ma'gus 14D1 14D3; må'ges 20Q1; må'gis 15P4; må'kis 8L4; må'gis 8L1 (note that -g- occurs only in N and W Wisconsin and E Minnesota). Cpd: Indian-; -støvlar (boots).

molasses n. a syrup 49. N *sirup* m. 12R1 19A1. E [məlæ′səz] > (1) mala′ses m., def. -la′sesen or -la′sien 4; -la′sis 3; -las′ses 4Q1 20Q1; -las′sis 6Q2 7G1; -læ′sis 17Q2; mela′sis 13N2 8L4; -læ′ses 1K1 2C2; -læ′sis 2C1; måla′ses 17Q4; -las′sis 9Q1 17Q4; mola′ses 4; -la′sis 8M1; mal′lasses 14D3 4L2 25A1; mol′lasses 22F1; mol′lasis 14C2; (2) mal′lasi m. 11 (all EN, esp. Wiota and Coon); malas′si 4 (esp. Valders); -la′si 8L2; målas′se 4N1; mola′si 20C1; mal′la′si 19A2. Cpd: lønn- (maple); -cake, -jug, -dalen (valley), -øl (beer). Quot: å så bryg′ga dei av malas′ses — de va′ kje beru′sende 5L1.

monkey wrench n. wrench with adjustable jaw 74. N *skifte-nykkjyl* m. 8L3; *skruenøkkel* m. 8F1; cf. *skruverensj* 8M3. E [mʌŋ′kirɛn′tsh] > (1) mån′ki- 21; mån′ki- 8; mon′ki- 18; mon′ki 7; man′ki- 4P1; (2) mån′ke- 9; mån′ke- 5G1; mon′ke- 7; mon′ke- 19A1; mon′ka- 15P2; for second part see **wrench**.

mortgage n. security in property for repayment of loan 65. N *hefte* n. 4L4. E [mɔr′gɪdzh] > (1) mår′gidzh m. 12; mår′gidzh 5; mår′gidzh 13N1; mår′gidsj 7; mår′gidsj 4P1; mår′gitsj 2; mår′-gitsj 3C1; mår′gitkj 18B2; mår′gitkj 4P1 15P1; mår′gitkj 13N2; mår′gitkj 18C2 22F1; mår′gidj 4; mår′gidj 5L1; mår′gets 9G3; mår′gits 7H2; mår′gisj 17P1; mår′gej 25A1; (2) mår′get m., pl. -ar 8; mår′get 6; mår′git 7; mår′git 6; mår′gis 7H1; mår′gis(e) 8L4 8M2. Der: -a v. Quot: [det heter] mår′git på nårs′k 18C1.

mosquito n. insect of family Culicidae 71. N *myhank* m. 13 (esp. Tel. Vald. So. Hard. Num.); *mygg* m. 3; *mitt* m. 3C3. E (1) [mɪs′kɪt] > mis′kit m., pl. -ar 38; mis′kit 4; mis′ket 7; mes′ket 20J1 19A1; mis′ket 4; mis′ke′t 3; mis′ket′ 9Q1; mus′ke′t 24A1; muskitt′ 8M1; mos′kit 8L1; mus′kite 8M2; mus′kit 8L4; (2) [məski′to] > meski′to m., pl. -s 2C2; moski′to 17P1 8F1; måski′ten 7G1; måski′tes 5H3; mes′kito 5C1; mis′ki′ta f. 15P1. Cpd: -bar. Quot: mis′kiten æ så lei′.

necktie n. decorative band 94. N *halsklut* m. 4L4 5L1 8M2 20F18; *halsplagg* n. 11C2; *sløyfa* f. 20C1; *slips* n. 13N1. E [nɛk′ta′i] > (1) nekk′tai′ n.m. (n. 60, m. 16), pl. -s 60; (2) nekk′tøy′ n. (f. 12R1) 9; nekk′ty′ n. 5N1; nakk′ty′ n. 1K1 (second part is a N substitution). Cpd: -sociable. Quot: du må ha kvi′t kra′ge å nækk′tai på′, sa n Ei′jel, ska du få′ fis′k 10C2.

next a. immediately following 77. N *nest* a. given by 36 in questionnaire responses, compared to 22 for **next**. E [nɛk'st] > nek'st a. Quot: ka va' dæ du vilde ha' nek'st 15P1; dei dan'sa te dak'sens ly's nek'ste mår'go 5H2; åver nek'ste blåf'fa 20E1; e æ nek'st den gam'last 19A2; tell nek'ste vi'ku 14C2.

no interj. negative 65. N *nei* appears to be less common, though both are in use. E [no'] > nå' interj.; cf. N *nå* 'well'. Quot: nå', in'kje så e'g håi'rde 20Q2; nå', han sa' han hadde jort' dæ æi'n gong' 14D15; nå', me bruk'te kje ju'letre¹ 20Q1; nå', de' kan du it'te 20F7; væ'l, nå', e tru' kje e sa' de 25H1; næi', itt' etål', nå' 8G2; næi', nå' 8L8; nei'da, nå' 10C12.

note n. promise of payment 50. N no equiv. E [no't] > no't f., pl. nø'ter; form identical with N *not* f. 'large fishing net'. Quot: han jo're ut ei no't på væ'rfa¹r sin 4Q2; no'ta er du' (due) 14D2; in'kje nå'ken no't å in'gen ting' 12Q2.

of course adv. certainly, obviously 18. N no equiv. (cf. *sjøl-sagt*). E [ekɔr's] > (1) (e)kåssj' (= kårs) adv. 8; (å)kå'sj 20J1 8C2 25A1; kår'sj 20F17; kåsj't 8L1; (2) (e)kår̩'s adv. 5. Quot: kåsj nå' får ti'en så syng'er dæm my'e på sko'*l*en 18C4; kår̩'s, viss dæ va'r non jen'ter run't 12Q4; kåsj nå' binner dæ å b*l*i' ro'liere 14D11; kåsj vi' hælt itte på' i mang'e da'er 14F3.

office n. (1) business place; (2) position of trust 41. N (1) (*kontor* n.); (2) *embede* n. 15P3. E [ɔ'fɪs] > å'fis m., pl. -ar 22; å'fis 4; åf'fis 11; åf'fis 3; åfi's 4N1. Cpd: county-, doktor- (doctor), påst- (post), town-, township-; -jenta (girl), -kar (holder). Quot: poli'tiske åf'fis 4Q3; nep'på åf'fisa ha'as 25A1.

oven n. baking chamber in stove 82. N *brødrom* n. 33; *bakaromn* m. 13; *bakarrom* n. 7; *trommelt* m. 14D2 (old); *steikeomn* m. 2C1; *steikerom* n. 7G1. E [ʌv'ən] > N *omn* m. 'stove'; forms with *m* (åmn, ømmen etc.) 12 (Gbr. Num. Hadel. Toten Solør Tr.); with *v* 24 (some by E influence, others in dial., esp. Tel.); with *b* 4 (all So.). Quot: så ba'ker je dæ førs't i åv'ven 18C5; brø'ro'mi kal'la dei ov'nen 5L1; om'nen er in'ni 14D4.

overall n. trousers with breast-piece 102. N *blåbuksur* 4L1. Several E pronunciations are reflected: [o'vərɔ'l], [o'vərhɔ'l], [o'vərɔ'lz], and [o'vərhɔ'lz]. The first part is usually N å'ver- or å'ver-, but 26 have E o'veɾ-. The second part is -å'l 23, -a'l 17, -hå'l 17, -ha'l 16, -ål's 7, -al's 8, -hål's 8, -hal's 1; the gender is m. except for f. 5, n. 2 (7G1 9Q1). Quot: ain ny'e o'veɾål's 15P6; e kun'ne ikke bru'ke å'verhå'l 11R2.

overcoat n. outside coat 85. N *ytrefrakk* 8L3; *overfrakk* 7G1; cf. uttapåkot 4H1 4P1; vinterkot 18B2 6Q1. First part is nearly always N *åver-* (So. aover-, yve- etc.); second part is **coat**, q.v.

pail n. round container with bail 78. N *bytta* f. 8. E [pe'l] > N *pei'l* m. 'half pint, liquid measure', used in Norway before introduction of metric system. May be regarded as a morphemic substitution because the form in some dialects differs from that which phonemic substitution would give. The forms are: pei'l 3 (11C1 15P2 5Q1); pai'l 12 (all So. Vo. Hard.); pæ'l 46 (most dial.); cf. pæ'*t* Hedd.); pæ'dl 3 (Suldal); pe'l 13 (Solør and various other dial.). Cpd: dinner-, mjølk- (milk), pappir- (paper), slabb- (slop), swill-, tin-, vatn- (water), tre- (wooden). Quot: ain fem'-seks pai'la mæ vat'ten 6P2; eit pa'r pæ'ler mæ vat'ten 5E1.

parlor n. room for reception and entertainment 36. N *stova* f. 9; *storstova* 4; *finstova* 22F1; *finrum* n. 8; *daglegrum* 20J1; *staserum* 15P2; *framrum* 1K1 6Q1. E [par'lər] > (1) par'leɽ m. most inf.; pa'ɽleɽ, paɽ'leɽ, par'ler; (2) pa'ler m. 5 (4L1 quot. 5L2 5L5 6P1 14C2); pa'lar 4Q1; pai'leɽ 10C6. Cpd: beer-; -suite. Quot: me læut nes'ten spyr'ja um lå'v te å få å'pna dø'ri å skå'a inn' 6Q3. Cf. **front room**, **living room**, **sitting room**, and the discussion of these terms by R. I. McDavid Jr. in *Social Forces* 25.171 (1946).

party n. social gathering 22. N *gjestebod* n. 5; *lag* n. 2. E [par'*t*i] > pa'ɽti n. (m. 3C3 20J1), pl. -s or -(e)r 8; paɽ'ti 7; paɽ'ti 3C1; par'ti 6; the form is partly that of N *parti* n. political group. Cpd: hus- (house), jule- (Christmas), quilting-, skule- (school), surprise-, Democratic-, Republican-. Quot: [det er] itte mange pa'ɽtier 14D14; en stør're paɽ'ti tå sko'g 20J1.

pasture n. land for grazing (all primary inf.). N no equiv. (cf. *beite* n., *hamnegang* m. for unenclosed pasture). E [pæs'tər] > pas'ter n., pl. —. Cpd: grise- (pig). Der: pastra v. Quot: gått' pas'ter 4F2; i pas'tre mæs'ta tå ti'en 14C2.

peddler n. itinerant merchant 53. N *kræmar* m. 14C1 (cf. *kramkar* m.). E [pɛd'lər] > (1) ped'lar m., pl. -ar 31; pæd'lar 2; ped'ler 13 (EN); pæd'ler 2; pedla'ri 8M1; (2) pel'lar m. 10C3 10C5 11C2 19A2; heard also by 10C1 22F1.

pencil n. implement for writing 51. N *blyant* m. 33 (20 give both words). E [pɛn'səl] > pen'sel m., pl. pen'slar; pæn'sel 16; pæn'sjel 10C3; pen'sedl 6Q1 12Q1 17Q2; there is a N *pensel* m.

'small paintbrush', prob. not widely used in the dialects. Cpd: lead-. Quot: han hadde bræk't pen'seln sin 25A1.

pieplant n. rhubarb 83. N *barbarot* f. 14C2. E [pa'iplæ'nt] > (1) pai'plæn't m.f. (m. 17, f. 6), pl. -ar 29; -pɫæn't 7; (2) pai'plan'te f., pl. -r 8; -pɫan'te 5H1; -plan'ta 6Q1 15P4 17Q4 13N1 9Q1; (3) pai'plen'te f., pl. -plen'tor 11; -pɫæn'te 14; -plen'ta 8. Note that there is a N *planta* f. and a *plenta* f. which are substituted in stems 2 and 3; three inf. use stem 1 as a generic name, 2 or 3 for individual plants. Cpd: -plante (plant), -rot (root), -sauce, -vin (wine).

pigpen n. enclosure for pigs 38. N no equiv. E [pɪg'pɛn'] > first part N gri's- 11; gri'sa- 9 (So. Hard. Vo.); gri'se- 19 (esp. Vald. Tel. Hall.); pig'- 25A1; second part N *penn* m. 'implement for writing' (also pænn'); f. 14D1 14D3; n. 4H1 9G1. Other cpds. with **pen**: bull-, hog-, kalve- (calf), ku- (cow), saue- (sheep).

pile v. stack, often with **up** 51. N *brota* v. 19A1; *la opp* v. 3C4 3C2; *legge* 2C2; *laga* 9G1 9G3. E [pai'əl] > pai'la v., pt. — or -te 6 (14D1 14D3 12Q1 12R1 17Q2 17Q4) 34; pei'la 17. Quot: å pæi'le lom'ber 8F1; pei'le dem opp 8G1; pæi'le den ve'en 8C2.

plate n. food dish 63. N *tallik* m. 52; (*bord*)*disk* m. 7H1 4L4. E [ple't] > plei't m., -ar; ple't 11 (Midl. WN Tr.); plett' 5 (esp. Vo.). Cpd: home-, pie-, silver-. Quot: nåke smø'r på ain plei't 20Q1.

play v. engage in a game 37. N *spela* v. 6; *leika* 19A1. E [ple'] > plei'a v., pt. — 14, plei'de 6, pleid'de 16; ple'a 8M1. This lw. partly coincides with the DN *pleie* v. 'care for'. Cpd: -hus (house). Der: -ing. Quot: da plei'de vi bå'l 10C12; vi bru'ker på å plei'e bå'l 14D22; så plei'de dom gei'mer 14F3; di plei'de gei'ms 4F3; vi spæl'te bå'l 14D1; vi pleid'de bå'l 20F18.

plenty n., a., adv. more than enough 25. N *nok* 14D3. E [plɛn'ti] > plen'ti 10 (WN Midl.); pɫen'ti 5; pɫæn'ti 5; pɫein'ti 4 (Solør). Quot: pɫein'ti å jæ'ra 14D20; plen'ti ma't å drik'ke 4L4; plen'ti gått' lann' 4L4; pɫæn'ti brænn'vi'n 8L; dæ går pɫæn'ti fort' ætte mi'n fårstann' 20J1; så me hadde plen'ti vat'ten 20P1; pɫen'ti jøs'sel 8C5; me har plen'ti rum' 20Q2; hu va'r visst pɫen'ti gɫa' 5E1.

plier, pliers n. small pincers 49. N *tong* f. 28; *hovtong* f. 10 (a somewhat larger pincers); *hovty* n. 3C2 10C2; *klypa* f. 5 (EN); *klypetong* f. 4F2 6P1; *klemma* f. 8M1; *knipetong* f. 5L1. E [plai'ər(z)]

> plaiꞌeŗ m., pl. -s 22; plaiꞌeŗ 4; plaiꞌer 7H2 12R1; płaiꞌer 7H1 9G3; preiꞌer 4L2 (also pl-); pleiꞌer 3; plaiꞌeŗs 10; plaiꞌeŗs 5; pleiꞌeŗs 4F1.

poker n. (1) card game 30; (2) fireplace implement 28. N no equiv. E [poꞌkər] > in meaning (1) poꞌkeŗ m. 24 (some have Eng. [o]); poꞌker 6; (2) poꞌkeŗ m. 12; poꞌker 7; poꞌkeŗ 5; poꞌkar 1K1 4N1 4Q1 9G1. Only 7 inf. make a phonetic distinction between the two meanings. Cpd: (1) stud-; (2) stove-. Quot: å so toꞌk o poꞌkern å so groꞌv inn i åsꞌka liꞌte grann' 20Q1.

porch n. veranda 42. N *tram* m. 13 (esp. Midl. EN); *sval* f. 4L1 4L4; *veranda* m. 3C1. E [pɔrꞌtsh] > poŗꞌtsj m. 9; poꞌrtsj 5; poŗꞌtkj 2; poꞌrtkj 2; påŗꞌtsj 6; påꞌŗtsj 2; påŗꞌtkj 3; påꞌŗtkj 3; poŗꞌtkj 4; poꞌrtkj 11C1; poŗꞌtsj 3; påŗꞌtsj 6Q1; poŗt' 25A1. Cpd: front- (q.v.), sleeping-. Cf. **stoop** n. usually smaller, often uncovered.

post office n. building for mail 39. N *posthus* n. 8. E [poꞌstɔˈfɪs] > påsꞌtåˈfis m. 27; påsꞌtåfiˈs 12. The first part is N; for the second see **office**. Quot: gåꞌr du på påsꞌtåfiˈsen, så fåꞌr du meꞌlen din — påsꞌten din 14D2.

pumpkin n. Cucurbita pepo 84. N no equiv. E [pʌngꞌkɪn] > (1) panꞌki m., pl. -ar 47; pånꞌki 5; ponꞌki 5; pʌnꞌki 3; paonꞌki 3; pønꞌki 3; panꞌk 15P2; (2) pånꞌkin m., pl. -ar or -s 6; pånꞌken 5; ponꞌken 6Q5; ponꞌkin 4; pʌnꞌkin 8F1; (3) ponꞌkis m., pl. -ar 6 (all Ind.land). Cpd: -dævel (devil), -øl (beer). Quot: så fann' dæm påˈ å så skaꞌr høꞌt i en panꞌki, å så sætꞌte dem en liꞌs inn i panꞌkien 14D4; so fann' [han] noko kådꞌnakˈs, å soꞌ noko pånꞌkin 4P4.

quarter n. (1) 25 cents; (2) 160 acres. N no equiv. E [kwɔrꞌtər] > (1) kvarꞌter m. (only in meaning 1) 30 (EN dialects and Suldal); (2) N *kvart* m. 'one fourth, esp. of a mile' (used in meaning 1 by some, in 2 by all exc. 11B4). Stem 1 is infl. by N *kvarꞌter* m. 'one fourth, esp. of a barrel or an ell'. Quot: for sangꞌen blott' en kvarꞌter eꞌr, vi konˈtant ham' betaꞌler 14D7.

quilt n. coverlet for bed 68. N *kvitel* m. 4P1 4Q2 6P1 15P3 (referring to homemade quilts). E [kwɪlꞌt] > kvilꞌt m., pl. -ar. Cpd: piece-, ull- (wool). Quot: æ du fæꞌri mæ kvilꞌten? 26P2.

rabbit n. a lagomorph mammal 39. N *hare* m. most inf. (some use *hare* for a larger animal); *jase* m. (all upper and lower Tel. and

Suld.). E [ræ'bɪt] > (1) rab'bit m., pl. -ar 11 (EN); ra'bit 9 (WN Midl.); (2) ræb'bit m. 8; ræ'bit 6; ræ'bet 6Q5; ræ'bet 15P4; ræ'bit 6Q3; ræb'bet 2. Quot: ræb'biten e grao' jamt, å min'dre [enn haren] 4Q2.

rail n. (1) wooden bar in fence; (2) steel bar in track 40. N (1) no equiv.; (2) *skjena* f. 16. E (A) [re'l] > ṛei'l m., pl. -s 5, n., pl. — 2; ṛei'l 3; rei'l 2; re'l 2; ræ'le f. 21H1; (B) [re'lz] > rel's m., pl. -ar or — 7; f., pl. -er 20J1; n., pl. — 12; rel's 13; ræl's 9; ṛei'ls 14D3; rei'ls 6; reil's 10C2; rel'sa f. 17Q3; rel'se f. 12R1. Cpd: -fence, -road. Quot: å so' um dai [the logs] va får kjuk'ke, so split'ta dai dai å fekk' so' å so' man'ge ræl's 20Q2; kro'kfæn'se da to'k man'ge, man'ge ræl's i kå'r kro'k 20Q2; å så måt'te dei ha rei'ls 5F1; sæk's å kju'e ræi'ls 5L1; så to'k han rel'se or ve'jen 4L4; rei'ls, låg'gar såm va split'ta i to' 5L1.

railroad n. railway 88. N *jernbane* m. 7H2. E [re'lro̩'d] > (1) rei'lrå̩'d m. 44; ṛe'l- 4; rei'l- 4N1; rai'l- 8 (So. Vo. Hard. Vald.); re'l- 3; ræ'l- 13N2; ræi'- 8M2; (2) rell'rå'd m. 18; ræll'- 2; ræll'- 10C1; rill'- 4 (So.). Cpd: Milwaukee-; -arbei (work), -åtti (eighty), -tie, -track. Quot: føs'te vek'ko e va på re'lrå̩'den 11R2; eg har fai'ra på rei'lrå̩'den 26P3; eg fekk ar'bai på ræi'lrå̩'den 15P1; så kom' vi te Læk'kråss, væit du, på ræll'rå̩'den 10C1.

ranch n. type of stock-raising farm 16. N no equiv. E [ræ'ntsh] > ren'sj m.f.n. (m. 9 f. 7H1 n. 23A2 3C2) 2; ræ'nsj 3; ræn'sj 2; ṛæ'nsj 3C2; ræ'ntsj 2; ṛein'tsj 13N3; ṛen'tsj 14D1; ren's 17Q4; ræn's 9G3; ren'tkj 4L2; ren'tsj 2C1.

rattler n. rattlesnake 11. N cf. **rattlesnake** below. E [ræt'lər] > ra'tel m., pl. rat'lar 9; ræ'tel 14D2; rat'tel 10C3 15P4 4L4 (also ra'tel); rat'lar 9Q1; ræt'lar 13N2. Cpd: -orm (snake) 7H2.

rattlesnake n. a venomous snake 60. N orm m. 1K1; *huggorm* m. 18B1; *grasorm* 6Q1; *klapperslange* m. 24A1 4N1; *giftslange* m. 6Q1. E [ræ'təlsne'k] > (1) ræ'təlsnei'k m., pl. -s 19; ṛæ'tel- 9; ræt'tel- 7; (2) ra'tel- 10 (incl. ra'telor'm 2); rat'tel- 8; rat'tel- 2; rat'le- 12Q1 15P1 17Q1 17Q4; ras'sjel- 14C1. Second part: -snei'k 40; -sni'k 3; -sne'k 5; -snekk' 8M1; -snikk' 8L1.

reap v. harvest grain 74. N *skjera* v. 17P1. E [ri'p] > (1) ri'pa v., pt. — (ri'fte 10C5) 48; ry'pa 5L3 5L5; re'pa 15P2 15P4; (2) rip'pa v. 18; (3) ri'p*t*e v. 5L2 5H3 20J1; rip'*t*e 4K1 20C1 21H1 (?). Quot: me ṣe'la upp ok'sane likaso dai jo're mæ hæs'tane å sæt'te dai fy rip'paren å rip'pa kvai'te å bygg' mæ ok'sa 6P2; så rip'pa dai de 12R1; da rip'per dom grø'ne 14D14.

reaper n. machine for reaping grain 95. N no equiv. E [ri'pər] > (1) ri'per m., pl. -ar 21; ri'per 17; ri'per 21; ri'per 2; ry'per 5L3 5L5; ri'par 9 (incl. all Beav. Cr.); ry'par 4Q1; (2) rip'per m. 6; rip'par 6Q3 6P1 6P2; (3) ri'pert m. 5L2 8M1; ry'pert 4Q1; (4) rip'pert m. 10 (all from Blair and Spr. Grove; 4F3 quotes). Quot: de va'r itte bin'nara den ti'a, de va rip'pert 11B2; så kåm' me så lang't at me fekk se' ein ri'per 5L; så bin'ne n å kåm'ma så lang't så n bin'ne å få høu'ste mæ en rip'per, da' vart dæ rek'ti svæ'rt 14D4; den fys'te ri'pern di had'de va ein hæ'ndrei'k 4L4.

ripe a. ready for harvesting 32. N *skjær* 46; *gjord* 6 (So. Vo. Hadel.); *mogen* 8 (Tel. Vald. Holt Gjerp.); *moden* 5; *ferdig* 6Q1 15P3; *moi* 11C1; *staen* 15P4. E [rai'p] > rai'p a. (15 add -t for neut., rest omit) 16; rai'p 7; rei'p 8; rei'p 4N1. Quot: ner' bli køn'ne rai'pt? 14D20; (dei] har'vesta grø'ne så sna'rt da blir rai'pt no 17P1; må set'ta bort røm'men da ma te n bli' liksåm rai'p såm vi bruk'te å kal'le dæ 3C4.

rising n. leaven 20 (cf. DAE 1833: the wife of a Canadian settler 'must know how to manufacture hop-rising and salt-rising for leavening her bread.') N *gang* m. 3 (cf. **yeast**). E [rai'zən] > rei's f.m. (f. 5, m. 2) 14; rai's 4P1 12Q1 12R1 20Q1; rei'-sing 4L4 10C6. Cpd: brød- (bread), humle- (hop), salt- (salt). Quot: mi' mo'r brukte brø'rei's — kjøp'te jis't å had'de i hom'le å suk'ker å litt sal't å pote'tes å pote'tvat'n; da måt'te de stå' å gå' å'ver ein da'g å ei natt'; den ki'pa se når ein sett' den i kjel'-leren 10C3; sal'treis var ei flau'rrø're — sjå kånn' sto de på åv'ns-pla'ta 4L4.

risk n. hazard 27. N no equiv. (cf. *risiko* m., *vågnad* m.) E [rɪs'k] > ris'k m. 16; res'k 9; røs'k 14C2. Der: -y. Quot: vi må røn'ne res'ken 23A2.

river n. large stream 98. N *elv* f. 3C4 1K1. E [rɪv'ər] > (1) rø'ver m., pl. -ar 37; rø'ver 2; rø'var 15P3; rø'var 12R1; ry'ver 3 (So. Hard.); rø'ver 2 (Vald); re'ver 2; ri'ver 2; (2) røv'ver m. 23; røv'ver 16; rev'ver 2; rev'ver 2; riv'ver 3; riv'er 2C2. Cpd: Kickapoo-, Mississippi-, Trempealeau-, Red-, St. Lawrence-; -bank. Quot: en by på Mississippi røvern 20P2 (written); krås'se en rø'ver 14D4; fårel'drene på beg'ge si'er kåm' te Quebec' å opp' Saint

Law'rence-rø'veren 15P3; ivi re'veren 4P1; kråss' rø'vern 14D; neri røv'*t*a 14D7; ne me rø've*r*n 20Q2.

road n. highway (all prim. inf.). N *veg* m. (some use this for minor roads only). E [ro'd] > rå'd m., pl. -ar; ro'd 3 (Eng. [o]). Cpd: cross-, dirt-, gravel-, oiled-, rail-, shale-; -bas (boss), -cart, -dragger, -gang, -map, -sign -tax, -arbei (work). Quot: ho (merra) kun'de no flu'ge nåk'så gått' ette rå'den 5L3; fame'lien lik'te itte at je skulle va'ra på rå'den he'le ti'a 20F2; så ar'bett je my'e på rå'den 12Q7; vi dri'v å save'rer ut rå'd da vet du 14D9; æi mi'ls rå'd 4Q2; ein ve'g va dæ'r dæ jekk' te fot's 15P2; dæ va'r omtræn't to' mi'l å kjø're å brak'ket å lei' væ'g 10C2.

rough a. rude, disorderly 16. N no equiv. (cf. *rå, strid, vill*). E [rʌf'] > råff' a., neut. -t or —, pl. -e. Quot: de må væra mi'e råf'fe få*t*'k dæ'r run't 14D4; en li'ten råff' by' 12Q4; dæ va snø' å sø'*t*e ette ve'gen, så dæ va tæm'meli råff' 5C1; da e' no litt råff' te snak'ka den ve'gen 6P1; dæ va råf't oppi dæ'r 8F1; dem sa' at e va rek'ti en råff' e'n 23A3.

rug n. carpet 55. N *matta* f. many inf. E [rʌg'] > rågg' m., def. råd'djen (Suld.), pl. -s 24; *r*ågg' 6; ragg' 4; røgg' 2; *r*øgg' 6; ròrg' 4; rʌgg' 4; råg'ge f. 1K1 12R4; rug'ge f. 7G1 (cf. Aasen NO *rugga* f. coverlet of rough cloth). Cpd: fille- (rag).

run v. direct, conduct; be a candidate (with **for**); in various phrases: run across, run down (criticize), run short, etc. N no equiv. E [rʌn'] > røn'na v., pt. — (rann', run'ne 8M4); rån'na 4Q1 6P2 5L3. Cpd: home-, over-; -about, -away. Quot: hann røn'ne bin'nern 14D22; såm røn'ner far'men 14D14; han rån'na ein blain'pigg' 5L3; han røn'na he'le me'nihe'ta 25A1; je øn'ske du ville røn'ne får kao'nti etår'ni 20F12; eg rån'na fý konstå'bel 6P2; han hadde ŕun'ne kråss 8M4; dai ran sjå'rt av ma't 8M4; rån'na ne¹ 4Q1; så røn'na vi på¹ ait sjæ'r [in the ocean] 4Q2.

saloon n. (pre-Prohibition) tavern 84. N no equiv. E [səlu'n] > salo'n m., pl. -ar 26 (esp. Tel. Set. Voss Holt); salu'n 4L4 11C2; sa'lon 22 (esp. So. Vald. etc.); sal'lon 35 (most EN); plur. sa'loar 1K1 (implying a sing. sa'lo). Quot: dai kad'la da sal'lon 6P2; di snak'ka kje um salu'n 4L4.

schoolmam n. female teacher 49. N *lærerinna* f. 4N1 7H2. E [sku'lma'm] > (1) sku'lemamm' f.m. (f. 14; m. 4); (2) sku'le-mam'me f. 35 (-a in the dialects having -a in the wk. fem.). The first part is N *skule;* the second coincides in some dialects with *mama.* Quot: de va ei sku'lmam'me såm bor'da sjå åss'... 'Ha du møtt' sku'lmam'ma vår du da, Kare'les?' 18C2; æ'g så kåm' mæ hen'dena mine frå Sjika'go, nett' så på æi sku'lemam'ma 15P1.

schoolteacher n. schoolmaster 31. N *skulemeistar* m., *skulelærar* m. many inf. First part is N *skule* m.; second part is **teacher**, q.v. Quot: bæi'nt åver hæ'ren [the shoulder] på sku'ltit'kjeren 26P3; vi had'de en fårfær'dele streng' nårs'k sku'ltit'kjer dær 10C4.

schottische n. a dance 61. N *skottisj* m. 6Q1 7G1. E [sha'tɪsh] > (1) sjat'tis m. 35; sja'tis 8; sja'dis 2; sja'tis 2; sja'tis 3; sja'tisj 3; (2) sjåt'tis 3; sjåt'tisj 12Q4.

screen n. protective wire mesh on window openings 82. N no equiv. E [skri'n] > N *skri'n* n. 'small chest', pl. —; skri̧'n n., pl. -s, def. pl. -sa 9. Cpd: -dør (door), -glas (window), -væv (web).

seed n. germ cell 49. N *frø* n. 5; *frøkorn* n. 3C1; *såkorn* n. 10C2. E [si'd] > si'd m.n.f. (m. 43; n. 5; f. 7H1). Cpd: kløver- (clover), korn- (corn), timothy-, tobakk- (tobacco). Quot: si'den æ så dy're 5N1; så må vi så' si'd eller frø' 12Q7; sprao'ta si'den 15P6; så dåi'r si'den 12Q7.

separator n. machine for separating cream from milk 59. N *separator* m. (sep'pera'tor 3C1; seperato'r 7H2). E [sɛp'ərei̯tər] > sep'perei'ter m., pl. -s; the first part: (1) sep'pe- 23; sep'pe- 5; seppe- 4; sepp'- 5; (2) såp'pe- 4L2; såp'pe- 4H1; såppe- 2; søp'pe- 6; søp'pe- 4Q2; søppe- 21H1; søpp'- 5; søpp'- 13N3; sup'pe- 2; sup'pe- 4K2; supp'- 18C2; the second part (accents not shown): (1) -reiter 19; -reiter 3; -̧reiter 6; -̧reiter 12; -reter 3; -̧reter 4L1; (2) -reitar 8 (So. Vo. Hard. Rog.); -̧reitar 2; -retar 2; -rator 7H2 7H3; -retter 8L4. Cpd: cream-, mjølke- (milk), rumme- (cream). Quot: e la'ga bræk'fæst å så vas'ke e søp'̧reiter[n] 19A3.

settle v. decide, fix; take up residence 18. N no equiv. E [sɛt'əl] > set'la, pt. —. Der: -ment, -r. Quot: no' e da set'la fy ida'g 6P2; set'le døs'ta 5H2; så set'la han i Sjika'go 4L4; så set'la e her i Blæ'r 14L2; da set'le vi i Sjika'go å lev'de dær en fem'-seks å'r 11C3; he'r sæt'la e ne' å he'r he e vo're 11R2; de vart opp'set'la fort' he'r 19A1; han kåm' te Gud'ju Kau'nti, da'r setla an ne' 20Q2.

shade n. roller curtain 19. N no equiv. E [she'd] > sjei'd m. (n. 3C2), pl. -s 15; sje'd 4. Cpd: vindu- (window).

shanty n. cabin, lean-to, often used for summer cooking 35. N no equiv. E [shæ'nti] > (1) sjan'ti n.f. (n. 20, f. 3); sjan'ti 4F2; (2) sjan'te f. 6 (n. 14D3); sjan't n. 6P1; (3) sjæn'ti n. 4L4 15P1; sjæn'te 4L1. Cpd: koka- (cook), log-, sleeping-. Quot: i den an'dre sjan'tia 8B2; i li'ta sjan'ti 18C1.

share n. part of proceeds in farming 36. N no equiv. (cf. *lott* m.). E [shæ'r] > sjæ'r m. (n. 14D3). Cpd: -brukar (holder) q.v., -mann (man), -del (part). Quot: å rei'sa tob'bak på sjæ'r 25P2; ha've på sjæ'r 14F1; ar'bett på sjæ'r 4K2; en far'm på sjæ'r 14F3.

shareholder n. tenant paying a share as rent 17. N *brukar* m. 4L3; *hælningsmann* m. 8L4. E [shæ'rho'lder] > sjæ'rhol'der m. 9G3; most inf. use an AmN creation sjæ'rbru'ker m. 9 (-ar 7), from 11 different communities (not incl. Koshk. and Suld. where shareman was in use); the model is N *gardbrukar*.

shed n. storage house 93. N *skjul* n. 2. E [shɛd'] > sjedd' m.n. (m. 44, all from Vernon and Crawford Cos.; n. 43, all from Tremp. and Waupaca Cos.), pl. — or -er. Cpd: høy- (hay), krøtter- (cattle), maskin- (machine), saue- (sheep), tobakks- (tobacco), ved- (wood). Quot: sum'me so vil'de no væra li'kare, so vil'de dai ha opp' sli'ke sjedd', veit du, ao lom'ber 20Q2; bort'i sa styg'ge sjed'de 11B6; ja', åsså ha'r vi sjæd'der da 14D21; in'ni e sjedd' 11B2; [tobakken] ku'rast i sjed'den 8B1.

shilling n. 12.5 cents (only in multiples of 2) 7. N no equiv. E [shɪl'ɪng] > N *skilling* m. 'about 1 cent'. Quot: father said to' sje'ling for 25c, ti' sje'ling for $1.25 4L4; heard to' sjil'ling, six, ten, father telling of things bought at store 5C1; to' sje'ling, seks sje'ling, never used four 4L1.

shivaree n. mock wedding serenade 26. N no equiv. E [shɪvəri'] > (1) sjøv'ri 4; sjøv'ri 2; sjø'vri 2; sjøv'eri 12Q2; sjø'veri 2; sjø-veri' 3; sjøveri' 5; sjøvri' 17Q1; (2) sjiv'eri 8L; sjev'eri 25A1; sjyv'eri 7G1; sjyveri' 7H2; sjæ'vri 9F1; sjæu'reri 14C11; sjev'ring 10C6.

shivaree v. conduct a shivaree 31. N no equiv. E [shɪvəri'] > (1) sjøv'era v., pt. — or -idde or -te 17; sjøv'era 3; sjæu'ere 10C5; (2) sjøv'eri'a v., pt. -dde or — 2; sjiv'eri'a 5; sjiv'eria' 241A; sjev'eri'a 4; sjøveri'a 17Q4 13N1; sjeveri'a 6P1 6P2; sjiv'eri'a 9F1; sjuv'ria 20Q1; sjøv'ria 21H1; (3) sjøv'ere'ra 4; sjev'ere'ra 20F9; sjæu'ere'ra 18C1 22F1. Der: -ar 3. Quot: dæ va sæk's å tju'ge såm sjev'ere'rte 20F9; ain hai'le bån'tsj a sjiveri'ar 6Q6.

shock v. set up grain in shocks 15. N no equiv. E [sha'k] > sjak'ka v., pt. —. Quot: so sjak'ka eg upp al't so va' på far'men 15P4.

shop n. working place or sales establishment 81. N no equiv. (cf. *verksted* n.). E [sha'p] > (1) sjapp' n.f.m. (n. 56, f. 12, m. 3); (2) sjap'pe f. 7 (Set. Tel.); cf. N *sjapp* f. 'saloon'. Cpd: balber- (barber), smiu- (blacksmith), slaktar- (butcher), hatt- (hat), kjøtt- (meat), sko- (shoe), tool-, vogn- (wagon).

shovel n. broad implement for removing earth, snow, etc. 65. N *reka* f. 4L2 8L3; *skuffa* f. 8L3; *snøskuffel* m. 4N1 8L3. E [shʌv'el] > N *skyffel* m. 'iron implement for cleaning weeds from garden paths' NRO; form in AmN: sjyf'fel 21, sjøf'fel 29; m.f. (m. all EN and Midl.; f. all WN exc. 15P3); sjøv'vel 11 (mostly younger inf.); sjif'fel 4 (Solør etc.). Cpd: scoop-, steam-. Quot: mik'sa de hei'ma me sjøf'lo 13N1.

sickle n. small implement for cutting grain, grass etc.; cutting edge on a mower 20. N *skjera* f. 10; *sigd* m. 9; *grasljå* m. 2 (Hedm.); *snidel* m. 6Q1; *kornkniv* m. 5L4. E [sɪk'əl] > (1) sik'kel m., pl. sik'lar; (2) sir'kel m. 4Q1 5H3 14D3 21H1 (cf. N *sirkel* m. 'circle'). Quot: skø'ri mæ sik'la 11C1; to' sik'la på kål'tive'tarn 4P2.

sidewalk n. surfaced walk beside a street or road 92. N no equiv. E [sai'dwɔ'k] > sai'dvå'k m.f. (m. 60, f. 23 incl. all Lyster and Valders, n. 3C4) 44; sai'dwå'k 13; sai'dvå'k 4; sai'dvå'g 4N1; sei'dvå'k 16; sei'dwå'k 8M1; sei'dvå'k 13; sei'lvå'k 25A1 (quot). Cpd: tre- (wooden). Quot: li'ke på sei'dvå'ka 14D7; en lang' sai'dvå'k 20F9.

sign n. inscribed board or space 53. N *skilt* n. 4; *plakat* m. 3. E [sai'n] > sai'n n. (m. 3C3 1K1) 40; sei'n 13. Cpd: veg- (road); -bord (board). Quot: e sto'rt sai'n 11C2.

silo n. tower for preserving fodder 20. N no equiv. E [sai'lo] > sai'lo m., pl. -ar; sei'lo 5E1 11B3. Cpd: -chute, -filler, -filling. Quot: så må du bin'ne mæ al'falfa å så fil'le sai'loa mæ kłø'ver 14D4; nå' skal vi tæll' å plei'e [plow] å så fil'le sai'loer 14D21; je måtte læ're me te' å...fil'le sæi'lo 5E1; dein' ti had'de vi itte sai'loer 14D4.

singletree n. pivoted crossbar to which are fastened the traces of a harness 18. N *humul* m. 7G1 7H2; *tverhumul* m. 11C1. E [sɪŋ'gəltriˈ] > sing'eltreˈ n. Second part is N *tre* n.; cf. **whipple-tree** n.

sitting room n. parlor 20. N *stova* f. etc. (cf. **parlor** n.). E [sɪt'ɪŋgruˈm] > sit'tingromˈ n., exc. sit'teromˈ 4K2. Second part is N *rom* n.

slipper n. light shoe 56. N *tøffel* m. 16; *ladd* m. 6 (EN and Midl.); *hudsko* m. 3C1 4L4 6P1; *filtasko* m. 5Q1 6Q1; *labb* m. 11C4 15P3. E [slɪp'ər(z)] > (1) slip'peṛs m., pl. -ar or — 21; slip'-pers 19; slip'pesj 8; (2) slip'peṛ m., pl. -s or -ar 6; slip'per 13N2 13N4. Cpd: bedroom-.

slop pail n. pail for liquid refuse 16. N cf. **swill pail**. E [sla'ppeˈl] > (1) slap'peiˈl m. 6; slap'peiˈl 3; (2) slabb'peiˈl m. 7 (4 from Coon area; 7H2 16C1 22F1); first part is N *slabb* n. 'slop'. Second part is N *peil* m.; for forms see **pail** n.

slough n. marsh 91. N *myr* f. 17Q2; *myrland* n. 7H2. E [slu'] > slu'e, slu'a f., pl. -or (most inf.); slu' 17Q2 20J1 11C4; slu've 11C2; slu'vu 11C1; slu'se 7G1. Cpd: stor- (big); -høy (hay), -høl (hole). Quot: han lev'de…ne'ri i slu'e ni en da'l 14D4; je jikk tvært' åver slu'a da åt na'boen 14D21; gå' å slå' på slu'a 14D11.

small grain n. grains other than maize 15. N *korn* n. 8L3. E [smɔ'l gre'nz] > små'grøˈn n. First part is N *små* 'small'; second is N *grøn* n. substituted for **grain**, q.v. Quot: naor da kjem' te har'ves'ten, so e' da te å kat'ta smao'grøˈne fys't då 6P4; små'-grøˈn — hav're å bygg' å li'te kvei'te 20Q1; me må sao' smao'gre'ne 4Q2.

smart a. clever, shrewd 18. N no equiv. E [sma'rt] > smar't a. 10; sma'rt 8 (EN, usually ṛ). Cpd: -weed. Der: -ing n. Quot: dæ va sma'rt ka'r 14D21; når dæ va' nå slaks bru'k får n, så va n sma'rt 5F1.

spider n. large frying pan 20. N *panna* f., *steikjepanna* f. most inf. E [spai'dər] > spai'der m. 12 (EN); spai'dar 7 (Vo. So. Hard.); spei'dar 6Q2.

spoke n. radiating rod in wheel 45. N *stikel* m. 1K1; *pinna* f. 10C5. E [spo'k(s)] > (1) spåk's n.m.f. (n. most inf., m. 15, f. 4), pl. — 16; spok's 9; spå'ks 10C6; spo'ks 3; (2) spo'k n., pl. -s 14; (3) spå'ke f. 3C4, m. 3C1.

spring n. (1) issue of water 58; (2) elastic piece of steel 35. N (1) *olla* f. 1K1; *uppkoma* f. 7H2; (2) *fjør* f. 4K1. E [sprıng'] > N *spring* m. 'fountain, pump, tap'. Cpd: (1) -høl (hole), -vatn (water); (2) seng- (bed), buggy-, stål- (steel), vogn- (wagon); -seat, -tooth, -vogn (wagon). Quot: (1) di byg'de attme ain plass' so va sprin'g 20P1; ain plass' dai kadla Sprin'gen 20Q2; spring' te å van'ne krø'tra 18C1; spring'en ve krik'ken 5L5; (2) [han] satt' på spring'e 11B5.

square dance n. dance for four couples 54. N no equiv. E [skwæ'rdæ¦ns] > skvæ'ṛdan¦s m. 18; skvæ'ṛ- 6; skvæ'ṛ- 8; skvæ'r-7; skwæ'ṛ- 14D4; skwæ'ṛ- 11; skæ'r- 4Q1; skæ'ṛ- 8L4 16C1. Second part is N *dans* m.

squire n. judge, justice of peace 13. N no equiv. E [skwai'ər] > skvæ'r m. 10; skvæ'ṛ 3C1 3C4 14D2. Word occurs in communities 3, 4, 6, 9, 13, 14, 17. Quot: dar set'te han' å In'jebjø¦r se up'pao å kjåi're te Mækfar'len, te æin skvæ'r — dei ha' kje pres't 4P1.

squire v. refl. be married by a squire 23. N no equiv. Derived from skvær m. in AmN: skvæ'ra seg, pt. —; skvæ'ṛa 7. Used in communities 3—9, 14, 16, 17, 21 (some younger inf. do not know it). Quot: de va kje almin'dele at dei skvæ'ra seg 5L1; han var sta' skvæ'ra seg 4F1.

squirrel n. bushy-tailed rodent 63. N *ikonn* n. 24; *grå-ikonn* n. 8L3; *trebjønn* m. 4P1; *eikun* m. 7G1. E [skwʌr'əl] > (1) skwø'ṛel m., pl. -s 26; skwø'ṛel 5; skvø'rel 11; skwø'ṛil 3; skvø'ṛel 5H4; skvø'dl 17Q3; skø'redl 17Q2; (2) skvæ'ṛil m., pl. skvær'lar 6 (EN); skwæ'ṛil 10C2 14D2; skvæ'ṛel 22F1 10C4; skvæ'rel 15P2 20Q1; skvæ'ridl 6Q1; skvæ'ril 3C1; skva'ril 4L1. Cpd: -kjøtt (meat), -skinn (fur). Quot: æin tamm' skwø'ṛel 5E1; han¦ska tå skvø'ṛelsjinn¦ uppå'ver ar'men 5H4.

stable n. building for horses, cattle, etc. 65. N *fjøs* n. 4L4 11B4. E [ste'bəl] > stæ'bel m., pl. stæ'blar 45; def. stæ'bedl 17Q3 17Q4; ste'bel 12; stei'bel 4; steb'bel 14C2 14D1 14D4 20Q2. Cpd: ku- (cow), høy- (hay), heste- (horse-), livery-, log-, saue-(sheep), sod-; -dør (door). Quot: bud'deiene lå'g i ste'beln [in Norway] 4L4; å så va dæ stæ'bel — nei, fjo's kal'la dem de no' [a seter in Norway] 11B4; han byg'de ste'bel 4F2; ba're noko gam'¦le stæ'blar 4K1.

stanchion n. upright bars enclosing cow's head 67. N no equiv. E [stæ′nshən] or [stæ′nshəl] > (1) stæn′sjen m., pl. -s or -ar 17; stæ′nsjen 9; stæn′tkjen 10C5; stan′sjen 3C2; (2) stæ′nsjel m., pl. -lar 9; stæn′sjel 2; stæ′nsel 4L3; stæn′tkjedl 13N2; sten'sel 4N1; (3) stæng′sel f. 2C1 14C1, m. 8L4, n. 8L1 14C2; this stem is N *stengsla* f. and *stengsel* n. 'bar, barrier'. Cpd: ku- (cow).

start v. begin 15. N *begynda* v. 14D3. E [sta′rt] > sta'ṛta v., pt. — 8 (all EN); star'ta 7. Quot: e star'ta No′ra Stå′r 4Q2; så sta'rta vi et dø*l*alag 10C2; dar va star'ta ai når′sk lin'ja 4Q2; da sta'rte je inn¹ 14D11; etter fæk'trie sta'rta 5G1; når dæi sta'ṛta u¹t 5F1; sta′rt på sku'*l*en 20F13.

stoop n. porch, esp. without roof 37. N *tram* m. 13 (Midl. EN) etc.; cf. **porch** n. E [stu′p] > stu′p m. most inf.; stupp′ 4F1 8M2 (quot.); stru′p 20Q1 (quot.). Cpd: bak- (back), fram- (front), front-. Quot: stu′pen — dæ′r har du dæ når′ske 5H3; stu′pen er re′gular når′sk 4L2.

stop v. stay 30. N (*overnatte, stogga* etc.) E [sta′p] > N *stoppa* v. 'come to a halt'. Quot: [han] fekk′ ikkje ståp'pe no'en sta 5F1; me ståp'pa i Milevå′ki ai vi'kes ti′ 8M2; han ståp'pa pao so djil't ta'van 5Q1; du sku ståp'pe dæ′r i tre′ u'ker 11C2; han′ såm vi ståp'te hos ha sko′stå′r 4Q2; di måtte ståp'pa y′ve nat′tæ 4P4.

store n. sales establishment 56. N *butikk* m. 5P1. E [stɔ′r] > stå′r n., pl. —. Cpd: department-, drug-, drygoods-, furniture-, general-, grocery-, hardware-, sko- (shoe-), tisent (tencent); -bill, -gang, -keeper. Quot: gå′ på stå′re 5G1; to′ sto're stå′r 10C2; et li'te stå′r 4Q2; ar'be på stå′re 20F1; e stå′r i Sæng′krikk¹ (Sand Creek) 18C4.

storekeeper n. merchant 83. N *kjøpmann* m. 4H1 4L3. E [stɔ′rki¹pər] > (1) stå'rki¹per m., pl. -ar most inf.; -ki¹par 35 (WN Midl. Tr.); (2) stå'rkip¹per m. 10C8 14D1 14D2; -kip'par 18B1 18B2; stå¹rki′pari 8M2. Quot: fai′r henni, han va′ en stå'r-ki′pari 8M2.

stove n. heating apparatus 105. N *omn* m. 6Q2 5Q1; *kakelomn* m. 5L2 8M1; *komfyr* m. 5N1 8L3; cf. kak′keloms-stå¹ve 8F1 (quot.) E [sto′v] > stå′v m., pl. -ar most inf.; sto′v 8 (Suld. Setesd. Tel.). Cpd: baka- (baking), køl- (coal), koka- (cooking), hetar- (heating), kjøken- (kitchen); -dør (door), -handle, -pipe (pipe), -poker, -ved (wood). Quot: stai'kja da på stå′ven 25P2;

nø're i stå'ven 5H2; de va no'e vi skull var'me på stå'ven 11R1; åska ottur ståven 4K1 (written).

street n. road in city or village 42. N *gata* f. 16. E [stri't] > stri't m. (n. 9G1 25A1), pl. -ar. Cpd: bak- (back); -car, -corner. Quot: li'ke ut i stri'ten 14D21; ne på stri'ta 14D2; etter stri'ta 14D2; så ræis't eg ut pao ga'ten 25P3.

streetcar n. conveyance on rails 34. N no equiv. E [stri't-ka'r] > (1) stri'tka'r m., pl. -s 5; stri'tka'r 5 (int. unmarked 4); stri'tka'r 3 (Vo.); (2) stri'tka'rs m., pl. -er 2; stri'tka'rs 2 (int. unmarked 2); stri'tka'sj 6; strit'ka'sj 2 (int. unmarked 2). Cpd: -conductor. Quot: ta stri'tka'ren ut ti Sjen'ks Kår'na 25P3.

suit n. (1) set of garments; (2) case at law 58. N (1) *klædning* m. 18; *klæde* n. 4P1 4P2; (2) *sak* f. 21 (cf. **lawsuit**). E [su't] > su't m. (f. 7H1 7H3). Cpd: klæ- (of clothes); -case; (2) law- q.v. Quot: eg vilde fao' meg en su't 4Q2.

supper n. evening meal (all prim. inf.). N *kveldsmat* m. 13; *kveldsverd* m. 9 (EN Tel. Biri); *kvelds* 5Q1 12R1; *nattverd* m. 8L3. E [sʌp'ər] > søp'per m., pl. -s or -ar (all EN and Tr.); såp'per (WN); såp'per (about half the WN inf.); sòp'per (Tel.); sʌp'per 4. Cf. N *søppel* f. 'refuse', which caused 18B1 to object to this lw. Cpd: chicken-, lutefisk-, midnight-, oyster-; -tid (time). Quot: da had'de vi søp'per dæ'r 14D21; vi...hadde søp'pers, — lu'tfisk-søp'per å rømm'grøtsøp'per å åis'tersøp'per å slik't 10C4; it'te me hadde vas'ka åss dao', vait du, å fått' såp'pern 20Q1.

surprise n. astonishing occurrence 76 (incl. those for **s. party**). N no equiv. E (1) [səprai'z] > sup'prais m. 5; sup'prais 4; suprai's 7; suprei's 2; suprai's 5; suprei's 1; søp'prais 6; søp'preis 1; søp'prais 4; søprai's 2; søprai's 5; sub'breit 4L4 (quot.); (2) [sərprai'z] > sør'prais 17; sørprai's 8; sør'prais 3; sørprai's 4. Cpd: -party. Quot: den suprai'sen 6P1; dem ha sup'prais på n 25A1.

surveyor n. one who surveys land 94. N *landmålar* m. 7H1 7H2. E [sərve'ər] > (1) sørvei'er m. 12; -ve'ar 9Q1; sør'vei'er 4; -vei'ar 24A1; sør'- 3; -vei'er 4; -vei'er 2; -ve'ar 2; sørvei'er 3; sørvei'ar 15P3; ser- 5H1; se- 4L3; -ve'ar 3; -vei'er 7G1; (2) save'r m. 5; sa've'r 6; seve'r 3; sev've'r 10C1; sav'ver 10C3; savæ'r 8M2; sørve'r 7H2; (3) save'rar m. 13; sa've'rar 4; sav've'rar 22F1; seve'rar 18C2; sørve'rar 13N1; save'rer 5G1; sa've'rer 4; sav've'rer 3; sev've'rer 2; søv've'rer 2; søu'e'rer 10C2; sær've'rer

2; sev'rer 10C5; sa'gave'r 4P1 (quot.). Quot: [han] sa've'rer ut rå'd 14D9.

swill pail n. pail for liquid refuse (cf. **slop pail**) 15. N *skuli-bytta* f. 3C1 11C1 11C2; others, who have substituted *peil* for *bytta*, use other N words for the first part: skuli- 12 (EN Vald. Tr.); sukke- 10 (Midl. WN); sukle- 8L3; sutre- 5 (Tel. Set. Suld.); suppe- 8M1; grisa- 4; søle- 24A1; skrap- 1K1. E [swɪl'pe'l] > svill'pei'l m.; svill'- 5G1.

tavern n. (1) inn, hotel (obs.); (2) saloon (since prohibition) 61. N (1) *hotell* n. 14C1 14F2; (2) no equiv. E [tæ'vərn] > meaning (1) ta'van n., pl. — 42; ta'van 4L4 5L1; ta'vande 4P1 17Q2; tava'n 7H2; (2) tæ'vern m., pl. -s 9; tæ'vern 6; tæv'vern 10C6; ta'varn 14D2. Quot: (1) så kåm' dær ain dan'shå'l å ait ta'van, å noe slik't, å dæ' lik'te ikkje kjær'ringa å in'kje e'g hel'le 15P1; ta'vane, de va'r en *pl*ass' di jekk' å fekk sei mid'dag 8F1; eit ta'van va ein min'dre *pl*ass' hell et hot'tel 10C2; ta'vane [har jeg] hø'rt av gam'lare fål'k 10C3; ta'van — de va plass' te ståg'ga 12R1; (2) desse tæ'verna 14D2.

teach v. instruct 53. N *læra* v. 9 (some use only for informal instruction); *skula* v. 6Q2 15P3; *halda* (skule) v. 10. E [ti'tsh] > ti'tsja v., pt. — 22; ti'tkja 20; tit'sja 8; tit'kja 3. Quot: han læ'rte åss te å syng'e...å så ti'tkja n sko'*l*e 8C2; [eg] byn'te å ti'tsje sku'*l*e 4H1; ho ti'tkja sko'*l*e 8L8; han va' itte så han ti'tkja den ti'a 19A2; note opposition: han tit'sja ve Luther [College] vs. bes'temor lær'de meg katekis'men 6Q1.

teacher n. instructor 55. N *(skule)lærar* m. 10; *skulemeister* m. 23. E [ti'tshər] > ti'tsjeɽ m., pl. -ar or -s 6; -tsjer 3; -tkjer 12; -tsjar 4Q1; ti'tsjeɽ 2; -tkjer 4; tit'sjer 13; tit'kjer 9; tit'kjer 2; -kjar 3. Cpd: kar- (male), music-, skule- (school), kvinnfolk- (woman). Quot: da ket'kje ti'tkjern døm 14D22; vi had'de både ka'rti'tsjer å kvinn'fålkti'tsjer 14D21; då'rlie tit'kjerer 14F2; han ha våre sku'letit'kjer 17P1.

team n. pair of animals 69. N (cf. *par* n., *spann* n.). E [ti'm] > ti'm n., pl. —. Cpd: bobsleigh-, heste- (horse), livery-, ukse- (ox). Der: -ster. Quot: vi bru'ke fæm' ti'm 14D1; så'nen hennes hit'kja opp ti'me te lum'bervång'ni 20Q1; når e bejyn'da å dri've ti'm i fi'la, så va eg sæk's å'r ga'målj 12R3; e ti'm mæ hæs'ter 10C14; fi'de ti'me 14F3.

thrashing crew n. men engaged to trash grain 37. N no equiv. E [thræ'shɪng kru'] > trøs'karkru' f., with N substitution in both parts; the first part has such forms as tres'sja-, trøs'sje- etc; for the second part see **crew** n. Quot: når trøs'karkru'e fann' al'kåhå'len, så byn'te dæm å drakk' tå n 19A2; tres'sjarkru'en besto' av åt'te mann' 5H3.

tie n. crossbeam to which rails are fastened 36. N no equiv. E [ta'i(z)] > (1) tai's m.f.n. (m. 19, f. 3, n. 2), pl. — 22; tei's 9; (2) tai' m. (n. 19A2), pl. -s 4 (10C6 13N1 14D3 20C1). Cpd: cross-, neck-.

timothy n. a grass (Phleum pratense) 14. N *timotei* m. 2C2. E [tɪm'əthi] > tim'moti m. 6; ti'moti 14D21; timo'ti 5L2 6P2; tim'oti 5 (WN Midl.). Quot: tim'moti, de va gam'melfi'den dem bruk'te 5L2; so kun'de me fik'sa dan rip'paren so at me kunde slao' håi' so sto' up'pe, so so klø'ver å tim'oti 6P2.

tip v. upset (often with **over**) 17. N *velta* v. 24; *bikka* v. 18B1; *rulla ivi* 4L4. E [tɪp'] > tip'pa, pt. —. Cpd. -over. Quot: [han] tip'pa å'ver 5F1.

tongue n. wagon pole (all prim. inf.). N *(vogn)stong* f. 8L3 8M2. E [tʌng'] > N *tong* f. 'pliers, tongs', pl. *tenger*.

tool n. implement 73. N *reidskap* m. 9 (Gbr. Tel. Mjøs region); *ambod* m.f.n. 3 (So. Vald.); *verktøy* n. 9G1; *handivle* n. 4P1. E [tu'l(z)] > (1) tul's m., def. -en, pl. —, def. pl. -a 44; tu'ls 26; tu'lz 9G2; to'ls 8M1; (2) tu'l m., pl. -s 4L4. Cpd: små- (small); -box, -shop. Quot: så pik'ka han upp tu'lsæ mine å så ga'v han meg tu'lsæ 15P1.

tough a. (1) difficult to chew; (2) trying, troublesome; (3) rowdy 16. N no equiv. E [tʌf'] > tåff', neut. — or -t, pl. -e. Quot: (1) ha'r je får my' fłøu'r, så blir lef'sa tåff' 18C5; (2) dæ gan'sje tåff' får di gam'le nårs'kera hæ'r 17P1; dæ va tåf't i fystnin'jene 12R5; da va tem'male tåff' da fys'te 5Q1; ti'en blai tåf'fe 12R1; tåff' jabb' å kåm'må inn 20C1; de sin'tes je va tåf't 14D1; (3) han va tåff' 8M1; dæ så'g gan'ske tåff' u't 20C1.

towel n. cloth for drying 54. N *handklæ* n. 46; *turkeplagg* n. 7 (Hall. So. Nfj.); *turkefilla* f. 4P1. E [tau'əl] > tao'l n.m. (m. 4F1 5G1 21H1) 37; tæu'l 13; tao'əl 4P1; ta'vel 11B1; ta'l 14D4. Cpd: bath-, dish-, turke- (drying). Quot: et re'nt tao'l 19A3.

town n. township (in Wisconsin) 66. N no equiv. (cf. *herred* n.). E [tau'n] > tao'n n. 55; tæu'n 11. Cpd: -bord (board), -clerk, -hall, -office, -program, -treasurer. Quot: i det'te tao'ne 5H6; i et an't teu'n 5N1; tao'n åv Al'bien 4F2; tao'n åv Li'ds 6P2.

township n. administrative division of a county 24. N no equiv. (cf. *herred* n.) E [tau'nship'] > tao'nsjipp' n. (m. 4N1); tæu'n- 9G1. Cpd: -embede (office). Quot: i det'te tao'nsjip'pe 5F1; kasse'rar fy tao'nsjip'pe 4P1.

tractor n. motorized vehicle 14. N no equiv. E [træ'ktər] > træk'ter m. 4 (Solør); træk'ter 3; træk'ter 3 (Spr. Grove); træ'kter 8F1; trek'ter 2; trek'ta'ri 8M1. Cpd: -plog (plow). Quot: eg bru'kar itte træk'ter 14L1; træk'tern fækk je kjø're 14D22; en trek'ta'ri te å dra'ge n 8M1; no' har me trek'ter 4P2.

train n. locomotive and cars 89. N *tog* n. 18B1; *træn* n. was also in general use in 19th century Norway, as appears from Larsen DNEO and Falk-Torp. E [tre'n] > trei'n n., pl. — 68; trei'n 3; tre'n, tri'n 15 (esp. So. Suld. Hard. Midl.); træn 3 (Tr.). Cpd: frakt- (freight), freight-, through-; -lass (load). Quot: dæ'r måtte di bi'te [change] trei'n 20P2; vi jikk' oppi blåf'fa å så trei'na gå' 14F2; trei'ne kun'de kje gao' ijøno kat'ta [the cuts] 20Q2; me to'k tre'ni 8M2.

tramp n. vagabond 81. N *fant* m. 4N1 6Q1; *tiggar* m. 4H1 6P1. E [træ'mp(s)] > (1) træm'p, trem'p m., pl. -s or -ar 44; træ'mp 12; træ'mp 4; tram'p m. 6; (2) trem's, træm's m., pl. — or -ar 14 (mostly from Coon and Spr. Grove areas); trem'ps 11C2; tram'ps 11C1.

trap n. device for catching animals 37. N *soks* f. 26 (EN Midl.); *glefsa* (*glepsa, gleksa*) f. 12 (WN Gbr. Tr.); *fella* f. 18. E [træ'p] > (1) træpp' f. m. (f. 14, m. 9 esp. EN) 14; trepp' 6; træ'p 3; træ'p 4Q1 21H1; (2) trapp' f. 5 (Set. Hadel.); trep'pa 17Q4; træp'pe 4L1; træ'pa 13N1; trap'pe 7G1; (3) træp's f. 18C2 22F1; stræ'ps 14D2. Stem 2 shows contamination with N *trapp* f. 'stairs'. Cpd: mink-.

travel v. walk (opposed to 'ride') 66. N *ganga* v. also used. E [træ'vel] > trav'la v., pt. — 30; tra'vla 10; trav'la 3; trav'le 11B1; træv'le 8L5 21H1; træ'vle 8L. Quot: han måtte tra'vle omtrent to' å tre'dve mi'l 12R6; så jekk' e da, trav'la to' mi'l u't te plas'sen te bro'r min 25P3; han kan gå' i ei vång'n, trav'le de e å bru'ke be'na 18B2; de e my'kje dei kal'la de trav'la når dei gå'r 5G1; [dai sa] trav'la naor dai mai'na jekk' te fot's — da bruk'te aldri me' i vaor't hai'm, pa'pa va so fårår'ga pao da' o're... [quoting a relative:] "be'bien e' so flin'ku, han e al't bjyn't å trav'la" — me høyr'de "trav'la" hel'stu tao ha'ringa å nåk're vås'singa so kom inn' i sai'nare ao'ræ 4P1; e sa' te gu'ten, "Ska' itte e' få væ're me å kjø're?" Så sa' n te mei', "Na'i, du' kainn tra'v*l*e" 11B1; fø'r i ti'a så bru'ka vi å træ'vle runt da, men nå' i sis'te å'ra så ha dm hatt ka'ṛa 8L.

trouble n. difficulty 20. N *bry* n. E [trʌb'əl] > trub'bel n.m. (n. 5, m. 4K2; most inf. no gender) Der: -some. Quot: dom hadde hatt' nå trub'bel mæ bå'ten 18C1; litt trub'bel me pres'ten 11B2; dai had'de noko trub'bel dao 6Q4.

truck n. automobile for carrying heavy loads 73. N no equiv. E [trʌk(s)] > (1) trøkk' m. f. (m. 30, f. 5L3 5Q1 6Q3; trøkk' 5; trakk' 17Q2; trukk 4N1; (2) tråkk' m. f. (m. 29 esp. WN Midl., f. 4P1 7H1 17Q3 17Q4); tṛåkk' 2. (3) trøk's m. 10C3; (4) tråk's m.f. (m. 13N1 13N4, f. 4Q1 13N2 13N3). Cpd: fire-. Quot: kjøre en trøkk' 20F11; di hær're trøk'kene 8F1; hy're en trøkk' 11C1.

trunk n. chest 73. N *kuffert* m. 7H2 8M3; *klækista* f. 4L4; *kista* f. 4L1. E [trʌng'k] > tron'k m., pl. -ar; trån'k 9. Quot: potret'te va ne'lakka i trou'kjen min 12R5; tron'ken min 20F1.

tub n. large, open vessel 96. N *stamp* m. 5N1; *vaskebal* m. 5L1. E [tʌb] > (1) tåbb' m. (f. 4L4), pl. -ar; tøbb' 9G1; (2) tåb'be m. 4K2 17Q3, f. 10C3. Cpd: bada- (bath), vaska- (wash), vass- (water). Quot: en tåbb' mæ vat'ten 20C3; de'r sto tåb'bi 4L4.

turkey n. bird (Meleagris) 49. N no equiv. E [tər'ki(z)] > (1) tør'ki m., pl. -s or -ar 19; tøṛ'ki 13; tur'ki 10C6; (2) tør'kis m., pl. — or -ar 16. Cpd: -hane (cock). Quot: me læu't fårtel'ja mo'r vaor at me vilde slak'ta den tør'kien...so rais'te me bur't å dra'p den tør'kien å fiksa han' upp' 6P1; å så va' dær ein tør'ki, tør'ki-ha'ne 4L4.

upstairs adv. to or on an upper floor 92. N *uppå loftet* 12; *uppå lemen* 5 (So. Vo. Suld.); *uppå treve* 5L3; *uppover* 14L1 11B1. E [ʌpstæ'rz] > upp'stæ*l*rs adv.; upp'stæ'rs 10; oppstæ'rs 13N2. The first part is N *upp* adv. 'up'; the second part: (1) -stæ'ṛs 19; -steṛ's 14; -stæ'rs 14; -ste'rs 3; -ste'ṛs 4; -stær's 4; (2) -stæ'sj 11; -ste'sj 2; -stesj' 8; -stæsj' 4K2; (3) -stæ's 5 (Nfj. So. Tel.); -ste's 6Q1; -stess' 18B1 18B2 6Q3; -stiss' 4N1; (4) -stet'tæ 8M1 8M2 (cf. Set.

stett f. 'stairs'). Cpd: -tropp (steps), -glas (window). Quot: e hør'de dæ opp'ste'r̩s e 10C2; så' raiste me' å' opp'sters' 6P1; ne're å opp'-stær's 20Q2; å pakk' dekkan ne' nå, ifrå opp'ste'r̩sen 20C2; eit pa'r vin'trar ståp'pa han jå kånn', liv'de upp'stæ'rs 4L4.

washtub n. tub for washing clothes 65. N *stamp* m. 5N1; *vaskebal* m. 5L1. First part N: vas'ke- 52, vas'ka- 14C2 14D3; vas'kar- 11 (Vald. Hall. Tr. Gbr. EN); second part like **tub**, q. v.

watermelon n. Citrullus vulgaris 34. N no equiv. E [wa'tər-mɛl'ən] or [wɔ-'] > (1) wå'termel'en m., pl. -s 9; va'termel'len 3 (Wiota); va'termelo'n 8L1; va'tmelo'ne f. 8L4; (2) va'termøl'le f., pl. -ur 12; vat'ter- 6; va'ter- 16C1; wå'te- 14C2; the second part is N *mølle* f. 'mill', with the following forms: -møl'le 10 (EN Tr.); -myl'le 4L3 8M1 14C1; -myl'da, -møl'da 5 (So.); myl'na 4L2 15P4. Quot: ai sto're pet'kj mæ va'termyl'de 20Q2; de e' nå møl'la anyway: mos'møl'la [muskmelon] 9Q1; je kun'ne itte sjå' når n sta't vat'termøl'ler 14D1.

well interj. expressing hesitation, surprise, etc. 61. N *å, ja, nei* etc. E [wɛl'] > (1) we'l, well', wæ'l, wæll' 12; (2) vell', væll' 22; væ'l 24 (incl. all Solør). Stem 2 is N *vel* adv. 'well' in various pronunciations. Quot: well', ti'dene har vært go'e 25P4; wæll', vi læ'rte nå vå'r de'l 20C5; væ'l, dæ umtren't såm hæ'r ve Ma'-disen 17P1; vell' sør, bai' smutt' 11C1; væ'i, en hall' mi'l kansje 20C3; væ'l, dem bruk'te pil's 4K2; well', dæ ai jam'naste tåll' fo't 12R1; væ'l, han fa'r va svæ'r te å dri've mæ my'e nytt' 10C2.

whip n. implement for striking animals 55. N *svepa* f. 8; *sveipa* f. 3 (8F1 8M2 18C1); *svippe* f. 14D4. E [hwɪp'] > hyp'pe, hyp'pa f., pl. -or. Cpd: -snert (lash). Quot: han to'k hyp'pa 8C1; så sto' e på tæn'ken me hyp'pa 10C2.

whippletree n. crossbar or crossbars to which are fastened the traces of a harness (distinguished from singletree by some inf., used to mean combination of two singletrees and a doubletree; cf. McDavid in *Social Forces* 25.170 (1946)) 77. N *humul* m. 7G1 7H2; *tverhumul* m. 11C1. E [hwɪp'əltri'] > hyp'peltre' n. most inf.; vip'pel- 16C1 22F1; wip'pel- 8F1; høp'pel- 9G1 9G3 10C2; hip'pel- (all dialects lacking *y*); the second part is N *tre* n. Quot: hyp'pel-tre' va'r når de var kånek'ta dåb'beltre' mellom to' sing'eltre' 5H3.

wrench n. tool for twisting 71. N *skruenøkkel* m. 8F1; *skifte-nykkjyl* m. 8L3. E [rɛntsh] > (1) ren'tsj m.f.n. (m. exc. f. 4 So.

Gbr. Vald., n. 9 So. Set. Vo. Vald. Hadel.) 17; ŗen'tsj 5; ren'sj 15; ŗen'sj 5; ren'tkj 4F1; ŗen'tkj 2; ren'kj 14D1; ren'ts 11C1; ren's 5; ŗen's 4; (2) rin'tsj 6Q3 8L1; rin'sj 3; ŗin'sj 2; rin'tkj 3; rin's 5 (So. Set. Vald.). Cpd: monkey- q.v.

yankee n. an American, a speaker of English; the English language 56. N no equiv. E [jæ'ngki] > jen'ki m., pl. -ar or -s (sing. used collectively) 32; jæn'ki 10; jæ'nki 3; jein'ki 10C5; jin'ki 9G3; djen'ki 5; djæn'ki 3; djæ'nki 2. Cpd: -kjering (woman), -namn (name), -nabo (neighbor), -skule (school), -språk (language), -hus (house), -sprengt (-fied). Quot: [ho] fekk ar'bai jao ain jæn'ki 4P1; denne jen'kien fen'sa imo't han 4Q2; da' e vi jen'kiar att (when mixing in English words) 8L3; djæ'nki, da e' no nåkså bra' når me in'kje noko an't kan snak'ka 4P1; naor me' va smao', kun'de me ik'kje snak'ka jen'ki 6Q4; min'dre du sei'er dæ pao jæn'ki 12Q1.

yard n. (1) 3 feet; (2) enclosure around house or barn 65. N (1) no equiv.; (2) *tun* n. 17; *gard* m. 15 (esp. EN); *tomt* f. 4H1. E [jar'd] > jar'd m.n. (m. all exc. n. 5, f. 21H1), pl. — 26; jaŗ'd 21; ja'ŗd 5; jær'd 8L4 8M1 13N1 15P3; jær'd 7G1 9G1 9G3 9Q1; jaŗd'de 9Q1. Cpd: (1) -stikka (stick); (2) barn-, brick-, grav- (grave), hus- (house), ku- (cow), lumber-, skrap- (scrap). Quot: fem'ti sent jar'den 5G1; tåll' jar'd 6P2.

yeast n. cells for fermentation 53. N *æst* m. 23 (EN Gbr.); *gjest* m. 12 (Set. Hedd. Vald. Gjerpen 9G2 22F1); *kveik* f. 4L1 5L1; *gang* m. 4P1 5N1 19A1; *as* n. 5Q1; *surdeig* m. 4H1 5G1 5H2 5L2; *gjær* f. 8F1 18B1 14D2; *emt* 15P2; *esning* m. 4K1. E [ji'st] > (1) ji'st m. 22; dji'st 7; jis't 17; djis't 6Q4 15P2; (2) is't m. 4K2 11C4 12Q1 18C2 24A1. Cpd: brød- (bread), humle- (hop). Quot: vi kjøp'te jis't å had'de i hom'le å suk'ker å litt sal't å pote'tes å pote'tvatn 10C3. See also **rising** n.

yoke n. frame joining draft animals, esp. oxen 41. N no equiv. (cf. *ok* n. Ryfylke etc.; DN *åg, åk* n.) E [jo'k] > (1) jo'k n. (m. 3, all Hedd.), pl. — 20; djo'k 13N3 14C1 17Q4; jokk' 3C1; jokk', jukk' 12Q1; jå'k 7G1 10C6; (2) jo'g n. 4L4 9G1 9G2; djo'g 6Q2 17Q2; jogg' 4L2 8L4 21H1 20Q2 14D2; ju'g 6P1 6Q1 9Q1 17Q3. Cpd: neck-, ukse- (ox). Quot: ista'nfy te ber're bru'ka æi'na jo'ke, så la'ga han te¹ æit jo'k fy ko'r [okse] 20Q2; dæ va ok'sejo¹g han had'de 14D4.

Appendix 1.

COMMUNITIES AND INFORMANTS.

Information is here submitted in as compact form as possible concerning the primary sources of the oral linguistic material analyzed in the preceding chapters. Relevant facts are given for each informant and community studied. The names used for the communities correspond in a general way to those found in histories of Norwegian immigration, though some have had to be improvised by the writer. The historical data are based on available sources, with some additional material gathered from the interviews. The communities are presented in the arbitrary, roughly geographical order in which they are numbered on the maps in this book: see plates 2, 7, and 9. The Norwegian communities from which the dialects stem are shown on plate 8.

I. COMMUNITIES

(A) *Southern Wisconsin.*

1. *Jefferson Prairie*, Rock County (1838). S. of Clinton, in twp. of Clinton, spilling across into Illinois. Founded by settlers from Numedal (chiefly parish of Rollag). One Lutheran church; area strongly mixed, with Norwegians a minority. Little Norwegian spoken; informant one of youngest still capable of speaking the language. Prevalent dialect Numedal (Vossing south of state line).[1] Primary informant: 1K1.

2. *Rock Prairie*, Rock County (1839), now known as Luther Valley. S. of Orfordville, W. of Beloit; twps. of Spring Valley, Avon, Newark, and Beloit. Founded by settlers from Numedal,

Hallingdal, and Land, but to-day dominated by speakers from Biri. Lutheran churches at Beloit, Orfordville, and Luther Valley. Middle generation still speaks a good deal of Norwegian, particularly in the central part of the Luther Valley area.[2] Primary informants: 2C1, 2C2; occasional informants: 2C3, 2C4.

3. *Wiota*, Lafayette County (1841). Extends from Argyle to near South Wayne, with the heaviest concentration in Wiota Twp., which includes the villages of Wiota and Woodford. There are Lutheran churches at Argyle, and in the countryside at Yellowstone, Wiota, and Apple Grove. The East Wiota Church is said to be the oldest Norwegian church in America still in use. The prevailing dialect in Wiota Twp. is from Land, while in Argyle Twp. is heard more Hadeland dialect. North of Argyle there are Valdres people from the settlement of Blue Mounds. Many of the earliest settlers came by way of Rock Prairie. Norwegian is still used very much by the oldest generation and quite a few in the middle age group, but has been completely discarded by the young generation. Occasional services are held in Norwegian in most of the churches.[3] Primary informants: 3C1, 3C2, 3C3, 3C4.

4. *Koshkonong*, Dane County (1840). Roughly an area bounded by the villages of McFarland, Cottage Grove, Deerfield, Cambridge, Rockdale, and Edgerton, and the city of Stoughton. The most heavily Norwegian townships are Albion, Christiana, Deerfield, Cottage Grove, Pleasant Springs, Dunkirk, Dunn, and Rutland, in Dane County, with adjacent parts of Jefferson County. Founded by settlers pushing north from other Norwegian settlements: Vossings from Fox River, Illinois; Numedalers from Jefferson Prairie; Rogalanders from Fox River; Telemarkings and Sognings began coming in 1843 and 1844. This large and prosperous farming community (tobacco, corn, milk) was broken up into several Lutheran congregations, East Koshkonong, West Koshkonong, and Liberty Prairie, plus one or more church in each of the villages mentioned above. Little Norwegian is spoken there today, though the middle generation generally understands it. Each dialect group has tended to concentrate in certain areas, but the settlement as a whole has had a strongly mixed character. An idea of the relative distribution can be gained from the Koshkonong church register of 1844-50; the members listed there came from Upper

Telemark (36.8 %), Lower Telemark (10.7 %), Sogn (17.5 %), Voss (11.8 %) and Numedal (8.6 %); the rest of them (ab. 15 %) were scattered.[4] Primary informants: 4F1, 4H1, 4K1, 4L1, 4L2, 4L3, 4L4, 4N1, 4P1, 4Q1, 4Q2; secondary: 4F2, 4F3, 4G1, 4K2, 4N2; occasional: 4C1, 4F4, 4P2, 4P3, 4P4, 4Q3.

5. *Blue Mounds*, Dane County (1844). An elongated north-south strip from near Black Earth to Blanchardville, with its heaviest concentration in the Twps. of Vermont, Springdale, Blue Mounds, Perry, Primrose in Dane Co., York in Green Co., and Moscow in Iowa Co. The chief trading center of this fertile but hilly region is Mt. Horeb; dairying and cheesemaking are typical occupations. Two locales with originally Norwegian names are Daleyville and Hollandale. The prevailing dialect is Valdres, from Bagn and Aurdal, particularly in Vermont, Springdale, and Blue Mounds; in Perry there are also many Telemarkings, in York many from Hadeland, and in Primrose there is a mixed population. Many of the early settlers had first spent som time in other settlements, e.g. Muskego or Koshkonong.[5] Primary informants: 5C1, 5E1, 5G1, 5H1, 5H2, 5H3, 5H4, 5J1, 5L1, 5L2, 5L3, 5L4, 5L5, 5Q1; secondary: 5F1, 5N1; occasional: 5H5, 5H6, 5H7, 5H8, 5H9, 5J2, 5P1.

6. *Norway Grove—Spring Prairie*, Dane and Columbia Counties (1845). An area centering around the village of DeForest, extending northwest to Lodi and northeast to Keyser and Rio (in Columbia Co.), with the heaviest concentration in the township of Vienna. Settled by the overflow from Koshkonong. Overwhelmingly dominated by Sognings, except for a Hardanger group east of Lodi, a Vossing group at Spring Prairie in Leeds and Hampden Twps. (Columbia Co.), and some Telemarkings at Bonnet Prairie, south of Rio. Lutheran churches at Lodi, Norway Grove, DeForest, Keyser, Spring Prairie, Bonnet Prairie, and Rio. Fertile dairying and grain raising region. Norwegian is little spoken today, but is familiar to most of the middle generation.[6] Primary informants: 6P1, 6Q1, 6Q2, 6Q3; secondary: 6P2, 6Q4, 6Q5; occasional: 6F1, 6P3, 6P4.

(B) *Eastern Wisconsin.*

7. *Valders—Gjerpen*, Manitowoc County (1846). Immediately west of Manitowoc, centering around the village of Valders, where the prevailing dialect is Valdres; immediately to the east is a congregation named Gjerpen, where an EN dialect is spoken. Norw. is in a very weak position here, since the Norw. population is not isolated nor dominant, being surrounded both in the village and in the rural areas by other nationalities, particularly Germans. Only the oldest generation ever uses Norw. Most of the early settlers came directly from Norway. The region is a gently rolling one, once heavily forested, now devoted to grain raising and dairying.[7] Primary informants: 7G1, 7H1, 7H2, 7H3.

8. *Indianland*, Waupaca County (1850). An area bounded by the villages of Waupaca to the south, Wittenberg to the north, Amherst and Nelsonville (in Portage County) to the west. The townships of Iola and Scandinavia, with the villages of the same name, are almost entirely Norwegian. The dominant dialects are: *Lower Telemark* (around Skien: Gjerpen, Siljan) between Scandinavia and Iola, and west to Nelsonville; *Setesdal* south of Scandinavia (now greatly reduced); *Heddal* (in Eastern Telemark, formerly known as Hitterdal, here used as the name of a congregation) north of Iola; *Gudbrandsdal* (particularly Gausdal) north and west of Iola; *Holt* (near Tvedestrand, an EN dialect) scattered. Bordered on the west by Poles and on the East by Germans, with heavy woods immediately to the north, this area has retained Norwegian with more tenacity than most other Wisconsin regions. Norwegian is still spoken on the streets of the villages, and even the youngest generation often employs it. This is a rocky, hill-strewn country, still in part resembling a pioneer region. Dairying and grain raising are the chief occupations, with some timbering still left. Waupaca and Stephens Point are the chief trading places. There are Lutheran churches in each of the villages of the area, in addition to rural churches at Hitterdal, New Hope, and Alban.[8] Primary informants: 8F1, 8L1, 8L2, 8L3, 8L4, 8M1, 8M2; secondary: 8B1, 8L5, 8M3; occasional: 8B2, 8B3, 8C1, 8C2, 8C3, 8C4, 8C5, 8E1, 8G1, 8G2, 8L6, 8L7, 8L8, 8M4.

9. *Wautoma—Mt. Morris*, Waushara County (1850). A small

settlement around the village of Wautoma, scattered through Mt. Morris, Wautoma, and Marion Twps. Originally one congregation bearing the name Holden, now split into three with one pastor. The name Holden refers to the community in Norway now called Holla, from which some of the earliest settlers emigrated (by way of the Muskego settlement). The prevailing dialect, however, is that of Holt; there are a number of people from Sogn also, but their dialect seems to have been forced back. According to Helgeson, who included it with the Indianland of Waupaca County, 31 early settlers were from Sogn, 20 from Holt, and only 10 from Holla (cf. his FIL 1.14). Norwegian is spoken only by the oldest generation, except for occasional first-generation immigrants. The Norwegians are not concentrated, but intimately in contact with other nationalities.[9] Primary informants: 9G1, 9G2, 9G3, 9Q1; secondary: 9E1, 9F1; occasional: 9G4.

(C) *Western Wisconsin.*

10. *Coon Prairie*, Vernon County (1848). Extends from near Cashton southwards to near Viroqua; on the west it is bounded by Coon Valley, on the east by non-Norwegian settlements in Clinton Twp. Westby is its chief trading center; it includes all of Christiana Twp., with adjacent parts of Coon, Jefferson, and Viroqua. One of the largest and best-known compact settlements of Norwegians in the state. First settled by overflow from Koshkonong. The prevailing dialect is that of Lower Gudbrandsdalen, particularly Biri; this is often referred to as 'Westby Norwegian.' In the area between Viroqua and Westby there are many from the SW coastal region around Flekkefjord; these are called 'Flekkefjordings', though very few of them came from the town itself. Norwegian is still actively spoken, even by many of the youngest generation, particularly on the farms. There are several Lutheran congregations, in and around Westby, and the name Coon Prairie is still preserved by one of the leading churches. Tobacco is one of the chief crops, though there is also much grain raising and dairying in this fertile area.[10] Primary informants: 10C1, 10C2,

10C3, 10C4, 10C5, 10C6; secondary: 10N1; occasional: 10C7, 10C8, 10C9, 10C10, 10C11, 10C12, 10C13, 10C14, 10F1, 10N2.

11. *Coon Valley*, Vernon County (1849). A long, winding valley extending from Stoddard to Cashton, with the Norwegians particularly concentrated around the village of Coon Valley in Hamburg, Coon, Christiana, and Portland Twps. Around the village of Coon Valley the prevailing dialect is that of lower Gbr., particularly Biri; farther up the valley, in Timber Coulee (Norw. Skogdalen) the dialect is that of upper Gbr., particularly Fron. Norwegian is still spoken very widely on the secluded farms of this region, even by the youngest generation. There are Lutheran congregations at Chaseburg, Coon Valley, and Timber Coulee. Tobacco is raised, but dairying is the chief occupation.[11] Primary informants: 11B1, 11C1, 11C2, 11C3, 11C4; secondary: 11B2; occasional: 11B3, 11B4, 11B5, 11B6, 11C5, 11C6, 11C7, 11E1, 11R1, 11R2.

12. *Viroqua*, Vernon and Crawford Counties (1851). This name is here used in lieu of a better for the region extending south and west from the city of Viroqua; in some accounts it is taken as part of Coon Prairie, but it has had little contact with the Coon Prairie settlement proper. From Viroqua it extends as far south as the villages of Ferryville, Mt. Sterling, and Gays Mills. It includes the southern parts of Viroqua and Jefferson Twps., plus all of Sterling and Franklin Twps. in Vernon Co., Freeman and Utica Twps. in Crawford Co. The prevailing dialect is that of inner Sogn, the overwhelming majority of the population being from Aardal and Lyster; in Utica Twp. there is also a sizable group of people from Nordfjord, the earliest of whom arrived in 1868. SW of Viroqua the area is known as West Prairie, with two Lutheran churches; there are other Lutheran churches at Soldiers Grove, Gays Mills, Utica, Mt. Sterling, Kickapoo, and Freeman. The chief occupation is dairying and tobacco raising. Norwegian is little spoken, particularly by the youngest generation.[12] Primary informants: 12Q1, 12R1; secondary: 12Q2, 12R2; occasional: 12F1, 12Q3, 12Q4, 12Q5, 12Q6, 12Q7, 12R4, 12R5, 12R6.

13. *Suldal*, Juneau County (1850). A small settlement mostly comprised within the triangle formed by the villages of Elroy, Mauston, and New Lisbon, in the townships of Lisbon, Lindina,

and especially Plymouth. Plymouth Church, five miles west of Mauston, is known in everyday speech as 'Suldal', because the overwhelming majority of the members came from that place in Norway. Other dialects appear to have been displaced by this one. The youngest generation does not speak Norwegian, but in the middle and oldest generation there are many who can and do. There are eight Lutheran congregations in the area, divided among three pastors; very few Norwegian services are now held. There has been much intermarriage with neighboring Germans. Grain and tobacco are the chief crops.[13]   Primary informants: 13N1, 13N2, 13N3, 13N4; secondary 13N5.

14. *Blair*, Trempealeau and Jackson Counties (1854). This village is located in the largest area of concentrated Norwegian settlement in Wisconsin, bounded by Galesville on the south, Whitehall on the west, Eleva and Osseo on the north, Hixton, Taylor, and Black River Falls on the east. Many different dialect areas are found within this region. In Blair and the area immediately adjacent to it on the west in Preston Twp. the dominant dialect is that of Solør (near the Swedish border in Southern Norway). On many farms Norwegian is spoken by the youngest generation; to the middle generation it is still the favorite language, except in the villages. There are two Lutheran congregations at Blair. The area is primarily a dairying region. Most of the informants interviewed here represent the dialect of Solør; with them has been included an informant using the West Toten dialect from Pigeon Valley, northeast of Blair between Pigeon Falls and Hixton.[14] Primary informants: 14C1, 14C2; 14D1, 14D2, 14D3, 14D4; secondary: 14D5, 14D6; occasional: 14D7-22, 14F1, 14F2, 14F3, 14F4, 14L1, 14L2, 14Q1.

15. *Beaver Creek*, Trempealeau and Jackson Counties (1857). Between Blair and Ettrick, and extending into Jackson County in the direction of Taylor, there is a settlement along the course of Beaver Creek in Preston, Ettrick, Franklin, and Springfield Twps. The dominant dialect is that of Hardanger; up the valley are a number of "Stril" (from the fishing districts near Bergen). First settlement made from Koshkonong. There are two Lutheran congregations. Norwegian is widely spoken by members of the middle generation; but it is dying among the youngest. The chief

occupation is dairying and raising of small grains.[15] Primary informants: 15P1, 15P2, 15P3, 15P4; occasional: 15P5, 15P6.

16. *Strum*, Trempealeau Co. (ab. 1870). Village in northern part of Trempealeau Co. located in a settlement centered in Albion and Unity Twps. The prevailing dialects are EN, including people from Toten, Solør, Hedmark, and Gudbrandsdal. Four miles north there are a number of Trønders. There are two Lutheran congregations in Strum.[16] Primary informant: 16C1.

17. *Lyster*, Buffalo Co. (1856). The name of a congregation which is the core of a large settlement of people from Sogn, extending from Mondovi to Nelson, and southeast to Lookout and Gilmanton. Within it lie the villages of Urne and Modena, in Modena Twp. The prevailing dialect is that of Lyster in Sogn, though there have been a few settlers from other parts of Norway as well. Even the youngest generation understands Norwegian and can speak it; but as a normal means of communication it is limited to the middle and oldest generation. Chiefly a grain raising and dairying area.[17] Primary informants: 17Q1, 17Q2, 17Q3, 17Q4; occasional: 17P1.

18. *Dovre*, Barron County (ab. 1870). SE of Chetek, in the twp. named Dovre, there is a congregation by the same name, composed largely of immigrants from upper Gudbrandsdal. There are also settlers from Hedmark. This is a late-settled region, originally cleared by timbering, but now devoted to grain raising and dairying, to which has been added a flourishing resort industry. Much Norwegian is still spoken, even in the middle generation, though one seldom hears any one of the youngest generation who can speak it.[18] Primary informants: 18B1, 18B2, 18C1, 18C2; occasional: 18B3, 18C3, 18C4, 18C5.

(D) *Eastern Iowa.*

19. *Waterloo Ridge*, Allamakee County (1855). A congregation in Waterloo Twp. south and east of Spring Grove, Minnesota. Norwegian is universally spoken by the middle generation, and is frequently understood by the youngest. The people of the region are referred to by others as 'Rørosinger', referring to the Norwegian

city of Røros. Actually, very few if any of the first settlers came from Røros itself; they were mostly from Ålen and Holtålen, valleys in Trøndelagen a short distance north of Røros. This is a hilly region, with dairying and grain raising the chief occupations.[19] Primary informants: 19A1, 19A2; secondary: 19A3.

(E) *Southern Minnesota.*

20. *Spring Grove*, Houston County (1852). The Norwegian settlement of which Spring Grove is the trading center includes primarily the twps. of Spring Grove, Wilmington, and Black-hammer, but extends also into adjacent parts of Iowa. It is the oldest settlement of Norwegians in Minnesota; the earliest settlers came by way of Wisconsin, many from Muskego, Rock Prairie, and Koshkonong. The use of Norwegian has here been preserved in a remarkable degree, even in the village itself. Many of the youngest generation can still speak the language, and it is widely used in the middle generation. The prevailing dialect, 'Spring Grove Nor-wegian,' is an indefinable EN dialect, probably based on the Hade-land dialect which was brought over by a large section of the settlers, possibly also on the Sigdal dialect. But others also speak the more deviant Halling dialect. In Blackhammer Twp. north of Spring Grove the prevailing dialect is Sogning. There is one con-gregation in Spring Grove proper, another in Wilmington 7.5 miles SE, and another in Blackhammer 5 miles N. There is an active Sons of Norway lodge in the village of Spring Grove.[20] Primary informants: 20C1, 20J1, 20Q1; secondary: 20C2, 20P1, 20Q2; occasional: 20C3, 20C4, 20C5, 20E1, 20F1-18, 20J2, 20P1.

21. *Vang*, Goodhue County (1855). In the NW corner of the county, where the Vang congregation was organized in 1862 by settlers from Vang, Valdres. Other N dialects surround this area without any sharp boundaries, including Telemarkings to the east, Hallings to the south. Not visited for this investigation; informa-tion entirely derived from word list of Nels Flaten in *Dialect Notes* 2.115-19 (1900-04) and his Valdris-Rispo in *Maal og minne* 1939, 30-50.[21] Primary informant: 21H1.

(F) *Northern Minnesota.*

22. *McIntosh*, Polk County (ab. 1871). Community in the Red River Valley region. Mixture of dialects—Trønder, Romerike, Valdres, Setesdal. Not visited for this investigation; informant living in Wisconsin at the time of interview. Primary informant: 22F1.

(G) *South Dakota.*

23. *Irene—Volin*, Yankton County (ab. 1869). Fertile region devoted chiefly to raising corn and cattle. Settled predominantly by people from Trøndelag. Norwegian still in active use as late as the early 1930's, but declining since that time. Not visited for this investigation, but earlier interviews made. Primary informants: 23A1; secondary: 23A2, 23A3, 23A4.

(H) *North Dakota.*

24. *Walcott*, Richland County (ab. 1870). Farming region, predominantly settled by Norwegians, including people from Trøndelag, Gudbrandsdal, Hallingdal. Not visited for this investigation; informant lived in Wisconsin at the time of the interview. Primary informant: 24A1.

(I) *Urban*

The only cities represented by interviews during this investigation were Sioux City, Iowa, where the author was born, and Madison, Wisconsin, where he lives. The study of urban speech is a separate problem, which would require a different kind of investigation from the one here conducted. City speech lacks the kind of stability which rural has had, and its forms generally disappear in the second generation. Primary informant: 25A1 (the author); secondary: 25H1, 25L1, 25P1, 25P2, 25P3, 25P4.

(J) *Miscellaneous.*

A small group of occasional informants were recorded briefly during the interviews made of others; they included 26A1, 26P1, 26P2, 26P3, 26P4., 26P5.

II. INFORMANTS.

The informants have here been identified by a code number only, in order to avoid personal embarrassment. The code number consists of (1) a number identifying his American community, (2) a letter identifying the dialect spoken, and (3) a number distinguishing the informant from others having the same community and dialect. The American communities are numbered as in the preceding list. The letters for the dialects have the following significance:

A Nordland, Trøndelag,   J Hallingdal
    Nordmøre
B Upper Gudbrandsdalen   K Numedal
C Lower Gudbrandsdalen and   L Upper Telemark
    the Mjøs region (Opland)
D Solør—Østerdal   M Setesdal (and nearby valleys)
E Lower EN (Romerike, Vest-   N Rogaland and Vest-Agder
    fold, Østfold, etc.) 'Vikske
    mål'
F EN-BL (urban speech)   P Hordaland (Voss, Hardanger)
G Lower Telemark (Bamle etc.)   Q Sogn
H Valdres   R Fjordane-Sunnmøre-Roms-
                    dalen

The code number is placed at the beginning of each description; it is followed by abbreviated statements about each informant. Wherever information was available, the following facts are presented: (1) *Generation:* 1 means born in Norway, 2 in the U.S. of parents born in Norway, etc.; a following A means 'immigrated after age 14', B means 'immigrated before age 14'; Ger means 'of German ancestry'; where two numbers appear, the first refers to the father's family, the second to the mother's; (2) *Year of Birth:* only the last two digits are given; if they are under 35, they are 1900's, otherwise they are 1800's; (3) *Immigration:* for those of generation 1, the year of informant's immigration is given; for later generations, the year of father's or paternal grandfather's immigration is given; when not known, the immigrated ancestor is indicated by F (father) or FF (father's father); (4) *Sex;* m is male, f is female; (5) *Dialect spoken:* a general indication is given when possible of the region in Norway reflected by the speaker's forms; when a specific community is known, it is given in parentheses after the region; but these are not to be taken to mean that the dialect is always identical with that of the mother community; EN means that it is some kind of East Norwegian dialect as yet unidentified; (6) *Community represented:* the township, congregation, or nearest postoffice is given, according to the information available; Pr. means 'prairie', V. 'valley', Co. 'county', Twp. 'township' etc.; the community chosen for each informant is that in which he grew up in this country, or with which he became most closely identified after his immigration; (7) *State;* (8) *Rank as informant:* the terms primary (P), secondary (S), and occasional (O) are explained in Chapter 12; they refer to the kind and amount of information secured from each informant; (9) *Interviewer:* EH is the author; MO is Magne Oftedal; (10) *Year of interview;* (11) *Questionnaire:* 36, 37, and 42 refer to different versions of the questionnaire devised by the author (cf. Chapter 12); S is Storm's Kortere Ordliste; WL is a word list compiled by the informant himself; absence of mark here means that the questionnaire was not used; (12) *Minutes recorded:* this is included to show which informants were recorded by mechanical means and to what extent; (13) *Occupation:* Ret. means 'retired'; other abbreviations will be self-explanatory; usually only the major occupation is included; (14) *Remarks:* miscellaneous comments on the quality and relationships of the informants.

Other informants than the ones here listed have been observed and even recorded; but these were not considered either important enough or relevant to the present investigation. More information is available in the writer's files about these informants, but space did not permit its presentation.

Informant	Generation	Year of birth	Immigration	Sex	Dialect spoken	Community represented	State	Rank as inf.	Interviewer	Year of interv.	Questionnaire	Min. recorded	Occupation	Remarks
1K1	3/2A	03	FF	m	Numedal	Jeff. Pr.	Wis.	P	MO	48	42	40	Ret. farmer	Lively, fluent
2C1	1B	75	77	f	Ø. Toten	Luther V.	Wis.	P	MO	48	42	30	Farm widow	Fluent
2C2	3/4	29	FF	m	Biri	Luther V.	Wis.	P	MO	48	42	30	Carpenter	Intelligent; group leader
2C3	1A	63	81	m	Vardal	Luther V.	Wis.	S	EH	39	—	12		
2C4	1B	69	72	m	Biri	Luther V.	Wis.	S	MO	48	42	—		Uncommunicative; reliable
3C1	2A	78	51	m	Land	Wiota	Wis.	P	MO	48	42	28	Farmer	Fluent
3C2	2A	87	79	m	Hadeland	Wiota	Wis.	P	MO	48	42	43	Farmer	Teacher's tr.; weak in N
3C3	2B/3	89	72	f	Toten?	Wiota	Wis.	P	MO	48	42	20	Housekeeper	
3C4	2A	70	53	f	Land	Argyle	Wis.	P	MO	48	42	30	Housekeeper	Fluent; modified dial.
4C1	1B	66	74	m	Hadeland	Stoughton	Wis.	O	MO	49	—	10	Ret. farmer	
4F1	2A	61	45	m	EN	E. Koshk.	Wis.	P	EH	37	37	15	Ret. farmer	Dial. modified by BL
4F2	2A	56	36	f	EN	Rockdale	Wis.	S	EH	37	37	10	Farm widow	Dial. modified by BL
4F3	2A/3	73	F	f	EN	Jefferson Co.	Wis.	S	EH	37	37	—	Farm wife	F is 4F4
4F4	1A	46	71	m	BL	Jefferson Co.	Wis.	O	EH	37	—	—	Schoolteacher	From Kvitseid, Telemark
4G1	1A	74	91	m	Siljan	Jefferson Co.	Wis.	S	EH	37	37	—	Farmer	Selected questions
4H1	2A	52	47	f	Valdres	Rockdale	Wis.	P	EH	36	36	10	Farm widow	Fluent

													Miscellaneous	customs
4K2	1A	53	69	m	Numedal	Co. Rockdale	Wis.	S	EH	36	36	—	Farmer	Poor inf.
4L1	3	76	FF	m	Telem. (Flatd.)	Pleasant Spr. Twp., Dane Co.	Wis.	P	EH	37	37	—		2 yrs. college; excellent inf.
4L2	1A	63	85	m	Telem. (Mo)	Burke Twp., Dane Co.	Wis.	P	MO	48	42	28	Ret. farmer	Fluent
4L3	2	74	F	f	Telem. (Lårdal)	Pleas. Spr.	Wis.	P	MO	48	42	30	Farm widow	Husband of Halling and Sogn stock
4L4	2B	50	43	m	Tel. (Morg.)	Lib. Pr.	Wis.	P	EH	37	37	90	Ret. farmer	Outstanding inf.
4N1	2A	06	65	f	Rogaland (Høle)	Koshkon.	Wis.	P	MO	48	42	14	Housewife	Fluent, but uses N little
4N2	1A	65	83	m	Rogaland (Bjerkreim)	Stoughton	Wis.	S	MO	48	—	15	Ret. farmer	F of 4N1
4P1	2B	69	41	f	Voss	Lib. Pr.	Wis.	P	EH	37-8	37	70	Housewife	Brilliant inf.
4P2	2A	63	50	m	Voss	Deerfield	Wis.	O	EH	41	—	5	Farmer	Bro. of 4P2
4P3	2A	69	50	m	Voss	Deerfield	Wis.	O	EH	41	—	5	Tobacco buyer	
4P4	1A	?	?		Hardanger	Koshkon.	Wis.	O	EH	41	—	10	Farmer	
4Q1	2B	71	44	m	Sogn (Aurland)	Utica	Wis.	P	—	—	—	—	Professor	Geo. T. Flom, print. articl.
4Q2	1A	57	77	m	Sogn (Sogndal)	Cottage Gr.	Wis.	P	EH	36	36	20	Farmer, storekeeper	Well-informed valuable inf.
4Q3	2A	69	54	m	Sogn (Sogndal)	Cambridge	Wis.	O	EH	42	42	10	Judge	
5C1	2B	70?	57	f	Hedal	Springdale	Wis.	P	EH	36	36	7	Farm wife	Uses little N; wife of 5H2
5E1	4	11	57	m	Romerike	Daleyville	Wis.	P	EH	36	36	10	Music teacher	M.A., U. of Wis.; valuable inf. (see Romerike 1948)

Continued.

Informant	Generation	Year of birth	Immigration	Sex	Dialect spoken	Community represented	State	Rank as inf.	Interviewer	Year of interv.	Questionnaire	Min. recorded	Occupation	Remarks
5G1	2A	57	52	m	Sannidal	Perry Twp.	Wis.	P	EH	37	37	—	Farmer	Dial. modif. EN
5H1	2B	06	62	f	Valdres (Aurdal)	Black Earth Twp., Dane	Wis.	P	EH	36	36	—	Librarian	Grad. U. of Wis.; interv. Storm's Kortere Ordliste
5H2	2A	72	68	m	Valdres (Bagn)	Springdale	Wis.	P	EH	36	36	7	Farmer	Fluent, though he uses N little
5H3	2A	72	49	m	Valdres (Aurdal)	Perry Twp.	Wis.	P	EH	37	37	—	Ret. farmer	Refused to be recorded
5H4	2B	62	44	m	Valdres (Bagn)	Springdale	Wis.	P	EH	36	36	10	Farmer	Good inf.
5H5	1B	65	67	m	Valdres (Bagn)	Perry Twp.	Wis.	O	EH	37	—	—	Farmer	Speaks little E; many lws.
5H6	1A	?	Age 19	m	Valdres (Aurdal)	Perry Twp.	Wis.	O	EH	37	—	—	Farmer	
5H7	1A	59	83	m	Valdres (Aurdal)	Perry Twp.	Wis.	O	EH	37	—	—	Farmer	Speaks little E
5H8	3	02	68	f	Valdres	Springdale Twp.	Wis.	O	EH	36	36	—	Teacher	Speaks little N; dau. of 5H2, 5C1
5H9	2A	76	76	f	Valdres	Perry Twp.	Wis.	O	EH	37	—	—	Farm wife	Wife of 5H5
5J1	1A	46	61	f	Halling	Mt. Horeb	Wis.	P	EH	35	S	—	Farm widow	See Hallingen, March 1933

Code				Sex	Dialect	Community	State		EH				Occupation	Notes
5J2	3	10?	?	f	Halling	Perry Twp.	Wis.	O	EH	36	—	12	Teacher	U of Wis grad; Americanized dial.
5L1	2A	58	50	m	Telemark (Nissedal)	Brigham Twp. Dane Co.	Wis.	P	EH	37	37	40	Farmer	Intelligent inf.; local historian
5L2	1A	60	82	m	Telemark (Tinn)	Blue Mounds	Wis.	P	EH	37	37	—	Ret. farmer	Poor inf.
5L3	2B	76	50	m	Telemark (Kvitseid)	Perry Twp.	Wis.	P	EH	36	36	15	Attorney	U of Wis grad; dial. modified
5L4	1B	79	84	m	Telemark (Treungen)	Perry Twp.	Wis.	P	EH	37	37	—	Farmer	Wife speaks Valdres
5L5	2A	65	50	f	Telemark (Bø)	Perry Twp.	Wis.	P	EH	37	37	—	Seamstress	Prefers N to E
5L6	2A	55	50	m	Telemark	Perry Twp.	Wis.	S	EH	38	—	50	Ret. farmer	Ancestors EN; fluent
5N1	1A	64	91	f	Jelse	Vermont Twp., Dane Co.	Wis.	P	EH	37	37	—	Farm wife	Urban Stavanger speech
5P1	1A	?	02	m	Voss	Mt. Horeb	Wis.	O	EH	41	—	5	Farmer	Fluent; one of four bro. and sisters
5Q1	2A	66	57	f	Sogn (Leikanger)	Springdale	Wis.	P	EH	37	36	10	Farm woman	
6F1	2A	86	?	m	Book Lang.	Norway Grove	Wis.	O	EH	42	—	2	Pastor	
6P1	3	77	47	f	Voss	Leeds Twp. Columbia Co.	Wis.	P	EH	36-7	36	10	Housewife	Fluent, valuable inf.; dau. of 6P2
6P2	2A	54	47	m	Voss	Spring Pr.	Wis.	S	EH	37	—	27	Ret. farmer	Fine narrator; personality
6P3	2A	07	97	m	Voss	Sun Pr.	Wis.	O	EH	41	—	10	R. estate brok	Son of 6P4
6P4	1A	76	97	m	Voss	Sun Pr.	Wis.	O	EH	41	—	5	Farmer	

Continued.

Informant	Generation	Year of birth	Immigration	Sex	Dialect spoken	Community represented	State	Rank as inf.	Interviewer	Year of interv.	Questionnaire	Min. recorded	Occupation	Remarks
6Q1	3	88	FF	f	Sogn (Balestr. ?)	Spring Pr.	Wis.	P	EH	36	36	10	Housewife	Good inf.; fluent
6Q2	2A	67	61	f	Sogn	Lodi	Wis.	P	MO	48	42	11	Farm woman	Enfeebled; taciturn
6Q3	2A	75	66	m	Sogn (Balestr. ?)	Lodi	Wis.	P	EH	36-7	36	10	Attorney	U of Wis. grad.; good storyteller
6Q4	3/2B	83	FF	m	Sogn	Norway Gr.	Wis.	S	EH	38	37	25	Farmer	Uses little N
6Q5	2A	96	94	f	Sogn (Hafslo)	Norway Gr.	Wis.	S	EH	42	42	—	Farm wife	Learned N at work
6Q6	3/2B	89	FF	f	Sogn	Norway Gr.	Wis.	O	EH	38	—	5	Housewife	Good inf.; rarely uses N
7G1	2A/3	88	ab. 70	m	Gjerpen	Cato Twp. Manitowoc Co.	Wis.	P	MO	47	42	—	Farmer	Switches from BL to dialect
7H1	1A	74	91	m	Valdres (V. Slidre)	Valders	Wis.	P	MO	47	42	—	Farmer	Good inf.
7H2	1A	70	90	m	Valdres (Hegge)	Valders	Wis.	P	MO	47	42	—	Ret. farmer	
7H3	2A	76	48	m	Valdres (Vang)	Valders	Wis.	P	MO	47	42	—	Business man	Unwilling inf.
8B1	1A	72	01	m	Gudbr. (Ringebu)	Iola	Wis.	S	EH	42	—	—	Ret. farmer	
8B2	2A	80	01	m	Gudbr. (Ringebu)	Iola	Wis.	O	EH	42	—	11	Janitor	Lived among Heddal sp.
8B3	2A	20	05	m	Gudbr. (Ringebu)	Iola	Wis.	O	EH	42	—	7	Farmer	

ID			Sex	Origin								Occupation	Notes
8C1	2A	71	48	m	Gudbr. (Gausdal)	Iola	Wis.	O	EH	42	—	3	Farmer	
8C2	2A	88	ab. 75	m	Gudbr. (Gausdal)	Iola	Wis.	O	EH	42	—	12	Farmer	
8C3	3	01	48	m	Gudbr. (Gausdal)	Iola	Wis.	O	EH	42	—	3	Office worker	
8C4	1B	79	81	f	Gudbr. (Gausdal)	Iola	Wis.	O	EH	42	—	5	Housewife	Wife of 8B2
8C5	3	15	FF	m	Gudbr. (Gausdal)	Iola	Wis.	O	EH	42	—	3	Farmer	
8E1	1A	03	22	m	Lardal	Iola	Wis.	O	EH	42	—	3	Farmer	
8F1	2A	66	Bef. 61	m	EN	Scandinavia	Wis.	P	EH	42	42	11	Ret. farmer	Infl. by BL
8G1	3	05	FF	m	EN (Nesverk)	Iola	Wis.	O	EH	42	—	05	Barber	
8G2	2A	71	48	m	EN (Nesverk)	Iola	Wis.	O	EH	42	—	11	Farmer	
8L1	2A	99	83	f	Telemark (Heddal)	Hitterdal	Wis.	P	MO	48	42	27	Farm wife	Fluent inf.; uses N much
8L2	2A	03	92	m	Telemark (Heddal)	Hitterdal	Wis.	P	MO	48	42	10	Farmer	Excellent inf.
8L3	1A	72	93	m	Telemark (Heddal)	Norske	Wis.	P	EH	42	42	22	Farmer	Uses little E; helpful inf.
8L4	2A	00	51	m	Telemark (Heddal)	Hitterdal	Wis.	P	MO	48	42	20	Laborer	Fluent; not always reliable
8L5	3/2	05	FF	f	Telemark (Heddal)	Hitterdal	Wis.	S	MO	48	—	25	Farm wife	Wife of 8L4
8L6	3/4	30	51	m	Telemark (Heddal)	Hitterdal	Wis.	O	MO	48	—	5	Farm boy	Son of 8L4, 8L5
8L7	2B	75	46	m	Telemark (Heddal)	Iola	Wis.	O	EH	42	—	11	Farmer	

Continued.

Informant	Generation	Year of birth	Immigration	Sex	Dialect spoken	Community represented	State	Rank as inf.	Interviewer	Year of interv.	Questionnaire	Min. recorded	Occupation	Remarks
8L8	2A	09	?	m	Telemark (Heddal)	Big Falls	Wis.	O	EH	42	—	11	Farmer	Fluent
8M1	3	93	49	m	Setesdal (Bygland)	Scandinavia	Wis.	P	EH	42	42	14	Farmer	Eager, talkative
8M2	2A	84	61	m	Setesdal (Bygland)	Scandinavia	Wis.	P	EH	42	37, 42	22	Business man	Excellent inf.; academy educ.
8M3	2A	63	49	m	Setesdal (Bygland)	Scandinavia	Wis.	S	EH	42	—	—	Farmer	
8M4	2A	58	ab. 52	f	Setesdal (Bygland)	Scandinavia	Wis.	O	EH	42	—	—	Farm widow	Mother of 8M1
9E1	3/4	98	FFF	f	EN (Røyken)	Mt. Morris	Wis.	S	MO	48	—	18	Housewife	
9F1	1A	90	04	m	EN (Drammen)	Wautoma	Wis.	S	MO	48	42	9	Clerk	Husband of 9E1
9G1	2A	68	52	m	Holt	Mt. Morris	Wis.	P	MO	47-8	42	30	Sheet metal worker	Good inf.; speaks little N
9G2	3/2A	00	FF	m	Holt	Mt. Morris	Wis.	P	MO	48	42	30	Farmer, town clerk	BL influence; little N
9G3	2B	76	44	m	Holt	Mt. Morris	Wis.	P	MO	47	42	27	Farmer	Reliable; indistinct speech
9G4	2A ?	66	?	m	Holla ?	Mt. Morris	Wis.	O	MO	47	—	6	Ret. farmer	
9Q1	2A	70	ab. 52	f	Sogn	Marion Twp Waushara Co.	Wis.	P	MO	47	42	47	Farm wife, ex-school teacher	Modified by BL; hesitant

10C1	1B	60	67	m	Hedmark (Stange)	Coon Pr.	Wis.	P	EH	42	42	22	Ret. farmer	Helpful inf.
10C2	2B	74	57	m	EN	Coon Pr.	Wis.	P	EH	42	42	22	Insurance agent	Fluent, helpful inf.
10C3	3	94	54	m	Gudbr.	Coon Pr.	Wis.	P	EH	42	42	—	Farmer	Slow, slightly unwilling
10C4	2A	76	68	f	Gudbr.	Coon Pr.	Wis.	P	EH	42	42	11	Housewife	Wife of 10C2; good inf.
10C5	2A/3	80	60	f	EN (Land)	Coon Pr.	Wis.	P	EH	42	42	—	Teacher	Talks N with mother
10C6	3	27	FF	m	Gudbr.	Coon Pr.	Wis.	P	MO	47	42	—	Student	"Westby dialect"
10C7	2A	68	57	m	EN (Land)	Coon Pr.	Wis.	O	EH	42	42	—	Unknown	F from Gausd.
10C8	2A	63	57	m	Gudbr.	Coon Pr.	Wis.	O	EH	42	42	10	Unknown	M from Biri
10C9	1B	?	?	m	Hedmark (Stange ?)	Coon Pr.	Wis.	O	EH	42	42	5	Unknown	
10C10	2A	53	50	f	EN (Land)	Coon Pr.	Wis.	O	EH	42	42	—	Farm widow	M of 10C5
10C11	2	?	?	m	Gudbr.	Coon Pr.	Wis.	O	EH	42	42	5	Barber	
10C12	2A	66	56	f	Gudbr. (Gausdal)	Coon Pr.	Wis.	O	EH	42	42	11	Housewife	
10C13	2A	77	58	m	Gudbr. (Øyer)	Coon Pr.	Wis.	O	EH	42	42	10	Unknown	"Westby dialect"
10C14	Ger.	94	ab. 61	m	Gudbr.	Coon Pr.	Wis.	O	EH	42	42	10	Farmer	Of German parentage
10F1	2A	81	59	m	BL	Westby	Wis.	O	EH	42	42	5	Secretary, translator	Community leader;
10N1	1B	49	57	m	Jæren (Sokndal)	Coon Pr.	Wis.	S	EH	42	42	55	Ret. farmer	dial. modif. BL
10N2	2A	73	65	m	Finnøya	Westby	Wis.	O	EH	42	42	5	Hotelkeeper	

Continued.

Informant	Generation	Year of birth	Immigration	Sex	Dialect spoken	Community represented	State	Rank as inf.	Interviewer	Year of interv.	Questionnaire	Min. recorded	Occupation	Remarks
11B1	2A	79	55	f	Gudbr. (Fron)	Coon V.	Wis.	P	EH	42	37	11	Farm woman	Fluent, valuable inf.
11B2	1A	55	66	f	Gudbr. (Fron)	Coon V.	Wis.	S	EH	42	—	22	Farm widow	Vivid personality; mother of 11B1
11B3	1A	?	?	m	Gudbr. (Fron)	Coon V.	Wis.	O	EH	42	—	2	Farm worker	
11B4	1A	88	?	m	Gudbr. (Fron)	Coon V.	Wis.	O	EH	42	—	11	Farm worker	
11B5	2A	?	?	f	Gudbr. (Fron)	Coon V.	Wis.	O	EH	42	—	5	Farm wife	
11C1	2A	69	49	m	Gudbr. (Biri)	Coon V.	Wis.	P	EH	42	37, 42	33	Farmer	Unusually valuable inf.
11C2	2A	64	49	f	Gudbr. (Biri)	Coon V.	Wis.	P	EH	42	37	40	Nurse	Dial. modif. by BL; intelligent; sister of 11C1
11C3	2A	70	49	f	Gudbr. (Biri)	Coon V.	Wis.	P	EH	42	37	5	Housewife	Sister of 11C1 and 11C2
11C4	3	11	FF	f	Gudbr. (Biri)	Coon V.	Wis.	P	EH	42	37, S	10	Student	Excellent inf.; U of Wis M.A.
11C5-7	No biogr. inf.				Gudbr (Biri)	Coon V.	Wis.	O	EH	42	—	18	Farmers	Recorded and observed
11E1	2	?	?	m	EN	Casht	Wis.	O	EH	42	—	11	Farmer	F from Eidsv.

No.	Type			Sex	Community (origin)	Community	State		F.W.				Occupation	Remarks
11R1	1A	92	ab. 10	m	Romsdal (Erisfj.)	Coon V.	Wis.	O	EH	42	—	—	Farm wife	F from Nordfjord
11R2	1A	92	10	m	Romsdal	Coon V.	Wis.	O	EH	42	—	10	Farmer	
12F1	2B	92	52	m	BL	Utica Twp. Crawford Co.	Wis.	O	EH	42	—	22	Attorney	
12Q1	2A/3	84	66	m	Sogn (Inner)	Utica Twp.	Wis.	P	EH	42	42	—	Farmer	Good inf.
12Q2	1B	55	57	m	Sogn (Årdal)	Gays' Mills	Wis.	S	EH	42	—	77	Ret. farmer	Community leader; good storyteller
12Q3	2	12	ab. 90	f	Sogn (Inner)	Soldier's Grove	Wis.	O	EH	36	—	5	Student	
12Q4	2A	72	66	m	Sogn (Inner)	Utica Twp.	Wis.	O	EH	42	—	22	Ret. business man	Dial. modified by BL
12Q5	1A	80	08	m	Sogn (Lyster)	Viroqua	Wis.	O	EH	42	—	15	Business man	
12Q6	2A	19	06	f	Sogn (Eivindvik)	Ferryville	Wis.	O	EH	42	—	5	Farm wife	Dial. modified by BL
12Q7	1A	86	06	m	Sogn (Eivindvik)	Ferryville	Wis.	O	EH	42	—	15	Farmer	Father of 12Q6
12R1	2A	81	60 ff.	m	Nordfjord (Innvik)	Utica Twp.	Wis.	P	EH	42	42	15	Farmer	Limited in experience
12R2	1A	66	01	f	Nordfjord (Hornindal)	Utica Twp.	Wis.	S	EH	42	—	24	Farm wife	Speaks little E
12R3	2B	—	F	m	Nordfjord (Svorstad)	Ferryville	Wis.	O	EH	42	—	10	Well digger	
12R4	2A	83	76	f	Nordfjord (Randabygd)	Mt. Sterling	Wis.	O	EH	42	—	8	Farm wife	
12R5	1A	62	92	f	Nordfjord (Breim)	Gays' Mills	Wis.	O	EH	42	—	—	Farm woman	Unusually high degree of borrowing

Continued.

Informant	Generation	Year of birth	Immigration	Sex	Dialect spoken	Community represented	State	Rank as inf.	Interviewer	Year of interv.	Questionnaire	Min. recorded	Occupation	Remarks
12R6	2A	78	71	m	Nordfjord	Ferryville	Wis.	O	EH	42	—	16	Farmer	Dial. modified by BL
13N1	1A	90	08	m	Suldal	Elroy	Wis.	P	MO	47	42	10	Miller	Reliable, intelligent inf.
13N2	2A	71	64	m	Suldal	Lindina Twp. Juneau Co.	Wis.	P	MO	47	42	55	Farmer	Valuable inf.
13N3	2B	88	62	f	Suldal	Mauston	Wis.	P	MO	47	42	30	Farm woman	Cousin of 13N2
13N4	2A/3	18	08	m	Suldal	Plymouth Twp. Juneau Co.	Wis.	P	MO	47	42	30	Milkman	High school, normal sch.; N anglicized; son of 13N1
13N5	2	91	—	f	Suldal	Wood Co.	Wis.	S	MO	47	42	17	Housewife	Wife of 13N1
14C1	2A	78	ab. 60	f	Toten	Hixton	Wis.	P	MO	48	42	45	Farm widow	Lively, active; uses lws. freely
14C2	3	05	71	m	Vardal	Preston Twp. Tremp. Co.	Wis.	P	EH	42-3	42	11	Farmer	Fluent; E strongly accented; N mother's dialect
14D1	2A/3	98	ab. 78	m	Solør	Preston Twp. Tremp. Co.	Wis.	P	EH	40-2	37	11	Farmer	Fluent speaker
14D2	1A	60	82	m	Solør	Blair	Wis.	P	EH	42	37	—	Ret. farmer	Good story-teller; uses little E

No.	Type			Sex	Dialect	Community	State	St.	Rec.	Yr.	Yr.	No.	Occupation	Remarks
14D4	2A	80	78	m	Solør	Twp. Tremp. Co.	Wis.	P	EH	40-2	37	22	Farmer	word list of dial.; later took Ph.D. at U. of Wis.; nephew of 14D1
14D5	2A	86	71	f	Solør	Preston Twp. Tremp. Co.	Wis.	S	EH	40	—	—	Farm wife	Unusually valuable inf.; fiddler
14D6	1B	73	76	m	Solør	Franklin Twp. Jackson Co.	Wis.	S	EH	40	37	—	Farmer	
14D7	2A	87	78	m	Solør	Blair	Wis.	O	EH	42	—	10	Farmer	Also recorded music
14D8	2A	93	82	m	Solør	Blair	Wis.	O	EH	42	—	11	Farmer	Son of 14D4
14D9	3	11	—	m	Solør	Blair	Wis.	O	EH	42	—	3	Farmer	
14D10	2B	84	71	m	Solør	Blair	Wis.	O	EH	42	—	5	Farmer	
14D11	2	81	53	m	Solør	Blair	Wis.	O	EH	42	—	7	Hotel keeper	
14D12	3/2B	—	69	m	Solør	Blair	Wis.	O	EH	42	—	11	Farmer	
14D13	2A	—	FF	m	Solør	Blair	Wis.	O	EH	42	—	4	Farmer	Brother of 14D4
14D14	2	98	71	m	Solør	Blair	Wis.	O	EH	42	—	11	Farmer	
14D15	2A	—	F	m	Solør	Blair	Wis.	O	EH	42	—	5	Farmer	
14D16	1A	79	69	m	Solør	Blair	Wis.	O	EH	42	—	5	Farmer	
14D17	3/2B	13	—	m	Solør	Blair	Wis.	O	EH	42	—	3	Farmer	Brother of 14D12
14D18	3	—	FF	m	Solør	Blair	Wis.	O	EH	42	—	11	Farmer	Son of 14D4
14D19	2A	—	71	m	Solør	Blair	Wis.	O	EH	42	—	4	Farmer	Brother of 14D8
14D20	2	01	F	m	Solør	Blair	Wis.	O	EH	42	—	5	Farmer	
14D21	2A	00	82	m	Solør	Blair	Wis.	O	EH	42	—	16	Farmer	Son of 14D2
14D22	3	27	FF	m	Solør	Blair	Wis.	O	EH	42	—	7	Farm boy	Son of 14D14

Continued.

Informant	Generation	Year of birth	Immigration	Sex	Dialect spoken	Community represented	State	Rank as inf.	Interviewer	Year of interv.	Questionnaire	Min. recorded	Occupation	Remarks
14F1	2	00	F	m	EN	Blair	Wis.	O	EH	42	—	3	Farmer	
14F2	1B	47	51	f	EN	Blair	Wis.	O	EH	42	—	—	Farm widow	Born in Sweden; but dial. Norw.
14F3	2A	73	ab. 69	m	EN	Blair	Wis.	O	EH	42	—	11	Farmer	Parents from Telemark
14F4	2B	09	F	m	EN	Whitehall	Wis.	O	EH	42	—	7	County Clerk	Bookish speech
14L1	1A	90	12	m	Telem. (Brunkeb.)	Blair	Wis.	O	EH	42	—	8	Farmer	Dial. modified by BL
14L2	2A	—	F	m	Telem.	Blair	Wis.	O	EH	42	—	11	Policeman	
14Q1	1A	97	15	m	Sogn (Aurl.)	Blair	Wis.	O	EH	42	—	5	Farmer	
15P1	1A	66	87	m	Hardanger (Odda)	Beaver Cr.	Wis.	P	EH	42	37	22	Ret. farmer	Valuable inf.
15P2	1B	65	67	f	Hardanger (Øyfjord)	Beaver Cr.	Wis.	P	EH	42	42	—	Farm widow	Slow, unwilling inf.
15P3	2A	78	54	m	Hardanger (Ulvik)	Franklin Twp., Jackson Co.	Wis.	P	EH	36-7	37	20	Engineer	Grad. U of Wis; chm. State Planning Board
15P4	2A	71	54	f	Hardanger	Beaver Cr.	Wis.	P	EH	42	42	25	Farm widow	Lively, interested inf.
15P5	2B/3	03	69	m	Hardanger	Beaver Cr.	Wis.	O	EH	42	—	6	Farmer	Son of 15P4
15P6	2B/3	15	69	m	Hardanger	Beaver Cr.	Wis.	O	EH	42	—	6	Farmer	Son of 15P4

	3		FF		EN	Sirum	Wis.	F	MO				Nurse	Unlocalized dialect; partly anglicized
17P1	2A	08	89	m	Voss	Mondovi	Wis.	O	EH	41	—	15	Farmer	
17Q1	2A	74	ab. 69	f	Sogn (Lyster)	Mondovi	Wis.	P	MO	48	42	15	Farm wife	Fluent speaker
17Q2	2	73	F	m	Sogn (Lyster)	Mondovi	Wis.	P	MO	48	42	25	Farmer	Poor inf.; uses little N
17Q3	2A	90	ab. 77	m	Sogn (Lyster)	Nelson Twp., Buffalo Co.	Wis.	P	MO	48	42	25	Farmer	Good inf.; uses little N
17Q4	2A	86	70	f	Sogn (Lyster)	Mondovi	Wis.	P	MO	48	42	21	Farm wife	Outstanding inf.
18B1	2A	75	ab. 68	f	Gudbr. (Heidal)	Dovre Twp. Barron Co.	Wis.	P	EH	42	37	33	Farm woman	Reliable inf.
18B2	2A	86	ab. 68	m	Gudbr. (Heidal)	Dovre Twp. Barron Co.	Wis.	P	EH	42	37	11	Farmer	Fluent, valuable inf.
18B3	3	13	FF	f	Gudbr. (Heidal)	Dovre Twp. Barron Co.	Wis.	O	EH	36	—	20	Housewife	Outstanding inf.; B of 18B1
18C1	3	00	57	m	Hedmark	Sand Cr. Twp. Dunn Co.	Wis.	P	EH	42	37	11	Farmer	Poor inf.; dialect anglicized
18C2	2A	99	ab. 85	m	EN	Dovre Twp. Barron Co.	Wis.	P	EH	42	37	11	Electrician	Of Heidal ancestry; dial. modified
18C3	1A	86	01	m	Hedmark	New Auburn	Wis.	O	EH	42	—	11	Farmer	
18C4	2	87	ab. 70	f	Hedmark	New Auburn	Wis.	O	EH	42	—	11	Farm wife	Wife of 18C3
18C5	3	01	FF	f	EN	New Auburn	Wis.	O	EH	42	—	11	Farm wife	Wife of 18C2

Continued.

Informant	Generation	Year of birth	Immigration	Sex	Dialect spoken	Community represented	State	Rank as inf.	Interviewer	Year of interv.	Questionnaire	Min. recorded	Occupation	Remarks
19A1	2A	61	54	m	Trønder (Røros)	Waterloo Twp., Allamakee Co	Ia.	P	EH	42	42	—	Ret. farmer	Prefers N to E; son of early settler
19A2	2A/3	94	ab. 75	m	Trønder (Holtålen)	Waterloo Twp.	Ia.	P	EH	42	42	22	Farmer	Fluent, helpful inf.
19A3	3	90	FF	f	Trønder (Holtålen)	Waterloo Twp.	Ia.	S	EH	42	—	22	Farm wife	Lively inf.
20C1	2B/3	78	67	m	EN (Hadeland)	Spring Grove	Minn.	P	EH	42	42	5	Farmer	Prefers N to E
20C2	3	00	FF	f	EN (Hadeland)	Spring Grove	Minn.	S	EH	42	—	22	Housewife, photographer	Lively inf.; dial. modif.
20C3	2B	63	F	f	EN (Hadeland)	Spring Gr.	Minn.	O	EH	42	—	11	Farm widow	Mother of 20C2
20C4	2A	75	64	m	EN (Hadeland)	Spring Gr.	Minn.	O	EH	42	—	7	Caretaker	
20C5	2A	90	64	m	EN (Hadeland)	Spring Gr.	Minn.	O	EH	42	—	8		Bro. of 20C4
20E1	3/2A	08	54	m	EN (Hadeland)	Spring Gr.	Minn.	O	EH	42	—	5	Farmer	
20F1	2A	77	58	m	EN (Ringerike)	Spring Gr.	Minn.	O	EH	42	—	5	Merchant	No biog. inf.; chiefly recorded for music (27 min.)
20F2	—	—	—	m	EN	Spring Gr.	Minn.	O	EH	42	—	5	Worker	

No.	Code	Yr.	Age	Sex	Origin	Community	State	Type	FW	Int.	2nd	Sess.	Occupation	Remarks
20F3	2B	83	50	m	BL	Spring Gr.	Minn.	O	EH	42	—	5	Merchant	
20F4	2A	04	80	m	EN	Spring Gr.	Minn.	O	EH	42	—	3	Teacher	
20F5	3	02	54	m	EN	Spring Gr.	Minn.	O	EH	42	—	5	Farmer	
20F6	2A	79	61	m	EN	Spring Gr.	Minn.	O	EH	42	—	5	Housewife	
20F7	Ger.	92	ab. 77	f	EN	Spring Gr.	Minn.	O	EH	42	—	5		Wife of 20C5
20F8	2A	—	F	m	EN	Spring Gr.	Minn.	O	EH	42	—	5	—	
20F9	2B	98	54	f	EN	Spring Gr.	Minn.	O	EH	42	—	8	Housewife	
20F10	3	80	ab. 51	f	WN ?	Spring Gr.	Minn.	O	EH	42	—	2	Farm wife	
20F11	2A	08	86	m	BL	Spring Gr.	Minn.	O	EH	42	—	3	Farmer	
20F12	2A	65	54	m	BL	Spring Gr.	Minn.	O	EH	42	—	—	Merchant	
20F13	3/4	25	FF	m	EN	Spring Gr.	Minn.	O	EH	42	—	11	High school student	
20F14	2A	—	F	m	EN	Spring Gr.	Minn.	O	EH	42	—	7	Banker	
20F15	3/2	98	FF	m	EN	Spring Gr.	Minn.	O	EH	42	—	3	Farmer	
20F16	2/3	93	84	m	EN	Spring Gr.	Minn.	O	EH	42	—	12	Farmer	Comic dialogue with 20J2
20F17	2	14	F	m	EN	Spring Gr.	Minn.	O	EH	42	—	5	Farmer	
20F18	3	30	FF	m	EN	Spring Gr.	Minn.	O	EH	42	—	11	Farmer	
20J1	2A	70	52	m	Hallingdal	Spring Gr.	Minn.	P	EH	42	42	8	Lumber merchant	Able, willing inf.
20J2	3	99	FF	m	Hallingdal	Spring Gr.	Minn.	O	EH	42	—	5	Truck driver	
20P1	2A	72	61	m	Stril	Pleasant Twp. Winneshiek Co.	Ia.	O	EH	42	—	7	Farmer?	
20P2	2A	82	71	f	Voss	Blackhammer Twp. Houston Co.		S	EH	42	—	35	Farm wife	Valuable stories; dial. modified
20Q1	3/2A	89	49	m	Sogn (Aurland)		Minn.	P	EH	42	42	11	Farmer	Fluent speaker

Continued.

Informant	Generation	Year of birth	Immigration	Sex	Dialect spoken.	Community represented	State	Rank as inf.	Interviewer	Year of interv.	Questionnaire	Min. recorded	Occupation	Remarks
20Q2	1B	59	70	f	Sogn (Aurland)	Black-hammer	Minn.	S	EH	42	—	48	Farm widow	Outstanding narrator; old-fashioned dial.
21H1	1B	67	—	m	Valdres (Vang)	Goodhue Co.	Minn.	P	—	—	—	—	College prof.	Nils Flaten, printed list
22F1	2A	87	ab. 81	m	BL	McIntosh	Minn.	P	EH	42	42	7	Pastor	BL mixed with dial. forms
23A1	2	—	—	f	Trønder (Ekne)	Yankton Co.	S. D.	P	EH	36	S	—	Farm wife	A preliminary interview
23A2	1A	46	69	m	Trønder (Opdal)	Irene	S. D.	S	EH	30	—	—	Ret. farmer	Stories noted; NASR 6.89-121 (1931)
23A3	1A	49	70	m	Trønder (Opdal)	Volin	S. D.	S	EH	30	—	—	Ret. farmer	Notes made on speech; bro. of 23A2
23A4	1A	51	73	m	Trønder (Opdal)	Irene	S. D.	S	EH	30	—	—	Ret. farmer	Extensive narrative
24A1	2A	00	ab. 88	m	Trønder (Rennebu)	Walcott	N. D.	P	EH	36	36	—	College teacher	Childhood bi-lingual
25A1	2A	06	99	m	Trønder (Opdal)	Sioux City	Ia.	P	EH	30	WL	—	Univ. Prof.	The writer
25H1	1A	64	90	m	Valdres (V. Slidre)	Madison	Wis.	S	EH	41	—	20	State worker	Tells narrative of own comp.

No.													Occupation	Notes
25L1	1A	69	91	f	Telemark (Fyrisdal)	Madison	Wis.	O	EH	36	—	10	Housewife	Also 10 m. music (Hard. viol.)
25P1	1A	72	04	m	Voss	Madison	Wis.	S	EH	36	—	10	Carpenter	Historian of the Vossings in America
25P2	1A	72	93	f	Voss	Madison	Wis.	O	EH	41	—	3	Housewife	
25P3	1A	85	11	m	Voss	Madison	Wis.	O	EH	41	—	5	Machinist	
25P4	1A	74	93	m	Voss	Mpls.	Minn.	O	EH	41	—	5	Contractor	Dial. modified by BL
26A1	1B	77	88	f	Nordland	Baldwin	Wis.	O	MO	48	42	—	Farm wife	
26P1	2	—	—	f	Voss	Freeborn Co.	Minn.	O	EH	41	—	2	Housewife	
26P2	1B	—	68	f	Voss	Hanlontown	Ia.	O	EH	41	—	2	Farm wife	Sister-in-law of 26P1
26P3	2/3	02	91	m	Voss	Lake Mills	Ia.	O	EH	42	—	5	Farmer	
26P4	1A	—	84	m	Hardanger	Ottawa	Ill.	O	EH	39	—	15	Lay preacher	
26P5	1A	—	08	f	Voss	Billings	Mont.	O	EH	41	—	3	Housewife	Dialect modified by BL

Appendix 2.

SYMBOLS AND ABBREVIATIONS.

1. *Abbreviations (languages and book titles).*

Aasen NG	Aasen, Ivar. Norsk Grammatik. Christiania, 1864.
Aasen NO	Aasen, Ivar. Norsk Ordbog. Christiania, 1873.
ACLS	American Council of Learned Societies.
AmE	American English, when necessary to distinguish it from British English.
AmG or AmGer	American German speech.
AmN	American Norwegian speech.
AmPort	American Portuguese speech.
AmSocRev	American Sociological Review.
AmSp	American Speech (a magazine)
Anderson FC	Anderson, Rasmus B. The First Chapter of Norwegian Immigration (1821—1840), its causes and results. Madison, Wisconsin, 1895.
APhSc	Acta Philologica Scandinavica (Copenhagen, Denmark).
Billed-Magazin	Billed-Magazin, Et Ugeblad til nyttig og belärende Underholdning. Ed. Svein Nilsen. Madison, Wis., 1869—1870.
BL	Book Language (used for the written DN, where its forms differ from those of colloquial DN).
Blegen NM	I: Blegen, Theodore C. Norwegian Migration to America, 1825—1860. Northfield, Minn., 1931. II: Blegen, Theodore C. Norwegian Migration to America. The American Transition. Northfield, Minn., 1940.

Blegen and Ruud Blegen, Theodore C. and Martin B. Ruud,
  NESB   Norwegian Emigrant Songs and Ballads. Min
              neapolis, 1936.

Bloomfield,
  Language   Bloomfield, Leonard. Language. New York, 1933.

CanFr   Canadian French.

DAE   Dictionary of American English.

DN   Dano-Norwegian (used for such N words as
              riksmål, dansk-norsk, bokmål to designate the
              cultivated urban spoken language of Norway).

D-P   Decorah-Posten (newspaper published in Decorah,
              Iowa).

E   English, usually as spoken in the American Middle
              West.

EN   East Norwegian (usually refers only to the dialects
              of the eastern lowlands, from the Oslo Fjord
              to Lillehammer; but is sometimes used to in
              clude all dialects not WN).

Flom NI   Flom, George T. A History of Norwegian Immi
              gration to the United States From the Earliest
              Beginning down to the Year 1848. Iowa City,
              Iowa, 1909.

FoE   Fædrelandet og Emigranten (newspaper published
              in La Crosse, Wis.).

Gbr.   Gudbrandsdalen.

Hall.   Hallingdal.

Hard.   Hardanger.

Haugen NWS Haugen, Einar. Norwegian Word Studies. 2 v.
              Madison, Wis., 1942 (mimeo.).

Hedm.   Hedmark.

Helgeson FIL Helgeson, Thor. Fra Indianernes Lande. 2 v.
              Iola, Wis., n.d.

Holand CP Holand, Hjalmar R. Coon Prairie. En historisk
              beretning om Den Norske Evangeliske Lutherske
              Menighet paa Coon Prairie. Minneapolis, Minn.,
              1927.

Holand CV Holand, Hjalmar R. Coon Valley. En historisk

	beretning om de norske menigheter i Coon Valley. Minneapolis, Minn., 1928.
Holand NSH	Holand, Hjalmar R. De norske Settlementers Historie. Ephraim, Wis., 1908.
inf.	informant.
IJAL	International Journal of American Linguistics.
JEGP	Journal of English and Germanic Philology.
Johnson NSG	Johnson, O. S. Nybyggerhistorie fra Spring Grove og omegn, Minnesota. Minneapolis, 1920.
KNVS Forh.	Kongelige Norske Videnskabers Selskab (Trondheim), Forhandlinger.
Kurath HLG	Kurath, Hans. Handbook of the Linguistic Geography of New England. Providence, R. I., 1939.
Lange's NTVL	Norsk Tidsskrift for Videnskab og Literatur.
Larsen DNEO	Larsen, A. Dansk-Norsk-Engelsk Ordbog. Kbh. og Kra., 1910,
Larson CW	Larson, L. M. The Changing West and other Essays. Northfield, Minn., 1937.
lbl.	loanblend
lsh.	loanshift
lw.	loanword
lws.	loanwords.
Mencken AL	Mencken, H. L. The American Language. 4th Ed., New York, 1936.
Midl.	Midland (dialects of the interior valleys from Telemark to Valdres).
N	Norwegian.
N-A	Norwegian-American (limited to institutions and certain social phenomena; otherwise AmN).
NAHA	Norwegian-American Historical Association.
NASR	Norwegian-American Studies and Records (Northfield, Minn., 1926—).
NFLH	Det norske folks liv og historie gjennem tidene. Oslo, 1930—35. 10 v.
NN	New Norse (used for the written *landsmål* or *nynorsk*, esp. as created by Ivar Aasen).
Nordfj.	Nordfjord.

Norlie HNPA	Norlie, O. M. History of the Norwegian People in America. Minneapolis, Minn., 1925.
Norlie NLM	Norlie, O. M. Norsk Lutherske Menigheter i Amerika 1843—1916. 2 v. Minneapolis, Minn., 1918.
NRO	Norsk Riksmålsordbok, ed. Trygve Knudsen and Alf Sommerfelt. (Oslo, 1937 ff.).
NTS	Norsk tidsskrift for Sprogvidenskap.
Num.	Numedal
P	Portuguese.
PaGer	Pennsylvania German
P-AS	Pap, Leo. Portuguese-American Speech. New York, 1949.
PMLA	Publications of the Modern Language Association.
Qualey NS	Qualey, Carlton C. Norwegian Settlement in the United States. Northfield, Minn., 1938.
Rene HUV	Rene, K. A. Historie om Udvandringen fra Voss og Vossingerne i Amerika. Madison, Wis., 1930.
Rohne NAL	Rohne, J. Magnus. Norwegian American Lutheranism up to 1872. New York, 1926.
Ross NB	Ross, Hans. Norske bygdemaal. 5 v. Chra., 1905—09 (Vid.-selsk. skr. II. Hist.-Filos. Kl.)
Set.	Setesdal
SIL	(University of Illinois) Studies in Language and Literature.
Sk or Skand.	Skandinaven (Chicago, Ill.).
So.	Sogn.
SoA	Skandinaven og Amerika (newspaper published in Chicago).
Sondresen NA	Sondresen, S. Norsk-amerikanerne. Bergen, 1938.
SoS	Språk och Stil.
SS	Scandinavian Studies (earlier Scandinavian Studies and Notes).
Stene ELN	Stene, Aasta. English Loan-words in Modern Norwegian. London, 1945.
Suld.	Suldal.
SyS	Syn og Segn.
TAPA	Transactions of the American Philological Association.

TCLP	Travaux du cercle linguistique de Prague (Prague, 1929—39) 8 v.
Tel.	Telemark.
Tr.	Trønder (dialects north of the Dovre mountains from Nordmøre to Namdalen).
Ulvestad NIA	Ulvestad, Martin. Norge i Amerika (Minneapolis, Minn., 1901)
v.	Voiced.
Vald.	Valdres.
vl.	Voiceless.
Vo.	Voss.
VSS H-F. Kl.	Videnskabs-Selskabet i Oslo, Skrifter, Historisk-Filosofisk Klasse.
WMH	Wisconsin Magazine of History.
WN	West Norwegian (dialects west of the mountains, counting from Setesdal to Sunnmøre).

2. *Phonetic symbols (the system of pronunciation).*

The two systems of transcription used in this book for N and E words represent a compromise between the practice of linguists and the standard spellings of the two languages. Special phonetic symbols are kept to a minimum, but an effort has been made to represent accurately all significant shades of sound as far as this can be done with the usual aphabet. Phonetic respellings of E words are always placed between square brackets [ ]; the values of the symbols are given below. Native N words are usually given in some kind of standard or normalized spelling, either that of DN or NN, which covers several varieties of local pronunciation. AmN words, however, having no spelling norm, are always understood to be written in an approximation to the actual pronunciation noted by this writer. Such spellings usually follow an arrowhead > which is to be read 'is reproduced as'; they are also characteristically marked by accents for stress and tone.

A. *English.*

The symbols written between square brackets have the same value as in John S. Kenyon's modification of the International Phonetic Alphabet, with certain changes made in order to avoid the use of special phonetic symbols. The phonetic values are those of general North Central American.

1. ACCENTS. Stress is marked by accents placed after the stressed vowel, or in the case of short vowels, after the first following consonant. Primary (loud) stress is marked by an acute accent ['], secondary (reduced) stress by a perpendicular accent ['], weak stress by the absence of an accent mark. Example: fanning mill [fæ′nɪngmɪll'].

2. VOWELS. The phonetic symbols correspond to the italicized spellings.

[a] c*a*r, h*o*t, f*a*ther (low central)

[ai] l*i*ne, tr*y*, s*igh*t (low central to mid front glide)

[au] l*ou*d, c*ow*, b*ough* (low central to mid back glide)

[æ] h*a*t, c*a*re, b*ea*r (low front)

[e] h*a*te, *eigh*t, p*ay* (mid front upglide)

[ɛ] y*e*t, d*e*bt, d*ea*d (mid front)

[ə] sof*a*, pap*er*, b*i*rd (mid central)

[i] mach*i*ne, c*e*de, pit*y* (high front).

[ɪ] b*i*t, w*i*ng, b*ee*r (high front relaxed).

[o] n*o*, d*ough*, s*ew* (mid back round upglide).

[ɔ] f*o*r, b*ough*t, l*aw* (low back round)

[ɔi] j*oi*n, b*oy* (low back round to mid front glide)

[u] r*u*le, b*oo*t, fr*ui*t (high back round)

[ʊ] b*u*sh, g*oo*d, sh*ou*ld (high back round relaxed)

[ʌ] c*u*t, s*o*n, fl*oo*d (mid central retracted)

3. CONSONANTS.

[b] b*o*b (v. bilabial stop)

[d] d*i*d (v. alveolar stop)

[dh] *th*is, o*th*er (v. dental spirant)

[dzh] *j*ug, *G*eor*g*e, e*dg*e (v. alveolar affricate)

[f] *f*ife, rou*gh* (vl. labiodental spirant)

[g] *g*a*g*, *gh*oul (v. velar stop)

[h] *h*ot (vl. glottal breathing)

[j] *y*ou (v. palatal semivowel)

[k] kit, cat (vl. velar stop)
[l] *l*ily (v. alveolar lateral)
[m] *m*a*m*a (v. bilabial nasal)
[n] *n*u*n* (v. alveolar nasal)
[ng] si*ng*i*ng* (v. velar nasal)
[p] *p*a*p*a (vl. bilabial stop)
[r] *r*oa*r*, bi*r*d, bette*r* (v. retroflex semivowel)
[s] *s*ister, *c*edar, *sc*ience (vl. dorsal sibilant)
[sh] *sh*oe, *Ch*icago, na*ti*on (vl. apical sibilant)

[t] *t*a*t*, s*t*one (vl. alveolar stop)
[*t*] ci*t*y, fi*tt*ing (v. alveolar flap)
[th] *th*ink, *th*ree (vl. dental spirant)
[tsh] *ch*urch (vl. alveolar affricate)
[v] *v*i*v*id (v. labiodental spirant)
[w] *w*omen (v. bilabial semivowel)
[z] *z*ero, bu*s*y, rai*s*e (v. dorsal sibilant)
[zh] a*z*ure, plea*s*ure, rou*g*e (v. apical sibilant)

B. *Norwegian.*

The Norwegian transcription is not strictly phonetic in the same sense as the English, and is therefore not enclosed in brackets. It is more elastic, since it accommodates several possible values, according to the dialect of the speaker. But for any given dialect, it should indicate with sufficient clarity just which sound is meant. The symbols are those of standard N orthography (except for the accents), and the principle has been to make the word images as similar to those of native Norwegian as possible while still rendering the pronunciation. When applied to native N words, this has made some of them look a bit unfamiliar, e.g. *å* for *og*, *får* for *for*, *hær* for *her* etc.; but this was necessary to make a distinction e.g. between dialects which pronounce *oss* 'us' as *åss* and those which really use an *o*. Some English sounds frequently occurring in lws. are also included.

1. ACCENTS. Stress, stress tone, and length are marked simultaneously by means of accents after the stressed vowels or immediately following consonants. If the accent follows the vowel, the vowel is long; if it follows the next consonant, the vowel is short (note that it may follow two consonants when these represent a single phonetic entity). If there is no accent, the vowel is short and unstressed. Primary stress is marked by an acute accent (') when it is accompanied by stress tone 1 ('simple' tone), a grave

accent (´) when it is accompanied by stress tone 2 ('complex' tone). Secondary stress is marked by a perpendicular accent (ˈ). Example: *baˈgaˈte* 'back street'; *unˈderverˈk* 'miracle'.

2. VOWELS. The various systems of vowel qualities (here distinguished as EN, Midland, and WN) are described in chapter 16. The approximate range for each symbol is here indicated, with EN values given first.

a j*a*, f*a*r, m*a*nn (low back to central); cf. E [a]
ai k*ai*, h*ai* (low back-high front glide); used for *ei* in some dialects; cf. E [ai].
ao g*ao*, p*ao* (low central-mid back round glide); only in So. Vo. Hard. dialects; cf. E [au].
e tr*e*, l*e*tt, b*e*st (mid front to lower high front); cf. E [ɪ] or [ɛ]; unstressed, as in stor*e*, it is mid central, like E [ə].
ei n*ei*, l*ei*t, b*ei*st (mid or low front to high front glide); cf. E [e].
i sk*i*, f*i*nt, kv*i*tt (high front, in some dialects with marked upglide); cf. E [i].
o sk*o*, *o*st, f*o*rt (high back overround, in Mdl. mid back round, in WN diphthongized); cf. E [u] or [o].
ó g*ó*tt, *ó*ss (mid central round); only in Telemark dialect; cf. E [ʌ].
u h*u*s, m*u*nn, b*u*st (high central overround, in Midl. high back round, in WN with marked upglide); not like E [u].
y l*y*t, sk*y*, b*y*tta (high front round); cf. Ger. ü, Fr. u.
æ f*æ*r, l*æ*t, l*æ*rd, h*e*rre (low front; in WN often lower mid front); cf. E [æ].
æi n*æi*, s*æi*n, s*æi*nga (low front to high front glide); a dialectal variety of ei; between E [e] and [ai].
æu s*æu*, r*æu*te, r*æu*st (low front to mid central round glide); has various values in the dialects, some beginning with ø or ö; cf. AmE [au] as spoken in the Southern states.
ø b*ø*, m*ø*tt, h*ø*st (mid front round); cf. Ger. ö, Fr. eu.
ö h*ö*l, sm*ö*r (low central round to front round); used in some dialects; cf. E [ʌ], Fr. eu in peur.
øy h*øy*, kl*øy*va, l*øy*ste (mid front round to high front round glide); cf. AmE b*i*rd as pronounced by some New Yorkers.

å l*å*t, s*o*v, *å*tte (mid back round, in Midl. low back round); cf.
   E [o] or [ɔ].

åi oh*oi*, h*oi*ra (mid ·back round to high front round glide); rare in
    DN, used instead of øy in some dialects; cf. E [ɔi].

3. CONSONANTS.

b *b*era, la*bb*en (v. bilabial stop); cf. E [b].

d *d*ag, ha*dd*e (v. postdental stop); cf. E [d].

f *f*å, sto*ff* (vl. labiodental spirant); cf. E [f].

g *g*od, be*gg*e (v. velar stop); cf. E [g].

h *h*a, *h*eim (vl. glottal breathing); cf. E [h].

j *j*a, g*j*era, g*i* (v. palatal semivowel); cf. E [j].

k *k*an, ta*kk*a (vl. velar stop); cf. E [k].

kj *kj*enne, *k*irke, t*j*ære (vl. palatal spirant; affricate in some Midl.
    and WN); cf. Ger ch, E [tsh].

l *l*ot, a*ll*e (v. postdental lateral; often vl. before vl. stops); cf.
   E [l].

ɭ fo*ɭ*k, da*ɭ* (v. cacuminal spirant, often with final tongue flap);
   only in EN (incl. some Midl. dial., Tr. and some Nordland
   dial.); cf. E [r].

m *m*at, ko*mm*e (v. bilabial nasal); cf. E [m].

n *n*ei, ma*nn* (v. dental nasal); cf. E [n].

ng sa*ng*, le*ng*e (v. velar nasal); usually written *n* before *k* and *g*;
    in some WN includes a velar stop; cf. E [ng].

p *p*ar, ho*pp*, s*p*å (vl. bilabial stop); cf. E [p].

r *r*o, fa*r*e, he*rr*e, ko*r*t (alveolar trill, uvular in some areas;
   may be unvoiced before vl. stops); in EN the trill is often
   lost before dentals, drawing the latter back to the alveolar
   position, a change which is usually not marked in the phonetic transcription, unless the r remains as a retroflex semivowel
   (cf. below); cf. Italian r (in some dialects French r) and E [r].

ṛ *ṛ*entsj, søp*ṛ*ei*ṛ* (v. retroflex semivowel); used for the E
   sound when occurring in N loanwords, also for cacuminal
   r before t, d, n, l in some N dialects; cf. E [r].

s *s*e, di*ss*e (vl. dorsal sibilant); cf. E [s].

sj *sj*el, *sk*jær, *sk*i, ve*rs* (vl. apical sibilant); cf. E [sh].

t *t*a, si*tt*e, s*t*å (vl. postdental stop); cf. E [t].

v *v*era. ha*v* (v. labiodental spirant); cf. E [v].

Appendix 3.

A SAMPLE QUESTIONNAIRE (1942).

BIOGRAPHICAL INFORMATION

1. Name . . . . 2. Address . . . .
3. Place of birth . . . . 4. Year of birth . . . .
5. Father's name. . . . . 6. Mother's name . . . .
7. Date, place of father's   8. Date, place of mother's
   birth . . . .   birth . . . .
9. Date of immigration to America; which members of family came to America and when . . . .
. . . .
10. Place(s) of origin in Norway . . . .
. . . .
11. Name of wife or husband, age, place of birth. . . . .
. . . .
12. When was or is Norwegian spoken. . . . .
. . . .
. . . .
13. What type of Norwegian (dialect) heard from (1) parents. . . . .
    (2) schoolmates. . . . . (3) wife or husband. . . . .
    . . . . (4) neighbors. . . . .
14. Which dialect do you speak. . . . .
15. Which dialect or dialects of Norwegian do you like best, if any. . . .
. . . .
16. Have you gone to Norwegian parochial school, or other Norwegian school
. . . .
17. Were you confirmed in Norwegian. . . . .
18. Do you read Norwegian. . . . . if so, what kind of reading. . . . . . .
. . . .
19. Do you write Norwegian. . . . . if so, to whom. . . . .
. . . .
20. Do you subscribe to Norwegian newspapers. . . . . if so, to which ones
. . . .
21. Origin of family name, if known; has your family gone by any other name than the present one . . . .
. . . .
22. Names of children, if any. . . . .
. . . .
. . . .
23. Can your children speak or read Norwegian. . . . .
. . . .

Name............ Dialect.......... Amer. Community...... Date....

(1) *Nouns*		Singular			Plural		
		Indef-inite	Def-inite	Dative	Indef-inite	Def-inite	Dative
Masc. 1.-a	kalv hund, by kniv (rygg)						
2.-i	sau sekk(benk) vegg(legg) (gris)*						
3. cons.	fot, bror (nagl) (mann)						
4.-n	hane(hare) fole(slede) stige(unge) hage(bakke) skugge						
Fem. 1.-a	øks (kvern) (kjering)*						
2.-i	skei, seng (bru) (oksl)						
3. cons.	bok, tå syster (klo) (geit)*						
4.-n long stem	visa, kyrkja (gjenta) (vogga) (kista)						
5.-n short stem	vika fluga (hosa) (gata)						
Neut. 1.-a	kne, horn (hus)* (lamb)*						
2.-n	eple auga øyra						

MORPHOLOGICAL SYSTEM   *Page 3.*
(2) ADJECTIVES, (3) PRONOUNS, (4) VERBS

Name............ Dialect............ Amer. Community.... Date....

(2) *Adjectives*	Singular		Plural	
	Indefinite	Definite	Indefinite	Definite
stor fisk				
gamal mann				
liten gut				
stor geit				
gamal kjering				
lita ku				
gult hus				
gamalt egg				
lite lamb				

(3) *Pronouns*   eg   meg   du   deg   me   oss   vår

dykk	dykk	dykkar	hann	honom	hans	ho	henne
(Nom.	(Acc.)			(Dat.)			(Dat.)

ho	dei	deira	den	denne	who	which	one
(Acc.)			det	dette	what	where	
hennar			de	disse			

(4) *Verbs*	Infinitive	Pres. Sing.	Pres. Plur.	Pret. Sing.	Pret. Plur.	P. Participle
Strong						
bita skjota						
drikka hogga						
sitja sova						
lesa mala						
slå gråta						
Weak						
drøyma høyra						
kjøpa spyrja						
sovna smaka						
liva						

page 4

B HOME AND FAMILY LIFE

1 this is my *home*
1a a *homestead;* he *homesteaded*
*3 *grandfather;* ask for *godfar, besten*
*4 terms of address for *father, mother*
13 *uncle*
14 *aunt*
*16 *bachelor*
16a he *baches it*
17 *cousin* (s.pl.)
17a *brother-in-law*
27 customs of courtship
29 customs of *wedding*
29a *squire* (justice of the peace); *squire* v.
*31 a *baby* in the *cradle* (if barn and vogga are unrecorded)
*33 a *widow* (sogn, voss, hard.set. tel.).

C THE HUMAN CONSTITUTION

2 I have a *headache*
5 a *fly* on your *nose*
*9 thick lips
*11 the *chin*
*16 *blind*
*19 *neck* (nakke)
*20 *throat* (hals)
21 the *shoulder,* -s; *on my shoulders*
22 the *elbow*
24 *left hand*
26 the *thumb*

page 5

C 27 *fingers*
27a verse on fingers
*28 the *fist*
33a I shall *tickle* him
*38 he is *awake,* she is *awake*
39a she didn't *feel* well
42 he *caught* a *cold*

43 a *boil*
*44 what were the most common diseases; any epidemics?
44a the *ague*
50 healers, wise women (disc.)
54 *died*
55 *dug* a grave
56 funeral customs
58 *graveyard*
61 *remember*
67a it's a big *risk*
68 he didn't *care* (for money)
69a it doesn't *sound* good
72a he should *mind* his own business (never mind; the children won't mind)
74 good *sense,* little *sense* (vit) (stort hode, lite vett)

D HOUSEHOLD LIFE

*4 *sunday*
tuesday
saturday
(older people: mækedag)

page 6

D 7 in the *evening*
9 in *summer*
in *fall*
10 in *winter*
11 *next* month is *July*
*20 *what time is it* (clock)
*21 *quarter* of nine
22 name the meals; *breakfast, dinner, supper; lunches* between the meals
26 *milk*
29 specifically Norw. foods: grøt, lefse, flatbrød, lutefisk, mølse, klubb, goro, fattigmann etc.
*30 ask for recipe, method of preparation of one
31 when these foods are used
32 cheeses—kinds?

33 difference between *øl* and *beer?*

33a *that beer* (is good)

34 prevalence of drinking now and formerly

35a *molasses*

36 flour

36a *midling*

36b *bran*

36c *corn meal*

38 *yeast;* was it ever homemade

38a *brødreis* (salt-, humle-)

40 *cooky, cookies*

40a *crackers*

44 *churn butter* (customs)

page 7

D 46 *sour cream;* rjome vs. fløyte

*47 *sugar* (only people from midl. and gbr.)

*48 *sausage*

49 *hungry*

*50 *thirsty*

51 *let's sit down*

*54 we've *sat* at the *table* a whole *hour*

55 *help* yourself to the *gravy*

*59 *swallow* v

64 *forks* (at table)

66 *plate* (def. and pl.)

67 *jug* (def. and pl.)

67a *basin* (beise) (s. pl.)

67b *dipper*

68 *basket* (g. and pl.)

69 *brush* n

70 *breadbox*

72 *stove*

72a *baking oven* (omn, brødrum)

73 *washtub*

73a *barrel*

79 stove *handle* kettle *handle*

81 *broom*

81a *clean house* (pt.)

*84 ever heard [sasa] for *skål*?

85 *frying pan*

86 *slop pail*

89 *faucet*

*91 *separator*

93 she's *knitting socks*

*95 *thimble*

page 8

D *100 use of loom or spinning wheel

101 a *cap*

*105 *ball of yarn*

106 *necktie*

107 *iron* n

*111 a *hole* in the *stocking*

*112 *slippers*

112a *moccasin* (s. and pl.)

*115 (man's) *suit*

119 (man's) *overcoat*

123 *overalls*

*125 *brown*

*128 *yellow*

129 *white*

132 *this* is not *the same color* as *that*

*133 *corset*

*136 *apron*

*138 *suspenders*

E BUILDINGS AND GROUNDS

1 name the various rooms in the house
living r., parlor, dining room, kitchen, *pantry, buttery*, bedroom

*2 the *floor*

4 the *ceiling*

*7 close *the door*

9 the *key*

12 *curtains; shades*

*18 *book case*

19 *carpet, rug*

20 *pictures* (on walls)

E *23 the *mirror*
  28 *bedspread* (g.)
  29 blanket (*g.pl.*)
 *30 *pillow case*
 30a *quilt* (kvitel)
 30b *sheet*
  32 *towel*
  33 *alarm clock*
  34 *dresser, commode*
  35 *clothes closet*
  38 *upstairs*
  39 *attic*
  40 *cellar*
 40a church *basement*
  46 *light* a *fire*
 *48 *light*, not dark
 *49 *dark* a.
 *50 kind of light used
 51a *lantern* (s. pl.)
 *53 *battery*
 *54 how did you first get water,
    how now (*brunn, spring*)
  55 cow *yard*, house *yard*
  56 *garden*, distinction from hage
  58 the *front porch*
  59 *screen* (s. pl.)
  61 *brick*
 *61a *frame house* (dial. using ai
    for ei)
 *62 *lumber*
 *66 *hammer*
  69 *tongs, pliers*
  71 *monkey wrench*
  72 *tools*, implements

E 73 *barn* (s. pl.) — list its com-
    partments; *history of devel-
    opment
 73a *hay bent* (s.pl.)
 73b *stanchion* (s.pl.)
  76 list other buildings on farm
    stable
    corn crib

granary
toilet
shed (tob. mach.)
*83 *gate*
 85 *fence post*
85a *rail* (s. pl. def.)
85b *ties* (s. pl.) r.r.

F FARMING

 1a *share, share-bruker*
  4 the *cornfield* (s.pl.)
 4a field names
  5 *wheat crop;* a good *crop*
 5a the *chinch bug*
  6 name principal crops; *pro-
    cess of cultivation
 7a (small) *grain*
 7b *seed* (s. and coll.)
 *12 *clover*
 *13 *alfalfa*
  15 *potatoes*
  18 *shovel* n
 *19 *hoe* (ask of all from Sogn Voss
    Hard.)
  20 *harrow*, drag
  22 *fork* (hay, manure, potato)
 *23 *scythe*
  25 *cultivator, corn plow*
 *26 *våronn*
  27 *harvest* v
  28 (grain) *ready to cut*

F 29 *cradle* n (implement)
  31 *reaper*
 30* *reap*
  33 a big thrashing *crew*
 33a *fanning mill*
 34a *husk* v
 34b *corn shredder*
  39 50 *bushel* per *acre*
  41 *beans*
  42 *peas*
  45 *lawnmower, mower*
 *47 *pine*

52 *hickory nuts*
52a *black walnuts*
53 a *pumpkin*
53a *watermelon*
*54 *forest* (ask only East Norw., incl. Gbr.)
56 *brush* (underbrush)
56a *pile* v (pt.)
56b *cordwood*
56c the *grove*
58a *grapes*
59 *rhubarb* (s. pl.)
62 (gasoline) *engine*
*63 (cheese) *factory*
*64 *wheelbarrow*
69 *bull, ox* (difference)
69a left and right ox (or horse): *near one, off one*
69b *yoke* (s. def.)
69c *ranch* (g.)
70a the *chores*
70b *chore(s)* v.
72 *manure*
80 *crows* pr.
80a a *turkey*

page 12

F 85 she *got bit* by a *dog*
*86 *barks* v
88 do cows have names; give all you can recall
*92 call the cat
*94 call the hens
*96 *feed* (ask only diphthongizing dial.)
101 *mosquitoes*
102 *squirrel*
103 *gopher*
104 *rattlesnake*
107 *rabbit* (s. pl.); dist. from hare
112 *trap* n
113 *fishpole*
114 *bait* n
117 is any fishing done; what kind of fish

G WEATHER AND TOPOGRAPHY
1 *river*
3 *lake*
4 *slough*
4a the *creek*
7 *snow*
*10 *it lightnings*
*15 *a flood*
16 an *island*
*24 *stars* in the *sky*
*26 the *rainbow*
*28 *it's cold*
*28a it's *warm*
31a *bluff* (g.pl.)
31b *map* (g.)
31c names of hills, valleys etc. in community
35 *dust*
41 *in the country* (contrast to city)

page 13

H TRAVEL AND COMMUNICATIONS
2 the *railroad*
3 a *train*
3a *freight* (train)
5 the *depot*
*6 my *trunk* (for speakers with -kj-)
10 he *brought* the *mail*
*13 *drive* (kjøre, aka)
15 *walk* (contrast to drive: gå, travle)
16 *gravel road*
17 *road* vs. *vei* (any difference)
23 *where are you going?*
24 over to the *corner*
*25 a big *sign* (for dialects with ei)
26 *buggy* (s. pl.)
26a a *cutter* (s. pl.)
27 a *whip*, the *whip*
27a *team* of horses (s. pl.)
28 the *tongue* (on a wagon)
28a *fills* (s. pl. def.)
28b *spokes* (s. pl.)

29 *reins*
30 *bridle*
30a *bit* (on bridle)
31* *harness*
32 *clevis* (s. pl.)
33 *whiffle tree*
34 *car*, automobile
38 the *brake*
*39 *oil* n
40 the *truck*
*50 between

page 14

H 58 names of nearby towns and villages as pronounced by Norwegians
59 a *block* (s.pl.)
60 the *sidewalk*
61a the *street* (s. pl.)

I BUSINESS, TRADE, GOVERNMENT

3 he *made* ten *dollars*
4b a (financial) *note* (s. pl.)
5a a *mortgage*
5b *insurance*
5c *cash*
8 can you *change;* he has *changed* his address
12 she *kept house*
18 I'll *bet* you a *nickel*
23 a *quarter* (25 cents; ever heard 'two shillings')
24a a *gallon*
26 a *barbershop*
27 *tavern* (tavan), *saloon*
29 a *storekeeper*
31 a *clerk*
31a *office, post office*
*34 *both* of us
37 *seven*
38 *eleven*
twelve
**twenty*
39 *forty*

eighty
40 **third*
fourth
41 a *half pound*
43 the *assessor*
44 a *county*
45 the *surveyor*

page 15

I 46 the *town*
*47 a *horse thief*
*49 a *fine*
50 the *judge*
51 a *lawyer*
52 a *lawsuit*
53 in *court*
53a *license* (g)
55 name of community group
55a which various dialect types are found in community
55b has there been any antagonism, rivalry, mimicry between these groups

J SOCIAL AFFAIRS AND INSTITUTIONS

1a how long and where gone to school
1c *school ma'm, school teacher*
*1d *teach school*
1e *common school*
4a did you know of any Norw. in community who could not read or write?
5a what games did you play at school
5b *played games*
*6 *arithmetic*
10 *ink well*
11 *pencil*
12 *blackboard*
12a *crayon* (kreant)
17* which Norw. newspapers have you or your family subscribed to in former days

page 16

J 19 have you read any Norw.
books
19a feeling about recent spellings of Norw., or Landsmål
*20 know any Norw. songs
23 when was parochial school
held in Norw.
23a does any one in community
talk 'book language'; what is
general attitude to it
*24 did children prefer to talk
Norw. or Eng. when you went
to school
25 name of pastor and congregation
27 are there any Norw. services
in your church
27a comment on change from
Norw. to English
27b does any one give children
Norw. names; what changes
have been made in names by
persons baptized with Norw.
names
33 name for sunday service
(messe, preik, miden)
*40 swear words
41 ghosts; stories
42 trolls; stories
43 witchcraft
43a Norw. proverbs
43b Norw. riddles
44 gå julebukk
45 christmas customs (food,
gifts, tree, time)

page 17

J 51 a *surprise party*
51a *parties* (kind, frequency)
52 *shivaree, horning*
54 go to the *fair*
54a the *circus*
55 have you ever danced

56a instruments used at dances;
fiddle
*58 objections to violin playing
60a can you play an instrument
62 *accordion* (if not written under 56a)
62a dances danced
schottische
square dance
*67 cardplaying (how much;
games played)
67a a *deck* of cards
68 *jack* of *clubs*
*69 *queen* of *diamonds*
*70 *king* of *hearts*
71 *ace* of *spades*
73 *poker* (game)
poker (instrument)
74 *deuce*
75 *baseball*
*78 *skates*
*79 *skis*

K HUMAN RELATIONSHIPS

3a characters in community;
odd or droll people
3b nicknames
4a an Indian (s. pl. def.)
4b an Irishman (")
4c a Yankee (")

page 18

K 14 the *hired man*
15 a tramp
15a a peddler
30 hello, *how are you*
33 *goodbye*
45 *talk:* snakke vs. tala
55 very, extremely, awfully (oie,
modig, faderlig)
61 I'm *busy*
62 *fight*
65 now we're *through*

FOOTNOTES TO VOLUME II.

Chapter 12.

METHODS OF INVESTIGATION.

[1] Zeitschrift für neufranzösische Sprache und Litteratur 10.199 (1888).

[2] For a fuller discussion see the writer's Problems of Linguistic Research among Scandinavian Immigrants in America, in ACLS Bulletin No. 34, 35-57 (1942); Om en samlet fremstilling av norsk-amerikansk sprogutvikling in Avhandlinger utgitt av det Norske Videnskaps-Akademi i Oslo. II. Hist.-Filos. Klasse 1938. No. 3. (Oslo 1939).

[3] See the full account and bibliography in Adolf Bach, Deutsche Mundartforschung, ihre Wege, Ergebnisse und Aufgaben (Heidelberg, 1934); also in Jos. Schrijnen, Essai de bibliographie de géographie linguistique générale (Nimegue 1933).

[4] 32 fascicules, Paris 1902-10. Supplement, vol. 1, Paris 1914. The most voluminous linguistic atlas hitherto appearing in Europe is the atlas of Italian dialects by the Swiss scholars Karl Jaberg and Jakob Jud, Sprach- und Sachatlas Italiens und der Südschweiz, Vols. 1-4 (Zofingen, 1928-32). In Scandinavia the only attempt to map the dialects of a whole country has been the Danish dialect atlas of V. Bennike and M. Kristensen: Kort over de danske folkemål (Copenhagen, 1898-1914); cf. also Johs. Brøndum-Nielsen, Dialekter og dialektforskning (Copenhagen, 1927).

[5] It was entitled Cirkulære (Spørgeliste); cf. Halvorsen, Norsk Forfatterlexikon (Kristiania, 1901) 5.486ff.

[6] Norsk Ordliste til Lydlæren. Kra. 1882.

[7] Kortere Ordliste med Forklaring af Lydskriften (Kra., 1884).

[8] Norsk Lydskrift med Omrids af Fonetiken. In Norvegia 1.19-132 (Oslo, 1884-1902).

[9] See the account of its history in Kurath HLG x.

[10] Ann Arbor, Mich., 1949.

[11] Cf. Kurath HLG 147ff. where the entire questionnaire is printed.

[12] Cf. Bloch in Kurath HLG 122ff, where the alphabet is described in detail.

[13] George T. Flom, English Loanwords in American Norwegian, as spoken in the Koshkonong Settlement, Wisconsin, AmSp 1.541-58 (1926) was the most important of these. Cf. also Prof. Nils Flaten's list from the Valdres dialect in Minnesota in Dialect Notes 2.115-26 (1900).

[14] A recent one is by Anders Bjerrum, Über die phonematische Wertung von Mundartaufzeichnungen in Bulletin du cercle linguistique de Copenhague 5.29-51 (1940) and Fjoldemålets Lydsystem in APhSc 18.5 (1945-8).

[15] Furnished by the Research Committee of the University of Wisconsin.

Chapter 13.

DIALECTS IN DISPERSION.

[1] Ord och Bild 1932, 259.

[2] 14D2.

[3] For further information about dialect study see Leonard Bloomfield, Language, 321-45 (NY, 1933), bibliog. 519-20; Johannes Brøndum-Nielsen, Dialekter og Dialektforskning (Copenhagen, 1927); Adolf Bach, Deutsche Mundartforschung (Heidelberg, 1934); A. Dauzat, La géographie linguistique (Paris, 1922).

[4] For details on the Norwegian dialects see Hallfrid Christiansen, Norske Dialekter (Oslo, 1946ff.); Amund B. Larsen, Oversigt over de norske bygdemål (Kristiania, 1907); Hans Ross, Norske Bygdemaal (Christiania, 1905-09). Extensive bibliographies were compiled by the present writer in his articles Analysis of a Sound Group: sl and tl in Norwegian in PMLA 57.879-907 (1942) and Norwegian Dialect Studies since 1930 in JEGP 47.68-79 (1948).

[5] Cf. figures in Blegen NM 1.138-9; for the later decades 1.357-61.

[6] Cf. Blegen in NASR 1.110-25; Qualey NS 29.

[7] Cf. Ole Rynning, Sandfærdig Beretning om Amerika 12 (Chra., 1838).

[8] Cf. reprint of list in Flom NI 314-30.

[9] Figures calculated from list of 327 early settlers in Holand CP 127ff.

[10] Social Adjustment among Wisconsin Norwegians, AmSocRev 14.780-7.

[11] Holand NSH; Ulvestad NIA.

[12] Holand NSH 435.

[13] 15P3.

[14] 5L1.

[15] 8L3.

[16] 15P5; 15P1.

[17] 22F1.

[18] 20F1.

[19] 8B1; 5Q1.

[20] 4K1.

[21] 11C1.

[22] 5Q1.

[23] 20P2.

[24] Denied e.g. by 3C4 8L4 20F6; but recorded by 2C1, 4L1, 5L1, 10C, 10C2, 4F1, 9Q1 and many others.

[25] Kakka pao baoten 6P1.

[26] 15P3.

[27] 14D13.

[28] 20F10.

[29] 4L1.

[30] Holand asserts that they are the most numerous of all dialect speakers in America; see NSH 125.

[31] Printed in Yust for Fun, Norwegian-American Dialect Monologues by Eleonora and Ethel Olson (Minneapolis, 1925); recorded by Victor, record 72183-A.

[32] 20F17; 5L2; 11C4; cf. also 9Q1.

[33] 12Q5.

[34] 4L4.

[35] Nils M. Holmer, Studies on Argyllshire Gaelic 13 (Uppsala, 1938).

[36] 5L4 brother from Telemark to Voss; 6Q3 father from Gudbrandsdal to Sogn; 10C1 father from Gudbrandsdal to Hedmark; 10C5 father from Nordland to Gudbrandsdal; 4H1 wife reports talking more like Numedal after living with husband's family.

[37] Like their mothers: 20F15 father died young; 20F16 Numedal vs. Trønder; 4L4 Morgedal vs. Vinje; 4P1 Vossevangen vs. Evanger; 11C2 Biri vs. Halling; like their fathers: 8L8 DN vs. Gudbrandsdal; 8C1 Gausdal vs. Larvik; 5G1 Sannidal vs. Treungen; 14F2 Solør vs. Swedish; 26P3 Voss vs. Telemark; 8F1 Kragerø vs. Gausdal.

[38] 14F2.

[39] 20Q2.

[40] 11B6.

[41] 4P4.

[42] 20F13.

[43] 5H4; 4L1; similar reports from 17Q3, 8L4.

[44] 10C7; cf. 10C2.

[45] 5H42.

[46] Written communication from 20P2, also on record D-23; cf. similar account from Spring Grove by 20F1.

[47] 4G1; cf. also 5N1 and 8M1 'når du snakkar mæ andre, så ska du dreie på dæ'.

[48] 20F14.

[49] 22F1.

[50] 10C7.

[51] 5L1; 5L2.

[52] 6Q4.

[53] Cf. 8L3 4L4; 4P1 6P1; 10C3.

[54] 5H3; 6Q1.
[55] 14D4; also 14D24.
[56] 26P2.
[57] 14D2.
[58] 4K1.
[59] 8L3.
[60] 12Q2.
[61] 5L1.
[62] 10C10.
[63] 14D21.
[64] 8G2.
[65] 5Q1.
[66] Cf. 11C4; 18B3; 25P3; 12Q7 etc.
[67] 13N1.
[68] 6Q3.
[69] 19A1; cf. also 17Q; 13N5.
[70] 8C2.
[71] 19A2.
[72] 10C4; 4H1.
[73] The word was used by several, e.g. 10C5, 22F1, 11C3, 11C1.
[74] Cf. 11C3.
[75] Progressive Norway 22-3 (Washington, D. C., 1939).
[76] Speaker from Iola: 8F1.
[77] Cf. the remark by 10C4 about a woman from Norway who had declared that they talked 'modi stykt', 'men vi synes dæ æ ålrait'.
[78] 15P3.
[79] 6Q3.
[80] 12F1; the same inf. noted a split between Mt. Sterling (Sogning) and Utica (Nordfjord) in 1906, along approximately dialectal lines.
[81] 12Q2.
[82] 14L2.
[83] 25L1.
[84] 11C2.
[85] Nordfjordlagets Aarbok 1920, 20-26.

Chapter 14.

BILINGUALISM AND BORROWING.

[1] The Grammarian and his Language, American Mercury 1.149-55 (1924), here cit. from Selected Writings 152 (Berkeley and Los Angeles, 1949).
[2] Cf. the present writer's articles, Problems of Bilingualism, Lingua 2.271

-90 (1950); The Analysis of Linguistic Borrowing, Language 26.210-31 (1950).

[3] Kurt M. Stein, Gemixte Pickles (N.Y., 1927).

[4] Prinzipien der Sprachgeschichte², Chap. 22 (Halle a. S., 1886).

[5] Cf. Paul, Prinzipien 338; Meillet, La méthode comparative 82 (Oslo, 1925); Meillet, Linguistique historique et linguistique générale 76 (Paris, 1921).

[6] Kurath in ACLS Bulletin No. 34 (March, 1942).

[7] For a complete bibliography to the date of its appearance see Otto Springer, The Study of Pennsylvania German in JEGP 42.1-39 (1943).

[8] There are 517 words in Lambert's dictionary; see A. F. Buffington in Studies in Honor of J. A. Walz, 66 (1941).

[9] Buffington, loc. cit., 80.

[10] M. D. Learned, The Pennsylvania German Dialect (Baltimore, 1889), 111ff.

[11] AmSp 17.94-101 (1942).

[12] AmSp 17.25-9 (1942) and 23.239-44 (1949); cf. also Carroll E. Reed (w. introd. by Lester W. Seifert), The Pennsylvania German Dialect Spoken in the Counties of Lehigh and Berks: Phonology and Morphology (Seattle, Washington, 1949).

[13] AmSp 23.121-34 (1948) and Symposium 3.114-29 (1949).

[14] In monograph cited in footnote 12, p. 11.

[15] Hans Kurath in Monatshefte für Deutschen Unterricht 37.96-102 (1945); Struble in AmSp 10.163-72 (1935); Tucker in Language 10.1-6 (1934).

[16] Leo Pap, Portuguese-American Speech. An Outline of Speech Conditions among Portuguese Immigrants in New England and elsewhere in the United States (New York, 1949).

[17] Pap, 7.

[18] Pap, 13.

[19] Pap, 27.

[20] Pap, 84.

[21] Pap, 122.

[22] Edward H. Spicer in American Anthropologist 45.410-26 (1943).

[23] Language, Culture, and Personality (Menasha, Wis., 1941), 66-74.

[24] Aasta Stene, English Loanwords in Modern Norwegian. A Study of Linguistic Borrowing in the Process (London-Oslo, 1945).

[25] Stene, 204.

[26] Stene, 33.

[27] See the writer's comment on these in his review in Language 25.63-8 (1949).

[28] Prinzipien, ch. 22.

[29] Cf. the recent studies by Bertil Malmberg, which have corrected earlier misconceptions, Studia Linguistica, 2.1-36 (1948).

[30] Slawo-Deutsches und Slawo-Italienisches 81 (Graz, 1884).

[31] Zum Fragenkreis ums Fremdwort, JEGP 38.42-63 (1939).

[32] Lis Jacobsen has pointed out for Danish that many of the LG words borrowed in the Middle Ages, such as svoger, frue, blive were quite unnecessary'; she concluded that they were borrowed simply because they were available due to historical circumstances. Cf. Dansk Sprog (Copenhagen 1927), reprinting essays Kvinde og Mand (1912) and Bevægelser inden Ordforraadet (1915).

[33] Emigranten, Feb. 1, 1859.

[34] 5H4.

[35] 11C2.

[36] 14D2.

[37] 6P2

[38] 6Q3.

[39] 15P3.

[40] 11C2.

[41] 20F10.

[42] Cf. Lis Jacobsen, Dansk Sprog 310: Hjemmeordene degraderes, fordi Fremmedordene...bruges i Tale og Skrift af 'de sagkyndige.'

[43] 'Meaning,' in Monatshefte für deutschen Unterricht 35.101-106 (1943).

[44] Pap P-AS 96.

[45] Language 208 (New York, 1921).

Chapter 15.

THE PROCESS OF BORROWING.

[1] TCLP 4.80 (1931).

[2] Cf. Ivar Alnæs, Bidrag til en ordsamling over sjømandssproget (Christiania, 1902); R. Iversen, Lånord og lønnord hos folk og fant (Trondheim, 1939); A. Larsen og G. Stoltz, Bergens bymål (Christiania, 1912). Unfortunately no full-scale study of E loans in the dialects has been made.

[3] Evidence on this point was gathered for the writer from the N dialect archives in Oslo by Magne Oftedal and in Bergen by Olai Skulerud.

[4] Skulerud, Telemaalet 73 (Christiania, 1918) and Tinnsmaalet (Halle a. S., 1922); cf. similar reports from Sweden and Swedish Finland in Folkmålsstudier 2.137-40 (1934) and Svenskbygden 1932.3-5.

[5] Wright, English Dialect Dictionary.

[6] Aasen NO² from Sogn 'og fler'.

[7] Language 26.210-31 (1950).

[8] Cf. Alva L. Davis and Raven I. McDavid, Jr. 'Shivaree': An Example of Cultural Diffusion, AmSp 24.249-55 (1949).

9   Cf. Paul Schach, Hybrid compounds in Pennsylvania German, AmSp 23.121-34 (1948).

10 Kr. Sandfeld-Jensen, Die Sprachwissenschaft 69 (Leipzig and Berlin, 1915).

11 The classification attempted here is somewhat different from that in the writer's article in Language; cf. his article on The Impact of English on American-Norwegian Letter Writing, in the Sturtevant volume of the University of Kansas Studies.

12 G. Trager, IJAL 10.146 (1944); Pap, P-AS. 94.

13 TCLP 4.79-96 (1931).

14 Paul, Prinzipien 340-1; Geo. Hempl, Trans. Am. Phil. Assn. 29.37; Bloomfield, Language 446.

15 IJAL 10.145 (1944).

16 V. Mathesius, Eng. Studien 70.23 (1935-6).

17 Harry Hoijer, Language 15.110-5 (1939).

18 Spicer, Am. Anthr. 45.410-26 (1943).

19 English Loan-Words in Modern Norwegian 164 (London—Oslo, 1945); hereafter cited as ELN.

20 Stene ELN 163 (her opinion that borrowed verbs are for this reason fewer than nouns seems insufficiently founded); Pap P-AS 106.

21 Pap, P-AS 96.

22 Paul Schach, Symposium 3.120 (1949).

23 W. Betz, Deutsch und Lateinisch, Die Lehnbildungen der althoch-deutschen Benediktinerregel (Bonn 1949).

24 Pap 87.

25 Pap 87; reference should here be made to a valuable article by Paul Schach, Semantic Borrowing in Pennsylvania German, AmSp 26.257—67 (1951).

26 Sandfeld-Jensen 69.

27 Pap 89.

28 Deutsch und Lateinisch 25.

29 Bloomfield, Language 455.

30 Language, culture, and personality 66-74 (Menasha, Wis., 1941).

31 Spicer, Am. Anthr. 45.410-26.

32 Paul Schach, Symposium 3.115 (1949).

33 A. Menarini, Al Margini della Lingua 145-208 (Firenze, 1947).

34 Schach, Symposium 3.115 (1949).

35 W. D. Whitney, On Mixture in Language, TAPA 12.5-26 (1881).

36 TCLP 8.85 (1939).

37 Otakar Vočadlo, Some Observations on Mixed Languages, Actes du quatrième congrès international de linguistes 169-76 (Copenhagen, 1938).

38 Op. cit. 176.

39 Cf. Stene ELN 5.

40 J. I. Kolehmainen, Am. Soc. Rev. 2.62-6 (1937).

41 Private communication from Professor Knut Bergsland of Oslo, 13. Sept. 1950.

42 Cf. Stene ELN 5; the writer's review, Language 25.63-8 (1949).

Chapter 16.

THE PHONOLOGY OF LOANWORDS.

1 Prinzipien der Sprachgeschichte² 340-1.

2 Cf. E. Haugen, Phoneme or Prosodeme?, Language 25.278-82 (1949).

3 On N stress see Johan Storm, Norsk Lydskrift 37-40 (Oslo, 1884); Broch and Selmer, Håndbok i elementær fonetikk 112-8 (Oslo, 1930); Ivar Alnæs, Norsk Uttale-Ordbok 22-26 (2 ed., Oslo, 1925); C. Hj. Borgstrøm, Zur Phonologie der norwegischen Schriftsprache, NTS 9.250-73 (1938); C. Hj. Borgstrøm, De prosodiske elementer i norsk, Festskrift Broch 41-8 (Oslo, 1947).

4 On English stress see John S. Kenyon, American Pronunciation 76ff. (6th Ed., Ann Arbor, 1935); Bloch and Trager, Outline of Linguistic Analysis, 35 (Baltimore, Md., 1942).

5 Cf. Kenyon, 78, 87.

6 For a bibliography of Scandinavian tones see N. C. Stalling, Das Phonologische System des Schwedischen I (Nymegen, 1935); precise information for N is to be found in Johan Storm, Norsk Lydskrift 42-56 (Oslo, 1884); Ivar Alnæs, Norsk Uttale-Ordbok 27-34; Ivar Alnæs, Norsk Sætningsmelodi 33-48; Ernst Selmer's several kymographic studies of the tones in Oslo, Bergen, Stavanger, and Sunnmøre; C. Hj. Borgstrøm in Festskrift Olaf Broch 41-8 (Oslo, 1947); Olaf Broch, in TCLP 8.116-29 (1939) and Mélanges Holger Pedersen 308-22 (1937); A. Western, MM 1937, 174-82. See now also E. Haugen and M. Joos, Tone and Intonation in East Norwegian, APhSc 1953.

7 On English pitch see Rulon S. Wells, The Pitch Phonemes of English, Lang.21. 27-39 (1945); Kenneth Pike, The Intonation of American English (Ann Arbor, Mich., 1947).

8 Cf. a more detailed treatment of the problem in one AmN dialect, Einar Haugen, Intonation Patterns in AmN, Language 17.40-8 (1941).

9 Stene ELN 120ff.

10 Morgenbladet (Oslo), April 11, 18, 1897.

11 On N sentence tone see Ivar Alnæs, Norsk Sætningsmelodi (Kra., 1916); Ernst W. Selmer, Satzphonetische Untersuchungen (Kra., 1917).

12 Cf. Ernst W. Selmer, Satzphonetische Untersuchungen 32ff (Kra., 1917), where slow and rapid speech are compared and the length of each sound has been measured.

13 On N quantity see Johan Storm, Norsk Lydskrift 56-67; Ivar Alnæs, Norsk Uttale-Ordbok 15ff.; Broch and Selmer, Håndbok 125ff.

[14] Lehmann's pronunciation, reported by Heffner and Lehmann, cf. Language 18.231 (1942).

[15] Cf. the analysis of American vowels by Bloch and Trager in An Outline of Linguistic Analysis 47, also Lang. 17.223-46 (1941); the only previous treatment of AmN quantity substitution is in M. Oftedal, A Norwegian Dialect in Wisconsin, Lang. 25.261-7, cf. p. 266.

[16] Cf. Einar Haugen, On the Stressed Vowel Systems of Norwegian, Scand. Studies Presented to Geo. T. Flom 66-78 (Urbana, Illinois, 1942).

[17] On the N vowels see also the handbooks listed above.

[18] Ann Arbor, Mich., 1935.

[19] Cf. E. Haugen, Phonological Shifting in American Norwegian, Language 14.112-20 (1938).

[20] On e and æ in N dialects see O. Skulerud, Tinnsmålet 681ff.

[21] Cf. E. Haugen, Notes on Voiced t in American English, Dialect Notes 6.627-34 (1938).

[22] Cf. E. Haugen, Lang. 14.112-20 (1938).

Chapter 17.

THE GRAMMAR OF LOANWORDS.

[1] Language 453.

[2] Cf. George T. Flom (Norwegian), JEGP 5.1-31 (1903); Albert W. Aron (German), Language Monographs 7.11-28 (1930); Carroll E. Reed (Pennsylvania German), AmSp 23.239-44 (1949); Ernest F. Haden and Eugene A. Joliat (Canadian French), PMLA 55.839-54 (1930); Leo Pap (Portuguese), P-AS 102-4 (1949); A. Senn (Lithuanian), Studi Baltici 2.48-55 (1933). Cf. also Daniel K. Dodge for Danish (in Denmark) in Americana-Germanica 2.27-32 (1898), C. B. Wilson (German), Americana-Germanica 3.265-83 (1899-1900); Aasta Stene (Norwegian), ELN 155-7; N. Bergsten (Swedish), Språk och Stil 15.86 (1915).

[3] Counted in E. Haugen, NWS vol. 2 (Madison, 1940).

[4] Aasen NG² 130.

[5] PMLA 55.844-5.

[6] JEGP 5.25.

[7] Cf. Aasen NG² 129.

[8] Aasen NG² 126.

[9] Stene ELN 161-2.

[10] Note that rälls was an early English loan in Sweden, but apparently not in Norway; N. Bergsten SoS 15.68 (1915) and Langfeldt SoS 15.90 (1915).

[11] Scand. Studies to Flom 89 (1942).

Chapter 18.

NATIVE FORMS FOR FOREIGN: LOANBLENDS AND LOANSHIFTS.

[1] Slang in America, in Complete Prose Works 407 (NY, 1914).
[2] Mencken AL[4] 665.
[3] Stene ELN 170.
[4] Cf. Stene ELN 170; Christiansen Gimsøymålet Par. 210; Ansteinsson, Sekundær t etter er-suffiks, KNVS Forh. 13.24-6 (1940).
[5] Cf. Leo Pap in P-AS 90.
[6] P-AS 88-9.
[7] Oral communic. from Herbert Paper and Yakira Frank.
[8] Privately communicated by Åse Gruda Skard.
[9] Cf. the discussion by B. H. Hibbard in The History of Agriculture in Dane County, Wisconsin 172 (Madison, Wis., 1905).
[10] Bjarne Guttormsen, Norge i Oslo 8 (Oslo, 1949).
[11] Cf. above, chapter 8, section 8.
[12] Clipping in Olson Scrapbooks in Wis. Hist. Society, signed Fridtjof (prob. R. B. Anderson himself).

Appendix 1.

COMMUNITIES AND INFORMANTS.

[1] Blegen NM 1.114, 119ff; Qualey NS 44; Flom NI 130; Holand NSH 123-4; Anderson FC 237; Norlie NLM 124.
[2] Blegen NM 1.124; Qualey NS 46; Flom NI 138 etc.; Holand NSH 128; Anderson FC 258; Norlie NLM 123; Billedmagazin 1.154, 182; Luther Valley 90th Anniversary Program; Luther Valley, Lutheran Church of Rock County, Wisconsin, Church Book 1931, compiled and written by L. O. Anderson (1934); Dr. J. S. Johnson, Rock Prairie, Samband 2.6ff (1911-12), 3.4ff. (1912-13).
[3] Norlie NLM 1.117; Rene HUV 177, 815; Holand NSH 176; Flom NI 302; Qualey NS 59; Wiota Lutheran Church 1844-1937; Landingsbogen 270-282 (Decorah, Iowa, 1924).
[4] Figures calculated from the printed church register in Flom NI 314-30. Anderson FC 326, Qualey NS 52, Holand NSH 145, Flom NI 259, 271, 305, Blegen NM 1.142, Rene HUV 240.
[5] Blegen NM 1.141; Qualey NS 58; Holand NSH 185; Rene HUV 468; Flom NI 340; A. L. Lien, Bluemounds settlementet, Samband 3.255ff (1912-3), 4.20ff (1913-4); A. O. Barton, The Story of Primrose 1821-95

(Madison, Wis., 1895); Bjorn Holland, History of the Town of Moscow (Hollandale, Wis., 1919).

[6] Flom HNI 331; Holand NSH 158; Rene HUV 304 (with map); Qualey NS 57 (erroneously dates settlement to 1842-3); Norlie NLM 1.130.

[7] Holand NSH 215; Qualey NS 64; A. A. Veblen, Valdressettlementet i Manitowoc County i Wisconsin, Samband 1928, 65-73; Helge Høverstad, En tur til Valders, Wisconsin, Samband 1934, 93-6; D. G. Ristad, In Remembrance of the 75th Anniversary, Manitowoc—Gjerpen—Valdres Congregation. Sep. 6, 1925 (Decorah, Iowa, 1925).

[8] Thor Helgeson, Fra Indianernes Lande is the chief source of personal information about this region; Holand NSH 201; Qualey NS 67; Olaus Duus, Frontier Parsonage, ed. T. Blegen (Northfield, Minn., 1947); Alfred O. Erickson, Scandinavia, Wisconsin, NASR 15.185-209 (1949); Malcolm Rosholt, Town 25 North (Rosholt, Wisconsin, 1948).

[9] Helgeson FIL 1.13ff; Holand 208-14.

[10] Holand CP is the chief source of detailed data about the settlement; also Holand NSH 268; Qualey NS 70; Norlie NLM 1.152; Blegen 1.141; a recent sociological study is Peter A. Munch, Social Adjustment among Wisconsin Norwegians, Am.Soc.Rev. 14.780-7 (1949).

[11] Holand CV is the chief source book on the settlement; also Holand NSH 269; Qualey NS 70; Norlie NLM 157.

[12] Holand NSH 271; Norlie NLM 152, 163; J. D. Korstad and Dr. Kolset, Settlementet i Crawford Co., Wis., Nordfjordlagets Aarbok 1918, 28-31; Jacob Aaland, Nordfjordsettlementet i Crawford County ved Ferryville, Wis., Nordfjordlagets Aarbok 1927, 34-40; Jacob Aaland, En gjesteferd til nordfjordingene i Ferryville-settlementet, Ibid., 41-50; see also the article cited above by Peter A. Munch.

[13] Norlie NLM 1.166; Holand NSH 261.

[14] Holand NSH 292; Norlie NLM 1.231.

[15] Norlie NLM 1.219; Holand NSH 294.

[16] Norlie NMH 1.229; Holand NSH 297.

[17] Holand NSH 298; Norlie NMH 1.251.

[18] Norlie NLM 1.275; Qualey NS 74.

[19] Norlie NLM 1.334; Waterloo Ridge Kirke og Waterloo Ridge Kvindeforenings Historie (1927); Waterloo Ridge Norwegian Lutheran Church, Allamakee County, Iowa (1942).

[20] Johnson NSG is the chief source of detailed information about this settlement; also Holand NSH 359; Norlie NLM 1.454; Qualey NS 115, also his article in NASR 9.54-66 (1936).

[21] Qualey NS 118; Holand NSH 483-97; O. I. Flaten, Valdris Settlementet i Goodhue County Minn., Valdris Helsing 1904-5, 85-90, 111-19.

[22] Einar Haugen, Norwegians at the Indian Forts on the Missouri River during the Seventies, NASR 6.89-118 (1931); for detailed biographies of many settlers of this region see Opdalslagets Aarbok, ed. for many years by Kristine Haugen and others.

INDEX.

The Norwegian letters *æ*, *ø*, and *å* are alphabetized as if they were *ae*, *o*, and *a*. The index includes all loanword models referred to in the text, marked by their part of speech. Italicized page numbers refer to special or detailed treatment.

Ronjat, Louis 9, 295
Rønning, N. N. 151
roof n. 82, 376
Roosevelt, Theo. 254
rooster n. 80
rootbeer n. 426
rope n. 80, 448
Røros dialect 348, 613
Rosendahl, P. J. 186
Rosholt, Malcolm 664
Rosing, Svend 51, 298
Ross, Hans 303, 639, 655
rouge n. 409, 435
rough a. 92, 368, 417, 428, 454, *592*
rub v. 93, 428
Rudie, K. K. 168
rug n. 62, 83, 428, 451, *592*
Rugby 122
Ruge, Herman 301
run v. 67, 75, 93, 134, 428, 460, 473, *592;* r. down v. 458, 474
runaway n. 67
Ruud, Martin 298, 308
Rynning, Ole 37, 297, 655

sabbaterian n. 453
Sæter, Johannes O. 172
Sætre, Allan 50
St. Ansgar, Ia. 227
St. Olaf 227
St. Olaf, Minn. 231
St. Olaf College 34, 137, 140, 142, 196, 259; given names of students 213—4
saloon n. 86, 152, 396, 425, 434, 453, *592*
salt rising n. 49, 84, 453
Sandfeld-Jensen, Kr. 660
sandwich n. 365
Sangerhilsen 148
Sapir, Edward 361
Sargent, J. Y. 304
satchel n. 461
sauce n. 56, 85
saucer n. 84, 435, 461
Saude og Nesherringer i Amerika 184

save v. 86, 122, 426
saw n. 77
saxophone n. 88
Scandinavia, Wis. 215, 346, 609; dialects in 341; origin of name 231
Scandinavian teaching at American institutions 137
scared a. 67
sceptic n. 409
Schach, Paul 364, 365, 660
Schneider, J. A. 308
school n. 465; s. district n. 467; s. fund n. 126, 130, 131; s. teacher n. 89, *593*
schoolmam n. 89, 422, 446, 448, 466, *592*
schottische n. 88, 418, 422, 430, 436, 462, *593*
Schøyen, D. M. 314
Schrijnen, J. 654
Schrøder, Johan 51, 55, 298
Schuchardt, Hugo 8, 295, 362, 373
sciainatore n. (AmIt) 404
screen n. 82, 435, 444, 468, *593*
screwdriver n. 467
scythe n. 78
seat n. 83
Seattle, Wash. 27
second a. 92, 418, 427, 454; s. cousin 92, 414, 457
section n. 76, 386, 469, s. boss n. 456; s. crew n. 387
seed n. 78, 425, 433, 438, 450, *593*
seedbed n. 97
seeder n. 78, 462
Seifert, Lester W. viii, 292, 364, 459, 658
Seip, Didrik Arup vii, 302, 308, 337, 419
Seland, Hans 175, 246, 308, 314
Selbulaget 184
self-binder n. 79, 467
self-rake n. 466
self-raker n. 435
sell out v. 474
Selmer, Ernst W. vii, 661

KEY TO INFORMANTS

This identification of informants by name is added in the Second Edition because it is valuable to the historical record and no longer seems likely to embarrass anyone.

1K1 Newhouse, Lawrence
2C1 Haugen, Mrs. Albert (Juline Starum)
2C2 Hegge, Merlin
2C3 Fossum, Ben
2C4 Haugen, Olaves M.
3C1 Johnson, Augustin
3C2 Johnson, Hjalmar
3C3 Ommodt, Laura
3C4 Nelson, Sophia
4C1 Smittbakk, Albert
4F1 Lien, Joseph Randolph
4F2 Tellefson, Mrs. Sina
4F3 Abrahamson, Mrs. Isak (Amanda Eriksen)
4F4 Eriksen, Tarje
4G1 Abrahamson, Isak
4H1 Moen, Mrs. Gilbert G.
4K1 Ellickson, Mrs. Edward
4K2 Burns, Ole (orig. Bjøraas) Andersen
4L1 Drotning, (Thomas) Alvin
4L2 Juve, Andrew
4L3 Asleson, Mrs. Albert (Joronn Holtan)
4L4 Stephens, O. B. (Hustvedt)
4N1 Gilbertson, Mrs. Morris (Tina Hovland)
4N2 Hovland, Enok
4P1 Reque, Mrs. Stark (Julia Anna Lee)

4P2 Berge, B. J.
4P3 Berge, Nicolai
4P4 Spilde, Nels N.
4Q1 Flom, George T.
4Q2 Thorstad, Jens
4Q3 Severson, Judge Herman Johan
5C1 Bang, Mrs. Halvor (Ingeborg Aline Anderson)
5E1 Grender, Abner H.
5G1 Davidson, David Abrahamson
5H1 Amble, Alva Theoline
5H2 Bang, Halvor Johannes
5H3 Haadem, Sever
5H4 Spaanum, Tore Sveinson
5H5 Boley (Bøle), Anton
5H6 Grøndahl, Henrik
5H7 Halvorsen, Knut (Jorde)
5H8 Bang, Myrtle Alvira
5H9 Boley, Mrs. Anton (Gjertru Øyhus)
5J1 Jeglum, Mrs. Guri (Guri Torsdatter Trøo)
5J2 Paulson, Hazel
5L1 Grimstad, Aslak
5L2 Haakeness, Hans
5L3 Stolen, Ole Andreas
5L4 Peterson, P. V. (Petter Vraal)
5L5 Jensen, Tine (Anne Kristine)
5L6 Dalby, Ole
5N1 Moe, Mrs. Erik (Johanna Margrete Larsdatter Skimling)

5P1 Bystol, Mikkel Larsen
5Q1 Eggum, Carrie (Kari)
6F1 Holum, Rev. J. O.
6P1 Nelson, Mrs. Robert
6P2 Pederson, John (Hosaas)
6P3 Sherven, John
6P4 Sherven, Ola
6Q1 Knudtson, Mrs. Oliver (Emma
    Bergum)
6Q2 Jameson, Karen Marie
6Q3 Nelson, Robert Nikolai
6Q4 Grinde, Leonard
6Q5 Quam, Mrs. Christ (Sara Solheim)
6Q6 Bergum, Mrs. Ben (Ida Grinde)
7G1 Pederson, Clarence
7H1 Qualley, John (Jens Kvale)
7H2 Berg, Knut
7H3 Berge, Otto G.
8B1 Stamstad, Gilbert (orig.
    Gulbrand)
8B2 Thulien, Gilbert
8B3 Wolberg, Harold
8C1 Wesley, Christian
8C2 Amundson, Harris
8C3 Wesley, Hanford
8C4 Thulien, Mrs. Gilbert (Emma
    Kolden)
8C5 Olson, Willard
8E1 Bergan, Ole
8F1 Hartvig, Theodor
8G1 Helgeson, Arnold
8G2 Jacobson, Henry
8L1 Williams, Mrs. McKinley (Anna
    Goli)
8L2 Loken (Løka), Elvin Theodor
8L3 Barikmoe, John
8L4 Flaata, Melvin
8L5 Flaata, Mrs. Melvin (Frances
    Solum)
8L6 Flaata, Corrin
8L7 Selmer, Fred
8L8 Aronson, Raymond L.
8M1 Gunnstein, Arthur
8M2 Krostue, Winfield
8M3 Gunnstein, Neri (known as Neil)
8M4 Gunnstein, Mrs. Gunne
9E1 Norlin, Mrs. Oscar (Charlotte)
9F1 Norlin, Oscar
9G1 Thompson, Reinert

9G2 Anderson, Sever W.
9G3 Thompson, Torge L. (Tørje)
9G4 Arveson, Andrew (Andreas)
9Q1 Arveson, Anne Marie
10C1 Nottestad, Even
10C2 Sveen, Emil O.
10C3 Thorsgaard, Ernest
10C4 Sveen, Mrs. Emil O. (Johanne
    Rudrud)
10C5 Dahl, Mrs. Millie (Larsen)
10C6 Lien, Walter
10C7 Hagen, Carl J.
10C8 Jefson, John
10C9 Nottestad, John
10C10 Larson, Mrs. Christine
10C11 Iverson, Oscar
10C12 Nottestad, Mrs. Even (Hanna
    Emilie Shærve)
10C13 Grimsrud, Richard M.
10C14 Von Ruden, Waldemar
10F1 Hektoen, Marie
10N1 Bentson, Reinert
10N2 Hage, Julius
11B1 Baglien, Paula
11B2 Baglien, Mrs. Kari (Engum)
11B3 Volden, Anton
11B4 Bakken, Iver
11B5 Beinerud, Mrs. Chris (Milli
    Baglien)
11B6 Torgersen, Tobias
11C1 Brye, Adolph C.
11C2 Brye, Martha M.
11C3 Evans, Mrs. Matilda (Karine
    Mathilde Brye)
11C4 Sanding, Ruth (Mrs. Albert J.
    Bonady)
11C5 Lunde, Archie
11C6 Brye, Milnor
11C7 Brye, Mrs. Milnor (Mabel
    Midtlien)
11E1 Beinerud, Christian
11R1 Nauste, Mrs. Severin (Ane
    Margrete Borvik)
11R2 Nauste, Severin
12F1 Langve, D. M.
12Q1 Quamme, Andrew B.
12Q2 Sime, T. T.
12Q3 Morkved, Cora
12Q4 Stevlingson, H. O.

12Q5 Vigdahl, J. P.
12Q6 Severson, Mrs. Nordal (Dina Chellevold)
12Q7 Chellevold, Ole
12R1 Froiseth, Alec
12R2 Hopland, Mrs. Mons (Marie Mælem)
12R3 Williams, Carl
12R4 Quigne, Mrs. John (Amanda Skrede)
12R5 Langve, Mrs. Rakkel
12R6 Moldrem, Robert B.
13N1 Roalkvam, Jacob
13N2 Larsen, Lars O.
13N3 Gugdal, Magle
13N4 Roalkvam, Tilmar
13N5 Roalkvam, Mrs. Jacob (Emma Nilsen)
14C1 Helom, Mrs. Nils (Karoline Gilbertson)
14C2 Nyen, Victor
14D1 Anderson, Goodwin
14D2 Halvorsen, Martin (Harberget)
14D3 Anderson, Odin
14D4 Nyen, Oscar
14D5 Storley, Mrs. Ole (Johanne Amundsen)
14D6 Johnson, Ole C.
14D7 Halvorsen, Almar
14D8 Austad, Albert
14D9 Nyen, Basil
14D10 Peterson, Bennie
14D11 Hanson, E. C. (Edwin)
14D12 Bergum, Farrel
14D13 Nyen, Helmer
14D14 Berk, Iver O.
14D15 Thompson (Taraldsen), Iver
14D16 Shelley, John
14D17 Bergum, Lawrence
14D18 Nyen, Odell
14D19 Austad, Omer
14D20 Dahl, Philip
14D21 Halvorsen, Selmer
14D22 Berg, Stanley M.
14F1 Rude, Albert
14F2 Olson, Mrs. Martha
14F3 Lysdahl, Tom
14F4 Matson, Roy H. (Mathison)
14L1 Kvaalset, Aslak

14L2 Mickelson, Edwin
14Q1 Underdahl, Peter
15P1 Seljestad, Jacob T.
15P2 Haugen, Mrs. Karlot
15P3 Torkelson, Martin (Wilhelm)
15P4 Odegard, Mrs. Nellie
15P5 Odegard, Chester
15P6 Odegard, Glenn
16C1 Kinderman, Mrs. (Thelma Gulliksrud)
17P1 Gray, Norman
17Q1 Ede, Mrs. John (Bertha Eriksen)
17Q2 Munson, Ole J.
17Q3 Ness, Christ B. (Kristoffer)
17Q4 Wulff, Mrs. Joseph (Kari Ødegaard)
18B1 Carlson, Marie
18B2 Carlson, Sigurd (Alfred)
18B3 Mathiesen, Mrs. John
18C1 Peterson, Juel
18C2 Harelstad, Richard Arthur
18C3 Bendiksen, Alfred
18C4 Bendiksen, Mrs. Alfred (Kristine)
18C5 Harelstad, Mrs. Richard (Thelma Peterson)
19A1 Lassesen, John
19A2 Overhaug, Olaf
19A3 Raaen, Mrs. Iver (Marie Louise Evenmo)
20C1 Gjerdingen, Carl Wilhelm (Willy)
20C2 Muller, Mrs. Gilmar
20C3 Gilbertson, Mrs. Addie (Bentson)
20C4 Kjos, Bernt O.
20C5 Kjos, Carl
20E1 Gubberud, Arnold
20F1 Quinnell, E. L.
20F2 Ellingson, Gus
20F3 Hallan, Henry A.
20F4 Peterson, James M.
20F5 Myrah, Lorentz
20F6 Selness, M. Albert
20F7 Kjos, Mrs. Carl (Kate Eusch)
20F8 Glasoe, Martinus
20F9 Gilbertson, Mrs. Gerhard (Olga Kinneberg)

20F10 Peterson, Mrs. Olaf (Emma
           Bjørgo)
20F11 Torvick, Olaf E.
20F12 Dahle, Olaus K.
20F13 Myhre, Odell
20F14 Halland, Oscar S.
20F15 Onstad, Otto
20F16 Lane, Reinhard
20F17 Haugland, Selmer
20F18 Loftsgordon, Willard
20J1   Storlie, Martin K.
20J2   Tollefsrud, Leonard
20P1   Akre, John J.
20P2   Opheim, Mrs. John (Synneva
           Jøssendahl)
20Q1   Berkvam, Jens
20Q2   Otternes, Mrs. Martha
21H1   Flaten, Nils
22F1   Haagenson, Rev. Helmer

23A1   Bjørlo, Mrs. Martin
23A2   Aune, Halvor
23A3   Lee, Ole
23A4   Mellem, Sivert
24A1   Meslow, Edwin
25A1   Haugen, Einar
25H1   Qualley, R. N.
25L1   Quisling, Mrs. Andrea (Veum)
25P1   Rene, Knut
25P2   Vethe, Mrs. Ole
25P3   Shelvik, Sivert
25P4   Setre, T. K.
26A1   Anderson, Matilda
26P1   Monsen, Mrs. Ingeborg
26P2   Monsen, Carrie
26P3   Rygh, Thorbjørn Lars
26P4   Foss, Knut
26P5   Arestad, Mrs. Oline (Oline
           Haga)